David D. Allsup
Ranger, Texas

THE FOUNDATIONS OF
MODERN EDUCATION

John Amos Comenius

1592-1670

The Foundations of Modern Education

Elmer H. Wilds

Late Professor of Education

WESTERN MICHIGAN UNIVERSITY

and

Kenneth V. Lottich

MONTANA STATE UNIVERSITY

THIRD EDITION

9817

Holt, Rinehart and Winston, Inc., N.Y.

To

Robert Ulich

*"For he who can view things
in their connexion is a dialectician...."*

Book VII, THE REPUBLIC

PREFACE

The years that have elapsed since the publication of the earlier editions of this book have been crucial ones in our history, and the crises through which we have passed—greatly influencing American life and institutions—have consequently produced a modified educational thought and practice. Although it is not an easy task to interpret and evaluate that which is so close in point of time, the present edition is such an attempt.

This volume still represents—as it did at the time of its first publication—a method of treatment which is held to be distinctively different from that found in other books dealing with the history and philosophy of education. It is the purpose of this study of the evolution of educational theory from the time of primitive man down to the present age not only to relate the history of education but also to illuminate the significance of contemporary movements and problems.

Through an analysis of the various conceptions of education found in the writings of outstanding educational thinkers and reformers it points out the implications of each phase of current educational opinion. By tracing the influence of changing social, political, economic, and religious views upon the development of educational thought it seeks to provide a sound basis for the interpretation and evaluation of present-day theories and practices.

In recent years the emphasis in history of education courses has shifted from a detailed development of educational institutions and practices to the foundations of the educational theories that underlie changing practices. There is a growing tendency to subordinate matters such as school legislation and school administration and to emphasize the educational philosophies that have influenced educational practice through the centuries in order to study their effects upon all phases of education under various conditions. The authors believe that this tendency should be furthered and it is hoped that their work will be of value in encouraging the movement.

When the first edition was prepared our intent was to write not merely another factual textbook in the history of education, but primarily a history of educational thought—with only a secondary emphasis on the history of educational practice. The philosophies and concepts of education that have developed in over three thousand years were presented in as unbiased and objective a manner as possible. In this new edition the conflict between progressivism and essentialism—and indeed the new recourses to idealism and reconstructionism—are discussed; the student is thus acquainted with each point of view so that he will be able to evaluate and to adopt the philosophy of his choice, or—should it seem preferable—to accept what he believes to be the best elements from several in the creation of his own eclectic philosophy.

The contemporary vogue for a treatment of comparative education likewise is recognized throughout the later sections, and Chapter XX is devoted to a quick survey of educational ideologies around the world. The contemporary ideological schism is observed and the relationship of new totalitarian influences on education is examined. The new recourses to nationalism—in both the older and the newer areas of the globe—are considered in the light of their meaning to educational practice.

By retaining the chronological order in the presentation of the varying philosophies the authors have attempted to preserve the historical approach and to avoid swinging too far in the direction of the conventional treatment of educational philosophy—through the isms. Thus the type of organization chosen—it is maintained—makes this book suitable for the orthodox course in the history of education as well as for the newer arrangement that combines the history and philosophy of education. Furthermore, the text may be used as a supplement to materials appropriate for courses in introduction to education, principles of teaching, or philosophy of education.

The subject matter of this volume is organized on the basis of selective continuity. Each chapter (except the last) presents a separate treatment of each of the following phases of education: (1) aims; (2) types; (3) content; (4) agencies; (5) organization; and (6) methods. Consequently, the history of the curriculum, the history of school organization, the history of method—any or all of these—may readily be traced from their beginnings down to the present.

The material offered—ordinarily a semester's study at the rate of approximately one chapter per week—is presented in twenty chapters. Each one aims at the mastery of some particular period or movement in the development of educational theory and practice, including special emphasis upon the application of this knowledge to contemporary needs. Obviously, this plan permits the use of the text through appropriate selection of chapters in courses which may continue for but one quarter and, should a year's program be desired, it will be found adequate when the basic volume is supplemented through utilization of the many references for further study placed at the conclusion of each chapter.

Specifically, each chapter contains:

A. An overview, which includes a summary of the geographical, social, political, economic, and religious influences underlying the period, motive, or movement under consideration; the relationship of this chapter to the preceding one; and a brief survey of the subject matter treated in the chapter.

B. An exposition, through which the concept or philosophy under consideration is studied in its application to the six aspects of education mentioned above: aims, types, content, agencies, organization, and methods. By this arrangement each one of these important foci may be emphasized and their significance to the pattern of education being discussed heightened.

1. Under *aims* the underlying purposes of education, its philosophy or ideology, the historical determinants, and tribal or national goals are stressed.

2. *Type* considers the various forms in which education appears within a given society or culture, for example, religious or moral instruction, vocational training, physical education, military or civic training, the liberal arts, esthetics, and the like.

3. *Content* emphasizes the selection of traditions, experiences, learnings, skills, crafts, or group activities thought to be valuable within a culture and made the basis for formal or informal education.

4. By *agencies* is meant the specific influence of the clan, the tribe or nation, the home (including parental instruction), the church or other religious orientation, apprenticeship, the formal school, or the society itself.

5. *Organization* refers to the various gradations, age levels, or special plateaus (usually of formal education) within the educational system. In contemporary situations *organization* may refer also to single ladder or multi-track, common or elite systems, academic, vocational, or polytechnical education, etc.

6. *Method* includes the devices, procedures, or direction of the formal school as well as the more informal influences of the society, culture, or polity. It may involve—and usually does—participation (actual or vicarious), initiation, emulation, imitation, and the various forms of discipline. *Method* itself represents an entity that may be either concrete or abstract.

It is the authors' belief that such a plan of utilizing a six-pointed attack on each of the main topics within a chapter presents a greater opportunity for summarization and comparison —essential features in contemporary educational analysis.

C. A compilation of complementary or collateral readings, carefully selected to supplement or expand the discussion in the text.

D. A table of questions for class discussion or for individual use. These have been designed to relate the material of the chapter to contemporary educational problems or developments but should not be thought of as ends in themselves. Consequently, they are for practice only and both instructor and students are urged to construct additional items or to expand those supplied.

The authors wish to acknowledge their debts to the late Dean Ellwood P. Cubberley of Stanford University, the late Dean Henry Wyman Holmes, Dean Francis Keppel, and Professors Robert Ulich and William H. Burton of the Graduate School of Education, Harvard University, and their appreciation to the many colleagues, friends, and students, contact with whom has served to catalyze, clarify, and encourage their thought about educational theory and practice.

Grateful appreciation is extended likewise to those authors and publishers who so courteously granted permission to use copyrighted materials as acknowledged in various footnotes in the text.

Missoula, Montana
February 1961

K. V. L.

CONTENTS

THE FOUNDATIONS OF
MODERN EDUCATION

CHAPTER I

EDUCATION FOR TRIBAL CONFORMITY

HOW EDUCATION BEGAN

The path by which man has progressed from what he was originally to what he is now has been a long hard climb, and the process has taken hundreds of thousands of years. Sometimes by accident, more often by conscious effort, he has gradually learned to adapt himself to nature and to harness it for his service, thus increasing his control over his environment; he has gradually learned to multiply his powers of communication through the development of the great communicating agencies and institutions of society such as language and transportation; he has gradually learned to dream dreams and see visions of a better life through the creative development of such ideals and aspirations as are expressed in art, literature, and religion. Man's changing conceptions of how this learning is to be achieved constitute the history of educational thought.

The thought processes of men are determined by the situations in which they find themselves. With an advancement of civilization there comes advancement in ideas about education; with the application of these theories to practice comes a still further advance in civilization. Thus, man's advancement in the practice of social living is an evolutionary process through which he has passed from aboriginal stages to our present highly complex stage of civilization. Certain phases of this evolution are accidental, involuntary, and undirected by man; much of it is conscious, voluntary, and directed by human control. The conscious or voluntary control of our evolution constitutes our educational thinking. In this chapter we shall attempt to discover the beginnings of such thinking among primitive peoples.

It is indeed difficult to say just when education itself began. Education is as old as life itself; it also antedates man, for even the animals of prehistoric ages must have passed on to their offspring, consciously or unconsciously, the tricks by which they were able to survive against the dangers of starvation and the attacks of their enemies. Education, conscious or unconscious, organized or unorganized, has always existed, playing an increasingly important role in the drama of human progress.

The making of man went on for a long time before man himself deliberately began to take a hand in the process. There was a period, lasting for thousands of years, in which education was conducted chiefly on the organic plane. Nature taught through a highly selective process. Those individuals and groups equipped with characteristics and traits favorable to survival in the environment in which they found themselves passed and were thus able through their survival to reproduce their kind and perpetuate these favorable traits. Those not so equipped flunked out and disappeared from the scene. This is one explanation of the so-called reflexes and instincts still a part of man's psychological equipment.

Education took place long before anyone thought about it; people thought about education long before anyone wrote about it; there were writings about education long before there was a problem of education. We shall see that primitive education is education reduced to its simplest terms.

But before we consider even primitive education the process by which man passed from lower to higher forms of existence must be mentioned. This advance was made possible through the development of culture. The generally accepted definition of culture, by the British anthropologist Edward B. Tylor, is "that complex whole which includes knowledge, belief, art, morals, law, custom, and any other capabilities and habits acquired by man as a member of society." [1] Many centuries were required for the evolution of so much as a simple culture.

One of our difficulties in the study of this chapter is the fact that it covers thousands and thousands of years. Primitive man passed through many stages in his development, just as the development of civilized man passes through many stages. Certain phases in this development from the primeval are often distinguished: (1) the eolithic stage, when the only implements were those of wood, horn, bone, or rock, picked up from the ground and used as they were found, and the only shelter was that of the appropriative type, the bushes and caves as supplied by nature;

---

[1] Edward B. Tylor, *Primitive Culture*. A reprint of the first edition. (New York: Brentanos, 1924.) P. 1.

(2) the paleolithic stage, when implements of stone were used, roughly knocked into shape as spearheads, arrowheads, axes, and hammers, and the shelter was of the adaptive type, stones and bushes worked over into rough dwelling places; (3) the neolithic stage, when the stone implements were polished and sharpened to keen edges far better than their rude prototypes, and shelter was created out of materials changed from their natural state. There is much difference between the way of life of the Neanderthal man, poor, grimacing, chattering, ape-like, squatting and trembling in his draughty cave, and that of the neolithic man as represented by the American Indian, skilled in shelter making, hunting, fishing, agriculture, and the domestic arts. Yet both are classed as primitive. We cannot in brief space treat fully the part education plays at each of these stages. We shall have to strike an average and discuss primitive life in general.

In our study of other chapters, we shall draw the most of our material for discussion from the writings of the great thinkers and philosophers who first developed and presented the ideas involved in that section. In our consideration of the educational concepts of primitive peoples, however, we must depend upon other sources.

Whatever ideas primitive man had concerning education were handed down by word of mouth from generation to generation. Usually these ideas were part of the secrets of the medicine men and priests, revealed only to the novitiates of the select circle. We must get our knowledge of primeval life from the archaeologists who study the tangible relics of extinct communities in the shape of buildings, weapons, utensils, and articles used for personal adornment or attire; from the anthropologists who, as anthropometrists, study comparatively the various skeletons found in the graves of long-vanished races, or, as ethnologists, study savage tribes that still exist in their primitive state in isolated and remote sections of the world today. These students of earliest man have given us all the knowledge we possess of his educational practices and ideas.

Recently Dr. Ruth Benedict produced a comparative study of three diverse primitive peoples, the Pueblos of New Mexico, the Dobus of Melanesia, and the Kwakiutl of the Northwest Coast of North America.[2] Although the culture pattern in each of these societies is quite different, common bonds exist in their need for complex systems of rules and regulations and for rudimentary educational practices.

ATTITUDES OF PRIMITIVE EDUCATION

AIMS   Primitive education is almost unconscious of its own aims. The objectives, goals, and ideals of the aborigine were few in number.

---

[2] Ruth Benedict, *Patterns of Culture.* (Boston: Houghton Mifflin Company, 1934.) Also published as a Mentor Book by the New American Library, New York, 1946.

His educational system, if indeed it may be called a system, did not need to be very elaborate to develop in the individual those characteristics and traits conceived as necessary for his own well-being and the welfare of the group. At first early man thought little, except about immediate things—how to satisfy his hunger, how to protect himself against the elements, how to avoid injury and death. He was tied to the present and neither understood nor anticipated the future. "Sufficient unto the day is the evil thereof" was his simple philosophy of living. He gave little thought to where he was going or whence he had come. Aboriginal man was only dimly conscious of his entity and his ends, of things to be done, the need of doing them, or the ways of doing them. Most of his activity was on the instinctive level, and whatever education there was may be considered as unconscious imitation.

Security was the basic aim of primitive education; for the basic problem of primitive peoples was how to get a living and protect themselves and their families from the destructive forces of nature and from enemies, both animal and human. Fear was undoubtedly the stimulus for most of their actions.

"In the beginning there was fear; and fear was in the heart of man; and fear controlled man. At every turn it overwhelmed him, leaving no moment of ease." [3]

Fire, storms, thunder, and death placed in the mind of primitive man a feeling of fear which stimulated him to action and caused him to pass on to his offspring those actions which proved effective. Fear was the earliest motive for education. Early man was a slave to his own needs and to his dread of unseen powers. His educational aim—if indeed, he was conscious of an educational aim at all—was to prepare the individual (1) to obtain the necessities of life for self and family and (2) to propitiate the unseen powers supposed to be active in nature.

For the primitive feared inanimate objects more than animate ones because to him all objects were animate—trees, rocks, storms, and everything else. All things could be angry or pleased; could destroy him or let him alone. This is the earliest religion, the religion of animism.

"Back of every material existence or phenomenal reality, the savage posits an immaterial power, a spiritual entity, a 'double' which controls the material object, explains its being and its resistance to the will of man and makes it an abode of consciousness no different in kind from the consciousness which he himself possesses." [4]

This conception of a dual world of body and spirit probably came to primitive man through his own dream experiences. At first he

---

[3] Lewis Browne, *This Believing World*. (New York: The Macmillan Co., 1926.) P. 27. Reprinted with the permission of the publisher.
[4] Paul Monroe, *Textbook in the History of Education*. (New York: The Macmillan Co., 1933.) P. 2. Reprinted with the permission of the publisher.

was conscious of only two kinds of spirits; those that were neutral, demanding no attention, and those that were hostile, therefore to be driven away or deceived. Later the possibility occurred to him that some spirits might be friendly, or that hostile spirits might be placated and thus made friendly. Security from the dread unseen powers came when man conceived the possibility of exploiting the spirits through the ceremonies and rituals of "magic." Security was the first purpose back of these ceremonies, restraints, taboos, and customs imposed upon the younger generation by the elders among the group.

Conformity was the second aim of primitive education, for conformity is a requisite of security. The fear of danger brought early men together to unite in families, clans, and tribes. With such groupings came the oldest problem of social life, that of conformity. Fitting the individual to the group constituted the major part of his education. The individual must conform to the group for his own safety and the safety of the group. Group consciousness rather than individual consciousness is the outcome emphasized in primitive education. The welfare of the group rather than the recognition of any individual rights is the chief concern.

At first this process of developing conformity was carried on without any definitely conscious aim in view. Man engaged in the process at first unconsciously and certainly without theorizing about it. With individuals naturally gathering into social groupings, for gregariousness was one of the traits essential to survival, likenesses among those of the group were necessary for the comfort and satisfaction of both the individual and the group. Therefore, without any conscious effort, the grouping became an educational force, stamping out eccentricities, forcing each individual into shape, and thus preserving a condition of likeness. When the individual reached the group standard, his education was complete. General social approval or disapproval was a sufficiently potent force to keep each one within the limits of the general status of the group.

When primitive man did begin to be conscious of education it was no problem to him, and so he did little thinking about it. He merely continued to do consciously what had been going on naturally: to adjust the individual to his material and spiritual environment through fixed ways of doing the things involved in his work and worship. The primitive tended not to encourage but to repress every individual variation, and to keep all the members of the tribe on one monotonous level of adherence to tradition and the customs of the tribe.

"Each new child was a task to be dealt with as occasion arose; but the elders of the group knew what to do with him. They knew what their job was; they were to break him in—to the uses and ways of life—or they were to throw him out. They had no alternative, no choice, and no problem. The matter was never questioned; either this youth came in—all the way in—with all his being and both his feet, or else he went out—all the way out—without mercy, and no questions asked."[5]

For centuries, therefore, education was nothing but the imposing of group characteristics upon the children. The object of all primitive organization was to create what has been called the cake of custom. Choice determined scarcely anything. The guiding rule was the rule of *status quo*. The dominant aim was to kill out variations at birth or in early childhood. For a member of his group to deviate from the old customs and usages of his tribe was unpardonable.

TYPES Primitive education contained, in rudimentary form, the two general types of education to be found among all peoples: (1) education with reference to the seen, or practical education; and (2) education with reference to the unseen, or theoretical education.

The practical education of primitive man included—in their simpler forms to be sure—such types of education as we now designate by the terms vocational training, domestic training, military training, physical training, and moral training. These types of education, when they are freed from the primitive standard of nonprogressive adjustment to environment and become the agencies for an ever-developing progressive adjustment, provide the basis for our economics, ethics, sociology, and politics. They educate us for all our work activities—those which deal with the material aspects of life.

The theoretical education of primitive man covered the types of education now designated by such terms as religious education, medical education, art education, musical education, literary education, and intellectual education—all those types that form the basis of our religion, medicine, art, music, literature, philosophy, and science. They originally had to do with the so-called worship activities, those which deal with the spiritual aspects of life.

It must be remembered, however, that although these forms of primitive theoretical education dealt with the spiritual and unseen forces, they were applied to the practical efforts through which security was attained. In fact, many of the activities that were worship activities for them have become work activities for us. Worship among aborigines was as practical as work. In a sense, then, all their education was practical; their education was a fitting for life, but it fell short of being a fitting for an abundant life.

CONTENT The education of primitive man consisted of three processes: (1) the training necessary to satisfy the physical wants; (2) the ceremonial and sacramental training necessary to propitiate the

---

[5] Joseph K. Hart, *Creative Moments in Education.* (New York: Holt, Rinehart and Winston, Inc., 1931.) P. 1. Reprinted with the permission of the publisher.

spirits; and (3) training in the customs, taboos, and restraints necessary for the harmonious living together of the members of the social group.

Boys were taught to hunt, to fish, to fight, and to make and wield the weapons for these pursuits. Girls were taught to care for children, to prepare food, to make clothing and the utensils and implements needed in their tasks, and to construct and care for the dwelling. All these tasks were simple and could be learned by simple methods.

The acts of worship were much more involved, and the training in the magic rites by which the spirits were to be placated became more and more complex. Naïve animistic explanations of sun, moon, stars, storms, seasons—all the ordinary processes of nature as well as the extraordinary—were handed on, the beginnings of science and philosophy. Ability to tell about and explain the unusual experiences that befell them, to decorate and embellish these stories, to repeat them in attractive forms, was developed as the beginnings of history and literature.

The ceremonies and rituals by which the gods were appeased were largely concerned with symbols. There were two types of symbols, the audible and the visible. As the spoken symbols increased in number we find the beginnings of language and music. With the development of the visible symbols in the forms of totem poles, statues, and altars we find the beginnings of art, architecture, and picture writing. To primitive man the symbol, instead of merely representing the spirit, contained its very essence; the symbol was as much the thing as the thing itself. To destroy the statue of a spirit was to destroy the spirit itself; to eat the symbol of a spirit in the form of a cake was to partake of the essence of the spirit; to pronounce the name of the spirit was to breathe the very essence of the spirit. Usually the name of a spirit was taboo and was not to be uttered except by a holy man at a holy moment.

Fetishes were commonly used. These were natural or manufactured objects in which the essence of the spirit happened to dwell, and the mere possession of which gave to the owner power to control the spirit. To learn all the magic rites involved in animism, fetishism, totemism, and tabooism soon became a very complicated procedure.

For example, Benedict tells how the sorcerers of Dobu use witchcraft and incantations to control the sweet potatoes growing in the gardens of the islands. These are thought of as persons; the islanders believe they have the ability to wander at night from garden to garden. The sorcerers' charms are designed to keep the yams at home.[6]

Medicine and religion were one among primitive peoples. Disease was caused by evil spirits, and the important thing was to know how to drive them out. The usual practice was to make the body so uncomfortable that the evil spirit no longer cared to dwell therein, but charms and incantations also were used. The evil spirit must be driven out or coaxed out, and the means for doing this constituted medical

---

[6] Ruth Benedict, *op. cit.*, pp. 131-140.

training. It is only within the last century that medical education has passed beyond this stage.

But early man did not neglect his physical condition, and the history of physical education begins here. Since one of his greatest problems was the protection of himself and his family from enemies, man and beast, it was necessary to develop a strong, able body. Physical exercise was carried on in various ways by different tribes. Means were devised to develop the physical constitution of the young, to give strength to their limbs and dexterity to their motions, to rouse their martial spirit and excite them to deeds of daring. Even from babyhood they were instructed in the art of dodging and swaying the body to and fro with agility to enable them later to avoid the missiles that might be aimed at them. Babies were taught to strike their parents for fear they might grow up as cowards. Youths were often compelled to endure their fathers' blows without flinching.

AGENCIES   The practical education of primitive man was imparted by the primary social group, the family. The women of the family would teach the girls those duties pertinent to a girl's work in household management and in the rearing of offspring. The men of the family would instruct the boys in the duties of men—hunting, fishing, fighting, making tools and weapons, and propitiating the gods.

"The boy imitates the work of the father, and the girl learns household duties by imitating her mother. The end to be attained in both cases is the same, the exact reproduction of the knowledge or skill of the parents. Variation has no place in this scheme of education, for the children are not supposed to make any advance beyond the attainments of their parents."[7]

When the youth knew as much as his father his education ceased; when the girl's knowledge was equivalent to her mother's her education stopped.

There gradually grew up in this social situation, however, a certain degree of specialization, wherein one or more persons in a group came to be able to do one thing better than anyone else could do it. One savage learned by accident or by trial and error to make a sharper spear, another an ax, a more shapely piece of pottery, or a more useful basket. Often these were clever enough to keep their secrets to themselves or pass them on only to their own children. More often, children of other members of the group came to them for instruction. Thus we find developing a more definite division of knowledge and skill, and a trend toward the impartation of this knowledge and skill as a specialized technique.

At first, all religious education was in the hands of the family. The spirits which gave greatest concern were the spirits of departed

---

[7] F. C. Spencer. *Education of the Pueblo Child.* (New York: Columbia University Press, 1899.)

members of the family. These still held an interest in the family, were friendly toward it as a rule, and thus provided the motive for family worship. The responsibility for placating these family gods rested upon the shoulders of the father of the family, he being the oldest, the most experienced, and the closest to the spirits that had passed on. Upon him rested the responsibility of training the young so to conduct themselves that the spirits would remain friendly. Hence the father taught the children the value of work, the necessity of fighting, the advantages of living together harmoniously, the proper relations of the sexes, the taboos and restraints, and all other things necessary to living well and thus pleasing the family spirits.

As families united into tribes, and tribal customs became a part of the social inheritance, it was felt necessary and wise to worship not only in families but also as tribal units. For this, there must be a tribal leader. He might be chosen for his strength, his age, his appearance, or his ability. He might be termed the medicine man, the wizard, the witch doctor, the shaman, or the priest. Primarily his duty was to propitiate the spirits, especially the evil spirits; to develop the dances, ceremonies, rituals, incantations—all the wild, bewildering forms of worship found among primitive peoples.

With the formation of such a priesthood, there came another differentiation in the educational scheme of early man. At first, the priest merely taught when and where the act was to be performed and the exact method of performing it. Soon came the question of why. The priesthood needed a special type of knowledge dealing with the reasons for such performances, and this knowledge forms our first distinct body of intellectual subject matter.

In order to carry from one generation to another this special knowledge, classes were organized to train the youths of the tribe who were to become priests; and the priests began to formulate systematically this body of knowledge, which they kept to themselves and did not permit the lay members of the tribe to know. This inquiry of the priests into the why and wherefore of things stimulated the first intellectual development and the first intellectual differentiation. Out of such inquiry grew a large body of theoretical knowledge; and with this knowledge the need to find a means of permanent retention. Next came the growth of an alphabet and written language and literature.

Obviously, this formation of a priestly class advanced the functions of education in respect to: (1) the formation of a definite body of subject matter, (2) the rise of a teaching class, and (3) the development of a language and a literature. These advances in educational functioning constitute the first distinct educational institution.

METHODS The earliest method of education was the method of organic education. Jean Baptiste de Lamarck (1774–1829) first offered the theory that all organisms including man evolved gradually and in response to conditions which affected their growth. He contended that new structures arose as adjustments or adaptations to environment, and were developed through use or disappeared through disuse. Someone learned to scowl and show his teeth; someone learned to clench his fist; someone learned to throw a stone; someone learned to hold and throw a club; someone learned the efficacy of a cry or a gesture. Such acquired mechanisms were so satisfying that they became fixed in the individual and were passed on to his descendants and thus became ingrained in the race.

"All that has been acquired or altered in the organization of individuals during their life is preserved by generation and transmitted to the new individuals which proceed from those which have undergone the change," said Lamarck, and thus promulgated the theory of evolution through the inheritance of acquired characteristics.[8]

In 1859, Darwin advanced a different explanation of the origin of traits and characteristics. He thought that these traits arose as chance variations in individual organisms. Those traits that were valuable in the struggle for existence enabled the individuals possessing them to survive until they could reproduce their kind and pass the traits on to future generations. Those individuals that possessed negative traits failed to survive and reproduce, and so the unfavorable traits disappeared. De Vries extended Darwin's idea of chance variations by pointing out the possibility of mutations, unique pronounced accidental variations, which would account for decided changes in organic evolution. These biological processes cover what we mean by the term organic method.

Next came the method of unconscious imitation, in which man took a certain share in the process, but did so unconsciously and certainly without any theorizing about it. Long before man made any conscious attempts to educate his children, the children began to educate themselves through unconscious imitation of the activities of their elders. Much of this unconscious imitation was carried on as play. The child's amusements and games were imitations of the activities of adult life. His toys were miniatures of the implements used by adults. Indian children played with a log in the water, paddling about as if it were a canoe. The boy constructed tiny bows and arrows and shot at a mark; the girls made tiny utensils and played at preparing food. Most of their sports were imitations of this type.

Even when the aboriginal father and mother enlisted the child in the performance of the many little chores involved in the life of the group, they were not conscious of the fact that they were really educating the child. Both imitation through play and imitation through work, effective as they might be, were largely on the unconscious level.

At later stages of primitive development, there arose the method

---

[8] Although Lamarck's theory generally has been rejected, a similar explanation, proposed by T. D. Lysenko, a Soviet agronomist, was accepted by the Central Committee in 1948 as the basis for biology teaching in the U.S.S.R. Since Lysenko's theories are in line with Marxist ideology they found great favor in the Soviet Union for a number of years.

of conscious imitation, or, viewed from the standpoint of the teacher rather than of the learner, the method of example. Early man watching his neighbor obtain the necessities of existence, or the youth watching the older men of the tribe, consciously attempted to imitate their activities in order to satisfy his own wants. The older members of the tribe, not being able to use as yet the methods of instruction by precept developed by historic peoples, consciously attempted to direct the attention of the youth to their own example.

Primitive education, like most complex modern education, is but the initiation of the individual into the ways of society through the acquisition of its cultural possessions, now expanded into many subjects requiring years for their acquisition. This instruction is of the purely imitative character; for the youths must accept without any variation or any questioning the traditions of their trible as transmitted by the only teachers they have. Custom once determined, the duty of the individual is implicit obedience through imitation.[9]

Another preliterate means of training was the trial-and-error method. This, however, could be used only in the few cases where the action did not conflict with any of the existing tribal customs, taboos, restraints, or rites. When the trial was successful, it could be repeated satisfactorily; when the results were painful, it was wise to refrain from that type of procedure. Thus reasoned the early learner. Any procedure that resulted in even a little success would be continued indefinitely. One recalls the story of the origin of roast pig as told by Charles Lamb; it is not unlike the early methods of potterymaking whereby the clay was molded in wicker baskets and the baskets then burned, that being the method someone had hit upon for burning clay.

When the first teaching class arose, with the turning over of much of the education of the young to the priests, the method used was largely one of indoctrination. The instruction for the most part dealt with the formal activities of worship, the what to do and how to do it. Even where the reasons for conduct were taught—this type of teaching usually being present only in the training of the recruits for the priesthood—the education was always of the type that taught what to think and not how to think.

Man's development is a record of his uniqueness. Since he represents the only organism with a true language, this permits him alone to store his accumulated knowledge and through education pass it on beyond individual memory. This extraordinary quality (plus the fact that he has developed a moral sense) stamps him as vastly different from the most highly trained animal.

ORGANIZATION   There was little organization in primitive education in the sense in which we use the term. There were no grades of instruction or levels of schooling. Most of the training was given in a

---

[9] Paul Monroe, *op. cit.,* p. 13. Reprinted with the permission of the publisher.

rather random fashion incidental to the other activities and duties of the family and tribe.

We find but one definitely organized step in primitive education, and that is the very important ceremony of initiation, by which the adolescent youth graduates into full manhood and tribal membership. Usually at the onset of puberty, the boys were taken apart by the priests or other elders of the tribe and put through a series of ceremonies as an initiation into full-fledged membership in the tribe. During these ceremonies they were taught the ancient secrets of the tribe, the proper relationship of the sexes, and all the practical and theoretical training deemed essential for their own well-being and the welfare of the group. Often they were tortured to show their strength and willingness to suffer for the tribe, and to prove their ability to keep the tribal secrets. Their elders grasped the importance of employing this moment of emotional and intellectual awakening to inculcate useful lessons.[10]

After the initiate has passed through all the ceremonials, he becomes a perfectly developed member of the tribe. The natives themselves say that the ceremonies have the effect of strengthening all who pass through them. They impart courage and wisdom, make the men more kindly natured and less apt to quarrel, in short, 'very good and great' men. Evidently the main objects are (1) to bring the young men under the control of the old men, whose commands they have to obey implicitly, (2) to teach them habits of self-restraint and hardihood, (3) to show to the younger men who have arrived at mature age the sacred secrets of the tribe.

The purpose of the ceremonies is evidently to make the youths of the tribe worthy members of the community, according to their lights. Certain principles are impressed upon them for their guidance through life—for instance, to listen and obey the old men; to share the fruits of the chase generously with others, especially with their kindred; not to interfere with women of the tribe, particularly those who are related to them, nor to injure their kindred, in the widest sense, by evil magic. Before the novice is permitted to take his place in the community, marry and join its councils, he must possess the qualifications which enable him to act for the common welfare.[11]

Participation in the rituals and ceremonies of the society together with an incidental apprenticeship to the daily and seasonal activities of the family and tribe constitutes the only educational program found in primitive cultures.[12] This is enough, however, to set the "cake of custom" firmly and usually to insure the perpetuation of the tribe. For this reason conformity in work and worship is the means whereby group security is secured and is the only goal of education in primitive and preliterate societies.

---

[10] See Benedict, *op. cit.*, pp. 22-27, for a further description of *rites de passage* in primitive societies. In some cultures girls as well as boys are included and must pass through certain ceremonies attendant on their newly achieved womanhood.

[11] Joseph K. Hart, *Creative Moments in Education.* (New York: Holt, Rinehart and Winston, Inc., 1931.) Pp. 15-16. Reprinted with the permission of the publisher.

[12] The educational system of each tribe or nation is unique and it is only by close observation and comparison that its real significance and goals are revealed. More than

FOR FURTHER READING

Adams, John, *Evolution of Educational Theory*. London: Macmillan and Co., Ltd., 1912. Pp. 104-127.

Barnes, Harry Elmer, *An Intellectual and Cultural History of the Western World*. New York: Random House, 1937. Pp. 27-61.

Benedict, Ruth, *Patterns of Culture*. Boston: Houghton Mifflin Co., 1934.

Breasted, James Henry, *The Conquest of Civilization*. New York: Harper and Brothers, 1926. Pp. 3-39.

Browne, Lewis, *This Believing World*. New York: The Macmillan Co., 1926. Pp. 27-65.

Butts, R. Freeman, *A Cultural History of Western Education*. New York: McGraw-Hill Book Co., 1955. Pp. 1-6.

Childe, V. Gordon, *Man Makes Himself*. London: Watts and Company, 1936.

Davidson, Thomas, *History of Education*. New York: Charles Scribner's Sons, 1900. Pp. 18-23.

Dawson, Christopher, *The Age of the Gods*. London and New York: Sheed and Ward, 1933. Pp. 3-107.

————, *The Dynamics of World History*. New York: Sheed and Ward, 1957. Pp. 3-110.

Eby, Frederick, and Arrowood, Charles F., *The History and Philosophy of Education Ancient and Medieval*. New York: Prentice-Hall, Inc., 1940. Pp. 1-35.

Frazer, Sir James G., *The Golden Bough* (One Volume Edition). New York: The Macmillan Co., 1922. *Passim*.

Hart, Joseph K., *Creative Moments in Education*. New York: Holt, Rinehart and Winston, Inc., 1931. Pp. 1-26.

Keesing, Felix M., *The South Seas in the Modern World*. Revised. New York: John Day Co., 1945.

---

a century ago Marc-Antoine Jullien de Paris (1775-1848), in a call for a greater comprehensiveness in the study of education, wrote: "Education, as other sciences, is based on facts and observations, which should be ranged in analytical tables, easily compared, in order to deduce principles and definite rules. Education should become a positive science instead of being ruled by narrow and limited opinions, by whims and arbitrary decisions of administrators, to be turned away from the direct line which it should follow, either by the prejudice of a blind routine or by the spirit of some system and innovation." (*L'Esquisse et vues préliminaires d'un ouvrage sur l'Éducation Comparée*, Paris, 1817. As quoted in Pedro Rossello, *Marc-Antoine Jullien de Paris*, Geneva, 1943). Arthur Henry Moehlman suggests a morphology consisting of the philosophy, people, the geography, historical determinants, and technology for use in the study of a system of education in its own culture pattern. (*Comparative Education*, Arthur Henry Moehlman and Joseph S. Roucek (Eds.). New York, Holt, Rinehart and Winston, 1952). The authors of the *Foundations of Modern Education* recommend such a comparative approach to the study of the educational records of the past and present and have attempted to utilize it in this work.

Kroeber, Alfred Louis, *Anthropology*. New York: Harcourt, Brace and Company, 1948.

Mayer, Frederick, *A History of Educational Thought*. Columbus, Ohio: Charles E. Merrill Books, Inc., 1960.

Mead, Margaret, *Coming of Age in Samoa*. New York: William Morrow & Co., Inc., 1928.

Messenger, James F., *Interpretative History of Education*. New York: Thomas Y. Crowell Co., 1931. Pp. 9-16.

Monroe, Paul, *Textbook in the History of Education*. New York: The Macmillan Co., 1933. Pp. 1-16.

Mulhern, James, *A History of Education*. Second Edition. New York: The Ronald Press Co., 1959. Pp. 1-54.

Shaw, Charles Gray, *Trends of Civilization and Culture*. New York: American Book Company, 1932.

Smith, William A., *Ancient Education*. New York: Philosophical Library, Inc., 1955. Pp. 254-294.

Tylor, Edward B., *Primitive Culture*. (A Reprint of the First Edition, 1871.) New York: Brentanos, 1924.

Ulich, Robert, *The Human Career, A Philosophy of Self-Transcendence*. New York: Harper and Brothers, 1955.

Wissler, Clark, *Man and Culture*. New York: Thomas Y. Crowell Co., 1923. Pp. 1-20, 47-72.

Woody, Thomas, *Life and Education in Early Societies*. New York: The Macmillan Co., 1949. Pp. 10-43.

QUESTIONS FOR CLASS DISCUSSION

1. How do modern methods of seeking security differ from those of primitive or prehistoric man?
2. Mention some present-day survivals of primitive animism, tabooism, and fetishism. What attitude should teachers take toward them?
3. Define culture as used in the anthropological sense. In what other ways may the word be used?
4. In what stages of civilization does fear still persist as a motive for religion?
5. To what extent is social approval or disapproval a sufficiently potent educational force in modern society to secure conformity of the individual to the customs of the group?
6. In what respects is there still a close relationship between religion and medicine? Healing in general?

CHAPTER II

THE PRESERVATION OF SOCIAL STABILITY

EARLY CIVILIZATIONS

Several thousands of years ago, barbarian tribes began to emerge
from their primitive state into the first ancient cultures. What marks
this transition from savagery to civilization? Some claim that early cultures began at the point where men first learned to control the forces of
nature, such as fire, water, and wind, and to apply these forces directly
to the satisfaction of their desires and needs through such developments
as the forging of iron implements and weapons, the irrigation of lands
for agriculture, the utilization of sails on their boats. Many such thresh-
olds may be identified in the search for the positive means whereby man
lifted himself from the simpler primitive societies to the more complex
stages of group living.[1]

Other writers, however, say that civilization first arose when
social classes and castes developed; when the blood ties that held primitive tribes and clans together were weakened and those persons having
common occupations and duties were brought together in closer relationships. As conditions changed differentiation developed. Differentiation
between the sexes, between families, between individuals—these were the
origins of the class system. The oldest caste grew out of the priesthood of

[1] See Kenneth V. Lottich, "Some Distinctions Between Culture and Civilization," *Social
Forces,* Vol. 28, No. 3 (March, 1950), pp. 240-250.

7. How do the educational functions of the modern family as an tution compare with those of the primitive family?

8. How did teachers as a special class first come into existence? trast the responsibilities of those of today's teaching class with th of the first teaching class.

9. To what extent do the primitive methods of imitation still pla part in modern education?

10. Compare the initiation ceremonies of fraternities, sororities, other fraternal groups with those of primitive or preliterate tribe

11. To what extent has modern education improved upon the method of vocational instruction used by primitive peoples?

primitive tribes; the priests became a group set aside from the common people. Individuals or families able to make the best implements paved the way for an artisan class. The strength and vigor of the warriors set them apart as a fighting and ruling class. Thus there arose the three great social divisions, known as castes or classes, that have played their part in so much of the world's history: the *soldiers,* protecting against visible enemies; the *priests,* protecting against supernatural enemies; the *producers,* protecting against the dangers of hunger and cold.

Next to the utilization of fire in the practical and esthetic arts, the invention of writing was the most important factor in the rise of ancient cultures. Although at first it was wholly pictorial (alphabets of symbols developing only through a long and interesting evolution), this writing made possible the compilation and retention of the sacred traditions and laws hitherto handed down by word of mouth. These sacred writings became the first curriculum and constituted the first textbooks. Furthermore, in order to provide a specific, systematic instruction in these sacred writings, the institution which came to be known as the school had to be established.

It is difficult to determine exactly where the first ancient civilizations arose, but it is generally agreed that Asia is their birthplace. Probably civilization was born either in the fertile valleys of Mesopotamia or in Central Asia; from thence it spread eastward, southward and westward. The earliest civilizations—all of them Oriental—are usually classified as: the Aryan, including the Hindus and the Persians; the Turanian, including the Mongolians and the Chinese; the Semitic, including the Hittites, Babylonians, and Assyrians; the Hamitic, including the Egyptians and the Minoans.

In the eastern hemisphere civilizations developed earliest in the fluvial valleys. Thus four early homes of man were located along the Tigris-Euphrates, the Hwang Ho, the Indus, and the Nile. Other strong groups developed in the plateau regions adjacent to the rivers and the sea, on nearby islands, and in the Fertile Crescent, an upland area stretching from the Mediterranean to the Persian Gulf. Indeed, a little later, important groups learned how to inhabit the semiarid lands of central and western Asia and even the desert itself.

We shall not need to study all of these early Oriental civilizations in order to determine the status of education in the eastern world; it will suffice to consider ancient China, India, Persia, and Egypt as typical.

ORIENTAL CONCEPTS OF EDUCATION

In general, what were the attitudes of these early Oriental nations toward education? Oriental education represents a progression from that of primitive peoples but lacks the freedom of later cultures.

Its aims and processes were controlled and dominated by external authority. Individuality was entirely suppressed; the individual counted for nothing. Oriental education dictated to the individual what he should do, what he ought to feel, what he should think. As a rule, it recapitulated the past, summing up in the individual the life of the past in order that he might not vary from it or advance beyond it. An omnipotent authority of tradition, varying in the different nations, determined the character of man's education and thus controlled his destiny. In China the authority of ancestral traditions ruled; in India, the authority of the traditions of caste; in Persia, the authority of military tradition and national destiny. In Egypt religion, as reflected through its priesthood and the deity of the Pharaoh, became the motif.

The general purpose, then, of early Oriental education was not to build up ideal men and women but rather to prepare them to fit into their place in the established order of things. They were taught to know their place and to play their part. There was much in their teachings about duties and obligations, but nothing about rights and privileges.

Our study of the history of educational thought will be unified and illuminated if the various theories of education are considered in relation to this problem of harmonizing individual development with social demands and needs—the conflict between individual progress and social stability. What was the attitude of Oriental nations toward this problem?

In the several Oriental programs of education discussed in this chapter we find, as a common characteristic, that education is concerned with fixing existing standards and perpetuating national ideals—not with individual development. It is a matter of building and maintaining an accepted national life. These systems were exceedingly successful in attaining this objective. The Chinese and the Hindus, for example, have preserved their national cultures for more than four thousand years. Not to develop the individual, not to secure social progress, but to secure social stability—stability of society, perpetuity of empire and family, conservation of the past—these were their aims. This negative or static character of their goal is the explanation of their success. "A stationary target is more readily hit than a moving one."

It may be well to compare their aims and ideals with American aims and ideals. We have looked to the future and emphasized progress. They have looked to the past and emphasized stability. The advantages are not all on the side of progress. We have strong inclinations toward individualism and personal liberty. These have their advantages, but it is difficult to combine them with stability. The effort to preserve things as they are, to keep to the sure and tried instead of running to the new and untried, affords a steadying influence. . . . They are held together by the power of their ideals rather than by the power of government. Our job is to establish an enduring social order, while preserving as much as we can of individualism.[2]

---

[2] J. F. Messenger, *An Interpretative History of Education*. (New York: Thomas Y. Crowell Co., 1931.) Pp. 19-20. Reprinted with the permission of the publisher.

The tendency to be satisfied with the *status quo* and to follow blindly and stubbornly the traditions of the past is always a barrier to social advancement. The philosophy of complacency which prevailed among Oriental peoples is the earliest of all educational philosophies. But it has been a dominant influence in most of our organized education, and it is still one of the greatest obstacles to the building of an educational system that will serve as a real force in the direction of social improvement and individual development.

ATTITUDES OF THE CHINESE TOWARD EDUCATION

Although China is one of the oldest nations in the world, dating back at least four thousand years, its development until well into the twentieth century was far different from that of the Western world. Dynasty followed dynasty; but the life of the people remained crystallized in fixed forms, and their ideals and beliefs continued to be very much the same from generation to generation. Their dominating motives were summarized by CONFUCIUS (551–478 B.C.) in the sixth century before Christ. His writings—probably representing the accumulated wisdom of many hundred years—became the guide for centuries to follow. It is from the writings attributed to Confucius and his disciples and those of other Chinese philosophers that we get our knowledge of what the Chinese have thought about education. Many of the early Chinese educational practices, too, survived until the end of the Second World War in 1945.

AIMS   The traditional ambition of the Chinese was to remain as they were and to seek to preserve the past. Deviation from ancestral customs was looked upon with extreme disfavor; every effort was made to mold the future upon the past. Formal education was confined to study of their ancient classics.

The teachings of Confucius center upon the idea of noble living. They make human relationships, order, duty, and morality, matters of prime importance. They stress the value of five fundamental relationships: (1) between sovereign and subject, (2) between father and child, (3) between husband and wife, (4) between brother and brother, (5) between friend and friend. These relationships are based upon a doctrine of submission: the subject must submit to the ruler, the child to his father, the wife to the husband, brother to brother, friend to friend. He also set forth as the five cardinal virtues: (1) benevolence, or universal charity; (2) justice, or impartiality; (3) order, or conformity to established usages; (4) prudence, or rectitude of heart and mind; and (5) fidelity, or pure sincerity.

Confucius' precepts frequently remained aphoristic but presented for his followers statements of purpose and indeed pearls of universal wisdom. For example:[3]

> At fifteen I was bent on learning;
> At thirty I stood fast;
> At forty I had no doubts;
> At fifty I knew the will of God;
> At sixty my ear was open to the truth;
> At seventy I could follow my desires without transgressing the square
(i.e. the bounds of right).

A man's character is formed by the Odes, developed by the Rites, and perfected by Music.

The princely man thinks of virtue; the mean man of gain.

Do not unto others what you do not like done unto yourself.

Rotten wood cannot be carved, and a dung wall ought not to be whitewashed.

The princely man is catholic, not narrow; the small-minded man is narrow, not catholic.

Observe a man's actions; scrutinise his motives; take note of the things that give him pleasure. How then can he hide from you what he really is?

When you see a good man, think of emulating him; when you see a bad man, examine your own heart.

Virtue cannot live in solitude: neighbours are sure to grow up around it.

We ought to have wholesome respect for our juniors. Who knows but that by-and-by they may prove themselves equal to the men of today?

It is only when the cold season comes that we know the pine and cypress to be evergreens.

He who requires much from himself and little from others will be secure from hatred.

It is the man that is able to develop his virtue, not virtue that develops the man.

The real fault is to have faults and not try to amend them.

Where there is education, there is no distinction of class.

Men who differ in their principles cannot help each other in their plans.

Men's natures are alike; it is their habits that carry them far apart.

Only two classes of men never change: the wisest of the wise and the dullest of the dull.

There are nine traditional volumes with which the name of Confucius is usually associated. Five of these are called Classics and are: (1) the *Shu King,* or *Book of History,* an outline of history before the time of Confucius; (2) the *Shi King,* or *Book of Odes,* an outline of poetry; (3) the *Yi King,* or *Book of Changes,* an outline of prophecy and augury; (4) the *Li Ki King,* or *Book of Rights,* an outline of social etiquette; and (5) the *Hsiao King,* or *Book of Filial Piety.* Some of the

---

[3] As arranged by Professor Donald G. Tewksbury, Teachers College, Columbia University. (An unpublished manuscript.)

material in these Classics was undoubtedly written by Confucius himself, but most of it he merely compiled and edited. The Four Books mostly come from a later period and were written by the disciples of Confucius. They are (1) the *Ta Hsio,* or *Great Learning;* (2) the *Chung Yung,* or *Doctrine of the Mean;* (3) the *Lun Yu,* or *Sayings of Confucius;* and (4) the *Meng-tze,* or *Sayings of Mencius.* These Four Books consist of reports of conversations between Confucius and his disciples, together with various maxims and doctrines of an ethical and political nature. These writings make up the Chinese Bible, the guide to their daily conduct. Thorough familiarity with all of it formerly was necessary in order to hold any official position.

Much of the teaching of Confucius was not original, but a reiteration of the ideas that had developed in the centuries before him. How great a debt he owed to LAO-TZU (604–517 B.C.?) we cannot be sure. At any rate, Taoism or "The Path of Reason," a second Chinese philosophy for living, is associated with the latter in much the same fashion that Confucianism is attributed to Confucius. There is a story—doubtless a myth—that the two great sages once met, although their philosophies remain, in essence, poles apart. The chief (and only) work attributed to Lao-tzu, the *Tao-teh-Ching,* consists of eighty-one stanzas, or brief aphorisms, which scrutinize life and the purposes of life. A free translation of the title reads: "The Book of the Way and the Virtue that comes therefrom." Many strange tales are told of Lao-tzu including his virgin birth, sixty-two-year gestation, and white hair at infancy. His very name is said to signify "Old Boy" or "Old Philosopher." His stanzas breathe contentment and preach a creative quietism.[4]

6. The breath of life moves through a deathless valley
   Of mysterious motherhood
   Which conceives and bears the universal seed,
   The seeming of a world never to end,
   Breath for men to draw from as they will:
   And the more they take of it, the more remains.

17. A leader is best
    When people barely know that he exists,
    Not so good when people obey and acclaim him,
    Worst when they despise him.
    "Fail to honor people—they fail to honor you"
    But of a good leader, who talks little,
    When his work is done, his aim fulfilled,
    They will all say, "We did this ourselves."

33. Knowledge studies others,
    Wisdom is self-known;
    Muscle masters brothers,
    Self-mastery is bone;

---

[4] These verses selected from *The Way of Life according to Lao-tzu,* Witter Bynner translation (New York: John Day Company, 1944), pp. 28, 34-35, 46, 53, 60-61, 75. (Reproduced by special permission.)

Content need never borrow,
Ambition wanders blind:
Vitality cleaves to the marrow—leaving death behind.

43. As the soft yield of water cleaves obstinate stone,
    So to yield with life solves the insoluble:
    To yield, I have learned, is to come back again.
    But this unworded lesson, this easy example,
    —Is lost upon men.

56. Those who know do not tell,
    Those who tell do not know.
    Not to set the tongue loose, but to curb it . . .
    Has attained the highest post in the world.

79. If terms to end a quarrel leave bad feeling,
    What good are they?
    So a sensible man takes the poor end of the bargain without
       quibbling.
    It is sensible to make terms, Foolish to be a stickler:
    Though heaven prefer no man, A sensible man prefers heaven.

But whereas Lao-tzu pursued a policy of withdrawal and in-
action, Confucius strove by writing, by teaching, by counseling with
rulers, by actual administration to bring his teachings into the life of the
people. Confucius never claimed that he was an innovator, but regarded
himself as a conservator of ancient truth and ceremonial propriety.
Nevertheless, many Chinese became followers of Lao-tzu; indeed, it is
alleged that more than a few were able to subscribe to both doctrines,
strange as this may appear to Western thinking.

Yet actually the difference between Confucius and Lao-tzu is one
that may be composed quite easily; Confucius emphasizes the good citizen while Lao-tzu stresses the spirit that makes the good man. It is not
too much to say that these qualities should be reconcilable.

AGENCIES   The center for most of the training under the
Confucian philosophy of duty naturally was the home. Most of the relationships discussed by Confucius are centered around the life of the
family. Although the Chinese developed the school as an educational
institution, the family continued to be the agency for the practical training of the child, as had been the case in primitive times. The practical
and domestic activities were all taught within the confines of the family
and imposed by the sanctions of ancestral worship.

No national system of schools was established, but private schools
were encouraged, and almost every village came to have an elementary
school. These schools were supported by tuition charges and taught by
the unsuccessful candidates for official posts. There were no specially
erected schoolhouses; the school was held in the home of the teacher, in
the home of some wealthy patron, in an old pagoda or temple, or in any
other available place. No attempt was made to add attractiveness to the
schoolroom. The schools were poorly attended because they fitted one

only to prepare for the governmental examinations leading to official positions; they did not fit one for everyday vocations.

Theoretically, the private schools and the public examinations were open to the males of all classes; actually, since the schools were private and since preparation for the examinations necessitated much leisure time, as a rule only sons of the higher classes were privileged to attend.

ORGANIZATION   Chinese education was organized on two levels: (1) elementary education, exceedingly formalized and rigorous; and (2) higher education, training for the governmental tests, which formed the highest stage of the educational process.

The child started to school at the age of seven. School began at sunrise and lasted until about five in the afternoon, with an hour off about ten for luncheon. School sessions were held throughout the year. Beyond the elementary level the pupil continued his education by himself. This higher education was marked by a series of examinations conducted by the government and leading to degrees. These degrees, with their distinctions and privileges, however, were bestowed only on the very few successful candidates. Yet theoretically the poor as well as the wealthy received an opportunity to "leap through the Dragon's Gate" as the gaining of high public office was called.

In the mind of the Chinese truth was what had been agreed upon in the past, and virtue was the observance of those fixed ideas and customs. Morality therefore became for them merely a matter of knowledge, and thus their ethical system was the result of instruction in the ancestral traditions. As their religion was largely that of ancestor worship, so their education began with training the child in the path of duty, in all the minutely prescribed details of life's occupations and relationships—details which had not varied for centuries and therefore had the ancestral approval of many generations. Because anciently Chinese education was designed for the maintenance of that which exists, without change or modification, it became the function of education to train the leaders in the knowledge of the classical learning—all the traditional rules governing the order of society and covering the proper relationships in life—and to train the masses in the proper modes of conduct with respect to every interest and every activity throughout their entire lives.

From a civic standpoint, the continuity of the empire was assured by placing the official duties of government only in the hands of those who had best mastered the traditions of the past as found in the sacred books. The evaluation of such knowledge was not to be left to chance but was systematically determined through the governmental program. Thus the leaders were to be trained in the ancient knowledge of the approved order of society, and the masses were to be trained so as to conduct themselves in accord with the requirements of duty.

Every motion and position of the body, in every detail of life, was prescribed in a complex system of rules. They had almost no religion beyond the veneration for their ancestors; their aim was to attain a well-ordered conduct rather than a strong, deep morality. The whole aim of education was to prepare the individual to fill a place in a fixed order of society.[5]

TYPES   The type of education outstandingly emphasized by the Chinese was moral training. We are using the term moral here in its derivative sense, for the word comes from the Latin *mores,* meaning manners, customs, conduct. Their education was essentially a training in customs, duties, and the regulations of conduct. Vocational training, domestic training, military training, civic training—all these types of training were provided, but in every case they were reduced fundamentally to the common basis of morality. Perhaps it would be better to use the term social training were it not for the fact that the term has been used with such diversity of meaning.

Practically no provision was made for physical training. The emphasis has always been placed upon the pursuits of peace rather than of war, and a sound mind has been reverenced above a sound body.

CONTENT   The basis of all the formal education of the Chinese—up to the new era initiated by ideological concepts produced through two World Wars—has been in the philosophy and teachings of CONFUCIUS, LAO-TZU, MENCIUS and others of their great philosophical figures. Of these Confucius probably was the most influential and after his death a system of thought and manners bearing his name developed. Confucianism is not a religion, in the truest sense of the word, for it does not offer a deity, a theological creed, or a ritualistic worship. It is a philosophy of social and civic ethics. Confucius was the founder of a system of utilitarian morality to be inculcated into the life of each individual through the authoritative sanctions of the family and the state. From his own time to World War I, the writings attributed to Confucius have been the principal subjects of study in all the schools of China. For the most part, these writings are devoted to an exposition of details of conduct having to do with every conceivable relationship and occasion of life. Chinese literature thus was the chief item used in testing.

The lowest examinations were held in each county, and those who successfully passed these preliminary examinations were awarded honors (*Hsiu Ts'ai*), somewhat similar to our Bachelor of Arts degree, and were elected to the ranks of nobility. Later on, these scholars could take another examination conducted in the various provinces. Upon successfully passing these tests, they were awarded a degree (*Chu-jen*), somewhat similar to our Master of Arts degree, and they rose still higher in the social scale. The final examinations, corresponding roughly to our modern doctorate examinations, lasted for thirteen days and were given in the capital. The successful candidate (whose attainment was called

---

[5] Mabel I. Emerson, *Evolution of the Educational Ideal.* (Boston: Houghton Mifflin Company, 1914.) P. 5. Reprinted with the permission of the publisher.

Chin-shih) had a right to public office at once and, if he conducted himself worthily, could rise to the great distinction of being a member of the imperial cabinet.

METHODS   Confucius himself was a master teacher. He attracted pupils from far and near and bound them to him with ties of loyalty and devotion. His methods resemble somewhat those employed by Socrates in Greece two centuries later. He walked "about from place to place accompanied by those who were absorbing his views." Evidently he wished his students to reason about his teachings. "Learning without thought is labor lost," he said, "and thought without learning is perilous." He also expected practical application of his teaching. "Although a man may be able to recite three hundred odes, if he know not how to act, of what use is his learning?"

Like all great teachers, Confucius respected his students. "A young student," he said, "may be worthy of veneration. Who knows but his knowledge may yet equal mine." He also adapted his teachings to the needs and capacities of the individual. When two pupils asked whether they should immediately put into practice something they had learned, he said to the one, "Ask the advice of your father and brother"; but to the other he said, "Act immediately." Asked why he gave such different answers, he said, "The first has more than his share of energy; therefore I kept him back. The second is retiring and slow; wherefore I urged him forward." And yet there are those who think that adjustment to individual differences is a modern method in teaching!

Another story is told of Confucius, who with his class was making a field trip. They came upon a woman weeping bitterly for her dead husband. When she explained that he had been slain by a tiger as had his father and grandfather before him, Confucius asked her reasons for remaining in such a perilous location. "In this state," she replied, "the laws are just."

The sage then spoke, "From this, you see, students, bad government is more to be feared than a tiger."

Modern educators who urge that children be taken out of the schoolroom and brought into contact with the actual conditions of life are really returning to the method of Confucius; for Confucius' teaching activity was not confined to a classroom. Another indication of his instinctive use of the principles of good teaching lies in the fact that he seems to have maintained close personal relations with his pupils. He never turned away a boy who really wished to learn; all he required was a studious and virtuous spirit.

But, as we shall see it happen again and again, the followers of Confucius soon departed from the example set by the master. Schools became formalized and meaningless. The development of reasoning was never an aim. The object of the teacher was to compel the child to remember, and thus learning became merely a laborious cramming of the memory. Direct and exact imitation was insisted upon; and discipline often was harsh. All the pupil's time was consumed in memorizing words, for he would be disgraced if he participated in labor or amusement.

The first years of a child's education were devoted to learning reading and writing of the Chinese language, a difficult process because of the intricacies of the characters used. The school was a loud school, as each child shouted the passages aloud until he had memorized them. Then he handed the book to the teacher, turned his back, and recited. He had to repeat the characters in exact order and at the highest possible speed. Writing was taught by the use of tracing paper, the characters being formed with a small brush. The children first traced the characters and then tried to reproduce them.

The sacred books were committed to memory. At the higher stages some attempts were made at interpretation, and essays were written, modeled after the sacred writings. In this essay writing, the method was that of conscious imitation. The more closely the form, the construction, and the thought paralleled the original, the more highly prized was the essay.

Such methods do not provide for symmetrical training of the mind. Their use may develop mastery of detail, retentive powers, and ability to imitate but it will not develop initiative, inventiveness, adaptability, or creative functioning.

ATTITUDES OF THE HINDUS TOWARD EDUCATION

The peninsula of India was settled about four thousand years ago by a branch of the Aryan race, a proto-Nordic people of the same stock from which modern Europeans arose. The climate, then as now, was enervating and prevented the development of the physical energy essential for strenuous activity. Fortunately, the rich and fertile valleys made it possible to get a living without much labor; but they attracted other peoples, and this in time made necessary a powerful soldier class to defend the country against aggression. The soldiers were not the dominant class, however, being under control of the priests.

The torrid climate and the natural inactivity of the people conditioned a mystical, other-worldly philosophy. Population increased, and with it the prevalence of suffering from disease, of misery from poverty. These burdens and the vicissitudes of life beyond human control tended to develop a religion of fatalism and mysticism. The prevailing religion of India has always been Brahmanism. It teaches that the world is an illusion; that Brahma, the world spirit, the all-pervading spiritual presence, is the only real entity; that the end of life is the loss of individual personality and absorption into Brahma. Since Brahma was conceived to be present in everything, the masses came to practice a form of polytheism, in which various objects of nature were worshiped as particles thrown off from Brahma. Among the upper classes, religion was a philosophy of mysticism; among the lower classes, it was superstition.

Very early the Hindu populace became assorted into its four main classes, each of which has been subdivided at times into other minor divisions. At the top of the social ladder were the Brahmans, the priests and teachers and intellectual rulers; next below were the Kashatriyas, the soldiers and rulers of war; below these were the Vaisyas, the artisans, merchants, and moneylenders; and at the bottom, the Sudras, the menials and serfs. In addition to these recognized social classes, there was a great mass of submerged and helpless outcasts, or untouchables, the Pariahs. Accident of birth determined an individual's caste, and thus his life and educational opportunities.

Nowhere else in the world has there developed as rigid a caste system as that in India. This complicated system of social differentiation prohibited members of one group from eating, sleeping, or intermarrying with a member of another group. Any Hindu disobeying one of the numerous and complex rules relating to caste might lose his position in the society. No one was allowed to rise above his caste although it was possible to sink to a lower level or to become an outcast. (The most severe feature of this system, untouchability, is now outlawed by the Republic of India government but old habits are difficult to change.)

AIMS   Hindu education has been dominated by these religious beliefs and this caste system. The two aims of its teaching have been: (1) to prepare for the life to come rather than for the activities of this life—to prepare for absorption into the infinite and universal spirit; and (2) to preserve the caste system.

The educational system, therefore, has been concerned with developing emotional attitudes rather than stimulating the acquisition of knowledge. The ultimate goal was the attainment of nirvana, a blissful state of perfection to be attained through worthiness as exemplified in self-control. The priestly class alone needed intellectual education; and what they most needed was to be able to recite the ancient national religious hymns, intone the sacred prayers, and perform the established sacraments. The Brahmans, as the official representatives of religion, had evolved an elaborate system of rites, in which each priest had to be trained. The other castes, believing that these rites were so potent that the gods were practically at the beck and call of the priests, were utterly dependent upon the Brahmans for salvation. Only by the priestly rites could they have any hope for happiness in this world or in the hereafter.

The Brahmans, through their teachings, did all in their power to preserve the special privileges and class prerogatives which accrued to them through the caste system. As the highest caste—benefiting most and enjoying the greatest prestige—they were the sustaining influence of the system. They allowed each individual the training needed in the religious observances suitable for his caste and, through his own efforts or that of his family, the specialized vocational training needed for playing his part in life, the artisan in his craft, the farmer in his field, the merchant in his business.

TYPES   The education of the Hindu is predominantly religious—we use the word in its broader sense. Their education is moral in the same sense as that of the Chinese: it imparts the customs and traditional modes of conduct that fit one for his proper place in life. It is largely ethical and ascetic in its emphasis upon self-discipline.

Intellectual education, which, until recently, was confined to the highest classes and forbidden to at least 95 percent of the people, was purely theoretical, limited to the knowledge of ancient tradition and lacking in practical applications to the betterment of living conditions or the scientific advancement of the race. There was no intellectual education for the lower classes or for women. Women were supposed only to minister to men and to bear children.

As in China, no provision was made for physical education or health training. Vocational training, domestic training, and military training were all to be acquired by the primitive methods of imitation and practice.

CONTENT   The chief content of Brahman education has been instruction in the body of sacred literature, written in Sanskrit, the language of learning. The Brahmans studied the Vedas, the *Rig Veda,* the *Sama Veda,* the *Yajur Veda,* the *Atharva Veda,* collections of ancient religious knowledge; the Angas, books of scientific and philosophical knowledge; and the *Code of Manu,* a book of ethics and traditional customs. In the Brahman parishads, or training colleges, the course of study has included such knowledge as we now designate by the terms history, grammar, poetry, law, mathematics, astronomy, and medicine.

The ancient Hindus gave much attention to speculative and mathematical science. Our numerical notation in arithmetic, including the symbol zero, originated in India. During the fifth century before Christ, the Hindus devised an algebra that was superior to that used by the Greeks. They had some knowledge of medicine, and they built up a science of grammar and rhetoric.

The Hindus have never emphasized the active virtues of ambition, self-reliance, and personal responsibility. Rather they have cultivated the passive virtues of patience, resignation, peaceableness, gentleness, and docility. They have been taught to be polite, respectful to their parents and elders, and obedient to authority.

AGENCIES AND ORGANIZATION   Education for the most part was received through the medium of the family in the home. There were some elementary schools but, like all Oriental schools, they were very simple. The boy started to school at about the age of seven. His teacher was a Brahman who was paid for his services by voluntary gifts, since it was deemed a disgrace to accept a salary. The teacher was highly respected, however, often receiving more reverence than the parents. Schools were often held in the open air under a tree.

Higher education was represented by the parishads, in which the Brahmans were educated, the course of study usually requiring twelve years for completion. At first only the Brahman class was admitted to the parishads, but later members of the soldier and merchant classes were sometimes admitted.

METHODS   Memorizing and imitation were the chief methods of learning. The sacred books were written in a rhythmic, metrical form so that they might be readily memorized. The lines were shouted by the pupils until they were memorized without a single error. Writing was learned by imitation of the teacher, the pupil first writing in the sand and then on palm leaves.[6] We quote here a description of their oral method of teaching:

"The teacher must himself have passed through the recognized curriculum, and have fulfilled all the duties of the Brahman student, before he is allowed to become a teacher, and he must teach such students only as submit to all the rules of studentship. He should settle down in a proper place. If he has only one pupil or two, they must sit on his right side; if more, they must sit as there is room for them. At the beginning of each lesson the pupils embrace the feet of their teacher and say 'Read, Sir.' The teacher then proceeds to pronounce words which the pupils repeat after him until the words are learned. In this manner they go on until they have finished a prasna (three verses of about forty syllables). After the prasna is finished, they have all to repeat it once more, and then go on learning it by heart, pronouncing every syllable with high accent."[7]

The practical result of this venerable system of mnemonic learning is to be recognized in the carefully preserved purity and integrity of the Sanskrit language. The texts of the Vedas have been handed down to us with such accuracy that there is hardly a variable reading or even an uncertain accent in the whole of them.

Discipline was mild. "Good instruction," says the *Code of Manu,* "must be imparted to the pupil in an agreeable manner, and a teacher must use sweet, gentle words."

Lest Western students imagine that the schools described were ineffectual in their preparation for life, it may be said that their concern was with the values of the Hindu culture rather than with training of any vocational or professional kind. Hindu life was but a reflection of these values; if the Hindu personality and that of a member of a Western civilization differ—as of course they do—this does not mean that

---

6 This probably is the origin of our expression "leaves of a book."
7 Sonnenschein, "Schools of Antiquity," *Cyclopedia of Education.* P. 382.

the more mechanistic culture of the West can sit in judgment on that of the East; indeed, when judged by the standards of the Hindu culture, Western life is clearly shown to be both worldly and materialistic.

ATTITUDES OF THE PERSIANS TOWARD EDUCATION

The Persians were the branch of the Aryan race which migrated westward and settled on the high tablelands south of the Caspian Sea originally, as presently, known as Iran but once called Persia. Here they found a bracing climate and a relatively barren country, and so the essentially aggressive characteristics of the Aryan race were not lost as they were in India. As population increased they preyed upon their various neighbors, especially those to the west; and thus a strong motive for conquest and a world empire arose. Stern conditions produced a warlike people who absorbed surrounding territories and built up a great civilization. Because of these national ambitions, the warrior class, rather than the priestly class, came to be of supreme importance among them.

Since Persian life was a struggle, from both the economic and the military standpoint, it is natural that its religion and philosophy should be militant and proselyting in character. ZOROASTER (c. 500 B.C.),[8] their great religious leader, was ever a fighter; and after his death his soul went marching on in militant Zoroastrianism which, like the fire which was its sacred symbol, spread with incredible rapidity. Vast armies, inspired by his religion, made the empire of the Medes and Persians one of the greatest the world has known. The teachings of Zoroaster became the law of the Medes and Persians; and, just a century after Zoroaster's death, a Persian king was thundering at the gates of Athens. From India to Greece the faith of the prophet of Iran was the religion of the East.

At first glance Zoroastrianism appears to be dualistic. It was the first religion to give us a personal devil as well as a personal god; it gave us the concepts of heaven and hell and the last judgment, which have played such a tremendous part in the history of religion. Evils and virtues were personified into demons of evil and archangels of light; a synthesis was made of life's problems, both practical and theoretical. But the thing that saved Zoroaster from dualism and kept him essentially monotheistic was his sublime faith that Ahriman and his dark hosts of evil would finally be overcome by the righteous Ahura Mazda and his legions of light. The final triumph of good over evil would come eventually; meanwhile, the struggle must be carried on in individual lives as well as on a cosmic plane. "He who does not fight for me is against me"

---

[8] The Persian name is Zarathustra, familiar to us in Nietzsche's *Thus Spake Zarathustra.*

was Zoroaster's characterization of the role Ahura Mazda assigned to man in this great conflict. This concept placed a strong moral element in Persian philosophy and was a dominant influence in Persian education.

AIMS   Persian education aimed at the strength rather than the refinement of culture. The predominant aims of its teaching were practical rather than literary or scholastic. The Persians wished to produce no great body of science or literature; they wished to produce a nation of soldiers, physically fit and brave, with all the virtues implied in the term "a good soldier." Their education was military rather than priestly in its fundamental purposes. It aimed at fixing and spreading national ideals; it was a matter of building national life. The virtues to be inculcated were much like those stressed by the Protestant Puritans or the Catholic Jesuits, and the religious motives used for the purpose were also much the same.

The emphasis upon the preservation of caste as a function of education is not found here as in India. With the exception of the hereditary royalty and the hereditary priesthood, class distinctions were in terms of wealth rather than of birth. Individual freedom was exercised to a degree not found in other Oriental countries. Through contacts with other peoples and the growth of the empire there developed a favorable attitude toward change.

Unlike the Eastern cultures previously described, material wealth assumed a greater importance in Persia. The ultimate goal of the Persian was the acquisition of property and empire and his feeling of success was equated with this. Perhaps that is why his civilization was short-lived in comparison with that of India and China. Persian culture was based too completely on the gaining of material possessions, and when these were taken away it seemed that life had lost much of its meaning. If the Hindu lost his possessions he still had his mystic goals; if the Chinese lost his possessions there still remained the unchanging traditions of his family and the Chinese society; but when the Persian was stripped of his possessions he felt that all was lost.

Persia, which might have proved the first type of Aryan progress, was forced to hand the torch to the Athenian Greeks.[9]

TYPES   As a result of these materialistic and nationalistic ideals, military training and physical training were the all-important types of education. These were made compulsory for every boy, especially of the aristocratic classes. There was a systematic religious education for the Magi, as the priests were called. Moral training in the modern sense of character building was accentuated through the authority of their religious beliefs. Every child was taught the virtues of the good life essential to salvation in the final judgment.

---

[9] F. P. Graves, *Education Before the Middle Ages*. (New York: The Macmillan Co., 1909.) P. 102. Reprinted with the permission of the publisher.

Vocational training for the work activities of life was provided for the boys of the lower classes, and domestic training was given to the girls in their household duties. Women were subordinated as in most Oriental countries and excluded from all formal education. One type of education that was sorely neglected was that of avocational training; the Persian became impatient in time of peace.

CONTENT   The most important items in the Persian curriculum were physical exercises and athletic sports to develop endurance, self-denial, and self-control. Running, slinging stones, shooting with the bow, throwing the javelin—all were practiced zealously. The boy was taught to ride and hunt, to swim, to bear extremes of cold and hunger, to make long marches, to sleep in the open air, to be content with simple meals, to forage from the country as he passed through. All this was to prepare for the qualities and skills needed in war.

Next in importance were the moral qualities to be developed. Truthfulness, justice, gratitude, courage, piety, honesty, purity, and industry were developed through the teachings of Zoroastrianism, as found in its sacred literature. These writings constituted the *Zend-Avesta,* the Bible of the Parsees, consisting of the *Vendidad,* a collection of laws and tales, the *Visperad,* a litany of rituals, and the *Yasna,* a collection of hymns. The boys were given religious ideas and some moral knowledge through the medium of these writings.

The Magi had their own system of education which, in addition to the mastery of the *Zend-Avesta,* included training in astrology, divinations, medicine, and law. The Magi were the wise men of the realm and were often consulted by the kings and nobles in regard to important undertakings.

AGENCIES   The family was the chief school for all classes. Until the age of seven, the boy was trained at home by the women, unseen by his father. The girl's only education was the domestic training of the home. Even after the age of seven the boy received much of his religious and moral education in the family. Military training was provided by the state—the first example we have of state control of education for the greatness and glory of the state. There was a high degree of cooperation between the home and the state. Authorities have agreed that the Persians took great pride in educating their sons well, at least to the extent of making them virtuous men and good soldiers.

ORGANIZATION   The Persians did not develop any specific educational institution. The boy's physical and military instruction was usually given at the courts of the nobility under the direction of the ruling class. After the boy was taken from his mother's care at the age of seven, he was regarded as belonging to the state and entered on a long period of public training. Until the age of fifteen, he was given physical training and taught practical military virtues and obedience by the older men. After fifteen, he saw actual service in the field, performing the duties involved in armed guardianship of the state. When he reached maturity at the age of twenty, he assumed the privileges of a full-grown man and was eligible for foreign service and public office.

METHODS The methods used in training were largely those of observation, imitation, and participation. Activity rather than reflection was always emphasized. The boy acquired physical and military skill and the desirable moral virtues by imitating his elders. Among the lower classes apprenticeship was used for teaching the practical vocational activities. Example rather than precept was emphasized.

Reading and writing—if taught at all—were taught in limited measure. It seems to have been no part of the essential training of the Persian youth that he should learn to read. He was given religious and moral notions by means of the legendary poems in which the deeds of gods and heroes were celebrated. These tales his teachers recited or sang in his presence and afterwards required him to repeat what he had heard or, at any rate, to give some account of it. This, in a way, was merely another type of learning by example.

ATTITUDES OF THE EGYPTIANS TOWARD EDUCATION

Egypt was settled by a Hamitic people who, according to some archaeologists, inhabited the valley of the Nile as early as 18,000 B.C. Their recorded civilization is one of the oldest and reaches back to the fifth millennium before Christ.

The land of Egypt is—in the happy phrase of Herodotus, the Greek historian—the "gift of the Nile." Situated partly within the Torrid Zone the entire area possesses an exotic climate, which partially accounts for its civilization. This, too, is chiefly dependent upon the activity of the Nile and its peculiar shaping force on the life and customs of the people. Overflowing periodically and regularly at approximately June 20 of each year, the receding waters leave an alluvial deposit which is of great assistance in agriculture. The necessity for irrigation during the growing periods helped the development of engineering; the science of prediction and the creation of a calendar may likewise be attributed to the behavior of the Nile. A system of government became necessary as the increasing population and the complexity of group living demanded much more than the simple community life which at first obtained.

The earliest groupings of population, known as nomes, were sufficient for governmental control; later these were combined into larger units and strong monarchies developed both in the north at Memphis and in the south at Thebes. In 3400 B.C. these areas were united under MENES; to the period of the Roman Empire Egypt then was ruled by a series of dynasties—usually indigenous—of Pharaoh-kings whose power was absolute. Since the country was virtually surrounded by desert, invasions were fewer than in other countries; the Mediterranean and the Nile itself offered means of communication and trade; camel trains brought products overland from the Near and Middle East. The result produced a highly developed civilization, in many respects as fully evolved as that of the contemporary age (without, of course, the machine culture and inventions of modern times).

The nature of this civilization was such that both a well-organized priesthood and a strong military group flourished. Although the area under control was extensive—somewhat larger than Texas—the agencies of government were not as highly organized as in many other imperial states. The personal rule of the Pharaoh, his presumed divinity, and the existence of a large corps of officials accountable to him alone for the creation of public works, the collection of taxes, and the general preservation of law and order produced a government in which there was not the slightest tinge of democracy.

Correlative to the government (and a support to it) was the Egyptian religion. Again—conditioned by the unique situation—the gods bore attributes quite relative to their geographical setting and the developing conceptions of morality of the Egyptians. Although there were indeed many gods—even those of primitive and savage origins—Re, Ra, or Amon-Ra was the chief; he was a personification or deification of the sun, or of its influence on fruition in Egypt. His insignia, the winged sun-disk, is a familiar item in Western culture; Osiris and Isis represented symbolically the Nile itself and the land of Egypt—thus the male and female principles; their son Horus was the god of day and usually was represented as hawk-headed. Osiris' evil brother Set appears to be a prototype of the Judaeo-Christian Satan. His domain was the desert; he also waged war against Osiris the good. Thoth was the god of wisdom and magic—the scribe; it is said of him that he wrote 20,000 volumes of scientific lore and thus fostered the development of science and the arts in Egypt.

Osiris was the judge of the dead. Fanciful and elaborate ritual and custom surrounded the funerary rites of Egypt. Since the Egyptians had confidence in an afterlife and the existence of the *Ka* (soul), death represented for them merely an opportunity of preparation for the future. The body was carefully embalmed and generally laid to rest in a more or less elaborate tomb (depending on the circumstances of the deceased). All manner of pictures, books, and objects (sometimes including the bodies of dead slaves) likewise accompanied the remains to the tomb. These, they thought, would be of service in the afterlife.

After death the deceased's soul or double made its way to the great judgment hall of Osiris. Here certain religious texts were recited and the *Ka* was weighed in the balance, the opposite mass being a feather—the symbol of truth. If the scales did not balance the favor of a blissful afterlife in the presence of the good Osiris was denied.

While the beauty and symbolism of this religion is apparent, it actually affected only the higher levels of society; on the lower the worship remained a superstition frequently involving degraded practices. The existence of a priesthood was a necessary concomitant to Egyptian religion and the hierarchy learned to wield power as well. Preoccupation of the Egyptians with the afterlife is revealed by the extensive remains of temples to the gods, the pyramids (which, of course, were the tombs of Pharaohs), and the immense series of crypts cut into rock ledges bordering the upper Nile. Because of the unique climate much more of Egyptian antiquity has been preserved than can usually be the case; both the land itself and the leading museums of the world contain vast deposits of Egyptology.

Religious texts were a necessity and these generally—as well as the business of education—were in the hands of the priests. The texts included the moral content suggested above as well as practical suggestions for behavior in this life; that the religious belief and practices buttressed the power of the state and the rule of the Pharaoh (himself thought to be a descendant of Amon-Ra) is obvious. Education thus became a means for the preservation of social stability and the preservation of the *status quo*.

AIMS   Egyptian education truly represented the foundations of the state. In this it was both moral and practical. It aimed primarily at inculcating the proper respect for the gods, including the Pharaoh; secondly, the development of the Egyptian civilization entailed the creation of artistic and practical forms of expression together with the recognition of commerce and trade. Writing and account-keeping were indispensable; the training of a large group of scribes for the transaction of official business likewise was an important goal. Many accounts have been left which suggest the respect with which Egyptians viewed writing and communication.

Scriveners were in great demand; to be a scribe was considered a responsible position: writers held preferred status in the Egyptian community. A father is found advising his son to become a scribe, pointing out the advantages of this profession over all others!

The mystical and magic secrets of the priesthood were imparted to neophytes in the Temple Colleges; this too insured the preservation and perpetuation of Egyptian society as well as the priesthood. Religious truth was a necessity for the Egyptian. If Egyptian society was not moral it certainly was well bound by moral rules and regulations. The "Negative Confession before Osiris" cited many more than ten faults that had been avoided by the supplicant!

Since several systems of writing were in vogue all had to be learned in order to communicate properly; foreign tongues and writing symbols had to be assimilated since Egypt played an extensive role in commerce. Systems of account-keeping and all sorts of vocational and professional preparation were mandated. In Egypt the rewards of learning were great.

Thus the aims of education were both cultural and utilitarian. In keeping with all educational systems it strove to perpetuate the culture but in Egypt, as in Confucian China, education was intolerant of change. It shunned innovation.

TYPES   Many types of education were in existence. Religious training and the vocational-professional predominated. There also were military schools for the sons of the nobility as well as apprenticeship for the children of the poor. Always there was training in the home. The important religious doctrines were firmly inculcated and probably no country has been more successful in institutionalizing the forms of living. Spengler considered the "Egyptian" a special culture type because of the thoroughness of its integration and the rigidity of its pattern.

Training for public administration was a necessity since the government was no more than the lengthened shadow of Pharaoh. The handing down of the wonderful achievements in engineering and architecture was another must as was the perpetuation of the artistic skill that embellished the temples and other public works.

The education of women was largely vocational although the daughters of the aristocratic class underwent a thorough tutoring. The position of women in Egypt was unique (females could inherit the throne as did Hatshepsut and Cleopatra) and placed the sex on a higher level than did any other oriental empire. Even women of the poorer classes had their family association and apprenticeship, sometimes in the royal household, to provide them with experience and a greater knowledge.

CONTENT   The content of Egyptian education was classical and vocational. Reading and writing were stressed as was the language of commerce. The literature—both religious and secular—was studied. In the professional and vocational sphere the content was particularly rich. Egypt's superiority here was traced to the beneficence of the great god THOTH, deity of wisdom. He was reported to have written thousands of volumes of scientific and mathematical lore. (Yet one does not need to attribute Egypt's splendid progress in the practical arts to the supernatural; the results of their labors show immense talent.)

The duties of the apprentice were ordained by time. Egypt's history was a long one and much development had already accrued in preliterate days. The semiskilled and skilled artisan in metals and lapidary had trade secrets of the highest quality to pass on. Thus there were vocational matters of all kinds to be perpetuated as well as the more formal content of the culture.

The literature is especially interesting for many Egyptian schoolbooks have been recovered. Aphorisms, proverbs, moral judgments, and the like, comprised the fare of an Egyptian boy's copybooks. Abridgements of religious texts appeared and admonitions of the seers were included. Such an influential one was "Old Seer," Птанноteр (2883–2855 b.c.). His advice and observations strike a parallel with those of Shakespeare's Polonius, although here one series is history, the other fiction. Popular accounts such as the story of an Egyptian "Sinbad the Sailor" were included and songs and ballads were likewise the diet of schoolboys on the Nile.

Mathematical subjects also had their place since the annual recovery of the land from the floodwaters of the Nile presented problems to be handled through mensuration and surveying. Geometry was a prominent subject. As mentioned above, architecture and engineering were predominant in technical education and astronomy brought aid both to religion and science. Medicine, including dentistry, flourished. Sports and physical education assumed an important role; hunting and fishing both on the vocational and avocational levels obtained. The Egyptians were much concerned with health practices and made a great deal of bathing and internal cleanliness. In the temples members of the priesthood shaved their bodies daily.

The skill and knowledge necessary for the remarkable achievements of the Egyptians could not have been devised with each generation but represents an accumulation of thousands of years of experience and practical ingenuity. These achievements were transmitted through education.

AGENCIES   The home began the education of the Egyptian child. Family duties as well as important precepts in the religious and moral world were impressed on young minds. Little boys played with toy crocodiles and girls with dolls. At the age of five the boy attended (if his parents were able to pay the fees charged) reading and writing schools organized—and sometimes taught—by the priests. Many of these schools were located in or near the temples and when lay teachers were utilized the program was under the general supervision of the priesthood.

The importance of reading and writing in Egyptian society cannot be overemphasized. As indicated above, various types of writing were utilized for different levels of thought or communication; the position of scribe was very important in Egypt and royal scribes commanded great prestige and even power.

Apprenticeship was a frequent device for the semiskilled (and sometimes the skilled) professions. Military schools for the sons of the elite offered opportunity for practical instruction in the arts of war and perpetuated an officer class. A School of Government attached to the royal treasury trained graduates of the reading and writing schools for public administration. Commerce and industry demanded specialized education for foreign trade and account-keeping. The foreign languages, including the Babylonian language and its calligraphy, cuneiform, were studied as were the various types of mathematics. Secular teachers as well as priests were utilized but education may be said to have been under the control of religion. This was an essential part of the Egyptian culture pattern.

Vocational schools (not far removed from apprenticeship) existed for the perpetuation of the simpler arts and crafts. Professional schools produced the proficiency needed in engineering, architecture, and medicine. Law was not a separate profession in Egypt; the legalities were handled by Pharaoh's corps of public officials and law—so closely connected with religion—was, in part, a function of the priesthood. Astronomy, likewise, was largely their province. Probably the highest level of instruction in Egypt was the work of the Temple College where, after ten or twelve years of basic preparation in reading, writing, and the literature of Egypt, young men were admitted to study for the priesthood and were instructed in the sciences and mysteries known only to them. Much of this was esoteric and forbidden to the laity and included the intense formalism of the religion and the ritual for the dead.

ORGANIZATION   The home was the first school. Since women held an unusually high position in Egypt the instruction and guidance by the mother was considered important. Apprenticeship at an early age was the route taken by the poorer classes; a boy's might be under his father as a continuation of home training or with a worker in metals, stone, or lapidary.

The reading and writing school began at age five. "High schools" dealt with the professions, public service, or commerce. Military schools instructed for war. But the most significant school for the perpetuation of the Egyptian culture was the Temple "College." Here, at approximately age seventeen, youths entered the priesthood. Vocational schools of various types flourished—although these were not too far removed from the system of apprenticeship.

The entire organization (although the various agencies described should not be thought of as comprising an articulated system in the modern manner) was controlled either directly or indirectly by the priesthood, since Egypt was, in the final analysis, a theocracy—Pharaoh himself being considered a deity.

METHODS   The methods used in the Egyptian schools would have been quite familiar to European students in the Middle Ages. Dictation, memorization, and the copying of texts were the chief devices. Imitation and repetition of stories, myths, and legends firmly fixed the history of the country along with the appropriate moral precepts from religion.[10] Observation and participation occurred in certain

---

[10] See James Henry Breasted, *The Conquest of Civilization*. (New York: Harper and Brothers, 1926), pp. 85-89, for examples of Egyptian scrolls used in the schools of over 4000 years ago; Will Durant, *Our Oriental Heritage*. (New York: Simon & Schuster, Inc., 1935), pp. 170-179, describes Egyptian literature and the schools.

areas, especially physical education. These activities served a double purpose—the strengthening of the body and preparation for war. To the Egyptian bodily hygiene was of the utmost importance; rules and rites concerning sanitary measures were learned and practiced.

On the vocational level practice was the method. Internship as well as theory prepared for public administration and military students participated in war games which simulated actual conditions.

Among the Egyptians the inculcation of religious doctrines and precepts was of the utmost importance. Such learnings—as well as those of a secular nature—were subject to memorization. Failure to learn usually was penalized by flogging. A well-known story relates an Egyptian boy's appreciation to his teacher for what he considered to have been his opportunity for character development, "Thou didst beat my back and I didst learn."

FOR FURTHER READING

Barnes, Harry Elmer, *An Intellectual and Cultural History of the Western World*. New York: Random House, 1937. Pp. 63-112.

Breasted, James Henry, *The Conquest of Civilization*. New York: Harper and Brothers, 1926. Pp. 43-110, 187-211.

Browne, Lewis, *This Believing World*. New York: The Macmillan Co., 1926. Pp. 75-89, 119-165, 169-196, 199-219.

Butts, R. Freeman, *A Cultural History of Western Education*. Second Edition. New York: McGraw-Hill Book Co., 1955. Pp. 6-18.

Davidson, Thomas, *A History of Education*. New York: Charles Scribner's Sons, 1900. Pp. 24-74.

Dawson, Christopher, *The Age of the Gods*. London and New York: Sheed and Ward, 1933. Pp. 141-165, 287-308.

————, *The Dynamics of World History*. New York: Sheed and Ward, 1957. Pp. 111-147.

Durant, Will. *Our Oriental Heritage*, Part I, *The Story of Civilization*. New York: Simon & Schuster, Inc., 1935. Pp. 112-823.

Eby, Frederick, and Arrowood, Charles F., *The History and Philosophy of Education Ancient and Medieval*. New York: Prentice-Hall, Inc., 1940. Pp. 36-107.

Emerson, Mabel I., *Evolution of the Educational Ideal*. Boston: Houghton Mifflin Company, 1914. Pp. 5-14.

Good, H. G., *A History of Western Education*. Second Edition. New York: The Macmillan Co., 1960. Pp. 6-17.

Goodrich, L. Carrington, *A Short History of the Chinese People*. New York: Harper and Brothers, 1943. Pp. 49, 116, 131, 150, 174, 194, 212, 214.

Graves, Frank P., *Education Before the Middle Ages*. New York: The Macmillan Co., 1909. Pp. 55-102.

Huntington, Ellsworth, *Mainsprings of Civilization*. New York: John Wiley & Sons, Inc., 1945.

Knight, Edgar W. *Twenty Centuries of Education*. Boston: Ginn & Co., 1940. Pp. 33-40.

Latourette, Kenneth Scott, *A Short History of the Far East*. Third Edition. New York: The Macmillan Co., 1957. Pp. 37-77, 78-189.

Lin Yutang, *The Wisdom of India and China*. New York: Random House, 1942.

Mayer, Frederick, *A History of Educational Thought*. Columbus, Ohio: Charles E. Merrill Books, Inc., 1960. Pp. 28-73.

Messenger, James F., *An Interpretative History of Education*. New York: Thomas Y. Crowell Co., 1931. Pp. 17-28.

Monroe, Paul, *A Textbook in the History of Education*. New York: The Macmillan Co., 1933. Pp. 17-49.

Mulhern, James, *A History of Education*. Second Edition. New York: The Ronald Press Co., 1959. Pp. 55-128.

Painter, Franklin, *A History of Education*. New York: Appleton-Century-Crofts, Inc., 1904. Pp. 11-27.

Smith, William A., *Ancient Education*. New York: Philosophical Library, Inc., 1955. Pp. 3-49, 50-68, 69-87.

Toynbee, Arnold J., *A Study of History* (One Volume Edition by D. C. Somervell.) New York and London: Oxford University Press, 1946. Pp. 12-47.

Ulich, Robert, *Three Thousand Years of Educational Wisdom*. Cambridge, Mass.: Harvard University Press, 1954. Pp. 3-13, 14-28.

Woody, Thomas, *Life and Education in Early Societies*. New York: The Macmillan Co., 1949. Pp. 47-194.

QUESTIONS FOR CLASS DISCUSSION

1. Suggest modern instances of the effect of geographical location and climate upon the educational attitudes and practices of peoples.

2. What present-day social conditions in India and China are due to their traditional attitudes and educational practices?

3. In what ways have the educational attitudes and aims of ancient Persia influenced the practices of certain contemporary nations?

4. Mention several ways in which Egyptian religious practices affected their schools.

5. How has the recent history of the Near East proved that static con-

ditions in Oriental cultures have been a consequence of educational practice rather than race?

6. To what extent have class discriminations been eliminated from contemporary educational systems?

7. Compare the attitudes of Oriental peoples of the past with those of today in regard to manual labor and vocational training.

8. To what extent has the method of memorization which formerly prevailed in all Oriental education been supplanted by other methods of teaching?

9. What classics in English literature and philosophy have had influences in our education similar to that of the sacred writings of China, India, Egypt, and Persia?

10. In what manner does the writing of compositions and themes in high school and college differ from the essay writing of early Chinese education?

CHAPTER III

MORAL TRAINING FOR NATIONAL IDEALS

THE HEBRAIC CONCEPT OF EDUCATION

The development of the Hebrew nation marks a transition between Oriental and Occidental attitudes toward education. This unique people developed ideals that were quite different from those of all other Eastern peoples. Western civilization has received from them many contributions to its religious and social thinking which have profoundly influenced its educational theories and practices. We are directly indebted to the Hebrews for (1) the basis of our monotheistic religious conception—the one and only God, (2) the basis of our system of ethics—the Ten Commandments, and (3) the basis of much of our literature—the Bible. Thus Hebrew education forms one of the most important foundations of modern educational theory.

Four thousand years ago a group of wandering Semitic tribesmen, living off their flocks and herds driven from oasis to oasis in the Arabian Desert, made their appearance in history. Their minds were filled with fear, for their religion was still that of primitive animism; their lives were full of hardship, for the desert was a cruel and bitter place of abode. To the north was a land of which they had often heard—the Fertile Crescent, stretching from the Mediterranean coasts on the west, to the Persian Gulf on the east, and envisaged as an Eden, a Paradise, a Promised Land, by these wanderers of the desert. Again and again the nomad tribes tried to break into these fertile territories. Sometimes they gained a precarious foothold, only to be driven out. Perhaps at a very early period they dwelt for a while in the far eastern tip of the crescent.[1] Later, under a tribal chieftain named Abraham, they tried their fortunes in Canaan and still later, under Jacob and Joseph, in Egypt at the extreme western tip. Escaping from a condition of slavery in Egypt, they wandered for many years in the desert wilderness under the leadership of Moses, until finally they were able to enter again into Canaan.

Here at last they were able to stay, and to build a great nation and a great culture which reached its golden age under David and Solomon. Dissension, however, ultimately divided the kingdom and weakened it to such an extent that Israel, the northern part, was conquered by the Assyrians,[2] and Judea, the southern part, by the Babylonians. As a result of these conquests, most of the Hebrews were carried off into captivity. The remnant, repatriated by Cyrus the Great after the Persian defeat of Nebuchadnezzar, the Babylonian king, continued largely under the political domination of stronger nations until the final destruction of Jerusalem and the Temple by the Roman Titus. This, in brief, is the story of this unusual people and indicates the three great crises in their history: (1) the Exodus from Egypt (c. 1250 B.C.); (2) the Exile to Babylon (586 B.C.); (3) the Destruction by Titus (70 A.D.).

The unique character of the Hebrews began to develop at the time of the Exodus. Before that, their social customs, their religious ideas, and their educational practices differed little from those of other Eastern peoples. MOSES (c. 1250 B.C.), however, was not only the Great Deliverer of his people from bondage but was also their Lawgiver. We recognize him as another of the great thinkers and reformers of antiquity. At first under his influence, and later under the influence of the prophets, who thundered their forceful messages before and during the Captivity, the Hebrews developed the national, religious, and social ideals upon which their educational conceptions were based.

The cultural history of the Jewish people extends for more than thirty-five hundred years. They have experienced the joys of prosperity and the pains of adversity; but whatever the character of their outward circumstances, whether exercising a wide dominion from the splendid capital at Jerusalem or wandering among all nations, they have clung with the utmost tenacity to their national feeling and to their national ideals and customs.

This cultural and civic consciousness, which has given to this people a unity of customs and aspirations such as no other people possesses, has been built upon the foundation of three outstanding concepts: (1) the concept of an omnipotent, righteous creator God who has selected the Hebrews as his chosen people upon earth; (2) the concept of a Mes-

---

[1] This may have been the origin of the story of the Garden of Eden.
[2] The ten "lost" tribes of Israel were completely dispersed and never returned to Palestine.

siah to restore them to this exceptional position which, through faithlessness, they have lost; (3) the concept of holiness on their part as a condition of this restoration. This holiness or righteousness they believed could be attained only through continuous educational emphasis. Thus, education has been the prime force in their cultural existence.

The greatest lesson to be drawn from the history of this people is that a strict adherence to an educational system based on a peculiarly high religious and moral ideal has preserved their unity in a way that no political system could approximate. The salvation of this people, at least, has been due to its education.

One lesson, above all, Jewish education has to teach us, that the most important element in all education is moral discipline. The Greek with his art and his philosophy, and the Roman with his law and his statesmanship, have vanished from the face of the earth; but the Jew, with his moral discipline, his Torah and his Talmud, is still with us, as strong and ready for life's struggle as ever.[3]

ATTITUDES OF THE HEBREWS TOWARD EDUCATION

AIMS   The educational aims of the Hebrews mark a distinct advance upon those of the other Eastern nations we have been discussing. Though the individual is still subject to an external authority, it is no longer that of ancestor, of caste, of the state, but the authority of Jehovah himself. It is perhaps this phase of their educational concept, more than anything else, that gives to the Hebrews their unique place in the educational history of antiquity.

Theocracy controls and dominates as well as motivates both the theory and the practice of their education. The end of education from the time of Moses has been to make faithful and obedient servants to a personal and living God, and thereby to assure harmony and cooperation in civic life and a glorious future for this, God's chosen nation. The sense of national destiny was stronger in Palestine than in Persia or even in Rome. The aim of education was to prepare the people for this great destiny; it would prepare each succeeding generation to fulfill faithfully its part in the great work.

Did ever a people hear the voice of God speaking out of the midst of the fire, as thou hast heard, and live? Or hath God assayed to go and take him a nation from the midst of another nation, by trials, by signs, and by wonders, and by war, and by a mighty hand, and by a stretched out arm, and by great terrors, according to all that Jehovah your God did for you in Egypt before your eyes?

---

[3] Thomas Davidson, *A History of Education.* (New York: Charles Scribner's Sons, 1900.) P. 85.

Unto thee it was showed, that thou mightest know that Jehovah he is God; there is none else beside him. Out of heaven he made thee to hear his voice, that he might instruct thee; and upon earth he made thee to see his great fire; and thou heardest his words out of the midst of the fire. And because he loved thy fathers, therefore he chose their seed after them, and brought thee out with his presence, with his great power, out of Egypt; to drive out the nations from before thee greater and mightier than thou, to bring thee in, to give thee their lands for an inheritance, as at this day.

Know therefore this day, and lay it to thy heart, that Jehovah he is God in heaven above and upon the earth beneath; there is none else. And thou shalt keep his statutes, and his commandments, which I command thee this day, that it may go well with thee, and with thy children after thee, and that thou mayest prolong thy days upon the land, which Jehovah thy God giveth thee, forever.

—Deuteronomy 4: 33-40 [4]

The dominating feature of the whole educational system was this: the Jew was taught to make holiness before the Lord the aim of his daily life. Although education in Jewish principles began in childhood, the work did not end there. Throughout life a Hebrew was to consider his relationship to Jehovah his primary purpose.

Remember also thy Creator in the days of thy youth, before the evil days come, and the years draw nigh, when thou shalt say, I have no pleasure in them. . . . This is the end of the matter; all hath been heard: Fear God, and keep his commandments; for this is the whole duty of man. For God shall bring every work into judgment, with every hidden thing, whether it be good, or whether it be evil.

—Ecclesiastes 12: 1, 13-14 [5]

Moses gave to the Hebrews a concept of Jehovah as a national deity who would protect his people if they would obey his commandments. It was a concept of one god—for the Hebrews. For other nations there might be other gods, but for the Hebrews there was only Jehovah. Through Moses, a solemn covenant was entered into, a contract binding the Hebrews to obey the commandments of Jehovah and binding Jehovah to favor them with divine protection. The God of Moses was anthropomorphic, jealous, vengeful, terrible, and often cruel. It was natural then that at first the function of worship should be to appease and placate this "Thunderer of the Wilderness." So an elaborate ritual of religious ceremonies, social relationships, and domestic customs was contrived by Moses, assisted by the priesthood, and superimposed upon the decalogue. This body of rules and regulations was rapidly built up and transmitted as the Torah, or Law. Religion became an institution; worship became a formalized observance of the external requirements of the law. Education became a training in these ritualistic observances. Early Hebrew religion was more largely monolatry than it was monotheism.

---

[4] American Standard Version.
[5] American Standard Version.

As the Hebrew nation achieved a more powerful position in the world grave dangers began to offer themselves. Tendencies to neglect their great heritage and to behave as other nations did were observable.

Then came the prophets. They saw Hebrew civilization advancing through changing political and economic conditions. They saw new relationships developing with the nations and peoples round about them. They saw the Hebrews, attracted by the sensuality of the religions of their neighbors, continually in danger of falling from the worship of Jehovah. Somehow there developed in Israel and Judea creative thinkers who could interpret these changes as an opportunity for teaching new and broader ideals and a more abundant life. They started out to restore the faith of the fathers, and they ended by presenting to the world a new idea of righteousness and a new concept of God—a God of Justice, a God of Majesty, a God of Love, a God of all the Earth. They presented to the Hebrews a new covenant, new commandments, new moral standards.

> I hate, I despise your feasts—
> I have no delight in your solemn assemblies.
> Yea, though ye offer me your burnt-offerings and meal-offerings,
> I will not accept them;
> Neither will I regard the peace-offerings of your fat beasts.
> Take thou away from me the noise of thy songs,
> For I will not hear the melody of thy viols.
>
> But let justice roll down as waters,
> And righteousness as a mighty stream.
>
> —*Amos* 5: 21-24 [6]

> Wherewith shall I come before Jehovah,
> And bow myself before the high God?
> Shall I come before him with burnt-offerings,
> With calves a year old?
> Will Jehovah be pleased with thousands of rams,
> Or with ten thousands of rivers of oil?
> Shall I give my first-born for my transgressions,
> The fruit of my body for the sin of my soul?
> He hath showed thee, O man, what is good:
> What doth Jehovah require of thee,
> But to do justly, and to love kindness,
> And to walk humbly with thy God?
>
> *Micah* 6: 6-8 [7]

> Behold the days come, saith Jehovah,
> That I will make a new covenant
> With the house of Israel, and with the house of Judah,
> Not according to the covenant that I made with their fathers,
> In the day that I took them by the hand
> To bring them out of the land of Egypt;

---

[6] American Standard Version.
[7] American Standard Version.

> Which my covenant they brake,
> Although I was a husband unto them
> And rejected them, saith Jehovah
> But this is the covenant that I will make with the house of Israel:
> After those days, saith Jehovah, I will put the law in their inward parts,
> And in their hearts will I write it.
>
> —*Jeremiah* 31: 31-33 [8]

In such radiant words spoke the great prophets of Israel, but most frequently their seed fell upon stony ground.

A prophet is one who sees the new trend, the promise of a new life, in the confusions of the present, and who is courageous enough, even at great personal peril, to teach to men the new way of life that is indicated. But institutions do not like prophets, and the institution usually has possession of the field. Hence, about all the prophet can do is to speak the speech that is in his soul and wait for the future to judge him and his work.[9]

These religious seers and reformers set up a new goal for educational endeavor. They wanted it to deepen religious insight and fervor, to teach a better knowledge of Jehovah and a richer, truer righteousness. But this new aim was seldom realized in the later education of the Jews; the school continued to devote most of its attention to the superficial observances of the older formal and institutionalized religion. Prophecy was always subordinated to the Law in Hebrew education: "—over and above all else was, is, and shall be ever the Law."

TYPES   It is difficult to determine whether the outstanding type of education among the Hebrews was religious training or civic training. The fact is that the two were practically one; religion was synonymous with patriotism. Jehovah was the God of Israel; loyalty to him was loyalty to the nation. By teaching her children to obey the commandments of God, the greatness and glory of the nation was being preserved. This was also moral training in the highest and best sense, in that all customs and relationships were directed toward the common welfare.

During the earlier period of Jewish history the chief characteristic of education was its domestic simplicity. In primitive society, before the notion of the state is fixed, family life is in control. Among the patriarchial Hebrews God was the real king.

If the child was to become the faithful servant of Jehovah it was only essential that he be taught—by precept and example—the moral judgments and religious beliefs of his people. It has been wisely said that

. . . among all nations the direction impressed on education depends on the idea which they form of the perfect man. Among the Romans it is the

---

[9] Joseph K. Hart, *Creative Moments in Education.* (New York: Holt, Rinehart and Winston, Inc., 1931.) P. 110. Reprinted with the permission of the publisher.

brave soldier, inured to fatigue, and readily yielding to discipline; among the Athenians it is the man who unites in himself the happy harmony of moral and physical perfection; among the Hebrews the perfect man is the pious, virtuous man, who is capable of attaining the ideal traced by God himself in these terms: "Ye shall be holy, for I the Lord your God am holy!"[10]

Education was democratic in that all were trained upon an equal basis. The Hebrews held that education should be for everyone, regardless of class status. Since all were equal before God, the law was laid on each one, and the ceremonies and sacraments were not the secrets of a class. They not only recognized this principle in theory but put it into practice. Education in Palestine thus was universal. It was considered essential for everyone to be educated if the nation was to survive. The ignorant man suffered civil disfranchisement and social ostracism; for the ignorant man could not be religious, and the irreligious were a detriment to the nation. It is interesting to note that the Jews were the first to insist upon the education of the whole people and were willing to establish schools for this purpose.

Vocational training was always considered most essential. It was the duty of every father to teach his son a trade. "Whosoever does not teach his son a handicraft, teaches him to be a thief." They honored manual labor, and the greatest scholars were artisans as well. Recall that Jesus of Nazareth was a carpenter, and Saul of Tarsus was a tentmaker.

Domestic training was raised to a new level. The Jews developed a much more beautiful home life than that of other countries. Woman was believed to have been created, not to be a slave to man, but as a helpmeet. The mother had a high place in the Jewish home and assisted the father in inculcating in the children their first lessons in the meaning and practice of the religious ceremonies and rites. Girls were trained by the mother in all the household duties, some of which were exceedingly complex. Various foods were prescribed and had to be prepared in definite ways. Directions for the treatment of relatives, strangers, and servants were minutely laid down. A glance through the many regulations of the law having to do with the life of the home soon reveals how necessary it was that the housewife should be carefully trained for her tasks and duties.

These Hebrews made little provision for physical education, although the Mosaic law included some laws of hygiene, and fathers were urged to teach the children how to swim.

CONTENT   The content of education was fundamentally the history of the Hebrew people and of Jehovah's dealings with them; the explanation of the festivals of the Passover, Pentecost, and the Tabernacles as they recurred; the Jewish law, the psalms, and the proverbs.

---

[10] Quoted from J. Simon, *L'éducation et l'instruction chez les anciens Juifs.* Paris, 1879, p. 16. In Gabriel Compayre, *The History of Pedagogy* (W. H. Payne, trans.) (Boston: D. C. Heath and Company, 1889.) P. 7.

In the main, it consisted of the Mosaic law, or Torah, and the Talmud. The latter originated about the time of the return from Babylon. By this time the Hebrews had been changed from a nomadic, pastoral people to an agricultural, trading people. Partly on account of their travail and partly because of the thunderings of the prophets, they now became exceedingly strait-laced. Yet the Mosaic law had to be re-interpreted to meet new conditions and new attitudes.

These interpretations of the law, with the commentaries written upon them in later times by the scribes, form the Talmud, which, after the dispersion, came to be of almost equal importance with the law itself. Education consisted mostly of instruction in the knowledge and practice of the law and its interpretation. Jewish law was a mixture of criminal, civil, sanitary, domestic, and ceremonial law; and instruction was based upon the assumption that all important truth had been revealed in the law, which had only to be understood in order to meet all exigencies. Hence every line, word, and letter of it was submitted to microscopic investigation by the scribes and made to yield a maximum of meaning. In fact, the Talmud has been the basis of all Judaic scholarship for hundreds of years. This code of endless prescriptions and minute ceremonials lies at the basis of their whole educational curriculum. It was applied to every act in the daily life of the people.

Music was a part of the education of the Hebrew people. Their psalms were written in rhythmic form for singing or chanting; and they learned to play several musical instruments, though their music was somewhat undeveloped.

In the schools, established in the second century before Christ, reading, writing, and simple arithmetic were taught. The chief reading texts were the Pentateuch and the Talmud. The cumbersome notational system that they used prevented them from pursuing any kind of advanced mathematics.

AGENCIES   In the beginning, the family was the sole educational institution, with the father acting not only as patriarchal ruler and priest but also as teacher, and with the mother sharing in the burden of instruction. Throughout all Jewish history, the mother has remained the teacher of the girls.

Only boys learned to read and write. Girls were taught to spin and weave, to prepare food, and to superintend the work of the household; also to sing and dance.

Intellectual culture, in the early days, was but an incident in the education of the Hebrews; love of country and moral and religious instruction were the major aims in Hebrew education. Fathers taught their children the nation's history, thus emphasizing the great events such as the Passover, the escape from Egypt, the work of Moses the lawgiver, and the building of the temple under Solomon; these things, they believed, marked their destiny as children of God.

The series of events celebrated by the periodic feasts, which were renewed annually—and in which the young also participated—served to fill their hearts with gratitude toward God and to deepen their love of country.

This zeal for instruction was intensified during the Roman period and especially after the advent of Christianity. Operated under domestic auspices up to this time, now Judaic education became public. It no longer seemed sufficient merely to indoctrinate children with good principles and sound moral habits. They must also be instructed in the wider areas—knowledge of the world and the learnings valuable in commercial pursuits. From the beginning centuries of the Christian era, the Jews approached our modern ideal: that of making education compulsory and universal.

It is reported that, in the year 64, the high priest Joshua Ben Gamala imposed on each town—under penalty of excommunication—the obligation to support a school. Moreover, there could be no technical evasion of this rule; if a town was divided by a river and there was no safe transit by means of a bridge, schools must be established on both sides.

Yet today we have hardly realized—as relates to the number of schools and teachers—the rule so clearly stated in the Talmud that, if the number of children does not exceed twenty-five, the school may be conducted by one teacher; if greater than twenty-five the town must employ an assistant; and if the number of children exceeds forty, then two schoolmasters must be employed.

"Like every brave nation that has been vanquished, whose energy has survived defeat, like the Prussians after Jena, or the French after 1870 [or the Germans after Hitler], the Jews sought to defend themselves against the effects of conquest by a great intellectual effort; and to regain their lost ground by the development of popular instruction." [11]

After the Exile the scribes, whose duties had hitherto been clerical, began to assume also the duties of a special teaching class. Besides serving in a judicial capacity as interpreters of the law, and in a priestly capacity in the synagogues as expounders of the law, they now began to function also as teachers in the elementary schools that were being established. These schools were attached to the synagogues in most of the villages, and their necessity came to be universally recognized. They were accepted as a requisite as important as the synagogue itself, and to live where there was no school came to be forbidden.

Both the school and the teacher—scribe or rabbi—were regarded reverently. In the Talmud we read:

He who studies and teaches others, possesses treasures and riches.

He who has learned and does not impart his knowledge to others, disregards the word of God.

---

[11] See Compayre, *op. cit.,* pp. 8-9.

It is not permitted to live in a place where there is neither master nor school.

Your teacher and your father have need of your assistance; help your teacher before helping your father, for the last has given you only life of this world, while the former has secured for you the life of the world to come.

High qualifications were required for teaching. All teachers were carefully selected and well trained and had to be of the highest moral caliber. They had to be married, mature, and able in every respect. Usually they pursued some other vocation besides teaching and received no regular salary, although they were allowed to accept whatever parents cared to contribute.

ORGANIZATION   During the period from the Exodus to the Exile, the organization of Jewish education was still in terms of the family just as it had been in earlier times. Another of the chief educational influences was the Temple and its worship. Three times each year —at the time of the Passover, at the time of Pentecost, and at the feast of the Tabernacles—all males were required to visit the Temple in person. These occasions had the same educational influence upon the Jews that the Olympic games had upon the Greeks—the development of a strong national unity.

Higher education, for the training of priests and scribes, was organized before elementary education. Just before the Exile, there arose institutions known as the "schools of the prophets," which were used to prepare the lay prophets for their work. These schools taught the theological interpretation of the law, the arts of sacred music and verse, and, beyond all else, the principles of holiness and righteousness. Much later there developed training schools or colleges for the scribes, called houses of instruction. These were first established in the homes of the most prominent scribes and were devoted to an intensive analytical study of the Torah and the Talmud. The virtues of prudence, chastity, temperance, charity, truthfulness, and diligence, were emphasized in this training. At a much later time some instruction in astronomy, mathematics, foreign language, and geography was given in these schools.

When formal elementary education was established, the organization was in terms of the synagogue or elementary school for the boys and the home for the girls. The work in the elementary schools was organized on three levels: one for the ages of six to ten, another for the ages of ten to fifteen, and still another for those over fifteen. The first two levels were compulsory for all male children, and rich and poor attended and studied together. From six to ten the Pentateuch was the chief text; from ten to fifteen the *Mishna,* or first part of the Talmud, was covered; if the boy continued his education beyond the age of fifteen he gave his attention to the *Gemara,* or second part of the Talmud.

METHODS   The method, as was usual in all Oriental countries and to be expected because of the lack of writing materials, was largely oral. In learning to write, a wax tablet and stylus were used. Even in higher education the method was largely that of exposition on the part of the master, with questioning and disputation afterwards on the part of the students. This was the type of school in which Jesus was found by his parents at the age of twelve, "in the temple, sitting in the midst of the doctors, both hearing them, and asking them questions." There was nothing unusual about the method; the only amazing thing was the extreme youth of the pupil.

In the elementary schools, the method was oral, with the emphasis upon memorizing. The pupils sat on the floor or on benches facing the teacher, who was supposed never to have more than twenty-five in the group. The pupils repeated the passages aloud, with careful articulation; for "to speak aloud the sentence which is being learned fixes it in the memory." Judaic teachers were skilled in the correlation of various types of memory—visual, auditory, and kinesthetic—and made extensive use of mnemonic devices. They had a grasp of some of the principles of method that are considered quite modern:

> The teacher should strive to make the lesson agreeable to the pupils by clear reasoning as well as by frequent repetitions until they thoroughly understand the matter and are able to recite it with great fluency.
>
> One learns much from the teacher, more from his school fellows, but most of all from his pupils.
>
> Only those pupils should be punished in whom the master sees capacity for learning; if they are dull and cannot learn, they should not be punished.

These precepts from the Talmud show that they had some comprehension of the principle of interest, the principle of socialization, and the principle of individual differences.

The school day was long, for it lasted from early morning until evening with a recess at noon, and the only vacations were the religious holidays. The discipline was somewhat rigorous, with corporal punishment recognized as a valid method of control. Severity, however, was tempered with kindliness, as is shown by the maxim, "Punish with one hand, and caress with two."

"What a singular spectacle is offered us by that people, which, dispossessed of its own country for 1800 years, has been dispersed among the nations without losing its identity, and has maintained its existence without a country, without a government, and without a ruler, preserving with perennial energy its habits, its manners, and its faith! . . . If ever a people has demonstrated the power of education, it is the people of Israel." [12]

---

[12] Quoted from J. Dittes, *Histoire de l'éducation et l'instruction* (translated by Redolfi). Paris, 1880. P. 49. In Compayre, *op. cit.*, p. 6. The re-establishment of Israel in 1948 serves to validate this tribute.

FOR FURTHER READING

Barnes, Harry Elmer, *An Intellectual and Cultural History of the Western World.* New York: Random House, 1937. Pp. 78-102.

Breasted, James Henry, *The Conquest of Civilization.* New York: Harper and Brothers, 1926. Pp. 212-234.

Browne, Lewis, *This Believing World.* New York: The Macmillan Co., 1926. Pp. 223-253.

Butts, R. Freeman, *A Cultural History of Western Education.* Second Edition. New York: McGraw-Hill Book Co., 1955. Pp. 11-12, 16-18.

Cubberley, Ellwood P., *Readings in the History of Education.* Boston: Houghton Mifflin Company, 1920. Pp. 41-42.

Davidson, Thomas, *A History of Education.* New York: Charles Scribner's Sons, 1900. Pp. 77-86.

Duggan, Stephen P. *Student's Textbook in the History of Education.* New York: Appleton-Century-Crofts, Inc., 1936. Pp. 7-13.

Eby, Frederick, and Arrowood, Charles F., *The History and Philosophy of Education Ancient and Medieval.* New York: Prentice-Hall, Inc., 1940. Pp. 108-159.

Graves, Frank P., *Education Before the Middle Ages.* New York: The Macmillan Co., 1909. Pp. 110-136.

Hart, Joseph K., *Creative Moments in Education.* New York: Holt, Rinehart and Winson, Inc., 1931. Pp. 106-120.

Hitti, Philip K., *Syria: A Short History.* New York: The Macmillan Co., 1959.

Knight, Edgar W., *Twenty Centuries of Education.* Boston: Ginn & Co., 1940. Pp. 40-44.

Laurie, Simon S., *Historical Survey of Pre-Christian Education.* New Impression. New York: Longmans, Green & Co., Inc., 1915. Pp. 65-100.

Marek, Kurt W., *The Secret of the Hittites.* New York: Alfred A. Knopf, 1956.

Mayer, Frederick, *A History of Educational Thought.* Columbus, Ohio: Charles E. Merrill Books, Inc., 1960. Pp. 73-78.

Monroe, Paul, *Cyclopedia of Education.* New York: The Macmillan Co., 1925. Pp. 542-545.

Mulhern, James. *A History of Education.* Second Edition. New York: The Ronald Press Co., 1959. Pp. 55 ff.

Painter, Franklin, *A History of Education.* New York: Appleton-Century-Crofts, Inc., 1904. Pp. 27-33.

Payne, W. H., editor, *Compayré's History of Pedagogy.* Boston: D. C. Heath & Co., 1889. Pp. 6-11, 16.

Shaw, Charles Gray, *Trends of Civilization and Culture.* New York: American Book Company, 1950. Pp. 99-124.

Smith, William A., *Ancient Civilization*. New York: Philosophical Library, Inc., 1955. Pp. 197-253.

Ulich, Robert, *History of Educational Thought*. New York: American Book Company, 1950. *Passim*.

————, *Three Thousand Years of Educational Wisdom*. Cambridge, Mass.: Harvard University Press, 1954. Pp. 643-668.

QUESTIONS FOR CLASS DISCUSSION

1. To what extent do the great state papers of the United States play the same part in American life and education that the books of Moses did in Jewish life and education?

2. What qualifications are required in present-day teachers beyond those demanded for teaching in the Judaic schools?

3. Do you believe that modern education demands maturity in its elementary school teachers to the same extent that this was required by Hebrew education?

4. Do you think that teachers in our modern schools are as esteemed and reverenced as were the Hebrew rabbis?

5. To what extent do contemporary teachers still require pupils to memorize selections from the great classics of literature? Of what value is such a practice?

6. Do you believe that modern schools teach and develop as high a standard of character and morality as did the schools of the ancient Jews?

7. What differences do you find between the civic education taught in the Judaic schools and that taught in today's American schools?

8. What is the place of religious education in the American public school of today? Do you agree or disagree with this?

9. In what ways does education under a theocracy differ from educational practices in contemporary totalitarian states?

10. Cite the position of the Jew in present-day civilization. To what extent do you feel that his educational system and educational practices have been responsible for this?

CHAPTER IV

THE DEVELOPMENT OF INDIVIDUALITY

GREEK CONCEPTS OF EDUCATION

The classical nations of Greece and Rome were the first representatives of Western civilization. These two peoples were somewhat different in their ideals, attitudes, and practices, and each made its own distinct contributions. The Greeks contributed more elements to modern culture than any other ancient people; they bequeathed to us art, literature, philosophy, science, and politics. The Roman mind was practical and the Romans excelled in engineering, law, and government. They were responsible, too, for spreading the Greek culture throughout western Europe.

In art, Greece produced individual masterpieces in sculpture and architecture that have become models for the ages, and developed standards and forms upon which much of later art has been based. Some of the finest classics in all the world's literature have come down to us from Greek writers, and we are indebted to them for most of our literary types and forms, such as epic poetry, lyric poetry, drama, oratory, and history. Greek thinkers were the first in the field of philosophy, developing specific systems, such as the Platonic, the Aristotelian, the Stoic, the Epicurean, destined to play a large part in the thought life of the world, and formulating some of the basic philosophical problems that are still subjects for speculation. Many of our present-day social and political theories originated with the Greeks and were applied in their experiments toward the first democratic governments. Many of the specific scientific conceptions of the Greeks have long since been exploded; but they are the earliest representatives of the scientific spirit, the spirit of research and investigation. The work of EUCLID (c. 400 B.C.) in mathematics, of ARCHIMEDES (287–212 B.C.) in physics, of ARISTOTLE (384–322 B.C.) in logic—all are still found as basic elements of our curriculum. PLATO (428–348 B.C.) is famous for his blueprint of the scientifically created state as well as for his philosophical "idealism."

It is to be assumed, then, that the educational conceptions and ideals of this virile and cultured people made many important contributions to the development of educational thought. Here for the first time we see education conceived of as a progressive adjustment, with recognition of the desirability of the development of individual personality.

The significance of Greek education lies in the fact that here is found a developing conception and standard of life, consequently a conception of education which enlarges through successive periods and in which change is tolerated and development of the individual provided for. Growth in social standards results from variations by individuals from social customs; progress comes when such variations are not only tolerated but seized upon and made permanent. For the first time, then, in Greek education is found a type in which the individual is neither unconsciously nor consciously suppressed. On the contrary some expression of individuality is thought compatible with, even desirable for, social stability and welfare.[1]

In Greece, we have the first creative moments in education. With a departure from the philosophy of complacency and its belief in the preservation of the *status quo,* we have the beginnings of an educational philosophy. With the acceptance of the principle of progress and growth, we have the first recognition of education as a problem.

What were the conditions and influences that made possible these contributions? What is the secret of the greatness of this people?

Sometime before 1200 B.C., the Aryan ancestors of the Greeks journeyed southward from the steppes north of the Black Sea into the peninsula now called Greece. This peninsula is mountainous, and these mountains lack passes and other means of easy transportation and communication. The result was that the Greeks become isolated in small city-states with little or no connection with each other. This early separation of the people into numerous small political units tended to establish a difference of interests. "Therefore, in consequence of the numerous centers of civic life, that rapid growth of independence and of the spirit of freedom which characterized the Greek, and which was the beginning of the idea of liberty for the whole human race, developed."[2]

---

[1] Paul Monroe, *A Textbook in the History of Education.* (New York: The Macmillan Co., 1933.) P. 52. Reprinted with the permission of the publishers.
[2] Simon S. Laurie, *Historical Survey of Pre-Christian Education.* (New York: Longmans, Green and Co., 1915.) P. 279. Reprinted with the permission of the publishers.

All the Greeks, despite the fact of special interests in their own city-states, spoke the same general language and worshiped the same gods, so that they felt themselves distinct from all other peoples around them, whom they called barbarians. This tribal pride is one of the significant influences of their history. In contrast to other peoples of southern Europe, the early Greek was fair in color, with regular and handsome features. He grew up more slowly than his neighbors, his vigor was more lasting, and his old age more protracted. The excellent climate of the country, along with their temperate habits and outdoor physical exercise, made the Greeks a very healthy folk. As we might expect of people in good health, they were happy in temperament and ever ready to enjoy themselves; while their own natural beauty, together with good taste, made them keen judges of beauty in other things and highly intolerant of ugliness.

The Greek state was wholly under the city organization and within the city limits; hence it is called a city-state to differentiate it from the modern territorial state.[3] There were hundreds of these little city-states at first, but some of them gradually combined into religious and political leagues under the leadership of the most powerful city of the league. Thus all the petty kingdoms of Attica were united in one city-state under control of Athens, and Sparta became the head of a similar state even larger than Athens. These two states are usually studied as typical of the two types of Hellenic culture: Athens as the best example of the Ionian branch, and Sparta as the best example of the Dorian branch.

Since Greek education changed as did political and social conditions, it is necessary to study it at different periods in order to understand its development. Therefore we shall divide our discussion as follows: (1) Homeric education, lasting from prehistoric times down to 776 B.C., and common to all the Greeks; (2) Spartan education, lasting throughout the entire history of Greece; (3) early Athenian education, lasting from the first Olympiad to the close of the Persian Wars in 479 B.C.; (4) later Athenian education, lasting from the close of the Persian Wars to the Macedonian conquest in 338 B.C. This last period is often called the Periclean age—the golden age of Greece.

HOMERIC ATTITUDES TOWARD EDUCATION

We can best learn of the character and customs of the Greeks of the Epic Age from their minstrels, who traveled about from court to

---

[3] An interesting, although fictional, account of the rise and fall of such a Greek state is the subject of George R. Stewart's *The Years of the City*. (Boston: Houghton, Mifflin Company, 1955.)

court and sang to the kings and nobles of the heroic deeds of gods and heroes. These wandering bards were the makers of the two great epic poems, the *Iliad* and the *Odyssey,* usually attributed to HOMER (c. 800 B.C.). It is these two Homeric epics that are our chief sources of information concerning the education of this period.

AIMS   We can hardly say that the Greeks ever had a religious aim for their education. The religion of the Homeric Greeks was founded largely on a pleasant, light-hearted myth making. When their minstrels sang of the gods, they sang of glorified men—gay, lustful, brawling heroes, who dwelt upon Mount Olympus and engaged in deeds of courage, craft, wisdom, and cunning. The early Greeks did not love their gods; neither did they fear them. Homeric tales reveal little terror of the gods; there is a measure of fondness, even a measure of respect, but beyond all else, a desire to imitate them, to be godlike. Deities were like men, differing only in their greater stature and strength and in their immortality.

Since the gods were only magnified men, they had both good and evil qualities; thus the influence of religion was both moral and immoral. The gods set an example of justice, kindliness, hospitality, and forbearance; but with equal readiness they taught men to lie and steal and kill. Neither was there a promise in their religion of a glorious reward in the hereafter to furnish a motive for right living. The realm of Hades (not to be confused with Christian ideas of hell) was cold, dark, and lifeless; the very thought of death was hideous, while life was full of beauty and joy. Their aim was to live a happy godlike life while on earth, not because the gods demanded it but because that was the type of life the people themselves approved.

These earliest Greeks seemed to have a twofold ideal of the perfect man. The first ideal was the man of wisdom, as exemplified by Odysseus. He was the man of judgment, sagacity, insight, shrewdness, and eloquence—an invaluable aid in the councils of peace and war. The second ideal was the man of action, as exemplified by Achilles.[4] His primary virtues were strength, courage, bravery, and endurance—the qualities needed for deeds and exploits. The aim of education, therefore, was to develop in every nobleman a combination of these two ideas, each to be tempered to avoid one-sidedness—action by reverence for the gods; wisdom by whole-mindedness or control of the appetites by reason. No attention was given to the countrymen, the menials, who had to learn their unskilled pursuits by imitation of their parents, much in the primitive fashion. Greek education had from the first this aim of individual excellence or worth, often named "fair-and-goodness" from its component

---

[4] The qualities of Achilles are recounted in the *Iliad,* the Homeric epic narrating the Greek attack on Ilium, or Troy; the *Odyssey* tells of the wandering of Ulysses, or Odysseus, on his long voyage home to Ithaca following the sack of the city, entrance having been effected through Ulysses' strategy of the wooden horse.

elements: perfection of body in strength and beauty, and perfection of mind in wisdom, temperance, fortitude, and justice. This aim was practical and social, for the ideal of individual excellence was never separated from that of public usefulness. Individual worth was worth for public ends, for social and political life in peace and war. Welfare of the group was the primary consideration.

TYPES   Homeric education, therefore, was primarily practical and social. All the qualities, traits, and skills needed for a happy and satisfying group-living were developed: training in the practical arts of war and peace, including training in military skill and craftsmanship, for the men; and training in the domestic arts for the women. Education was not democratic as we consider it today, since the people were divided into classes with different ways of life and, consequently, different types of training were needed.

CONTENT   The nobles owned the land, with its farms, orchards, vineyards, and cattle. While slaves and hired men tended these estates, the lords lived in the city with their fellows or went on long expeditions of war, thus sharing in the religious, social, and political life for which they were destined. Trained for this higher calling, they looked upon themselves as the brave, the mighty, and the best, contrasting themselves with the base and cowardly men of the lower untrained and unskilled working class who were living miserable lives in the country performing the menial tasks of the farms.

Skilled workers, trained in their special duties, were more highly honored. In fact, the lords and ladies themselves often shared in their tasks. Skilled female slaves were trained in dyeing, weaving, and embroidery. Among the skilled men was the smith who busied himself in making armor and weapons; the potter sitting at his wheel; the leech curing a wound by sucking out the blood and spreading on soothing ointments; the seer consulting the oracles and prophesying; the minstrel delighting with his song and lyre. All these the Greeks of the time called craftsmen and held in high esteem. Youths and maidens were taught to dance and to play upon musical instruments, thus adding to the pleasure of life at court. Conversation was deemed an art, and men were trained to reach decisions through the medium of group discussion.

AGENCIES AND ORGANIZATION   No formal educational institution existed in Homeric times. The organization was in terms of the family and the clan, the home of the lord and the council of the nobles. The minstrel bard taught the virtues of good living by singing of the deeds of gods and heroes; the crafts and handiwork were taught by those skilled in these arts. Family life was beautiful; and women—within the home—were the equals of men. The matrons taught the household crafts;

the queen herself "sat among her serving women and appointed brave handiwork for her handmaidens."[5]

METHODS   In such an educational scheme of things, the methods depended upon were those of example and imitation. The boys learned the approved virtues through hearing of the example set by the gods and the heroes of old, and acquired the practical skills through actual participation in the campaigns of the wars, the crafts of the home, the councils of the elders. The girls in similar manner learned the skills of the household through sharing in its tasks.

SPARTAN ATTITUDES TOWARD EDUCATION

We have already seen that one of the most forceful influences in political, social, and educational history is that of geographic location. Many of the educational concepts of various peoples are due to the geographic conditions in which they find themselves. Sparta is a good illustration of this. The Spartans were a branch of the Dorian Greeks who settled in the Peloponnesus—the southern section of the Greek peninsula —about the eleventh century before Christ, bringing under subjection the tribes then occupying the land.

By the ninth century, the Spartans constituted about nine thousand families surrounded by almost thirty times that number of subject peoples, known as Perioeci and Helots, who did all the manual work. The Perioeci, or "dwellers-around," were the occupants of adjacent lands and were subject to military duty; the third class, the Helots, were outright slaves and the threat of death was continually held over their heads. Threatened with constant danger of attack from without and of insurrection within the state, the Spartans called upon LYCURGUS (c. 800 B.C.) to devise a new constitution and develop a system of law. The laws of Lycurgus form the basis of the Spartan educational system, and from them we get our best knowledge of the attitudes of the Spartans toward education.

AIMS   The constitution drawn up by Lycurgus—a legendary figure—aimed at training a powerful body of soldiers; it aimed at making Sparta a perpetual training camp and armed garrison. Education aimed at group welfare, the group in this case being that of the Spartan state. In a way, this was in accord with the Greek ideal of individual excellence for state usefulness; but individual excellence here meant

---

[5] Penelope, the wife of Ulysses, has long been considered the epitome of wifely virtue. Confident of her husband's return from the Trojan War, she thwarted the many suitors for her hand and kingdom by an ingenious and amusing device.

military excellence, and state usefulness meant usefulness in time of war. The Spartans followed the Homeric ideal of the man of action rather than of the man of wisdom. Their aim was to give each individual such physical perfection and habits of complete obedience that he would make an ideal soldier.

To have developed strength, courage, endurance, cunning, patriotism, and military efficiency—that was the Spartan's ideal of good citizenship. Sparta sacrificed all the nobler qualities of its people to the perfection of the body as the supreme goal in life. Its aim was to rear a nation physically invincible, capable of enduring hunger, thirst, torture, or even death without flinching; a people unequaled in military skill, and with absolute devotion to the state.

Spartan education was simple in its objects; it was not the result of any general view of human nature, or of any attempt to unfold its various capacities; it aimed at training men who were to live in the midst of difficulty and danger and could be safe themselves only while they held rule over others. The citizen was to be always ready for the defense of himself and his country, at home and abroad; and he was, therefore, to be equally fitted to command and to obey. His body, his mind, and his character were formed for this purpose and for no other; and hence the Spartan system, making directly for its own end, and rejecting all that was foreign to it, attained, within its own sphere, to a perfection which it is impossible not to admire.[6]

Sparta is, indeed, an early example of totalitarianism. Laudable though the qualities mentioned above are in the abstract, present-day democracy cannot consider the Spartan system one to imitate—or even to condone.

The educational system based upon this aim continued for seven hundred years with little change; and in all this time—as a result of this narrow concept of life—Sparta contributed nothing to the world except her rigid doctrine of devotion to a single purpose, which has made the word "Spartan" a synonym for all the qualities characteristic of such a single-track objective.

Types   With this objective the types of education stressed were physical training and military training. Since these were for the benefit of the Spartan general welfare, the education could be called social in its broadest sense; and since it was for the preservation of the state, it could be called civic. All Sparta's moral training also was a phase of training for military preparedness. Even instruction in music and dancing was a form of physical training.

Domestic training likewise was subordinated to the needs of the state; a family life was suppressed in the interest of war preparedness. Moreover, most of the practical duties of the household were performed

---

6 Franklin Painter, *A History of Education*. (New York: American Book Company, 1905.) P. 45. Reprinted with the permission of the publishers.

by slave women. Among the Spartans themselves there was no vocational training, since all the manual tasks were performed by the slave class who had to prepare themselves for their labor, which was largely of the unskilled type.

Intellectual training had little attention and was limited to the memorizing of the laws of Lycurgus and a few selections from Homer.

CONTENT The Spartan curriculum consisted almost entirely of gymnastic and military exercises and practice in the moral and social habits essential to living a life of devotion and service to the state. The boys were taught to maintain absolute control over their appetites, to observe temperance in all their habits, and to be obedient and reverent to their elders. They were taught to be modest and retiring until time for action, and then to be aggressive and fearless.

The education of girls was not neglected in Sparta, for it was felt that the women should be equally strong and courageous. The girls too were given gymnastic exercises, in which modesty was never a concern, in order to make them more capable of bearing strong, healthy children and to prepare them to endure the hardships of dangerous living. While the boys struggled to develop a reverential demeanor, a reserved conduct, a stoicism under pain, and a habit of blind obedience, the girls strove to achieve vigor and womanly dignity.

Reading and writing were taught to a very limited extent, if at all; but the boys had to learn the laws of the state and the tales of the heroes of old, and to listen attentively to the conversations of their elders. Drills were given in the art of speaking to the point without wasting words; this is the origin of the expression "laconic reply," [7] as the territory of the Spartan city-state was called Laconia; the Spartans themselves are sometimes called Lacedaemonians after the name of the founder of the city.

Music was taught, though the songs were always serious and moral, usually in praise of men who had died for their country; yet the stately Doric measures had a martial rhythm that inflamed the mind and stirred it to enthusiasm and fervor for action. Likewise, their stress of dancing was not for esthetic values or for the development of grace and beauty, but—like their gymnastic exercises—was designed to build bodily strength and vigor.

AGENCIES AND ORGANIZATION The one dominant educational agency was the state, and the state controlled the education of the individual from birth until death. All family life was dictated by the state; marriage was controlled by the state and made compulsory; all children were considered as belonging to the state, and the state council decided at birth whether a child should be permitted to live. The weak

---

[7] A Spartan legend tells that the Persian king had threatened the city saying "If I come to Greece I will lay your city in the dust." The Spartan reply, "If."

or defective child was ordered exposed to the elements. Some died or were devoured by wild beasts. Others were rescued to be raised as slaves.

The healthy boy was given over to his mother until he was seven years old, but even then his education was controlled by the demands of the state. The discipline of self-control began from the day of his birth. He was trained to overcome fear by being left alone in the dark; he was made hardy by fasting; he ate simple coarse food, wore scanty clothing, had plenty of sleep and open-air exercise. At this early age, he learned to cultivate habits of silence, respect, obedience, and reverence toward his elders.

When the boy was seven years old, he entered a public educational institution in the form of barracks where he was to live, under the supervision of older boys and a state official called the *paidonomus*, until he should reach the age of eighteen. Here he was under severe discipline and exacting rules of conduct. He had a bed of straw or hay, no blankets, no shoes, and scanty clothing. His food was plain and limited in quantity at that. The boys were encouraged to steal, but were severely punished for their lack of skill if they were caught at it.[8] In these public barracks the boys were rigorously trained through games, exercises, and drills; they participated in jumping, running, wrestling, spear throwing, and quoits. All these practical and military exercises were used solely for the purpose of developing qualities serviceable in war. Through discussion at the public mess tables, they were instructed in moral and civic issues and in the affairs of state. They learned to converse in an intelligent and agreeable manner and early acquired a dignity of bearing and a practical wisdom far beyond their years.

The next two years (eighteen to twenty) were spent by most of the boys in professional war training. Those who had demonstrated qualities of leadership remained in the barracks to supervise the younger boys. At the age of twenty, all took the oath of allegiance to the state and were sent to various army posts and on military campaigns for war maneuvers and actual warfare. At the age of thirty, every man became a full-fledged citizen, was compelled to marry and to take a seat in the public assembly or council.[9] At times he had to go to the public barracks to act as mentor and example to the boys there; in this respect, every citizen was a teacher.

The home was the school for girls. There was no institution for girls corresponding to the public barracks for the boys; they were, however, organized into packs. The purpose of these girls' packs was to furnish a means for giving physical education, develop a group spirit, and to produce healthy bodies for the bearing and rearing of sturdy and patriotic sons for the Spartan military state.

---

[8] A famous story is that of the Spartan youth who, having stolen a fox, placed it under his tunic. During cross-examination he allowed himself to be clawed to death rather than admit the theft.

[9] It has been suggested that Plato borrowed much from the Spartan system in the creation of *The Republic*.

METHODS   The method of education in Sparta was one of training rather than of instruction. Learning was carried on through participation in activities under the leadership of older boys and with citizens as mentors and examples. It was entirely an activity method, and there was nothing bookish in its nature. Periodic testing was carried out, but this was not for the purpose of testing memory but to test moral habits and physical capacities.

Discipline was most severe and cruel. Corporal punishment was used both for moral delinquencies and for mental inattention and lack of alertness. Every adult citizen was expected to punish any boy caught in the act of violating one of the rules of proper conduct, and fear of public disapproval was used as a strong motivating influence. Emulation and rivalry also were used extensively as means of stimulating learning.

EARLY ATHENIAN ATTITUDES TOWARD EDUCATION

In the Homeric age, the Ionian Greeks had been simple farmers and herdsmen without commerce, manufactures, or money. After the first Olympiad (776 B.C.), however, a change began to take place. In Attica,[10] especially, industry and commerce developed, and the tribal custom of barter gave way to the use of coins. These changes brought about serious economic, social, and political problems; and the Athenians were involved in perplexing difficulties when Solon was called upon to take charge of affairs.

SOLON (639–559 B.C.), the great Athenian lawgiver, belonged to one of the noblest families of Athens, and because of his wisdom is reckoned as one of the Seven Sages. He was no mere theorist, but a clear-headed, sober-minded, practical statesman. "Nothing to excess," a maxim of his, sums up his character and political principles. He instituted reforms in the government of Athens that made it a true democracy, drawing up a set of laws that solved many of the distressing economic and social problems of his people and guided the life of Athens for several centuries. The prosperity of Athens dates from the time of Solon, and early Athenian education was largely the result of his influence. He encouraged learning and formulated the ideals upon which it was to be based.

AIMS   Early Athenian education had little in common with that of Sparta except in the simplicity of its aim and in the directness with which that aim was achieved. Here again the Greek ideal of individual excellence for public usefulness was stressed; but in this case

---

[10] Attica was the territory in which Athens was located.

individual excellence meant a fully rounded development of mind and body, and public usefulness meant the ability to take an active part in all the affairs of state in times of peace as well as war. In Athens the man of wisdom was emphasized more than the man of action. While the Spartans aimed at strength and endurance, and often developed coarseness of body and manner, the Athenian sought beauty and grace of body, mind, and spirit.

The Athenians believed that the best prerequisite for citizenship was a broad individual development. They conceived of education as a protection for the state; but they believed that the best preparation for citizenship was development of the individual through participation in the religious, social, political, and military activities of the state, always with a rigid public opinion upholding traditional ideals of morality. Reverence, loyalty, and temperance were upheld rather than mere intellectual cleverness. The whole purpose of early Athenian education was the development of virtue, but the virtues were always civic virtues. The Athenians aimed at developing all sides of individual personality useful for public welfare; their sense of proportion was evident in their education as well as in all the other concerns of their life. In opposition to Spartan totalitarianism, the Athenian government did not try to control the education of its youth completely; the stronger sense of Attic individuality left more in the hands of the parents.

TYPES   Civic training was the dominant type of training in early Athenian education, and all other types were subordinated to this end. Physical training was carefully organized, but this was for the purpose of developing grace and harmony rather than mere strength and brawn. Moral training emphasized the old virtues of the Homeric heroes and also the virtues essential to the service of the state. Intellectual training was of the type needed for the activities of the assembly and the market place. Music, poetry, and dancing were taught not as a means of pleasure and amusement, but as an ennobling influence on intellect and morals; as a means of developing personality and elevating the soul, of providing a type of good cultural training. The early Athenians believed that, "in union with poetry, music leads the soul to virtue and impresses it with courage."

Domestic training and vocational training were neglected. Out of the half-million people of Athens there were four hundred thousand slaves; and practically all the manual work, which was despised by the free citizens, was performed by these slaves. Formal education was, therefore, a class education, limited to male citizens, the girls as well as the slaves being excluded.

CONTENT   The Athenian boy first learned reading by the alphabet method, and then writing by the use of a wax tablet and stylus. As much arithmetic was learned as was necessary for the reckonings of the market place. Selections from Homer, HESIOD (c. 776 B.C.), Solon, and AESOP (c. 560 B.C.) were taken from dictation, memorized, and chanted. Music played on the lyre and flute was taught as a sister art to poetry; and accompaniments were often improvised to go with the chanting of poetry.

Gymnastic drills, interspersed with sports and games were much used. The exercises and games were varied and interesting, with little importance attached to winning. Leaping, running, jumping, wrestling, throwing the javelin, hurling the discus, and quoits were all engaged in, with special attention given to the art of swimming. Later, the boy acquired military skill, practiced civic virtues and all else necessary for playing his part as a free citizen in a democratic state.

AGENCIES   Education in Athens was supervised by the state, but was not compulsory. It was, however, a matter of family pride; and if a father neglected to give his son the proper training, he could not hold the son responsible for support in his old age.

At school the boy was instructed by private teachers, and the social position of these teachers was rather low. When he was very young, he was placed under the care of a *paidagogos* (pedagogue), usually an aged and trustworthy slave, and remained under his charge throughout the period of his education. The pedagogue was valet, servant, guardian, counselor, and moral censor; and usually he was the chief moral influence in the life of the boy. Often he was chosen for this duty because he was not fit for anything else—in these cases an influence hardly wholesome. In his later training the youth was under the supervision of state officials, who acted as his drillmasters and moral censors.

There was no real family life in Athens, and the home as an agency of education was of slight account. Women of the home were so illiterate that children were usually rather badly brought up, and bad habits were invariably formed. The little training acquired by the girls was given sometimes by the mother, but usually by slave nurses. Women were not held in as high esteem as in Sparta. The only educated and cultured women in Athens were the *heterae* (courtesans)—a special class who participated in the social life and philosophic discussions of the upper ranks.

After the boy's basic schooling was over, his further education depended upon incidental participation in the activities of the city's life. All the Athenian institutions were highly educative. The young man learned much in the assembly, where he listened to the debates and discussions; on the juries, where he saw the laws interpreted and applied; at the theater, where he listened to the great tragedies and comedies; at the Olympic games, where he came in contact with all that was best in Greek culture. All the throbbing life of the great city was in itself an agency for education. The Athenian youth learned by living.

ORGANIZATION   In Athens, the father himself rather than the state determined whether the infant was to live or be exposed to death. Until he was seven years of age the boy lived at home, usually under the care of slave nurses. His childhood was easy and pleasant.

From the age of seven to sixteen the boy divided his time between two schools, which he attended accompanied by his slave attendant, the pedagogue. In the *didascaleum* (music school) he learned reading, writing, arithmetic, poetry, and music. In the *palaestra* he engaged in gymnastic exercises, sports, and games. It is difficult to determine whether the boy went to the music school for the first few years and then entered the *palaestra* or spent part of each day in each of the two types of schools. The latter is more probable.

From the age of sixteen to eighteen the youth was freed from all literary and musical studies but continued in the public gymnasium the physical education begun in the *palaestra*. Here he associated freely with other youths and older men. He was trained in exercises, mostly athletic and military, by a state drillmaster, called the *paidotribe,* and was under the supervision of a state moral censor, called the *sophronist.* The censorship of his morals was quite strict in this early period of Athenian history, and the exercises and drills were more severe and rigorous than in the *palaestra*.

Having completed these two years of preliminary training, and having demonstrated to the state officials that he was physically and morally qualified for citizenship, he took the following pledge of allegiance to the state, known as the Ephebic Oath: "I will not bring reproach upon our sacred arms, nor desert the comrade at my side, whoever he may be. For our sanctuaries and laws I will fight, alone or with others. My country I will leave, not in a worse, but in a better condition. I will at all times submit willingly to the judges and established ordinance, and will not consent that others infringe or disobey them. I will honor the established religious worship. The gods be my witness."

The next two years, as an *ephebos* (a youth from the age of eighteen to twenty), the young man spent in the military service of the state. He was placed on guard at the frontier posts where he was subjected to the severest military discipline. At the age of twenty he was given the privileges of full citizenship, assumed definite duties in the assembly and on the juries, and entered fully into the pleasant and agreeable life of the city. He spent most of his time in public and in the open and was seldom at home. His female intellectual companionship was largely with the brilliant *heterae* of whom we have already spoken.

METHODS The Athenian youth learned much by imitation and through the example of the living model. He imitated his master in learning to write, and his musical and physical training was largely a matter of imitating his teachers. As in Sparta, the method was one of training rather than instruction. Parts of his readings were memorized, but no great emphasis was placed upon this type of exercise. Most of his education came from actual participation in the activities of life:

his civics was not learned from books but through attendance at places where civic activities were going on. Examinations were not for the purpose of testing knowledge but for testing physical and civic capacities and skills. Emulation was often used as a motive for learning.

Discipline was exceedingly severe. Corporal punishment was used extensively, even the *paidagogos* having the power to use it upon those in his charge. Although the classes in the school were small, there was no bond of affection between the teacher and his pupil. Every effort was made to "bring up the child in the way he should go."

As soon as one understands what is said, nurse, mother, pedagogue, and father himself vie with each other in this, how the boy may become as good as possible, in every word and deed teaching and pointing out to him that this is just and that unjust, this is honorable and that base, this is holy and that unholy, and this you must do and that you must not do. And if the boy obeys willingly, it is well, but if not, like a tree twisted and bent, they make him straight by threats and blows.[11]

LATER ATHENIAN ATTITUDES TOWARD EDUCATION

In 500 B.C. circumstances developed that resulted in conflict between Athens (and the other city-states of Greece) and Persia, the leading Asiatic empire of that day. The struggle lasted until 479 B.C., and in the process Athens herself became an empire.

The successful outcome of the Persian wars brought many important changes in the political, economic, and social life of the Athenians; and these changes were reflected in their educational views and practices. Athens had been the chief factor in the victories over the Persians and now became the center of Greek life as the head of the Delian Confederation. As imperial master of the surrounding states and islands, the great city of Athens began to take on a more cosmopolitan character; interchange of ideas with traders, travelers, and other foreigners developed wider interests and a more diversified community life.

These new and broader contacts with the world induced criticism, modification, and abandonment of the older traditions and basic ideals of the early Athenians. The activity of the trading and commercial class brought prosperity and the possibility of an accumulation of individual wealth hitherto undreamed of. The amassing of wealth led to more opportunities for the pursuits of pleasure and the patronage of the cultural arts. Greatness was measured in terms of wealth and power, not in terms of birth or of genuine service to the state. Political skill was no longer restricted to the local assembly, but could now be utilized

---

[11] Plato, in *Protagoras.*

in the larger realm of imperial diplomacy and statesmanship. Citizenship was opened to all free inhabitants, and new opportunities for personal aggrandizement developed on every hand for the ambitious young men of the city.

AIMS With the old civic ideal of devotion to the public good dying out, with the old religious and moral ideas being rejected on every side, and with desire for fame, fortune, and personal gratification becoming dominant, new demands were made upon education. The goal of education for this new age was preparation for personal advancement. The aim of the young men of Athens now became individual excellence for individual success. The older objective of social service and public usefulness was changed to one of selfish and rugged individualism. The youth of Athens wanted a training that would free them from the hampering restrictions of the older standards of life and develop within them the skills most useful for personal advancement and political preferment.

These new demands were met by the Sophists, a group of teachers who came to Athens from the colonies, bringing with them a new type of education, adapted—so they maintained—to the changed conditions of the times. The Sophists set up a new sanction for human conduct to replace the old external authorities of tradition—family, caste, gods, or state. The new authority was the individual himself. PROTAGORAS (481-411 B.C.), one of the most upright of the Sophists, expressed this idea in the words, "Man is the measure of all things"; that is, all things are to a man just what he believes them to be. All knowledge comes through the senses; there are no universal principles of truth; each individual must determine for himself what his attitudes and conduct toward his fellows, the state, and society should be. Furthermore, the Sophists—as teachers of practical wisdom—aimed through their instruction to prepare their students for an active and successful life, especially in the realm of political and public affairs.

The educational standards and practices of the Sophists were deplored by the older and more conservative members of the community. These faithfully attempted to stem the tide of eclectic individualism, which they believed was carrying Athens to ruin, and to return the youth to the old idea of service to the state. Prominent leaders in this conservative group were ARISTOPHANES (448–380 B.C.), who held the Sophists up to ridicule in his comedies, and XENOPHON (434–355 B.C.), who called the attention of the Athenians to the Spartan and Persian devotion to their states in his *Cyropedia*. But it was too late to reverse the current; new conditions made new demands, and Athens could not turn back to the good old days.

Three great Greek educational philosophers, SOCRATES (469–399 B.C.), PLATO (428–348 B.C.), and ARISTOTLE (386–322 B.C.), sought a solution for the ever-recurring problem of the reconciliation of individualism and social stability. These mediators realized that the old educational aims were inadequate to meet the changed conditions; but they were equally convinced that the selfish individualism of the Sophists could not suffice as a basis either for morality or for education. Thus each demanded more enduring sanctions for morality and broader and nobler objectives for education.

SOCRATES found his solution in a morality based upon knowledge. Rejecting the Sophist position that the individual is the measure of all things, he declared that there were universal concepts, such as piety, temperance, and justice, upon which all men could agree, since the elements of these concepts existed in the consciousness of every man and could be grasped and understood by clear and rigorous thinking. The knowledge and application of these concepts in the lives of men is virtue, and this virtue is the goal of education. The aim of Socrates' teaching was to develop the power of thinking, to enable man to arrive at these fundamental concepts, or moral principles, of the universe. He taught that "the unexamined life is not worth living." His maxim was "Know thyself." Truth was his ultimate objective.

Plato, pupil of Socrates, insisted that the type of knowledge demanded by Socrates could be had only by men of high intellectual capacity, whom he called philosophers. He maintained that this knowledge consisted of abstract ideas of universal validity, supersensual ideas after which earthly existences are patterned. Not all men could grasp these abstractions; only the philosophers could see behind the visible manifestation and grasp the reality.

Plato's ability to use vivid imagery as well as to strike a moral concerning reality and education is well illustrated by the allegory of the cave described in his chief educational work, *The Republic.*

> Behold! human beings living in an underground den, which has a mouth open towards the light and reaching all along the den; here they have been from their childhood, and have their legs and necks chained so that they cannot move, and can only see before them, being prevented by the chains from turning round their heads. Above and behind them a fire is blazing at a distance, and between the fire and the prisoners there is a raised way; and you will see, if you look, a low wall built along the way, like the screen which marionette players have in front of them, over which they show the puppets. . . . And do you see, I said, men passing along the wall carrying all sorts of vessels, and statues and figures of animals made of wood and stone and various materials, which appear over the wall?
>
> You have shown me a strange image, and they are strange prisoners.
>
> Like ourselves, I replied; they see only their own shadows, or the shadows of one another, which the fire throws on the opposite wall of the cave. . . . [12]

Plato's social system, also presented in the same volume, would be controlled by an intellectual ruling class, each individual being edu-

---

[12] Plato, *The Republic,* Book VII, (Jowett trans.) (Cleveland: World Publishing Co., 1946.) P. 249.

cated for the place in society and the kind of work for which by nature he was best fitted. He believed that there were three dominant human traits: intellect, passion, and appetite; and he would divide society into corresponding classes of rulers, soldiers, and workers, a man's place in this classification depending upon which trait was predominant in his personality. According to Plato, the aim of education is both the happiness of the individual and the good of the state; and the business of education is to achieve these ends by a determination of the social office for which each individual is fitted, by a process of selection, sifting, and testing. Plato's goal was justice.

Aristotle, a pupil of Plato, declared that the purpose of education was to produce rational living. He wanted an educational system that would enable the individual, in association with others, to guide all his conduct by reason. The highest function of man is to be rational in thought and conduct; the highest function of the state is to direct society in such a way as to effect the greatest good of mankind. Wellbeing and well-doing, on the basis of sound reasoning, constitute true virtue and the ultimate goal of all education. These educational ideas Aristotle set forth for the most part in his *Ethics* and in his *Politics*.

Aristotle's greatest goal was happiness—although this was never to be reached save through the best relationship of the individual to his state and to himself. The golden mean, a realization of moderation in all things, was one of his most important concepts.

These great educational thinkers of Greece, though they have had a lasting influence on the thought life of the world, had little effect upon the educational practices of their own times. Their insistence upon sanctions transcending individualism could not stem the currents of selfishness that were—in a day of plebeian democracy—vitiating the life of Athens. The people as a whole, though superficially acquainted with their teachings, were little influenced by them; while most of the enlightened and educated class were already thoroughly corrupted. The rascality and moral worthlessness of the so-called "better class" proved a greater misfortune to Athens than all its military defeats. The lack of ethical standards developed by this individualistic education ultimately brought the Athenians to ruin. The philosophers could not undo the damage done by the ambitious schemes and gross mismanagement of the politicians and the popularly controlled generals.

TYPES   All the educational leaders and theorists during this period were much concerned with the problem of moral training. The Sophists discussed moral questions and settled them, not from a religious, social, or civic point of view but from the standpoint of a pragmatic and utilitarian philosophy. The basis of their morality was so individualistic and rationalistic that to the conservative Greeks they seemed to be teaching actual immorality. Their ideas of morality placed an unprecedented emphasis upon individual choice. They taught that the individual was to determine his own ends in life, his own standards of conduct, his own services to the state, his own adjustment to the group customs and moral traditions.

Much disturbed by such an individualistic solution, Socrates, Plato, and Aristotle each contemplated profoundly this problem of morality and moral education. Although they differed in their definitions of virtue and the good, they equally advocated educating for the virtuous and good life. Socrates urged a type of training that would bring about, through the dispelling of error and the discovery of truth, the attainment of the perfect life. Plato said, "Education is nurture. It can determine whether a nature shall be wild and malevolent or rich with benefits to mankind." He considered the development of character most important. Aristotle said, "The end of life, and therefore of education, is the attainment at once of intelligence and moral virtue, which bring with them the truest pleasure of which man is capable."

The intellectual training of this period was of a higher type than any we have encountered up to this point. Although the thinking developed by the Sophists frequently was superficial, it did represent an increased intellectual acuteness in discrimination between words and an increased cleverness in meeting the practical problems of life. Socrates, on the other hand, trying to stimulate a thorough and deep intellectual discipline, developed a type of intellectual training that has hardly yet been surpassed in its effectiveness. Although Plato would limit intellectual training to those who had natural aptitudes in that direction, he set forth a thorough system for accomplishing this. Aristotle advocated the training of reason through the study of the sciences and philosophy; he developed in his *Organon* the deductive method of reasoning upon which much of our later intellectual activity has been based; and first gave a vocabulary of logic to the world.

Consequently, although the general tone of political morality was low,

> The entire period was one of great intellectual activity, with probably a higher average of intellectual attainment than has ever been reached by any people, certainly a period unsurpassed in its intellectual products. The mental vigor of the entire people was stimulated, their intellectual horizons were broadened, and the content of their thought was much enriched.[13]

Vocational education of the professional type was now added to the older vocational training in manual labor. The Sophists strove to train public speakers at a time when the ability to speak convincingly and persuasively was an open sesame to positions of personal advantage. Plato also believed that there would be the greatest justice in the state when those best fitted to be artisans were trained as artisans, those best fitted to be soldiers were trained as professional soldiers, and those best fitted to be public officials were trained as professional rulers of the state.

---

[13] Thomas Davidson, *Education of the Greek People.* (New York: Appleton-Century-Crofts, Inc., 1904.) P. 30. Reprinted with the permission of the publishers.

The emphasis upon physical, military, and civic training as a preparation for state service was lessened in the actual educational practice, although the philosophers all urged these types of education as agencies for the attainment of their ideals. Domestic training for women continued to be neglected, although Xenophon advocated a system of education for girls in which for the first time a regular course of instruction in the household arts is provided. Plato, too, urged the necessity of all types of education for women—the same as for men—including intellectual education and even training for the army.

Esthetic, or cultural, education during this period made much progress. Literature was studied, not only from the grammatical and rhetorical standpoint but also for the pleasure it gave. More leisure created a demand for esthetic enjoyment; and art, music, literature, and sports were looked upon as a satisfaction of this need. This concept of education for personal enjoyment encouraged the development of new instruments and forms in music, a widening of the range of literary forms, and the utilization of sports and games for amusement and pleasure. The philosophers generally deplored this use of the arts for esthetic enjoyment and tried to elevate them again to their former place as agencies for moral education, but with little success.

CONTENT   The content of elementary education remained somewhat the same as during the earlier period, with reading, writing, arithmetic, chanting of poetry, and gymnastic exercises as the basic studies of the curriculum, but with certain changes in emphasis and approach. At the higher levels, however, physical and military exercises gave way to literary and intellectual subjects. The Sophists introduced grammar, rhetoric, declamation, and argumentation, together with the study of human nature and practical rules of conduct. The core of the whole Sophist curriculum was the art of public speaking. In fact, there is a great resemblance between the emphasis placed upon the psychology of selling in the postwar prosperity period in the United States and the emphasis placed upon public speaking by the Sophists.

With the development of secondary and higher schools to take the place of the physical training and military drill of the earlier period, geometry, astronomy, drawing, grammar, and rhetoric came to be taught at the secondary level; and philosophy, mathematics, and science at the higher levels.

Socrates apparently did not believe in formal education content. He himself did little, if any, reading. He believed in gaining knowledge through direct contact with people and by personal observation and experience. He felt that in such ways knowledge revealed itself through the soul. Socrates thus put the emphasis upon the essential content of learning and had little interest in the forms and tools, such as the rules of grammar and rhetoric, or the skills of speaking and writing.

Plato advocated, for the lower stages of training, the traditional Athenian content of reading, writing, chanting of poetry, gymnastics, and military training. For the more advanced level, he recommended four subjects which later came to be called the Quadrivium—arithmetic, astronomy, geometry, and music. For the highest stage, he advocated the study of philosophy.

Aristotle favored for the lower level the formation of physical and moral habits. For the secondary stages he recommended the training of the emotions through gymnastics, music, and drawing. For what would now be considered the collegiate plane he advocated civic training, and the development of the reason through mathematics, logic, and the sciences. Aristotle was a prolific writer on a wide variety of subjects, especially scientific and philosophical. He sought the truth everywhere, both in the world of nature and in the world of man.

Although considered the father of deductive thought, Aristotle's use of the inductive method of discovering truth made him one of the greatest thinkers that has ever lived; he laid the foundations of logic, physics, physiology, and politics and contributed much to the curriculum of later education.

AGENCIES   The *palaestra* and music school continued as the agencies of primary education in the later Athenian period, but underwent certain changes in emphases and standards. In these private schools, taught by private teachers, known as grammatists in this period, emphasis was now placed upon formal literary exercises and hair-splitting discussions. New musical instruments and new forms of music were introduced to give more subjective pleasurable effects. The severity of physical training was relaxed, and exercise was made aesthetic.

However, it was in the agencies for higher education that the most striking changes took place. The period, from the age of sixteen on, which in the older Greek education had been devoted to physical, military, and, indirectly, to political training, was now given over to purely literary and intellectual training. At first no formal schools were organized by the Sophists; the organization was in terms of informal meetings between the teacher and those who paid to hear him. Thus, in private rooms, on the street, or in the gymnasia and surrounding groves, the Sophist collected his body of adherents and gave the instruction desired.

The Sophists were well-traveled and clever, and through wide contacts and careful observation of commercial, social, and political life in various parts of the world, had picked up the practical wisdom that they taught. They were non-Athenians who had been drawn to the metropolis by the opportunities to teach for high fees, and they attracted great numbers of students.

Socrates, Plato, and Aristotle taught in much the same informal manner, although they were inclined to frequent certain places more than others. Because of the fact that Plato usually taught in the grove known as the Academy, the school of philosophy later organized by his followers came to be known as the School of the Academy. Likewise, because Aristotle frequented the Lyceum, the school that developed from his teaching came to be known as the School of the Lyceum. Similar philosophical schools were developed by ZENO (336–264 B.C.), the Stoic, and EPICURUS (342–270 B.C.), founder of the Epicurean school of philosophy.

Thus the educational urges introduced by the Sophists ultimately developed two agencies for higher education in the Mediterranean area. One stream flowed through Socrates and eventuated in the establishment of institutions known as the "philosophical schools"; the other proceeded through ISOCRATES (436–338 B.C.) and resulted in established institutions called the "rhetorical schools." After a few years these two bodies more or less fused, and to the organization thus formed some modern writers have given the term University of Athens, although at that time the word university certainly was not used. A similar development at Alexandria after the Macedonian conquest of Egypt gave rise to the University of Alexandria, which likewise became a great center of learning that persisted for hundreds of years.

ORGANIZATION   Later Athenian education came to be organized into four levels: (1) home education, usually under slaves, from birth until the age of seven; (2) primary education, in private schools, from the age of seven to the age of thirteen; (3) secondary education, in private schools, from thirteen to sixteen; (4) higher education, in the rhetorical and philosophical schools, from the age of sixteen onward.

Plato advocated distinct changes in this organization.[14] He wanted a rigid system of state-controlled public education, with the slave population excluded from all educational opportunities, but with women educated the same as men. The home was to be abolished, and children were to be considered the property of the state. He proposed the following divisions in the school organization: (1) from birth to ten years of age primary education in play, exercise, games, and tales; (2) from ten to twenty years of age secondary education in music, gymnastics, and military skill; (3) from twenty to thirty years of age higher education in mathematics, astronomy, dialectic, and philosophy. At the age of ten all those best fitted for artisans were to be eliminated; at the age of twenty all those best fitted for soldiers were withdrawn; and only those fitted for ruling over the others were to be given higher education. This was to continue, with periods of practical application, until the candidate reached the age of fifty. It was only then that Plato considered him a philosopher-king and ready to rule.

Aristotle suggested an organization in which home and state should each play a part. From birth to seven the home should train in good physical and moral habits; he condemned the usual practice of relegating the child to the care of ignorant slaves. From seven to puberty he advocated training the emotions; and from puberty to the age of

---

[14] See Book VII of *The Republic.*

twenty-one he prescribed a training in civic virtues and in reasoning. Both Plato and Aristotle believed that for the most intelligent few there should be a still higher education—one preparing for a life higher than that of civic participation: a life of study and contemplation.

METHODS   The methods of the elementary schools continued very much as they were in the earlier period. The Sophists, however, introduced into higher education a new method, that of the lecture, a method most likely to develop the habit of ready acceptance rather than of individual thinking. Their discipline consisted of acquiring information and of memorizing set speeches on a variety of topics; and, even with the best of the Sophists, mere form—pretentious argument, and word-quibbling—frequently played an important part. The lecture method continued as the prevailing method in the philosophical and rhetorical schools. In general, education tended to emphasize bookish and schoolroom tactics, in which rote learning or memorization was superseding the activities of the earlier period.

The greatest contribution toward the development of a theory of method was made by Socrates, one of the master teachers of all time. Although he himself used it continuously and with great success, the method was little followed by those of his own time and is just now beginning to find wide acceptance.

As a teacher, Socrates was critical, skeptical, patient, sympathetic, and good-natured. His method was to get the pupils to think for themselves and to see things as they really are. He believed the spirit of the learner was the one thing the teacher should produce in the pupil. The teacher's function was merely that of stimulating the mental activity of the pupil, by giving suggestions and guidance. The aim of his "Socratic method" was to bring the pupil to the place where he would be able to see his own ignorance and acquire the attitude of the true learner. He thus applied what has come to be one of the fundamental principles of modern teaching method.

This conversation or question method is sometimes called the dialectic method; and, as developed by Socrates, it has two stages: (1) the ironic[15] or destructive stage, in which, by interrogation, the pupil is brought from unconscious ignorance to conscious ignorance; (2) the maieutic[16] or constructive stage, in which, by further questioning, the pupil is led from conscious ignorance to clear and rational truth. Socrates called the teacher the "gadfly of thought" and the "intellectual midwife." If only the method of Socrates had been followed by many more of the teachers who followed him!

Of course, in education, method alone is insufficient; it is no panacea for all educational ills. Socrates has sometimes been accused of emphasizing method without enough attention to content and it is

---

[15] Ironic, from the Greek *eiron,* a dissembler in speech.
[16] Ma-ieu'tic, from the Greek *maia,* a midwife.

claimed that he overdeveloped mere discussion. And, in a way, he laid the foundations for the later development of the disciplinary concept of education. Nevertheless, in spite of these few shortcomings—as a thought-stimulation device—the method of the Socratic dialogue has never been surpassed although, in the use of the parable by Jesus Christ, we find a similarly effective teaching method.

FOR FURTHER READING

Barnes, Harry Elmer, *An Intellectual and Cultural History of the Western World*. New York: Random House, 1937. Pp. 117-193.

Breasted, James Henry, *The Conquest of Civilization*. New York: Harper and Brothers, 1926. Pp. 237-481.

Brubacher, John S. *A History of the Problems of Education*. New York: McGraw-Hill Book Co., 1947. Pp. 23-30, 96-106.

Burnham, William, *Great Teachers and Mental Health*. New York: Appleton-Century-Crofts, Inc., 1926. Pp. 10-36.

Butts, R. Freeman, *A Cultural History of Western Education*. Second Edition. New York: McGraw-Hill Book Co., 1955. Pp. 19-71.

Cole, Luella, *A History of Education*. New York: Holt, Rinehart and Winston, Inc., 1950. Pp. 8-42.

Davidson, Thomas, *Education of the Greek People*. New York: Appleton-Century-Crofts, Inc., 1904. Pp. 103-176.

Dawson, Christopher, *The Age of the Gods*. London and New York: Sheed and Ward, 1933. Pp. 343-361.

————, *The Dynamics of World History*. New York: Sheed and Ward, 1957. Pp. 148-166.

Duggan, Stephen P., *A Student's Textbook in the History of Education*. Revised Enlarged Edition. New York: Appleton-Century-Crofts, Inc., 1936. Pp. 15-50.

Durant, Will, *The Life of Greece*. New York: Simon & Schuster, Inc., 1939. Pp. 37-671.

Eby, Frederick, and Arrowood, Charles F., *The History and Philosophy of Education Ancient and Medieval*. New York: Prentice-Hall, Inc., 1940. Pp. 160-514.

Good, H. G., *A History of Western Education*. New York: The Macmillan Co., 1960. Pp. 18-41.

Graves, Frank P., *Education Before the Middle Ages*. New York: The Macmillan Co., 1909. Pp. 138-229.

Hart, Joseph K., *Creative Moments in Education*. New York: Holt, Rinehart and Winston, Inc., 1931. Pp. 27-85.

Knight, Edgar W., *Twenty Centuries of Education*. Boston: Ginn & Co., 1940. Pp. 46-71.

Mayer, Frederick, *A History of Educational Thought*. Columbus, Ohio: Charles E. Merrill Books, Inc., 1960. Pp. 81-101.

Messenger, James F., *An Interpretative History of Education*. New York: Thomas Y. Crowell Co., 1931. Pp. 29-46.

Monroe, Paul, *A Textbook in the History of Education*. New York: The Macmillan Co., 1933. Pp. 55-174.

Mulhern, James, *A History of Education*. Second Edition. New York: The Ronald Press Co., 1959. Pp. 129-177.

Painter, Franklin, *A History of Education*. New York: American Book Company, 1905. Pp. 39-77.

Reisner, Edward H., *Historical Foundations of Modern Education*. New York: The Macmillan Co., 1927. Pp. 1-104.

Shaw, Charles Gray, *Trends of Civilization and Culture*. New York: American Book Company, 1932. Pp. 125-157.

Smith, William A., *Ancient Education*. New York: Philosophical Library, Inc., 1955. Pp. 88-149.

Thut, I. N., *The Story of Education*. New York: McGraw-Hill Book Co., 1957. Pp. 41-73.

Ulich, Robert, *A History of Educational Thought*. New York: American Book Company, 1950. Pp. 1-43.

————, *Three Thousand Years of Educational Wisdom*. Cambridge, Mass.: Harvard University Press, 1954. Pp. 31-89.

Woody, Thomas, *Life and Education in Early Societies*. New York: The Macmillan Co., 1949. Pp. 197-472.

QUESTIONS FOR CLASS DISCUSSION

1. What Greek contributions to the modern world are still valuable?
2. What Greek conceptions of education were reflected in the educational views and practices of Nazi Germany and Fascist Italy?
3. Which educational system, Spartan or Athenian, would be more effective in meeting present-day conditions and problems in American life? Why?
4. To what extent are modern ideas concerning the education of girls and women similar to the views held by Plato? To those held by the Spartans?
5. Give your own interpretation of Plato's famous allegory of the Cave or "Den."

6. What plans or devices are used in American schools to serve functions similar to that of the Grecian Ephebic Oath?

7. Compare the emphasis placed today upon participation in extra-curricular activities in high schools with that placed upon participation in community activities by the early Athenians. What are the educational values of such participation?

8. Contrast the games and sports of Greek education with the athletic programs of American schools and colleges. What evils in American athletics were not present in the Greek games?

9. Contrast the place of music in Grecian schools with that in American schools. Are the motives similar?

10. Compare or contrast contemporary family life in America with that of early Athens.

CHAPTER V

AN ACCENT ON UTILITARIANISM

THE ROMAN CONCEPTS OF EDUCATION

With the continued development of the Greek philosophical schools and the rise of great centers of learning in certain cities, especially Athens, Alexandria, Antioch, Pergamum, and the Island of Rhodes, Hellenistic education withdrew more and more from the practical affairs of life. Education as a leisure pursuit and as a life of contemplation replaced the old ideal of education for service to the state and to society.

Education became theoretical rather than practical. Although theorizing about life, the scholars in these schools kept themselves cloistered and aloof from its actual problems. Where at first the Greek philosophers had sought practical ideals for expression in life, later philosophers were interested chiefly in intellectual speculation for its own sake, and in the circulation of their theories among their disciples.

There was need for a new force in education, an influence that would return it again to the actualities of life as the early Hellenes had regarded them. This influence came from the fresh and vigorous civilization of Rome, which had been gradually developing for the past several hundred years across the Ionian Sea on the peninsula of Italy.

Athens is a point of light in history. But the world needs more than light. It needs solid foundations under its feet. The primitive world had not much light, but it did have solidity. Greece destroyed for a time the legend of that solidity. It was the business of Rome to bring back some part of that legend, and to do what could be done to give to men, once more, a feel of permanent security.[1]

Founded—according to legend—in 753 B.C., the tiny city-state of Rome had grown until her power dominated first the whole peninsula of Italy, then the entire Mediterranean world. Her success may be traced mainly to two circumstances: the geographical location and the character of the Roman people.

Rome did not make many intellectual or artistic contributions to modern civilization. The contributions of the Romans were along the lines of organization and administration. They were a practical people and rendered their great service to mankind by building up the institutions through which the aspirations of other peoples might be realized. The value system of modern life has been taken largely from Greek and Hebrew sources, but for the institutions of modern life we are indebted largely to the Romans. The Romans judged all things by their usefulness; they were essentially a utilitarian people.

Passing from Athens to Rome is as passing from poetry to prose, from an artists' picnic to a business house; from a people seeking to make the present beautiful and to enjoy it rationally and nobly, to a people that subordinates present enjoyment to future gain; from a people that lives by reason to people that lives by authority.[2]

The Roman genius for organization showed itself particularly in its military and political institutions, through the effectiveness of which Rome was able to achieve a great world empire—surpassing even the empires of Persia and of Alexander. The Romans took the religion of a despised and persecuted sect and, through the power of their organizing ability, transformed it into the closely knit administrative structure of the great Roman Catholic Church. The Romans organized a body of civil law which even today lies at the basis of the legal systems of most of the Western world.

The Roman talent for adaptation and application was far superior to its genius for originality. This was manifest in the Roman contributions to art and literature, although it is true that certain specific literary contributions made by such writers as Cicero, Vergil, and Horace have influenced literature even to this day. In the sciences, Rome's contribution has been in the field of applied science such as mechanics and engineering rather than pure science; she took the mathematics and logic of the Greek philosophers and applied them to the building of roads, bridges, and aqueducts, and to the development of agriculture. Similarly, in education, although Rome contributed little that was

---

[1] Joseph K. Hart, *Creative Moments in Education.* (New York: Holt, Rinehart and Winston, Inc., 1931.) P. 86. Reprinted with the permission of the publishers.
[2] Thomas Davidson, *A History of Education.* (New York: Charles Scribner's Sons, 1900.) P. 106.

original or unique to the development of educational thought, she was able to build up an educational pattern which—from the standpoint of organization and effectiveness—was superior to any that had preceded it.

What were the influences that produced these Roman characteristics? What made it possible for Rome to make its peculiar contributions to civilization in general and education in particular? What were the origins of this virile nation?

The Italian peninsula was settled for the most part by three general groups: (1) the Italians, (2) the Etruscans, and (3) the Greek colonists. The Italians, the chief people of the peninsula, consisted of various Aryan tribes who had pushed their way from eastern and central Europe across the Alps and down into central Italy. The most important of these tribes were the Sabellians, the Umbrians, and the Latins. Ultimately, city-states developed among them as in Greece, with the Latin city-state of Rome emerging finally as the most powerful and significant. Who the Etruscans were or whence they came is unknown; but when we first hear of them they were far in advance of the Italians in all that relates to security, comfort, and refinement. They made vases and sculptures, paved roads, dug canals, built massive walls, towers, and arched gateways. They had religious leaders and sacred laws; and the Italians— particularly the Latins—must have learned much from this advanced Etruscan culture. But, as teachers of the Italians, the Etruscans were in the end outrivaled by the Greek colonists who, about the middle of the eighth century before Christ, began to settle the shores of southern Italy and Sicily.

From the mingling of these various peoples came the strong, energetic Roman nation. Italy is extremely long in proportion to its breadth, and near it in every direction are alien lands from which enemies can easily come. Thus, it was a logical development for the remaining city-states of Italy to be united under Rome, her strongest commonwealth. Even when united, the country was unsafe while neighboring nations remained powerful enough to assail it. Consequently the desire for self-preservation forced Rome—the leading power of the peninsula—to adopt her great imperial career of foreign conquest.

The Apennines, extending throughout the length of the peninsula, slope to the eastern shore; and the country is thus closed to the east and open to the west. Turning its back upon the East, with its decaying politics, ancient Rome faced the fresh vital peoples of the West and found her chief interest in giving them her institutions. It is due to the influence of Rome that the vigorous peoples of central and western Europe developed into modern nations. There is abundant reason for looking upon the Roman as the last of the ancients and the first of the moderns. Geographical conditions, climate, and the self-sufficiency of the peninsula were favorable for promoting the well-being, happiness, and prosperity of its people. It is not surprising that Dionysius, a Greek writer on Roman history, should call Italy "the best and most favored country in the ancient world."

Politically, the history of Rome covers many periods; but, from the standpoint of educational development, we can divide the whole history into two: (1) the early or purely Roman period, lasting from the founding of the city of Rome (753 B.C.) to the burning of Corinth and the annexation of the Greek city-states, in 146 B.C.; (2) the later or Graeco-Roman period, lasting from 146 B.C. to the closing of all pagan schools by the Christian emperior Justinian, about 500 A.D.[3]

ATTITUDES OF THE EARLY ROMANS TOWARD EDUCATION

The story of the beginnings of Rome—as it has come down to us—is a mixture of fact and fiction. Of the many legends of the founding of Rome, the familiar myth of Romulus and Remus was the one that came to be accepted by the Romans themselves, who wanted to connect their history with that of Greece—the country from which they had derived so much of their culture. No one really knows by whom or under what circumstances Rome was founded. It was merely one of several early towns of Latium. Even the traditional date of its founding, 753 B.C., can be taken only as approximate.

At first Rome consisted of a federation of clans, or *curia,* governed by a war chief, the king; by a senate, composed of the heads of the patrician families; and by a popular assembly, the *comitia curiata,* made up of all freemen who could bear arms. The commoners were called plebeians, the multitude; and the nobles were called patricians. About 509 B.C., the kings were expelled, and the power was transferred to the aristocratic senate, in which the plebeians had no part. Then began a great struggle on the part of the common people for recognition. The greatest reform was the codification of the laws by the *Decemviri,* elected for that purpose. The ten original laws were established in 451 B.C., and later two more were added. These are the famous laws of the Twelve Tables, codified and set up in the market place. Through these laws and other political reforms, the plebeians gradually won their rights, and the Roman republic became a democracy.

What were the attitudes of the Romans toward education during this early period including the rule of the kings and the beginnings of the republic?

---

[3] Within this latter era occurred a remarkable period which is known in history as the "Roman peace." From the beginning of the reign of Augustus (27 B.C.) through that of Marcus Aurelius (d. 180 A.D.), with the exception of border skirmishes on its far-flung frontier, the empire remained at peace. "There was nothing on which the people of the empire prided themselves more than this universal peace—the *pax Romana* as they called it. The regions devastated by the wars of the republic were restored to prosperity, commerce and industry flourished on every hand, and wealth increased. Never before in history had peace and contentment been so general over so large an area as during the first two centuries of the empire." (McKinley, Howland and Dann, *World History in the Making,* New York: American Book Company, 1927.) P. 257. Reprinted with the permission of the publishers.

AIMS   The aim of early Roman education was to repress the freedom of the individual in the interest of the state—to make a nation of brave warriors and of dutiful citizens. The Roman concept of the good life was quite different from that of the Greeks. In contrast to the subjectivity of the Greeks, the Roman was objective, striving for the accomplishment of some concrete purpose lying outside of his own thought life, some excellence or achievement of concrete and tangible worth to his fellows. Early Roman education was distinctly a training for practical life. Its aim was the development of the *vir bonus*—the good citizen, the good soldier, the good worker. The *vir bonus* was the man possessed of all the virtues essential for the exercise of his rights and the discharge of his duties and obligations. The virtues chiefly prized were piety, obedience, manliness, courage, bravery, industry, honesty, prudence, earnestness, sobriety, dignity, fortitude, and gravity.

Utility—rather than harmony or grace—was most important to the early Romans. The Roman virtues are in sharp contrast to those praised by the Greeks: personal satisfaction, esthetic enjoyment, happiness, and intellectual activity for its own sake. The Romans looked upon the Greeks as a visionary and impractical people; for they themselves judged everything by its serviceability and effectiveness. Even religion with the Romans remained a practical means of getting on in the world, a means of regulating everyday life, closely connected with the family and with political and business affairs. It consecrated love of country, hallowed the family relation, preserved the sanctity of the oath, developed a sense of duty—in fact gave authority and sanction to most of the goals of their education. In fact, the educational aim of these early Romans was to train men to be active and efficient in daily life; to be conquerors in war, wise in politics, and to have reverence for the gods.

TYPES   This education was essentially practical training for the affairs of life. There was no attempt at intellectual or esthetic training; and poetry, music, and gymnastics, so prominent in Athenian education, were conspicuous by their absence. Early Rome had no use for what they thought were the passing fashions of education. "Life was real and life was earnest," and so emphasis was placed upon physical training, military training, civic training, and vocational training.

The Romans had a moral view of life as well as a practical, and most of their education had the coloring of ethical training. Moral rights and duties were clearly defined by law, and for every right there was a corresponding obligation. Youths were trained to obey the moral law, for the moral law and the civil law were in practice one and the same.[4]

---

[4] Many legends or perhaps myths were used to assist in the moral indoctrination. For example there were the stories of Mucius and Cloelia, brave representatives of both sexes who so impressed an invader with their courage that he gave up the attack; of Marcus Curtius, who sacrificed himself for the city; of Camillus, the upright general; and, of course, of Cincinnatus, who willingly laid down the dictator's power; and—unnecessary to relate—of the Horatius who kept the bridge.

Religious training was tied up with moral and civic training. Roman religion was a religion of duty in contrast to the Greek religion of beauty. A good citizen of early Rome was obedient to authority, pious, frugal, and generally honest. His religion and morals were, however, always of a practical sort; for, though he was willing to sacrifice his life for the good of the state, he was equally willing to enrich himself at the expense of his neighbors. Vocational education, a training for a livelihood, disdained by the Greek freeman, was given a respected place in early Rome.

CONTENT   The content of early Roman education, therefore, was distinctly practical and moral in character. Children were taught home life, citizenship, and ancestral traditions. There were no books at first. The children memorized and chanted legendary ballads glorifying the traits esteemed by the Romans, religious songs, and the laws of the Twelve Tables.

The children were trained in religious ceremonies and usages. Every activity of life, such as plowing and harvesting, marriage, and birth, was under the auspices of some deity to whom it was necessary to give homage. In this early Roman period, the deities were conceived of as stern and inexorable; they were to be propitiated by sacrifices and ceremonies, and must be if family relations, court procedures, national campaigns were to be well begun and fortunately carried out; religion had an intimate relation to private and public conduct. Jupiter, the chief deity, was a generalization of Roman manhood and was supreme guardian of Rome; Juno, wife of Jupiter, was the generalization of noble Roman womanhood; Janus, twin-faced, blessed the beginnings and ends of all activities; Saturn blessed seed-sowing; Minerva warned "the husbandman in time of the works to be undertaken"; Mars guided the destiny of battles; Vulcan blessed the forge and was the god of industry; Venus was the garden deity until identified later with Aphrodite, the Greek goddess of love. The first religious education of the child was in the home, where he gave offerings to the *Lares,* spirits of his ancestors, and to the *Penates,* spirits of the household. The shrine was the hearth, and Vesta was goddess of the hearth. Sacrifices were given each morning, and special ones on holidays.

The laws of the Twelve Tables formed a large part of the content of education in this early period. What the laws of Moses were to early Hebrew education, the laws of Lycurgus to Spartan education, the laws of Solon to the early Athenian education, the laws of the Twelve Tables were to the early education of the Romans. These laws defined private and public relationships and made clear the human and property rights of each person under Roman control and protection. The rights recognized were: (1) the right of a father over his children, (2) the right of a husband over his wife, (3) the right of a master over his slaves, (4) the right of one freeman over another through contract or forfeiture, and (5) the right of a man over his property.[5] The youth was supposed to memorize these laws as a practical guidance for his later life. This was his training in citizenship.

In the home, the child played and romped; and games were encouraged for younger boys and girls, to help give them strength and vigor. Specific military exercises for the boys were given later in the military camps. Physical education apart from training for war was an idea unfamiliar to the mind of the Roman. As the boy grew older, he went about in the company of his father and learned the efficiencies of life from his father and the other men he met. If a patrician he accompanied his father to banquets and to the forum, where he learned by listening to discussions of affairs of state. If a plebeian he joined with his father in the duties of farm and shop.

The girl was trained at home by her mother in the domestic arts and the moral virtues. She learned to spin and weave and perform the other household tasks. She too was taught to be devoted to the state and to be ready to serve it at all times. Reading and writing were little needed and so were seldom taught—not until late in the third century before Christ, when Greek elementary schools began to be set up by private teachers.

AGENCIES   The family was the significant institution in early Roman life, and to its continuance as such was due largely the greatness of Rome in the best days of the republic. The father, the *pater familias*, was supreme, but the mother likewise was held in high esteem. The father had the right to exposed weak or defective children to die, and those whom he spared usually grew up healthy and strong. Though early custom placed the wife in the power of her husband, in contrast to the position of wives in Greek society, she went about freely, taught her children, and sometimes aided her husband in his career. Her position as matron of the household commanded respect from the state as well as from society in general. The phrase "Roman matron" was a synonym for all that was fine in womanhood in the days of ancient Rome. Both parents were equally careful to train the children in the stern, simple virtues which made good soldiers and good citizens. The father had teaching as well as priestly functions in these earlier days, and the mother was his able assistant. The home, then, was a strict moral school in which youth was disciplined for private and public life.

In a conception of education that for the most part has to do with the formation of moral character, schools can have but a minor place as an educational means. Their place was to be taken by other institutions, above all others, the home.[6]

---

[5] It will be noted that these Roman rights were "rights over," which corresponds to the strictness with which they viewed the social relation. They are in contrast to the obligations stressed by Confucius which represented mutual relationships.
[6] Paul Monroe, *A Textbook in the History of Education.* (New York: The Macmillan Co., 1933.) P. 185. Reprinted with the permission of the publishers.

The military camp and the forum, as well as the farm and the shop, were agencies in the education of the boy; but the girl received all her education in the home, under the mother. Toward the middle of the second century before Christ, many cultured Greeks were brought to Rome as slaves, and these sometimes acted as tutors to the children of wealthy families. And not long after, some Greek teachers opened schools in Rome and taught the rudiments of intellectual education to those who were able to pay their fees; but they were scorned by the conservative practical-minded Romans and for the time being made little headway.

ORGANIZATION The organization, then, was largely in terms of the home, where the mother supervised the early training of both boys and girls; and from which, later, the boy accompanied his father to the farm and the shop, where he learned to work, or to the forum, where he learned his future role in public affairs by hearing practical questions of state business discussed.

When the boy reached the age of sixteen, he became a citizen of the state. He now took on the *toga virilis* of manhood, in place of the *toga praetexta* of his youth, solemnized through the performance of domestic ceremonies and religious rites, temple sacrifices and family festivals. He then entered the camp, an institution for specific military training. Thus he was prepared for his duties in life, both civic and military.

METHODS The method of early Roman education was mainly that of direct imitation. The Roman was convinced that the proper way to learn any activity or to acquire any virtue was through imitation and, by practicing the activity or virtue often enough, to develop it into a fixed habit. Great stress was placed upon habit formation. Thus education was essentially training—not instruction; to give instruction in the rational bases of habits was never even considered. The boy learned by imitating his father, the girl, by imitating her mother. And they were urged to imitate the heroes of the past who had served Rome, and whose exploits were recorded in song and story. Thus biography as well as living examples provided models for imitation. Plutarch's *Lives,* although written at a much later period, are typical of the form and substance of this material. These biographical stories were not usually read by the boys themselves, but were told or recited in their presence. When the father helped his boy get the little ability considered necessary in reading, writing, and counting, he did it by example and imitation.

The laws of the Twelve Tables were memorized along with certain ballads and religious songs. Although the laws were recognized as a source of practical guidance for later life, they were not studied critically; the intellectual element in early Roman education was slight.

Discipline was exceedingly rigorous. Corporal punishment and even death could be inflicted by the father at will. This was possible under the power known as *patria potestas,* granted to the father by the ancient law.

ATTITUDES OF THE LATER ROMANS TOWARD EDUCATION

In the early period of Roman history, as we have noted, educational ideals and practices were purely Roman. In the later period, however, Greek influence becomes more and more pervasive, and education becomes composite and cosmopolitan. Owing to the conservative and stable nature of the Roman personality, change from the early to the later attitudes was much more gradual than in Athens; and it is difficult to fix a dividing line between the two periods.

In some areas the influence of the Greeks was felt rather early. Rome drew its alphabet from Greece, and certain elements in its religion and laws were typically Grecian. But there were no outstanding social or educational changes derived from Greece until about the middle of the second century before Christ. In education, these changes were along the line of agencies and institutions; and the somewhat radical innovations were indebted, for their acceptance, to the lack of any organized system of educational institutions in Rome to be displaced.

As Rome extended her political and military power outside the Italian peninsula, through the Punic[7] and Macedonian wars, her people came in contact with other civilizations, especially the Greek, with consequent widening of their intellectual horizon. As early as 267 B.C., cultured Greeks were brought to Rome as slaves. One of these was LIVIUS ANDRONICUS; after obtaining his freedom, he became a teacher of the Greek language to Roman youths. Andronicus translated the *Odyssey* into Latin and thus made Homer available in Roman education. Many other Greeks opened tutorial schools in Rome to teach both the Greek language and Greek literature in Latin translations. Soon, Roman youths were journeying to Greek centers of learning to study rhetoric and philosophy, and some Greek philosophers and rhetoricians appeared in Rome.

Early in this era of gradual transition, elementary schools were set up by private teachers to teach reading, writing, and counting. The name given to these schools, *"ludi,"* from *ludus,* meaning sport or play, indicates that their function was merely supplementary, and that they were not essential to the real education of the Roman youth. In no way

---

[7] Punic comes from Phoenician and these wars, beginning in 264 B.C. and ending with the destruction of Carthage—a Phoenician colony—in 146 B.C., completed the sovereignty of Rome in the Mediterranean.

was the emphasis upon family training in the habits and duties of the man and the citizen lessened by these early *ludi*.

These schools established thus early under Greek influence were all private undertakings and were attended by only the few children and youth of the upper classes. They were held in private homes and in certain unfrequented nooks or porches of the temples or other public buildings. Even by those who patronized them, these schools were evidently looked upon at first as diversions from the essential training of the purely Roman tradition. Indeed the Latin word for school, *schola,* signifies leisure and it seems the early Greek schools were so considered.

The native conservatism of Roman character made a sudden transition impossible. The leader of the opposition was CATO THE ELDER (234–149 B.C.), who for years strenuously opposed the growth of Greek ideas and customs, because of his conviction that the Greeks were decadent. In warning his fellow citizens against what he considered a pernicious influence, he said:

> Believe me, the Greeks are a good-for-nothing and unimprovable race. If they disseminate their literature among us, it will destroy everything; but still worse if they send their doctors among us, for they have bound themselves by solemn oath to kill the barbarians and the Romans.[8]

Through his efforts and at his instigation, the senate in 161 B.C. decreed the expulsion of all philosophers and rhetoricians from Rome.

But with the death of Cato and, three years later, the final conquest of Greece through the destruction of Corinth (146 B.C.), the floodgates were opened to foreign influences. Shiploads of art treasures were brought in as plunder from the cities of Sicily and Greece. Without appreciation of real beauty, the wealthy nobles nevertheless took pleasure in adorning their houses and villas with stolen statues. Along with foreign art came the ideas, the religions, and the morals, of the conquered strangers. It is not surprising that, along with other plunder, Greek scholars, Greek literature, and even complete libraries were transferred to Rome by the conquerors. There was also imported the system of education upon which all this culture was based, although the system was greatly improved in its organization by the institutionally minded Romans. The final triumph of the Greek influence upon Roman education was marked by the publication of CICERO's *De Oratore* in 55 B.C., for this book is the first formulation by a Roman of the Greek educational ideal. By this time, the Graeco-Roman educational system was fixed as it was to remain until the close of the empire. Truly "captive Greece took captive her rude conqueror."

What were the educational attitudes prevalent during this Graeco-Roman period? In what respects did Greek influence shape the aims, types, content, agencies, organization, and methods of later Roman education?

---

[8] Quoted by Pliny, *Natural History,* XXIX, 7. 14.

Aims   The aim of later Roman education was mainly in the direction of intellectual development. Language ability and success in public speaking and debate became the main purpose of training. But at first the purely Roman emphasis upon moral character was retained; the *orator,* who was considered the ideally educated man, must be *vir bonus* first and after that the skilled speaker. The function of education was to produce a good man skilled in speaking and thus able to be of practical service to the state. Only such a man was the true orator. The aim included three factors: (1) moral character, (2) wide culture, and (3) ability to speak convincingly.

The Romans attempted to introduce the new wine of Greek culture and intellectual activity and individualism into the old bottles of Roman institutional life. Never before, perhaps never at any time, has one people attempted to appropriate so thoroughly the intellectual life of another. The native vigor of the Roman character made it possible to do this without a complete surrender of their own characteristics and consequently rendered some modification of the Greek intellectual and educational characteristics necessary. The Romans never acquired the intellectuality, versatility, or the originality of the Greeks; at most, they succeeded in mastering the external; at best, they perfected the forms of literature; at worst, in the later centuries, their education became one of pure form possessing little content or real value.[9]

The aim of the Roman-organized school system was to prepare the student for the life of public affairs. Cicero (106–43 b.c.) in his *De Oratore,* Tacitus (55–117 a.d.) in his *De Oratoribus,* Quintilian (35–100 a.d.) in his *De Institutione Oratoria,* set up the orator as the ideally educated man. All conceive of the true orator as one who uses his learning by putting it to the practical use of public service. All agree that he should have a wide background of basic culture and be primarily a "good man."

Thus, during the republic and early empire, training for service to society was the ideal, and such training was carried on vigorously and effectively, especially in the rhetorical schools. But in the later imperial period—the three hundred years just prior to Rome's loss of political sovereignty—the aim of education degenerated: the old elements—the *vir bonus* and the concept of state service—dropped out, and rhetorical training was sought for mere affectation and personal display. Indeed this shallow interpretation of what formerly had been a rigorous and meaningful training was to remain current in education for many of the years that followed the fall of Rome.

Types   Education was intellectual and yet largely practical. Speech training was the outstanding type of training demanded. In terms of its ultimate goals, and when carried on at its best, the education of this period was civic education.

---

[9] Paul Monroe, *op. cit.,* p. 197. Reprinted with the permission of the publishers.

Although Roman education of this period was not democratic or universal, great men were produced under such an educational system—men whose names are known everywhere for their service not only to Rome but to the world. Cicero, Vergil, Caesar, Seneca, Quintilian—these men could think, talk, and write well, and believed that such talents should be used for the benefit of their fellow men. But it never occurred to the Roman leaders that Rome could endure only by raising the intelligence and culture of the whole mass of the people. While a few leaders were getting a high type of broad intellectual training, the great mass of the population were getting the narrowest vocational training, and with less and less attention to their moral training. As a result, the Roman people as a whole became more and more decadent, interested only in the material things that gave satisfaction to their senses and their appetites, and the efforts of the intellectuals all went for naught in the end. Rome decayed, declined, and eventually even lost those powers of government which had been the reason for her early greatness.

AGENCIES AND ORGANIZATION   As one would expect, the organizing genius of the Romans expressed itself in a perfected system of schools. The construction of a carefully organized educational ladder is the striking contribution of imperial Rome. The Romans appropriated the educational institutions of the Greeks, but perfected them into a system such as the Greeks never thought of developing.

For the elementary level, they developed the school of the *litterator* (the school of the teacher of letters). This was the outgrowth and successor of the earlier *ludus* and was attended by both boys and girls from the age of seven to ten. For the secondary level, they developed the school of the *grammaticus* (the school of the teacher of grammar), for boys only, from ten to sixteen. This school existed in two types: (1) the Greek grammar school for the study of Greek grammar and literature, and (2) the Latin grammar school for the study of Latin grammar and literature. The Roman boy attended both, but Quintilian advocated that he should go to the Greek school first and afterwards attend the Latin school. For the higher level there was developed the school of the *rhetor* (the school of the teacher of rhetoric), providing a course of two or three years for boys from the age of sixteen on.

At first there was no institution in Rome beyond the schools of the *rhetors;* and any Roman youth who wished to obtain a "university" education had to study abroad, at Athens, Alexandria, or Rhodes. But the practice of bringing manuscripts to Rome as part of the war plunder led to the establishment of a library by VESPASIAN in 75 A.D.; and around this library there developed a center of learning called the *Athenaeum,* which was to serve the purposes of what today would constitute higher or university education.

All the schools were at first privately controlled and supported by tuition fees paid to the teachers, and attendance was voluntary for the well-to-do. The Roman never regarded the school of the *litterator* as an important part of the system; and the teachers in these schools were held in low esteem, and their fees were very irregular and uncertain. As no qualifications for teaching were demanded in this school, it was usually presided over by a freedman. The teaching generally was poor, and the equipment was of the same quality. Many Roman boys never went to it, but received their elementary training from a tutor at home. A *custos,* similar to the Greek pedagogue but more carefully selected, accompanied the child to and from school. As in Athens, this *custos* generally replaced the father in the direct oversight of the child. The teachers in the grammatical and rhetorical schools were of a higher class and received much better pay.

During the later imperial period, a movement in the direction of state control and support began—particularly of the schools of the *grammaticus* and *rhetor* and of the university. Quintilian, in a lengthy argument, shows the superiority of the public school over the private school and advocates the establishment of a complete public school system. Vespasian (69–79)[10] began the payment of salaries out of the public treasury to Greek rhetoricians in Rome; Trajan (98–117) provided for public scholarships in the schools; Antoninus Pius (138–161) exempted many teachers from taxation, army service, and the obligation to support soldiers, and Marcus Aurelius (161–180) instituted the payment of salaries to teachers in the university.

CONTENT   Even in this later period, elementary education never attempted to give more than the merest rudiments of reading, writing, and calculation. The laws of the Twelve Tables continued to be used as reading texts, but by the time of Cicero these had given way entirely to the Latin translations of Homer and versified moral maxims. Arithmetic was very elementary because of the cumbersome Roman notation system.

In the secondary school curriculum, grammar was the chief study. But grammar had a wider meaning for the Roman than it has now for us; it included the study of literature as well as language. Many Greek and Latin authors were read in a study of the content and form of literature; and minute attention was given to the style of those who were used as models for writing and speaking. Geography, history, natural sciences, and mythology were studied rather superficially to enable the student to understand allusions to these subjects in literature. In the grammar school, the practical character of Roman life was always considered, and only subjects of functional value were presented. Gymnastics and dancing were never introduced into the schools. The former was used in connection with military training, and the latter was taught, if at all, in the home. Music was introduced in connection with speaking, as an aid to the improvement of intonation in oratory.

---

[10] The dates in this paragraph refer to reigns of emperors.

In the higher school rhetoric was the outstanding study. This consisted of declamation, extempore speaking, and debates on points of Roman law and moral principles. At their best, these schools of *rhetors* also emphasized ethical and cultural content. CICERO insisted that the orator must not only develop his natural gifts for speaking, but must acquire knowledge in many fields as a cultural background. He held to a high moral standard; philosophy to him was the crown of all learning, the school of virtue. Pupils must know the history of their country, he said; he cared little for natural sciences, yet he called politics the queen of sciences. In his *De Oratore* he declared that the orator must have the philosopher's knowledge of things and human nature, but must have also the power to make such knowledge effective by influencing his fellow citizens through speech.

According to QUINTILIAN, just as the grammar school should acquaint the boy with all literature, so the rhetorical school should give him knowledge of music, arithmetic, astronomy, geometry, and philosophy. He enumerated the following as essential elements in the training of the orator: (1) a knowledge of things, (2) a good vocabulary and ability to make a careful choice of words, (3) gracefulness and urbanity of manners, (4) knowledge of history and law, (5) good memory, (6) a good delivery. Beyond all else he stressed ethical content in education; for, in his estimation, no one could be a good orator unless he was a good man. Practice in the schools, however, perhaps fell far short of these standards set by Cicero and Quintilian.

The curriculum of the Roman university varied from that of the Greek higher schools. Neither philosophical speculation nor pure science appealed to the practical Romans. It was science in the applied form which claimed their attention; thus in higher education there developed professional preparation for law, medicine, architecture, and mechanics. What philosophy was to the Greeks, medicine and law were in the Roman culture—the highest intellectual goals.

METHODS   At the elementary level, the methods were those of memorizing and imitation. Material was meager. The pupils sat upon the floor or upon stones and rested their tablets on their knees. School hours were long, lasting from sunrise until sunset; but there was no school in summer, and holidays were numerous. The pupils were taught the names and order of the letters of the alphabet, generally without learning anything in regard to their forms.[11] All the possible combinations of syllables were then learned by rote. Next, writing and reading were taught by means of exercises dictated by the teacher. Pronunciation, enunciation, and intelligent expression received special attention.

---

[11] Quintilian, however, in Book I of his *Institutes of Oratory* recommended the following: "As soon as the child has begun to know the shapes of the various letters, it will be no bad thing to have them cut as accurately as possible up on a board, so that the pen may be guided along the grooves. Thus mistakes such as occur with wax tablets will be rendered impossible for the pen will be confined between the edges of the letters and will be prevented from going astray."

Writing was taught by copying and tracing on a wax tablet with the stylus, as in Greece. Counting was done on the fingers, with pebbles, or with the abacus. Discipline was severe; the rod and the whip were used frequently.

At the secondary level, the method was largely one of drill in good literary and moral habits. There was usually intensive drill on parts of speech, syntax, inflections, and other grammatical elements. There were elaborate exercises in paragraphing, composition, and verse-writing. A favorite method was for the teacher to dictate a quotation from some writer, to be taken down verbatim and used by the pupil as the basis of an elaborate theme, which was organized according to the following outline: (1) a panegyric on the author, (2) an expansion of the thought, (3) an explanation and defense of the principle underlying the thought, (4) a comparison of the thought with similar ideas of other authors, (5) a collection of confirmatory quotations of incidents, and (6) a statement of the moral lessons to be drawn from the passage, and a suggestion as to how the principle is to be put into practice.

At the higher level, there was much declamation of memorized passages, with attention given especially to intonation, articulation, and other elements of delivery. In addition, there were frequent debates in which the fine distinctions of Roman law and morality were developed. Practice was given in funeral orations and eulogies, pleas for plaintiffs and defendants, and all other types of speaking. The *rhetor* used the lecture method in presenting the wide range of subjects considered necessary for the cultural background of the orator.

While both Plato and Aristotle wrote of theoretical methods of education and Socrates taught with the greatest skill, Quintilian's *De Institutione Oratoria* is the first practical exposition of the entire field of education, and is also the first real approach to a solution of the problems of educational methodology. It is the first treatment of the principles of educational procedure, and anticipates many of our so-called modern principles of teaching. Thus, Quintilian (1) condemns the use of physical force and emphasizes the necessity of making studies attractive, taking the position that proper methods of teaching will remove the necessity for corporal punishment; (2) emphasizes the fact that different natures demand different treatments, and urges that teachers study the dispositions of their pupils; (3) points out the proper attitudes that teachers should take toward their pupils; and (4) indicates the importance of careful selection of teachers, setting forth the qualifications that they should possess. *De Institutione Oratoria* probably reflects the methods of only the very best of the Roman schools, but it was considered the standard authority for the guidance of the teacher throughout the later centuries of Roman history. Quintilian, of course, was not only a writer on education, but a most successful teacher himself—having been the first of the *rhetors* subsidized by the Emperor Vespasian. He was therefore no dreaming theorist but a most practical educational worker.

Roman utilitarian education did not rival the originality and genius of the Greeks of the Golden Age but it did produce, in the precepts of Cicero, Seneca, and Marcus Aurelius, some excellent standards; and, in the methodology of Quintilian and through the opportunity for moral inculcation offered by Plutarch in his famous *Parallel Lives,* it served to influence both the medieval and the modern world.

FOR FURTHER READING

Barnes, Harry Elmer, *An Intellectual and Cultural History of the Western World.* New York: Random House, 1937. Pp. 195-256.

Breasted, James Henry, *The Conquest of Civilization.* New York: Harper and Brothers, 1926. Pp. 482-693.

Browning, Oscar, *A History of Educational Theories.* New York: Harper and Brothers, 1905. Pp. 18-34.

Brubacher, John S., *A History of the Problems of Education.* New York: McGraw-Hill Book Co., 1947. Pp. 173-178.

Butts, R. Freeman, *A Cultural History of Western Education.* Second Edition. New York: McGraw-Hill Book Co., 1955. Pp. 72-115.

Clough, Shepard B., *The Rise and Fall of Civilization.* New York: McGraw-Hill Book Co., 1951. Pp. 118-162.

Cole, Luella, *A History of Education from Socrates to Montessori.* New York: Holt, Rinehart and Winston, Inc., 1950. Pp. 43-90.

Dawson, Christopher, *The Age of the Gods.* London and New York: Sheed and Ward, 1933. Pp. 363-384.

Duggan, Stephen P., *Student's Textbook in the History of Education.* Revised Enlarged Edition. New York: Appleton-Century-Crofts, Inc., 1936. Pp. 51-66.

Durant, Will, *Caesar and Christ.* New York: Simon & Schuster, Inc., 1944. Pp. 1-672.

Eby, Frederick, and Arrowood, Charles F., *The History and Philosophy of Education Ancient and Medieval.* New York: Prentice-Hall, Inc., 1940. Pp. 515-577.

Good, H. G., *A History of Western Education.* New York: The Macmillan Co., 1960. Pp. 42-57.

Graves, Frank P., *Education Before the Middle Ages,* New York: The Macmillan Co., 1909. Pp. 230-270.

Hart, Joseph K., *Creative Moments in Education.* New York: Holt, Rinehart and Winston, Inc., 1931. Pp. 86-105, 121-139.

Knight, Edgar W., *Twenty Centuries of Education.* Boston: Ginn & Co., 1940. Pp. 72-86.

Mayer, Frederick, *A History of Educational Thought.* Columbus, Ohio: Charles E. Merrill Books, Inc., 1960. Pp. 103-113.

Messenger, James F., *An Interpretative History of Education.* New York: Thomas Y. Crowell Co., 1931. Pp. 47-53.

Monroe, Paul, *A Textbook in the History of Education.* New York: The Macmillan Co., 1933. Pp. 176-218.

Mulhern, James, *A History of Education.* Second Edition. New York: The Ronald Press Co., 1959. Pp. 178-212.

Painter, Franklin, *A History of Education.* New York: American Book Company, 1905. Pp. 83-142.

Reisner, Edward H., *Historical Foundations of Modern Education.* New York: The Macmillan Co., 1927. Pp. 105-222.

Shaw, Charles Gray, *Trends of Civilization and Culture.* New York: American Book Company, 1932. Pp. 158-186.

Smith, William A., *Ancient Education.* New York: Philosophical Library, Inc., 1955. Pp. 150-196.

Ulich, Robert, *A History of Educational Thought.* New York: American Book Company, 1950. Pp. 44-60.

————, *Three Thousand Years of Educational Wisdom.* Cambridge, Mass.: Harvard University Press, 1954. Pp. 90-123.

Woody, Thomas, *Life and Education in Early Societies.* New York: The Macmillan Co., 1949. Pp. 475-756.

QUESTIONS FOR CLASS DISCUSSION

1. In what period of American history was the American boy trained in ways similar to those used in the rearing of the early Roman youth? What changes have occurred?

2. How do contemporary ideas of the "good man" resemble or differ from the Roman conception of the *vir bonus?*

3. Do you believe that the problem of juvenile delinquency would be less serious today if parents and the home played the same part in education that they did in ancient Rome? Explain.

4. In what respects is the organization of American education more like that of the Greeks or more like that of the Romans?

5. Compare the use of biography in today's schools with its use by early Roman teachers.

6. In what periods of American history did public speaking play as important a part as it did in the republican era in early Rome?

7. In what respects does the curriculum of the American college resemble or differ from that of the rhetorical school of Rome?

8. To what extent do American political leaders reflect the character attributed to Roman and Greek figures by Plutarch?
9. In what respects did Quintilian advocate educational principles and practices similar to those some contemporary educational leaders favor?
10. Compare present-day attitudes toward vocations and vocational life with those of the Roman freeman.

CHAPTER VI

THE CHRISTIAN CONCEPT OF EDUCATION

THE ROMAN PEACE

In the reign of the Augustus, when imperial Rome had brought into subjection practically all of the known civilized world, had reached the greatest height of its military and political power, and had brought the *pax Romana* to the far-flung dominions of its empire, there was born to Jewish parents of the Galilean village of Nazareth, a child to whom was given the name JESUS. His fellow countrymen were groaning under the oppression of their Roman overlords, and the zealots among them were fomenting insurrections that were to lead a few years later to the destruction of the temple and the ultimate dispersal of the Jewish nation by the emperor Titus. In this travail, they were looking forward longingly to the coming of their Messiah and a new and glorious day for the chosen children of Israel. In the meantime, they were following the teachings of their rabbis and observing scrupulously the minute prescriptions of the Mosaic law. Thus they were attempting to attain the holiness and righteousness required by the God of their fathers as a condition of their release from the bonds of oppression. Under such circumstances and into such an environment this lowly Nazarene destined to become the founder of Christianity [1] was born.

---

[1] See Will Durant, *Caesar and Christ*. (New York: Simon & Schuster Inc., 1944) for a graphic account of conditions in Judea just prior to the advent of Jesus, pp. 528-549.

In an out-of-the-way corner of this Universal Empire, in the days of its greatest glory, the Creative Spirit once again broke through all the repressive bonds of custom and tradition and once again offered new hope to the world. . . . Christianity was a new creative spirit of life—not alone in the spiritual realm, but in every phase of experience, soon or late. Its influence upon, its contributions to, education cannot be estimated.

To be sure, as with Socrates, what its originator aimed at could not be accomplished; it was defeated in the hands of its professed friends, as Socrates was defeated in Athens. Humanity has not the courage to be creative for more than a moment at a time. But even in that moment, enough creative virus may be released to keep the old institutions on the defensive, reconstructing themselves or apologizing for themselves, for a thousand years to come. This was the similitude—and the fate—of Christianity.[2]

Christianity was one of the greatest creative forces in all history. For twenty centuries it has dominated the civilization and culture of the Western world, persistently affecting the theories and practices of its education. Although it has fallen far short of its potentialities, its contribution to civilization in general and education in particular cannot be ignored.

The story of Christianity is long and bewildering, for it stretches through twenty centuries and is written in a hundred tongues. In part it is a story of almost incredible rapacity and bitterness, of incessant war and intrigue, and low, greedy self-seeking. But in far larger part it is a story of wondrous kindness and saving grace. Though the Church of Christ may stand guilty of untold and untellable evil, the teaching of Jesus, which is the light glimmering beneath the ecclesiastical bushel, has accomplished good sufficient to outweigh that evil tenfold. For it has made life livable for countless millions of harried souls. It has taken rich and poor, learned and ignorant, white, red, yellow, and brown—it has taken them all and tried to show them a way to salvation. To all in pain it has held out a balm; to all in distress it has offered peace. . . . And therein lies Christianity's highest virtue. It has helped make the weak strong and the dejected happy. It has stilled the fear that howls in man's breast, and crushed the unrest that gnaws at his soul. In a word, it has worked—in a measure.[3]

The problem that Christianity attempted to solve was the same problem that had confronted the various pagan civilizations—the problem of harmonizing individual freedom, in the attainment of personal desires and aspirations, with social stability for the preservation of the race or of the nation. The problem was essentially one of establishing an ethical standard for the relationships of the individual to society. The solutions to this problem, as offered by the Athenian mediators, Socrates, Plato, and Aristotle, were based on the intellectual nature of man and possible only to the few. The Stoic philosophy, which attracted so many of the

---

[2] Joseph K. Hart, *Creative Moments in Education*. (New York: Holt, Rinehart and Winston, Inc., 1931.) P. 140. Reprinted with the permission of the publishers.
[3] Lewis Browne, *This Believing World*. (New York: The Macmillan Co., 1926.) P. 301. Reprinted with the permission of the publishers.

educated intellectual class in Rome, also claimed that reason was the proper rule of life, that virtue was its own reward. It, too, was so intellectual that it satisfied only the few. What was needed was an ethical system based upon the emotions and the natural moral nature of man, a system that could touch all mankind with its inspirations to goodness and virtue. Such an ethical system was given to the world by the teachings of Christianity. Christianity, by first appealing to the emotions rather than to the intellect, entered into the lives of people of every class and of every type.

Christianity gave to the world a new ethical force, a new motive for releasing the effective energies of all mankind; a new humanitarianism that provided a basis for the education of all and the consequent establishment of a sound social organization. The imaginative, artistic, and creative Greeks had placed emphasis upon political and personal freedom and individual initiative, and as a result had developed a literature, an art, and a philosophy that constitute one of the great heritages of modern times. The practical, aggressive, and systematic Romans had stressed law and government and the practical arts, and as a result had imposed law and order and the institutions of government upon an unruly world. The weakness of one was the strength of the other, and Christianity combined and harmonized the best elements of each, and developed an ethical standard by which the claims of both personality and society could be met and satisfied. The ethical contributions of Christianity were twofold: (1) an ideal of personal morality, including such virtues as sincerity, honesty, truthfulness, and chastity; (2) an ideal of social responsibility, based upon motives of brotherly love—neighborliness, loyalty, kindness, generosity, altruism, and unselfishness. As a result of these ideals, class distinctions and racial prejudices have been lessened, womanhood has been elevated to a higher place and a new dignity, and childhood has become more sacred. Rights have come to be recognized as well as duties and obligations.

The development of the early Christian concept of education is a history of the struggle between the basic teachings of Jesus and the amplifications, constrictions—and even misapprehensions—of these teachings by his own followers. Christians—as the adherents of Jesus soon began to call themselves—found themselves in a state of confusion between the simple preachings of the Master on the one hand and the interpretations and interpolations of his disciples and apostles on the other.

As a result the religious beliefs and practices of the ancient church were considerably altered from those of the unassuming Galilean; similar changes likewise occurred in educational attitudes and practices. The original gospel of Jesus was institutionalized by St. Paul and other early leaders of the apostolic and patristic periods, as well as by the converts themselves; thus elements of theological doctrine and religious ritual drawn from the Greek philosophies, the Hebrew moralities, and the various eastern mystery sects prevalent at this time were soon added.

Organized Christianity is particularly indebted to Mithraism, the worship of Tammuz, and the mother-goddess cults of Egypt and Lydia.

It is our purpose, therefore, to consider the early Christian conceptions of education under two headings: (1) the educational attitudes and practices of Jesus; and (2) those of the early Christian church during the first two centuries of its existence.

EDUCATIONAL ATTITUDES AND PRACTICES OF JESUS

In this study we are not concerned particularly with Jesus' contributions to the history of religion. Jesus is to be considered here as a teacher; we are not discussing him as a divine being but simply as an educator who played his part in the tremendous drama of educational history. It is to be regretted, perhaps, that, just as the real teaching personality of that great Hindu teacher of the sixth century before Christ, Gautama, the Buddha, has been distorted, and obscured by later Buddhism, so the burning and magnetic personality of this penniless teacher, who wandered about the dusty sunlit country of Judea, has been sadly ignored and misrepresented.

Jesus has rightly been called "The Great Teacher." He was one of the three greatest masters of the teaching art: Socrates, Gautama, and Jesus. In method, his teaching resembles that of Socrates; in aim and content, it is like that of Gautama. The parable method of Jesus is as effective as the dialectic method of Socrates; the Sermon on the Mount is very similar to the Sermon in the Deer-park; the Beatitudes of Jesus approximate closely Gautama's Eight-fold Path of "right views, right intentions, right speech, right action, right occupation, right effort, right mindfulness, right concentration." Each of the three had an intense consciousness of a mission to be fulfilled, and the radiant personality of the effective teacher.

In his personality, in his life, in his teachings, Jesus represents the ideal teacher. His personality was compelling, his preparation was complete, his aims were lofty, his methods were effective. He was "a man who really lived the best truth he knew, who took what he had read and thought and interpreted it to humanity by embodying it in his own life." [4] When men hereafter bow to him, it should be in recognition of a superior craftsmanship in the art of living and in the art of teaching that life to others.

AIMS   The aim of Jesus' teaching may be summed up in his words, "Seek ye first the Kingdom of God and his righteousness,

---

[4] C. F. Potter, *The Story of Religion.* (New York: Simon & Schuster, Inc., 1929.) P. 232.

and all these things shall be added unto you." What Jesus himself meant by this statement and what the Christian church afterwards attributed to it for centuries to come are two different things. It was the church's interpretation which most affected our educational thought and our educational systems; it is the true interpretation of Jesus' own words that must come to influence the educational philosophy and practices of the future if the teachings of Jesus are ever to attain their highest possibilities as an influence in education. Jesus taught a new and simple and profound doctrine—the universal loving Fatherhood of God and the coming of a Kingdom of Heaven on earth based on the principle of universal brotherhood. This is certainly one of the most revolutionary doctrines that ever stirred and changed human thoughts. The Kingdom of Heaven on earth as an ultimate objective of education has never been surpassed in its nobility and grandeur.

Jesus advanced two basic principles as fundamental to this kingdom in the hearts of men: (1) respect for human personality and the rights of the individual, and (2) social efficiency in all human relationships. He aimed at giving the individual the greatest satisfactions of life, the "peace that passeth understanding." He taught that every human being is sacred in the sight of God. There are few who would deny that most of our movements in the direction of a greater humanitarianism have been influenced by the teachings of Jesus.

But Jesus also advanced a new social gospel; taught new principles to govern human relationships and social organization. The Golden Rule had existed before his day, but its application had been limited to the relationship of friends, relationship within families, and relationship among the peoples of one nation. Racial hatreds, national pride, fear, suspicion, antagonism, and prejudice had limited its scope. Jesus taught a new and a great commandment, "Love thy neighbor"; and, in the parable of the good Samaritan, he interpreted neighborliness in a way that no one could misunderstand.

Not only did Jesus strike at the traditional conceptions of patriotism and of family ties, but his teaching of God's universal Fatherhood and the brotherhood of humanity clearly condemned all the artificial gradations of the economic system of his day; all personal privilege and advantage. He denounced riches and the selfishness of private ambitions. He taught not only a moral revolution in the individual but a revolution in society as well. He said that his kingdom was not one of geographical bounds ruled from a throne, but a kingdom in the hearts of men. To the extent that his kingdom was set up in the hearts of men, to that very extent would the world be revolutionized.

The problem of the wealthy young man whom Jesus advised to sell all his property, give to the poor, and follow him was different only in degree from those of his disciples. H. G. Wells shows how the broad gulf between absolute purity and the call of this world must have affected even the greatest of his admiring group:

He was too great for his disciples. And in view of what he plainly said, is it any wonder that all who were rich and prosperous felt a horror of strange things, a swimming of their world at his teaching? Perhaps the priests and the rulers and the rich men understood him better than his followers. . . . He was like some moral huntsman digging mankind out of the snug burrows in which they had lived hitherto. In this kingdom of his there was to be no property, no privilege, no pride and no precedence; no motive indeed and no rewards but love. Is it any wonder that men were dazzled and blinded and cried out against him? . . . Is it any wonder that the priests realized that between this man and themselves there was no choice but that he or priestcraft should perish? Is it any wonder that the Roman soldiers, confronted and amazed by something soaring over their comprehension and threatening all their discipline, should take refuge in wild laughter and crown him with thorns and robe him in purple to make a mock Caesar of him? For to take him seriously was to enter upon a strange and alarming life, to abandon habits, to control instincts and impulses, to essay an incredible happiness. Is it any wonder that to this day this Galilean is too much for our small hearts?[5]

TYPES Jesus emphasized moral training in the loftiest meaning of the term; his was the highest type of ethical education. The authority for conduct was the sanction of brotherly love. The authority of ancestors, caste, state, Jehovah—all now gave way to the authority of a great moral principle in the universe, the principle of love. "For God so loved the world." "As the Father hath loved me, so have I loved you; continue in my love." "This is my commandment, that ye love one another as I have loved you." "A new commandment I give unto you, that ye love one another." "Thou shalt love thy neighbor as thyself." Social education and moral education were one to him.

But Jesus was concerned also with religious training in its truest sense, the development of the right relationships between man and his God. His first and great commandment was: "Thou shalt love the Lord thy God with all thy heart, and with all thy soul, and with all thy mind." He was not concerned with teaching the observances of the minute prescriptions of religious rites and ceremonies, but never ceased to emphasize the necessity of developing an abiding trust and confidence in God and a true reverence for Him. This is religious education at its best. He also recognized the obligation of citizenship, but reduced it to his fundamental principle of morality. "Render unto Caesar the things that are Caesar's."

Education based on the teachings of Jesus must of necessity be a universal and democratic education. He himself taught all who came to him in their need for instruction. In teaching that God is the common Father of all mankind, he removed education from the fetters of national limits and racial prejudice. With this tremendous truth he swept away

---

[5] H. G. Wells, *The Outline of History.* (New York: Doubleday & Co., Inc., 1949.) Pp. 425-426. Reprinted with the permission of the publishers.

the distinctions of class and caste which had weighed so heavily in Oriental education and in the education of Greece and Rome. By making everyone a child of God, stamped with the divine image, he abolished all forms of slavery—slavery of workers, slavery of women, slavery of children—attached due importance to every individual, overthrew the injustices and oppressions of society, and thus stressed the necessity of and paved the way for a universal and common education for every man, woman, and child.

The teaching of Jesus stresses the necessity of the education of the young child—elementary education. "Suffer the little children to come unto me and forbid them not, for of such is the kingdom of heaven."

CONTENT   The essence of the teaching of Jesus is to be found in the few pages of the Sermon on the Mount. He taught his disciples not to retaliate for injuries received, but to forgive as their loving Father would forgive them; not to worry about food, clothes, shelter— for if God provided for even the birds and flowers, he would care for his own children. They were to seek first the kingdom of God. He so practiced what he taught and so lived his exalted conception of what God would do if he were a man, that his own life was his curriculum.

The content of his teaching had to do with human conduct, yet he was not interested in the formation of specific habits and skills nor in the memorizing of rules and regulations. A large part of his recorded utterances is aimed against the meticulous observance of the rules of the pious and puritanical Pharisees. He flouted the habits of the formalist; he endeavored to develop in his disciples an individual and social behavior that was based on the acceptance of broad and deep general principles of human relationship.

It is noteworthy that Jesus seems to have concentrated all his efforts on teaching the essentials. Only a few things really mattered to him; he dealt only with fundamental universal truths. One finds in his program neither belles-lettres nor courses in theology, and yet he was successful in developing the most efficient humanitarian and religious workers the world has ever known.

AGENCIES AND ORGANIZATION   Jesus did not organize a school or develop any special institution for the promulgation of his teachings. The Christian church itself was organized by his later followers; Jesus himself organized no such institution. Like Socrates, he wrote no books; he used no textbooks, although he was familiar with the literature of his people and quoted extensively from it. He merely talked to people wherever he found them. The home, the seashore, the riverbank, the highway, the hilltop, the social gathering, the religious service —all these were his agencies for education. He taught whenever and wherever a situation arose of which he could make effective use.

Jesus, like Socrates, considered the teacher an agent of education.

He probably would have been in sympathy with President Garfield's definition of a college as "Mark Hopkins on one end of a log and a student on the other." He never took the role of a professional teacher. He expected no pay for his services. To him teaching was the giving of a transcendent gift of knowledge and wisdom and the setting of a noble example, and remuneration for such a service was far from his thoughts. Here was a very human, very earnest, very capable man—clearly a teacher with personal magnetism. He attracted his disciples and filled them with wisdom, love, and courage. The most effective agency of his instruction was his own radiant personality.

METHODS   The most helpful lessons that modern education can draw from the work of Jesus as a teacher are along the lines of method. The teaching procedure of Jesus is, without a doubt, as effective as any yet contrived. In his manner of instructing his disciples and the multitudes that gathered around him, he has set us an excellent example in educational methodology. He seemed to have an intuitive grasp of the laws of learning and of the principles of teaching that are now accepted as basic to teaching effectiveness.

Jesus prepared his hearers for the truths to be taught by presenting concrete examples of their application in life and in human relationships. He drew extensively upon their previous knowledge by frequent reference to the various books of the Old Testament—the Law and the Prophets. He continually adjusted his lessons to the common experiences of those he taught by referring to the familiar phenomena of nature and to the institutions and practices of social life. He made effective use of the simile, the metaphor, the analogy, and the parable. The parable especially—there are fifty-three of these allegories found in the gospels—not only made the lesson concrete and interesting, but drove home the truth to be taught so that no one could miss its meaning. In these parables he made reference to such familiar experiences as sowing, shepherding, and husbandry, and such familiar objects as vines, sheep, and coins. He used concrete, everyday incidents for his examples. He used the simplest language to teach the most profound truths; he used the phrases, idioms, and expressions current among the common people.

Jesus also recognized the principle of activity in his teaching. He urged his disciples to be "doers of the word and not hearers only." He encouraged questions, and gently rebuked his followers for entertaining questions which they did not ask. He appealed to the imagination and made use of the power of suggestion to stimulate the thought processes of his hearers. He recognized the principle of individual differences and adjusted his teaching methods to the needs, conditions, and capacities of those with whom he came in contact. His treatment of the woman taken in adultery is different from his treatment of the rich young ruler. His approach was always determined by the nature of the occasion and the needs of the individual or of the group.

Motivation also was often exemplified in the method of his

teaching. His words and demonstrations were full of interests and attracted and held the attention of his listeners. The power of his motive is easily understood. The common man needs a motive that appeals to the feelings rather than to the intellect, and this Jesus always recognized. He made no use, however, of such motives as competition and acquisition. Love was the only aim offered as a stimulus to goodness. Later—as we shall see—a system of rewards and punishments in an eternal heaven or hell was developed from Zoroastrianism by the early church and set up as a motive for righteousness, but Jesus himself reached people by the simple motive of love—love for God and love for man.

The method of Jesus was objective, direct, and personal. He directed attention to the external world and objective activities. He used oral instruction—either the sermon method, used in speaking to large numbers, or the dialectic method, used in the intimate circle of a few friends. Beyond all else, he taught by example. His own life was the best advertisement for his teachings. His obedience to authority, his observance of the spirit of the law, his humility, his mercy, his charity—all were continual examples set before the disciples for their guidance. He always practiced what he preached, and where can one find a better way?

EDUCATIONAL ATTITUDES OF THE EARLY CHRISTIAN CHURCH

The history of Christianity during the first two centuries following the crucifixion is somewhat obscure. The record found in the Acts of the Apostles and the Epistles of St. Paul and other early Christian leaders presents a patchwork rather than a systematic account; it does, however, produce a revealing picture of the trials and tribulations of the ancient church. St. Peter, we are told, traveled to Rome and was largely instrumental in establishing the church in the eternal city. Paul likewise journeyed to Rome and to many other Mediterranean cities; he made a remarkable address at Mars Hill in Athens.[6]

Many consider Paul to be the founder of the organized religion; it was he probably more than any other who set the doctrines and worked out a system of theology. Under his inspiring leadership the movement was internationalized until it spread into every corner of the Roman world. Yet in this early period the creeds and dogma had not crystallized and there were wide variations in tenets and church practices among those who accepted the new faith.

Despite local differences in doctrine and ritual, there is reason to believe that everywhere during these early days the Christians were

---

[6] See Will Durant, *op. cit.*, pp. 575-595, for a moving account of the place and influence of Peter, Paul, and John in the formation of the Christian religion.

carrying out much of the true spirit of Jesus in their daily lives and were practicing those virtues of simplicity, purity, and unselfishness that contrasted so strikingly with the vices of the pagan world. The persecutions and oppressions that the early Christians had to endure are evidence of their strength. If the faith had not been deemed a menace to government Christians would not have been persecuted. But these persecutions, instead of weakening the church, strengthened it still more, as Constantine observed. So in 311 A.D., three years before his accession as head of the Western Empire, Christianity was legalized; that is, granted the same protection as the pagan worship. Under the Emperor CONSTANTINE (272–337) it was not only tolerated but encouraged, and, with his own conversion, became the state religion of the Western Roman Empire.[7] This was a fine thing for the growth of the church organization, but it is an open question whether it was equally favorable to the continuation of the early emphasis upon Christlike living on the part of the whole membership of the church.

During this period certain elements from other religions and from pagan philosophies were being fused with the original teachings of Jesus. Alexandria at this time was the great melting pot of religion and philosophy, and the Alexandrian school of thought contributed much to Christianity. The early church apostles and fathers came from different backgrounds and brought from their own earlier environment and experiences distinct contributions to the growing Christian faith. By combining with the original teachings of Christ certain elements from the ceremonies and rites of Hebrew morality, concepts from Graeco-Roman philosophy—especially from Stoicism and Neoplatonism—and ceremonies from some of the popular mystery religions of the eastern Mediterranean world, Christianity was gradually adapted to the temperaments and customs of the diverse peoples to whom its message was carried.

Many centuries passed before the synthesis was complete and Christianity had assumed a fixed form. Bitter controversies, such as that over the nature of the deity of Jesus between the Arians, led by ARIUS (280–336), and the Trinitarians, led by ATHANASIUS (296–373) (settled finally in favor of the latter by the Council of Nicaea), shook the church. It was not until the beginning of the fifth century that the structure of orthodox Christianity was completed by the work of AUGUSTINE (354–430), the first to build a complete and coherent system of theology for the Roman Catholic Church, in his *De Civitate Dei*.

In such a formative period as this, Christian education was little concerned with intellectual theology but confined itself to the training of children, converts, and clergy alike, in the fundamental and commonly accepted doctrines and practices of the early church.

---

[7] While a contender for the imperial crown Constantine in a vision beheld a flaming cross bearing the inscription *In hoc signo vinces*—in this sign, conquer. Successful, he favored Christianity.

AIMS   The primary aim of early Christian education was the moral regeneration of the individual. Early Christianity was distinctly a reform movement; it had as its ultimate goal the moral reformation of the world and the destruction of the corrupt society of pagan civilization. But the church realized that the reform of society could come about only through the transformation of the individuals that make up society; so it devoted itself to the moral training of its own membership and of the converts won over to the cause of the Christlike ideal.

The Christian protest was directed especially at the looseness and debauchery prevalent in the empire, especially at Rome. Attention to the early Roman virtues had flagged; the government was corrupt; the armies were no longer victorious. The upper classes and even the proletariat of Rome had fallen into vicious customs and habits; the abundance of slaves made it unnecessary for much of the population to work; surfeited by leisure, the common people demanded bread and circuses which political leaders and aspirants to public office were only too glad to supply; during the second and third centuries civil war raged frequently and "barrack" emperors reigned more often than not.

The Roman concept of the *vir bonus* seemed to have been forgotten in the urge to pleasure and self-gratification. Divorce became frequent and common to all strata of society; infanticide and child exposure were practiced; the Roman family—the strength of the early republic—deteriorated as its members no longer were guided by the ancient morality. Cruel and bloody gladiatorial shows, public ceremonies of the most immoral type practiced under the cloak of religion, and licentiousness in private life contributed to the decay in society that the Christian viewed as an evidence of Satan's work and power.

To combat these evils, the Christian church had a new set of virtues to take the place of the vices of the pagan. Simplicity instead of luxury, purity instead of licentiousness, temperance instead of indulgence, humanitarianism instead of brutality, brotherly love instead of selfishness—these were the virtues required for entrance into the church; and in these, therefore, training must be given.

The world, the flesh, and the devil—these were the sources of evil and corruption. Men should be taught to renounce the world, to subdue the flesh, and to escape the devil; to serve God by living pure and simple lives, and thus to obtain eventually the heavenly reward of the faithful. As the difficulty of reforming the world became more and more obvious, the Christian's aim ultimately became that of saving his own soul and the souls of as many of his fellow men as he could convert to the faith. But the early Christians of the first two centuries had not yet reached these conceptions of unworldliness and other-worldliness. They still had hopes of reforming the world through the regeneration of human souls.

TYPES   To satisfy such an aim, only two types of training

were needed: moral training and religious training. If sufficient moral and religious training was given to prepare the child or the convert for baptism, the aim of Christian education was fulfilled.

There was no intellectual education at first, for early Christianity was based on feeling rather than on reason; and at first, and particularly in the West, it was considered unnecessary to give intellectual training even to the clergy. Later, especially in the East, where Christianity had attracted the attention of the learned pagan world and had made converts from among the intellectual and educated classes, intellectual education was introduced if for no other reason than to train controversialists to meet the arguments of opponents from without the church and heretics from within. But even in these later schools, moral and religious training always took precedence over intellectual training.

Physical training and esthetic training were despised by the Christians, and the only musical training tolerated was in connection with the psalmody and hymnology of church worship. There was no recreational training, since sports and amusements of all kinds—because of their association with Roman life and paganism in general—were looked upon as sinful.

CONTENT The curriculum of early Christian education was limited by the suspicion and distrust with which Christians looked upon learning of the intellectual and worldly type. They were bitterly opposed to the subjects taught in the pagan schools and blamed pagan culture for the vices and corruption of pagan society. To them its literature was full of impurities; its art depicted immoralities and was associated with immoral religions; its philosophy undermined and destroyed Christian faith because it led to trusting one's own wisdom. "I will destroy the wisdom of the wise and will bring to nothing the understanding of the prudent. Hath not God made foolish the wisdom of the world?"[8] Therefore the pagan school was the enemy of the church and its curriculum was to be despised by all true believers. Moreover, early converts to Christianity were from the lower classes and would have none of the learning that differentiated their masters from themselves. Physical training, literature, art, science, rhetoric, philosophy—all were eliminated from early Christian education; and subjects quite foreign to the later pagan schools, moral and religious training, took their place.

At first the instruction purposed only to fit candidates for baptism for membership in the church. The pupils were converts from Hebraism and paganism and the children of believers; so the simple elements of church doctrine and church ritual, and the moral virtues of Christlike living, made up the brief course of training.

But during the second century a more advanced curriculum was introduced into church education by pagan teachers who had been converted to Christianity. These teachers opened schools primarily to give

---

[8] *I Corinthians* I:19-20.

elementary training in Christian faith and doctrine to prospective church leaders and workers; but grammar, literature, rhetoric, and even philosophy were taught as "handmaidens to the Scriptures." This type of curriculum flourished, particularly in the East where it first arose. For the most part, the church in western Europe continued to oppose all pagan learning and excluded it from Christian education. It was such Greek fathers as CLEMENT (150–220), ORIGEN (185–254), BASIL (329–379), and GREGORY (325–389) who favored the use of pagan studies in the training of Christian youth. They contended that if proper selection were made pagan culture could contribute to the understanding of the Scriptures, and that it was justifiable to "spoil the Egyptians." On the other hand, such Latin church fathers as TERTULLIAN (160–230), JEROME (340–420), and AUGUSTINE, although they themselves had been deeply learned in classical literature and philosophy before their conversions, feared the effect of pagan culture on Christian morality. The *Confessions* of Augustine express this antagonism. The Western point of view finally prevailed in the church; and, at the Council of Carthage in 401 A.D., the clergy were forbidden to read the pagan literature.

AGENCIES AND ORGANIZATION   Upon the death of Jesus, his followers began to come together at stated times to read, study, take communion, and plan the future of the organization of which his teachings were the seed. The church itself was thus the first agency of Christian education. The Christian home, which was far more rigid and close-knit than the contemporary pagan home, was also an efficient agency, the mother occupying an honored place and joining with the father in the moral and religious training of their children.

Very early, however, and universally throughout the church, there grew up an institution known as the catechumenal school. This school was organized for the instruction of those who desired to become members of the church but who lacked the requisite knowledge of church doctrine and ritual and the requisite moral stability. These probationers were called *catechumens* and were divided into two groups, those who had expressed a desire to become members of the church and those who were considered to be worthy of full membership. At stated intervals these *catechumens* met in some part of the church, usually the porch, for instruction in religious discipline, moral virtue, and psalmody. The organization was informal, the teachers at first being merely able members of the local church and only later deacons and priests. Both sexes were admitted to this instruction, but no one was received into full communion or given the sacrament of baptism until he had received this training. The length of the training was usually about two years, but later this was extended to four years for the children of the believers. These schools continued for centuries as the elementary schools of the church.

When Christianity began to make converts among the grammarians, rhetoricians, and philosophers, a new type of school was organized. At first it was private and unconnected with the church. But in 179 A.D., PANTAENUS, a converted Stoic philosopher—one of the Apologists who were attempting to reconcile Christianity with Greek philosophy— became head of the catechumenal school in Alexandria. His school and those patterned after it came to be known as catechetical schools because of their use of the catechetical or question-and-answer method. They were used especially for the training of church leaders and were in a way rudimentary theological schools, but they included virtually the entire gamut of pagan studies as supplementary to the religious training.

Later in this period, when the church began to perfect its organization, and bishoprics were established, theological training schools for the education of the clergy were organized in each bishopric. These were called episcopal or cathedral schools. With the final victory of Christianity over paganism, the catechetical schools disappeared, particularly in the West, and the cathedral schools remained as the higher schools of Christian learning. These schools were located in the cathedrals and were under the direct instruction of the bishop himself or of a cathedral canon delegated to that function.

METHODS   The methods of early Christian education frequently fell far short of the standards set by Jesus, the Great Teacher. In the beginning, inspiration of the voice of the spirit was depended upon more than learning or instruction. Prophesying, or impromptu exposition and exhortation, was a common method of spreading the gospel in the early days when the church itself was the sole agency of education. In the home the method of example continued to be used.

In the schools that were later established, the catechetical method prevailed. The pupil memorized the answers to set questions and recited these answers to the teacher when the question was asked. Little attempt was made to learn the meaning of the words; it was enough if the words could be recited by rote. This method continued in use throughout the Middle Ages and is still used extensively in some parochial education.

Yet to speak of methods in connection with the dissemination of the teachings of Jesus seems somehow to miss the spirit of the real Christianity. Those who heard the Great Teacher himself *caught* his vision. Robert Ulich has expressed this subtlety in a few simple words:

> But there inheres in Christ's gospel a deeper educational claim than can be expressed in merely didactic terms. It rests on the combination of two closely interrelated tenets of Christianity. . . . One of them is the conviction that the dignity of man imposes on him the duty of considering the human soul as an end in itself, not to be submitted to alien purposes. The other idea is that of love or charity. It springs from the same metaphysical root as the idea of dignity and ends in the same demand to respect one's fellow man.[9]

---

[9] Robert Ulich, *A History of Educational Thought.* (New York: The American Book Company, 1950.) P. 70. Reprinted with the permission of the publishers.

FOR FURTHER READING

Barnes, Harry Elmer, *An Intellectual and Cultural History of the Western World*. New York: Random House, 1937. Pp. 267-325.

Browne, Lewis. *This Believing World*. New York: The Macmillan Co., 1926. Pp. 255-301.

Burnham, William, *Great Teachers and Mental Health*. New York: D. Appleton-Century Company, 1926. Pp. 39-69.

Butts, R. Freeman, *A Cultural History of Western Education*. (Second Edition). New York: McGraw-Hill, 1955. Pp. 81-84; 94-115.

Cole, Luella, *A History of Education, Socrates to Montessori*. New York: Holt, Rinehart and Winston, Inc., 1950. Pp. 91-111.

Cubberley, Ellwood P., *A History of Education*. Boston: Houghton-Mifflin, 1920. Pp. 82-105.

Durant, Will, *Caesar and Christ*. New York: Simon & Schuster, Inc., 1944. Pp. 552-672.

Eby, Frederick, and Arrowood, Charles F., *The History of Education Ancient and Medieval*. New York: Prentice-Hall, 1940. Pp. 578-629.

Good, H. G., *A History of Western Education*. New York: The Macmillan Co., 1960. Pp. 58-63.

Graves, Frank P., *Education Before the Middle Ages*. New York: The Macmillan Co., 1909. Pp. 272-296.

Hart, Joseph K., *Creative Moments in Education*. New York: Holt, Rinehart and Winston, Inc., 1931. Pp. 140-166.

Mayer, Frederick, *A History of Educational Thought*. Columbus, Ohio: Charles E. Merrill Books, Inc., 1960. Pp. 115-132.

Messenger, James F., *An Interpretative History of Education*. New York: Thomas Y. Crowell Company, 1931. Pp. 54-62.

Moore, Ernest C., *The Story of Instruction: The Church, the Renaissance and the Reformation*. New York: The Macmillan Co., 1938. Pp. 1-91.

Mulhern, James, *A History of Education* (Second Edition). New York: Ronald Press, 1959. Pp. 213-227.

Reisner, Edward H., *Historical Foundations of Modern Education*. New York: The Macmillan Co., 1927. Pp. 169-194.

Shaw, Charles Gray, *Trends of Civilization and Culture*. New York: American Book Company, 1932. Pp. 187-211.

Ulich, Robert, *A History of Educational Thought*. New York: American Book Company, 1950. Pp. 61-88.

————, *Three Thousand Years of Educational Wisdom*. Cambridge, Mass.: Harvard University Press, 1954. Pp. 127-171.

QUESTIONS FOR CLASS DISCUSSION

1. Do you believe that teaching today would be more effective if use were made of parables similar to those used by Jesus? Give examples of modern parables.
2. Discuss the part played by Greek philosophy in the formation of the early Christian doctrines.
3. In what ways was the organization of the early Christian church conditioned by the structure of the Roman Empire?
4. Can you find any parallels between the pattern of life suggested by Plato for his ideal *Republic* and that adopted by the early Christian church?
5. Mahatma Gandhi is reported to have said, "Give me your Christ, but keep your Christianity." What do you suppose he meant?
6. What present-day agencies of church education are performing the same function as the catechumenal schools of the early Christian era?
7. What tendencies in contemporary American society appear to be similar to conditions in Rome at the time of the birth of Christianity?
8. In what respect does the modern Sunday School perform functions similar to those of the early Christian schools?
9. Compare the present struggle between religion and science as it affects the Christian church with the clash between the Eastern and Western churches over pagan culture.
10. In what respects do the differences between the fundamentalists and the modernists in present-day religion resemble the differences between the Eastern and Western churches?

CHAPTER VII

SPIRITUAL DISCIPLINE FOR THE
SOUL'S SALVATION

MEDIEVAL CONCEPT OF EDUCATION

The date of the deposing of Romulus Augustus, the little emperor, by the barbarian Odoacer (476 A.D.) is usually considered to mark
the end of the Roman Empire in the West—and, consequently, the transition from ancient to medieval civilization. For, the sovereign having
been removed and the imperial ornaments sent to Constantinople in
token of the presumed reunion of the Empire, the collapse of the western
sector of the great Roman Empire of Augustus and Trajan was complete. Although there was as yet no similar collapse in the East (nor
would there be for a thousand years more), the West was henceforth to
be controlled by the Teutonic invaders; and so began the development
of a new Western civilization founded on the traditions and standards
of life of these immigrants from north and eastern Europe, modified
and redirected—to be sure—by the strong influence of the successor to
the imperial power of Rome, the organized and militant Christian
church.

Medievalism thus was the result of a fusion of three dominant
elements: (1) the decaying social and moral conditions fostered throughout western Europe by the nature of the Roman government and the
Roman economic structure under the later Caesars; (2) the individualistic feudalism of the Germanic barbarians who had swept down from
the north and had gradually undermined the power of the Roman

Empire; and (3) the enterprising, formalized, and hierarchically ordered Christian church. Two of these components have already been noted. Teutonic feudalism, however, must be described, as this unique institution represents still another foundation stone in the development of educational theory and practice.

In turning from the Romans to the Teutons, we pass from ancient to medieval history. The Teutons, or Germans, together with the Celts and the Slavs, belong to the same European branch of the Aryan race to which the Greeks and the Italians belong and originated in the same regions north of the Black and Caspian seas. The Celts earlier had moved westward and occupied Britain, Ireland, Gaul, and a part of Spain, where in time they were conquered and civilized by the Romans. The Teutonic tribes had wandered here and there over the plains of central Europe until their desire for better homes impelled them to move westward and southward into the provinces of imperial Rome.

One need not doubt that these Teutonic peoples were inherently as capable as the Greeks and the Italians; in their geographical location in Europe, however, they had fewer means of learning the arts and institutions of higher civilization. They therefore remained barbarians for a much longer time, but they were far from being savages. They had developed, but they had developed along different lines from the people of the South, with fewer intellectual complications, more personal dignity, and a more intimate contact with the rigors of wind and sky and sea. Their culture at the time they began to move in upon Rome was at the nomadic agricultural level, very similar to that of the early Hebrews under Moses. The morals of marriage and of the family were pure among them; they respected womanhood more than the later Greeks and Romans. Their sense of personal dignity would not permit these early Teutonic peoples—as had the Spartans and early Romans—to yield their liberty to the iron discipline of a state, to make themselves an unthinking part of a social machine. Caesar, in the *Commentaries,* speaks of the Germans with great respect, and Tacitus lauds their virtues in his *Germania* and *Annals.*

Before they were Christianized, the Teutons worshiped the powers of nature—gods of war, of harvest, of the home, of waters, woods, and seasons, of various living things and natural forces. Priests attended to the public worship in sacred groves, for there were no images or temples. They were a fierce and warlike people, adventuresome and bold. Each tribe followed an hereditary king or a temporary duke elected to lead it in war or in migration. The chieftain rode in the midst of his mounted retainers, who were pledged to loyal service—this "Teutonic following" as it is sometimes called being the prototype of the lord and vassal relationship of the medieval feudal system.

These various Teutonic groups—the Franks, the Anglo-Saxons, the Alans, the Burgundians, the Lombards, the Visigoths, the Ostrogoths, the Vandals—were powerfully to harass the Romans and eventually to establish the many petty kingdoms and principalities of feudal medievalism.

The organized Christian church attempted to build out of these diverse tribes something in the nature of a religious empire, and succeeded to a large degree; but the church had shared in the general degradation of Roman civilization and was prone to compromise, to act on expediency rather than on principle. It had been diverted from its nobler aims and its higher life by long devastating struggles over forms of worship, creeds, doctrines, and governmental organization; and its complete uniformity of belief and practice had been gained at a great price. Bitter persecutions of the unorthodox and heretical had left a blight on the true spirit of Christianity. Furthermore, church adherents had entered into the secular life of the time and were more inclined to emphasize the acceptance of religious creeds and the practice of church ceremonies than the living of the Christlike life. The obligations of morality sometimes were ignored, and leaders as well as laymen indulged in practices forbidden by the Christian church of the second century.

It is not surprising that under such circumstances learning and education should decline and the spirit of inquiry should become virtually extinct in Europe. Most of the parish priests were only superficially trained, and many church leaders advanced themselves by intrigue more often than by humanitarian service or scholarship. Nevertheless, it is true that in some of the Irish monasteries there was preserved a shining flame of piety and learning which was later to kindle similar light in other places; and in the monastery of Jarrow in England, BEDE THE VENERABLE (673–735), by his stainless life and ardent love of knowledge, redeemed the church from the curse of utter intellectual barrenness. Compared, however, with the earlier centuries of the history of the church, with such distinguished intellectual leadership as that furnished by Jerome and Augustine, most of the medieval period can justly be characterized as a "mournful sterility of sanctified erudition."

Yet out of this moral degeneracy, this political disorganization and confusion, this feudal economic system, the Middle Ages developed four institutions which must be recognized as fundamental in the evolution of modern educational concepts and practices. They are (1) Monasticism, (2) Scholasticism, (3) Chivalry, and (4) the Guild System. The remainder of this chapter will offer a discussion of the educational implications of each of these medieval institutions in terms of aims, types, content, agencies, organization and methods.

EDUCATIONAL ATTITUDES AND PRACTICES OF MONASTICISM

Monasticism did not originate with Christianity and is not confined to Christianity. In most of the early Oriental religions, there were ascetics who devoted themselves to the solitary and contemplative life apart from the affairs of the world. This practice was especially common among the Hindus because of the mystic character of their religion. Undoubtedly the development of Christian monasticism was influenced to some degree by these earlier monastic practices.

In the beginnings of the church, all Christians considered themselves a people apart, a separate community within society but participating as little as possible in the political and social activities of the world which they judged evil and immoral. After Christianity was officially tolerated and became fashionable large numbers entered the church for reasons of expediency; prompting a desire in many of the more spiritually minded to differentiate themselves from the ordinary membership. Believing that the perfection of soul necessary to eternal salvation was only to be secured by keeping apart from worldly pleasures and the secular activities of society, these ascetic spirits fled from the centers of population, subjected their bodies to rigorous discipline, and endeavored to develop the "habit of the presence of God." Even before this, many Christians, fugitives from persecution, had fled into the desert, the mountains, or the wilderness, where they could worship in safety. There were also millennists who believed that the second advent of Christ was near at hand, and that if one had no interests in the life around him he would be better prepared for the coming.

The term monasticism comes from the Greek *monos,* meaning alone, and the earliest form of monasticism was true to this root meaning. From almost the very beginning of the history of the church, ascetics had retired into the deserts where, like the famous ANTHONY (251–356) of Egypt, they lived entirely alone as anchorites, or hermits. But the social instinct eventually prevailed; and we discover that about 330 A.D. a hermit named PACHOMIUS organized a community form of monasticism on an island in the valley of the Nile. Here the monks lived apart in separate cells for contemplation and meditation, but came together for meals, prayers, and religious ceremonies. This cenobitic type of monasticism was introduced into Greece by BASIL about 350, and soon afterward ATHANASIUS and JEROME transferred the idea to Rome.

For nearly two centuries, each monastery was organized under its own system of rules, which varied widely; but in 529 the organization of community monasticism became definite and uniform with the formulation of the Rule of Benedict. BENEDICT (480–543) founded the monastery of Monte Cassino in southern Italy and drew up a code of seventy-three articles which covered in detail the organization and administration of the monastery and the daily life of its members. Eventually the Rule of Benedict was adopted by all the existing monastic orders of the West; and every succeeding order that has been established has based its code upon it.

At first thought it might seem that such a movement could have but little influence upon education. It is indeed true that the anchoritic form of monasticism made no educational contributions. The cenobitic form, however, developed the monastery as an educational institution and made large contributions not only to the Middle Ages but to later times. We owe much to the Christian monasteries for preserving and spreading learning and culture. They not only preserved ancient knowledge but they brought forth chronicles and religious writings of their own, and made copies of the sacred writings of the early church. We must rely on the works of the monks for much of our knowledge of the Middle Ages. The monasteries stood out against the vice and corruption of the medieval world; and they were an influence in taming the warlike spirits and refining the crude customs of the Teutonic peoples. Through the monasteries, Europe acquired industrial skills and a conception of the true dignity of manual labor. The poor, the sick, and the hungry found succor within their gates and at the hands of the mendicant friars. The monasteries were the schools, the libraries, the publishing houses, the literary centers, the hospitals, and the workshops of medieval times. Their educational influences were very significant.

The wide extent of the monastic schools geographically—ranging from Scotland to the Nile—and their long life chronologically—stretching from the fourth to the sixteen century (with some few even to the present day)—renders generalization a difficult task. The salient features of monastic education, however, are as follows.

AIMS In general, the ultimate aim of monastic education was the same as the ultimate aim of monastic life—the salvation of individual souls. The primary idea of monasticism was asceticism, the disciplining of all bodily desires and all human affections and aspirations so that the mind and the soul might be devoted to the interests of the higher life. The immediate aim is physical and moral discipline.

Certain elements in the monastic ideal are not new but are to be found in the religions and philosophies of Jews, Persians, Hindus, Egyptians, and Greeks. Stoic contempt for pain and death and indifference to the vicissitudes of fortune; Pythagorean silence and submission to the forces of physical nature; Brahman rejection of the material world and absorption in the infinite spirit; Zoroastrian concern with the eternal struggle between the forces of good and evil and cynic neglect of the obligations and responsibilities of society—all these are to be found in monasticism. Together with the Christian desire to live according to a higher code of morality, monasticism fused all these and organized them into a system based on two principles: (1) bodily mortification, and (2) world renunciation.

One aim of monasticism was to deny all the claims and desires of the body. The virtue of a monk was often measured by his ingenuity in devising new ways of punishing the body—by fasting or insufficient and inappropriate foods, by going without sufficient sleep, by wearing insufficient and coarse clothing, by assuming unnatural and painful bodily positions, by enduring all forms of physical torture. Any method that could produce bodily suffering was used as a mortification of the flesh. All this physical discipline was for the sake of spiritual growth and the moral improvement of the penitent.

The second principle, world renunciation, meant denying all the claims of social and human institutions. The Rule of Benedict imposed upon the monk three vows: chastity, poverty, obedience. (1) The ideal of chastity included condemnation of the family and all the human relationships and affections growing out of the institution of the home. For family ties and responsibilities, were to be substituted purely religious relationships and spiritual interests, expressed in meditation and continuous devotion and worship. (2) The ideal of poverty included rejection of all the economic relationships and material interests of life. Upon entering the monastery, one must give up all his property and all claims to inheritance. Within the monastery all things were held in common; and, although the monastery itself could acquire property and become very wealthy, the individual monk could make no claim to any personal share in the wealth. It was because of this ideal of poverty that charity and alms-giving was exalted in the Middle Ages as the highest Christian virtue, later paving the way for modern Christian philanthropy and benevolence. (3) The ideal of obedience included the renunciation of all power and rank and distinction. When one entered the monastery, he must give up all rights of personal choice, of disposing of his own time, of satisfying his own individual interests. He must subject himself to the will of his superiors and the wishes of his brothers. He must give up all allegiance to other institutions. This meant surrender of the last vestige of individual personality as well as negation of all political and social affiliations. Monasticism, then, renounced completely the three great aspects of social organization: the domestic home, the economic structure, and the political state. The aim of monastic education was to prepare not for this world but for the next.

With the exception of this lack of interest in the political aspects of living much of the organization of monastic life—as well as the organization of the governmental structure of the church—may be traced to Plato's picture of the ideal state in *The Republic*.

In the monastic ideal there was often an element of mysticism or transcendentalism. Most medieval mystics were also monks, though mysticism was to be met with outside the monasteries and far beyond the monastic period. The aim of the mystic or of the transcendentalist was to attain the highest spiritual knowledge and the purest spiritual satisfaction through appropriate training in the arts of meditation, contemplation, and inspiration. It was an attempt to grasp through intuition the ultimate reality of the "Divine Presence" and thus be in direct communication with God. To the mystic, God was an experience, not an object of reason; and there was a distinct possibility of the realization of the Divine to such an extent that he could lose himself wholly in this realization, while the material world and all human relationships became as nothing. Monastic mysticism, then, aimed at a life of contemplation and of devout and direct communion with God. To the extent that the monks were mystics, monasticism was a spiritual discipline as well as a physical and moral discipline.

TYPES   With such aims, the work of the monastic schools was restricted to literary training and manual training, both of which were looked upon as phases of moral and religious education. But, since the human relationships of the monk were so few in number, the moral education was not of a very broad character; and only in the case of the mystic was there religious education in its truest sense.

Article 48 of the Rule of Benedict declares: "Idleness is the great enemy of the soul, therefore the monks shall always be occupied, either in manual labor or in holy reading." The rule specified seven hours of manual work each day, and that each monk should read the sacred literature of the church for two hours daily. The requirement of manual labor was to keep the monks in good physical condition, and to keep them active so that they would have no time for temptation or brooding. They became skilled artisans in wood, leather, and metal; skilled farmers trained in agriculture and horticulture. Through the agency of the monasteries, swamps were drained, forests cleared, desert regions reclaimed, hillsides terraced with vineyards, and large areas developed for agriculture. The peasants were taught better methods of agriculture, provided with agricultural information, and taught various types of practical arts and crafts. In the convents for women—corresponding to the monasteries for men and operating under similar rules—the requirement of manual labor was carried out in weaving church hangings and embroidering altar cloths and church vestments, and these arts had to be taught to the novices. Everywhere under this dignifying of manual labor, the Teutonic barbarians were raised to a new level of practical civilization.

The reading requirement led to the collection of manuscripts in monastery libraries and the copying of manuscripts to provide duplicate copies for themselves and for exchange with other monasteries. The work in the scriptorium, or copying-room, was done to a large extent by those incapable of hard manual labor. They were allowed to spend their seven hours of work time in this occupation. But the monks did not confine their literary labors to mere copying. They also produced many original (though frequently mediocre) writings of a religious, moral, or historical nature. Thus both the manual and literary training needed to carry on the activities of the monasteries were always directed toward moral and religious purposes.

CONTENT   The subject matter used by the monastic schools was eventually incorporated into a fixed curriculum of the so-called Seven Liberal Arts, consisting of (1) the Trivium—grammar, rhetoric, and dialectic; and (2) the Quadrivium—arithmetic, geometry, astronomy, and music. In the earlier monasteries, the educational content was very rudimentary, intended to prepare merely for the essential duties of the monastic life. The novitiates were required to learn to read in order to study the sacred books; to write in order to copy manuscripts; to sing in order to take part in the religious ceremonies; and to calculate so that they could compute the time of the church festivals.

Later, in the more advanced monasteries, certain elements from Greek and Roman classical culture were introduced. The subjects were usually studied from compendia (or encyclopedias) rather than from direct source material. Those most popular were CAPELLA's *The Marriage of Philology and Mercury;* BOETHIUS' *Consolations of Philosophy;* CASSIODORIUS' *On the Liberal Arts and Sciences;* and ISIDORE OF SEVILLE's *Origines.* It was Cassiodorus who gave to the world the term Seven Liberal Arts and Isidore who first used the terms Trivium and Quadrivium.

The content in this monastic curriculum is not well indicated by the names of the subjects as they had somewhat different meanings from those which they have today. *Grammar,* the study most emphasized in monastic education, was really an introduction to literature. The pupil first acquired some skill in the rudiments of reading and then read the various Christian authors and, in some of the stronger monasteries, Vergil and other pagan authors. *Rhetoric* was largely written composition; but, besides teaching how to write various kinds of church letters, documents, and reports, it included some knowledge of church history and canonical law. *Dialectic* was similar to the formal logic of today; and, although it played little part in the curriculum of the earlier monastic schools, it later became the major subject of the trivium under the Scholastic movement, which we shall discuss later.

Arithmetic consisted at first of little more than the calculation of church festivals and holidays; but, in the tenth century, with the introduction of columnal calculation and the Arabic system of notation, its content was enlarged to include the keeping of accounts. *Geometry* at first dealt with those geometrical and geographical elements useful in surveying, architecture, and map-making, but later included the complete system of Euclid. *Astronomy* was studied to determine the dates of festivals and fast days, and the proper time for planting and harvesting crops and engaging in other practical pursuits. *Music* was the study of the chants and other sacred compositions used in the church services.

AGENCIES AND ORGANIZATION   Aside from the cathedral schools, which provided very meager fare, and the parish schools, which were, quite superficially, carrying on the work of the earlier catechumenal schools, the monastic schools were the only agencies for education throughout most of the medieval era. Boys were customarily admitted to the monastic school at the age of ten and, after a course of training lasting for eight years, were admitted to the monastic order at eighteen. But in many of the monasteries and convents, particularly in the later centuries of the Middle Ages, boys and girls who did not intend to become monks and nuns were admitted as pupils. They were called *externi* to distinguish them from the *interni* or *oblati* who were to take the vows and enter the order. The head of the monastic school was the abbot.

Monastic schools probably reached their greatest efficiency under CHARLEMAGNE (742–814) in the eighth and ninth centuries. This Frankish German warrior was a strong advocate of learning and the perpetuation of the Latin culture as well as an ardent Christian. In his desire to effect cultural unity among the people of his kingdom, he brought about a revival of education. He developed the "Palace School" at the court for the sons of the nobility, in the hope of producing more intelligent leaders for the church and the state; and he sent to the cathedral school at York, England, for the greatest schoolmaster of his day, ALCUIN (735–804). Alcuin served not only as head of the palace school but as virtual head of Charlemagne's entire educational system.[1] The emperor issued official decrees, or capitularies, to the abbots of the monastic schools and to the bishops in charge of cathedral schools, calling for a better educated clergy and for the establishment of parish schools for the children, where they did not already exist. He also sent out *missi dominici,* or official messengers, to see that his decrees were enforced.

A little later the standards of the monastic schools in England were raised by King ALFRED THE GREAT (849–901), who was himself engaged in editing various religious and historical works and translating them into the Anglo-Saxon vernacular and was beginning the writing of the *Anglo-Saxon Chronicle*. He sent to the Continent for outstanding scholars, among them GRIMBALD, who came from Flanders to become abbot of the monastery school at Winchester, and JOHN THE SAXON, who came from Corbie to become abbot of Athelney. Under Charlemagne and Alfred the monastic schools of western Europe multiplied rapidly, and were strengthened and improved in organization and administration.

METHODS   In methods, the teachers of the monastic schools showed great interest and skill. The general method of teaching was the catechetical, or question-and-answer, method. Since copies of the manuscripts were scarce, the teachers resorted frequently to dictation. The instructor would dictate a passage to the pupils and they would copy it for memorizing. It must be remembered that no instruction in the vernacular was given, Latin being the only language used for learning; and that these schools were secondary rather than elementary in character.

In the mystic phases of monastic education, there was dependence upon the methods of quiet meditation and contemplation, since the mystics believed that the highest knowledge and the deepest experiences of life could be gained only through divine inspiration.

---

[1] See Eleanor Shipley Duckett, *Alcuin, Friend of Charlemagne* (New York: The Macmillan Co., 1951), for a sensitive picture of Charlemagne's efforts to bring the dispensation of knowledge to his Frankish court.

Discipline was very severe in the monastic schools, growing out of the general ascetic character of monastic life. Teachers made frequent use of the rod.

EDUCATIONAL ATTITUDES AND PRACTICES OF SCHOLASTICISM

Late in the medieval period—that is, during the eleventh and twelfth centuries—there was a stirring of new life in Christian scholarship; and the revised beliefs and logical methods of discussion of its proponents have been termed scholasticism. The early Middle Ages, from the sixth to the tenth centuries, had been an era of faith, in which men had accepted without question the creeds and dogmas established by the church. But with the cessation of the barbarian invasions of the North and the East, with Europe assured a period of comparative peace and quiet, there was time for intellectual activities. With the reception into Christian Europe of Saracenic Aristotelian science from Spain, and with the return of the crusaders from their sojournings among the Byzantine Greeks and Arabs, skepticism began to assert itself. Men speculated now concerning the validity of doctrines they had hitherto accepted unquestioningly. The result was that in certain monastic and cathedral schools the study of theology was pursued with new vigor; in the universities profound thinkers came to be recognized as leaders, attracting students from near and far.

There were great schoolmen before the eleventh century—Bede, Alcuin, and ERIGENA (John the Scot); but scholasticism received no important contributions until the treatises and teachings of ANSELM (1033–1109), after 1093 Archbishop of Canterbury, often called the father of scholasticism.

Scholasticism does not refer to any one set of doctrines, but is rather a general designation for the particular methods and tendencies of philosophical speculation that were encouraged within the monasteries and cathedral schools in the eleventh century. These attained a measure of perfection in the universities in the twelfth and thirteenth centuries, and declined rapidly after the fourteenth century. The most striking characteristics of scholasticism were the narrowness of its field of thought on the one hand and the thoroughness of its methods on the other.

Scholasticism began as a movement to rationalize the doctrines of the Church; it ended in an elaborate system of civilization and culture. A vine was planted, took deep root, and began to fill the land; the hills were covered with the shadow of it and it sent out branches into the rivers and boughs into the sea. This scholastic vine may have been more leafy than fruitful but it possessed life and showed itself capable of ramifying into all the nooks and crannies of Church and State.[2]

AIMS   The aim of scholasticism was to support the doctrines of the church by rational argument. It was an attempt to support authority by the intellect, to justify faith by reason, to substantiate theology by logic. It was assumed that the church held possession of all final truth, by divine revelation; and this "truth," diversely stated as truths, had been accepted on faith. The aim of scholastic education was to show that these truths were consistent with each other and in complete accord with reason. The origin of this aim is to be found in the fact that questions from the East and from heretics within the church made it necessary to promulgate this prescribed belief not on faith alone but on the basis of reason.

Up to this time, the medieval church had been hostile to the intellectual approach to theology; and when Erigena had ventured the assertion that all true philosophy was identical with church doctrine, his efforts met with little favor. It was felt that faith was sufficient and did not stand in need of any rational defense. But when, two centuries after Erigena, Anselm expressed the same attitude, his arguments met with approval. Anselm believed that reason was in accord with dogma, but maintained that faith must precede knowledge and that doubt as preliminary to belief could not be tolerated. His motive was *Credo ut intellegam;* and in his *Monologue on the Method in Which One May Account for His Faith,* he wrote the following explicit statements:

I do not seek to know in order that I may believe, but I believe in order that I may know.

The Christian ought to advance to knowledge through faith; not come to faith through knowledge.

A proper order demands that we believe the deep things of Christian faith before we presume to reason about them.

This aim was dominant throughout the period of scholasticism—to show the essential harmony between reason and faith.

Scholastic education sought also to develop the ability to formulate beliefs into logical systems and to defend these against any intellectual arguments that might be advanced against them. Never was any attempt made to examine critically the fundamental beliefs already formulated and accepted by authority. There was no attempt to stimulate the inquiring attitude based upon doubt and the absence of preconceived notions, which is the basis of all modern scientific thinking. The chief purpose of scholasticism was to establish in a carefully organized philosophical system the theology that had been accepted as inspired. The aim of scholastic education was essentially intellectual discipline.

---

[2] C. G. Shaw, *Trends of Civilization and Culture.* (New York: American Book Company, 1932.) P. 236. Reprinted with the permission of the publishers.

TYPES AND CONTENT   Scholasticism limited itself to religious and intellectual education, the content of which was entirely confined to theology and religious philosophy. The range of knowledge within which the scholastic mind was allowed to work was very narrow; scholars might defend only such things as the church held to be orthodox, and so had to work intensively on a few subjects or questions. As a result, the scholastics subdivided and systemized their material beyond all measure. Just as the church was imposing its language and ideals upon every other activity of medieval life—architecture, music, and literature—so it was imposing its restricting influence upon scholarship and thought. The curriculum of scholasticism, consequently, was not so much a new system of philosophy as it was a new system of philosophizing about theological beliefs.

In this task of devising a system, the scholastics divided into two camps or schools of thought. The great controversy was over the nature of universal concepts. Anselm, at Canterbury, was the chief representative of the realists, a term, by the way, which has a directly opposite meaning today to what it had then. Scholastic realism was based on Neoplatonism and perhaps would be better understood if we used the term Platonic idealism, which means belief in the reality of ideas. The realist believed that ideas, or concepts, are the only real entities, and that the objects known through the senses are only copies of these ideas, "specimens of the species," as it were. He contended that the human senses are deceptive, and that true knowledge can be reached only through an intellectual and abstract grasp of universals.

The year before Anselm's advancement to Canterbury, ROSCELLINUS, a canon of Compiègne, had been forced to retract his heresy of nominalism; and it was to combat the effect of this heresy that Anselm put forth his argument of realism. ROSCELLINUS (1050–1122) had based the position of the nominalists on the philosophy of Aristotle. He insisted that universal ideas and concepts are mere convenient names, abstractions, or symbols; that individual objects as known through the senses are the only true entities. This thesis was not very favorable to such religious concepts as God, man, original sin, and salvation, nor to the concept of the church itself; and the Council of Soissons saw to it that the heresy was suppressed.

In the twelfth century, PETER ABELARD (1079–1142), "the most independent, the most courageous, and the most relentless among the schoolmen,"[3] essayed the reconciliation of realism and nominalism in a position that is sometimes called conceptualism. He argued that, although a universal concept has no objective existence, it is not merely a name out of all relation to individual objects, but is an expression of the sum total of characteristics that a group of individual objects have in common. Abelard was too much interested in the practical aspects

---

[3] Alfred Weber, *History of Philosophy* (translated by Frank Thilly). (New York: Charles Scribner's Sons, 1925.)

and problems of living and teaching to believe with Anselm and his old teacher WILLIAM OF CHAMPEAUX that there was no reality in the individual;[4] and yet he was too much the sound and honest thinker to agree with Roscellinus that only individual objects are real. So he developed his theory that the universal is only a concept until it is expressed in the individual, when it becomes real.

Thus Abelard saved scholasticism from becoming purely metaphysical through the extreme position of realism; but, although his conceptualistic position was approved by the church, his insistence that reason was antecedent to faith and could be made the foundation of church doctrine brought charges of heresy against him and he was twice condemned.

In the thirteenth century scholasticism reached its zenith with the union of Aristotelian philosophy and Christian theology in a logical theological system. This was set forth by THOMAS AQUINAS (1225–1274), whose *Summa Theologiae* remains today the authoritative exposition of Roman Catholic theology.

AGENCIES   The earlier representatives of scholasticism were associated with cathedral and monastic schools—Anselm at Canterbury, Roscellinus at Compiègne, Abelard at Notre Dame in Paris. They presented their ideas both by teaching and by writing, and students flocked to their schools to hear their lectures. Their writings were widely read and copied, and many were used as textbooks in the schools, especially such popular works as the *Sententiae* by PETER LOMBARD (1100–1160), a pupil of Abelard; Abelard's *Sic et Non;* and Aquinas' *Summa Theologiae*.

In course of time, as the fame of certain schoolmen spread and caused large numbers of the more mature students to gather, a broader and more flexible educational institution developed. This was the medieval university. Awakening interest in such secular studies as civil law and medicine—influenced by the crusades and contacts with Saracenic culture—further stimulated the growth of universities. Almost simultaneously there grew up the University of Paris for the study of theology and the University of Bologna for the study of law, both civil and canonical. Usually Bologna is considered the older—in fact the first of the medieval universities. *Bonomia docet* on the university seal indicates her pride—Bologna teaches!

ORGANIZATION   The organization of the cathedral school and the monastic school continued as heretofore. The organization of the early university was quite different. It began as an association of teachers—in effect, a guild—which was chartered by pope, emperor, or

---

[4] See Helen Waddell, *Peter Abelard*. (New York: Holt, Rinehart and Winston, Inc., 1933), for a penetrating picture of his personal and professional life, especially the tragic story of his great love for Heloise.

king and was, therefore, more independent of local ecclesiastical authority than was the cathedral school under the bishop or the monastic school under the abbot. It was also independent of political or secular control. Many privileges, hitherto granted only to the clergy, were guaranteed to its members under the charter; among them, exemption from taxation, exemption from military service, special courts outside of civil jurisdiction, and immunity from arrest by civil authorities.

The complete organization was known as the *Universitas Magistrorum et Scholarium,* the term *universitas* being given to any chartered company or association. Thus this group was merely a corporation of teachers and students. The entire study body was the *Studium Generale;* but outside the lecture hall students grouped themselves into "nations" according to their place of origin, for they came to the university from almost every country in Europe. Each nation annually elected a councilor. Each group of masters teaching the same subject was called a *facultas,* and each of these elected annually a dean. The deans of the faculties and the councilors of the nations made up the university council, which annually elected a rector who served with delegated power as the chief executive officer of the university. In some of the Italian universities, the rector was a student, and the students virtually governed the institution.

When a student entered the university (at about the age of fourteen), he attached himself to a master under whom he studied until he could "define and determine" by which was meant until he was able to read, write, and speak Latin. When he could demonstrate by examination that he was adequately proficient, he was declared a bachelor. He then continued his studies under several masters for from four to seven years until he could "dispute," that is, until he could defend his thesis or masterpiece. The successful defense of his thesis entitled him to his *licentia docendi,* or license to teach. He was now admitted to the ranks of the masters and was allowed to enter into competition with the other masters for students and allowed to charge fees for his work.

By the end of the thirteenth century, most of the universities had become fully organized into four faculties: *Arts, Medicine, Law,* and *Theology.* By the arts faculty, the Trivium and the Quadrivium of the monastic schools were taught, amplified by EUCLID's geometry and PTOLEMY's astronomy. Upon completing the arts course, most of the students entered the course in theology, though some entered law and medicine. Law included both canon and civil law. Medicine at first made little headway until Saracenic culture influenced European universities, bringing with it the medical texts of Jewish and Saracenic doctors.

METHODS   Methods of teaching under scholasticism and in the medieval universities were devised to give the student knowledge of the subject matter studied and ability to reason and debate. Two distinct methods were used. First there was the lecture, in which the teacher read the text together with glossaries and annotations on the text, so that the student might make an authentic copy of the authoritative work. In a way, this was a form of dictation. The second method was that of disputation, or debate, in which a student or group of students was opposed by another. A thesis was proposed, the proof was given, objections were raised and refuted, the whole proposition being treated in a minutely logical procedure.

The method of scholasticism, as one of logical analysis, is exemplified in the writings of Thomas Aquinas and Peter Lombard. There is (1) a statement of the thesis or proposition; (2) its proof; (3) a citation of solutions other than the orthodox one, with a refutation of each; (4) a consideration of objections to the orthodox solution, with the answer to each. The method not only emphasized systematic arrangement but demanded precision of thought and definite conclusions.

Scholasticism sought mainly to supply deductions which could be drawn from general principles. The favorite form of argument was the syllogism, a form of reasoning made up of three propositions: a major premise, a minor premise, and a conclusion. For example:

> All men are mortal.
> John is a man.
> Therefore John is mortal.

There are three elements in a syllogism: a large class or term; a smaller class, the middle term; and a specific case. If the middle term can be placed entirely within the operation of the larger term in the major premise, and the specific case can be placed within the operation of the middle term in the minor premise, then the specific case comes under the operation of the larger term and the conclusion is valid.

Although the scholastic method was barren in its immediate results, it stirred mental effort and thus eventually contributed to a wider intellectual awakening and later intellectual development in Europe. The method, though often devoted to endless and profitless quibbling over nonessentials, did enhance intellectual activity, preparing the way for the Renaissance and the development of modern science.

There was little discipline in the medieval universities. The privileges granted to the students made them impatient of restraint and enabled them to indulge in excesses and frequent immoralities. Since these immunities covered a student while he was going to and from the university, students often wandered about from one university to another, begging their way and indulging in riotous and unconventional practices. Many Latin student songs which have come down to us witness to this reckless life.[5]

---

[5] See Helen Waddell, *Wandering Scholars*. Seventh Edition. (London: Constable and Company, 1949.) for a definitive picture of medieval student life.

EDUCATIONAL ATTITUDES AND PRACTICES
OF CHIVALRY

Society in the Middle Ages continued to be differentiated into the same three classes that had existed from the dawn of civilization: the priestly class, the warrior class, and the working class. Until the end of the twelfth century, there were in western European society—from Cordova to the far North—only the Christian clergy, the feudal nobility, and the landless serfs.

The two institutions that we have just discussed, monasticism and scholasticism, were direct outgrowths of the Christian church, and their educational agencies were primarily designed for the training of the clergy. Unfortunately little consideration need be given to the training of the lowest class, the medieval serfs, for it was limited and simple. Vocational training in the "tilling of the soil, the hewing of wood, the drawing of water" was achieved by direct imitation of the elders of the group; and the simple religious instruction needed for participation in the rites and ceremonies of the church was given by the priests in the parish schools. In the case of the nobility, however, a definite system of education was provided through a social institution that was a direct outgrowth of medieval feudalism. This was the institution of chivalry, dating from about the beginning of the ninth century, when the feudal system had become fixed in its main characteristics, until about the sixteenth century, when feudalism began to disintegrate.

To understand chivalry it is necessary to understand its feudal background. The term feudalism is of obscure origin. Some think that it comes from the Latin *fides,* meaning faith. But it more probably arose from the Germanic *fehu,* meaning cattle; for among the Teutonic peoples property was measured in terms of cattle, and feudalism is distinctly concerned with property. Feudalism has been described as "a complete organization of society through the medium of land-tenure, in which from the king down to the lowest landholder all were bound together by obligations of service and defense; the lord to protect his vassal, the vassal to protect his lord; the defense and service being based on and regulated by the nature and extent of the land held by the one or the other." [6] Since the turbulent and unsettled conditions of the times made it impossible for any king or lord to rule an extended domain, he would divide part of his estate among his warriors, giving to each the authority of a sovereign over his own lands; and, in return, the warriors would bind themselves to give military or other aid to their overlord whenever it was required. In such agreements is found the genesis of the institution which became a definite system about the ninth

---

[6] James Harvey Robinson, *Readings in European History.* (Boston: Ginn and Company, 1904.) Vol. I, p. 187.

century and a powerful political and social force in the eleventh, twelfth, and thirteenth centuries.

The feudal system was most thoroughly developed in France, Germany, Italy, England, and Scotland; its cradle was the empire of Charlemagne. Charles, when merely king of the Franks, had determined to build a great Christian empire to include all the Germans; and when he was crowned by the Pope "Emperor of the Romans" (800), he had truly succeeded. Already almost every sovereign of the West had become his vassal. Charlemagne's wealth was in land, not in money. So he had paid his loyal war leaders and civil governors in large grants of land and promises of protection; and these had pledged to him their own aid and service and that of their men-at-arms—as had also the nobles he had conquered. His empire had been welded by the bonds of feudalism. The method was not new with Charlemagne; it was a convenience to his Frankish predecessors and to many another landowner. But such an extensive, orderly, and effective use of it was new, and it established feudalism as the social system of the Middle Ages.

Feudalism developed rapidly in Europe after the breakup of Charlemagne's great empire. Because of the weak successors who ruled the divided empire, and because of the inroads of Saracens, Slavs, and Huns, the century after Charlemagne was an age of disorder, and all classes were glad to avail themselves of the protection the system offered. This was especially true of the subordinate classes, for the castles of the feudal nobles provided fortresses whether against invading lords or bands of marauding brigands. When the kings and princes gave of their lands to feudal lords, and these in turn granted sections to lesser lords, and so on down, the land so granted was called a "fief," or "feud"; the grantor was called "lord," or "liege"; and the one who received the grant was "vassal," or "retainer." The vassal made pledges of loyalty, military service, and other aid to his lord, and the lord in turn provided his vassal with counsel and protection. The great bulk of the population were serfs, who were bound to the soil and who passed with the land when it changed masters. Thus feudalism was a system of political and economic relationship. Political feudalism centered in the relation of the landlords or nobles to one another and ultimately to the monarch; economic feudalism centered in the relation of the lord to the serfs who toiled in his domain.

The essence of feudalism was service, expressed either in the tilling of the land or in fighting. Those whose service was of the military type were regarded as of noble character; those whose service consisted of cultivating the soil to which they were tied were deemed of base and common extraction. Thus there developed a warrior class made up of the nobles whose sole excuse for existence seemed that of fighting. The life of the typical lord was absorbed in his castled estate, war, and the chase. But out of this life—crudely bold—there evolved one of the most interesting of social developments—the system of chivalry. The rules and social usages that accumulated in connection with the life of the nobility constituted chivalry; and the preparation for this life, chivalric education. The term chivalry comes from the French *cheval,* horse, horsemanship being a basic accomplishment in the system. A noble who had gone through the prescribed training and taken the vows was made a knight; so chivalric education was largely a training for knighthood.

AIMS   As a system of education for the nobility, chivalry aimed to teach the best ideals, social and moral, that the Teutons could understand. Chivalry tried to take what good there was in a brutal, selfish, unprincipled fighting society, and make it over in accordance with the standards of Christianity. It sought a happy blend of barbarian warrior with Christian saint. It taught the protection of the weak, gallantry toward women, honesty in everything. Chivalry provided a definite system of training aimed to inculcate the "rudiments of love, war, and religion."

The greatest virtue of the times was courage. The most useful attainment was the ability to fight. The ideals and manners of life practiced and advocated by Christ and his followers could not be comprehended. They could understand being heroic. . . . If the courage and the fighting could be put to some good use, the world would be better. This made a good start, and it was the task of chivalry to find some virtues that would harmonize with these. The desire for glory is a powerful motive. . . . Chivalry offered something glorious to fight for. Something particular, tangible, and personal serves as an objective much better than does an abstract principle. Love, war, and religion are more spectacular than labor, thought, and morality.[7]

The ideals of chivalry were quite different from those of monasticism and scholasticism. Instead of asceticism and intellectualism, chivalry emphasized action. It was a life of high ideals and standards; the true knight was to be devoted to the service of his God, his king, and his lady. Before he could be knighted, he must take: (1) the vow of religion, expressing his loyalty to the church; (2) the vow of honor, expressing his loyalty to his feudal superior; (3) the vow of gallantry, expressing his loyalty to his lady. The aim of chivalric education was essentially one of social discipline to train the knight to play his part in the faithful observance of the social usages, customs, and ideals approved by his social class. The maxim by which the knight lived was: "Act as if the person for whom you have the highest regard were looking on." This produced in the knight courtesy, gallantry, generosity, and good manners—all of which had their refining influence upon society, even if these actions were performed mechanically rather than from the heart.

The ideals of chivalric education are depicted in the lyrics of the troubadours of France, the minnesingers of Germany, and the minstrels of England. Chaucer, Spenser, Scott, and Tennyson delighted in

---

[7] J. F. Messenger, *An Interpretative History of Education.* (New York: Thomas Y. Crowell Co., 1931.) P. 78. Reprinted with the permission of the publishers.

telling of the knightly deeds of courtesy and courage. There was, however, too much affectation and superficiality and Miguel de Cervantes
rendered a wholesome service in depicting its exaggerated sentimentality
in his delightful burlesque, *Don Quixote.*

The ideals of chivalry were probably not so effectively realized
in England as in an earlier France. J. R. Green, in a commentary on
the introduction of the tournament in England by Edward I, speaks of
"the frivolous unreality of the new chivalry," "the false air of romance,"
and, in connection with Edward himself, states that "chivalry exerted on
him a yet more fatal influence in its narrowing of all sympathy to the
noble class, and its exclusion of the peasant and the craftsman from all
claim to pity." [8]

TYPES   Chivalric education was a form of social training.
It emphasized manners more than morality, but as a training in social
etiquette probably has never been surpassed. It emphasized military
training; in fact, it made fighting a profession and devoted a large share
of its attention to the development of professional military skills. It
placed emphasis upon a phase of education that both monasteries and
universities neglected—that of physical training. Religious training was
of a rather superficial type: the knight was trained to take part in all the
religious rites and ceremonies of the church. There was some literary
training, but it was mostly oral and confined to the vernacular. Chivalric
education was essentially class education and was distinctly aristocratic.

CONTENT   The curriculum was one of activity rather than
intellect. The course of study was made up of physical activities, social
activities, military activities, and religious activities. At the earlier levels,
the content consisted of health instruction, religious instruction, training
in etiquette and obedience to superiors, in playing the harp, singing,
chess, and the development of skills in riding, jousting, boxing and
wrestling. Sometimes a little training was given in the reading and
writing of the vernacular. At the higher levels, the curriculum consisted
of the so-called "Seven Free Arts": (1) jousting, (2) falconing, (3) swimming, (4) horsemanship, (5) boxing, (6) writing and singing verse, and
(7) chess. Girls received a thorough training in social etiquette similar
to that of the boys, but physical and military training was omitted from
their course of instruction. Instead, they were given training in household duties and in such domestic accomplishments as sewing, weaving,
and embroidering. Chivalric education for girls differed from convent
education in that there was more emphasis upon the social and less upon
religious and intellectual content.

The most important change fostered by chivalry was the rapid
development of vernacular literatures and the practice of them as part

---

[8] J. R. Green, *A Short History of the English People.* (London: Macmillan & Co., Ltd.,
1929.) Chapter III, iii.

of the content of education. By the time of Charlemagne there were two distinct groups of spoken language, the Germanic and the Roman-derived Romance. English, a mixture of Germanic tongues slightly Latinized during the Roman occupation and more and more so after the Norman Conquest, told its earliest tales of chivalry in the odd conglomeration that we know as Middle English. Similarly, within the Germanic and Romance groups, there were differing vernaculars which had developed individually in different localities. The written vernacular practiced in the schools of northern France differed greatly from that of southern France. The Garonne valley from 1100 and 1300 was a land of verse and song, stimulated by chivalry. The singing poets, the troubadours, brought their own hero tales and love ballads to the court at Toulouse and, traveling over western Europe, helped greatly in the notable ascendancy of the French language. French soon replaced Latin as the language of secular culture of the Middle Ages.

AGENCIES   The earliest education of the child was in the hands of the mother in the home; later the lords and ladies of the castle of the father's feudal superior were the teachers. The castle, the tournament fields, and the fields of battle, were the schools for the education of the boy; the home and the court were the schools for the girl.

We should not fail to appreciate the importance of the troubadours, minnesingers, and minstrels as agencies of education during the earlier centuries of chivalry. The medieval age was, for the most part, one in which reading was done by few but monks and scholars (and sometimes merchants); in which travel was slow, difficult, and dangerous; in which diversions, aside from eating, playing games, hunting, and fighting, were few. Then, across the broad scenes, pass the traveling troubadours. They were the gazetteers, the spreaders of news, the providers of entertainment and amusement. It was their office to bear tidings from castle to castle, to sing the praises of beautiful ladies and gallant knights. They were living magazines, who acquainted the inhabitants of one district with the customs and manners evolving in another—matters of speech, dress, methods of hunting, habits of eating, rules of courtly etiquette; and sometimes they warned of impending danger from jealous rivals or robber bands. Even those troubadours who settled in a particular castle or remained in the castle of their birth exerted appreciable influence in the education of the youth of the estate. And all the while they were circulating the new vernacular, to which each area was contributing and upon which each was drawing.

ORGANIZATION   From birth until the age of seven, the children of the gentry remained at home where they were given the necessary physical, moral, and religious training by their mothers. At the age of seven, they went to the castle of the feudal overloard. (This custom probably began when the subordinate nobles sent their sons and daughters as hostages or pledges of their fidelity to the overlord.) Orphan children were sent as wards to the castle because the overlord legally was their guardian. Girls were sent to the court by their parents with the making of desirable marriages in view. Thus the castle became the center of chivalric education.

From seven to fourteen, the boy was a page and attended a noble lady of the court who directed his education both indoors and out. Between fourteen and twenty-one, the youth was a squire and attended a knight. He still waited upon his lady, with whom he sang, played upon the harp, and played chess, but his chief duty was to attend upon his lord. Many services were required of him; he served the lord at table, made his bed, groomed his horse, cleaned his armor, carried his shield. He accompanied him in the tournaments and in actual battle, and thus learned the arts of both peace and war.

At twenty-one his education was complete and he was ready for knighthood. He prepared himself for the ceremony by confession, fasting, and an all-night vigil. Elaborate religious rites were performed; and after promising to be faithful, to protect women and orphans, never to lie or slander, to live in harmony with his equals, and to protect the church, he received the accolade—a slight blow on each shoulder with the flat of the sword; his new sword and spurs were buckled on, and he thus became a knight.

METHODS   Since chivalric education was largely the acquisition of skills, the methods used were those of example and practice. Attendance upon his lady and his lord enabled the boy to develop the social behavior and accomplishments of chivalry through imitation. The color and action of the court life and the desire for social approval provided motivation for his learning. Ideals were acquired through the songs of love and war, praising beautiful virtuous ladies and gallant valiant knights, and through the pledges taken in impressive ceremonies. Discipline was maintained through the ideals of obedience and service, though at times these ideals had to be enforced by threats of mortal combat. Pupils learned by doing, were motivated by high ideals, and were restrained and controlled by an adherence to recognized social standards.

EDUCATIONAL ATTITUDES AND PRACTICES
OF THE GUILD SYSTEM

The medieval period contributed one more factor in the development of educational theory—the rise of the middle class and the organization of the guild system—which occurred toward the end of the Middle Ages. Largely as a result of the crusades, an increase in trade and commerce developed; as a result of this came the growth of free cities;

with the growth of free cities, there arose a new social class—the burgher, bourgeoisie, or middle class. Finally, there came a demand for a new type of school in which the children of the new class could be educated according to their needs.

The crusades, the most spectacular movement of feudal chivalry, were the chief cause of its demise. The knights of the Middle Ages were ever conscious of the medieval problem of personal salvation, and to them a solution offered in the scheme to redeem the Holy Sepulcher from the infidel Turk. The same spiritual force that had sent men into the monasteries now set in motion thousands of crusaders from every Christian country of Europe.

Although the crusades failed to achieve their avowed purpose, unsuspected results did follow—results that were ultimately disastrous to the system that brought them about. The narrow isolation of feudal life was broken down, and communication between countries stimulated. The necessity of transporting the armies of crusaders resulted in the development of seaport cities as centers of shipping, trading, and banking. The crusaders themselves became acquainted with new forms of food, clothing, and ornamentation, new luxuries and commodities; and this acquaintanceship bred a multitude of new wants. This stimulated the development of a system of banking, trade, and industry, to import, process, and distribute the commodities demanded. The towns in which the new commerce and industry were centered became free cities, with feudal immunity and independence from church and state. By purchase, by diplomacy, and even by force, these "city-states" obtained their rights of self-government and guarded their liberties. "The somber merchant on his mule won in the tilt with the gay knight on horseback." The burgher class which thus arose formed a new caste, distinct from clergy, nobles, and serfs. The needs of this new class were quite different from those of the older classes in medieval society, and demanded a different education for the burghers' children.

Much of the life in these medieval communities centered around the guild system. The guilds were organizations or associations of those engaged in commerce and industry and were of two types, the merchant guild and the crafts guild. The merchant guilds were the first to appear and flourished from the twelfth to the fourteenth centuries, especially in England. The members were all residents of the same town and included both merchants who bought and sold and artisan merchants who sold their own manufactured products. The guild usually had a monopoly of the retail trade in its town, with the privilege of taxing outsiders who brought in goods.

The craft guilds were associations of manufacturers, artisans, and skilled workers. In each town all who shared in a certain craft or trade, such as weaving, goldsmithing, or silversmithing, banded together to advance the standards of their work. These craft guilds were most prominent in the fourteenth and fifteenth centuries. Eventually they subdivided into two organizations. The skilled workers founded guilds,

which were the forerunners of modern trade unions; and the owners of
the shops, on the other hand, formed associations of capitalist employers,
which were the forerunners of modern trade associations. Around these
guilds, types of education adapted to their needs developed.

AIMS, TYPES, AND CONTENT   The primary need of this new
middle class was for an education of a practical type. Vocational training
was necessarily emphasized, for children were to be prepared for the
activities of commercial and industrial life. This is the unique contribution of this movement to education, a new emphasis upon a new type
of vocational training. Yet the burghers did not want a narrow type of
vocational or trade training with everything else neglected. Elementary
instruction in the rudiments of reading and writing the vernacular and
in arithmetic was always required as preparation for the industrial and
commercial training of the guilds. Masters were obligated to give instruction in the rudiments to their apprentices and required to see that
they received adequate religious instruction. Guild schools were usually
taught by priests. Nevertheless, these schools were much more secular
in spirit and in aim than the cathedral, monastic, and parish schools.
Usually the intellectual education of the guild class was on the elementary level; yet some guild schools later expanded into Latin schools, such
as Merchant Taylors' in London.

AGENCIES   New types of schools developed in these trading
cities for the education of the burgher children. The chantry schools
were founded out of bequests made by wealthy merchants or traders,
stipulating that special priests be employed to chant masses for the
repose of the souls of the deceased patrons. Since the special priests had
much unoccupied time at their disposal, many of these bequests provided that they devote some time to the instruction of children of the
city in the rudiments of elementary education. There were three hundred chantry schools in England alone at the time of the Reformation.
Sometimes, through a union of chantry foundations, strong schools
were developed in the larger towns.

Burgher schools also arose in the larger cities. These were supported and controlled by the public authorities and were often taught
by lay teachers as well as by priests. The usual type was the guild school,
for the children of craftsmen. These were taught by the same priests who
performed religious functions, such as baptism and marriage, for the
guild members. They usually provided the elementary education in the
vernacular, which was required as a foundation for the later vocational
education given in the guilds themselves.

ORGANIZATION   The only formally organized education in
the guild system was this vocational training. The members of the guilds
were divided into three classes: masters, journeymen, and apprentices.
The masters alone were entitled to own a shop, buy raw materials, and

sell the manufactured goods. They bought and sold at prices established by the guild, and their establishments were supervised by the guilds so that inferior articles would not be produced. The beginners in the craft were known as apprentices. By the terms of apprenticeship, the master furnished the apprentice with a home and taught him the trade in which the master was engaged. The apprentice was to obey the master and to give him his services as long as the apprenticeship lasted, and for this he was to receive only board and lodging. The term of apprenticeship depended somewhat upon the trade to be learned—usually about seven years.

The journeyman was not bound to one master, but could go about as he wished. He received wages from the master and lived in his home. He continued to acquire additional skill. Each journeyman was required to construct a masterpiece before being declared a master, just as the candidates for the degrees in the medieval universities were required to defend a thesis. After becoming a master, his education was considered complete, and he could set up in business for himself as soon as he accumulated sufficient capital.

METHODS   There is nothing particularly new in the methods of instruction and training used in these schools. In the chantry, bourgeois, and guild schools, they were actually much the same as those in the monastic and parish schools. The methods for apprenticeship were example, imitation, and practice used so often before. Discipline was no less severe than in other medieval schools. Masters were usually quite harsh in their treatment of apprentices.

FOR FURTHER READING

Barnes, Harry Elmer, *An Intellectual and Cultural History of the Western World*. New York: Random House, 1937. Pp. 326-440.

Butts, R. Freeman, *A Cultural History of Western Education*. Second Edition. New York: McGraw-Hill Book Co., 1955. Pp. 116-164.

Cole, Luella, *A History of Education, Socrates to Montessori*. New York: Holt, Rinehart and Winston, Inc., 1950. Pp. 114-200.

Davidson, Thomas, *A History of Education*. New York: Charles Scribner's Sons, 1900. Pp. 151-174.

Duckett, Eleanor Shipley, *Alcuin, Friend of Charlemagne*. New York: The Macmillan Co., 1951.

Durant, Will, *The Age of Faith*. New York: Simon & Schuster, Inc., 1950. Pp. 1-135; 421-1086.

Eby, Frederick, and Arrowood, Charles F., *The History and Philosophy of Education, Ancient and Medieval*. New York: Prentice-Hall, Inc., 1940. Pp. 630-815.

Good, H. G., *A History of Western Education*. New York: The Macmillan Co., 1960. Pp. 64-80; 88-110.

Graves, Frank P., *Education During the Middle Ages*. New York: The Macmillan Co., 1910. Pp. 1-39, 47-75.

Hart, Joseph K., *Creative Moments in Education*. New York: Holt, Rinehart and Winston, Inc., 1931. Pp. 157-185.

Knight, Edgar W., *Twenty Centuries of Education*. Boston: Ginn & Company, 1940. Pp. 87-149.

Mayer, Frederick, *A History of Educational Thought*. Columbus, Ohio: Charles E. Merrill Books, Inc., 1960. Pp. 133-151.

Messenger, James F., *An Interpretative History of Education*. New York: Thomas Y. Crowell Co., 1931. Pp. 63-99.

Monroe, Paul, *A Textbook in the History of Education*. New York: The Macmillan Co., 1933. Pp. 243-313.

Mulhern, James, *A History of Education* (Second Edition). New York: The Ronald Press Co., 1959. Pp. 227-293.

Reisner, Edward H., *Historical Foundations of Modern Education*. New York: The Macmillan Co., 1927. Pp. 195-363.

Shaw, Charles Gray, *Trends of Civilization and Culture*. New York: American Book Company, 1932. Pp. 212-258.

Ulich, Robert, *A History of Educational Thought*. New York: American Book Company, 1950. Pp. 89-101.

————, *Three Thousand Years of Educational Wisdom*. Cambridge, Mass.: Harvard University Press, 1954. Pp. 172-190.

QUESTIONS FOR CLASS DISCUSSION

1. What survivals of the Seven Liberal Arts may be found in the curriculum of the contemporary American high school? The college and university?

2. To what extent is knowledge still given in our schools by means of compendiums of information? By lecturing?

3. What modern American patrons of learning have played a part in the improvement of schools and colleges similar to that played by Charlemagne and Alfred the Great? Does this similarity extend to motives too?

4. What survivals of mysticism and transcendentalism may be found in the religious education of today?

5. In what respects are American universities superior to those of medieval days? In what respects inferior?

6. Do you believe that student life in contemporary American colleges and universities is on a higher or lower plane than that of medieval universities? Explain?

7. In what ways are the methods used today in high school and college debates different from the practices of medieval scholasticism?

8. To what extent is the apprenticeship system as developed by the guilds still to be found in American trade and industrial training.

9. How do the powers and practices of modern trade unions differ from those of the medieval guilds?

10. What types of schools today give training on a par with that taken under chivalry?

11. Compare the position of women under chivalry with that of women in modern American life. With those of India.

CHAPTER VIII

THE SARACENIC APPROACH TO EDUCATION

THE BIRTH OF ISLAM

Out of the Arabian desert,[1] that land of nomad shepherds, original home of the Semitic peoples, from time immemorial successive bands of nomads had shifted north, east, and west into the more fertile lands of Egypt, Mesopotamia, and the Mediterranean coast. We have noted how the ancestors of the Jews had thus left the Arabian desert to seek a more comfortable existence in the Promised Land of Canaan, but this was only one of many such Semitic migrations. Each emigration, however, left behind a nucleus of desert tribes, enough to raid and trade and exact tribute from caravans driven across their sands. The great empires of Egypt, Persia, Macedonia, Rome, and Byzantium in turn claimed some degree of sovereignty over these desert tribes. Now and then an Arab chieftain would rise to independent power and bring some trading city, such as Palmyra, Mecca, or Medina, into temporary prominence. In the writings of the Roman historian Marcellinus of the fourth century we find these Arabians first identified as Saracens, the word coming possibly from an Arab word meaning eastern. Its use then had nothing to do with Mohammedanism. As will be seen, we apply the

---

[1] See Chapter III, p. 47.

term Saracens here to those Mohammedans whose culture derived from Arabia originally, grew spectacularly, and waned suddenly—all in a short period of six hundred years.

Until the opening of the seventh century, A.D., there were no signs of any unwonted or dangerous energy in the Arabian deserts. The life of the country was going on as it had gone on for long generations. Wherever there were fertile patches, wherever, that is, there was a spring or a well, a scanty agricultural population subsisted, living in walled towns because of the Bedouin who wandered with their sheep, cattle, and horses over the desert. Upon the main caravan routes, the chief towns rose to a certain second-rate prosperity, and foremost among them were Medina and Mecca.[2]

In Mecca and Medina the religious movement of Islam began. It was in Mecca that MOHAMMED (570–632), the founder of Islam, was born; and it was the *Hejira,* or flight to Medina (622 A.D.), that marked the beginning of his power. Saracenic education began formally about 650, eighteen years after Mohammed's death, when the *Koran,* the sacred book of the Mohammedans, was compiled from the notes that had been made by his disciples while he talked. It reached its highest development in Spain in the hundred years before 1050—years during which intellectual Mohammedans, because of persecution by orthodox reactionaries of their faith in the East, had left Bagdad, Damascus, and other centers of their culture, and fled to the more liberal caliphates of western Africa and Spain. It closed its career of phenomenal culture about 1250, by which time the Mohammedan scholars had been driven from Spain before the Christian armies from the north.

The Saracenic movement, although it ran concurrently with the rest of medievalism, is so different in its educational concept from Christian medieval education and is of such significance in its educational implications that it deserves a separate treatment. No chapter in the history of educational thought is more colorful than that which records the rise of Saracenic culture in Spain. Not only was this civilization an intriguing phenomenon in itself, with a most interesting background, but it made astounding contributions to the modern world. Because of religious prejudice, these contributions too often have gone unrecognized.

The Saracenic culture in Spain is particularly striking because of its contrast with contemporary conditions in the rest of Europe. When Moorish Spain was most advanced, Christian Europe was still held back by the repressive tendencies of the Dark Ages; the humanities had not yet replaced the divinities. To the Saracens fell the privilege of preserving ancient learning, both in content and in spirit; and to the Saracens must go much of the credit for leading Europe out of medievalism.

Not only did the Saracens preserve learning, they improved upon it. Their greatness seems to have been due to their ability to assimilate

---

[2] H. G. Wells, *The Outline of History.* (New York: Doubleday & Co., Inc., 1949.) P. 476. Reprinted with the permission of the publishers.

the best in the intellectual culture of the peoples with whom they came in contact and to apply this heritage to their own practical needs. They took mathematical and medical knowledge from the Hellenistic world. They took the notation system of arithmetic and the algebraic forms from India. They developed the practical sciences and the mechanical arts. They created a civilization in which science ceased to be mere learned lore and was applied to the arts and crafts of daily living; in other words, they bent science to the immediate service of human life. We are indebted to them for the creation of the scientific spirit of investigation and experimentation, by which man has enlarged the "bounds of human empire over nature," and for the invention and improvement of tools[3] of science. They exerted a tremendous influence upon western Europe in the domain of philosophical thought. Although they developed no new schools of philosophy, they did assimilate the Grecian philosophy and elaborate upon it; and it was through the Saracens that Christian scholars were led to a revival of interest in Aristotelian science and logic. From Spain came the first complete knowledge of the writings of Aristotle that Christian scholasticism had.

Spain under the Saracens was the cultural center of the world in the tenth and eleventh centuries, although the seed of this culture had been planted among a scattered, simple, unlearned people in the deserts of Arabia only a few centuries before. This seed was Islam, and its growth is one of the most amazing movements in history. What is the story of this remarkable movement?

Mohammed—illiterate prophet though he called himself—while not above his fellow Arabs in intellectual learning, surpassed them in insight. As a trader and guide for caravans he had traveled through neighboring countries and had come into contact with the accepted religions and philosophies of his day. Convinced that what his illiterate, superstitious, and warring people needed was "a Book and a God," he undertook to provide them with both. He came to believe that certain revelations from Allah, the "Lord of the Worlds," had been granted to him. The result was the *Koran,* a chaotic book, in part tedious, in part beautiful, and strangely composed of a mixture of Jewish, Christian, and other religious elements. Under the stimulus of a little group of disciples, he developed his message, summed up in this phrase: "There is no God but Allah, and Mohammed is his prophet."

Mohammed (Arabic: "highly praised") began his ministry at the age of forty, his first convert being Khadijah, his faithful wife. His message was couched in terms that the Arabs could understand; he offered a paradise of surcease from toil—a realm of many rivers, with green oases and curious fountains from which there ran continually the life-giving fluid so necessary to the desert dweller's existence—to all who believed. For those who would not, he predicted a dwelling forever in continual fire, the breath of hot winds, and nothing to drink save boiling and

---

[3] "Tools" is used here in its abstract sense.

stinking water. His persistent theme, that God is one, that he himself was the prophet of God, and that truth was contained in his revelation from God is repeated over and over again (as the following selected verses show) in the *Koran*.

There is no doubt in this book; it is a direction to the pious, who believe in the mysteries of faith, who observe the appointed times of prayer, and distribute alms out of what we have bestowed on them, and who believe in that revelation which hath been sent down unto thee and that which hath been sent down unto the prophets before thee, and have firm assurance of the life to come; these are directed by their Lord, and they shall prosper.

Now in the creation of heaven and earth, and the vicissitude of night and day, and in the ship which saileth in the sea, leaden with what is profitable for mankind, and in the main water which God sendeth from heaven, quickening thereby the dead earth, and replenishing the same with all sorts of cattle, and in the change of winds, and the clouds that are compelled to do service between heaven and earth, are signs to people of understanding; yet some men take idols beside God and love them as with the love due to God; but the true believers are more fervent in love towards God.

There is no God but God, the living, the self-subsisting; he hath sent down unto thee the book of the Koran with truth, confirming that which was revealed before it; for he had formerly sent down the law, and the gospel a direction to men; and he had also sent down the distinction between good and evil. Verily those who believe not the signs of God shall suffer a grievous punishment; for God is mighty, able to revenge.

These are the signs of the book of the Koran: and that which hath been sent down unto thee from thy Lord is the truth: but the greater part of men will not believe. It is God who hath raised the heavens without visible pillars; and then ascended his throne, and compelled the sun and the moon to perform their service; every one of the heavenly bodies runneth an appointed course. He ordereth all things.[4]

The new religion had its expected effect and more. Because of its attractiveness to human nature and its satisfaction of human longings, it prospered. The nature of its faith made it imperative that its believers go forth and convert the heathen. This the Mohammedans under the unflagging and unflinching leadership of Abu Bekr, close friend of Mohammed and his successor, zealously set out to accomplish by conquest and the sword. Within ten years all Arabia was converted; and then Abu Bekr, with the faith that moves mountains, resolutely set himself to the task of bringing the whole world to the worship of Allah. The attempt came near to succeeding; if there had been many men like Abu Bekr, it probably would have succeeded. The Moslems advanced steadily across northern Africa and into Europe through Spain until they were finally checked by Charles Martel at the battle of Tours (732 A.D.).[5] Thereafter, the Pyrenees remained the boundary in the

---

[4] *The Koran (Alkoran)*, George Sale, Trans. (New York: A. L. Burt Company, 1902.) Chapters I-XIII, pp. 57-211.
[5] Called by the French, the battle of Poitiers.

West of their political power, though nothing could stop their intellectual influence from filtering into Europe. It is interesting to speculate how different the history of Europe might have been if this battle of Tours had turned out otherwise. In the East, the energy of the Moslem advance spent itself in conquering and assimilating Persia and Turkestan; if its first successful campaigns in Syria had been continued against Byzantium, there can be little doubt but that, by the eighth century, it would have entered Europe from the East as well. Wherever its conquests reached, Islam prevailed among the conquered, not only because of the religious zeal of its followers, but because of the social and political order it offered.

As long as Islam was confined to the unlettered Arabs, as long as it remained a mere faith, it needed no support from learning and called for no special education. The *suras,* or chapters, of the *Koran* could be communicated by mouth and committed to memory, and all truth not contained in the *suras* was vain and to be spurned. When, however, Mohammedanism advanced into Syria, Egypt, and other centers where ancient learning held sway, a change took place. Before Islam could hope for acceptance from the inhabitants of these countries, it had to attain to the dignity of a philosophy; it had to become Hellenized, but this does not seem to have been at all distasteful to its sponsors. Their fresh minds and newly aroused curiosity reached out after this culture and made it their own. Especial credit is due the Christian and Jewish scholars and physicians who were influential in converting the Moslem converters to Greek science and philosophy.

We have seen in an earlier connection that the catechetical schools of the East had shown a more liberal attitude toward Hellenic culture than had the schools of the West. But in the fifth century, the eastern church had shown itself narrowly orthodox when it denounced the Hellenized theology of NESTORIUS, Patriarch of Constantinople from 428 to 431, and procured his banishment to Egypt. His followers had fled to the cities of Syria—to Antioch, Nisibis, and Edessa—beyond control of the church. Here they had developed excellent schools where the study of Greek science and philosophy was continued. They preserved much Greek medical science, and added to it; medical skill, developed especially at their medical college at Gondesapore in Persia, made them popular with the Moslem caliphs.

The Nestorian Christians had been not the only teachers of the Arabs, however. In the various eastern cities, especially in Alexandria, the Arabs had been in contact with Jewish scholars with their distinctive literature and traditions, to the mutual advantage of both Arab and Jew. The Moslems, though on many occasions they had shown bitter hatred of the Jews, had despoiled them and exacted tribute from them, and reaped hatred in return, yet could—when circumstances prompted—induce friendliness again; especially if the circumstances involved scholarly discussion, agreeable and advantageous to both. The Islamites, in moving up from Arabia and drawing upon the centers of learning in Syria and Egypt, had been intellectually broadened and enriched; and soon they were to find another source of inspiration in India.

Yet the Arabs were assimilators rather than creators. Under the inspiration of the cultured peoples with whom they had come in contact, by travel or conquest, Mohammedan scholars began to translate into Arabic the Greek mathematical, philosophical, and medical writings. They applied themselves also to the mathematical lore of the Hindus. Greek libraries were established at the courts of the caliphs; and learned men—philosophers, poets, physicians, and mathematicians—were brought from the newly conquered countries to live at the courts. By the tenth century, schools rivaling the best in Syria had been established at Bagdad, Bassora, Bokhara, Cairo, Delhi, and elsewhere in the East.

One of the outstanding Saracen scholars was AVICENNA, or IBN-SINA (980–1037) of Persia, who was famous in Europe as a physician and interpreter of Aristotle, also as the author of the *System of Medicine*. It was largely due to his influence that a small group of learned men who called themselves the "Brothers of Sincerity"—their aim was to combat the fatalism and fanaticism of Islam with Greek philosophy—published the *Encyclopedia,* which was virtually a complete scheme for higher education directed toward a rational Moslem theology.

These efforts on the part of Saracen scholars to rationalize the doctrines of Islam tended to undermine its supernatural authority, and thus aroused the suspicion and antagonism of the fanatically orthodox Arabs. So those who would intellectualize Mohammedanism were compelled to migrate to the West, where—as we have said—they found refuge among the more liberal Moslems of western Africa and Spain. In these centers, the scholars continued their work, encouraged and supported by the liberal caliphs.

Brilliant as the Saracenic civilization in the East may have been, the student of the history of educational thought will find the culture and scholarship of the Saracens in Spain of greater interest; the more so, since it was these Moslems of the West who played so important a part in bringing back into Europe the lost spirit of learning. It was indeed a splendid culture that resulted from the introduction of this Hellenized Islam into Spain. The rulers distinguished themselves as patrons of learning and set an example of refinement strongly contrasting with the life of the European Christian princes. The palaces of the emirs and caliphs were luxuriously furnished at a time when Christian lords were living in draughty and gloomy castles. In the cities of Cordova, Seville, Granada, and Toledo, the streets were paved and lighted by public lamps seven hundred years before there were lights in London, and centuries before the citizens of Paris could step out into the streets on rainy days without sinking in mud up to their ankles.

It is not surprising that in a civilization such as this should be found a well-organized system of schools. A complete system of education spread throughout the Mohammedan dominions of Spain—an inspiring, but little heeded, example to the Christian countries of Europe.

ATTITUDES OF SARACENIC EDUCATION

AIMS   Education, as the Saracens in Spain conceived it, was primarily a search for knowledge and an application of scientific facts. The Saracens appreciated the sciences for their intellectual values; undoubtedly they derived much gratification from the study of science as such.

The Arabian mind found special satisfaction in the pursuit of the natural sciences. The exuberant fancy of the Arab, his love of wonder and mystery, intensified by a swiftly unfolding history, which surprised and flushed him, helped to make the powers and movements of nature an attractive study.[6]

But the primary aim of Moslem education was a practical, scientific one. The Saracens worked to develop arts and crafts. Their purpose was to adapt science to their needs, to devise the tools of science and use them in the everyday affairs of practical living. Saracenic education, therefore, aimed at the assimilation and development of the sciences, not merely for their own sake, but particularly for the services that they could render in man's manifold activities. The Moor did not disdain the hard work of the laboratory, and engaged in patient experimentation because he was working for practical results. He was turning out products and commodities to enrich the life of himself and his fellow men. He was deriving and utilizing scientific facts to further his civilization.

Here we find an education in which science was expected to play a new and important role; it was no longer to be mere intellectual gymnastics, but was to be applied to all the useful arts and crafts. Likewise, reading was not a mere accomplishment but a necessity for the man of affairs. Their emphasis upon philosophy was a natural outgrowth of their devotion to the applied sciences. Aristotle especially interested these people because there was scarcely an aspect of the world of nature and the world of man upon which he had not thought and written. His philosophy was objective and concrete and subject to useful applications; therefore they made Aristotle their own. They stressed medicine because it was a practical art and necessary for the preservation of life—life that was interesting and worth living. Chemistry was studied because of its applications to medicine and industry. Mathematics was indispensable to mechanics and industry as well as to other sciences. Astronomy was studied as an aid to geography and navigation.

Saracenic education was liberal in the truest sense of the word, since it aimed at the development of individual initiative and social welfare. All education began with religious education, the memorizing of the *Koran*. It was a simple religion and for the most part easily understood. An insistence upon kindliness and considerateness in daily life was one of the main virtues of Islam, and its monotheism had none of

---

[6] Hungerford, "The Rise of Arabic Learning," *Atlantic Monthly*, Vol. 58, p. 549.

the exclusiveness of the Jewish religion. It produced an unusual degree of tolerance within the faith, for Mohammed had decreed that all Moslems were brothers and equals. The theological elaborations that have confounded and divided Christianity were absent and no loophole was left for the development of a self-exalting or governing priesthood. Islam had (and still has) learned doctors, teachers, and preachers, but no hierarchy of priests and no monastic orders. Thus, except for those training to be teachers of divinity or philosophy, there was no need for extended religious education, and youth suffered few religious restrictions to hamper its educational freedom. The after life was taken care of by a simple faith, and education was free to devote itself to the improvement of life in this world.

The education of the Saracen was eminently successful in achieving its practical aims. It turned out men of affairs, and the Spanish Moors were able to improve the conditions of life on every hand. They developed a system of agriculture, regulated by codes of laws. They introduced into Europe such new plants as rice, sugar, cotton, spinach, saffron, and many of the edible fruits. They gave much attention to the breeding of fine cattle, horses, sheep, and poultry, and introduced the culture of the silkworm. They adopted the Egyptian system of irrigation, with floodgates, pumps, and water wheels. They manufactured paper, textile fabrics, earthenware, iron, and the steel that has made the name of Toledo, like that of Damascus, famous throughout the world. The cities of Cordova and African Morocco gave their names to the finest grades of leather. The Moors introduced gunpowder, invented the cannon and other types of artillery, and the mariner's compass. In the days of their prosperity, they maintained a merchant marine of more than a thousand ships. As a result of their inventive genius, their cities and homes were equipped with many facilities and luxuries not dreamed of by their European neighbors.

TYPES   Vocational education was stressed more than any other type; but this was for the professions and skilled trades and crafts and comprised instruction as well as training. In such preparation, skills were acquired on the basis of a knowledge of scientific facts and principles instead of through imitation of skills originally acquired through trial and error—a procedure different from anything we have found hitherto in this study. Intellectual training in the sciences is thus made the basis for vocational training for the professions and the mechanical and commercial trades. Commercial training was emphasized; and we find the beginnings of a science of economics as a basis for business and trade.

The representation of the human form was forbidden, so the Saracens provided no art education for sculptors and painters; but they did give training in architecture, artistic carving, repeating design, and color, that resulted in such structural gems as the world-famous Alhambra. Their artistic propensities were encouraged also in their textiles, pottery, and metal work. Religious education was in general limited to the study of the *Koran,* because of the simplicity of the Mohammedan faith and the absence of a governing and institutional priesthood.

We know less about the avocational training of the Moham-medans; but certainly reading was a form of enjoyment, and story-telling was highly developed; observe the entertainment in *The Thousand and One Nights*—old Moslem tales of Arabia and Persia, repeated orally until gathered into a book in Egypt in the fifteenth century. There was also much extemporizing of verse—for almost every Arab would be a poet— and music and dancing, though the latter was done usually by slaves. We may count, too, hunting with a falcon, which, both in the East and the West, passed from a means of livelihood to a fashionable sport.

Saracenic education was universal, although not entirely demo-cratic as Mohammed had decreed it should be. The wealthy had some educational advantages not generally available to the poor classes; but elementary education was free and open to boys and girls of all classes, and the doors of the higher educational institutions were open to all, rich or poor. Financial aid was often provided for advanced students who needed it. It was this great liberality which the Saracens displayed in educating their people—a development that was one of the most potent factors in the brilliant and rapid growth of their civilization—which so universally diffused learning that it was said to be difficult to find a Saracen who could not read or write.

CONTENT   The curriculum of the Saracen schools was the most complete and most carefully organized of any in ancient or medieval times. At the elementary level, it consisted of reading, writing, arith-metic, religion, grammar, and elementary science. At the higher levels, it consisted of algebra, geometry, trigonometry, physics, chemistry, geog-raphy, astronomy, anatomy, pharmacy, medicine, surgery, philology, his-tory literature, logic, metaphysics, and jurisprudence. In fact, the Sara-cens seem to have studied most of the subjects that we have in our schools today.

The system of education arranged at Basra[7] by the Brothers of Sincerity in their *Encyclopedia*[8] was a marvel of completeness. This monumental outline of education comprised fifty-one treatises arranged under four heads: (1) thirteen treatises on logic, (2) seventeen treatises on natural science, (3) ten treatises on metaphysics, and (4) eleven trea-tises on theology. This encyclopedia claims our interest for several rea-sons: (1) it sums up the best thought of a long period of culture; (2) it has roots in all the past of humanity and branches in all its future; (3) it is all-comprehensive, including nature and spirit, and shows that the former has its origin in the latter; (4) it does its best to harmonize

---

[7] A port on the Shatt al Arab in Iraq, about 60 miles from the Persian Gulf.
[8] The *Encyclopedia* which was valued so highly by the Christian schoolmen and credited by them to the authorship of al-Farabi of Bagdad was probably this same work.

reason with revelation; (5) it shows man his place in the universe, his origin, his destiny, and therefore his duty; (6) it thus furnishes a complete education, enabling its recipient to lead a rational, purposeful, and free life. This system was generations ahead of its time.

Saracenic education in Spain, moreover, had a rich content. Not only did its curriculum include many subjects, but each subject covered its field with surprising completeness.

The Arabians were proud of their language, and in their schools much attention was paid to the study of Arabic language and literature. Philology must have been a subject of vast interest to them. Not only grammars, but great lexicons and dictionaries were produced, one of which consisted of sixty volumes, the definition of each word being illustrated. To the Arabian language we are indebted for many of our common names—syrup, julep, elixir, admiral, alcohol, spinach, cotton, chemise, and chemistry. The Saracens had a considerable body of literature that, in addition to the *Koran* and the commentaries on it, must have been studied in their schools. The first Arab writers of distinction were historians and biographers, and romantic fiction and the short story soon followed. Their poetical productions embraced most of the modern forms and types—such as elegies, odes, and satires—but they never produced a really great epic or tragedy.

In mathematics, the Arabs built on the Greek and Hindu foundations. Arithmetic made great advances with the clumsy Roman numerals replaced by the figures which the Arabs had borrowed from the Hindus. It was an Arab mathematician who first used the zero and the decimal notation and gave the digits the value of position. Algebra, although it had its beginnings in India, was virtually the creation of the Arabs. They added very little to Euclid; but they developed trigonometry, inventing the sine, the tangent, and the cotangent.

Mathematics was applied to the study of physics and astronomy. The Arabians measured the size of the earth, calculated the angle of the ecliptic and the precession of the equinoxes. They made many applications of mathematics to the control of physical forces; for example, in hydraulics. They invented the pendulum clock. They made certain important discoveries in optics and other branches of physics, explaining refraction of light, gravity, capillary attraction, twilight, and other natural phenomena. While Christian scholars and navigators were declaring that the world was flat, the Saracens were teaching geography in their schools by means of globes and studying astronomy in observatories. They constructed many astronomical instruments which are in use today. To the knowledge of the heavenly bodies they added much that we now consider elementary but which was far in advance of a world devoted to astrology. The fate of one of their astronomical observatories in Spain is rather significant. After the expulsion of the Moors, it was turned into a belfry because—we are told—the conquering Christians did not know what else to do with it.

Although the Arabs took the beginnings of their medical science from the Greeks, they added much to it. They kept up intensive study of diseases, diet, drugs, and various phases of physiology and hygiene. Their *materia medica* makes a large part of ours today, and their pharmaceutics was well begun—with some understanding of the nature of chemical changes, they could make tinctures, essences, and syrups. They had surgeons who knew the use of anaesthetics and who performed difficult operations with surgical instruments of types still in use. Anatomy was studied by dissection. At a time when in Christian Europe the diseased and the crippled were seeking miraculous cures, in Saracen Spain physicians and surgeons were practicing their healing arts with some success. The Arabs knew also something of the scientific breeding of cattle and horses, and the horticultural secrets of grafting to produce new varieties of fruits and flowers.

The Arabs made strides in transforming ancient alchemy into chemistry; they discovered many new chemical substances, such as alcohol, potash, nitrate of silver, corrosive sublimate, nitric acid, and sulphuric acid. They applied their chemistry in many directions—to the working of metals and other substances, and to the cultivation of the soil. The former led to the development of metallurgy and ceramics. A large part of the population was engaged in contriving objects, as useful as they were beautiful, out of gold, silver, copper, bronze, iron and steel; and in making and shaping glass and pottery. Their skill in manufacturing fine steel enabled them to supply not only such famous products as the Damascus and Toledo blades, but also fine instruments for use by astronomers and navigators. Another application of chemistry, advanced and practical, was in agriculture: the scientific use of fertilizers and crop rotation. Much of this practical ability and skill, necessary for the carrying out of these agricultural, industrial, and commercial advances, was undoubtedly a goal of their education.

As a combination of art and applied science, Arab workmanship reached its climax in architecture in Spain. Moorish architecture was not only elaborately beautiful, with wood and stone carvings, and tile intricately patterned in colors, but it was practical and durable as well. The mosques and palaces of Cordova and Seville and that last triumph of the Moors—the fourteenth century palace, the Alhambra, at Granada— are world examples of thorough craftsmanship.

The sciences of business and trade were not neglected, and beginnings were made in the field of economic theory.

Not only did the Moor labor in his laboratory, turning out products and deriving scientific facts; he wrote about his discoveries. There was scarcely a subject left untouched in his literature. It is said that in the library connected with the university in one of the Saracen cities, there were over 400,000 books—most of them by Moorish writers. These books were not all of a scientific nature. Many were writings on philosophy. The Saracens, favoring as they did the philosophy of Aristotle, confined their philosophical works almost entirely to commentaries on Aristotelian thought. Chief among these philosophers was

AVERROES, or IBN-RUSHD (1126–1198), who taught at Cordova, and who became the authoritative commentator on Aristotle; he was especially so regarded by medieval Christian universities, where his works were diligently translated and copied.

AGENCIES   The caliphs of Moorish Spain, after the example set by the rulers of the East, proceeded to foster education and scientific achievement by every means that lay within their power, and were instrumental in founding elementary schools, academies, universities, and libraries.

As for the East, the courts of the early caliphs might themselves well be called educational institutions, and they were from the beginning the greatest agencies of education; for the caliphs of the East surrounded themselves with groups of learned Nestorian Christians and Jews and often became ardent scholars themselves. In connection with these courts, vast libraries were fostered, with manuscripts gathered from the far corners of the earth. The caliph HAROUN-AL-RASCHID of Bagdad, a contemporary of Charlemagne, and one of the first great patrons of Moslem learning, saw the need for elementary schools and established a school in connection with each mosque, in which reading, writing, simple numeration, and the precepts of the *Koran* were taught. This custom was handed down and became the pattern of such schools throughout all Moslem domains. The Moslems were well circumstanced to be patrons of learning in that they were a wealthy people. Immense sums of tribute money could be and were expended for the advancement of learning. Elaborate experiments could be made, and costly instruments could be constructed. Journeys were undertaken to far places, from which scholars brought back collections of rare manuscripts to be translated by learned Jews and Nestorian Christians under royal patronage. So, held back neither by lack of means nor lack of time, the Moslem made rapid strides in assimilation of scientific knowledge and philosophical thought.

The Saracens in Spain made similar expenditures of wealth to establish universities. Those at Cordova, Seville, Toledo, and Salamanca became world famous. The best instructors to be had were summoned, many of them being Jews and Christians; for so completely had the Arabs become imbued with the scientific spirit that they judged the teacher by his true learning, not by his religious views.[9] Indeed, the unlettered Mohammed himself had told his followers to respect the opinions of the people with the Book, meaning the sacred Hebrew writings, and in matters of scholarship at least this respect had persisted. The greatest of the universities, that at Cordova, had fifteen separate departments, each specializing in a different field of learning, and had beautiful buildings with the most complete equipment money could buy.

---

[9] The position of the Jews and Christians under Mohammedanism is fully discussed in David S. Margoliouth, *The Early Development of Mohammedanism*, Lecture IV, "The Status of the Tolerated Cults." (New York: Charles Scribner's Sons, 1914.) Pp. 99-134.

Libraries profited no less than universities from this wealth and generosity. The caliphs or emirs sent emissaries to all parts of the known world to collect manuscripts; and the results of these searchings and of the later literary activities of the Saracens themselves made possible voluminous libraries of carefully copied and richly bound books. Nor did these countless books lie idle; students were permitted to use them at will. Each university soon had an available library; moreover, it became the custom of wealthy men to open their valuable private collections to the students.

Such magnificent educational advantages could not fail to attract the attention of Europeans who wished to lift themselves out of the morass into which Christian education had fallen. In a time when the Christian schools of both eastern and western Europe were falling into decay, the schools of the Saracens were growing and attracting eager students. These Moorish universities served as models for some of the best features of the new Christian universities springing up in Europe.

ORGANIZATION   The educational system of the Saracens in Spain was definitely organized on three levels: elementary, secondary, and higher.

Following the custom of Haroun-al-Raschid, elementary schools were especially fostered and were to be found in every city and town of the Moors. These were usually attached to the mosque and were free, and open to both boys and girls of all classes. The children entered these elementary schools at the age of five years, remained three years if they were of the poorer classes, then went into some trade or industry. The children of the rich did not leave school until they reached the age of fourteen, after which they either entered the higher schools or traveled with a tutor. The elementary education consisted mostly of the study of reading, writing, arithmetic, grammar, religion, versification, and geography. The *Koran* was the chief reading text used at these lower levels.

For the wealthier students, there was a type of secondary school somewhat similar to the later boarding schools of England and America. These schools were arranged in twenty-four or thirty apartments each accommodating about four students, with a rector presiding over the school. Here learned, well-trained, and well-paid teachers—often Jews or Christians—instructed in Arabic literature, grammar, mathematics, astronomy, metaphysics, chemistry, and medicine. These schools for the wealthier youth were self-supporting.

The universities, which arose in all the chief Moorish cities of Spain, were colleges in the literal sense; for students and professors shared accommodations. Special departments, or schools, were created for the various sciences. There were medical schools with chemical laboratories, and finely equipped hospitals for clinical instruction. There were schools of astronomy which offered the use of observatories equipped with the most costly and most accurate instruments that could be constructed. Other schools specialized in mathematics, agriculture, music, navigation, physics, or some other branch of learning. The doors of these universities were open to all, rich or poor, native or foreign; and altruistic men often provided financial aid for those students who needed it.

METHODS   In the elementary schools, the methods were largely the catechetical methods that we have already seen used in the Christian schools. There were no particular advances made by the Saracens beyond the methods used in other countries, in which these elementary subjects were learned by memorizing and imitation. It was in the higher schools that the Saracens' genius was expressed in the development of new methods of learning. Although considerable use was made of the lecture method, the Saracen learned much of his science by experimentation and observation, actually exploring in an objective manner the field in which he was interested. Here we find the origin of the true, unprejudiced scientific method. Here we find laboratories and clinics used for the first time. Chemistry, physics, astronomy, and medicine were taught by experimental methods; and it was undoubtedly because of these methods that so many important discoveries were made.

FOR FURTHER READING

Barnes, Harry Elmer, *An Intellectual and Cultural History of the Western World.* New York: Random House, 1937. Pp. 494-499.

Browne, Lewis, *This Believing World.* New York: The Macmillan Co., 1926. Pp. 303-334.

Butts, R. Freeman, *A Cultural History of Western Education,* Second Edition. New York: McGraw-Hill Book Co., 1955. Pp. 118, 147.

Davidson, Thomas, *A History of Education.* New York: Charles Scribner's Sons, 1900. Pp. 133-158.

Duggan, Stephen P., *Student's Textbook in the History of Education.* (Revised Enlarged Edition). New York: Appleton-Century-Crofts, Inc., 1936. Pp. 91-94.

Durant, Will, *The Age of Faith.* New York: Simon & Schuster, Inc., 1950. Pp. 153-344.

Eby, Frederick, and Arrowood, Charles F., *The History and Philosophy of Education, Ancient and Medieval.* New York: Prentice-Hall, Inc., 1940. Pp. 668-669, 697-701, 710-711.

Good, H. G., *A History of Western Education.* New York: The Macmillan Co., 1960. Pp. 80-89.

Haines, C. Grove, and Walsh, Warren B., *The Development of Western Civilization*. New York: Holt, Rinehart and Winston, Inc., 1941. Pp. 106-117.

Hart, Joseph K., *Creative Moments in Education*. New York: Holt, Rinehart and Winston, Inc., 1931. Pp. 192-200.

Hitti, Philip Khuri, *The Arabs, A Short History*. Princeton, N.J.: Princeton University Press, 1943. 224 pp.

————, *History of the Arabs*. New York: St. Martin's Press, 1956 (Sixth Edition). 822 pp.

Knight, Edgar W., *Twenty Centuries of Education*. Boston: Ginn & Co., 1940. Pp. 157-158.

Mayer, Frederick, *A History of Educational Thought*. Columbus, Ohio: Charles E. Merrill Books, Inc., 1960. Pp. 152-160.

Mulhern, James, *A History of Education* (Second Edition). New York: The Ronald Press Co., 1959. Pp. 244 ff.

Moore, Ernest C., *The Story of Instruction: The Church, the Renaissance and the Reformation*. New York: The Macmillan Co., 1938. Pp. 247-300.

Randall, John H., *Making of the Modern Mind*. Boston: Houghton Mifflin Company, 1926. Pp. 208-210.

Ulich, Robert, *Three Thousand Years of Educational Wisdom*. Cambridge, Mass.: Harvard University Press, 1954. Pp. 193-201.

QUESTIONS FOR CLASS DISCUSSION

1. To what extent is the school system in the United States more democratic than that of the Saracens?
2. Why do you suppose that general histories and educational accounts frequently pay little attention to the culture and achievements of the Moslems?
3. Presuming that the Moslems had triumphed at the battle of Tours (Poitiers) and had conquered Western Europe, do you believe that we should be more advanced in science than we are at present? Why or why not?
4. To what extent did the Saracenic civilization of Spain resemble that of prewar Germany in scientific thought and technical achievement?
5. What branches of science have developed in modern times and thus were not studied by the Saracens?
6. Do you believe that modern universities are as tolerant as those of the Saracens were? Discuss the part played by religion and politics in the Moslem institutions.

7. Do you think that religion hampers or restricts education today to a greater or lesser degree than it affected education under Islam? Explain.

8. Compare the work of the various educational foundations that have developed in the United States of the twentieth century with the generous support given to education by the Mohammedan caliphs.

9. What scientific developments of the past two decades have carried us far beyond the achievements of Saracenic science?

10. Does the progress shown in Mohammedan countries today compare in any way with that of the earlier Saracenic culture? Discuss.

CHAPTER IX

THE STUDY OF THE HUMANITIES
FOR A MORE ABUNDANT LIFE

THE ORIGINS OF HUMANISM

Most authorities agree that modern times began with the movement known as the Renaissance; and, since education is always a reflection of the times, modern education and modern theories of education
also can be said to have begun with this same movement. The foundations upon which the various modern theories of education have been
built were established in ancient and medieval times; but it took certain
definite social, political, economic, and philosophical changes that occurred in western Europe during the fourteenth and fifteenth centuries
and thereafter to modify these foundational elements and crystallize
them into the educational theories that have become prevalent in recent
times.

The first of these modern theories of education was that known
as humanism. Humanistic education was the distinct outgrowth of the
Renaissance, and to understand its full significance we must realize that
the Renaissance is only one phase of a great general awakening in
Europe. H. G. Wells says:

The Renaissance was only a part of the Renascence of Europe. The
Renaissance was a revival due to the exhumation of classical art and learning;

it was but one factor in the very much larger and more complicated resurrection of European capacity and vigour. . . .[1]

What were the causes of this general reawakening? What were the factors that profoundly influenced the intellectual and cultural life of the fourteenth and fifteenth centuries and thus brought about the development of the educational philosophy known as humanism?

Yet the serenity of the age mankind was leaving also had its effect on the foundations of thought and on educational theory. This life is revealed in the parable of *The Castle and the Rock*.

There was, in these middle years, a valley broad and wide, well-watered and fertile whose inhabitants did indeed count themselves the most fortunate of men—men formed of the dust of the field in the image of their God. For their lives followed the rhythm of the seasons; they plowed and they sowed; they reaped and feasted; the drought came and the famine; yet the bounty of the olive tree nourished them and the vine refreshed them; and they were at peace.

When the wintry blasts roared from the North and when the scorching sirocco blew from the South they accepted these things—not gladly but hopefully for life was short and heaven held its bounty even to eternity. Thus their eyes were set on high and the two great configurations of the valley continually reassured them. For the Castle stood on its craggy eminence in the East and was ever visible though oft-times partially hidden by the mistiness of dawn and by the frosts of autumn. And, likewise, to the West, there stood the Rock, and when the morning sun first lighted the upper reaches of this great granite peak with a brilliance impossible to describe—or when in the beauty of the sunset its silhouette revealed that stairway etched in stone which stretched from earth to sky—the Rock offered a comfort that was so far beyond the simple pleasures of the soil that there is no telling of it.

And from the Castle issued great retinues of men, some with bright glorious banners, others carrying the holiest of objects, and as they wound throughout the valley their progress was beautiful to behold. For at their head rode Caesar and his raiment glittered. But of the valley folk they tribute took; fat sheep and grain, one sighed but then in vain; for better they than brigands bold that dwelt beyond the plain.

Yet the Rock was loftier than the Castle and indeed when one swept his gaze from the East to the West in the early dawn or rosy twilight he understood their meaning and marvelled that the mystery of earth and heaven should stand exposed before him. In truth man's life was encompassed by their comforting stillness. In the morning he was born, at midday he flourished, in the evening like the somber shades that fitfully fled across the valley, he was gone. But his happy spirit dwelt forever in the shadow of the Everlasting Rock.

So these men judged (and rightly too) that this their life had meaning only in these simple observances: their soil they tilled; their toll they paid; their lives they sped. He of the Castle came and went. But the Mighty Rock did not change; it prevailed in absolute silence and solace gave to him who sought its

---

[1] H. G. Wells, *Outline of History*. (New York: The Macmillan Co., 1921.) P. 699 n. Reprinted with the permission of the publishers.

peace. Man deemed this good, and praised the Rock; and looked to it for succor.[2]

It was, of course, impossible that medieval life could continue in isolation when winds of change were blowing all about it. The progress of the Saracen had hardly touched the man of the Middle Ages; industry and trade had been stilled; and thought itself—if not sterile—had been rigidly circumscribed. If medieval man was happy perhaps it was because he lacked the modern concept of progress.

Vast economic changes were taking place at this time. The crusades had their social and economic as well as their religious implications. The growth of free cities—such as Genoa and Venice—was tremendously stimulated by the necessity of equipping and transporting the thousands of crusaders who swarmed toward the East in the seven crusades that occurred in the century and a half from 1097 to about 1270. The crusaders found their tastes and desires greatly enlarged by their sojourns in the East where, they discovered, people had better things to eat and wear than the medieval European had ever possessed. These contacts with eastern civilization created a demand for the importation and processing of the commodities of the East; and so trade grew, and commerce and manufacturing were stimulated in the free cities of Europe. The city or burgher class—the merchants, bankers, and masters of the guilds—who supplied these new economic demands now rose to the importance of a Third Estate, a stratum distinct from nobles, clergy, and serfs. The needs and ideals of this new class were different from those of the established medieval classes and pointed the way to a new manner of living.

Expanding commerce sought new worlds to conquer and found them. The discovery of new routes to India by Marco Polo and others, and the discovery of the American continent by Columbus and his followers in their search for still shorter routes to the Orient, enlarged the scope of trade; and this in turn changed the conduct of trade. The free cities within their narrow limits were not sufficient to meet the new commercial problems, and trade became national in scope. This situation was one of the outstanding factors in the rise of the nations of western Europe, and was the forerunner of new conceptions and practices in education. "Princes of Trade" began to supersede the "Princes of the Church" in power and influence.

Thus, the crusades, the enrichment of free cities, the rise of a city class, the expansion of commerce, of industry, and of banking, the increasing importance of guilds and of apprenticeship in the trades, the growing spirit of nationalism, and the development of national languages and literatures—all these were factors in the revival of an interest in the things of this world to replace the provincialism and other-worldliness of medieval Christian civilization.

We are likely to consider great epochs in history as distinct and

---

[2] Suggested by Henry Adams' appraisal of the late medieval period in *The Education of Henry Adams*. (Boston: Houghton Mifflin Company, 1918.)

separate periods, cut off sharply from those that precede and follow. We forget that all advance is evolutionary; one period grows out of previous periods. The Renaissance was the natural outgrowth of certain developments in the later medieval centuries to which we referred in the discussions of medieval and Saracenic education.

The roots of the Renaissance are to be found in changed economic and social conditions. But the real meaning of the Renaissance is to be found in the new spirit of inquiry into knowledge which was undermining the structure of monasticism and scholasticism—undermining it just as surely as the new industry and the new trade were destroying the structure of feudalism. Scholasticism had fettered thought, had engaged in a quibbling play of words, until intellectual accomplishment was at a standstill; but it had supplied the foundation for intellectual advancement. It led students to see the advisability of analytical thought and furnished them with thought processes which, although at first used only to prove dogmas already accepted, later became the means by which scholasticism itself was destroyed and replaced by scientific inquiry. The universities, founded during the later years of the Age of Faith, began to stimulate a desire for intellectual achievement. With the rise of faculties of law and medicine to supplement the faculties of theology came more intellectual freedom, and more dissatisfaction with those institutions that restricted thought and suppressed inquiry. Moslem learning—gradually influencing Europe more and more through Spain—had prepared the way for the importation from Byzantium, the storehouse of Greek culture, of the writings of the great classical authors and of teachers of the new humanities.

Many material things came into European life to aid intellectual advancement. Paper was introduced from the Saracens; printing was invented to multiply the copies of classic manuscripts—discovered and brought into Europe by the early humanists. Thus the mad desire of the few to read spread to the many by the adequacy of the supply of books; and books becoming cheaper and more plentiful gave added motivation to intellectual activity.

The work of explorers and scientific discoverers quickened the spirit of inquiry and investigation. Magellan, sailing west to find the East, had verified the hypothesis that the world was round. Copernicus demonstrated that the sun and not the earth was the center of the universe. So the old unity of belief, the old dogmatic authority, had to give way under the force of an inquiring attitude demanding concrete proofs instead of metaphysical abstractions.

The church itself—because of a false sense of security—had suffered a decline, and many ecclesiastical courts had become corrupted. It was not unnatural therefore that some individuals should lose trust in the church, begrudge loyalty to its leaders, and at last stand out against the powers of the ecclesiastical domination. Men became less interested in ritual and more interested in the life of the contemporary world. Their attention passed from the divinities to the humanities. It was fixed upon the joys of living, the beauties and wonders of nature, the human relationships of life, and the desires, ambitions, and aspirations of individual human beings. There was less emphasis upon formalized church observances that led only to the one end of obtaining eternal life and of escaping eternal damnation, and more on every form of art, literature, science, and commerce that made life rich and pleasant, whether it was good for the soul or not.

Thus, the thought processes developed by scholasticism, the broadening of the universities, the incoming of Moslem learning from Spain, the increased supply of books, the findings of exploration and scientific discovery, the degeneration of the church—all helped to develop the intellectual freedom and individual personality that brought about the intellectual, artistic, moral, and spiritual rebirth of western Europe, provided the genesis of its modern culture, the emancipation of its will, and an enthusiastic delight in freedom of thought, speech, and action.

It has already been indicated that the Renaissance was much more than a revival of learning; that its influence was much more than literary; that it profoundly changed the moral, social, intellectual, and artistic life of western Europe. It should be emphasized also that the Renaissance was not limited to Italy where it began, but that the movement soon spread to every land of Europe. In Spain and Portugal, the Renaissance spent itself in exploration, in colonization, and eventually in the reform of the church from within. In France, the stimulative force of the movement was felt in literature and in art; in England, almost entirely in literature and learning. In Germany and Holland, however, the movement took deep root, stimulating not only scholarship and art, but also an interest in moral and social reform that eventually brought on the Protestant Revolt and Reformation.

In general, it is desirable to distinguish between the early Renaissance in Italy and the late Renaissance in northern Europe.[3] The Renaissance in Italy represents individual humanism: it stressed personal culture, individual freedom and development, as the best way toward full and rich lives; it produced a revival of classic learning and paganism, which eventually brought about a counter-movement under Savonarola; it went back to the writers of classical antiquity to revive the long-forgotten humanistic way of living and of looking at life; it was essentially aristocratic, limited to the few who had individual means for the desired culture. On the other hand, the Renaissance in the north represents social humanism: it stressed social and moral reform as the best means of providing rich and full lives; it preserved an interest in the church and was essentially religious in spirit; it emphasized Hebrew classics as well as study of Greek and Latin because of its additional interest in the original sources of Biblical and patristic church literature; it was essentially democratic, since it aimed at rich and full lives for the masses as well as for the favored few. Therefore, in our treatment

---

[3] See Wallace K. Ferguson, *The Renaissance.* (New York: Holt, Rinehart and Winston, Inc., 1940.) Pp. 1-8.

of the educational implications of humanism, it will be necessary for us to treat the subject under each of these headings. Furthermore—both in Italy and in the northern countries—humanism passed through two stages: the first a broad and true humanism; and the second a narrow and formal humanism, often designated by the term "Ciceronianism." Because of these different aspects of humanism, we shall discuss it under two divisions: (1) Italian Humanism; and (2) northern Humanism.

ITALIAN HUMANISM

Renaissance humanism began in Italy, where the quickening influences were felt earliest and more keenly than in the rest of Europe. The city-states of Italy were the first to increase their wealth and prestige as a result of the crusades and the accompanying growth of trade and industry. Their independence, the outcome of struggles against the ecclesiastical domination of the Holy Roman Emperor, offered splendid opportunities for personal advancement and individual fortune. Italy was the ancient home of Graeco-Roman culture, and the tradition of this culture had persisted more strongly among the Italians than among any of the other peoples of Europe. It was proper that they should strive with patriotic fervor to revive their cultural heritage from the past.

PETRARCH (1304–1374) and his co-laborer BOCCACCIO (1313–1375) may be taken as types of the early Italian humanistic scholars. Petrarch has been called the first modern scholar and man of letters. He attacked the medieval universities with their Aristotelian philosophy as "nests of gloomy ignorance"; he repudiated the other-worldly ideal of the monasteries and bitterly criticized the whole range of scholastic learning. Beginning with his first great discovery in 1333, he collected and copied ancient Latin manuscripts; and of these he took special pleasure in the orations of Cicero. He wrote in Latin to familiarize his contemporaries with the lives of great men of antiquity; but he wrote sonnets in the Italian vernacular designed to voice the humanistic emphasis on emotional life and to give the individual, personal, and esthetic keynote to the Renaissance. He was not a Greek scholar himself, but he inspired others to revive the Greek spirit at its best. He was influential in the introduction of humanistic studies at the University of Padua.

The desire of the early humanists to be able to read the masterpieces of Greek literature caused them to turn to Byzantium for an adequate supply of the writings of the great classic authors and for good teachers to teach them how to read them. A new day dawned when CHRYSOLORAS (1350–1415) came from Constantinople (1396) to become a professor of Greek at the University of Florence. Many distinguished humanists came to listen to this first and most famous of the émigré teachers, and they carried the seed to every university center in Italy.

Chrysoloras himself taught at other Italian universities and wrote his *Catechism of Greek Grammar,* which became the basic text for the study of the language; he also made a translation of Plato's *Republic* into Latin. He was the first of many Greek professors to strengthen the enthusiasm of Italian humanists for Greek culture, and to spread the knowledge of Greek language and literature throughout Europe.

Humanism in Italy was fostered and strengthened by the support of those great bankers and rulers of Florence, Cosimo de' Medici (1389–1464) and Lorenzo de' Medici (1449–1492), generous patrons of the humanities, who founded the Medicean Library in Florence, spending large sums for the collection and copying of manuscripts, and subsidizing the endeavors of such artists as Ghiberti, Donatello, Botticelli, Raphael, and Leonardo da Vinci.

Similarly, ruling princes of other Italian city-states, including those of Milan and Urbino, and some of the popes at Rome, notably Leo X (1475–1521), were ardent patrons of humanism, supporting literary studies in the universities, the establishment of libraries, and the maintenance of court schools.

Aims   This Italian, individualistic humanism is the very foundation of modern education. Freedom of thought, self-expression, and creative activity are fundamental bases. This new freedom is the aim of humanistic education, which strives for the expression of individual personality through art, literature, music, architecture, and nature.

Versatility is the keynote of this new conception of education— to be versatile in order to develop individual personality to the fullest extent, to receive life's greatest enrichment, and to live the abundant life. The aim of humanistic education is living luxuriantly. The humanist aims at getting the most out of life in a really satisfying way; he aims at the living of a fine, rich, full life.

The first objective of Italian humanism was the Greek ideal of a liberal education—the harmonious development of mind, body, and morals. The ideal personality to the Italian humanists was the individual with a fully rounded development in all the aspects of human life. The second fundamental was a renewed emphasis upon individuality; a return to the old Athenian emphasis upon individual excellence and personal self-realization. "This education aimed at the development of the free man possessing individuality of his own, and power of efficient participation in everyday life, based upon a wide knowledge of life in the past and an appreciation of opportunities of life in the present." [4]

Types   The humanistic aim in education relies upon literary and esthetic education. The education of the Italian humanists was practical in the sense that it prepared the young nobles of the court

---

[4] Paul Monroe, *A Textbook in the History of Education.* (New York: The Macmillan Co., 1933.) P. 369. Reprinted with the permission of the publishers.

for active participation in the everyday affairs of human life. It was not vocational in the modern meaning of the term—as a preparation for a definite profession. In fact, since the days of the early Greeks there has been a feeling that vocational education and liberal education are antagonistic to each other. The exponents of the liberal humanistic education have usually disparaged what they consider a narrow training.

With the Italian humanists, the literary and esthetic types of education were somewhat fused. The ancient literatures of Greece and Rome were studied not only for the knowledge they gave of the institutions and ideals of the Graeco-Roman world, but also for their beauty and as models for new creative literary effort. Esthetic education was of the broadest type, aiming at appreciation not only of literature, but also of art, architecture, music, and drama. This estheticism—which had been wholly absent from medieval education—was the outstanding new element in humanistic education, and has always been characteristic of it.

Another pronounced feature of individual humanism was the emphasis upon physical education. Physical training received great attention, not only in the form of swimming, fencing, boxing, riding, dancing, but also in matters of diet and hygiene. Social training in deportment and manners was emphasized as the most important aspect of moral education. The moral education of the early humanists was not limited to obedience to religious authority, but had a much more practical bearing upon life than had the moral teachings of the church. In practice, moral standards might often give way to license, as in the later stages of Graeco-Roman civilization; but the educational writers of the Renaissance always stressed the importance of good moral training. VITTORINO DA FELTRE (1378–1446) strongly emphasized moral and Christian influences at his palace school in Mantua.

CONTENT In the curriculum of the humanistic school, the humanities replaced the divinities that had so dominated the literature of medieval time. Instead of a content devoted to the other world, there was a turning to that devoted to the things of this world. Humanism took all human interests as its province. The individualistic humanist had two outstanding characteristics: (1) variety of interest, and (2) desire for light. The representatives of this movement had many and varied interests; they did many things and studied many different subjects. Leonardo da Vinci, for example, best known to the world as a great artist, was also an engineer, a musician, and a philosopher. Galileo, the famed physicist and astronomer, was also an artist and a musician. The humanist curriculum is almost as broad as life itself.

The studies of the Renaissance schools were most varied, opening up to the student three aspects of life that had remained almost unknown throughout medieval education. One of these new worlds was the vibrant life of the past, the life of the Greeks and the Romans with its variety of interest and wide knowledge. This life was reflected in the incomparable literature and arts of those who had lived it. The humanists believed that the charm of the classics lay essentially in their human-ness. Hence, classical literature and classical art were sought and studied as an expression of this life and were used as models and themes for a national art of painting and sculpture, and a national literature of poetry, drama, and romance; and the artistry developed soon came to rival the classic models. The humanistic course of study, when exempli-fied at its best, included facility in reading, writing, and speaking the basic Latin; extensive study of Greek and Roman prose writers and poets; and familiarity with the life of the ancients through a reading of history and biography.

A second world opened up to the humanistic student was the subjective world of the emotions. An attempt was made to develop the joy of living and the contemplative pleasures of speculation about things of this life; to inculcate an appreciation of the beautiful; and to foster an interest in introspective observation and analysis from the esthetic and human standpoint. This was done through participation in the activities and interests of life, through self-culture and improvement, and through the appreciation and creation of literature and art.

The third world opened up to the humanistic scholar was the world of nature, a world almost unknown to the medieval scholar, and, in general—regardless of his veneration for Aristotle—deemed by him ignoble and debasing in its effects upon mankind.

The humanistic curriculum, however, was not limited to literary and esthetic subjects. Instruction in morals, manners, and health was included. A wide range of physical exercises was utilized, combining both Athenian and chivalric elements. Maxims of morality were drawn from both church writers and classical writers; and manners were taught as an essential concomitant of moral education. Dancing and music were taught not only for their esthetic but also for their social values.

Although the medieval Trivium and Quadrivium were in part retained in the universities, the shift was away from the emphasis placed upon dialectic or logic by the medieval scholars back to an emphasis upon grammar, rhetoric, and mathematics.

AGENCIES AND ORGANIZATION   Humanistic education tri-umphed through the establishment of new schools founded in the new spirit and expressing the highest educational ideals of the humanists.

The important and outstanding educational result of the revival of learning by Italian scholars was that it laid the basis for a new type of school below that of the recently created universities, and one destined in time to be much more widely opened to promising youths than the cathedral and monastic schools of the Middle Ages had been. This new school, focusing its curriculum on the intellectual inheritance recovered from the ancient world by the Italian scholars, *dominated secondary-school training of the middle and higher classes of society for the next four hundred years.* This type of school was well under way by 1450, and it clearly controlled education until after 1850. Out of the efforts of the Italian scholars to resurrect, reconstruct, understand, and utilize in education the fruits of our inheritance from the Greek and Roman worlds, *modern secondary education* arose.[5]

The first classical secondary schools were the court schools in Italy; they furnished models for similar schools in other countries—the *collèges* and *lycées* in France, the *Gymnasien* in Germany, the Latin grammar schools in England and the early American Colonies.

The court schools were so designated because they were founded and maintained by the ruling princes and dukes of the Italian city-states. These sometimes dictatorial rulers endeavored to make their cities centers of humanistic learning, not only through the collection of manuscripts, and founding of libraries, and the subsidizing of scholars and artists, but also by the establishment of schools. Famous schools were located at Florence, Venice, Padua, Verona, and other cities; but the two most outstanding were those at Mantua and Ferrara—the school at Mantua, under the control of VITTORINO DA FELTRE from 1423 to 1446; and the school at Ferrara conducted from 1429 to 1460 by GUARINO DA VARONA. These two great teachers—who were among the greatest scholars of the Renaissance—were thoroughly committed to the ideals of humanistic education, and were skilled in the ability to construct a curriculum and devise methods effective in achieving the aims of the new learning.

Although most of the pupils paid fees, the children of the poorer court retainers were taught free at these schools. They were like modern boarding schools in that they admitted boys at the age of nine or ten and kept them until the age of twenty or twenty-one. Girls did not attend but studied at home under tutors. The boys lived at the school, and were educated both in and out of the classroom. The court schools at first rivaled the work of the universities which were still antagonistic to the new humanistic learning; but later, as the work of the universities became more liberal, and was raised to a higher level, court schools became in some degree preparatory. Such schools as those conducted by Vittorino and Guarino, with their broad intellectual, physical, and moral training, did much to establish the type of classical humanistic secondary school that has persisted down to the present day.

METHODS   With the establishment of the humanistic secondary schools, new teaching methods were devised. Texts became more plentiful and were made available for the students, thus obviating the necessity of continual lectures. Written themes displaced the oral disputations so common in the medieval schools. Although instruction aimed primarily at the development of linguistic ability, Latin and Greek were treated as living and not dead languages, and self-expression and self-activity were continually stressed.

Vittorino, for example—who has been called the first modern schoolmaster—made a genuine attempt to adapt the work of the individ-

---

[5] E. P. Cubberley, *Public Education in the United States.* (Boston: Houghton Mifflin Company, 1934.) P. 5. Reprinted with the permission of the publishers.

ual to his particular needs and capacities, thus anticipating by almost five centuries the emphasis upon adjustment to individual differences. Vittorino, in fact, marks the advent of the professional teacher. He was the first to formulate many of the important educational doctrines. He stood for the development of interest and of the power to think; he believed that development should be well-balanced, that mental activity is dependent upon physical activity, and that play is of educational significance. He contended that the subjects of the curriculum should be varied, and that there should be due alternation of subjects.

The methods of discipline in these schools were mild. Punishment and threats of punishment were not needed as motives for learning, and the stern repressive asceticism of the church schools was absent. Sufficient motivation was to be found in the fact that the higher posts of honor and activity in the life of the times were open only to those who had been thoroughly trained in the humanistic manner.

NORTHERN HUMANISM

The spread of the Renaissance movement into northern Europe was facilitated by the work of a nonmonastic order, founded in Holland in 1376, called the Hieronymians, or Brethren of the Common Life. Pious and humanitarian in spirit, they devoted themselves to the copying of manuscripts and the teaching of the poor and ignorant lower classes. They also helped to support worthy but indigent scholars and were so successful in teaching backward students that existing schools were placed under their supervision and they were encouraged to open new schools of their own. In these schools they rejected the formal and meaningless methods of early medieval education and attempted to satisfy the needs of their students. Their work soon spread from the Netherlands into northern France and Germany. Although their own schools were much superior to any of the others, the Brethren were open-minded enough to seek still further improvement. By the middle of the fifteenth century, when the Renaissance began to scale the Alps, they had schools in the Netherlands, France, and the German states ready to welcome it. Hieronymian scholars went to Italy to study the work of the court schools there; and wandering Italian scholars, visiting the countries of northern Europe where they were received enthusiastically by the Brethren, impregnated them with the spirit of the humanistic education. Northern humanism thus came to have a dual characteristic, combining the social piety of the Brethren, represented in the work of THOMAS À KEMPIS (1380–1471), and the broad literary spirit of the Italian Renaissance, represented in the work of that other great Hieronymian scholar, DESIDERIUS ERASMUS (1466–1536). Other outstanding products of the Hieronymian movement were Johann Reuchlin, Rudolphus Agricola, Peter Luder, Jacob Wimpfeling, Philip Melanchthon, and Johann Sturm, of whom we shall have more to say later.

Another influence in accelerating the Renaissance in the north was the attempt of the French kings Charles VIII and Louis XII to enforce hereditary claims upon certain cities in northern Italy. From a military and political standpoint they failed, but culturally by bringing the French people into contact with Italian humanism at its best sources and in bringing back to France humanistic scholars, who established *collèges* and libraries at such centers as Bordeaux and Paris they rendered a service. GUILLAUME BUDAEUS (1476–1540), the royal librarian of France under Francis I, was perhaps the greatest of the French humanistic scholars. He set up a royal press in Paris and greatly improved the *collèges* of France.

The origination of a method of printing from movable type by JOHANN GUTENBERG (1397–1468), the fall of Constantinople to the Turks, and the geographical explorations and discoveries of Dutch and English adventurers, gave additional momentum to the Renaissance in these northern countries.

AIMS   The educational aim of northern humanism was different from that of the Italians; it was more social than individual. The emphasis was less subjective and esthetic and more objective and moralistic. Education was aimed not so much at the attainment of individual happiness as at social reform and the improvement of human relationships. Education in the northern countries was not directed toward a breadth of interest in human life; these humanists had no interest in the pleasures and riches of life beyond practical religious and social life. The selection of the classics to be translated, edited, and used in education was determined by one goal, that of eliminating the ignorance of the common people and the greed, selfishness, and hypocrisy, and tendency toward exploitation of the social leaders—that is to say, of the leaders of churches, monastic orders, universities, and governments. WIMPFELING expressed this aim when he said, "Of what use are all the books in the world, the most learned writings, the most profound research if they only minister to the vainglory of their authors, and do not, or cannot, advance the good of mankind?"

From the standpoint of the development of personal character and individual freedom, the aim of the northern education was narrow; from the standpoint of the development of the general social welfare, it was broad. Instead of aiming at a rich and full life for the individual—as in Italy—northern humanism aimed at a rich and full life for society as a whole. ERASMUS, liberal humanist that he was, in discussing the aims of education, put piety ahead of learning, moral duty ahead of manners.

TYPES   These socially minded humanists of the north, therefore, stressed religious education, moral education, and social education far more than they did esthetics. Literary training was encouraged, but as a means to a religious and social end rather than for its own sake. Careful religious instruction was invariably coupled with the liberal classic training. (The Italian humanists took their religion lightly; thus there was little conflict with the church.) The social humanists took their religion seriously and bitterly attacked the moral evils in the church, even though they—at this time—accepted the current theological doctrines.

Instead of the aristocratic class education of the Italians, we find in the north an attempt to provide a more democratic type of education. In practice, chief stress was placed on secondary and higher education, but there was also an attempt to improve elementary schools.

CONTENT   In the curriculum of northern social humanism, there was a union of classical and Biblical literature. Erasmus provided for use in the schools a Greek edition of the New Testament, a new translation of the New Testament into Latin, and a paraphrase of the writings of such church Fathers as Jerome, in addition to editing a number of Latin and Greek textbooks. The content of the German schools consisted of the church catechism, the New Testament, and parts of Jerome, as well as an intensive study of Latin and Greek grammar, the reading of a few selected authors such as Cicero, and training in the speaking and writing of Latin after the model of Cicero's style. In the French *collèges,* the Hebrew language was taught along with Latin and Greek largely because it was the language of the Old Testament; and JOHANN REUCHLIN (1455–1522) introduced the same language into Germany. THOMAS ELYOT (1490–1546) in his *Boke Named The Governour,* an exposition of the humanistic ideal in education, advocated the study of Latin as a living language, Greek for its literature, and certain classical authors and selected parts of the Old Testament for ethical training. Erasmus urged the importance of the study of history, geography, and science as a help toward illuminating the classics. Although Elyot advocated drawing, music, dancing, and a wide range of physical exercises for the English humanistic schools, the physical training, music, and art of the Italian court schools found little place in the secondary schools of England, France, and Germany at this time. Sturm and Melanchthon had little use for such subjects.

AGENCIES AND ORGANIZATION   The Renaissance movement in the north organized appropriate institutions to carry out its educational aims. The court schools of Italy served as patterns for the early Teutonic *Fürstenschulen,* or princes' schools, even before the first German *Gymnasium* was established by JOHANN STURM (1507–1589) at Strassburg. Sturm's school was the most important school in Germany resulting from the humanistic influence, and it fixed the name and character of German secondary schools for centuries.

JOHN COLET (1467–1519), who had studied at Florence, with the help of Erasmus founded St. Paul's School in London as the beginning of the humanistic movement in English secondary education. We have already called attention to the establishment of the French *collèges* under the influence of such great French humanists as Budaeus and Corderius.

Not only in these secondary schools, but also in the universities of these northern countries, the humanistic studies were encouraged by the patronage of kings, queens, dukes, and princes. In Germany, the municipal authorities controlled and supported the *Gymnasien,* and this was also somewhat the practice in the cities of France. The universities of France broadened their work by adding chairs of Greek; Henry VIII and Elizabeth encouraged the colleges at Cambridge and Oxford to found royal professorships in the classics. Erasmus was the first teacher of Greek at Cambridge; and WILLIAM GROCYN (1446–1514), who had studied at Florence, introduced Greek learning into Oxford. In Germany, the existing universities gradually introduced humanistic studies; and new ones, like Wittenberg—humanistic from the start—were founded by PHILIP MELANCHTHON (1479–1560), and Reuchlin.

There was some variation in the organization of the northern secondary schools. The grammar schools of England were usually boarding schools, but the *Gymnasien* of Germany were mostly organized on a day-school basis. Tuition charges were levied in all these schools; and, as a rule, the school was arranged into nine or ten classes or forms, the beginning of the class-a-year practice still prevalent in our modern secondary schools.

These educational institutions—the humanistic secondary school and the university—were open only to boys and men (although Erasmus himself advocated that women should have the same educational advantages as men).

METHODS   The humanistic educators of the north were concerned with the problems of method, and in their writings advocated methods quite in advance of those actually used in the schools. Some of the methods suggested appear very modern. Perhaps the techniques actually used in the schools fell short of the ideals of the founders; but the fact that such advanced ideas were even thought of at this time is significant.

Erasmus wrote two great educational classics in which he presented constructively his views on educational methods: *The Liberal Education of Children* and *The Method of Study.* He emphasized the importance of a careful study of the child's nature and advised continual personal and individualized care and direction of studies. He stressed the important place of plays, games, and exercise in education and the importance of keeping education in close touch with social needs and the life of the times. He discussed many of the minor details of reliable and effective method, such as the value of repetition, of the mastery of small units of work at a time, and of the prefacing of study by preparation. He attacked the barbarous methods of discipline used in the medieval schools and advocated a more attractive system. He favored mild discipline. Praise and reward, he said, accomplish more than threats and blows. The business of the teacher was to help his students and not to display his learning, and he especially ridiculed those narrow teachers who mistook the form for the spirit of the new learning.

As time went on, the earlier broad humanism declined into a narrower formalized humanism. From the middle of the sixteenth century on this narrower humanism was distinctly in the ascendant. In its narrowest form this tendency was called "Ciceronianism."

Ciceronianism was the practice of laying emphasis upon the style and actual sentence construction of the Greek and Roman classic writers, especially Cicero, rather than upon the thought and important characteristics contained in their writings. It was largely a superficial imitation; for it was based upon the idea that, in order to create, one must first imitate the masters of style; and few ever got beyond the stage of imitation. Erasmus expressed the narrowness of this tendency when he said, "It is an apishness in which one discovers none of the virtues that have made the glory of Cicero, such as his happy inspiration, the intelligent disposition of his subjects, his large acquaintance with men and affairs, and his ability to move those who hear him."

Roger Ascham (1515–1568), teacher of Greek at Cambridge and later tutor to Queen Elizabeth, was the first Englishman to write a treatise on educational method in the vernacular. This book, *The Scholemaster,* has been given a place in literary as well as educational history. In his discussion of method, Ascham perhaps presents the best humanistic practices of the Renaissance schools in England. He particularly presented improved methods of teaching language; his book has been said "to contain perhaps the best advice that was ever given for the study of languages." His method of double translation—translating a passage into English and then an hour later retranslating it into the original for comparison with the original—was a considerable improvement in linguistic method over the older method in which the memorizing of meaningless forms and rules in the ancient tongue was stressed. In Ascham's method, grammar was learned incidentally in connection with the translation. Like Erasmus, Ascham bitterly opposed the brutal discipline of the times and argued for more humane methods. Instead of corporal punishment, he too advocated praise. "Where the child doth well, let the master praise him and say, 'Here ye do well,' for there is no such whetstone to sharpen a hard wit and encourage a will to learning, as is praise."

In the *Gymnasium* at Strassburg under Sturm, the method was from the start more narrowly humanistic. Sturm had a greater genius for thorough organization and carefully graded instruction than he had for the development of a good teaching method. His method stressed imitation and memory, called for utter neglect of the vernacular and for the use of Latin as the language of the classroom. Systematic study of words and phrases, the intricacies of grammar, syntax, and prosody, heavily burdened the pupil. Extensive use was made of pupil monitors, and classical study was motivated by the acting of plays in Latin and Greek. But the purely logical manner in which all instruction was organized killed interest, and it was necessary to resort to harsh disciplinary measures. The pupils in the German *Gymnasien* always have been trained such in an atmosphere of precision and regularity.

Thus, humanistic education became narrow and formal. Instead of calling for a wide reading of the ancient literatures, the curriculum was limited to a few selected classics. The aim of the school was to develop a fine style, a correct form of expression. The old rejected scholasticism with Aristotle as master and dialectic as content returned in another and no less narrow form with Cicero as master and linguistics as content.

Erasmus attacked this narrowing tendency in his essay *The Ciceronians*, but his was a voice crying in the wilderness. It was not until the time of the realists of the sixteenth and seventeenth centuries that we find any very effective reaction against this formalized humanism.

The genius of the new age had promised to lead men out of the cloister into the new world. In the end it led them only out of the cloister into the classroom. Pedantry resumed its sway under a changed form, and the present went back into the bondage of the past. Even the world 'humanities' soon lost its large and generous original meaning, and shrank into a synonym for Greek and Latin learning. These two dead languages became the sole instruments of culture, and the classical scholars were accepted as the only possible type of educated men. It is necessary to lay stress upon these absurd Renaissance ideas because their evil influence was destined to be far-reaching and long-enduring and to continue indeed right down into our own modern world.[6]

FOR FURTHER READING

Adams, John, *Evolution of Educational Theory*. London: Macmillan and Co., Ltd., 1912. Pp. 229-249.

Burnham, William H., *Great Teachers and Mental Health*. New York: Appleton-Century-Crofts, Inc., 1926. Pp. 1-119.

Butts, R. Freeman, *A Cultural History of Western Education*. Second Edition. New York: McGraw-Hill Book Co., 1955. Pp. 165-193.

Clough, Shepard B., *The Rise and Fall of Civilization*. New York: McGraw-Hill Book Co., 1951. Pp. 163-191.

Cole, Luella, *A History of Education from Socrates to Montessori*. New York: Holt, Rinehart and Winston, Inc., 1950. Pp. 202-220.

---

[6] Paul Monroe, *Thomas Platter and the Educational Renaissance of the Sixteenth Century*. (New York: Appleton-Century-Crofts, Inc., 1904.) P. 61. Reprinted with the permission of the publishers.

Duggan, Stephen P., *Student's Textbook in the History of Education*. Revised Enlarged Edition. New York: Appleton-Century-Crofts, Inc., 1936. Pp. 113-130.

Durant, Will, *The Renaissance*. New York: Simon & Schuster, Inc., 1953. Pp. 1-728.

Eby, Frederick, and Arrowood, Charles F., *The History of Education Ancient and Medieval*. New York: Prentice-Hall, Inc., 1940. Pp. 837-939.

Ferguson, Wallace K., *The Renaissance*. New York: Holt, Rinehart and Winston, Inc., 1940.

Good, H. G., *A History of Western Education*. New York: The Macmillan Co., 1960. Pp. 11-138.

Graves, Frank P., *Education During the Middle Ages*. New York: The Macmillan Co., 1910. Pp. 110-176.

Hart, Joseph K., *Creative Moments in Education*. New York: Holt, Rinehart and Winston, Inc., 1931. Pp. 201-221.

Knight, Edgar W., *Twenty Centuries of Education*. Boston: Ginn & Co., 1940. Pp. 152-165.

Laurie, Simon S., *Studies in the History of the Development of Educational Opinion*. New York: The Macmillan Company, 1903. Pp. 1-37, 58-85.

Mayer, Frederick, *A History of Educational Thought*. Columbus, Ohio: Charles E. Merrill Books, Inc., 1960. Pp. 165-178.

Messenger, James F., *An Interpretative History of Education*. New York: Thomas Y. Crowell Co., 1931. Pp. 119-126.

Monroe, Paul, *A Textbook in the History of Education*. New York: The Macmillan Co., 1933. Pp. 351-397.

Moore, Ernest C., *The Story of Instruction: The Church, the Renaisance and the Reformation*. New York: The Macmillan Co., 1938. Pp. 382-452.

Mulhern, James, *A History of Education*. Second Edition. New York: The Ronald Press Co., 1959. Pp. 297-308, 328-361.

Painter, Franklin, *Great Pedagogical Essays*. New York: American Book Company, 1905. Pp. 228-239.

————, *History of Education*. New York: Appleton-Century-Crofts, Inc., 1904. Pp. 140-153.

Quick, Robert Herbert, *Educational Reformers*. New York: Appleton-Century-Crofts, Inc., 1904. Pp. 1-32, 80-89.

Randall, John H., *Making of the Modern Mind*. Boston: Houghton Mifflin Company, 1926. Pp. 11-141.

Ulich, Robert, *History of Educational Thought*. New York: American Book Company, 1950. Pp. 102-113, 130-148, 156-161.

————, *Three Thousand Years of Educational Wisdom*. Cambridge, Mass.: Harvard University Press, 1954. Pp. 205-217, 250-271, 287-301.

Wender, Herbert, *The Growth of Modern Thought and Culture.* New York: Philosophical Library, Inc., 1959. Pp. 1-41.

Woodward, William H., *Vittorino da Feltre and the Humanist Educators.* Cambridge: Cambridge University Press, 1897. Pp. 1-93, 175-258.

QUESTIONS FOR CLASS DISCUSSION

1. Do you believe that the education called liberal today is as truly liberal as that of the humanists of the Italian Renaissance? Explain your point of view.

2. Have the scientific discoveries of the nineteenth and twentieth centuries influenced intellectual life in any ways similar to the influence of the great geographical discoveries of the fourteenth and fifteenth centuries?

3. To what extent do those who now consider themselves exponents of the New Humanism differ from, or resemble, the humanists of the Italian Renaissance?

4. Can it be demonstrated that the contemporary tendency to Biblical study known as the higher criticism is an outgrowth of northern humanism?

5. It has been alleged that vocational subjects have replaced the humanities in recent years to the same extent that the humanities replaced the divinities in the Renaissance. Agree or disagree with this statement.

6. Have you ever observed any antagonism between those who favor liberal education and those who advocate vocational training?

7. Can you mention any contemporary patrons of the humanities whose services to education and culture compare with those of the Medici?

8. Is it possible to make present-day teaching of ancient and modern languages more truly humanizing? Explain.

9. In what respects is the present-day high school different from Colet's Grammar School or Sturm's Gymnasium?

10. Do the curriculum and methods of modern liberal arts colleges reflect the spirit of broad humanism or that of Ciceronianism?

CHAPTER X

THE RELIGIOUS MOTIVATION OF MORAL CONDUCT

RELIGIOUS MORALISM

The educational history of the United States cannot be understood without knowledge of the religious forces and struggles released by the Reformation; and the development of one of our dominant educational theories—the theory of education for religious moralism—can be studied only in reference to this same movement. We soon discover that many of the ideas concerning educational theory and practice held by the Reformers, both Protestant and Roman Catholic, are embodied in the objectives of present-day leaders in education.

Present-day education in the United States owes a great deal to this revolutionary movement of the sixteenth century. Most of our American traditions of a religious and ethical nature were born out of the Protestant revolt and the concomitant Roman Catholic reaction, and were brought to our shores by the early settlers. Many came from religious motives: to secure religious freedom; to escape the struggles and persecutions that followed ecclesiastical schisms; to establish their churches and schools, and maintain their moral standards in this new land. The English Puritans of New England, the Calvinistic Dutch of New Amsterdam, the French Huguenots of the Carolinas, the Scotch Presbyterians of New Jersey and the Alleghenies, the English Quakers of eastern Pennsylvania, the Swedish Lutherans along the Delaware, the German Lutheran sects in the central valleys of Pennsylvania—all these were offshoots from the Protestant revolt; and their influences were to determine and fix strongly religious and ethical ideals upon which our national life was based and toward which so much of our education has been directed. Maryland was settled by Roman Catholics who had been persecuted in England by the Protestants. Roman Catholic teaching orders, particularly the Jesuits (fruits of the counter-Reformation), were a definite influence in fixing the religious and moral ideals of the French settlers to the north and in the Northwest.

No other era in modern history has created such advances and discords, virtues and evils, liberties and persecutions, as has this period. Many interesting and significant facts about it have been overlooked by those eager to present a one-sided picture. (We are not concerned here with the condemnation or defense of an eccelsiastical revolt; we are concerned with the effect of that movement upon the development of education.) Therefore we must study the movement from all its angles.

The revolution of the sixteenth century, usually termed the Reformation, was the most far-reaching, many-sided and profound awakening in the history of the western world. To think of the Reformation merely as a reform of church organization or religious doctrine, important as these were, is to misinterpret its deeper significance for human progress; no aspect of man's personality was untouched by it. The Reformation involved political, economic, religious, moral, philosophical, literary, and institutional changes of the most sweeping character; it was in fact, a Nordic revolt and reconstruction.[1]

We frequently have over-emphasized the religious and ecclesiastical phases of this revolution which led directly to the breaking apart of the church. From the Protestant viewpoint, the Reformation was intended to correct abuses in the church, primarily in connection with the sale of indulgences. From the modern Roman Catholic standpoint such a correction was thoroughly justified on moral grounds. The Roman Catholic of today has no defense for the corruption that had crept into the church. The question in his mind is whether such a justifiable moral motive should have led to revolt and schism.[2] If the church leaders of the time had assumed a more tolerant attitude toward the tendencies of their age, the history of modern life, and particularly of educational thought, might have been different. They did not assume this attitude, however; and whether we be Roman Catholic or Protestant should make no difference in dealing with the facts of history. The truth that history records is that the Protestants did revolt, and that the church governed from Rome did reform. To what extent the revolting was a stimulant to the reforming is an open question. Whether we believe that ZWINGLI,

---

[1] Frederick Eby and Charles F. Arrowood, *The Development of Modern Education.* (New York: Prentice-Hall, Inc., 1934.) P. 29. Reprinted with the permission of the publishers.
[2] See article on the "Reformation" in the *Catholic Encyclopedia.*

LUTHER, CALVIN, and KNOX were inspired men, leading the world to a truer faith; or whether we believe them to have been ambitious and selfish, history remains the same.

In 1517, MARTIN LUTHER (1483–1546), an Augustinian friar teaching philosophy at the University of Wittenberg, criticized certain practices of the church, later defied its authority, was excommunicated and forced into hiding. The German people, under the leadership of their princes, supported Luther's side of the dispute, and revolted from the authority of the church. The revolt spread to other countries of northern Europe; and the church, which had remained the great unifying force in Europe for centuries, now became permanently divided. Whether or not because of this disaffection, the Roman Catholic Church reformed its practices. We could most accurately call this period the period of Protestant revolt and Roman Catholic reformation. But our chief concern is with the ways in which this particular revolt and this particular reform have affected the development of educational concepts.

For centuries the German peoples had been subjected to the domination of Christian institutionalism. Their literature, the language of their learning, their laws, their theological doctrines, and their religious practices—all had come to them from Rome. The indigenous Teutonic characteristics had been modified and suppressed, but had never been completely destroyed. Under stimulus of the Renaissance humanism, they had been revitalized—these native elements of physical vigor, moral zeal, and free individualism—imparting new power and direction to the lives of the northern peoples.

The Reformation completed the work of the northern Renaissance. The critical tendencies of social humanism, once started, could not be stopped. Luther was right when he said that he had but hatched the egg laid by Erasmus; and Erasmus was right when he said that he had laid only a hen's egg but Luther had hatched out a gamecock. The humanist's zeal for social reform, for the improvement of human life here on earth, naturally and inevitably led to criticism of the church. Even this powerful institution, which had dominated human destiny for a thousand years, could not escape the critical spirit of humanism. Long before Luther, social humanists had attacked the moral evils of the church and had clamored for church reform. They had persistently demanded that the clergy lead purer lives, that ecclesiastical leaders earn their high incomes, that the monasteries make some useful contributions to human society. However, they made no doctrinal or theological attacks. But with the humanistic interest in the study of the sources of Biblical literature in the original Greek and Hebrew, it was inevitable that theological beliefs and ecclesiastical practice should be questioned and eventually attacked.

Not all the northern humanists went so far. While Sturm, Melanchthon, Bugenhagen, Corderius, Ascham, and Elyot followed Luther out of the church and aligned themselves with the reformers, men like Erasmus, More, Colet, and Wimpfeling remained within the church.

Although all the social humanists did not become reformers, virtually all the reformers were humanists. In a way, the new movement represented a broadening of the fusion of religion and humanism begun in the northern Renaissance.

It must be remembered, however, that the Protestant revolution developed because of oppressive political and economic conditions as much as because of religious and ecclesiastical evils. The need for religious and ethical reform seems to have furnished the immediate opportunity for revolt; the need for political and economic reform was the underlying cause. The social humanists of the northern Renaissance had been religious, reformatory, critical of moral evils; and now it seemed to the Teutonic peoples that their political, social, and economic desires could best be realized by separation from the church.

The prosperous free cities of northern Europe, particularly those of the Netherlands and the north German plain, were nurseries of the revolt against the church. The political autonomy of these free towns, the indomitable spirit of individualism in their citizens, the security of their economic independence, when strengthened still further by their organization as the Hanseatic League, made these cities influences to be reckoned with in political and economic affairs. At the beginning of the sixteenth century, Germany was still divided into many petty dukedoms, principalities, and elective states, more or less independent of imperial sovereignty. If it had not been for the sympathy and protection of the free cities, the electoral princes, and the minor nobility, Luther would probably have been burned at the stake, as were the noted heretics who preceded him, and his doctrines would have been relentlessly stamped out. Instead, the movement to which he had given such impetus spread from Germany, Switzerland, and the Netherlands to England, Scotland, and Scandinavia, where again it was a political as well as a religious revolution.

Luther's quarrel with the church began as a protest against certain economic injustices practiced in the church. That his protests should result in his being driven from the church and his founding a new institution was a thing he never anticipated or at first desired. Wealth had been concentrating in the control of churches, monasteries, and ecclesiastical courts for centuries, and this concentration had been made possible by very effective money-raising devices. Based on the doctrine that salvation comes from good works, gifts, endowments, and tithes flowed into the treasuries of churches, monasteries, and ecclesiastical princes, until it is reported that two-thirds of the wealth of Germany was in the hands of the church. Germany, as Charles A. Beard so aptly stated, was "the milch cow of the Papacy, which it at once despised and drained dry."

The immediate cause of Luther's challenge through the Ninety-five Theses—which he nailed on the church door at Wittenberg—was the presence of a Dominican monk, John Tetzel, commissioned by the pope to raise money to complete St. Peter's at Rome. The Germans felt that far too much of their money had already gone to Rome to increase the power and glory of the Vatican; so there arose in these northern countries a sympathetic and vigorous response to Luther's challenge opposing the economic exactions of the papacy.

Thus the movement came about through intellectual, religious, ethical, political, and economic influences. It is to be expected that a movement arising from such a complexity of causes should have widespread and profound effects upon educational theory and practices. These we shall now discuss with reference to each of the two opposing groups, the Protestant reformers and the Roman Catholic meliorators.

ATTITUDES OF PROTESTANT REFORMERS TOWARD EDUCATION

The Protestant reformers established certain principles that had profound educational implications. Regardless of their theological controversies and doctrinal divergences, they agreed upon certain fundamental issues: the authority of their interpretation of the Bible was substituted for the authority of the church as the infallible rule of faith and moral practice; individual judgment was substituted for collective judgment as sufficient for determining the truth contained in the Holy Scriptures, and thereby fixing Christian duty in belief and conduct; individual responsibility for salvation was substituted for collective responsibility. While accepting the doctrine of original sin, the reformers contended that only an abiding faith in God's mercy could effect salvation; and that masses, penances, and charitable works could be dispensed with as agencies of deliverance.

Ritualism gave way to inner piety; good works, to good will; blind obedience, to inner faith. Holiness was held no longer to be self-renunciation or world-renunciation, but rather the benevolent spirit which lives the normal life of the human being in social relations, without yielding to sensuality or selfish interest.[3]

The reformers formulated the principles that there should be close cooperation between church and state; that religion goes with the land; that the religious choice of the ruler should determine the religion of his subjects; that the state should be the servant of the church in insisting upon adequate educational opportunities for the preservation of the moral and religious character of its people. State, church, and home must work together in the task of educating the youth of the land.

---

[3] Frederick Eby and Charles F. Arrowood, *op. cit.*, p. 178. Reprinted with the permission of the publishers.

AIMS   Religious moralism as an aim for education was not original with the Protestant reformers. We have already seen that the education of primitive and ancient peoples was primarily religious and moral rather than intellectual. Even the education of the Greeks placed little emphasis upon the literary and intellectual element until after the time of Socrates. The philosophers of Greece and Rome tried to establish morality without the sanctions of religion. On the other hand— although Jesus himself had fused religion and morality in his teachings— the Christian church of the Middle Ages placed its reliance on an exclusive interest in theological doctrines and ritualistic observances. Of course, the reformers did not discontinue ecclesiastical control over education—evidence of their general belief in the essentially religious and moral character of education.

The object of Protestant education has always been a worthy life here as guarantee of a glorious life hereafter. Education, therefore, must provide adequate training in the duties of home, occupation, church, and state. Luther had a glimpse of the modern broad social purpose of education but narrowed his own aim by directing it to the end of religion. JOHN CALVIN (1509–1564), from Geneva, also advocated education as a training for society and state as well as for the church, and he added to this his insistence upon the necessity of education as a means toward liberty of individual conscience. Both Luther and Calvin considered religion the highest interest in life; as the basis of all worthy living.

The reformers conceived an educational ideal which would prepare Christian men and women to discharge any and all duties. They realized the close interdependence of character and religion, and advocated an education that would develop physical, mental, and moral powers to bring about not only personal salvation but the moral regeneration of society. Religion, morality, and education were to be man's major interests, the "fixities and verities" of life; and they deemed it impossible to consider them separately.

Luther insisted upon right training of children as a divine requirement. He was opposed to education according to the whims of the parents. He wrote:

> If we wish to have proper and excellent persons both for civil and ecclesiastical government, we must spare no diligence, time, or cost in educating our children, that they may serve God and the world. . . . Let every one know, therefore, that above all things it is his study and duty (or otherwise he will lose the divine favor) to bring up his children in the fear and knowledge of God; and if they have talents to have them instructed and trained in a liberal education, that men may be able to have their aid in whatever is necessary.[4]

Luther went so far as to say that the right bringing up of children was the straightest and most easily attained road to heaven; that hell could

---

[4] F. V. N. Painter, *Luther on Education*. (Philadelphia: Lutheran Publication Society, 1889.) Pp. 116-117. Reprinted with the permission of the publishers.

not be more deserved than by allowing children to run about freely, neglected, swearing, singing shameful words, and following only the dictates of nature.

The educational aim of the Protestants attempted to combine the best ideals of the past with religious morality. From the ancient Greek and Roman world—through humanism—it drew the ideals of elegant expression, of rational inquiry, and of public service. From chivalry, it took the ideals of good manners and of social service; from Christianity, the ideals of personal piety. These three ideals—intelligence, social virtue, and individual piety—were not stressed equally by all Protestant educators, nor were they fully attained in all Protestant schools, but an integration of these three elements was attempted wherever the Protestant influence was felt.

TYPES   From the standpoint of ultimate aims, Protestant education always was religious, but in attaining this ultimate goal, varied types of training were utilized.

Some Protestant educators would have called their technique "character education," because its ultimate purpose was the development of Christian character. But moral training, social training, civic training, vocational training, domestic training—all played a part in the attainment of the religiously motivated moral conduct emphasized as the objective of their educational efforts.

There was little esthetic training in Protestant schools. Physical and musical training were given for religious and practical reasons rather than for esthetic. Protestantism educated for work rather than for play. In fact, as Weber says, "The Protestant ethics which regards restless, continuous systematic work in a worldly calling as the highest means to asceticism functioned in a concrete way as the most powerful lever for the expansion of the spirit of capitalism." [5]

Practical training of professional, commercial, and industrial types was characteristic of Protestant education. Man was expected to work for the glory of God and fulfill the divine will by the constant exercise of the human one. Protestantism changed most of the traditional Roman Catholic holidays into work days and sanctioned a new commercial economy to replace the injunction of Jesus, "Lay not up for yourselves treasures on earth." (It is interesting in this connection to note that the first systematic defense of charging interest on money was made by John Calvin.) In "The Toiling of Felix," Henry Van Dyke expresses the Protestant ideal of work:

This is the gospel of labor, ring it, ye bells of the kirk!
The Lord of Love came down from above, to live with the men who work.
This is the rose He planted; here in this thorn-cursed soil;
Heaven is blessed with perfect rest, but the blessing of Earth is toil.

---

[5] Max Weber, *The Protestant Ethic and the Spirit of Capitalism.* (New York: Charles Scribner's Sons, 1930.) See also R. H. Tawney, *Religion and the Rise of Capitalism* (New York: Harcourt Brace and Co., 1937.)

The Protestant reformers advocated universal, compulsory, free education. Luther believed that all classes and both sexes should be educated, although he was in favor of a higher type of education for those destined for the ministry and the magistracy than for the masses. He advocated universal education because he realized that to fulfill the varied duties of life, different degrees of intelligence were necessary. Calvin urged that the laity be educated as well as the clergy. Both Luther and Calvin believed that if men were to save themselves by the exercise of faith and private judgment, based on the reading and study of the Bible, then all must be taught to read, study, and think. In other words, there must be universal education at the elementary levels, even though education at the higher levels might continue to be selective.

Luther should be recognized as the first modern educational reformer to recommend compulsory education. He not only insisted that the state authorities should establish schools themselves or require the people to do so, but went so far as to demand that parents should be compelled to send their children to school for the sake of the church and the state. In his *Sermon on the Duty of Sending Children to School,* he said:

> I maintain that the civil authorities are under obligation to compel the people to send their children to school. . . . If the government can compel such citizens as are fit for military service to bear spear and rifle, to mount ramparts, and perform other martial duties in time of war, how much more has it a right to compel the people to send their children to school, because in this case we are warring with the Devil.[6]

CONTENT The basic subject in Protestant elementary schools was the study of the Bible, and the basic skill to be acquired was the ability to read in the vernacular or common tongue. Religion was the heart of the curriculum, and the Bible the principal textbook. Luther, in his *Address to the Nobility,* says: "Above all, in schools of all kinds the chief and most common lesson should be the Scriptures, and for young boys the Gospels. . . . Should not every Christian be expected by his ninth or tenth year to know all the Holy Gospels, containing as they do his very name and life? . . . Everything must perish where God's Word is not studied unceasingly."

To make the Bible available for reading by the people at large, either the people must learn to read Latin, or the Bible must be translated from the Latin Vulgate into the language of the people. JOHN WYCLIFFE of Oxford (1320–1384), over a century before Luther, asserting that everyone should be able to read and study the Scriptures as a means to personal salvation, partially translated the Bible into the English vernacular. JACQUES LEFÈVRE (1455–1537), pioneer French Protestant, translated the Bible into the vernacular for his people. Luther's

---

[6] Reprinted in Frederick Eby, *Early Protestant Educators.* (New York: McGraw-Hill Book Co., 1931.) Pp. 149-150.

translation of the Bible not only made it available to the German people
in their own tongue but set the standard for the literary German of his
own and later times, just as Calvin's *Institutes of the Christian Religion*
and WILLIAM TYNDALE's translation of the New Testament set standards
for French and English prose.

Luther supplemented the Scriptures with other reading material,
religious and moral. He published two catechisms, one for children and
one for adults, and composed many hymns. He translated Aesop's fables,
which he considered next to the Bible in importance for moral instruction.

The Protestant schoolmaster early developed a simple course of
study for the teaching of reading. A child in learning to read began
with the hornbook, a thin board on which a printed leaf containing the
alphabet and the Lord's Prayer was pasted, covered over with a thin
sheet of transparent material to preserve it from wear. The child learned
his letters from this device until it was superseded by the primer. The
earliest primer was a simple A-B-C book, a sheet of cardboard folded to
form four or six pages, containing an illustrated alphabet with a verse
beneath each letter. From this developed the type of primer introduced
into the American colonies, containing the alphabet, the illustrated
alphabet with verses, the syllabarium, and short reading passages consisting of selections from the Psalter and the New Testament, and hymns.
Having learned to read, the child passed to the catechism, the Psalter,
and the Bible, which constituted the entire range of reading in the early
Protestant schools.

Singing and physical training were stressed as important subjects
in the curriculum of the vernacular primary schools. "Music," Luther
claimed, "drives away all care and melancholy from the heart, and gymnastics produce elasticity of the body and preserve the health." Not since
Plato, had an educator appreciated the educational values of music as
Luther did. He created a vernacular hymnology and encouraged others
to do likewise.[7] The first Lutheran hymnal was printed under his direction in 1524, and from that time on the people could participate in the
service of the Church in a language they could understand. Luther's
enthusiasm for music made religious music one of the chief interests of
the school, and to him may be given some credit for the almost universal
love of music found among the German people.

Luther was a firm believer in vocational training. He insisted
that every boy and girl should learn the practical arts of trade and home,
although he did not advocate these subjects as part of the school curriculum. In fact, most of his arguments are directed toward proving that
the acquisition of these practical skills need not, and must not, interfere
with school work. "My idea," he says, "is that boys should spend an

---

[7] Among Luther's hymns *"Eine feste Burg ist unser Gott"* (A Mighty Fortress Is Our
God) and the children's Christmas carol, "Away in a Manger," are especially well
known in America.

hour or two a day in school, and the rest of the time work at home, learn some trade, and do whatever is desired." Similarly, in speaking of the education of girls, he said, "In like manner, a girl has time to go to school an hour a day, and yet attend to her work at home; for she sleeps, dances, and plays away more than that."

Under the apprenticeship method, the practical arts were learned in the home. Luther, and the other reformers as well, approved this. In his discussions of practical training, Luther tried to show that school-work need not interfere with this apprenticeship in trade and home duties. He did not urge a return to the union of work and study as found in the medieval monastic schools, nor did he advocate the intro-duction of arts and handicrafts into the schools which others promoted at a later date.

Thus the curriculum for the common people, given to both sexes in the vernacular through the agency of the vernacular primary school and the home, included religion, reading, writing, singing, physi-cal training, trades and crafts, and household duties. It was imposed upon all by compulsion of church and state. This is the type found in the elementary schools established throughout northern Germany by JOHANN BURGENHAGEN (1485–1558) in carrying out Luther's educational ideas.

In the Protestant schools of England, reading, writing, catechism, manners, and morals were included in the course of study. Good man-ners as well as good moral conduct were greatly stressed by English teachers. Character training has always been a dominant feature of the English schools and is often provided for by law; the endowed schools in particular have been very effective in inculcating the manners re-quired of an English gentleman.

The curriculum of the Protestant secondary schools and univer-sities was largely a continuation of the humanistic subject matter. The alignment of such social humanists as the learned Melanchthon and the educator Sturm with the reformers marked the union of humanism and Protestantism in the learning of northern Europe. Luther and Calvin readily accepted humanistic studies as desirable for the training of Protestant teachers, preachers, and civic leaders. In the Protestant sec-ondary schools—used mainly as preparatory schools for the clergy—such humanistic studies as Latin, Greek, Hebrew, dialectic, and mathematics were taught. The ancient languages—Latin, Greek, and Hebrew—were continued in the curriculum mainly for their contribution to an under-standing of the Bible. In the Protestant churches, one who could not read the Bible in the original tongues could not qualify as a minister of the church. Logic, rhetoric, and eloquence were considered important as a preparation for sermon construction and theological discussion.

Luther, however, urged the inclusion of certain subjects in the secondary curriculum not usually found in the humanistic schools; namely, history, mathematics, natural science, music, and gymnastics.

The study of history was considered by the Protestant reformers of the greatest value in combating the claims of the papal hierarchy; and of use also toward understanding human nature and the growth of institutions, and as the bearer of moral lessons. "Historians," said Luther, "are the most useful of men, and the best teachers." Luther had a somewhat broad view of the training of youth. In one address he says, "I would have them learn not only the languages and history, but also singing, instrumental music, and the whole course of mathematics."

Since the Protestant revolt originated in the universities, it was natural that the curriculum of the northern university should undergo reform. Scholastic theology was replaced by Biblical interpretation. Although the faculties of theology became of first importance—training and examining candidates for the ministry, as they did—the faculties of law, medicine, and philosophy made some headway. The rising importance of the state gave prominence to civil jurisprudence, and interest grew in philosophical and scientific studies.

German philosophy and science, German literature and culture grew up in the soil of Protestantism, and they may be described as the result, although perhaps remote, of that spirit of freedom and independence of thought which the Reformation called into being.[8]

AGENCIES   The reformers always considered the home to be the basic agency for education; in their minds, the family was the educational institution of primary importance. Luther placed the fifth commandment, "Honor thy father and thy mother," at the foundation of his social order. He considered good home training, parental discipline, and sound family life as the very foundations of good government and social welfare, and he bitterly assailed lack of parental control and weak methods of home training. The Calvinistic home was supervised by the church authorities. Parents were obliged to teach the children the church catechism and the habits of Christian living. This instruction, and even the daily conduct of the parents, was strictly supervised by the local church, every home being inspected at least once a year to see that the regulations were carried out. Parents were obliged to see that their children attended the schools and became properly educated.

On of the most significant developments of the Reformation, at least as far as Germany was concerned, was the part played by civil authorities as agencies for the establishment and support of education. Luther placed both school and church under the guardianship of the state and thus laid the foundations for state and national control of education throughout Germany. However, Luther never contemplated a secularization of education. He appealed to the rulers on the ground that they derived their power from God and, as God's representatives, must care for the spiritual interests of their domains as much as for the material interests. In England, where the Protestant revolt was political

---

[8] F. Paulsen, *The German Universities*. (New York: The Macmillan Co., 1895.) P. 33.

as well as religious, the civil authorities had even greater control over the schools. In Calvinistic countries, however, the church and the state cooperated in the control. Very often, as in the Netherlands and later in Puritan New England, the civil authorities acted as "servants of the church" in passing laws for the support and management of the schools. Calvin believed that the state was obligated to make laws for the organization and support of schools in accordance with the ideas of the pastors. Church, state, and family must be welded into one great institution for the instruction and discipline of the entire citizenry. In other words, the state should be a theocracy, under the domination of the pastors of the church and this indeed became the pattern in New England.

Where the state would not or could not be utilized, the church should assume full responsibility for the support and control of the schools. JOHN KNOX (1505–1572), who carried Calvin's ideas to Scotland, recommended that each church support a schoolmaster, and, if that were impossible, that the minister teach the children. In the middle colonies of the American seaboard, where many sects were found, civil authorities played so little part in education that the church-controlled parochial school was the dominant agency of education throughout the entire colonial period.

The importance of the teacher as an instrument of education was always emphasized by the Protestant reformers. Luther deplored the low financial status of the teaching profession. He believed that an industrious and high-minded teacher, who faithfully trained and disciplined youth, could never be sufficiently recompensed. The Protestants believed in thorough training; consequently most of their teachers were university men as well educated as the ministers. In all Protestant countries and churches, close supervision was maintained over schoolmasters. The church leaders were held responsible for the attendance of the schoolmaster at the regular worship of the church, for his orthodoxy, and for his loyalty to the government.

ORGANIZATION The Protestant school system was organized into three types of schools: the common vernacular school, the classical secondary school, and the university. These schools, however, were not organized into a ladder sequence as we have them today in the United States. They constituted rather a dual system of education, providing one type of education for the masses, and another type for those destined to be leaders.

The vernacular primary school was organized for popular education. This part of the educational system was universal and compulsory. Girls as well as boys attended, although Bugenhagen's plans always included separate schools for girls. These Protestant vernacular schools were in many instances a modification and reorganization of the burgher schools of the free towns that had developed in the late Middle Ages to furnish boys of the commercial class instruction in reading, writing, and counting. Under Protestantism, this earlier school of the middle

classes was linked to a greater extent with religious instruction and became the elementary school of the common people. This was especially
true of the schools in the Netherlands. Much of the credit for the organization of the elementary school should be given to Bugenhagen, who has
been called the "father of the German *Volksschule*." John Knox also was
a firm believer in elementary education. He was instrumental in establishing in Scotland—under the control of the parishes—the free elementary schools which have done so much for the enlightenment of the
Scottish people. But, despite these wise and earnest organizers, many
Protestant reformers and educators were somewhat lukewarm to the
vernacular school—being primarily interested in the development of the
Latin schools.

Wherever the influence of the Protestant reformers spread the
humanistic classical school was taken over and reorganized into an instrument for the training of Protestant leadership. Humanistic elements
were retained, but new elements of religion and morals were added. In
this reorganization of the secondary schools men like Melanchthon,
Sturm, and Calvin played a leading part. Melanchthon was the greatest
scholar among the school organizers of the German reformation. He
made a thorough survey of school conditions in Thuringia and Saxony
in 1527—probably the earliest school survey ever made. As a result of
this investigation, he drew up the famous Saxony plan for the reorganization of the schools of that state.

This Saxony system was the first state school system of history,
although it must be remembered that it dealt only with secondary school
organization. According to this plan, the secondary schools, which were
to be established in every town under the support and control of the
civil authorities, were to be organized on three levels. The first level was
for beginners, who were to learn to read Latin; the second level was for
the study of Latin grammar; the third level was for the pursuit of more
advanced linguistic studies, reading of classic authors, exercises in rhetoric, and the study of logic. Sturm, in his *Gymnasium* at Strassburg,
greatly improved upon this system by projecting a ten-class organization,
a class-a-year plan, which was perhaps the first development of a graded
system of school organization. Sturm's school at Strassburg was also the
result of a survey of school conditions in that city, leading to a consolidation of three inefficient classical schools into one large institution,
which became the model for classical secondary schools throughout
Europe. This is perhaps one of the first examples of school consolidation.

John Calvin had a genius for organization. He drew up plans
for the religious and educational organization of the city of Geneva into
a religious city-republic. He reorganized several Latin schools into a
consolidated classical secondary school, which is sometimes known as
"Calvin's Academy." This school had seven classes, was under the supervision of the city, but was financed by tuition fees. The basis of the curriculum was humanistic, resembling that of Sturm's *Gymnasium*, although much greater emphasis was placed upon religious and moral

instruction. This school was one of the chief nurseries of Protestant preachers and teachers for many lands.

In England, after the Anglican revolt, the Latin grammar schools and the colleges were re-endowed by private gifts and by appropriations from the resources of dissolved monasteries and other ecclesiastical foundations. The Latin grammar schools—among which were some of the present so-called public schools of England—were modeled on Colet's St. Paul's School, and were humanistic-religious. By the Acts of Uniformity of 1662, all non-Anglican teachers were driven out of these schools. In the universities, religious restrictions were introduced; and no nonconformist could receive a degree from any of them.

The influence of the Protestant Reformation upon educational organization was outstanding. Wherever the Calvinistic and Lutheran points of view prevailed, foundations were laid which largely determined the organization of modern state school systems. The vernacular elementary school, the classical secondary school, and the universities for the training of leadership—these educational institutions as organized or reorganized in the sixteenth century under Protestant influence have remained the general models of educational institutions in Europe and the United States.

This educational drive fostered through the philosophy of religious moralism is easily discernible in the following excerpt from the great Northwest Ordinance of 1787 in the United States: "Religion, morality, and knowledge being essentially necessary to good government and the happiness of mankind, schools and the means of instruction shall forever be encouraged. . . ."[9] This expression of the Protestant educational ideal shows how the influence of the Reformation dominated early American education.

METHODS   Ciceronianism, or formal methods of instruction, which already had begun to shape the humanistic teaching, were continued and even extended by the Protestant schoolmasters. In the elementary schools, reading was usually a routine pronunciation of words; the memorization of answers to the questions of the catechism, of passages from the Gospels and Epistles, and of hymns and psalms, was substituted for intelligent comprehension of meaning. In the secondary schools, Latin grammar was largely a matter of learning rules and declensions, and long passages from the classics were memorized.

Many of the Protestant reformers were intensely interested in the study of the problems of educational method. In the same way that they turned to the ancient classics to throw greater light upon their theology, rhetoric, and moral conduct, so they turned to the ancient educational classics to seek information on pedagogical methods. Cicero's *De Oratore,* Quintilian's *De Institutione Oratoria,* and the educational

---

[9] Article 3, *An Ordinance for the Government of the Territory of the United States Northwest of the River Ohio,* Congress of the United States, July 13, 1787.

contributions of Plato and Aristotle were rescued from the oblivion of centuries. Many of the principles which they found they attempted to apply to their own schools. The educational ideas of Quintilian and Cicero (or Tully as he sometimes was called) appeared again in the writings of Luther, Calvin, Sturm, Melanchthon, Ascham, and Elyot.

Luther himself had advanced ideas concerning methods of teaching. The classroom should be attractive, and study made pleasant. Subject matter should be adjusted to the capacity of the child, and only the aptest pupils should go into the higher schools. There must be no lack of discipline, but the disposition of the individual must be taken into consideration in fixing punishment. "Our schools," he said, "are no longer a hell and a purgatory in which children are tortured with cases and tenses, and in which, with much trembling and flogging, they learn nothing."

But—probably because of Sturm's excessive formalism and the more severe Calvinistic theology—the Protestant classroom became a place of gloom and even of terror for children. Methods of teaching became even more rigid, discipline even more harsh, and the divorce of the life of the school from the life of the world even more complete than ever before. The freedom of individual thought promised by the Protestant revolt was seldom realized in the schools. The theory that the individual was to determine his beliefs and his conduct through his own interpretation of the Scriptures did not work out in practice. The church, through the school, closely guided the individual's thinking, and it was easy for this guidance to become domination. Children were taught not how to think, but what to think. Religious indoctrination became the chief method of the schools.

ATTITUDES OF THE CATHOLIC REFORMERS TOWARD EDUCATION

The Protestant revolts were not equally successful in all the countries of Europe. In Italy and Spain, all rebellion against the papacy was promptly and effectively checked. In France, the state church and the government had achieved a considerable degree of independence from Rome even before the days of the Huguenots and had forced concessions from the pope. Although the Huguenots were tolerated after the Edict of Nantes (1598), France remained predominantly Catholic. Generally speaking, Protestantism was adopted by the countries of northwestern Europe, while the peoples of the south, including even southern Germany, remained loyal to Roman Catholicism.

This loyalty was due in part to the Catholic reaction, a movement within the Church itself, a counter-Reformation accelerated by the Protestant revolts. Even before Luther published his challenge to such evils as those involved in the sale of indulgences, a movement to correct the abuses had begun within the Catholic Church. The counter-Reformation was an important influence in increasing the power and vigor of the church of Rome. Abuses were swept away by reforming popes and other high officials of the church, the reform movement culminating in the great Council of Trent—the sessions of which lasted from 1545 to 1563. This council did a great work in eliminating the most offensive abuses and in clarifying and defining the doctrines concerning which most controversy had arisen.

The Council of Trent enacted regulations of great importance to education. Realizing that the Protestant leaders were relying upon education as a most effective agency to advance their cause, the Catholic leaders determined to use the same instrument to root out heresy and win the dissenters back to Catholicism. Teaching orders and teaching congregations were encouraged; the parish schools were reorganized, and new institutions established for the training of Catholic children; theological seminaries were developed for the training of priests.

Most of this work of educational reform in the Catholic Church was carried out by various orders which were established during the sixteenth and seventeenth centuries. The most important of these was the Society of Jesus (popularly known as the Jesuits), organized in 1534 by IGNATIUS OF LOYOLA (1491–1556), a Spanish nobleman who had been converted to the religious life while recovering from a wound received in battle. Another outstanding teaching order was the Brethren of the Christian Schools, established by JEAN BAPTISTE DE LA SALLE (1651–1719) in 1684, and devoted to the gratuitous teaching of the poor in the vernacular. Both of these orders were concerned only with the teaching of boys.

Active in establishing Catholic schools for girls as well as schools for boys was a group of men and women, sometimes called Port Royalists and sometimes Jansenists. They were followers of a Dutch bishop named CORNELIS JANSEN (1585–1638), whose theological doctrines resembled somewhat those of Calvin. Led by the ABBÉ DE ST. CYRAN, a number of them settled at Port Royal, near Versailles in France, and there established in 1637 the famous schools known as the Little Schools of Port Royal. There were a number of orders of Catholic sisters devoted primarily to the teaching of girls. Some of the most educationally effective of these were the Order of Ursulines (1535), the Sisters of Notre Dame (1598), and the Sisters of St. Joseph (1650). The development of education for women among the Roman Catholics was greatly stimulated by the efforts of FÉNELON, Archbishop of Cambrai, whose treatise *The Education of Girls* gave him first place as a modern theorist on the education of women, and whose work as supervisor of teaching at the Convent of St. Cyr gave ample evidence of his worth as a practical schoolmaster.

AIMS   The aim of the new Roman Catholic education was—in its ultimate implications—religious moralism. Preparation for a pious and useful life here as well as a glorious life in the hereafter was the dominant objective. The motto of the Jesuits, *"Ad majorem dei gloriam"* ("All for the greater glory of God") expressed the ultimate goal of their educational efforts. But, although the ultimate goals of the Protestant and Roman Catholic reformers were not dissimilar, the immediate objectives were quite different. The avowed aim of the Protestant educator was to develop a religious and moral life through the individual's own interpretation of the Bible. The Catholic educator sought the same goal, but through the subjection of the individual to institutional control. The principle of the Protestant Reformation had been the exaltation of individual reason and faith; the principle of the Catholic reformers remained an unquestioning obedience to the authority of the church. But since the Protestant churches did not, in practice, long adhere to the principle their founders had proclaimed, the actual aims of their schools were after all not so very different from those of the Roman Catholic schools.

The Jesuit schools were designed primarily to train leaders to advance the cause of the church and of a pious Christian society. They provided a high type of spiritual and moral training; men who could read and speak Latin correctly and easily, who were disciplined and loyal to the doctrines of the church and the ideals of the order, who were competent to teach the Christian way of life, who were eager and able to perpetuate certain established ways of religious thinking and moral acting.

The aim of the elementary schools established by the Christian Brothers was to provide "Christian education, especially to children of artisans and the poor." These schools were impregnated with the ideals of religious asceticism. Similarly, the aim of the Jansenist schools was to bring about the spiritual salvation and moral reform of a few selected boys and girls. The aim of the convent schools was to prepare young women to perform their duties as guardians of Christian homes and as members of a Christian society. The first of these duties was to establish and maintain a chaste and pious moral character. Refined tastes and gentle manners, as well as skill in the management of their homes, were next in importance. The professed aim of the Catholic parish schools, convents, and academies has always been to prepare boys and girls to be faithful and loyal communicants of the church, to be moral and useful members of a Christian society, and to attain the salvation of their souls.

TYPES   In view of their aims, the Catholic schools placed religious and moral training before everything else; this was made to function through religious and moral instruction. Vocational training and domestic training were still left largely in the hands of the parents, although the virtues of honest labor and the ideals of a truly Christian home were impressed upon the pupils. In higher education, intellectual training was encouraged, but only as it assisted in the service of the church and never when it led to heresy. Among the Jesuits any type of training that prepared for preaching, for mission work, pastoral duties, ministering to the sick or to the poor, or teaching, was accepted as desirable. Literary work and scientific research were favored as long as the result contributed to the "glory of God and His Church."

The attention that the Jesuit teachers gave to physical training was a somewhat unique feature of their education. Their careful consideration of the health of the pupil and their encouragement of sports and games as an agency for physical welfare was unusual for this period.

One of the outstanding contributions of these Roman Catholic teaching orders was emphasis upon a better type of professional training. Graduate schools of law and medicine, as well as of theology, were developed by the Jesuits. But it was in the field of teacher training that these orders rendered their greatest service to education. The Jesuits became noted for the careful selection and training of their teachers; and the Christian Brothers established normal schools, with attached practice schools, to train the Brothers for their work of teaching.

CONTENT   The curriculum in the Roman Catholic schools was similar to that of the Protestants. In the elementary school taught by the Christian Brothers, the course of study covered the four R's—reading, writing, elementary arithmetic, and religion—with the emphasis always on religion. The atmosphere of the schools was deeply pious, the natural activity of the children being severely repressed.

The Jesuit fathers developed the broadest curricula in secondary and higher education of any of the teaching orders. The course of study in their lower colleges, the *studia inferiora,* corresponds roughly to that of the German *gymnasien* and the English Latin grammar schools; the course of study in their higher colleges, the *studia superiora,* to that of the Protestant universities. The lower college gave a humanistic-religious education similar to that of the Protestant classical secondary schools. The Latin language was considered the indispensable vehicle of all learning. The study of selected Latin classics was pursued in the formal manner. The Greek literature that was studied was in Latin translations. The textbooks were prescribed. The works of pagan authors were expurgated and also supplied with notes to adapt them to the training of Catholic youth. Latin texts by Christian authors were used wherever possible. History, geography, science, and mathematics were studied only as a means of understanding better the classical authors. The study of language, literature, and the other supplementary subjects was closely correlated with moral training and the activities and exercises of religious worship.

In the higher Jesuit colleges, the faculty of philosophy included scholastic philosophy as its nucleus, with Latin classics, logic, and rhetoric added. The faculty of theology emphasized theology, with philosophy and Oriental languages included. Aristotle was the basis of their philosophy; Thomas Aquinas, of their theology.[10]

The Port Royalists had a curriculum somewhat more advanced than other Catholic schools. Although they neglected physical training and science they went farther than the Jesuit schools in the literary studies. They insisted that instruction begin with the vernacular, and they gave an introductory survey of classical literature through the use of French translations. Latin grammar was studied only in so far as it was necessary for the reading of the classics, and a wide variety of authors was read for content rather than for style. Mathematics was taught, as well as logic, for the purpose of training the understanding. In these schools there was no specific instruction in religion or ethics: moral and religious training was sought through an atmosphere of piety and the continual good example set by the teacher.

In the convent schools for girls, the course of study was very much the same as in the boys' schools, with some slight additions adapted to the special needs of women. Fénelon believed that the content of the school for girls should begin with illustrated stories in the vernacular; should include writing, arithmetic, and grammar; and should provide in addition such subjects as domestic law, ancient and French history, music, art, and embroidery. Fénelon's views, unfortunately, had little effect upon the schools as a whole, and the content of the education for girls was usually much narrower and repressive than that for boys.

AGENCIES AND ORGANIZATION Three types of schools were utilized by the Catholic teaching orders: the elementary school, the secondary school, and the higher school. The Christian Brothers confined their efforts to the building up of elementary schools; the Jesuits and the Jansenists were concerned with the secondary school and the higher school. The elementary school was the school for the education of the poor; the secondary and higher schools were for the education of leaders. In each case, the school was church-supported and church-controlled.

The Catholic teaching orders—especially the Jesuits—showed a genius for organization, and the schools were most effective institutions of learning. The details of Jesuit organization were worked out gradually and finally set forth in the Constitution of the order, issued in 1556. This constitution was in ten parts, the longest of which dealt with education. In 1584, a commission was appointed to study the best educational systems of the times—Protestant as well as Catholic—and to submit recommendations for the approval of the teachers of the order. In 1599, as a final result of forty years of experience and investigation, the expanded educational section of the Constitution was published as the *Ratio Studiorum*. This plan of studies provided in great detail for the administration of the schools, the courses and programs of study, the

---

[10] See E. A. Fitzpatrick, ed., *St. Ignatius and the Ratio Studiorum*. (New York: McGraw-Hill Book Co., 1933.)

selection and training of teachers, the techniques of teaching, and the methods of discipline.

The Jesuit order is organized on the basis of a military hierarchy. At the head is the democratically elected Superior General of the order. Over each province is a Provincial appointed by the General. Over each school is a Rector appointed by the General, but under the supervision of the Provincial in whose province the school is located. Within each school are to be found in the order of their rank, the Prefect of Studies (appointed by the Provincial), the Prefect of Discipline, the House Prefects, the Teachers, and the Monitors.

There were two types of schools, secondary and higher, both free, for boys only, and open to both *interni* and *externi.* The secondary school (lower college) was divided into five classes: three grammar classes, *Infima, Media,* and *Suprema;* a fourth class, *Humanitas;* and a fifth class, *Rhetorica.* For prospective Jesuits, this was followed by two years of spiritual preparation (novitiate). In the higher school (higher college), there was a three-year arts course (faculty of philosophy), followed for prospective Jesuit teachers by two years of teacher training (juniorate) and five years of practice teaching in the secondary schools (regency). For prospective Jesuit priests, a four-year theological course (the faculty of theology) followed the regency, to be followed by ordination and a final year of spiritual preparation (tertianship). Colleges were opened only when there were endowment funds sufficient to support the number of teachers required to conduct the institution. There was close supervision over all matters of teaching, examination, and discipline. The careful selection and placing of the teachers and the close supervision of all instruction by the Prefect of Studies are noteworthy features of the Jesuit organization. The schools, however, were large; the classes usually included so many pupils that monitors were a necessity.

The organization of the schools of the Christian Brothers was set forth in the *Conduct of Schools,*[11] a manual corresponding to the *Ratio Studiorum* of the Jesuits. The organization of the order roughly corresponds to that of the Jesuits: an elected General Superior appointed Brother Visitors over each district, and appointed Brother Directors over each school. From the beginning La Salle organized special training schools for teachers, and no one was permitted to teach in the elementary schools unless he had attended one of the training schools. La Salle's first training school, established at Rheims in 1685, was the earliest forerunner of the normal school or teachers college.

Although the *Conduct of Schools* was rigidly prescriptive, it has been amended frequently. The Christian Brothers have been able to modify and expand their educational organization to keep pace with new conditions and new demands. They have expanded their educational activities to include industrial schools, reform schools, commercial

---

11 F. de la Fontainerie, *The Conduct of the Schools of Jean-Baptiste de La Salle.* (New York: McGraw-Hill Book Co., 1935.)

schools, secondary schools, and colleges. Their work has been especially successful in the United States.

The Jansenists at Port Royal organized two types of secondary schools: schools for boys under the instruction of "Gentlemen," and schools for girls under the instruction of nuns. There was a very loose organization among the teachers, and no special preparation was required. A most unique characteristic of the Jansenist school was its size. They were small, often called *les petites écoles,* and classes were limited to five or six pupils.

METHODS   These Roman Catholic teaching orders made distinct contributions to the development of educational method; in many respects their pedagogy was far superior to that used in the Protestant schools. The Jesuits, the Christian Brothers, the Jansenists—all used teaching devices and methods still worthy of study.

The Jesuits' methods were geared toward doing a small amount of work at a time, doing it well, and making sure it was retained. There were two steps in their teaching method: prelection and repetition. Prelection was virtually a lesson assignment; the teacher took his pupils over the work of the lesson to be next mastered. He would first explain the general meaning of the lesson; then explain matters of syntax and grammar; then all historical, geographical, literary, and other allusions; then the rhetorical elements; and finally point out the moral lessons involved. Prelection was always adapted to the abilities and interests of the pupils. In the lower classes the active participation of the pupils was enlisted by questioning; but in the higher classes the preparation was usually in the form of a lecture by the teacher.

The second step, repetition, was strongly emphasized. One of the mottoes of the Jesuits is *"Repetitio mater studiorum est."* The first part of each day's class period was given over to repeating the previous lesson; each week ended with a review of the week's work; the last month of the year was given over to a review of the year's work.

The Jesuits were pioneers in the development of devices for producing motivation. Besides utilizing the desire to please parents and teachers, and the sense of duty, they developed elaborate plans for stimulating the natural instinct of rivalry and emulation. Each pupil was paired with a rival of somewhat equal ability, with whom he was in continual competition; classes were divided into rival groups; schools were divided into competing camps. Honor societies were organized, in which students had to compete for membership.

The Christian Brothers were the first to grade elementary school pupils into classes according to their ability and to adopt the simultaneous method of teaching, in which the pupil recited, not to the teacher individually, but to the entire class. The Jansenists made great progress in teaching the reading of the vernacular by introducing the phonetic method of beginning with the pronunciation of the letter sound, instead of using the prevailing alphabetic method of beginning by naming the letters. The Jansenists also insisted that nothing be memorized except what was understood, and they wrote new textbooks applying this idea of appealing to the reason instead of solely to the memory.

The conduct of the pupils in all these schools was carefully supervised; all students were compelled to engage in daily public and private devotions and attend confession at regular intervals. Jesuit methods of discipline were firm, but were free from the brutality so common in other schools. Corporal punishment was used only as a last resort in extreme cases of misconduct and, when it was used, was never administered by the teacher but by a special teacher, the Corrector. There frequently was a delegation of disciplinary powers to various pupil officials —a forerunner of student government activities.

Corporal punishment was never used in the Jansenist schools. Unlike the Jesuits, the teachers of the Port Royal schools were opposed to all appeals to individual or group rivalry. They depended for motivation upon auto-emulation, or desire to surpass one's past efforts; and constant vigilance on the part of the teacher was the device invoked for controlling discipline. They relied upon the affection of the child and the zeal of the teacher as the best preventive of any disorder.

The discipline of the schools of the Christian Brothers differed from that of the Jesuits and the Jansenists in that corporal punishment was used, but the *Conduct of Schools* minutely prescribed under what conditions and to what extent it was to be administered. Thus in each of the Roman Catholic teaching orders some signal advance in the organization and practice of their educational system had been achieved. These were important contributions to the development of pedagogical theory.

FOR FURTHER READING

Bainton, Roland H., *Here I Stand: A Life of Martin Luther.* New York: Abingdon Press, 1950.

Barnes, Harry Elmer, *An Intellectual and Cultural History of the Western World.* New York: Random House, 1937. Pp. 546-596.

Butts, R. Freeman, *A Cultural History of Western Education.* Second Edition. New York: McGraw-Hill Book Co., 1955. Pp. 194-217, 240-266.

Cole, Luella, *A History of Education from Socrates to Montessori.* New York: Holt, Rinehart and Winston, Inc., 1950. Pp. 221-252, 296-326.

Cubberley, Ellwood P., *The History of Education.* Boston: Houghton Mifflin Company, 1920. Pp. 287-378.

Duggan, Stephen P., *Student's Textbook in the History of Education.* Revised Enlarged Edition. New York: Appleton-Century-Crofts, Inc., 1936. Pp. 131-155.

Durant, Will, *The Reformation.* New York: Simon & Schuster, Inc., 1957. Pp. 1-643, 751-940.

Eby, Frederick, and Arrowood, Charles F., *The Development of Modern Education.* New York: Prentice Hall, Inc., 1934.

Good, H. G., *A History of Western Education.* New York: The Macmillan Co., 1960. Pp. 139-369.

Graves, Frank P., *Education During the Middle Ages.* New York: The Macmillan Co., 1910. Pp. 179-237.

Hart, Joseph K., *Creative Moments in Education.* New York: Holt, Rinehart and Winston, Inc., 1931. Pp. 232-237.

Knight, Edgar W., *Twenty Centuries of Education.* Boston: Ginn & Co., 1940. Pp. 166-187.

Laurie, Simon S., *The Development of Educational Opinion.* New York: The Macmillan Co., 1903. Pp. 86-93.

Marique, Pierre J., *History of Christian Education.* New York: Fordham University Press, 1926. Vol. II, pp. 122-162.

McGucken, William J., *The Jesuits and Education.* Milwaukee, Wis.: The Bruce Publishing Company, 1932.

Mayer, Frederick, *A History of Educational Thought.* Columbus, Ohio: Charles E. Merrill Books, Inc., 1960. Pp. 180-196.

Messenger, James F., *An Interpretative History of Education.* New York: Thomas Y. Crowell Co., 1931. Pp. 127-140.

Monroe, Paul, *A Textbook in the History of Education.* New York: The Macmillan Co., 1933. Pp. 401-439.

Moore, Ernest C., *The Story of Instruction: The Church, the Renaissance and the Reformation.* New York: The Macmillan Co., 1938. Pp. 453-563.

Mulhern, James, *A History of Education.* Second Edition. New York: The Ronald Press Co., 1959. Pp. 308-327, 333-334.

Painter, Franklin, *Great Pedagogical Essays.* New York: American Book Company, 1905. Pp. 169-202.

————, *A History of Education.* New York: Appleton-Century-Crofts, Inc., 1904. Pp. 153-194.

Quick, Robert H., *Educational Reformers.* New York: Appleton-Century-Crofts, Inc., 1904. Pp. 32-62. .

Randall, John H., *Making of the Modern Mind.* Boston: Houghton Mifflin Company, 1926. Pp. 143-169.

Raup, Bruce, *Education and Organized Interests in America.* New York: G. P. Putnam's Sons, 1936. Pp. 73-98.

Reisner, Edward H., *Historical Foundations of Modern Education.* New York: The Macmillan Co., 1927. Pp. 364-501.

Ulich, Robert, *History of Educational Thought.* New York: American Book Company, 1950. Pp. 114-129, 149-155.

————, *Three Thousand Years of Educational Wisdom.* Cambridge, Mass.: Harvard University Press, 1954. Pp. 218-249, 272-286.

Wender, Herbert, *The Growth of Modern Thought and Culture.* New York: Philosophical Library, Inc., 1959. Pp. 41-57.

QUESTIONS FOR CLASS DISCUSSION

1. Give examples of American traditions that have become established as the result of Protestant Reformation influence.
2. Are the educational methods of the Roman Catholic reformers still used in the schools and colleges connected with the Roman Catholic Church today? Explain.
3. Do you believe that governments of today should revive the practice of appropriating money for the support of sectarian schools? Defend your position.
4. How do American reasons for universal education and for state-controlled schools differ from those advanced by Martin Luther?
5. Why is it impossible for the public schools in the United States to teach religion to the extent that it was taught in the schools of the Protestant and Roman Catholic reformers?
6. To what extent is the Bible used in American schools for educational purposes other than those of a strictly religious nature?
7. In what way does the contemporary aim in the study of history differ from that of Luther? From that of the Jesuits?
8. To what extent is the Jesuit plan of motivation still found in the schools of today—both public and private?
9. Which do you believe we should emphasize more in contemporary American education—the training of the masses in elementary schools or the education of leaders in higher schools?
10. How does the thoroughness of modern teacher education compare with that of the Jesuits and the Christian Brothers?
11. Do you believe that girls should be educated in the same schools as boys or in separate facilities? Explain your position.

CHAPTER XI

PREPARATION FOR PRACTICAL LIVING IN THE WORLD OF EXPERIENCE

THE REALISTIC MOVEMENT

The great awakening in western Europe expressed itself along three lines: (1) the Renaissance, (2) the Protestant revolt, and (3) the beginnings of scientific inquiry—a renewed interest in the practical realities of life. We have already inquired into the educational consequences of the first two movements; let us now examine the educational implications of the third. This aspect of the general renascence of European civilization, the so-called realistic movement, was in part synchronous with the Renaissance and the Reformation. The earliest realists were contemporaries of the humanists, and the work of the reformers was still vigorous when the later realists began to make themselves heard.

Realism came into existence as a protest against the narrowness of both the humanists and the reformers. The term realism—as used here—is applied to that point of view which holds that education should be concerned with the actualities of life. Whereas the humanists were individual and personal, directing their efforts toward literary and esthetic achievement, and the reformers were social and political, working toward religious and moral ends, the realists were both impersonal and nonsocial, with their attention fixed on a new objective determination. Italian humanism at its best had been overemotional and esthetic, too narrow and superficial in its interests. Northern humanism at its best had been to much engrossed in problems of social welfare and reform to the exclusion of other interests, while many zealots had been too insistent upon the limitations of doctrinal religious teachings.

Unhappily, many of the secondary schools that stemmed from the Renaissance (and the Reformation) had by now descended into a dreary and formal Ciceronianism—an excessive devotion to Latin linguistics and a deadening routine of meaningless exercises with words. The reformers—with their extreme religious fervor—had not only intensified the linguistic formalism of later humanism but had added to it a religious sanction—an authority and tradition entirely alien to a true and broad humanism as it had been conceived at the outset of the Renaissance. It was inevitable that a reaction should occur, that men should attack this sterile and narrow type of education. Ciceronianism, nevertheless, continued to dominate the schools for over three centuries more, but never without opposition from those who aimed at bringing education nearer to the meaning of and to the practical needs of life.

These protests were stimulated by the scientific investigations and discoveries that were being made outside the schools—made in spite of the antagonism of ecclesiastical authorities.

While churchmen were exhausting their powers in fiery controversies over matters which admit of no absolute settlement, and schoolmen were immersed in deadening routine and formalism, great scientists in various lands were making epochal discoveries, and explorers were adding treasures of new information, which largely discredited the meager knowledge of ancient writers.[1]

These explorers and scientists were interested primarily in the concrete objects which make up the material universe. This concern with the concrete and material was not new; it was as old as mankind itself. The observation of the phenomena of nature had been an everyday experience for many Greek philosophers from Thales to Archimedes.

As early as the thirteenth century, Roger Bacon had turned from the theological scholasticism of the medieval universities to inquire into natural phenomena and to experimentation. In the fourteenth century, the Renaissance curiosity of Leonardo da Vinci had led him to turn his remarkable abilities as a physicist and engineer to probing science and producing concrete and valuable results. Modern science, however, really began about the middle of the sixteenth century with the great work of COPERNICUS, to be followed soon by that of KEPLER and GALILEO. The publication in 1687 of the *Principia* by SIR ISAAC NEWTON, greatest vindicator of the new scientific method, laid a firm basis for studying physical science. What the philosophy of Aristotle was to the ancient world, what the theology of Aquinas was to the medieval world, the science of Newton was to the early modern world. These experimental scientists

---

[1] Frederick Eby and Charles F. Arrowood, *The Development of Modern Education.* (New York: Prentice-Hall, Inc., 1934.) P. 200. Reprinted with the permission of the publishers.

do not figure directly in the history of educational thought, yet the spirit directing their work was the same spirit that infused the realists and determined—even though indirectly—the direction of later education.

Most of the realists themselves exercised an influence outside the schools, and must be thought of as educational writers and thinkers rather than as educational workers. Most of them were primarily concerned with other interests. Yet at some time or other during their busy careers, seeing that education was out of touch with the realities of life, they took up this problem and left us their reactions in works that have become educational classics. Only in the case of some of the later sense realists, did they engage as schoolmen in the shaping of educational practices as well as in the development of educational theories.

While all the realists agreed that the schools developed by the humanists and the reformers were open to criticism, and that a new type of education should be developed to prepare boys and girls more adequately for the concrete duties of practical living, they were not agreed as to the methods by which such preparation should be given. This difference of opinion assumes three aspects: (1) humanistic or verbal realism, (2) social realism, and (3) sense or scientific realism. On the one hand, the movement reverted to the humanism of the Renaissance; on the other, it looked ahead—prophetic of the great scientific age of the nineteenth and twentieth centuries. Moreover, it should be thoroughly understood that the above classification is an arbitrary one and will be used only for convenience. Actually, the similarity of the realists to be described is considerably greater than any assumed differences.

VERBAL REALISM

Some of the earlier realists did not break away entirely from the concepts of the humanists; they may be called humanistic realists. They agreed with the Renaissance humanists that the classical languages and literatures were the only subjects worthy of study, the ideal means to a liberal education. They believed that the ancient writers had attained the highest achievement of which the human mind is capable and had included in their writings about all that was worthy of man's interest and attention. But they differed widely from the Renaissance humanists in the object of their study. Although their education was humanistic in content, it was realistic in aim and method.

In this group of verbal realists, we may place: (1) JUAN LUIS VIVES (1492–1540), Spanish scholar, friend of Erasmus and Sir Thomas More, who taught and wrote at Louvain, Oxford, and Bruges, author of *On a Plan of Studies for Youth, On the Instruction of a Christian Woman,* and *On the Teaching of the Arts;* (2) FRANÇOIS RABELAIS (1483–

1553), French monk, priest, scholar, physician, madcap, famous satirist, author of *Life of Gargantua,* and *Heroic Deeds of Pantagruel;* (3) JOHN MILTON (1608–1674), English Puritan and poet, author of *Tractate on Education.* Each of these writers is a typical exponent of verbal or humanistic realism.

AIMS   The verbal realists aimed at a complete knowledge and understanding of human society—human motives, nature, institutions, and relationships both to the world of man and to the world of nature—and with such understanding, to fit the individual to the environment in which he must live. This, they believed, could best be brought about through knowledge of ancient civilizations; and the most complete information concerning any subject of man's endeavor would be found in classical literature. So the purpose of the verbal realists was to seek out intelligently the meaning of the classic literature; to study it not for its own sake, but for the scientific, historical, and social information which it contained. They were not concerned with diction, structure, or style, like the Ciceronians, nor with religious and moral precepts, as were many of the reformers. They did not look upon the classic authors as infallible authorities, but only as convenient sources. Thus, the verbal realists believed in the utilization of classical literature as the best available means of preparing for the realities of life.

Vives, in all his writings, shows that—though favorable to humanistic studies—he is essentially a realist. He insists that education should develop personality, Christian virtues, and competence in business. Everything must be subordinated to religion, morality, and use. Literary study is to be the basis of learning; the goal is the development of character and ability. "This is the fruit of all our studies. . . . Having acquired our knowledge, we must turn it to usefulness, and employ it for the common good."

Rabelais, satirically protesting against—and ridiculing—all medievalism, scholasticism, and formalism in education, points out that there is no reason why real life values cannot be obtained from the study of the classics. The aim of learning, he says, is "the formation of a complete man, skilled in art and industry," "the development of the whole man, physically, morally, intellectually."

Milton reveals his belief that education is to prepare for actual living when he writes, "I call, therefore, a complete and generous education that which fits a man to perform justly, skillfully, and magnanimously all the offices, both private and public, of peace and war." In another connection he says, "Language is but the instrument conveying to us things useful to be known." These verbal realists conceived of education as a study of *words* in order to understand *things;* a reading of books to find out about the world in which we live and how to react to it. There are still many educators who have the same idea: that we can best learn how to live through reading.

TYPES   From the standpoint of content, the verbal realists stressed the literary type of education. It was essentially a bookish type of learning as far as agencies were concerned. When, however, we appreciate the breadth of their aims and the scope of the subject matter they advocated for use in their educational program, we see that they had in view many forms of education. In terms of aims, they were urging a very practical type of education, for all their learning was to be put to practical use. Their education is of a much more liberal type than that of the Renaissance humanists, for they would provide intellectual education, moral education, social education, religious education, and physical education—they advocated a type of education that would develop the whole man for all the practical needs of life.

CONTENT   The content of the educational course of study proposed by Vives, Rabelais, and Milton is encyclopedic. These men, extensive and thorough scholars, greatly overestimated the capacity of the average human mind for knowledge. In the completeness of the curriculum they proposed, they were a century or more ahead of their times; in many respects our modern curriculum has not caught up with theirs in enrichment and completeness.

Although Vives believed that all great knowledge was to be found in the Latin, he felt that a correct and fluent vernacular was a necessary tool of education. He said that it was the duty of the parent and the master to take pains that children speak the mother tongue correctly; that the master must be able to speak the mother tongue of the pupils fluently and correctly if he is to teach the ancient tongues effectively; that it was the duty of every scholar to purify and improve the vernacular speech of his country. The study of the vernacular, nevertheless, should be only incidental to the mastery of Latin, which, he believed, was necessary as a universal language to make possible (1) contacts between scholars of different lands, (2) a wide diffusion of books into many countries, and (3) the spread of the Catholic religion to all parts of the globe. In his study of the Latin language, he rejected the dialectic grammars used in the Middle Ages and advised instead the study of grammars based upon usage. In the reading of books in the ancient languages, he placed the study of content and meaning ahead of the study of form and style. Works on mathematics, natural sciences, and physical sciences were to be studied, as well as works in literature and philosophy. Works on history and geography were to find place in the curriculum. In the higher schools, the emphasis should be on technical and professional study of such subjects as theology, law, medicine, architecture, political science, and war. For women, Vives advocated training in the vernacular, in Latin, religion, moral conduct, care of children, and household management. He omitted the typical humanistic subjects for women—music, drawing, dancing—as well as mathematics, science, and history.

For the education of Gargantua and Pantagruel (his equally

gigantic son), Rabelais proposed a mighty curriculum. The subject matter mentioned is so extensive that he must have had in mind the mere sketching of a curriculum from each part of which selections were to be made. Rabelais presented a wide range of physical exercises, games, and sports; a rich program of Bible study and religious exercises; a long list of instrumental musical instruments; a wealth of intellectual readings from ancient authorities in science, history, mathematics, and astronomy, and of ancient literature proper in the Latin, Greek, Hebraic, Chaldaic, and Arabic languages. While Pantagruel was a student in Paris, Rabelais supposed that Gargantua wrote to him as follows:

I intend, and will have it so, that thou learn the languages perfectly; first of all, the Greek, as Quintilian will have it; secondly, the Latin and then the Hebrew, for the Holy Scriptures' sake; and then the Chaldee and Arabic likewise. And that thou frame thy style in Greek, in imitation of Plato: and for the Latin, after Cicero. Let there be no history which thou shalt not have ready in thy memory; and to help thee therein the books of cosmography will be very conducible. Of the liberal arts of geometry, arithmetic, and music, I gave thee some taste when thou wert yet little, and not above five or six years old; proceed further in them, and learn the remainder if thou canst. As for astronomy, study all the rules thereof; let pass, nevertheless, the divining and judicial astrology, and the art of Lucilius, as being nothing else but plain cheats and vanities. As for the civil law, of that I would have thee to know the texts by heart, and then to confer them with philosophy.

Now in matter of knowledge of the works of nature, I would have thee to study that exactly; so that there be no sea, river, or fountain, of which thou dost not know the fishes; all the fowls of the air; all the several kinds of shrubs and trees, whether in forest or orchards; all the sorts of herbs and flowers that grow upon the ground; all the various metals that are hid within the bowels of the earth; together with all the diversity of precious stones, that are to be seen in the orient and south parts of the world. Let nothing of all these be hidden from thee. Then fail not most carefully to peruse the books of the Greek. Arabian, and Latin physicians, not despising the Talmudists and Cabalists; and by frequent anatomies get thee the perfect knowledge of the microcosm, which is man. And at some of the hours of the day apply thy mind to the study of the Holy Scriptures; first in Greek, the New Testament, with the Epistles of the Apostles; and then the Old Testament in Hebrew. In brief, let me see thee an abyss and bottomless-pit of knowledge: for from henceforward, as thou growest great and becomest a man, thou must part from this tranquility and rest of study, thou must learn chivalry, warfare, and the exercise of the field, the better thereby to defend my house and our friends, and to succour and protect them at all their needs, against the invasion and assaults of evil doers.[2]

Milton, too, believed that the whole gamut of ancient learning should be studied. Not satisfied that the student should know only the content of Latin and Greek classics, he advocated the reading of books in Hebrew, Chaldaic, Syriac, and Italian. Great literary classicist though

---

[2] Rabelais, *Pantagruel*, Book II, Chapter VIII.

he was, he regarded no education complete without a wide acquaintanceship with scientific as well as literary writings—natural science, social
science, mathematics, philosophy—all the knowledge of all the ancients.
Milton condemned the study of formal grammar and the development
of an elegant and ostentatious style as a waste of time. Puritan in outlook, he differed from Rabelais in that he provided no free play or competitive games in his program, but he did advocate physical education
as a training for military service. Moral and religious instruction was to
be given, not only through a pious atmosphere in the school itself, but
by the reading of the ethical writings found in the Bible and in other
ancient literature.

Thus the content of the education proposed by the verbal realist
was to be found largely in books—books on all subjects and books in all
languages. Although a bookish curriculum, it was far from being narrow.

AGENCIES AND ORGANIZATION   While the verbal realists were
primarily concerned with the aims and content of education, they did
advance certain proposals, varying widely, for the organization and
arrangement of school work. Usually their suggestions were so idealistic
as to be impossible of accomplishment, at least in their time; and so
had a minor influence, except in the case of a few exceptional teachers
and of a few schools that kept alive their ideas. The work of the schools
continued to be carried on in the formal, artificial, perfunctory traditionalism that is always so hard to overcome. Our interest in these men
is not because of their influence upon the organization of the schools of
their own time, but because they advanced some ideas that we of the
present day could well use. The plans outlined may not be, as Milton
admits, "a bow for every man to shoot in," but they are rich in stimulating inspiration and offer practical suggestions.

Vives insisted that both parents should take part in the education of the child; the mother should be the child's first teacher, and the
father should oversee and direct all the child's training. In rare instances,
it might be necessary for the child to be taught privately by a tutor.
When this was the case, he should have at least one companion in his
studies. Ordinarily, the boy should enter a public day school at the age
of seven, living at home while attending the school. Vives believed that
schoolmasters should be men of sound scholarship and that their training should include much practice. These schoolmasters should be paid
from public funds, and no teacher should receive any money from his
pupils. Vives thought that the site of a school building should be selected
with the greatest of care, and that considerable attention should be given
to the planning, construction, and equipment of the building.

The organization of Rabelais' scheme of education is largely in
terms of a tutor—a private teacher who is to live with the boy and make
every hour of the day serve some educational purpose. This new type of
instructor is pictured in the education of Gargantua:

First he brought him into the company of learned men, which stirred in him emulation and desire to whet his wit and improve his parts and to bend his study another way, so that the world might have a value for him. And afterwards, he put himself into such a road, that he lost not any one hour in the day, but employed all his time in learning and in honest knowledge.[3]

While Gargantua was being bathed, dressed, and fed, the tutor carried on his teaching. During the hours of physical games and sports, during the time spent in playing cards, during evening walks and visits to lectures, courts, stores, and manufacturing shops, education went on under the guidance of the tutor. Life and all its manifold activities shared in the educative process.

Differing from both the tutorial idea of Rabelais and the public day school of Vives, Milton's scheme is based on the idea of a single institution of learning, which he calls the "Academy." Milton believed that the entire education of a boy could be given in this academy instead of being divided between the secondary school and the university. He says: "All this may be done between twelve, and one and twenty, less time is now bestowed in pure trifling at grammar and sophistry." Milton describes the organization of his academy in these words:

First to find out a spacious house and ground about it for an academy, and big enough to lodge a hundred and fifty persons, whereof twenty or there-abouts may be attendants, all under the government of one, who shall be thought of desert sufficient, and ability either to do all, or wisely to direct, and oversee it done. This place should be at once both school and university, not heeding a remove to any other house of scholarship, except it be some peculiar College of Law, or Physic, where they mean to be practitioners; but as for those general studies which take up all our time from Lilly [Lilly's Latin Primer] to the commencing [degree] as they term it, Master of Arts, it should be absolute. After this pattern, as many edifices may be converted to this use, as shall be needful in every city of this land, which should tend much to the increase of learning and civility everywhere.[4]

Verbal realism, combined with certain other influences, eventually brought about the establishment of new educational institutions, particularly on the secondary level. The Act of Uniformity, passed in England in 1662, excluded hundreds of nonconformist ministers from their parishes and closed the Latin grammar schools and universities to nonconformists. Many of these ministers turned to teaching for a livelihood and opened private secondary schools for the children of nonconformists. Influenced probably by the description of Milton's brainchild, these schools were called academies and patterned somewhat after the educational ideals of the verbal realists. But, retaining the highly religious character of the schools of the reformers, these academies placed greater emphasis upon practical preparation for actual life. Latin and

---

[3] Rabelais, *Gargantua,* Book I, Chapter XXIII.
[4] Milton, *Tractate on Education.* (London: Thomas Dring, 1673.) P. 5.

Greek were retained; but modern foreign languages were taught also, and all instruction was in the vernacular. History, geography, mathematics, and natural philosophy were subjects of their curricula.

METHODS   The verbal realists not only attacked the narrowness of the curriculum of the classical humanists but also the formalism of their methods. They advocated methods far in advance of their times. Vives, in particular, had some exceedingly advanced conceptions of methodology. In his writings, he drew upon the earlier educational theorists, especially Aristotle and Quintilian. He was a forerunner of the modern psychologists in his desire to make the study of the operations of the mind the basis of teaching method. His last essay, *De Anima* (Concerning the Mind), reveals a clear understanding of the function of sense-perception and of the natural growth of knowledge in the individual mind.

Influenced probably by Quintilian, he advocated that the masters should study each pupil individually and adapt the work each was to pursue to his particular interest and ability. He suggested that the pupils enter school a month or so early, so that their capacities might be studied thoroughly by the masters. His idea that at least four times each year all the masters should hold conferences, at which they could exchange observations concerning the progress and ability of their pupils, strikes a modern note.

Rabelais suggested a most informal system; today we would probably call it an incidental method of learning. All study was to be made pleasant; attractive rather than compulsory means were to be favored; spontaneity and interest were to be substituted for formalism and authority. He believed that learning could come best through natural, exuberant activities engaged in spontaneously in the open air; that knowledge could be attained best by the following of natural interests. Reference books were used to clear up discussions; a careful observation of nature and direct contact with the everyday activities of life supplemented and vitalized the reading of the classical authors. Reasoning was substituted for rote memorizing. "Learning truly becomes, not the drudgery of imprisoned schoolboys, but the sport of kings."

Milton bitterly assailed the existing grammar schools because of their excessive emphasis upon grammatical drill, and because of their stress upon the writing of compositions in imitation of classical Latin and Greek models. He said: "These are the fruits of misspending our prime youth at the schools and universities as we do, either in learning mere words or such things chiefly as were better unlearned."

The basis of Milton's method was reading—widely and thoroughly—for content and not for syntax and grammar. But this was to be vitalized through discussions with the teacher and through explanations and lectures by authorities on all subjects; these resource persons were to be brought to the academy to talk to the boys, whose education was to be further supplemented by travel in England and abroad.

SOCIAL REALISM

The social realists joined the verbal realists in their attacks upon classical learning; but whereas the verbal realists protested most against the narrowness and formalism of this learning, the social realists protested against what they thought its utter uselessness as a preparation of the individual for his life among other human beings, *e.g.*, its failure to fit the individual for social living and social adjustment. The social realists were aristocratic members of the upper classes, men of affairs interested in the training of their sons for active participation in public life. They sought an education that would develop the gentleman, the man of the world; and they believed that such an education could be had best by direct contact with people and their social activities rather than through books. They had little patience with the bookishness of the verbal realists who, they said, were preparing young men for the life of the past.

MICHEL DE MONTAIGNE (1533–1592), French aristocrat, Mayor of Bordeaux, lawyer, outstanding essayist, tolerant epicurean, and admirable gossip, was the most truly representative exponent of this educational position known as social realism. His educational views are set forth in detail in two of his famous essays, *On Pedantry* and *On the Education of Children*.

AIMS   Social realism was another reaction to Ciceronianism and was a step further on toward sense realism. The aim of the social realist was not to produce a scholar or a professional man, but to prepare the aristocratic youth for the life of a gentleman in the world of affairs. Montaigne said that education was the art of forming men rather than specialists. To him education meant a pragmatic utilitarianism. Like the Sophists of Greece, he advocated a highly individualistic education that would prepare the youth for individual efficiency and success in the social life of his day. The immediate aim was to develop a sound and practical judgment of men and affairs. Instead of cramming the memory with facts, education was to provide the basis for the making of sensible choices and decisions, to enable the individual to get along efficiently with his fellows and to enjoy his leisure hours. Actually, the only aim was to prepare the youth for a successful and pleasurable career.

To a gentleman born of noble parentage, and heir of a house that aims at true learning, and in it would be disciplined, not so much for gain and commodity to himself, nor for external show and ornament, but to adorn and enrich his inward mind, desiring rather to shape and institute an able and efficient man than a bare learned man. . . . I would rather prefer wisdom—judgment, civil customs, and modest behavior—than bare and mere literal learning.[5]

---

[5] Montaigne, *On the Education of Children*. (Translation by John Florio.) P. 7.

So social adjustment, the fitting of the individual for an efficient and pleasant life with other individuals, is the educational aim of the social realist. The development of a practical judgment and a social disposition is the best means to that end; not merely the acquisition of information. The art of living is the goal of learning; the pupil is to live what he learns.

TYPES   The social realist advocates a practical type of education, but not utilitarian in the sense of being vocational or professional. He is not interested in preparing for a specialized trade or profession, but he is concerned with the development of a practical man of affairs—the versatile man of the world. This is social education in the broadest meaning of the term, the development of the ability to get along smoothly and harmoniously with other people in all the activities of life. Montaigne proposed a broad education that would include physical training, moral training, and intellectual training. His physical training had in it a suggestion of the hardening process later developed more fully by Locke and Rousseau; his moral training was adaptation to the social customs of the gentleman, including the acquisition of such abilities as the capacity to drink gracefully and to make love romantically; his intellectual training was development of sound practical judgment and wise discrimination.

Montaigne's conception of education was essentially aristocratic. He was concerned only with the training of the upper classes and paid little attention to the other classes in European life. He was satisfied to have the apprenticeship system and the workhouse take care of the education of the children of the poor.

CONTENT   Montaigne advocated the use of an activity curriculum and scorned the idea that a mere study of books would provide an adequate education. To him experience was much more important than words and books. Where books were used, the most important results to be obtained from their reading was the vicarious participation in the experience of others that they provided. History was to be approached as a study of the experiences of others in the past, and philosophy was the study of human conduct and man's offices and duties.

Montaigne demanded the addition of new subjects to the curriculum. Latin was to be retained as a part of the education of a gentleman, but an overemphasis on Greek was to be rejected as the mere equipment of a scholar. French and contemporary foreign languages were considered much more important than Latin and Greek, because these were the languages needed for conversation with people at home and in travels.

Like Milton, Montaigne stressed travel as a most effective means of education, the best agency for gaining experience and becoming familiar with people and customs. Actual contact with people and places was considered much more valuable than reading about them. The world was to be the curriculum.

This great world, which some multiply as several species under one genus, is the true mirror wherein we must look in order to know ourselves, as we should. In short I would have this to be the book my young gentleman should study with most attention. Many strange humours, many sects, many judgments, opinions, laws, and customs teach us to judge rightly of our own actions to correct our faults, and to inform our understanding which is no trivial lesson.

AGENCIES AND ORGANIZATION   Montaigne had little use for schools and colleges as agencies in education. In speaking of the product of these institutions, he says, "Do but observe him when he comes back from school, after fifteen or sixteen years that he has been there: there is nothing so awkward and maladroit, so unfit for company and employment; and all that you shall find he has got is, that his Latin and Greek have only made him a greater and more conceited coxcomb than when he went from home."

Instead of the conventional institutions as agencies for education, Montaigne—as Rabelais had done earlier—urged the use of a tutor. He declared that the choice of a tutor was the most important and most difficult duty of the parents.

The charge of the Tutor, which you shall appoint your son, in the choice of whom consists the whole substance of his education and bringing up, on which are many branches depending . . . my desire is therefore, that the parents or overseers of such a gentleman be very circumspect, and careful in choosing his director, whom I would rather commend for having a well composed and temperate brain, than a full stuffed head, yet both will do well.

This private tutorial system, under which the education of the boy at home and abroad was closely directed and supervised, was not only adopted by many of the noble families of France but also became popular in England. The narrow classical formalism of the Latin grambar schools and the growing acceptance of the idea that the grand tour was an indispensable part of the complete education of a gentleman brought about the adoption of the tutorial type of training among the English upper classes.

Although Montaigne himself favored private tutors, some persons who came under the influence of his social realism demanded new types of schools to carry out its aims. Members of the French aristocracy demanded a school which should turn out a gentleman instead of a pedant, and a few such schools were ultimately established under the name of academies. Instead of the classics and religion stressed in the Renaissance and Jesuit colleges, these schools emphasized modern languages, mathematics, good manners, and military arts.

The development of such schools for the upper classes was much more pronounced in Germany. The Thirty Years' War (1618–1648) enhanced the position of the nobility and developed a class feeling between the bourgeoisie or burgher class on the one hand and the aristocracy on the other. Social differentiation led to educational differentiation. The sons of the noblemen were withdrawn from the classical *Gymnasien,* and schools were established for their exclusive use. This new type of second-ary school was called the *Ritterakademie.* The character of this school was determined not only by the desire of the nobleman for a school that would prepare for civil and military affairs, but also by the great in-fluence that French court life was beginning to have upon the German nobility. Therefore, French language and literature, physical training and social accomplishments, political history and geography, mathemat-ics and military science formed the backbone of the curriculum.

The schools that developed under the influence of social realism have their survival today in the finishing schools and military academies attended by the sons and daughters of the wealthier classes in American life, as well as in the Public Schools of England.

METHODS   The gist of Montaigne's conception of method is found in the famous quotation: "To know by heart only is not to know at all."

He believed in a method that emphasized understanding and judgment rather than mere memorizing. Knowledge should be assimi-lated, facts used, action imitated, ideas applied in conduct. Latin should be learned by speaking it; foreign languages should be learned by travel-ing through foreign countries and conversing with the people; informa-tion should be obtained through direct social contacts rather than from books. "What a man knows directly, that will he dispose of without turning to his book or looking to his pattern."

Montaigne urged that learning should be pleasurable and attrac-tive to the child. He condemned the harsh measures so often used in the schools of his day to secure attention and diligence.

Some never cease brawling in their scholar's ears to follow their books; yet is their charge nothing else but to repeat what has been told them before. I should have a tutor [show the pupil] how to choose and distinguish, without the help of others, sometimes opening him the way, other times leaving him to open it by himself. I would not have [the tutor] invent and speak alone, but suffer his disciple to speak when his turn comes. . . . "Most commonly the au-thority of them that teach, hinders them that would learn.". . . I would not only have him demand an account of the words contained in his lesson, but of the sense and substance thereof, and judge of the profit he hath made of it, not by the testimony of his memory, but the witness of his life. . . . I would have him make his scholar narrowly to sift all things with discretion, and harbour nothing in his head by mere authority, or upon trust.

Thus Montaigne advocates a method that is in accord with the best principles of teaching; he is encouraging discrimination, independ-ent thinking, and application on the part of the pupil himself and condemning too much authority and activity on the part of the teacher.

SENSE REALISM

The culmination of the realistic movement in education is to be found in the ideas of the sense realists. They bring to fruition the seeds sown by the verbal and social realists. Instead of a reality as found in books, instead of a reality experienced in everyday human relationships, they postulate a basic reality—the reality found in the forces and laws of nature. This phase of realism has been called scientific realism; it is the beginning of the scientific movement in education.

This realistic movement is the outgrowth of the scientific discoveries of the sixteenth and seventeenth centuries. The heliocentric theory of the solar system by Copernicus; the exploration of the motions of the planets by Kepler; the discovery of celestial phenomena through the invention of the telescope by Galileo; the development of logarithms by Napier, of analytical geometry by Descartes, and of calculus by Liebnitz; the discovery of the law of gravitation by Newton; the advance of theories of gases and of the vacuum by Boyle; the formulation of the theory of the circulation of the blood by Harvey; the invention of the barometer by Torricelli and of the compound microscope by Malpighi—these were the results of a new type of intellectual activity far removed from the traditional learning of the schools, and paving the way for a new conception of education. Practical men, looking upon these fruits of the new methods of observation and reasoning, of independent thinking and of free judgment, determined that training along such lines should find a place in the schools, began to think, write, and teach in this manner. They advocated a type of education in which scientific content was introduced and scientific method utilized.

Four great educational thinkers may be taken as typical exponents of sense realism: (1) RICHARD MULCASTER (1531–1611), headmaster of Merchant Taylors' School and of St. Paul's School in England, author of two texts on education, *Positions* and *Elementarie;* (2) FRANCIS BACON (1561–1626), English statesman, philosopher, and scientist, author of *Advancement of Learning, The New Atlantis,* and *Novum Organum;* (3) WOLFGANG RATKE (1571–1635), German founder of experimental schools, author of *Methodus Nova;* (4) JOHN AMOS COMENIUS (1592–1670), Moravian bishop, "prophet of modern education," philosopher, educator, and textbook writer, author of *Great Didactic, Gate of Tongues Unlocked, The Vestibule, The School of Infancy,* and *Orbis Pictus (The World in Pictures).*

AIMS   The ultimate aim of the sense realists was to develop a natural individual and a natural society—working in accord with sense perception. Natural conditions and natural laws—the only true realities —were the goals of education. Mulcaster said that education should not attempt to repress the natural tendencies and activities of childhood; that the "aim of education and training is to help nature to her perfection." Bacon believed that the ultimate goal of education was to give to man dominance over *things,* to increase human power through the utilization of scientific knowledge. Knowledge of the natural environment, its phenomena and its processes, was to be utilized as the new foundation for a practical and useful life. "Man is but the servant and interpreter of nature; it can be commanded only by being obeyed; thus do human knowledge and human power really meet in one." The chief purpose of education was to learn its laws and to control nature for the benefit of man. Bacon was a realist in that he made the end of scientific inquiry practical rather than metaphysical. He believed that learning had as its aim the mastery of *things* in order to further man's control over nature. He optimistically foresaw the use of the scientific method for the benefit of human welfare; he believed that the scientific study of nature was basic to all human progress. *The New Atlantis,* the plan for his model state, included the establishment of a research institution, a clearing house for scientific investigation called Solomon's House, which would apply its findings to the advancement of human welfare.

Bacon was not alone in this dream of a social order brought about through a new type of education. The scientific inventions and discoveries of the sixteenth century had fired the imagination of many enlightened minds to attempt great achievements in the transformation of human nature and human society. Utopian schemes (from the original *Utopia* of Sir Thomas More) were the expressions of a new faith in the improvability of human life, a faith in the possibility of reconstructing human society through the power of education. Most of these writers who presented their seventeenth century schemes for the reform of society agreed with Bacon that education was the essential agency for the betterment of both society and the individual. Although novel for this century the idea was not really new; Plato in *The Republic,* two thousand years earlier, had looked upon education as a means for reforming society and the state.

Comenius, with his combination of religious zeal and passion for knowledge, represents a transition between the religious moralists and the sense realists. His ultimate goal of education was "eternal happiness with God." But this, he believed, could come about only through the right kind of living on earth. Comenius was a firm believer in the power of education to regenerate human life. He insisted that there was no better way to raise the standards of sunken humanity than through the proper education of the young. This could be accomplished only through the teaching of all truth. The aim of education should be the teaching of all things to all men. He said that "charity bids us not niggardly to withhold from mankind what God has intended for the use of all, but to throw it open to the whole world." Although eternal happiness with God was the ultimate goal of education, the immediate aim of the school was to prepare for the activities of life through the utilization of a wealth of knowledge.

They will learn, not for the school, but for life, so that the youths shall go forth energetic, ready for everything, apt, industrious, and worthy of being intrusted with any of the duties of life.[6]

The sense realists aimed at the discovery and advancement of new knowledge rather than the mere learning from books. They sought this in the realm of nature. But they did not seek information about nature for the sake of knowledge as an end in itself, or to satisfy only curiosity. They were rather seeking power, with which to utilize nature's forces for the welfare of mankind. The sense realists—like the practical scientists of today—aimed at the discovery and utilization of the secrets of nature for the real and practical benefits they could bring to man in the everyday work of the world.

Nor did the sense realists limit their aim to the search for natural laws in the external world. They believed that the operations of the inner processes of the mind were also a part of the laws of nature. The immediate aims of Ratke and Comenius were to discover the laws of nature that governed the learning process. They aimed at an educational system that could be in accord with the natural order that the mind of a child followed in learning. Bacon's immediate aim was the development of a scientific method for the discovery and organization of scientific knowledge; the immediate aim of Ratke and Comenius was the development of a scientific method for the inculcation of that knowledge in the minds of youth.

TYPES The sense realists—as did all the other realists— emphasized a practical type of education as far as purposes were concerned. From the standpoint of content, most of them placed stress on the scientific type of training. Their education was liberal to a much greater degree than most of that which had preceded them, for they were all interested in a pansophic curriculum—one of which included practically all knowledge. Religious and moral types of training were still stressed (especially by Comenius), and linguistic and intellectual types of training were considered essential as tools for the gaining of knowledge.

One striking characteristic of the sense realists was their emphasis upon democratic education, and the vernacular. Comenius in particular had a profound sympathy for the common people and was a champion of education for all in the same schools. "As far as is possible, all should be educated together, that they may stimulate and urge on one another." Mulcaster thought that education should be widely diffused and adapted to the needs of all the people. Both Bacon and Comenius firmly believed that if knowledge were properly organized, it could be grasped by the common man.

---

[6] S. S. Laurie, *John Amos Comenius.* (Syracuse, N. Y.: C. W. Bardeen and Company, 1892.) P. 200.

CONTENT   The curriculum advocated by the sense realists was, as a rule, quite comprehensive. Of all the writers of this group, Mulcaster probably had the narrowest conception of the content of education; yet even he contended that learning should be wide in scope and adapted to the needs of all. In his six-year elementary schools, children were to be taught reading and writing as a necessary equipment for all citizens. The English vernacular was given first place in these schools, both as the only medium of instruction and as a subject of study in itself. Together with the reading and writing of English, drawing and music entered into the education of all. These were the only subjects offered along the lines of sense training or object study and no provision was made for the study of natural phenomena, the chief characteristic of sense realism and the one from which it derives its name. The usual emphasis of the other sense realists upon nature as an object of study was absent from Mulcaster's theories. He did insist, however, that games and physical exercise should have a prominent place in his schools.

Ratke was more interested in developing a natural method of teaching than he was in teaching nature. He placed greatest emphasis upon the languages, being chiefly interested in the rapid acquisition on the part of the pupil of the Latin, Greek, and Hebrew tongues. In the lower three grades of his school, the German vernacular was taught, and in the upper grades the other languages were approached through it. He hoped to train teachers "to impart to their pupils a thorough, good, and fluent knowledge of any language, especially of Hebrew, Greek, and Latin, in less time . . . and also with much less pains." In addition to this emphasis upon language, arithmetic, singing, and religion were included in the curriculum. Yet, as far as the content of instruction was concerned, Ratke can hardly be called a true sense realist.

Bacon was convinced that the knowledge of nature was the only real and fruitful knowledge and the only kind worth presenting in the schools. Education should be devoted largely to the study of natural phenomena. His great desire was to advance knowledge rather than to repeat what was already written. The true educator, he said, "Should labor as the bee, gathering where he can and working into a single structure all that he gathers." He should turn to nature, contriving experiments by which the secrets of nature are revealed. He should observe, weigh his observations, and relate his discoveries most carefully. From this scientific, inductive type of investigation come the generalizations that make up a real knowledge of natural laws and their applications—the true content of learning. Subject matter should come neither from tradition nor from the dogmatic assertion of authority—but only from a careful observation and experimentation directed toward a search for the truths of the natural world. In Solomon's House, the most important feature of his Atlantis, Bacon set up a research institution devoted to the scientific investigation of natural phenomena, the discovery of natural laws, and the harnessing of nature to man's needs.

According to Bacon the greatest task of education is to learn the laws of nature; the most important subject matter of education is science. Instead of the superstitions and false notions—the "idols" as he called them—of scholasticism and humanism, he planned to fill the curriculum with the true knowledge that comes from an inductive study of nature.[7] Bacon was more interested in educational content than in educational method: he concerned himself with the problem of discovering and classifying knowledge; he said that he had "taken all knowledge to be his province."

Bacon's greatest weakness was his failure to appreciate the place of mathematics in science. He rejected the work of Copernicus largely because he did not understand its mathematical implications.

Comenius proposed an even wider curriculum than did Bacon. As was the case with many other realists, he overrated the capacity of the human mind for knowledge. He proposed a pansophic curriculum—one that was all-comprehensive and encyclopedic in scope. Since the aim of education was "to know all things, to do all things, to say all things," every subject was to be taught in his schools. He accepted Bacon's principle of utility and demanded that all useful knowledge should be taught, if not in all its details, at least in its general outlines. He included all the older subjects of the Trivium and Quadrivium, grammar, rhetoric, dialectic, arithmetic, geometry, astronomy, and music, and in addition included physics, geography, history, morals, and religion. He especially emphasized the value of history as "the most important element in a man's education, the eye of his whole life, as it were." He was especially insistent that manual and industrial arts and play activities be included in the curriculum of the school. He was the first to recognize play as an agency for the building of a healthy body and a normal mind. He even advocated the use of humor and wit as a part of the content of education.

In regard to the linguistic content, he emphasized the vernacular but advocated the study of foreign languages for the sake of conversation with neighbors. He included Latin, Greek, and Hebrew in his secondary and higher schools, but was not enthusiastic about most of the classic authors. The languages were never to be learned as an end in themselves, but always as a means for the discussion of scientific and practical subjects. The Latin language was to be used as a supplement to the vernacular in acquiring a knowledge of the arts and sciences. In all his linguistic education, he shifted the emphasis from *words* to *things*.

In Comenius' "School of the Mother's Knee," the content was to be drawn from the various areas of the child's interest—interest in *things,*

---

[7] Renowned for his advocacy of the inductive method—and thus the spirit of scientific investigation—Bacon is famous likewise for his conception of the bar to clear and rigorous thinking which he calls the four idols. These preconceptions (or errors) in thinking Bacon labeled: (1) Idols of the Tribe (human lack of objectivity); (2) of the Cave or "Den" (ethnocentric, nationalistic, or other group inhibitions); (3) of the Marketplace (self-interest, the commercial aspect, or simply specious ignorance); (4) of the Theater (the mode, climate, or special context wrongly invoked).

interest in manipulation, interest in language, interest in people. In the vernacular and Latin schools, these interests were to be further utilized: the interest in *things* was to lead to a study of natural phenomena; the interest in languages was to stimulate the study of the mother-tongue and then of the Latin language through the vernacular; the interest in manipulation was to express itself in a study of the practical and fine arts; the interest in people was to motivate the study of history and literature. Thus the principle of curriculum organization was one of continuing at each higher level the studies begun in the level below.

AGENCIES   All the sense realists we are here considering were (with the exception of Bacon) practical schoolmen and interested in the development of schools as the ideal agency of education. Even Bacon, who wrote little about the applications of his theories to concrete educational practice, devotes a section of *The New Atlantis* to a description of Solomon's House—his model educational institution for scientific investigation, a forerunner of the modern research university.

Mulcaster believed that education in schools was much more effective than education by tutors. He insisted on the education of girls as well as boys. Although himself a secondary-school headmaster, he contended that as much attention should be given to the development of the elementary schools as to the development of secondary and higher schools. He drew up a detailed plan for a six-year vernacular elementary school open to all boys and girls. He was particularly interested in having school buildings so situated as to furnish plenty of light and air, and favored ample playground space in connection with every school plant.

Ratke, through the generosity of Prince Ludwig of Kothen, was able to demonstrate his educational theories in a model school. The state furnished him with buildings and all the equipment necessary to try out his ideas in a school which about five hundred boys and girls were compelled to attend. The school was doomed to early failure, but furnished a pattern for many of his followers to imitate.

Comenius also advocated schools as the best agency for education. He believed that educational objectives could be realized only by a carefully organized and clear-cut system. His was divided into four types of schools: (1) the School of the Mother's Knee, in every home; (2) the vernacular school, in every hamlet; (3) the Latin school, in every city; and (4) the university, in every province. He also mentions a "College of Light," similar to Bacon's Solomon's House, to be established for advanced research.

Comenius was a firm believer in the value of the textbook as an agency of instruction. Up to his time handbooks were scarce and expensive, and there was a serious lack of uniformity. Most schools were still following the medieval custom of each pupil reproducing his own from dictation by the teacher. Comenius wanted all pupils to have the same text covering the entire subject matter of the course. One of his greatest contributions to education was the writing of many textbooks.[8] Although he prepared manuals for his School of the Mother's Knee and the vernacular school, he is best known for his many Latin texts.

All sense realists emphasized the importance of the teacher as an agency in education. They believed in the possibility of a trained teacher who could study children and master the natural laws underlying sound educational practice. Mulcaster advocated the establishment of training schools associated with the English universities. He insisted that teachers of young children should be especially well trained (and well paid), since in their work the greatest teaching skill was required. Ratke and Comenius devoted most of their efforts to the development of methods of teaching so that teachers might be made more efficient in their work. They believed that the method of instruction used by the teacher in the classroom was the most important factor in educational success.

Early in the eighteenth century, certain new educational institutions were established in Germany embodying the conceptions of sense realism. The development of these new agencies for sense realism was largely due to the Pietists (dissenters from the Lutheran faith), and their chief educational representative, AUGUST HERMANN FRANCKE (1663–1727). Francke developed a group of institutions at Halle, including the new University of Halle, emphasizing scientific studies; a pedagogical seminar for the training of teachers for the new *Volkschule;* the *Pedagogium,* a secondary school combining the study of science and modern language with the older Latin and Greek classics. JULIUS HECKER (1707–1768), a pupil of Francke, later established a *Realschule* in Berlin, a secondary school in which the classics received little stress and in which the pure and applied sciences dominated. This was the first of the *Realschulen,* which came to be established throughout Germany and are now an alternative to the classical *Gymnasien* in preparing German students for the university.

ORGANIZATION   The sense realists believed that school organization should be based upon the natural capacities of the pupils and should follow the natural laws of child development. They advocated, for the first time, a ladder system of organization. Mulcaster was in favor of a six-year vernacular elementary school for children from the age of six to twelve. He insisted that this first stage of learning was of most importance; that all children were able to profit from this elementary training in the vernacular. Since reading and writing, at least, should be the common right of all people, he urged universal attendance in these schools by both boys and girls. He did not think that all could profit by higher education in the classical languages; only those should attend the

---

[8] See William Brickman, "Three Centuries of Comenius' Contributions to Education," *School and Society,* Vol. 86, No. 2131 (April 26, 1958), pp. 192-194, for comments on the tercentenary of Comenius' *Orbis sensualium pictus.*

secondary school and university who were fitted for such education. But elementary education was to be considered of as much—if not more—value than higher education, and the study of the vernacular should precede both in time and importance the study of Latin. Those who were to go on to the Latin grammar school and the university—as well as those who were not—were to be thoroughly trained in the use of their native tongue.

Ratke's experimental school at Kothen was also organized on a six-year plan. This school represented a fusion of elementary and secondary education. It was divided into six classes. In the first three classes, the vernacular was taught; in the fourth class, the study of Latin was started; and in the sixth class, the study of Greek. Ratke believed that the vernacular language should be the medium of all instruction and that all other languages should be approached through it.

Of all the sense realists, Comenius made the foremost contribution to the theory of school organization. He suggested a complete graded system based upon the natural psychological development of the pupils, a consistent ladder plan of organization, with each school leading to the next. According to his scheme, there should be four periods of six years each. Education was to begin at birth and the first six years was to be given in the home, or in the school of infancy—the School of the Mother's Knee. Comenius antedated the modern conceptions of preschool education by two centuries. He set forth in detail all that should be done in the training of the child during these formative years. For the next six years of childhood (6–12), Comenius advocated a vernacular elementary school for all children in every hamlet. For those who aspired to occupations higher than the farm or workshop, the next six years (12–18) were to be spent in a Latin school, one of which was to be established in every city. The vernacular school was to train the senses and to give sensory experience; the purpose of the Latin school was to train the pupil to understand and systematically organize information collected in the earlier period. The Latin school was not to be limited to the learned or higher classes but was to be open to all who had the aspiration and ability to profit by its instruction. Those who were of high moral character and who were able to pass rigid examination were to be admitted to the university for six more years (18–24). A university was to be established in each province. Like Bacon, Comenius believed that scientific research could best be achieved through the cooperation of the learned men of all nations. He therefore urged the establishment of a research institution, a College of Light, somewhere in the world, where the great scientists of all countries could assemble and carry on their investigations. He believed that university graduates of superior ability should not only attend the College of Light but also travel widely to have direct contact with human nature and institutions.

In the matter of internal organization, Comenius was equally advanced in his recommendations. He insisted that all schools should begin on the same date each year and that children should not be admitted except on the opening day. He believed in a very systematic organization of the schedule of class work—each year, each month, each week, each day, and each hour was to have a definite task assigned to it. Each class was to have a separate room, a separate teacher, and separate textbooks. The school day was to be organized in agreement with child nature. Older children were to study six hours a day; younger children were to study four hours. There was to be no homework and a half-hour period of relaxation was to follow each study period. The morning hours were to be devoted to the intellectual subjects; afternoon hours were to be given over to physical and esthetic subjects.

Thus Comenius suggested an educational ladder similar, though much superior in its organization, to the one that developed in American education more than two centuries later. He anticipated many modern principles of classroom organization and management.

METHODS   Of all the contributions of the sense realists to educational theory, the most noteworthy are those concerning methods of teaching. They expressed the belief that natural laws underlay the processes of learning, laws that could be discovered and formulated, and they paved the way for the later developments in child study and educational psychology. They insisted for the first time that knowledge comes through the senses and that the order of learning must be *"things, thoughts, words."*

Mulcaster urged that children be studied and their innate abilities respected. His psychological analysis of the three natural powers of children, "wit to conceive by, memory to retain, discretion to discern by" was not very penetrating, but was in the right direction. His desire to make use of the natural tendencies and activities of childhood, through the use of games, plays, and exercises, was pedagogically sound.

As far as classroom methods were concerned, Bacon had nothing better to suggest than the practices of the Jesuits. His prescription, however, of the inductive method for the advancement of learning was of great educational significance. Bacon did not invent the inductive method; it was practiced by Aristotle and really is as old as the human mind itself. What he did was to state the procedure under which inductive reasoning should operate, the removal of prejudices, the thorough observation by the senses, the careful tabulation of cases, the study of exceptions as a check, the formulation of the generalization. In his *Novum Organum,* Bacon justified the use of the inductive method, the controlled observation of the objective phenomena of the external world, as the only true source of knowledge. Although Bacon himself did not apply the inductive method to school procedures, his writings paved the way for the use of observation and experimentation as classroom procedures; for the study of facts as the beginning of the thinking process; for the selection, comparison, and classification of examples and instances; and for placing the emphasis upon the problem.

Ratke was the first educator to seek for the method of nature—

the natural order in which the mind develops. Although both Ratke and Comenius made the error of basing their conclusions concerning the growth of the child upon the analogies of external nature, they did establish the principle that the true basis of educational method should be the process of the natural growth. Ratke undertook to develop a teaching method upon the following principles: (1) everything in its order, the course of nature; (2) only one thing at a time; (3) each thing should be repeated often; (4) everything first in the mother tongue; (5) everything without compulsion; (6) nothing must be learned by rote; (7) similar subjects should be taught in the same way; (8) first the *thing*, and afterwards the explanation of the *thing*; (9) everything through induction and experimentation. By following these rules, Ratke believed that the work of education could be accomplished in a much shorter time.

In spite of the fact that Comenius accepted the psychology current in his day and for so long thereafter, and indulged in the dangerous practice of reasoning by analogy, his innumerable principles of method are amazingly modern in their conception. The underlying motive of all his teaching was that education should be according to nature. "Let our maxim be to follow nature in all things, to observe how the faculties develop one after the other, and to base our method on this principle of succession." [9]

Proceeding according to this basic principle, Comenius formulated many practical rules for teaching—rules which were embodied in all the many school texts which he wrote. Some of these may be stated as follows:

(1) Education should appeal to the child's natural interests.

(2) Whatever is to be known must be taught by presenting the object directly to the child.

(3) Whatever is taught should be of practical application to everyday life.

(4) Whatever is taught should be taught straightforwardly and not in a complicated manner.

(5) General principles should first be explained and details then considered.

(6) Order, positions, and connections of objects should be studied.

(7) All things should be taught in due succession and only one thing should be taught at a time.

(8) A subject should not be left until it is thoroughly mastered.

(9) Stress should be laid on the differences which exist between things so that knowledge may be clear and distinct.

(10) Senses, memory, imagination, and understanding should be daily exercised in conjunction.

---

[9] See *John Amos Comenius, 1592–1670, Selections.* Introduction by Jean Piaget. (Paris: United Nations Educational, Scientific and Cultural Organization, 1957.) Pp. 11-31. This work includes many passages from Comenius' less familiar *The Labyrinth of the World and the Paradise of the Heart* (1623), as well as *The Great Didactic, The Pampaedia,* and *The Panorthosia.*

(11) Learning should proceed from the known to the unknown.

(12) *Things,* objects, and actions should be associated with the words representing them in the vernacular.

(13) Instruction should be fitted to the comprehension of the child.

(14) Children must learn to do by doing.

(15) Words must not be repeated.

Such were the principles and rules of method set forth by Comenius in his greatest educational classic, *The Great Didactic.* He was not only a theorist, but a practitioner as well. He successfully applied his methods to classroom procedure and embodies them in his textbooks. His *Orbis Pictus* was the first illustrated school textbook, and his *Janua Linguarum Reserata* applied his new and better methods to the teaching of Latin.

Comenius believed that by the use of his methods the school would become a place of happiness and joy instead of a place of drudgery and gloom, and that interest in work would become the agency of good discipline instead of the rod. He recognized the distinction between moral infractions and backwardness in studies and believed that the latter should be dealt with only through reproof. Ratke also believed in a mild form of discipline. There was to be no constraint in his school; the teacher was to devote his entire efforts to teaching and the pupils were to keep order and good discipline.

There is an interesting story that Comenius was offered the presidency of Harvard College, founded a generation earlier in the American colonies of Great Britain, but this conceivably is myth.[10] It is clear, however, that the educational methods advocated by the Moravian bishop were greatly in advance of those of the religious moralists of colonial New England.

Another European-American tie of this realist period is the development of the new American secondary school—the public academy. Perhaps influenced from abroad (although this is debatable) this practical school first appeared in the colonies at the end of the seventeenth century. In 1751 the most famous of these was founded by BENJAMIN FRANKLIN in Philadelphia;[11] and within a few decades this became the prevailing type of secondary education for the American school system, rapidly replacing the Latin grammar schools. These academies were at first designed to prepare for the activities of life and not for college, and

---

[10] Yet no less an authority than Cotton Mather has recorded in his *Magnalia Christi Americana* (Hartford, Conn.: Silas Andrus, 1820) , Vol. II, P. 10, the following memorial and tribute: "That brave old man, *Johannes Amos Commenius,* the *fame* of whose worth has been *Trumpetted* as far as more than *three* languages (whereof everyone is endebted unto his JANUA) could carry it, was indeed agreed withal, by one Mr. *Winthrop* in his travels through the *Low Countries,* to come over into *New-England,* and illuminate their *Colledge* and *Country,* in the quality of a *President.* But the solicitations of the *Swedish* Ambassador diverting him another way, that incomparable *Moravian* became not an *American.*" The date was 1654 and the occasion the resignation of President Dunster.

[11] See James Mulhern, *A History of Secondary Education in Pennsylvania.* (Philadelphia: The Author, 1933.) Pp. 174-216.

were attended by those who desired a nonclassical education leading to business and trade. They were usually open to girls as well as boys. They were private educational institutions, although many were supported by generous endowment gifts, and some even succeeded in getting government subsidies. The curriculum was very broad, including modern languages, English, grammar and composition, the sciences, drawing, mathematics, history, and many subjects in practical arts. Until the establishment of the normal schools, these academies were the teacher-training institutions for the preparation of elementary school teachers.

FOR FURTHER READING

Adamson, John, *Pioneers of Modern Education*. Cambridge: Cambridge University Press, 1905. Pp. 46-79.

Barnes, Harry Elmer, *An Intellectual and Cultural History of the Western World*. New York: Random House, 1937. Pp. 669-705.

Browning, Oscar, *History of Educational Theory*. New York: Harper and Brothers, 1905. Pp. 51-85, 92-102.

Burnham, William, *Great Teachers and Mental Health*. New York: Appleton-Century-Crofts, Inc., 1926. Pp. 141-187.

Butts, R. Freeman, *A Cultural History of Western Education*. Second Edition. New York: McGraw-Hill Book Co., 1955. Pp. 217-239, 267-299.

Clough, Shepard B., *The Rise and Fall of Civilization*. New York: McGraw-Hill Book Co., 1951. Pp. 191-216.

Cole, Luella, *A History of Education from Socrates to Montessori*. New York: Holt, Rinehart and Winston, Inc., 1950. Pp. 328-355, 356-397.

Cubberley, Ellwood P., *The History of Education*. Boston: Houghton Mifflin Company, 1920. Pp. 379-427.

Eby, Frederick, and Arrowood, Charles F., *The Development of Modern Education*. New York: Prentice-Hall, Inc., 1934. Pp. 200-288.

Good, H. G., *A History of Western Education*. New York: The Macmillan Co., 1960. Pp. 170-200.

Graves, Frank P., *Great Educators of Three Centuries*. New York: The Macmillan Co., 1912. Pp. 1-51.

Knight, Edgar W., *Twenty Centuries of Education*. Boston: Ginn & Co., 1940. Pp. 188-209, 343-346.

Mayer, Frederick, *A History of Educational Thought*. Columbus, Ohio: Charles E. Merrill Books, Inc., 1960. Pp. 199-221.

Messenger, James F., *An Interpretative History of Education*. New York: Thomas Y. Crowell Co., 1931. Pp. 141-155.

Monroe, Paul, *A Textbook in the History of Education*. New York: The Macmillan Co., 1933. Pp. 442-502.

Mulhern, James, *A History of Education*. Second Edition. New York: The Ronald Press Co., 1959. Pp. 328-372.

Quick, Robert H., *Educational Reformers*. New York: Appleton-Century-Crofts, Inc., 1904. Pp. 63-79, 103-171.
Ulich, Robert, *A History of Educational Thought*. New York: American Book Company, 1950. Pp. 162-199.
————, *Three Thousand Years of Educational Wisdom*. Cambridge, Mass.: Harvard University Press, 1954. Pp. 305-346.
Wender, Herbert, *The Growth of Modern Thought and Culture*. New York: Philosophical Library, Inc., 1959. Pp. 59-82.

QUESTIONS FOR CLASS DISCUSSION

1. In what respect do realistic conceptions of education find expression in the contemporary emphasis upon activity curriculums?
2. Do you believe that modern education is still too bookish? Explain.
3. To what extent do the extracurricular programs of today's schools illustrate the ideas of the social realists?
4. Compare the illustrated textbooks prepared by Comenius over three hundred years ago with modern devices for visual education.
5. What recent reorganization in the American educational system is in line with the proposals of John Amos Comenius?
6. To what extent do present-day schools and universities follow the suggestions of Milton and Montaigne concerning the educational values of travel?
7. Do you believe that we still need to study classical literature in the ancient languages in order to get a knowledge of human society and human institutions? Defend your position.
8. Do you believe it wise or unwise for anyone today to aspire to Francis Bacon's goal of "taking all knowledge for his province"? Explain.
9. Interpret Bacon's four idols in contemporary terms. Can you illustrate with actual modern instances?
10. What modern principles of teaching were applied by Ratke and Comenius in their educational practices?
11. Do you consider the education of Gargantua practical or impractical? Defend this in contemporary terms.
12. Which should be emphasized more in the schools of today—the study of words or the study of *things*?

CHAPTER XII

FORMAL DISCIPLINE AND THE APPEAL TO REASON

DISCIPLINISM AND RATIONALISM

The first half of the eighteenth century was characterized by two reactions: the rise of the doctrine of formal discipline, and the development of an aristocracy of reason. Formal discipline in education arose as a new defense of the narrow classical humanism against the advances of realism. An aristocracy of reason appeared, and the movement toward a democratic and universal system of education was checked, as rationalism became a goal of education.

The humanists of the Renaissance had rejected the theological dialectic of scholasticism on the grounds that it had little value for the needs of life. They had turned to the classical literatures of Greece and Rome, because in them they found a content that enriched their lives; that acquainted them with the human activities and institutions that had contributed to rich and full careers in this world. But the study of classical languages and literature had degenerated into Ciceronianism, and the liberal spirit of the older broad humanism had been lost. Although the reformers had taken over the classical education as the accepted means for training their leaders in secondary and higher schools, yet, by the seventeenth century, this linguistic and literary course of study had become merely traditional, justified only by the authority of two centuries of use and by the details of classroom procedure and the techniques for instruction which had been developed to such a high degree of perfection.

It had not been difficult for the sense realists to demonstrate that this linguistic training in the classical languages had little practical value. Latin had ceased to be the language of religion among the Protestant churches. Services were conducted, and the Bible and other religious books read, in the vernacular, though the clergy continued to use Greek and Hebrew in their study of the original Biblical sources. Latin was retained as an official language only by the Roman Catholic Church. By the end of the seventeenth century it had ceased to be the sole language of the universities; it had become less and less the medium for scientific discussion; it was no longer the only approach to the knowledge of human achievement and human thought. Latin literature was rapidly being replaced in the interest of the people by the vernacular literature. Therefore the classical education could no longer be justified on the basis of practical values. If it were to survive, it must find a new justification and a new defense. Such a defense was found in the doctrine of disciplinism, or formal discipline.

Both the reformers and the realists had been instrumental in advancing the cause of popular and universal education. Although Luther had insisted on special classical training for those who were destined to serve the state and society as preachers, doctors, teachers, and civil magistrates, he also had demanded religious and vocational training for the masses. The Calvinists had insisted upon an elementary education for the common people. Especially in the cities and towns of the Netherlands, public efforts were made to require elementary education for all children; and upon the civil authorities was laid the duty of establishing schools where children of every class of society might learn to read. Among both Protestant and Catholic reformers, the movement for universal popular education grew slowly but surely. The realist philosophy added momentum to this development. Comenius, especially, advanced the most democratic conception of education formulated until recent years in his demands for the education of all children: "Not the children of the rich and the powerful only, but of all alike, boys and girls, both noble and ignoble, rich and poor, in all cities and towns, villages and hamlets, should be sent to school."

This movement for popular education found support not only among the Protestants, but also from some of the Catholic teaching orders. Impelled by a sense of duty and piety and a desire to build Christian character, philanthropic societies were organized and missionary teachers sent out to give education to the masses. The Protestant Pietists of Germany took great pains to educate the poor and give religious instruction to all classes. In England, the Society for the Propagation of the Gospel in Foreign Parts (Episcopal) carried popular education into the colonies, and the Brothers of the Christian Schools performed a similar function among the Catholics.

It is not surprising to find these democratic conceptions of education opposed by those who had aristocratic beliefs. The point of view held by the opponents of popular education was well expressed (1671) by Governor William Berkeley of the British colony of Virginia when he said: "I thank God, there are no free schools nor printing; and I hope we shall not have these for a hundred years; for learning has brought disobedience and heresy. . . . God keep us from both." The aristocratic view was presented also by Cardinal Richelieu for France, in these words: "Although the knowledge of letters is eminently necessary for a country, it is certain that they need not be taught to everybody. . . . If letters were profaned for all types of mind, one would see more people ready to raise doubts than to solve them, and many would be more ready to oppose truth than to defend it."

The most effective attack on universal education, however, was that of the rationalists, who advanced an aristocratic conception of education. They proposed as the goal of education, not the development of an aristocracy of birth or breeding, nor of wealth or power, but an aristocracy of brains—an aristocracy of the intellect. This conception of education is designated as the doctrine of rationalism.

We are now ready to discuss the implication of these two conservative movements: (1) the doctrine of formal discipline, and (2) rationalism. In considering these two movements, we shall give particular attention to the English Puritan, JOHN LOCKE (1632–1704), great philosopher, political economist, and educational theorist, in whose thinking so many currents mingle that he is often called an eclectic. In the encyclopedic content of the curriculum which he recommends, he resembles the humanistic realists; in his distrust of existing schools and his recommendation of the tutorial system and of travel, he resembles the social realists; in his emphasis upon sensationalism, he resembles the sense realists. But his most effective contributions to educational thought have been along the lines of disciplinism and rationalism. From his *Essay Concerning the Human Understanding,* his *Thoughts Concerning Education,* and his *Conduct of the Understanding* we can select his contributions to the disciplinary and rationalistic movements of the late seventeenth and early eighteenth centuries.

THE DOCTRINE OF FORMAL DISCIPLINE

It is desirable that we give considerable attention to the disciplinary conception of education, for it dominated schools from the time of Locke down to the middle of the nineteenth century and is still prevalent in many educational institutions, especially those at the secondary and higher levels.

This theory of formal discipline stressed the value of the processes of learning rather than the value of the things learned. In this respect it was but a revival and a new defense of the formalism of medieval scholasticism and of Ciceronianism. This new justification of narrow classical humanism was welcomed by all those who looked upon education from the religious viewpoint. The leaders of the church of Rome (and the Protestant moralists as well) had considered the realistic movements—especially that of sense realism—as irreligious and atheistic; and we find in their antagonism the beginning of opposition by the theologian to scientific education. The church was glad to have a new defense for the type of subject matter which realism sought to displace. The church was also very familiar with the idea of discipline in all its aspects. Monasticism had been a moral discipline; mysticism had been a spiritual discipline; scholasticism had been an intellectual discipline; chivalry had been a social and physical discipline. By emphasizing education as eradication of the essential evil in man and as development of high moral character, religious thought provided a background for the disciplinary theory of education.

The disciplinary concept of education was also in accord with the traditional psychological theories current at the time. Aristotelian faculty psychology, still accepted in the seventeenth century, held that the mind was made up of certain faculties, such as attention, memory, observation, and reason. One who had these faculties well trained could use them effectively. Education consisted of training the various faculties of the mind by appropriate disciplines or exercises.

The disciplinary concept of education has always been popular with many people. Church leaders have liked it because it adheres closely to their religious doctrines. Classical scholars have liked it because it gives them a justification of their favorite subjects. Teachers have liked it because it provides a simple technique for them to follow and a definite goal. Parents have liked it because it is something they understand, and because they think that its results are best for their children. Even the psychologists liked it until faculty psychology was dethroned by modern psychological investigations.

There is a difference of opinion as to whether John Locke formulated the doctrine of formal discipline. Most writers give Locke credit for the disciplinary theory and claim that he formulated and elaborated the doctrine. The truth seems to be that this many-sided thinker did develop and support certain aspects of the theory; but it must be admitted that he is by no means responsible for many of the ideas and practices that have been advocated under the name of formal discipline. Many who claimed to be followers of Locke have carried his educational doctrines to ridiculous extremes.

AIMS The ultimate aim of disciplinism, as set forth by Locke, is the formation of character, the word character being used in its broadest sense. It involves the cultivation of the whole man—moral, physical, mental. Locke believed that the development of the body was an essential concomitant of the development of mind and morals. Like the Greeks, his motto was, "A sound mind in a sound body." Physical, mental, and moral prowess comes as a result of rigorous exercises of body, of mind, and of self-control. The immediate aim of education is to provide these exercises. Locke gave expression to this aim in the following:

> The great work of a governor is to fashion the carriage and to form the mind, to settle in his pupils good habits and the principles of virtue and wisdom . . . to give him vigor, activity and industry. The studies which he sets him upon are but, as it were, the exercise of his faculties . . . to teach him application and accustom him to take pains.

The theory of formal discipline, therefore, maintains that it is not the thing learned, but the process of its learning that is the important aim of education. Locke stood for the belief that mental power is more important than knowledge acquired through study. Thus he set up, as the aim of mathematics, the making of reasonable creatures; as the aim of reading, the development of discrimination. He believed that all intellectual capacities were the result of practice.

> As it is in the body, so it is in the mind: practice makes it what it is; and most even of those excellencies, which are looked on as natural endowments, will be found, when examined into more narrowly, to be the product of exercise, and to be raised to that pitch only by repeated actions.

The aim of disciplinism is to provide the exercises or disciplines for the training of the mind as well as those for the hardening of the body and for the development of self-control. The aim of Locke is to develop by exercise the desirable physical, moral, and mental habits. His whole plan of education was to habituate the pupils to effective and desirable ways of thinking and acting. He believes that the mind of the child at birth is like an unwritten tablet, a *tabula rasa*. Development comes only through the formation of habits through discipline. The work of education is to form specific habits and to develop intellectual capacities through exercise. The educative process is for the purpose of increasing the powers of the individual rather than of enlarging his possessions.

TYPES   Locke emphasized three major types of education, physical, moral, and intellectual. He advocated: (1) vigor of body; (2) good breeding and wisdom in conduct; (3) mental power. He stressed character education—the education of the whole man. Locke believed in a broad type of education—he never confused education with mere instruction. There is a great divergence between Locke's view and the views of the later disciplinarians who thought of education only as an intellectual discipline. Locke himself started all education with bodily exercises. The first paragraphs of his *Thoughts Concerning Education* are devoted to a discussion of physical education:

Thus I have done with what concerns the body and health, which reduces itself to these few and easy observable rules; plenty of open air, exercise, and sleep, plain diet, no wine or strong drink, and very little or no physic, not too warm and straight clothing, especially the head and feet kept cold, and the feet often used to cold water and exposed to wet.

After physical education, Locke placed moral education—the control of the desires by reason. He speaks of virtue as "the hard and valuable part to be aimed at in education." Intellectual education is placed last in the order of importance by Locke, whereas the later disciplinarians have advanced it to a place of first, if not sole, importance.

CONTENT   The exponents of the doctrine of formal discipline are usually satisfied with a limited curriculum. They contend that the intellectual powers of memorizing and reasoning, developed through the study of the right kind of subject matter, can be used in mastering other subject matter or in meeting the experiences of daily life. Since they are confident that the classical languages and mathematics are best adapted to training the mental powers of memory and reasoning, they consider it unnecessary to waste time on the teaching of other subjects. They allege that the student who has developed his mind through the study of these subjects can readily master of his own accord the easier practical subjects and meet all the demands of vocational, political, and social life. The disciplinarian builds his curriculum on the theory that these few well-organized linguistic and mathematical studies, with their orderly arrangement of parts, their universality of principles, their perfected technique of method, are sufficient for a liberal education.

Locke himself did not favor the curriculum that the later disciplinarians advocated. In his discussion of the content of education as found in his *Thoughts on Education,* he seems to be in agreement with the realists, especially in the matter of the intellectual subjects. The content he recommended is quite different from that of the grammar school curriculum of his day. He considered intellectual study of less importance than physical and social training. Although he counted Greek essential to the scholar, he thought it quite unnecessary in the education of a gentleman. While Locke advocated the retention of Latin, he did not do so on disciplinarian grounds—such a justification of Latin was advanced by his followers. He was opposed to the linguistic exercises used by the humanists in their teaching of Latin; he was more concerned with developing the ability to read it than with speaking or writing. Locke emphasized the value of being able to speak and write the English vernacular; he said that French, as well as Latin, should be learned by the conversational method. He suggested certain additions to the curriculum, such as drawing, geography, history, anatomy, ethics, dancing, and a few practical and fine arts as hobbies and recreations. In view of such recommendations, it is difficult to see how the later disciplinarians came to use Locke as a justification for their narrow, formalized curriculum. Yet Locke really discusses the curriculum from two points of view. In his *Thoughts on Education,* where he is considering the kinds of information needed in the education of an English gentleman, he is speaking as a utilitarian and a realist; in his *Conduct of the Understanding,* in which he discusses the kinds of exercises and drills needed to train and develop the mind, he advocates disciplinism.

It is Locke's discussion of the place of mathematics in the curriculum that justifies us in calling him a disciplinarian; this probably had the greatest influence upon the later advocates of formal discipline. Again and again he emphasized the value of mathematics in the training of the reasoning faculty.

> Would you have a man reason well, you must . . . exercise his mind. . . . Nothing does this better than mathematics, which, therefore, I think should be taught to all those who have the time and opportunity; not so much to make them mathematicians, as to make them reasonable creatures . . . that having got the way of reasoning, which that study necessarily brings the mind to, they might be able to transfer it to other parts of knowledge, as they shall have occasion.[1]

Such statements led those who wished to keep the classic languages in the curriculum of the schools to use the disciplinarian theory to retain their hold upon education. They saw in the study of Latin and Greek the same training in reasoning and the same transfer of reasoning power that Locke seemed to see in mathematics. The justification that Locke used for the inclusion of mathematics in the curriculum, the classicists used for the continuation of the linguistic study of Greek and Latin. Even the later scientific realists, in defending the place of scientific studies in the curriculum, came to defend these subjects in terms of their value in the development of the mental powers.

In the elementary schools, the disciplinary concept gave a new stimulus to drill subjects such as spelling, arithmetic, and formal grammar, and postponed the addition of content subjects such as history, geography, and the elementary sciences. Instead of these drill subjects being looked upon from the standpoint of their value in the development of useful and practical habits of life, the disciplinarians valued them for their contributions to the development of the general powers of the mind.

AGENCIES AND ORGANIZATION The doctrine of formal discipline gave little in the way of new agencies or new organization of education; it tended to preserve the existing schools with their traditional organization. The fact that great minds had been developed by these traditional means was in itself a sufficient excuse for their con-

---

[1] John Locke, *Conduct of the Understanding,* pp. 6-7.

tinuation; and the established schoolmasters seized upon the doctrine and used it to perpetuate themselves and their institutions. The grammar schools of England and America, the *Gymnasien* of Germany, and colleges and universities everywhere found in this doctrine a defense for the continuation of their traditional organization and practices.

Locke distrusted the existing schools and, like the social realists, advocated the tutorial system as the best agency for the education of the young gentleman. He had the typical attitude of the English aristocrat toward the education of the common people; like Montaigne, he believed that any training they were to receive could best be obtained in the workhouse or by the apprenticeship system.

Locke's recipe depends on the proper selection of his tutor. "To form a young Gentleman as he should be, 'tis fit his Governor should himself be well-bred, understanding the Ways of Carriage and Measures of Civility in all the Variety of Persons, Times, and Places; and to keep his Pupil, as much as his Age requires, constantly to the Observation of them. This is an Art not to be learnt nor taught by Books. . . . Breeding is that which sets a Gloss upon all his other good Qualities, and renders them useful to him, in procuring him the Esteem and Good-will of all that he comes near. Without good Breeding his other Accomplishments make him pass but for proud, conceited, vain, or foolish." [2]

But it was not the tutorial system that became the great instrument of disciplinism; it was the humanistic secondary school and college and the religiously motivated church elementary school. These schools were organized entirely in terms of physical, moral, and intellectual discipline, and continued so until well into the nineteenth century. In the English secondary schools, the whole course of from six to nine years was given over to Latin and Greek prose composition and to the writing of Latin verse. The extent to which the early American Latin grammar school and college were organized and articulated on the disciplinarian philosophy is indicated by the following statement of the admission requirements of Harvard College in 1642:

> When any scholar is able to understand Tully [Cicero] or such like classical author extempore, and make and speak true Latin in verse and prose . . . and decline perfectly the Paradigms of Nouns and Verbs in the Greek tongue, let him then, and not before, be capable of admission into the College.

Until 1850 at Oxford and until 1851 at Cambridge, the subjects for entrance examination had to be chosen from the classics and mathematics alone.

The disciplinary conception was exemplified by the German *Gymnasien* until the twentieth century; by the great public schools of England until the end of the nineteenth century; by the Latin grammar

---

[2] John Locke, *Some Thoughts Concerning Education.* (R. H. Quick, Ed.) Cambridge, England: The University Press, 1902. P. 69.

schools in the United States until they were replaced by the academies in the nineteenth century. Even today in many countries we find school-men who are instruments for the preservation of the theory of formal discipline, defending the old formal grammar, Latin, algebra, and geom-etry as the most important subjects in the curriculum, on the grounds that they produce great minds through a training in logical thinking.

METHODS   As a rule, the disciplinarians continued the for-mal methods of the Ciceronians; for they had found new justification of these monotonous and uninteresting devices of learning. When it comes to the question of method, there is less doubt as to Locke's disciplinism than there is in the case of aims and content. He bases all his educational procedure on the laws of habit formation; his educational techniques are devised for the habituation of the pupils in desirable ways of thinking and acting. Learning, to him, is thus largely a matter of exercise and drill, whether it be physical, moral, or intellectual.

Yet Locke had a much broader conception of the educational process than did most of the later disciplinarians. He recognized three distinct steps in learning: (1) sensation, (2) memory, and (3) reasoning; and his idea of drill was an exercise of all three of these faculties. Sense impressions form the basis of learning, and so sense training is of first importance. Sense impressions and experiences make up the content of knowledge; but to be of any value, they must be retained through memory. Therefore, memory training must be stressed. The retained knowledge is the raw material for the higher and more important mental processes involved in reasoning. Reasoning is the crowning achievement of man; and the training of the reason is the most important aspect of the educational process.

The later disciplinarians soon began to overlook the importance of sense training, and concentrated their efforts upon drill in formal memorizing and formal reasoning. They retained the emphasis upon habit formation, but restricted their efforts—at least in the intellectual field—to the forming of habits of rote memorizing and logical associa-tions. Instead of drilling upon useful material, they concentrated upon subject matter that was merely difficult. They confused the uninteresting with the difficult; because a pupil fretted and groaned under a subject, they took it for granted it was valuable as an exercise in developing memory and reasoning. Locke himself urged that the educational process be made as pleasant as possible for the child, and was opposed to severity. He suggested pleasurable methods of study and play devices to make the drills interesting. Locke never meant to imply that a subject had disciplinary values just because it was hard and dry.

The disciplinary schools and schoolmasters, however, soon devel-oped a severe authoritative methodology. They believed that physical and mental powers, and powers of moral control, could come only as a result of rigorous exercises of body, mind, and conduct. The work of the schools became a process of physical, mental, and moral gymnastics, by which the body, mind, and conscience were to be strengthened and trained in the right directions. The body was to be trained by hardening exercises; the moral nature was to be developed by the constant checking of natural desires; the mind was to be developed by continual exercises in the memorizing of rote material and in reasoning with abstract and logical material.

In all the schools dominated by the disciplinary concept of education, the force of authority was exerted with the utmost severity. Corporal punishment was used extensively for even the slightest offenses and deficiencies. Not only did the masters themselves rule with the utmost severity, but pitiless fagging and hazing systems developed in the schools, in which the older boys undertook to discipline the younger.

Locke believed in utilizing the motive of approval rather than the motive of fear. He advocated the use of praise and censure, the former to be administered in public but the latter to be given only in private. Corporal punishment was to be used only in cases of obstinacy, which he considered the root of many later evils.

In the words of Robert Ulich, "One might ask how it came about that for two centuries or more the ideas of the Commonwealth educators (William Petty, John Durie, Samuel Hartlib, and John Milton, for example) and of Comenius were condemned to oblivion, whereas John Locke's treatise . . . became a classic."[3] The simplest answer is "that Locke provided for the educated Englishman of the eighteenth century the right mixture of progress and conservatism." Furthermore Locke's prestige in the areas of political science and philosophy secured a wider reading of his *Thoughts Concerning Education*.

Like the influence of Plutarch, Locke's conception of the English gentleman provided just the image eighteenth century England was seeking—in many respects close indeed to the Greek and Roman equivalents of the early Roman empire.

RATIONALISM

The original intent of rationalism was to offer a protest against arbitrary authority in church and state. Its ultimate results, however, led to a reaction against the newly awakening forces of democracy and universal education—the rise of downtrodden or neglected classes. In its appeal to reason—against the hampering restrictions of tradition and authority—the movement was praiseworthy; in its disregard of the needs of the masses and the right of the common man, it was reactionary.

Yet such a movement was sorely needed. The early part of the

---

[3] Robert Ulich, *A History of Educational Thought*. (New York: American Book Company, 1950). Pp. 200.

eighteenth century was a period of narrow bigotry in religious and social life and despotic absolutism in political government. After the first flush of the Reformation had paled under the hatreds of the religious wars, worship among both Protestants and Catholics had settled down to a rigid conformity to dogmas and practices, from which no divergences were allowed. Religious creeds and social conduct were based upon supernaturalism and revelation; the authority for all phases of life rested upon precedent rather than reason.

Political government was in the hands of sovereigns who ruled by "divine right," benevolent despots at their best, absolutist tyrants at their worst. England alone had achieved a limited constitutional monarchy through its Bill of Rights, but this was a victory for Parliament alone and not for the common people. In Prussia, Austria, Russia, and Spain, legislative asssemblies rarely met; but the benevolent despots in power, although they ruled autocratically, did make an attempt to improve the conditions of the masses in the interest of their nationalistic ambitions, giving expression to the oft-quoted statement, "Everything for the people, but nothing by the people." In France, absolutism—shorn of all benevolent interests in the common people—bore its most terrible fruits. The magnificent and luxurious court at Versailles, infested by hypocritical sycophants and extravagant idlers, rested upon an impoverished, overtaxed, submerged population of common people.

Two powerful social institutions, an arrogant church and a despotic state, had joined together to check the individual freedom that had been the fruits of the Renaissance; and to curtail the recognition of the needs of the common man that had first been made by the reformers. What was needed was a force powerful enough to break the bonds of an autocratic authority based largely upon custom and traditions, a force powerful enough to secure for the common man the right to think and act for himself. Such a force was found in rationalism; but in its limitation of the reasoning power to the aristocratic few it failed to realize fully its possibilities. It succeeded in attacking the political theory of absolutism and the arbitrary dogmatism of the contemporary Christian church, but it callously neglected the needs of the peasants and workers. Essentially an aristocratic movement, its results were limited to the attainment of rational freedom for the few.

Actually not a new conception, this questioning of all sanctions other than that of the intellect—an "autonomy of thought"—had proceeded from Stoicism and Cynicism through Cicero and the medieval gadfly, Abelard. Its esssence is that reason alone possesses the capability for discerning all truths, religious and moral as well as mundane; the view that thought can perceive, by its own volition, and without assistance from any supernatural agencies (or sense perception), a system of eternal verity.

Modern rationalism first arose in England. HERBERT OF CHERBURY (1583–1648) began a critical movement directed at revelation, which was later espoused by Locke and Newton and led to the growth of English deism. In Germany CHRISTIAN WOLFF (1679–1754), LESSING, MENDELSSOHN, and REIMARUS shared in rationalistic activities leading to the *Aufklärung,* a northern revival of interest in self-realization, emancipation from prejudice, general education and culture, although BARON GOTTFRIED WILHELM VON LEIBNITZ (1596–1716) is perhaps the best known of the German rationalist philosophers of this period. SPINOZA in the Netherlands accepted pantheism and, somewhat earlier, RENÉ DESCARTES (1596–1650) in France had used reason as a buttress for religious truth in the realm of faith.

In England, while rationalism fostered deism, its influence was largely political. Although Locke never renounced Christianity he did uphold reason as the chief faculty to be developed. In his zeal for the development and use of the individual's mind, he emphasized that rational freedom makes possible a reign of reason, and in this respect he is the first of the rationalists. His views influenced Hume and Berkeley in their philosophical speculations and helped to bring about the growth of English skepticism and deism.

It was in France that the worship of reason reached its zenith. Influenced by Locke's empiricism and the rationalistic philosophy of Descartes, which had glorified the supremacy of reason and provided an exact method of verifying truth and discovering the invariable laws of nature, FRANÇOIS VOLTAIRE (1694–1778) spearheaded the movement at Paris where it received a warm welcome. The rationalistic theory was more completely elaborated by a group of men usually known as the Encyclopedists. The leader was DENIS DIDEROT (1713–1784), editor of the French *Encyclopedia* being written at the time; other prominent members of the group were HELVETIUS, HOLBACH, MONTESQUIEU, TURGOT, CONDILLAC and LA METTRIE. These French rationalists, in their self-assurance and conceit, called themselves *illuminati;* hence the rationalistic movement is often spoken of as the "Enlightenment."

AIMS   The rationalistic aim of education was so to train those capable of reasoning that they could throw off the binding shackles of religious, political, and social authority which restricted their intellectual freedom. The objective was to enable men to think for themselves, to test all things human and divine by the power of their own reason. The ultimate purpose was to free the intellect from all repression. "The rationalists were determined to free the human mind from the control of supernatural terrorism and of traditional beliefs in religion, and to liberate the individual from the legal injustices and political tyranny of the state."[4]

Rationalism aimed at developing an individual who could control all the aspects of his life by means of a coldly critical reason and

---

[4] Stephen P. Duggan, *A Student's Textbook in the History of Education.* (New York: Appleton-Century-Crofts, Inc., 1936.) P. 195. Reprinted with the permission of the publishers.

suppress all spontaneous enthusiasm and feeling. The rationalist realized that this aim was attainable by few individuals; and so it was that the rationalistic philosophy of life and the rationalistic aim in education were applied only to the upper classes. In a sense, rationalism aimed at the education of the young gentleman as much as did disciplinism. It was directed toward teaching the youth to think for himself, to control his passions by reasons, to avoid all display of vulgar feeling, to live the reasonable life of a highly artificial society. It aimed at the intellectual education of the few; so that reason might replace tradition and dogmatism among those who controlled society, and so that the educated classes as a whole might be dominated by reason. The aim of the rationalist was to build up a new aristocracy of intelligence to replace the old aristocracy of family, of position, of the church; a new aristocracy of talent to replace the old aristocracy of blood.

Thus, the aims of Voltaire and the *illuminati* were negative and destructive rather than positive and constructive. While they attempted to prevent dogmatism, tradition, superstition, prejudice, passion, injustice, and privilege of ecclesiastical obscurantism and absolute despotism from adversely affecting the lives of intelligent people they did little to develop this reasoning power, which they praised so highly, to a point where it would become a guide to better living and a means for the solving of the many problems of private and institutional life. The movement partook more of the nature of a religious and political revolt than of a constructive attempt to remove social inequities.

Types   The education resulting from these aims was aristocratic because it was rationalistic. Voltaire and his co-workers were as unapproachable as were the aristocrats of the old régime that they opposed. They did not believe that the masses of men were amenable to reason; they could not accept the idea that the lower classes were capable of being educated. Voltaire himself referred to the common mass of mankind as *canaille,* needing a god and a king to keep them under control.

The Encyclopedists had a similar attitude. They had only an academic interest in the woes of the common man. They had no desire to share with the people their intellectual knowledge and reasoning powers; these advantages of the Enlightenment were only for the *illuminati* themselves—the higher classes endowed with the intelligence they exalted. The rationalists had no use for universal education.

Almost the entire emphasis of rationalistic education was upon intellectual training. Physical, esthetic, and vocational education were neglected.

Social education was recognized as essential; but it was of a formal, stilted, artificial type. Manners, language, and taste were developed and refined to the highest degree; but this so-called culture was heartless and artificial. Cleverness, brilliancy, and wit were glorified. Sparkling conversation, polished manners, and elegant taste were exalted,

Training in manners took the place of moral training. Never were morals at a lower ebb.

CONTENT   The content of rationalistic education consisted of everything that was reasonable, and all that was unreasonable was cast aside. The curriculum included the truth that was to make men free! Philosophical and scientific knowledge was the subject matter of greatest value. The textbooks of rationalism were to be found in the ever increasing tide of political, philosophic, economic, and scientific pamphlets and books—often written in a satirical as well as a critical vein—that were pouring from the printing presses. Scientific and philosophical arguments became the popular rage among the French intelligentsia. Aristocratic ladies discussed the latest theories in their boudoirs and fashionable salons. The knowledge of natural laws discovered by the scientists was supplemented by the knowledge of human laws discovered by the philosophers. Enlightenment replaced old traditions as the content of learning. Superficial though it was, the intellectual subject matter of the Enlightenment was more comprehensive than any since that of the ancient Greeks. Sensual, materialistic, and atheistic though it was, it had universality.

The rationalists' idea of educational content included philosophy, science, art, literature, and social refinement. There was no place for religion or for the actualities of the workaday world. Polished manners, formal artificial etiquette, the codes of self-interest—these were substituted for ethics and true morality. The old moral virtues were replaced by sexual looseness, immodesty, conjugal infidelity, voluptuousness, and extravagance—all adorned, to be sure, by wit and elegance. Manners became an art, and the traditional virtues of morality were looked upon as "unreasonable" and worthy only of cynical contempt. The artificialities of a coldly calculating society made up a large part of the individual's training.

AGENCIES AND ORGANIZATION   The rationalists were not schoolmen; they presented nothing of a constructive type concerning the agencies and organization of education. What they had to say about schools and schoolmasters was largely destructive in character. They criticized every educational institution that hampered freedom of thought, and so the colleges and schools came in for their share of abuse. Since rationalism was opposed to all that was arbitrary and organized, it gave little thought to the building up of educational institutions and organizations. It seemed to imply a sort of self-education through the reading of tracts and pamphlets and through discussions in the fashionable salons. The work of the *illuminati* in compiling their new *Encyclopedia,* embodying all the knowledge of science and philosophy discovered by man up to that time, is an indication of the type of agency the rationalists considered most helpful in the attainment of their ends.

The schools that were used were those secondary and higher schools already developed under the earlier humanistic movements. The dancing master seems to have been the chief agency for the education of the child of the aristocracy, instilling in him the artificialities of the drawing-room society of the time and attempting to convert him into a miniature adult.

METHODS   Since the chief aim of rationalistic education was to develop the reason, the rationalists applied the doctrines of sensationalism and disciplinism in their methodology. Materialistic and sensual in all their views, they believed that man was a machine and that all higher mental processes were the result of the impressions made by objects upon the physical sense organs. Nothing could be known except that which appeared to the senses; therefore all reasoning had to proceed according to the Baconian inductive method. There was no place in their method for revelation, imagination, or feeling. Everything must be approached through critical analysis.

Characteristic of their method was that requirement of applying the cold light of reasoning to every phase of human life and human institution, and cynically rejecting everything that could not stand their test. As a result of their exclusive concern with such a process, they neglected the emotional side of life and scornfully tossed aside all faiths and institutions as enemies of clear and logical thinking. The worship of reason as the sole means of enlightenment was exalted almost to a degree of fanaticism.

FOR FURTHER READING

Browning, Oscar, *A History of Educational Theory*. New York: Harper and Brothers, 1905. Pp. 102-118.

Butts, R. Freeman, *A Cultural History of Western Education* (Second Edition). New York: McGraw-Hill, 1955. Pp. 281-299.

Demiashkevich, Michael, *An Introduction to the Philosophy of Education*. New York: American Book Company, 1935. Pp. 227-288.

Duggan, Stephen P., *Student's Textbook in the History of Education* (Revised Enlarged Edition). New York: Appleton-Century-Crofts, 1936. Pp. 182-198.

Eby, Frederick, and Arrowood, Charles F., *The Development of Modern Education*. New York: Prentice-Hall, 1934. Pp. 386-440.

Good, H. G., *A History of Western Education*. New York: The Macmillan Co., 1960. Pp. 181-189.

Graves, Frank P., *Great Educators of Three Centuries*. New York: The Macmillan Co., 1912. Pp. 52-66.

Hart, Joseph K., *Creative Moments in Education*. New York: Holt, Rinehart and Winston, Inc., 1931. Pp. 246-252.

Mayer, Frederick, *A History of Educational Thought*. Columbus, Ohio: Charles E. Merrill Books, Inc., 1960. Pp. 222-230.

Messenger, James F., *An Interpretative History of Education*. New York: Thomas Y. Crowell Company, 1931. Pp. 156-163.

Monroe, Paul, *A Textbook in the History of Education*. New York: The Macmillan Co., 1933. Pp. 505-529.

Mulhern, James, *A History of Education* (Second Edition). New York: Ronald Press, 1959. *Passim.*

Noble, Stuart G., *A History of American Education*. New York: Holt, Rinehart and Winston, Inc., 1954 (Second Edition). Pp. 339-362.

Painter, Franklin, *Great Pedagogical Essays*. New York: American Book Company, 1905. Pp. 278-290.

————, *A History of Education*. New York: Appleton-Century-Crofts, 1904. Pp. 230-238.

Quick, Robert H., *Educational Reformers*. New York: Appleton-Century-Crofts, 1904. Pp. 219-238.

Ulich, Robert, *A History of Educational Thought*. New York: American Book Company, 1950. Pp. 200-210.

————, *Three Thousand Years of Educational Wisdom*. Cambridge, Mass.: Harvard University Press, 1954. Pp. 347-382.

Wender, Herbert, *The Growth of Modern Thought and Culture*. New York: Philosophical Library, Inc., 1959. Pp. 83-112.

QUESTIONS FOR CLASS DISCUSSION

1. What discoveries by modern educational psychologists have invalidated most of the claims of the disciplinarians?

2. To what extent do you agree with Locke that the mind at birth is a *tabula rasa?*

3. What secondary school subjects are today still usually justified in terms of formal discipline and transfer of training?

4. To what extent does the disciplinary function dominate instruction in American colleges and universities?

5. What elements emphasized in the contemporary study of grammar are results of the disciplinary concept of education?

6. How do present ideas concerning character training differ from those held by John Locke?

7. Do you agree with the rationalists that the masses cannot be allowed to think for themselves but must be taught to follow those who can do their thinking for them? Explain.

8. What have been the effects of excessive intellectualism upon the school curriculum—especially those phases dealing with the practical and fine arts?

9. To what extent is the current emphasis upon the education of the gifted child in accord with the ideas of the *illuminati* of eighteenth century France?

10. In what ways do the intellectuals of today resemble the representatives of the Enlightenment?

11. In what respects have those engaged in physical education abandoned Locke's view of physical training as a process of hardening the body through exercise?

CHAPTER XIII

EDUCATION IN ACCORD WITH NATURE

NATURALISM

The most influential educational movement of the eighteenth century was the development of the doctrine known as naturalism. Later educational theories owe much to this theory, which prevailed extensively toward the close of this fruitful century, not only in educational thinking, but also in economic, political, and social thought. The earnest student of education should give particular attention to it, not only because of its influence upon current educational theory and practice, but also because the concept of natural rights is the basis for our American political and economic structure—especially in its emphasis upon individualism and personal rights.

In a certain sense, naturalism was both an outgrowth and an antecedent. It was, in a way, a continuation of certain aspects of sense realism, and, at the same time, it was a forerunner of the psychological developmentalism of the nineteenth century. Naturalism stands for education in accordance with nature. Nature is a term so general that it is easy to become confused as to its meaning, especially when the term is used in discussions concerning education. To educate according to nature could mean discovery, formulation, and application of natural laws to the educational process. Such an aim was in the minds of the sense realists, though they really did very little in the way of achieving their

aim in actual practice. Bacon, Ratke, and Comenius believed that educators should "diligently observe nature and learn of her"—study her
methods and base their own upon them. Although we do not ordinarily
consider these educational thinkers as naturalists, in their advocacy of
the following of nature they had no peer. Their naturalistic theory
failed because it was based upon a faulty reasoning by analogy.

In the second place, to educate according to nature could mean
education in accord with the natural laws of human development. To
educate an individual, one must understand the nature of his growth.
Both the end and the process of education are to be determined by a
study of the nature of the pupil. This type of naturalistic approach to
education, later designated by G. Stanley Hall as the "paidocentric"
attitude, had been accepted by Plato, Quintilian, Ascham, and Comenius.
Although the idea did not reach its full expression until later—in the
work of the developmentalists—the eighteen century naturalists deserve
the credit for first popularizing the doctrine in the educational world.
(The later developmentalists recognized their debt to them in this
respect.)

In the third place, to educate according to nature can mean a
return to the natural as opposed to all that is artificial. This was the
naturalists' greatest contribution to educational thought, and this is the
sense in which we shall use the term naturalism. The specific target of
the naturalistic movement was the highly affected life of the upper
classes. They attacked especially the training of children in these artificialities. They condemned the repression of the natural spontaneity of
the child, the treatment of children as manikins, the hothouse type of
development—all those artificialities which were the dancing master's
stock-in-trade. They deplored the absence of the simple life of the home
and the prevailing tendency to relegate the care of children to nurses,
governesses, and tutors. Naturalism—as they saw it—meant a return to
the simple life of the peasant home and to the natural rearing of
the young.

Naturalism like rationalism placed its emphasis upon the rights
of the individual and rejected the absolute authority of the state and
the dogmatic authority of the church; but in other respects the two
movements were quite different. As we have already pointed out, the
rationalistic revolt of Voltaire and the Encyclopedists was aristocratic;
it aimed at the setting up of an aristocracy of reason to replace the aristocracy of birth and power. The naturalistic movement on the other
hand, was a revolt not only against the aristocracy of blood but also
against what the naturalists considered the cold and heartless oligarchy
of intellect. Naturalism opposed both autocratic and intellectual preten-
sions. Unlike rationalism, it rejected not only the medieval institutions
of authority, but also all the conventions and artificialities of a cultured
society based upon reason. It desired a return to the simple state ruled
by natural feelings. The rationalist glorified the intellect; the naturalist
worshiped feeling. Since feeling is an element common to all men, the

doctrine of naturalism is essentially democratic. Actually naturalism is not so much a special system as the holding of a point of view or tendency to look upon nature as the origin and basic source of all existence. Thus its adherents seek to explain everything in terms of natural phenomena.

The outstanding champion and exponent of eighteenth century naturalism was JEAN JACQUES ROUSSEAU (1712–1778). Not only did this great French thinker and writer have tremendous influence upon education, but it is difficult to over-emphasize his prodigious influence upon the very course of modern civilization itself. His writings on government, society, religion, and marriage revolutionized the prevailing ideas of his day; his doctrines have profoundly modified our modern political and social life. His great work, *The Social Contract*, formed the basis of modern democratic political theory; his *Profession of Faith of a Savoyard Vicar* influenced the development of a doctrine of religion based on nature and the rejection of the doctrine of innate depravity; *The New Héloise* inaugurated a conception of marriage based upon romantic love and conjugal fidelity. Yet it is his influence upon education with which we are concerned here; and certainly this is not the least of his potent contributions to modern life. His educational views were set forth in *Émile,* published in 1762—one of the greatest and most influential of all educational classics. The book was a sensation even at the time of its first appearance. It attracted the hostile attention of Catholic and Protestant leaders, who regarded it as the most godless and impious book of its day; countless others read it with pleasure and profit, greatly impressed with its doctrines. It is impossible to give here the fascinating details of Rousseau's life; it must be noted, however, that the convictions and ideas of the man were determined to a high degree by the tragic and quixotic events of his controversial career.

Rousseau himself was not a school practitioner; he was a theorist. He never attempted to put into practice any of his own educational theories and principles. In fact, he placed his own children in foundling homes as soon as they were born and gave no further attention to them. Like so many other educational theorists, he probably would have discovered the inconsistencies and weaknesses in his ideas if he had tried them out. Attempts to apply his theories were made by others, who soon discovered that certain modifications had to be made in his proposed program.

The first to put Rousseau's naturalistic doctrines into practice was JOHANN BERNARD BASEDOW (1723–1790), a German schoolmaster who was profoundly affected by the reading of *Émile;* Basedow raised money through writing *An Address to Philanthropists* in 1768 to establish a school, called the *Philanthropinum,* in which he attempted to put the plan into practice. In 1774 as a result of this experience he published *Das Elementarwerk* and *Das Methodenbuch,* in which he set forth his modification of Rousseau's ideas. Both of these books were received with considerable enthusiasm, and together with *Émile* they laid the foundation for the development of naturalism in the schools. Although Basedow's own *Philanthropinum* was short-lived, it stimulated the establishment of other schools that opened the way for further reforms in elementary education.

NATURALISTIC EDUCATION

AIMS   The doctrine of naturalism—as developed by Rousseau—aimed at the preservation of the natural goodness and virtues of the individual, and the formation of a society based upon the recognition of natural individual rights. The ultimate end of education was the attainment of a society in which what Rousseau considered the primitive virtues of equality, fraternity, simplicity, and liberty could be realized by all its members.

"Everything is good as it comes from the hands of the Author of nature; everything degenerates in the hands of man." In these opening words of the first book of *Émile*, one sees the point of view upon which Rousseau's educational aims are based. Education is conceived as a negative process, a matter of *laissez faire*, a hands-off matter. Rousseau aims at warding off the evils of artificial society so that the natural goodness of the child may be free to unfold itself in all its spontaneity. He proposes to give free play to the development of the natural endowments of the child, the cultivation of its own individual nature, its own natural capacities, its own natural inclinations. Since in his estimation the child at birth is naturally good, its instincts, inclinations, and feelings are to be given full and free expression.

It is a mistake to suppose that Rousseau was opposed to social organization; he aimed at the development of a new type of social order. He believed that the traditional organization of society had created artificial inequalities which made it impossible for man to realize his true self. He advocated a return to a social order based upon the state of nature. His objective was to prepare the individual to enter enthusiastically and effectively into all the human relationships of a society adjusted to his natural traits and capacities and one in which he could live to the fullest degree the life of a natural man. Rousseau did not want to abolish the institutions of civilization; he merely wanted to change such institutions as the church, the state, the family, and the school, in order to bring them into harmony with what he considered the fundamental principles of nature; to adapt them to the needs of his natural man. In his social writings, he contended that personal liberty and equality belong to man as a natural right. When men join together in a social state, they do so by mutual contract; they must "find a form of association which will defend and protect with the whole common force the person and goods of every associate, and in which each, while uniting himself with all, may still obey only himself and remain as free as before." Thus he aimed at the development of a society in which all cooperated for protection without any loss of individual liberty.

Yet the educational program set forth by Rousseau in *Émile* was directed toward the education of the upper classes. The poor man, he contended, had no need of education, since he was so close to nature that he was saved from the false and artificial training to which the children of the higher classes were submitted. The very nature of the peasant's life had developed in him all the natural virtues of equality, spontaneity, and unaffectedness. It was the children of the upper classes who had to be protected from the artificialities and insincerities of the society in which they found themselves. Instead of an education to adjust the child to the existing conventions, attitudes, and accomplishments of society, Rousseau proposed to remove the child from all such artificialities and take him into the country, where his natural inclinations could have free rein.

Rousseau's educational aim, therefore, was highly individualistic. He desired an education that would emancipate mankind from the trammels of an artificial society as well as from the restraints of human authority. Education was not a procedure to be imposed from without; it was a process of natural individual development, or growth. The ultimate goal of education was to be the maintenance of a natural stage wherein the rights of the individual, as found in the laws of his own nature, are preserved; wherein the simple tastes and wants of the untutored masses dominate; wherein the natural desires and interests of the individual are not hampered and restrained, freedom is not lost, and the artificial arts and sciences of a polite society are undeveloped and despised.

TYPES Naturalistic education is primarily general rather than specialized. Rousseau was opposed to the education prevalent in his day which aimed at producing workers, citizens, and members of society. He saw that the training of specialized powers and the building up of specialized occupations involved the subjection of certain individuals to others, and the growth of dependence of one upon another. Education, in making a worker or a citizen, made him less a man. Rousseau pleads for a generous and liberal cultivation of all the natural endowments of the child; a development of the whole man instead of a cramping, distorting specialization.

Not only does he consider the direct vocational type of training unnecessary and unwise, but he despises the direct civic type also.

Education by Nature will restore the natural unsophisticated man, whose sole function is to be a man. In the natural order of things, all men being equal, their common vocation is manhood; and whoever is well trained for that, cannot fail to perform any vocation connected with it. Whether my pupil be destined for the army, the church, or the bar, is of small consequence. Regardless of the calling of his family, Nature calls him to human life. To live is the craft I desire to teach him. When he leaves my hands, I admit he will be neither magistrate, soldier, nor priest; he will be, first of all, a man; all that a man may be, he will be able to be, as well as any one.[1]

While it is true that Rousseau advocates everyone learning an industrial trade this is not to be done for a vocational purpose. Émile— though an upper-class boy—learns a trade because this is the best preparation for understanding social relationships, raises him above any danger of parasitism, and overcomes any tendency to despise those who work with their hands. For similar reasons, Basedow recommended handicrafts for all in his *Philanthropinum*. Under naturalism, the pupil is not to be trained for a definite vocation and a definite social position or class. He is to be made adaptable, so that he can adjust himself to the changing fortunes of industrial life and the changing environment of society.

The naturalist stands for a democratic and universal type of education. Rousseau declared that education is the privilege of all free men, one of their natural rights. "Since all children, by the constitution of the state, are equal, they should be educated together and in the same way." Basedow also insisted that rich and poor should be educated jointly.

Naturalism particularly emphasizes the importance of physical education and health training. The aim is to make the child a healthy little animal, and that is accomplished best by letting nature take its course. Rousseau lays down many sensible—though mostly negative— health rules. The young child is not to be swaddled, confined, or rocked, but must be allowed the utmost freedom of limb and voice. Clothing should be loose and comfortable and limited to that which is necessary. The child is to be nursed and tended by its own mother and not by a foster-nurse. It must be exposed to a reasonable amount of cold, heat, and risk, in order that it may be hardened into a robust and courageous individual. Medicines and doctors should be avoided. All restraint on physical freedom should be removed; and the child should be allowed to run, jump, climb, and swim at will, playing naturally in the open country.

Although the need for moral education is recognized, it, too, is to be acquired naturally. Rational moral training is tabooed; ideas of right and wrong are not to be imposed, because the child is unable to understand them. Moral instruction through the use of precepts, through the use of history, fables, and similar devices, is to be avoided because these demand moral judgments of which the child, being unmoral, is incapable. Rousseau advocated a moral training through natural punishment; the natural consequences of a child's acts serving to inhibit those that are unnatural and therefore undesirable, and to cause a repetition of those that are natural and therefore desirable. Moral education is to be a matter of experience rather than of instruction. Basedow likewise

---

[1] J. J. Rousseau, *Émile*, p. 5. Quoted in Thomas Davidson, *Rousseau and Education According to Nature*. (New York: Charles Scribner's Sons, 1898.) Pp. 102-103.

contended that formal moral instruction was of little value, and insisted that all practical instruction was moral in that it led to the natural life.

Intellectual education is limited to the informal training of the senses; the development of sense discrimination; the free expression of the child's ideas; the acquisition of knowledge through natural curiosity and interest; opportunities for training in scientific observation, investigation, and inference. Books are to have little place in education; affected speech and the use of meaningless words are to be carefully avoided.[2]

Religious education is to be postponed until the child is past fifteen. Up to this time he is unaware of any deity, and he is now to learn of divinity through its manifestation in nature. Rousseau advocates a natural rather than a revealed religion. He favors a deistic, naturalistic explanation of life; stresses reverence instead of creeds and dogmas; and insists that every individual should be allowed to develop his own theology. He objects to the teaching of ritualistic forms and ceremonies, which he thinks makes for good sectarianism but does little to develop reverence for God or love for one's neighbors. Religion to the naturalist is a matter of heart rather than head; it is to be felt.

CONTENT   Since Rousseau's program relies chiefly on nature, the task of those in charge of education consists mostly of keeping the traditional subject matter away from the pupil. The content of the curriculum is made up of natural phenomena, presented in the order in which they become manifest to the child. Instead of the conventional habits and ideas of an artificial society, the curriculum consists of the budding activities and interests of the pupil's own nature. The habitual responses and skills of civilization and the body of knowledge and information built up by humanity through the centuries should be consistently avoided. The program of education is to be the natural unfolding of the child's powers to meet his natural needs. The activities which spring naturally from the needs of life make up the curriculum.

In place of the books which played so prominent a part in the traditional curriculum, Rousseau advocated the informal exercises of the senses, of the muscles, and of speech. Rousseau was opposed to the three R's because they dealt with artificial symbols. He had a hatred for books, because, as he said, "they merely teach us to talk of what we do not know," and because they "come between the child and the things of nature." He approved *Robinson Crusoe* as the only desirable textbook because it alone pictures the unfolding of a human being under natural conditions and emphasizes the advantages of simple living. The work of Basedow inspired the writing of the *Swiss Family Robinson,* conceived in the same vein and used for the same purpose, the forerunner of a new type of children's literature to replace the fairy tales and the fables

---

[2] See R. L. Archer (editor), *Rousseau on Education.* (New York: Longmans, Green and Co., 1912.)

which had been used for centuries. Rousseau was also opposed to the study of foreign languages. The boy is to learn to use only his mother tongue, and that in a natural, unaffected manner. Reading, writing, language, literature, history—all these are subjects that he would rigorously avoid.

The educational program of Émile as a young child consisted of sensory and motor activities motivated by his own curiosity. The physical activities of running, jumping, climbing, and swimming were encouraged. Sense discrimination was developed by counting and weighing things, measuring distances, drawing objects, and singing. Speech and drawing were used as means for the free expression of the child's own ideas. Agriculture and carpentry were introduced; the child learned to use the spade, the hoe, the lathe, the hammer, the saw, the plane—in fact, all the tools of the common trades—as a means toward the development of sense perception and practical judgment. Arithmetic and geometry were taught, not as formal studies, but as experiential activities in the natural life of the pupil.

As Émile grew older, intellectual subject matter was brought into his educational program. The phenomena of nature, however, rather than the facts of human relationships were to absorb his attention. Astronomy and geography were studied, not from books but directly from nature. The pupil should make his own apparatus from the study of the natural sciences; and geography was to be learned from the topography of the neighborhood, instead of from the customary maps and globes. The activities of agriculture and of the manual arts and trades were to be continued.

Knowledge of human nature and social institutions was not given to Émile until he reached the age of fifteen. At that time, he began his contact with actual social situations. He visited prisons, workshops, and hospitals, where human beings were grouped. He participated in play groups, where human characteristics were manifested. History, in the form of biography, was introduced as a means of learning how to live with one's fellows. As Émile reached maturity, a careful study of the economic organization, the political aspects, and the social classifications of Europe was made. The abstract and general study of the physical sciences, previously studied concretely, was now taken up. Ancient languages were learned to give a more thorough knowledge of the native tongue; and ancient literatures were now approached, with a glance at the modern literature as well. Philosophy, ethics, and religion were studied to develop the right kind of socially minded conduct and to enable Émile to play his part in bettering society.

Rousseau's conception of the educational curriculum for women is little advanced. Woman is to have no individuality; her duty is to please man; her whole life is supplementary to that of man. She is to be made physically strong in order to bear strong children. She is to be taught singing, dancing, embroidery, and designing in order to please man and be able to contribute to his comfort. She is to receive an early education in morals and religion so that she may provide a good home environment for her family. But she is never to be trained to think for herself.

It was Rousseau's attitude toward religion as a subject in the curriculum that drew down upon him the universal condemnation and opposition of the church—both Catholic and Protestant.

Rousseau believed that in trying to give children an idea of divinity when they are young, teachers give them a conception of God which is "mean, harmful, grotesque, and unworthy." When the youth approaches maturity, he should then—and not until then—be given a religion—a deistic belief which, Rousseau thought, discovers in the constitution of the universe a logical morality and a dynamic impulse to serve his fellows.

Basedow and his followers had very much the same ideas of the content of education as did Rousseau. In the curriculum of the *Philan-thropinum*, the views of Rousseau were everywhere in evidence. The early training of the child was dominated by motion and noise; that is, by activities. Physical exercises and games were employed for physical training and bodily development. Nature study and excursions were used to train the senses. The vernacular language, rather than the classi-cal languages, was the chief instrument of learning; and, when Latin was taught, conversational or natural methods were used. Every child learned a handicraft for educational and social reasons; and arithmetic, geography, physics, and geometry were taught from a practical stand-point.

AGENCIES Under the naturalistic theory of education, those who are to take charge of the child's education act chiefly to pro-tect the child from the dangers of an artificial society. Rousseau said that the father and mother, as the natural tutor and nurse of the child, must "stand guard over him from the moment he comes into the world, take possession of him and not leave him till he is a man." The parents must combine all their efforts to develop his inherent qualities. Rous-seau is to be commended for his admirable insistence on the duty of parents in connection with the education of their children, although he himself did not furnish a very good example.

Although Rousseau glorified the parents as the most effective agency of education, he did not insist that all education be in their hands. Some have claimed that Rousseau was inconsistent in his discus-sion of the agencies of education; that he sometimes advocated education as a family function and at other times as a public function. Probably Rousseau would not have admitted any such contradiction. He favored the agency best suited to achieve his purposes under the conditions in which the pupils he was discussing at the time had to live. In his model state, education would necessarily begin in the family, and would then be taken over by public authorities. In the *Discourse on Political Econ-omy* he advocated a universal system of public education.

Public education, under regulations prescribed by the government, . . . is one of the fundamental rules of popular or legitimate government. If children are brought up in common in the bosom of equality, if they are imbued with the laws of the state and the precepts of the general will; if they are taught to respect these above all things; if they are surrounded by examples and objects which constantly remind them of the tender mother who nourishes them, . . . we cannot doubt they will learn to cherish one another, as brothers.

In his discussion of the function of the family and of the state as agencies of education, Rousseau is concerned with the ideal family and the ideal state; here education is to begin in the family under close supervision and is then to be taken over by public authorities. In *Émile*, Rousseau is confronted with a different situation. Émile is a scion of wealth and aristocracy, and his problem is far removed from that of a child brought up in a natural family or in a state of nature. It is necessary to isolate Émile from his family relationships and the artificial society into which he was born.

Yet even in the case of Émile Rousseau declared that the father is the natural teacher for boys, as the mother is the natural teacher for girls; that Émile would be "better educated by a judicious though ignorant father" than by the most skillful teacher in the world. But Émile is an orphan; and so Rousseau uses another type of educational agency— the tutor—as the imagined practitioner of his educational theories. This model tutor is young, not only in years but in tastes and feelings, and he is above accepting pay for his service. Rousseau expressed his high opinion of the profession of teaching in these words: "There are professions so noble, that no one can pursue them for money without showing that he is unworthy to pursue them."

The tutor must be willing to remain loyal to his task and remain with his pupil for twenty-five years, for any change of tutors would affect the education of the pupil. The tutor chooses for his ward a nurse who is willing to remain with the child as long as it needs a nurse. The tutor and the nurse must be in complete accord, and both must follow the laws of nature. "The child at birth is already the pupil not of the tutor, but of Nature. The tutor merely understudies this first teacher and prevents her efforts from being balked."

Although Rousseau had little to say about the education of teachers, Basedow placed strong emphasis upon training teachers in the methods of naturalism; and teachers from the *Philanthropinum* at Dessau ultimately were distributed over all Germany, proving effective agents in the promulgation of the naturalistic aims and methods.

It must be remembered, however, that whether the naturalist accepts as agencies of education the parents or tutor in the home on the one hand, or teachers in private or public schools on the other, the one great agency and authority of education is nature. Under this philosophy, nature is supreme; all other agencies are merely instruments for the carrying out of her purposes and program.

ORGANIZATION   Naturalism entails a careful and systematic organization of educational procedures. Although Rousseau was not a schoolman and was therefore not concerned with the organization of a school system, he outlined a thorough gradation of education into definite periods or stages. He rejected the traditional attitude that education must be a procedure uniform in character throughout its course; that the child should be treated throughout his training just as an adult would be. He firmly believed that the development of the pupil proceeds through sharply defined periods having little connection with each other, and that the education of the child is to be determined by these various stages of development. Each of these stages has its own characteristic and dominant trait; this becomes the dominating factor in organizing the learning of that period.

Rousseau was the first to develop the recapitulation theory as the basis for educational organization. He believed that the child, in his progress from birth to maturity, lives over again the epochs through which the race passed in its progress from savagery to civilization—that "ontogeny repeats phylogeny." The child begins as an animal, then partly civilized, then a solitary Robinson Crusoe, then a rational thinking being, and finally a social being. Rousseau was also the first to advance the saltatory theory of development—that certain faculties arise with a leap at certain stages of the child's development. Education at each stage must be adapted to these newly awakened characteristics and functions.

The education of Émile was organized into four stages, and each of the first four books of Rousseau's great classic is devoted to one of these periods: (1) Infancy, (2) Childhood, (3) Boyhood, (4) Adolescence. The first period lasts from birth to five years; and during this period the infant is in a state of nature, an animal with few needs, with actions mechanical, with no power to reason, with feelings dominant but simple. The second period lasts from five to twelve years; and during this period the child is in a stage of savagery, says Rousseau, nonmoral and nonsocial, with needs still few, and feelings active and dominant. The third period lasts from twelve to fifteen years; and during this period the boy is in a Robinson Crusoe state of solitude, still nonmoral and nonsocial, with feelings less dominant, with reason and judgment emerging, with curiosity driving him to seek the meaning of things. The last period is from fifteen to twenty years; and during this epoch the adolescent becomes a social being, unable to satisfy his wants by himself, with sex life emerging and resulting in marriage, with abstraction arising, with imagination and reason developing. For each of these stages, Rousseau proposed a special curriculum and a distinct methodology.

METHODS   The supreme contribution of naturalism to educational method lies in its emphasis upon making the child the center of the process. The study of the nature of the child is to be the determining factor in all educational procedures. "Observe nature and follow the route which she traces for you"—this is Rousseau's slogan. In his insistence upon observing and obeying the laws of nature in all instructional methodology, he followed the lead proposed by the sense realists.

The child's nature and the child's growth are to determine the processes and techniques of teaching. Nature to Rousseau means the native instincts and predispositions of the child as opposed to those habits and conventions acquired through drill and social contacts. He demanded an educational process which would consist of the unhampered and unrestrained growth of the native powers and capacities of the pupil. Nature rather than nurture was his keynote. All the conscious processes of instruction were to be based upon a study of the native equipment, the instincts and interests, and the resulting natural expressions and activities of the child.

Rousseau firmly established three modern principles of teaching: (1) the principle of growth, (2) the principle of pupil-activity, (3) the principle of individualization—the fundamental laws that lay at the heart of the reforms of Pestalozzi, Herbart, Froebel, and other developmentalists.

It is easy to misunderstand and misjudge Rousseau. Many have insisted that he advocated a "soft" pedagogy, and certain of his followers have adopted easy-going methods of allowing the pupil to do exactly as he pleases. Some of Rousseau's statements seem to give support to this interpretation. Émile does not follow any set program; he is subjected to no regimen and no arbitrary commands; he is relieved of the harsh yoke of the conventional system of education. But Rousseau, in advocating the overthrow of the rigorous rule of the pedagogical martinet, does not go to the other extreme of a *laissez-faire* policy in education. He merely substitutes the commands and necessities of nature for the demands and compulsions of what he calls an artificial society. The driving powers of human development are the natural needs of life; the human faculties are developed through functioning, to supply these needs. The order of nature is: (1) need, (2) activity, (3) experience, (4) knowledge. The process of education should follow the same order. The work of the teacher is not to drive, but merely to guide learning in such a way that it follows the natural order.

Nothing must be done for the pupil that he can do for himself—this is the great principle of pupil-activity. The child is educated through his own activity. Not what the teacher does, but what the pupil does is the important factor. Rousseau said, "Do not give your pupil any sort of verbal lesson, for he is to be taught only by experience."[3] Again he said, "Without doubt we derive much clearer and more accurate notions of things which we learn for ourselves than of that we gain from the instruction of others." A basic principle of the naturalistic method, there-

---

[3] An excellent interpretation of the *Émile* is to be found in Gabriel Compayré, *The History of Pedagogy*. Translated and edited by W. H. Payne. (Boston: D. C. Heath and Company, 1889.) Pp. 278-310.

fore, is that nothing should be learned on the authority of others. Rousseau placed Émile in such circumstances that he was obliged to rely upon himself to an ever-increasing degree, to form his own thoughts and to reach his own conclusions; he is told nothing that he can discover for himself. He must construct his own apparatus for learning: he must make his own charts, maps, and globes, his own apparatus for the study of scientific and philosophical phenomena.

Another basic principle of Rousseau's was that each child be allowed to develop according to his own nature. The interests and needs of the individual must be placed above those of society; individuality must not be sacrificed for social stability. The child's individuality is not to be crushed by forcing him into the mold of social conformity. Man is not to be fitted for his station in life; his station is to be fitted to him. In the same way, the child is not to be adjusted to his education, but his education is to be adjusted to his needs.

Naturalism placed the authority of the school upon an entirely new foundation. Rousseau's attitude toward traditional methods of discipline is expressed in these words: "Discipline, the restraining or curbing of the natural impulses, is what confuses, degrades, and blasts human nature." Instead of attempting to control the conduct of the pupil through scolding or whipping on the one hand, or through praise and reward on the other, Rousseau merely permitted the pupil to suffer the natural results of his own acts. This doctrine of natural punishment has been discussed widely in connection with school discipline, and its advantages and disadvantages have been ably presented. It has been recognized that such a procedure removes the human element in the problem of discipline, and the child feels no resentment to the teacher or parent. Furthermore, when the child is old enough to reason, the recognition of the law of cause and effect is indeed valuable. On the other hand, there are many objections to natural punishment: it is sometimes too severe and sometimes not severe enough; it applies in varying degrees to different individuals; the "just are often punished with the unjust"; it often punishes others more than the child; finally, it may result in the development of a morality of mere prudence—a negative rather than a positive morality. This lack of an absolute standard is only one of the many dilemmas associated with naturalism.

Furthermore, the idea of education as merely affording opportunities for natural reaction and natural growth is not one that can be held by a person who realizes the complexities of modern life. Perhaps it would be theoretically desirable—as some claim—to return to a simpler and more natural way of life, under which instinctive impulses and reactions would regain their original usefulness; but this is practically impossible without bringing about great disaster. We cannot afford to go backward; we must go forward. We are committed to the complexities of modern civilization, and it is therefore necessary for us to adjust the child to its artificialities.

If the preservation of civilization is considered desirable, we must

train children in ways not natural to them. Self-direction and self-control
and originality are not possible to children unless they are developed
through carefully controlled education. Complete freedom does not train
an individual in the inhibition of natural but undesirable responses—a
training which is essential if the individual is to play his part in a cooperative endeavor toward the improvement of human society; and that—
it seems—was Rousseau's ultimate objective after all.

FOR FURTHER READING

Adams, John, *Evolution of Educational Theory*. London: Macmillan
and Co., Ltd., 1912. Pp. 250-282.

Archer, R. L. (editor), *Rousseau on Education*. New York: Longmans,
Green and Co., 1912.

Browning, Oscar, *History of Educational Theory*. New York: Harper and
Brothers, 1905. Pp. 135-150.

Butts, R. Freeman, *A Cultural History of Western Education* (Second
Edition). New York: McGraw-Hill, 1955. Pp. 290-291.

Cubberley, Ellwood P., *The History of Education*. Boston: Houghton
Mifflin Company, 1920. Pp. 530-538.

Duggan, Stephen P., *Student's Textbook in the History of Education*
(Revised Enlarged Edition), New York: D. Appleton-Century Company,
1936. Pp. 203-219.

Eby, Frederick, and Arrowood, Charles F., *The Development of Modern
Education*. New York: Prentice-Hall, Inc., 1934.

Good, H. G., *A History of Western Education*. New York: The Macmillan Co., 1960. Pp. 201-224.

Graves, Frank P., *Great Educators of Three Centuries*. New York: The
Macmillan Company, 1912. Pp. 77-121.

Hart, Joseph K., *Creative Moments in Education*. New York: Holt, Rinehart, and Winston, Inc., 1931. Pp. 252-261.

Knight, Edgar W., *Twenty Centuries of Education*. Boston: Ginn & Co.,
1940. Pp. 347-356.

Mayer, Frederick, *A History of Educational Thought*. Columbus, Ohio:
Charles E. Merrill Books, Inc., 1960. Pp. 231-244.

Messenger, James F., *An Interpretative History of Education*. New York:
Thomas Y. Crowell Company, 1931. Pp. 164-181.

Monroe, Paul, *A Textbook in the History of Education*. New York: The
Macmillan Co., 1933. Pp. 533-585.

Mulhern, James, *A History of Education* (Second Edition). New York:
Ronald Press, 1959. Pp. 411-422.

Parker, Samuel C., *History of Modern Elementary Education*. Boston:
Ginn & Co., 1912. Pp. 161-206.

Painter, Franklin, *Great Pedagogical Essays*. New York: American Book Company, 1905. Pp. 321-350.

Reisner, Edward H., *The Evolution of the Common School*. New York: The Macmillan Co., 1930. Pp. 151-178.

Quick, Robert Herbert, *Educational Reformers*. New York: D. Appleton-Century Company, 1904. Pp. 239-289.

Ulich, Robert, *A History of Educational Thought*. New York: American Book Company, 1950. Pp. 211-224.

————, *Three Thousand Years of Educational Wisdom*. Cambridge, Mass.: Harvard University Press, 1954. Pp. 383-425.

QUESTIONS FOR CLASS DISCUSSION

1. What has been Rousseau's outstanding contribution to modern education? Which of his ideas concerning education have been the least accepted?
2. What ideas of Rousseau concerning the nature of the child have been exploded by the findings of contemporary psychology?
3. Do you believe that present-day education depends more upon nature or upon nurture? Explain.
4. To what extent has Rousseau's suggestion that moral and religious education be postponed until the period of adolescence been followed?
5. Are Rousseau's ideas concerning the natural woman still current? Do modern coeducational schools and women's colleges buttress his belief?
6. In what respect is modern progressive education an expression of the doctrine of naturalism? To what extent do progressive educators follow the teachings of Rousseau?
7. Are school books today better than those which Rousseau viewed with such bitter aversion? In what ways better or poorer?
8. To what extent, and by what methods, do some modern educators attempt to provide the child with a more natural environment?
9. Do you believe that we should make greater use of the method of "natural punishment" in contemporary education? What dangers might follow if the "discipline of natural consequences" were adopted?
10. What features of the *Philanthropinum* were adopted by progressive education as it developed in the United States?

CHAPTER XIV

TRAINING FOR PATRIOTIC CITIZENSHIP

NATIONALISM

During the nineteenth century, both in Europe and in the United States, two educational theories were prevalent and exceedingly influential. The first of these was the nationalistic theory, which we are about to consider; the second was the theory of developmentalism, which will be taken up in the chapter immediately following. The influence of nationalism was felt equally in the external and internal organization of the educational system; the developmental influence was concerned mainly with the internal conditions of the schools.

The principle of nationalism has been one of the most powerful influences upon education in the entire evolution of educational thought. It was nationalism that stimulated the development of the state-controlled and state-supported public school systems that are to be found everywhere today throughout the world. Wherever there has been the growth of a strong nationalistic spirit, there "schools and the means of education" have been encouraged and utilized as powerful agencies for the preservation and honor of the nation. Monarchies and democracies alike have come to accept the establishment and maintenance of public schools as an essential national policy. Nationalization of education has taken place under both the totalitarian and republican forms of government. Under the one, education has been forwarded in order to produce obedient, contented, and efficient subjects; under the other, education has been fostered in order to equip its citizens with the knowledge necessary for the perpetuation of free representative government.

The nineteenth century was the period in which clear-cut and reasonably effective national systems of education were first built up but nationalism had been the guiding spirit in the political development of Europe for several centuries before. In fact, the foundations of nationalism may be said to lie in ancient civilizations. This growing spirit, which eventually flowered into national school systems, had an interesting evolution and was the result of several different influences. Early Egypt developed under the joint authority of religion and the crown; Pharaoh himself was considered divine and an object of national worship. In ancient Persia and Sparta, military authority was dominant, and national patriotism was the supreme virtue. Civic responsibilities and virtues reached their peak in ancient Athens and Rome; patriotism and loyalty to the state took the place of religion in the minds and hearts of men. The Jewish people are an interesting variant; nationalism and religion were one and the same with them; obedience to the commandments of God was the supreme obligation of patriotic citizenship. In the later Graeco-Roman period, the Empire was preeminently a secular organ and loyalty to the emperor and patriotic service to the state were the virtues most desired. Throughout antiquity, group loyalty was always a strong factor in survival and progress, and treason was considered a most serious offense.

During medieval times secular power was weakened, and the power of the priestly class rose again; this time in the name of Christendom. With few exceptions, kings and princes were subordinate to the commands of Rome. Religious authority was much stronger than any civil authority. Feudal lords, though maintaining some power over their retainers in temporal matters, were themselves under the authority of the pope in all matters of great importance. Despite local wars and struggles between rival nobles, the European world had achieved under medievalism a greater degree of internationalism than at any other period of history.

With the revival of commerce and the rise of cities in the eleventh and twelfth centuries, ambitious kings were able to establish their authority over the petty feudal lords. With the growing questioning of ecclesiastical authority, these kings were able to challenge the power of the church. In consequence of the Protestant revolts, the great power which the papacy had held over the secular activities of men during the Middle Ages was fragmented. By the sixteenth century, kings of national states were able to establish the superior strength of the nationalistic form of government over the claims of the international church-state. The seventeenth and eighteenth centuries saw the national state, with its compact area and its economic and military resources, the dominant form of organization in Europe.

In more recent times many influences have fanned this spirit of nationalism. Population pressure has been one of the most effective. The growing economic problem of finding food, clothing, and shelter for the enormously increased population of nations has brought into existence an industrial and commercial conflict which has intensified the earlier national jealousies and animosities. New areas of overpopulated nations have often been obtained only at the expense of the enmity of rival nations or by the dispossessing and exploitation of the original inhabitants. The great developments of commerce and industry through the application of modern science have furthered the interests of nationalism. Interchange of raw materials and world markets for finished goods have intensified the economic rivalries of large nations and the exploitation of weaker ones. The traditional economic theory has recognized the nation as the basic unit in an economic policy of manufacturing raw materials at home and selling finished products abroad in order to maintain a favorable balance of trade. In these tendencies toward expansion and nationalistic rivalry lie a great many of the causes of the wars that have kept the world in a state of nervous tension throughout most of the twentieth century.

Economic rivalries added to ideological enmities make the condition of any nation precarious. Military preparedness is not a sufficient guarantee of security. It is not surprising that in all nations schools have been used to stimulate loyalty to the nation and to prevent defection from its aims and ideals. Public education early came to be recognized as one of the most effective agencies of national defense. Even some of the benevolent despots of the eighteenth century realized that the economic and military prosperity of a nation depended, in the long run, upon the welfare and understanding of the common people, and attempted to improve their educational system.

In the nineteenth century, nationalism became the dominant note in education, and countries began the establishment of systems of schools to help achieve their national aspirations. It will suffice for our purpose to take three nations as typical of this movement—France, Germany, and the United States. These were the nations that first responded to this tendency, and the other states have duplicated their procedures. The great exponents of nationalism in education have been citizens of one or the other of these nations, but the influence of these leaders has been felt in countries other than their own. LA CHALOTAIS, ROLAND, DIDEROT, and CONDORCET, in France; FRANCKE, HECKER, and FICHTE, in Germany; JEFFERSON, MANN, and BARNARD, in the United States—these men stand out as advocates of nationalistic conceptions of education.

Nationalistic conceptions of education were influenced by earlier educational, political, and social theories. The naturalism of Rousseau had given rise to a deeper recognition of the rights of the individual man and of the significance of human personality. The rationalism of the Encyclopedists and the physiocrats had weakened the authority of the church and had developed a new idea of the function of the sovereign:

that of an intelligent and benevolent ruler who existed for the benefit of his people instead of forcing the people to exist for his benefit. The pietism and philanthropism of Francke and other German philosophers had developed a realization that the greatness of a nation depended upon a happy, contented people. These theoretical considerations, as well as the more practical considerations obvious to intelligent rulers, led to the widespread acceptance of this doctrine of national education.

NATIONALISTIC EDUCATION

AIMS   The objective of nationalism, in its ultimate analysis, is the preservation and glorification of the state. The state is usually conceived as a society organized for the primary purpose of protecting those who make up this society from the dangers of external attack and internal disintegration. Government is the instrument set up by the state to carry out this function. The nationalist looks upon education as an effective agency for assisting in the performance of this governmental function. The maintenance of education is looked upon as a patriotic duty. Education is used to develop military aggressiveness and preparedness, to develop national wealth and economic independence, to develop national unity through common ideals and traditions. Nationalism recognizes that education is an instrument which the state can use to maintain itself and to progress toward its national ideals. Nationalism believes that the state must depend upon education if it wishes securely to safeguard itself against disintegration. There is little questioning of the efficiency of a national policy of education in promoting national ends.

FRENCH NATIONALISM

Although not necessarily the first country in which the alliance between nationalism and education is observable, France offers an excellent example of the concentrated power of such a union. Here the conception of education for national ends arose as a defense reaction on the part of a threatened people. Following the great French Revolution, which began in 1789—the same year the United States constitution went into effect—the people of France were called upon to defend their newly won freedom against a combination of foreign powers. The kings of Europe saw in the French Revolution a threat to their own power, and hurled armies against France in order to restore the old system. As a result of this attack upon their liberties, a strong patriotism was born among the masses of the French people. The leaders of the Revolution, realizing the need of keeping the patriotic impulses alive, recognized the desirability of establishing a state system of education through which the people might be informed of the advantages of the new system of government and instructed in their rights and privileges under the new social order. They saw clearly that, in the education of the children, the Revolutionary government had an effective agency of social control and a guarantee of stability and permanence.

While successive regimes of the French Revolution did not succeed in establishing a workable system of state education, the various reports that were made to the assemblies, the bills that were introduced, and the laws that were passed set forth the aims and purposes that were to dominate national school systems during the entire nineteenth century. Although little was actually accomplished, the Revolutionary Convention gave much attention to the possibility of establishing a national system of lay education. The numerous Jesuit colleges had been suppressed in 1764, and in 1792 the National Convention had confiscated the church schools of other religious orders. Such actions left the French people virtually without schools. From 1763 down to the close of the century, such educational reformers as La Chalotais, Roland, Diderot, and Condorcet, and such political leaders as Talleyrand and Mirabeau formulated and presented plans for systems of national schools to replace the suppressed teaching orders of the church. These aimed at the centralization of all learning under public control for the sake of improving the state and maintaining the government. La Chalotais in his *Essay on National Education* (1763), Roland in his *Report on Education to the Parliament of Paris* (1768), Diderot in his *Provision on Education* (1791), recommended new educational systems dedicated to the purposes of national solidarity and to the service of the state. La Chalotais was especially influential in shaping subsequent political theory and prompting action regarding this relationship of education to the state. He believed that education was essentially a civil affair; that the real purpose of education was to prepare loyal citizens of France; that the government should make citizens efficient as well as content by educating them for their sphere in life. Roland said: "Education cannot be too widely diffused, to the end that there may be no class of citizens who may not be brought to participate in its benefits. It is expedient that each citizen receive the education which is adapted to his needs."

Condorcet's *Report on Behalf of the Committee on Public Instruction* (1792) proposed an educational system through which "each individual is to be taught to direct his own conduct and to enjoy the plenitude of his own rights and to insure the perpetuation of liberty and equality."

In the philosophy of these French liberalists, the objectives of education were completely and radically changed from what had been accepted in earlier centuries. Education was understood as aiming at civic virtues rather than the traditional religious and humanistic virtues.

These dauntless thinkers believed and asserted that instruction was a civil affair—aiming at the development of a national spirit, the ability to guard one's own rights, and the proficiency to serve the state in civil offices.

PRUSSIAN NATIONALISM

Yet the French Revolutionary assemblies contributed more to the objectives of nationalistic education than they did toward actual accomplishments. It remained for Prussia to implement the first embodiment of the nationalistic concept of education in a comprehensive state system of schools. Here again the recognition of the nationalistic function of education came in a time of crisis.

It was even easier for the nationalistic concept to flower in the Protestant states of Germany. From the time of the Protestant revolts, the church and its religiously motivated schools had received encouragement and support from the civil rulers. Although these rulers of the German states during the seventeenth and eighteenth centuries did not recognize the possibilities of the schools in the development of patriotic loyal citizenship, they did feel that it was part of their duty as benevolent despots to maintain schools for the teaching of literacy and religious faith, as a phase of the internal improvement of their realm. In 1642, near the close of the Thirty Years' War, DUKE ERNST of Saxe-Coburg-Gotha had issued his remarkable *Schulmethodus,* a program of school reform which aimed at the restoration of universal training in the "four R's" under church supervision, but by the authority of the state.

In Prussia particularly, the rulers had exhibited considerable interest in educational affairs, and the state had long exercised authority over the establishment of schools and had shown itself interested in their maintenance and improvement. As early as 1717, FREDERICK WILLIAM I (1713–1740) had issued decrees requiring compulsory school attendance and prescribing conditions for the building of schoolhouses, the support of teachers, the payment of tuition and fees, and administrative aid. FREDERICK THE GREAT (1740–1786), believing that the child belonged to the state and not to the home, laid the real foundation for a Prussian state system of public elementary education. Frederick, who is known as one of the most tolerant and humane of the eighteenth century European despots issued in 1763 the epochal *General Land-Schule Reglement* (General Regulations for Village Schools) as a part of his policy of internal improvement. These regulations aimed at securing "an education both scientific and Christian in true fear of God and in other useful things . . . to the end that ignorance so dangerous and unbecoming to Christianity may be prevented and remedied." These ordinances provided for the compulsory attendance of children, the maintenance of a full school term, the training and compensation of teachers, and the curriculum and methods of instruction.

Although these rulers of eighteenth century Prussia accepted the principles of FRANCKE and HECKER that it was the obligation of the state to foster and maintain schools, the aim was largely that of religious moralism, and the actual supervision of the schools was still left to the church leaders and the local pastors. Nationalism as the principal function of education did not dominate the schools of Prussia until after the defeat of the Germans by Napoleon at Jena, in 1806. Yet it is true that, as early as 1794, the twelfth chapter of the *General Civil Code,* drawn up by the Commission of eminent jurists appointed by Frederick the Great to codify the Prussian law, asserted the supremacy of the state over all education in these words: "Schools and universities are state institutions, charged with the instruction of youth in useful information and scientific knowledge. Such institutions may be established only with the knowledge and approval of the state. All public schools and educational institutions are under the supervision of the state and are at all times subject to its examination and inspection."

Nevertheless, Frederick's successor, Frederick William II, continued to appoint clergymen to the positions of educational leadership and supervision; the schools were secularized without eliminating the religious aim.

The crushing defeat administered by Napoleon revealed to Prussia the inadequacy of its social and economic order, the corruption of its government, the selfishness of its nobility, and the indifference of its oppressed common people. With the nation prostrated, Frederick William III inaugurated a series of reforms to bring the nation back to new life and vigor. In this effort he was assisted by liberal and able advisers, infused with the principle of nationalism. Among these no one was more influential than JOHANN GOTTLIEB FICHTE (1762–1814), a philosopher who saw education as the most effective of all national regenerative forces. In 1807–1808 he delivered a series of fourteen *Addresses to the German Nation,* in which he set forth the following ideas:

Individualism and self-seeking among the citizens and classes of Germany were the cause of her defeat and humiliation. Only when the individuals of the country are drawn together in common loyalty and service to a social organism can they discover the true meaning of their existence. For all Germans, the society in which each person has to find his larger self, and to which he owes full loyalty and love, is the German nation which has been placed on earth as a part of the divine plan and has a destiny to fulfill. The only way in which the individual can realize his complete selfhood is through identifying himself with the nation by serving and improving it. The subordination of self to society is to be accomplished through love of the fatherland. In order that all may be made to realize this sentiment, schools must be established in which children can be separated from the reigning social habit of self-seeking and be nurtured in the atmosphere of social service and co-operation. If Germany is to be saved, the nation must be taken as the unit of social organization, Germany must realize its character and destiny, and through a conscious control of education, it must liberate all its potentialities—moral, intellectual, physical, vocational—for national service, that exists within the children of all its people.[1]

In these words Fichte brought to Germany the conception of nationalism as the dominant aim of education and the conception of the school's function as that of building up and preserving the national welfare. To carry out this aim, during the quarter of a century following the Treaty of Tilsit, a series of laws was passed establishing a thoroughly efficient national system of education headed by a national Department of Public Instruction, with WILHELM VON HUMBOLDT (1767–1835) as its first head. In a General Order issued by one of Humboldt's successors, BARON VON ALTENSTEIN, we find an excellent statement of the nationalistic aim that was to dominate Prussian education for almost a century and a half:

And, to sum up all very briefly, [that the people] may know how to serve and wish to serve God, the king, the fatherland, and themselves, with strong, skillful bodies, awakened intelligence, and good conscience.

Another illuminating statement of the aim of Prussian education is found in a *Sketch of a General Education Law for Prussia,* prepared in 1819:

Loyalty to king and nation and unqualified obedience to the laws and legal ordinances are essential aspects of moral character. It is thereby declared that to awaken and strengthen these qualities in the youth and through all the means at the command of the school to work toward that condition when every school will be a nursery of blameless patriotism, is made the most sacred duty of all schoolmasters and mistresses.

AMERICAN NATIONALISM

A nationalistic concept of education has prevailed in the United States almost from the beginning of its history as a nation. Throughout the Colonial period there was only one real motive for the maintenance of schools—the religious idea, which sprang largely from the Reformation and counter-Reformation. With the demand for independence, which began about 1750 and ultimately resulted in the American Revolution and the Declaration of Independence, this religious motive began to wane. It required a half-century of battle before the ecclesiastical grip on the schools was broken and real public schools were created; but the theories upon which our public school system was ultimately erected

---

[1] Abstract of Fichte's *Addresses* by Edward H. Reisner, in the *Evolution of the Common School.* (New York: The Macmillan Co., 1930.) Pp. 218-219. Reprinted with the permission of the publishers.

were inherent in the political philosophy held by the fathers of our Republic and expressed in the Declaration of Independence and the Constitution of the United States. In this new nation, to be controlled for the people and by the people, education was to be considered an absolute necessity. A new motive was given to American education: the individual must be educated not only to save his soul but to save his country. If the people were to rule, they must be taught how to rule. In the words of Noah Webster, "to continue the form of education that had largely prevailed while the States had been colonies . . . was to miss the spirit of the Declaration of Independence." [2]

The leaders of the American Revolution held a philosophy of government derived largely from the teachings of the French. They believed that "all men are created equal"; that "they are endowed by their creator with certain inalienable rights"; that "to secure these rights Governments are instituted everywhere, deriving their just power from the consent of the governed." They believed that human life is capable of great improvement, and that government exists to effect this improvement. They believed that man had natural rights, such as "life, liberty, and the pursuit of happiness," and that such a government should be set up as would assure to the people the enjoyment of these rights. They agreed that education was a principal means by which a government could be assured that would secure these rights to the people and protect the general welfare of all the people. Two diverse conceptions of the relationship of government to education were possible—growing out of the conflicting political theories prevalent at the time. The Federalists, who believed that government should be highly centralized in a strong federal system, would insist that the federal government prepare its citizenship through a strong national educational system. Jeffersonians, who held that individuals and communities should manage their own affairs, would urge that education satisfy local needs, instead of being administered by the central government in a single system of national ideas.

When the Federal Constitution was adopted in 1788, education on a national basis had not yet been achieved in any European country. Moreover, weighty matters of state had to be cared for, and many problems had to be left for future consideration. One of these concerns was that of education, no mention of which occurs in our Constitution. It was not until the Tenth Amendment to the Constitution, providing that "powers not delegated to the United States by the Constitution, nor prohibited by it to the States, are reserved to the States respectively, or to the people," was ratified in 1791 that the status of education in the United States was clarified. Under the provision of this amendment, education remained a function of each state rather than that of the federal government and the control of the schools belonged (as one of the unmentioned reserved powers) to the people of the states to handle as they

---

[2] Quoted from Webster's *Essays, 1790*, p. 24. In Oscar Allen Hansen, *Liberalism and American Education*. (New York: The Macmillan Co., 1926.) P. 235.

saw fit. It was expected that each commonwealth would adopt the system best adapted to the needs of its citizens.

Such a dedication to general literacy is revealed in the phrases of the Ordinance of 1787 (cited in Chapter X) which—in the same year that the Constitution was written—provided the formula for the organization and government of the territory north of the Ohio and east of the Mississippi. It emphasized the need for "religion, morality, and knowledge," and encouraged "schools and the means of instruction."

And very early in our history, outstanding leaders of state and nation revealed their acceptance of the nationalistic conception of education. Again and again they expressed their belief in citizenship as the new motive for education. The following early American leaders all give voice to the theory that preparation for civic responsibilities is the primary aim of education.

THOMAS JEFFERSON, in a letter to James Madison, in 1787:
Above all things, I hope that education of the common people will be attended to; convinced that on this good sense we may rely with the most security for the preservation of a due degree of liberty.

GEORGE WASHINGTON, in his First Message to Congress, 1790:
Knowledge in every country is the surest basis of public happiness. In one in which the measures of government receive their impressions so immediately from the sense of the community as in ours, it is proportionally essential.

JOHN HANCOCK, as Governor of Massachusetts, in 1793:
Amongst the means by which our government has been raised to its present height of prosperity, that of education has been the most efficient; you will therefore encourage and support our Colleges and Academies; but more watchfully the Grammar and other town schools. Should the support of such institutions be neglected, the kind of education which a free government requires to maintain its force would be very soon forgotten.

GEORGE WASHINGTON, in his Farewell Address, 1796:
Promote then, as an object of primary importance, institutions for the general diffusion of knowledge. In proportion as the structure of government gives force to public opinion, it is essential that public opinion be enlightened.

JOHN JAY, in a letter to Dr. Benjamin Rush:
I consider knowledge to be the soul of a Republic; and as the weak and the wicked are generally in alliance, as much care should be taken to diminish the number of the former as of the latter. Education is the way to do this, and nothing should be left undone to afford all ranks of people the means of obtaining the proper degree of it at a cheap and easy rate.

THOMAS JEFFERSON, to Colonel Yancey, in 1816:
If a nation expects to be ignorant and free in a state of civilization, it expects what never was and never will be. There is no safe deposit for the

functions of government but with the people themselves; nor can they be safe with them without information.

JAMES MADISON, as President of the United States:

A popular government without popular information, or the means of acquiring it, is but a prologue to a farce or a tragedy, or, perhaps, both. Knowledge will forever govern ignorance; and a people who mean to be their own governors must arm themselves with the power which knowledge gives.

DANIEL WEBSTER, at Plymouth, Massachusetts, in 1822:

We do not, indeed, expect all men to be philosophers and statesmen; but we confidently trust, and our expectations of the duration of our government rest on that trust, that by the diffusion of general knowledge and good and virtuous sentiments, the political fabric may be secure, as well against open violence and overthrow, as against the slow but sure undermining of licentiousness.

DEWITT CLINTON, as Governor of New York, in 1826:

The first duty of government, and the surest evidence of good government, is the encouragement of education. A general diffusion of knowledge is a precursor and protector of republican institutions, and in it we must confide as the conservative power that will watch over our liberties and guard them against fraud, intrigue, corruption, and violence. I consider the system of our common schools the palladium of our freedom, for no reasonable apprehension can be entertained of its subversion as long as the great body of the people are enlightened by education.

ABRAHAM LINCOLN, in a letter to the *Sangamon Journal,* 1832:

Upon the subject of education, not presuming to dictate any plan or system respecting it, I can only say that I view it as the most important subject which we as a people can be engaged in. That every man may receive at least a moderate education, and thereby be enabled to read the histories of his own and other countries, by which he may duly appreciate the value of our free institutions, appears to be an object of vital importance.

THADDEUS STEVENS, to the Legislature of Pennsylvania, 1835:

If an elective republic is to endure for any length of time, every elector must have sufficient information, not only to accumulate wealth and to take care of his pecuniary concerns, but to wisely direct the Legislatures, the Ambassadors, and the Executives of the Nation; for some part of all these things, some agency in approving or disapproving of them, falls to every freeman. If, then, the permanency of our government depends on such knowledge, it is the duty of government to see that the means of information be diffused to every citizen. This is a sufficient answer to those who deem education a private and not a public duty.

DANIEL WEBSTER, at Madison, Indiana, in 1838:

On the diffusion of education among the people rests the preservation and perpetuation of our free institutions. I apprehend no danger to the country from a foreign foe. . . . Our destruction, should it come at all, will be from another quarter. From the inattention of the people to the concerns of government—from their carelessness and negligence—I must confess that I do apprehend some danger. I fear that they will place too implicit a confidence in their public servants, and fail properly to scrutinize their conduct. . . . Make them intelligent and they will be vigilant—give them the means of detecting the wrong, and they will apply the remedy.

The sentiments expressed above have come to be accepted by a large proportion of the American people, and today no motive is more prevalent in our education than this desire to use the schools to prepare our youth for citizenship in both state and nation.

It is difficult to evaluate results of the nationalistic aim in education. Some of its results have been good and some have been very bad. A fair analysis has been presented by Edward H. Reisner in his discussion of education for national ends.

Mass nationalism has meant competition among nations, all the keener because it involves the best resources of economic and military strength which the nations have possessed. It has produced wars, probably not so many as occurred in the seventeenth and eighteenth centuries, but certainly bigger wars, and besides it has kept nations stirred up to a tension of military preparedness which is bad enough in itself. On the spiritual side, it has fostered intense, restricted loyalties for their own country and violent hatred of other nations in the individual citizens. In this way the fact and the attitude of nationalism have operated against the development of co-operative relationships within the whole social order, embracing all national groups.

On the other hand, it must be observed that national interest has provided the effective dynamic of social reform and better human husbandry. In the interest of pack strength the individuals had to be made more intelligent, more productive, more loyal, and better contented. On the spiritual side it must be credited with a positive enlargement of human personality. The citizen, conscious of his identity with an historical tradition and a living cause and willingly devoting himself to his country's need, is more of a person than the peasant who knows nothing and cares nothing beyond his immediate and personal affairs. To lift the individual to the vistas of national consciousness and loyalty was a great human accomplishment. Perhaps it ought to be regarded as the necessary halfway station on the upward road to a lively consciousness of human kind.[3]

This nationalistic aim in education, developed early, as we have indicated, in France, Prussia, and the United States, has come to direct the educational thinking of practically all the nations of the world. Just prior to World War II Germany, Italy, and Japan, in order to further the extreme nationalist and totalitarian ideas then current in each, utilized their schools as indoctrination agencies for the creation of strong youth movements. Soviet Russia's use of education as a support to the Communist ideology will be discussed in a later chapter.

---

[3] Edward H. Reisner, *op. cit.,* pp. 230-232. Reprinted with the permission of the publishers.

Perhaps a distinction should be made between systems of education utilizing the schools for the simple nationalistic purpose of developing responsible citizenship and those totalitarian systems which in supernationalistic fashion actually prepare for war through school indoctrination.

TYPES   Nationalism demands certain types of education, and these naturally were the ones stressed as national systems of schools arose. The nationalistic ideal emphasized primarily secular and civic education. Where religious and moral types of education were preserved, these were considered as agencies in the promotion of patriotism. In all nations, law-abiding morality has been recognized as an essential element in patriotic citizenship. Nations have varied, however, in their attitude toward religious education. In Prussia, religious instruction was retained in the schools as a part of the training in patriotism. The German church has always been subordinated to the state and used as a national agency since the time of the Reformation, when the leaders had to depend upon the support of the German princes. In France the schools were more completely secularized. The French liberals believed that the schools must be taken out of the hands of the church and be wholly controlled by the state, with lay instructors substituted for religious teaching orders. As a result, religion has seldom played the part in French nationalism that it did in the Prussian. Yet even in pre-World War II Germany, Hitler fostered a distinct movement toward complete secularization. The issue of religious versus secular schooling was revived when the totalitarian government inaugurated a semi-official campaign to destroy both Catholic and Protestant schools.

The conditions under which the United States was founded, including a multiplicity of religious sects, made it impracticable if not impossible for the new nation to erect a state school system on a religious basis. The framers of our Constitution handled the problem in the only intelligent manner possible in a country with so many religious sects; they provided for complete religious toleration. The result was that religious education was left to the different churches, and the state schools confined themselves to secular instruction.

In the USSR, although churches still exist, the political ideology is the real religion and Communist Russia has realized the efficacy of a national policy of education in promoting national ends, and has established a system of mass education which aims at making the communistic concept of the state successful. The plans developed by the Kremlin include thorough indoctrination in the theories of government cherished by the Soviet and rigid exclusion of conflicting theories. The curriculum is controlled closely, and teachers must be approved politically as well as academically.

Physical education has usually been considered an essential element in a national school system. Under Frederick the Great in Prussia, the final authority over education in the nation at large was placed in a

Ministry of Religion, Education, and Public Health. The German schools have always placed emphasis upon training for health and physical vigor. In the United States, particularly since the two World Wars revealed the physical defects of our citizenry, both states and nation have encouraged more and better physical training.

Vocational training also has been given emphasis by national governments, especially for the rank and file of the people, who must be made vocationally efficient if the nation is to survive in its military and economic struggles with other nations. National leaders in both Europe and the United States have emphasized the necessity of having a body of contented citizens as a guarantee of national stability.

Nationalistic education is usually universal, compulsory, and free, although seldom common in the true sense of the word. The French reformers believed that education must be universal. Roland said: "Education cannot be too widely diffused, to the end that there may be no class of citizens who may not be brought to participate in its benefits." Most of them believed that instruction should be free even for professional training and for adults. Condorcet recommended that education be absolutely free. The Revolutionary liberals believed also that schooling should be compulsory and attendance obligatory. Aided by the census required for universal military service, Prussia very early succeeded in persuading her children to attend the schools regularly. Regular school attendance became a national habit in Germany, a half-century before England and three-quarters of a century before the United States achieved a like result. Toward the middle of the nineteenth century, the United States—largely as a result of the opinions of our leading statesmen, the extension of suffrage, the support of associations of workingmen, and the efforts of such educational reformers as HORACE MANN (1796–1859) and HENRY BARNARD (1811–1900)—established free and universal education on the elementary level.[4] This was later extended through the secondary and higher levels, so that the United States now has a complete system of public education, free and open to all.

Although the United States has not yet actually provided equal educational opportunities for all, the principle of a common school system organized after the ladder pattern has been accepted as the American ideal. The "American Dream" mandates equal opportunity for all the children of all the people at all the levels of education. This is quite different from the dual type of education generally prevalent in European countries. In Germany, France, and other European countries, a parallel system of folk and secondary schools developed, with a wide social and economic gulf between the parents who sent their children to the free elementary folk schools and those who paid fees for their children in secondary and higher schools. The European tradition has pro-

---

[4] For a well-integrated account of the activities of Mann, Barnard, and others see Newton Edwards and Herman G. Richey, *The School in the American Social Order.* (Boston: Houghton Mifflin Company, 1947.) Pp. 322-385.

vided for a type of public elementary school designed to serve the humble needs of the working class with secondary schools and universities maintained for the development of leaders from the more favored classes. In the United States, a ladder type of education favoring the rise of individuals, even from modest circumstances and minimizing social stratification, has evolved. Thus our entire educational system is more "common" than are those of most European countries.

CONTENT   One of the most important steps in the development of nationalism is the creation of a common culture and a unity of attitude. Nothing contributes more to this end than a common language spoken by all the elements in a nation's population. The leaders of the French Revolution realized this; and so their plans for education called for the teaching of a standard French in all the schools in order to eliminate as far as possible the use of other tongues and various local dialects by the inhabitants of certain regions. They even emphasized the necessity of teaching the French language and literature in the secondary schools and colleges, where Latin had always been the language of first importance. Likewise, in Prussia, special attention was given to German language and literature. In Germany, not only the *Volksschulen,* but the secondary schools and universities as well, were required to teach the German language and literature as a subject in the curriculum; German was, as a rule, the medium of teaching; and teachers and pupils were expected to use German as the extra-class language. In the teacher-training schools it was the patriotic duty of the prospective teacher to give special attention to the study of the German language and literature. In the United States, great emphasis has been placed on the teaching of the English language and literature.

One of the most important developments of the nineteenth century in both England and the United States was the rise of English grammar to popularity as a leading subject in the curriculum. Such orginal texts as LINDLEY MURRAY's *English Grammar* were used extensively in both England and America and rapidly replaced Latin grammar in importance. In the years during and immediately after World War I, the so-called Americanization movement stressed the teaching of English to the foreign-born immigrants who had continued the use of their native tongues. This movement, providing for the training of illiterate adults in the English language, as well as in the principles of democracy and the duties of citizenship was an obvious outgrowth of a nationalistic conception of education.

Next in emphasis to the teaching of the national language and literature comes the teaching of history and geography. The French revolutionists advocated instruction in the history and geography of their country, and for a long time these subjects have been required units in the curriculum of the French secondary schools. In the Prussian elementary schools, geography and history were taught, not only in their general implications, but with special reference to the German nation.

If the child was to be made conscious of his country, he needed to know its body—its towns and cities, mountains, and plains, and rivers, the make-up of its population, its products, its occupations, and its historic places. Thus to cause the child to connect the whole extent of his country with the little valley or the single town in which he lives and to identify his fortunes and his physical heritage with that of the millions of his fellow citizens, was an indispensable condition to the enlargement of his thinking on the national scale.

But this latitudinal extension of his interests was not sufficient. It was necessary that he should identify himself with the generations dead and gone and become conscious of membership in a social group that had a history and was to live on in the future. He must be made to see himself as the custodian of a whole heritage of heroism, suffering, and effort, which it was his duty to conserve and enrich. To this end, he learned the story of battles lost and won, and heard tales of heroic adventure and unselfish devotion to his country's cause. He came to revere the names of great men and of kings bold and good, the shepherds of the people. Likewise, he learned to know the enemies of his land and to hate them for the suffering and death which they had brought to his own.[5]

These are the ideals and purposes back of the study of geography and history in American schools as well as those abroad. Most states have laws requiring the study of the history of the United States and of the state itself.

The central feature of most nationalistic courses of study is government and the duties of citizens. The leaders of the French Revolution insisted that the "Declaration of the Rights of Man and the Citizen" be memorized, just as we in the United States have frequently emphasized the phrases of the "Declaration of Independence" and the "Preamble to the Constitution." The political doctrines of the Revolution were to replace the earlier stress on religion in the pupils' interest. In Germany, emphasis was still placed upon training for a moral and Christian life; but the pupils were also taught to love their rulers and their fatherland; be informed, according to the needs of their social position, of the social institutions and laws of their country; be contented with their social status and happy in their lot.

In the United States the teaching of civics has not only been emphasized but, especially in recent years, has been required by law. No subjects have been made the object of legal requirement as extensively as have the subjects of civics and American history.

No one whose sands of life have run one-half of the Psalmist's allotment will be surprised to learn of a considerable quantity of war legislation, and immediate post-war legislation, calculated to develop love of country and a lofty appreciation of the duties and responsibilities of the individual citizen.[6]

The spirit of the times may be reconstructed in part by noting

---

[5] Edward H. Reisner, *op. cit.*, pp. 228-229. Reprinted with the permission of the publishers.
[6] D. C. Shilling, "Legal Requirements for the Teaching of Civics," *Historical Outlook*, April 1933, pp. 181 ff.

the legislation passed in certain states widely separated and unlike in many respects. A Nevada Act approved March 21, 1917, reads as follows:

It is hereby made the duty of all school officers in control of public high schools in the State of Nevada to provide for courses of instruction designed to prepare the pupils for the duties of citizenship, both in times of peace and in time of war. . . . It shall be the aim of such instruction to inculate a love of country, and a disposition to serve the country effectively and loyally.

Iowa requires "each public and private school to teach the subject of citizenship in all the grades." A Connecticut statute of 1930 states that the "duties of citizenship, including the knowledge of the form of national, state, and local governments, shall be taught in all elementary schools." Maine stipulates that the youth shall be taught in all elementary schools "the cost, the object, and the principles of our government, the great sacrifices of our forefathers, the important part taken by the Union army in the war of eighteen hundred sixty-one to eighteen hundred sixty-five, and to teach them to love, honor, and respect the flag of our country that cost them so much and is so dear to every American citizen."

Ten days after the American declaration of war in 1917, New York passed a law requiring instruction in patriotism and citizenship. Its preface states: "In order to promote a spirit of patriotic and civic service and obligations and to foster in the children of the state moral and intellectual qualities which are essential in preparing to meet the obligations of citizenship in peace or in war, the regents of the state of New York shall prescribe courses of instruction in patriotism and citizenship, to be maintained and followed in all of the schools of the state."

Nationalism also emphasizes music as an essential part of the curriculum. Patriotic songs and martial orchestration particularly are used. Music was emphasized as a preparation for participation in the patriotic singing-societies and festivals which were organized at the time of the "Uprising of Prussia" in 1813. The singing of patriotic songs is not only a definite part of the exercises of all schools in the United States, but generally is prescribed. In Maryland, for example, it is mandatory that "any grammar school, high school, preparatory school, college, or university who have morning, afternoon, or evening exercises, open such exercises . . . with the singing of 'The Star-Spangled Banner.'"

The nationalistic curriculum invariably includes physical training designed to secure the health, vigor, and physical soundness of the people. In Prussia physical exercises were given an emphasis before unknown, because of their hygienic and military value. Religion was also retained—especially in Prussia—with the emphasis now placed upon moral earnestness, self-sacrifice, and obedience to authority rather than the earlier stress on the catechism and church doctrine.

AGENCIES   Those who hold to the nationalistic conception of education invariably believe in the public school as the best agency for instruction. As a rule, they adopt measures for the establishment of a school system that is publicly supported, publicly controlled, free, universal and nonsectarian. They may not always attain this ideal, but these characteristics are accepted as the principles underlying the school systems they attempt to build up. Such public school systems were first developed early in the nineteenth century in France, Germany, and the United States; and toward the close of the century in England, Italy, and other countries throughout the world. These public school systems—although not usually the exclusive agencies of education—are always recognized as the proper agencies of nationalistic education.[7]

As early as 1792, CONDORCET, in his *Report to the Legislative Assembly of the Committee on Public Instruction,* proposed the establishment of a completely democratic system of public schools. This report called for a primary school in every village, higher primary schools in the principle towns, secondary *collèges* in the larger cities, and secondary *lycées* in nine principal centers of France. A National Society of Sciences and Arts was to crown this public educational system. Although Condorcet's proposal was not put into effect, it became the basis for the gradual development of a French state school system, and had an important influence upon similar developments in other countries.

In 1802, Napoleon appointed COMTE DE FOURCROY (1755–1809) as Director of Public Instruction, and a law was passed which laid the foundations for a general organization of public instruction. Although the law provided that primary schools be established in every district, with a schoolhouse and a teacherage, the government gave no financial support to these schools and attendance was not compulsory. Napoleon was not particularly interested in primary schools but in *lycées* for the training of youth of superior ability for the executive duties of his autocratic government. The Law of 1802 placed emphasis upon secondary and higher education with a high degree of uniformity and centralized control. In 1808, Napoleon established the "University of France," not an institution for instruction, but a governing, examining, supervising, and disbursing body to control all educational institutions in France, public or private, primary, secondary, or higher.

VICTOR COUSIN (1792–1867), director of the Higher Normal School of France, was sent on a mission to study the school system of Germany in 1831. Upon his return he published his famous *Rapport sur l'état de l'instruction publique . . . en Prusse,* which was translated into English and published in London and New York where it had great influence upon British and American educational thinking. Based upon this report, the Law of 1833 laid the foundations of French elementary public schools and strengthened the public secondary and higher schools. Under this law, provision was made for teacher certification and school inspection. These beginnings proved effective and France gradually devel-

---

[7] See Frederick Eby, *The Development of Modern Education.* Second Edition. (New York: Prentice-Hall, Inc., 1952.) Pp. 532-545.

oped a complete system providing universal education at public expense and under close state supervision and control.

As early as 1713, under the organizing genius of FREDERICK WILLIAM I of Prussia, the foundations of a centralized state school organization were laid; and the encouragement, centralization, and control of education by the state was still further developed by FREDERICK THE GREAT. Frederick William's *Regulatory Code* of 1713 and *Fundamental School Law* of 1737, and Frederick the Great's *General School Regulations* of 1763 and *General Civil Code* of 1794, provided beginnings in the direction of publicly supported and publicly controlled schools. The *Code* of 1794, although it did not provide the free schools, prescribed the rates of tuition and provided means for state subsidies for those too poor to pay tuition. This *Code* also provided for a high degree of centralized state control. Fines were imposed upon parents who failed to send their children to school, teachers were required to keep accurate records concerning children, teacher qualifications were stipulated, uniform textbooks were designated, and annual clerical inspections required. In 1808, a Department of Public Instruction was created as a branch of the Ministry of the Interior.

In 1834, a system of "leaving" examinations was established for those graduating from the *Gymnasium*. These examinations, given by the states, were made requirements for entrance to the university and for nearly all branches of the state civil service. The closest analogy to this plan in our own country is the system of Regent's Examinations in the State of New York, though our whole system of college entrance examinations was somewhat influenced by this German system. These requirements tended to unify the whole secondary and university system of German schools, as well as the elementary, under one centralized governmental bureau. Thus evolved a German public school system existing for the purpose of preparing German subjects for faithful and efficient service to their state.

When the federal government of the United States established its Bureau of Education in 1867, it too made this agency a branch of the Department of the Interior. In 1817, the Prussian Department of Public Instruction became a Ministry; but, in the United States—although there has been much agitation in that direction—the Bureau of Education (now Office of Education) has never been raised to Departmental status, with its head a cabinet officer. Education is, however, now placed under the Department of Health, Education and Welfare rather than Interior.

It took almost a half-century of agitation and conflict before the issue of public education in the United States was settled in favor of the principle of universal education for all children at public expense. Although much remains to be put into practice that was agreed to in principle, by 1850 the proponents of state public schools had won their fight, and a public school system had been established as a definite American policy. Although the battle was fought along different lines in the various states, there were seven strategic aspects of the struggle. Cubberley lists these stages of the conflict for tax-supported, state-controlled, free, universal, nonsectarian schools as follows:

1. The battle for tax support.
2. The battle to eliminate the pauper-school idea.
3. The battle to make the schools entirely free.
4. The battle to establish state supervision.
5. The battle to eliminate sectarianism.
6. The battle to extend the system upward.
7. The battle to crown the system with a State university.[8]

Almost from the beginning of our nation's history, steps were taken in the direction of public secular schools. In 1779, Governor THOMAS JEFFERSON (1743–1826) advocated a complete scheme of universal education for Virginia based on the theory that a moderate education for all, and special advanced education for the most capable, should be offered at public expense. He proposed the establishment of free elementary schools in every "hundred" or township, a number of secondary schools over the state, and a state university as the capstone of the state's school system. His plan was too far advanced for the public opinion of his time; but in 1810 Virginia did establish a permanent fund, to be used to subsidize education for the poor. Through Jefferson's personal efforts, the University of Virginia was finally opened in 1820.

Napoleon's University of France was patterned after the University of the State of New York (1784), its closest parallel in the United States. Neither institution, however, is a university in the usual sense, but merely represents the authority of the state in educational matters.

Moreover, in 1812, New York became the first state to create a state officer to exercise supervision over its schools. In that year a law was passed providing for state aid for schools and establishing a State Superintendent of Common Schools. The first holder of the office, GIDEON HAWLEY (1785–1870), was so efficient that he was removed from office by the politicians, and the office abolished.

Michigan was the first state to establish permanently a state office for state school supervision and control. Under the influence of Cousin's Report, ISAAC CRARY (1804–1854) and other leaders in the constitutional convention of 1835 secured provision in the new state constitution for a state school system with a State Superintendent of Public Instruction at its head. JOHN D. PIERCE (1797–1882), the first to hold this office, did much to establish the position as a permanent factor in American education, the practice spreading to each of the states. Pierce reveals the origin of his belief in the function of the state as an educational agency:

About this time, Cousin's report on the Prussian system came into my hands and was read with much interest. Sitting one pleasant afternoon upon a log, General Crary and myself discussed, for a long time, the fundamental prin-

---

[8] E. P. Cubberley, *Public Education in the United States.* Revised Edition. (Boston: Houghton Mifflin Company, 1934.) Pp. 163-281.

ciples which were deemed important for the constitutional convention to adopt, in laying the foundations of a new state. The subject of education was the theme of special interest. It was agreed, if possible, that it should be a distinct branch of government, and that the [state] Constitution ought to provide for an officer who should have the whole matter in charge.[9]

These offices for state supervision were created to enforce the state requirements set up for securing special funds. This aid was provided from the growing state school funds, which had been developed largely under the stimulation of the land-grant policy of the federal government. The Northwest Territory, from which Ohio, Indiana, Illinois, Michigan, and Wisconsin were erected as states, was divided by Congress into townships and sections, and the land sold to the settlers. When Ohio was admitted as a state in 1803, the federal government granted the sixteenth section of each township as school-lands with the understanding that the state would not tax unsold public lands. With few exceptions, these grants were made to all states later admitted to the Union, and grants of public lands in the west were also made to the older states in the east.

The first State Board of Education in the United States was established in Massachusetts in 1837, largely as the result of the efforts of JAMES G. CARTER (1795–1849), one of the most outstanding leaders in the fight for the establishment of an American public school system. The State Board was empowered to appoint an executive secretary to act as state school officer. A similar organization was set up in Connecticut in 1839. But agitation, propaganda, or even legislation are not enough to bring about educational reforms. Men must be found to undertake the important and difficult task of putting the idea into practice, and through persistent effort make the reform a reality. HORACE MANN and HENRY BARNARD, chosen as the first secretaries in Massachusetts and Connecticut respectively were outstanding men. These educational leaders did most to establish workable public education by developing state systems of education which became the models for other states. Both deserve honor as pioneers in the struggle to establish in the United States a system of free schools for all the children of all the people. By 1861, there were *ex officio* state school officers in nine, and regular school officers in nineteen states. Ten states had also provided the office of County Superintendent of Schools, and twenty-six cities employed City Superintendents of Schools.

At first, state money was used only to pay the cost of schooling for paupers and orphans. Those who could afford to pay did so through tuition charges and rate bills. In state after state the battle was fought to eliminate these and make the schools free to all on the same basis. Certain influences made it easier to bring about this result. For years the

---

[9] For further illustration of Pierce's dedication to the concept of a statewide system of instruction at all levels see Allen S. Whitney, *A History of the Professional Training of Teachers at the University of Michigan for the First Half-Century.* (Ann Arbor, Mich.: George Wahr, 1931.) Pp. 1-11.

taxpaying public had become accustomed to paying for the education of the children of others through membership in such philanthropic educational agencies as the Sunday School Society, the Infant School Society, and the various city school societies such as the Public School Society of New York.

These philanthropic societies—based on the idea that schools contributed to the general public welfare and hence should be supported by public gifts—paved the way toward a willingness to have tax moneys used for the support of the schools. Furthermore, the monitorial type of schools, developed about 1797 by JOSEPH LANCASTER (1778–1838) and ANDREW BELL (1753–1832) in England, and popular in the United States during the first of the century (because of their cheapness), helped to develop a willingness to have the schools supported by taxation.

In 1821, in Boston, the first democratic public secondary school was established, a type of institution which spread throughout the country as the successor of the earlier Latin grammar school and academy. The Massachusetts law of 1827 made the establishment of such public high schools obligatory, and the decision in the Kalamazoo Case (1874) settled the question of the legal status of this tax-supported secondary school. In 1787, provisions were first made for state universities in Ohio, where land grants were set aside for the support of Ohio University at Athens and Miami University at Oxford. A few misguided efforts were made to convert existing denominational colleges into state universities, but such action was checked in the famous Dartmouth College Case by the Supreme Court of the United States in 1819. By 1860, however, sixteen states had established state universities, mostly aided by federal land grants. A great stimulus to the establishment of state-controlled higher education was the Morrill Act of 1862, which offered land grants for the establishment of state colleges of agriculture and mechanical arts.

Enthusiastic nationalists sometimes have attempted to stretch the power of the state beyond its limits. Oregon, a generation ago, endeavored to give the public schools a monopoly in the education of the children of the state. The legislature passed a law requiring all children to attend the public schools. This act, although it did not specifically so provide, had as its intent the elimination of all other agencies of education except the public schools. The question was carried to the Supreme Court of the United States, which in 1925 declared that the state has the right to determine the minimum educational standards to be enforced, but that the parent has the right to decide the agencies by which these standards are to be attained. Since then, many American states have taken action to inspect and supervise private and parochial schools. In 1904, France closed all convent schools, thus giving the state a virtual monopoly in primary education. Several other nations have moved in the same direction, but such action has seemed incompatible with the American conception of a free democracy.

Nationalism recognizes the teacher as one of the most important agencies in the achievement of its purposes. Cubberley—one of the most nationalistic of American educators—proclaims:

> Education in a democratic government such as ours is the greatest of all undertakings for the promotion of national welfare, and the teacher in our schools renders an inconspicuous but a highly important national service.[10]

In all national school systems, provision has to be made for the careful training and selection of teachers. Teacher-training institutions have been established under state control, and systems for the examination and certification of teachers have been developed. The Prussian government early realized that the success of their public schools depended more on the quality of the teachers than on any other single factor. Hecker had established a private seminary for training teachers as early as 1738. Under Frederick the Great it became the Royal Teachers Seminary with a government subsidy, and by 1800 there were a dozen of these pedagogical seminars. In 1809, as a result of Pestalozzian influence, a Teachers Seminary was organized at Leipzig, the first to be established as an integral part of the state school system. Prussia led the way among the European states in providing thoroughly trained and professionally enthusiastic teachers through the organization in every administrative unit of a teachers seminary, imbued with the tradition and atmosphere of patriotism. The qualifications of Prussian public school teachers were determined by examination, and no teacher could be chosen unless he held the royal ratification of his nomination. As a rule only those teachers were selected who had had training in the approved seminaries.

The Superior Normal School of France, established by the National Assembly in 1794, was soon abandoned, but it was reestablished by Napoleon in 1808. In France the normal school has been of great influence in providing teachers in sympathy with the aspirations of the nation. Since 1870, there has been a normal school in each of the eighty-one departments, in addition to the Superior Normal School in Paris. In the United States, New York made the first state provision for the training of teachers, granting aid to those academies which included teacher-training in their courses. James G. Carter was instrumental in establishing the first state normal school at Lexington, Massachusetts in 1839, under the principalship of CYRUS PEIRCE (1790–1860). A second was established in 1839 at Barre, and a third in 1840 at Bridgewater. The movement spread, and by 1860 there were twelve, some of them as far west as Minnesota. Today there are state teacher-training schools in every state of the Union, most of them having developed into teachers colleges or colleges of education. Teachers Institutes, first organized by Henry Barnard in Connecticut in 1839, have also been used as commonwealth agencies for the training and inspiring of public school teachers. Today, every state in the Union has a system of teacher certification, although

---

[10] E. P. Cubberley, *op. cit.,* p. 764. Reprinted with the permission of the publishers.

these systems vary widely in method of administration and extent of requirements.

All nationalistic governments have endeavored to see that the teachers in their public school systems are loyal and patriotic servants of the state. For example, several states have passed laws providing for the study of civics, United States history, and state and national constitutions, by all students in teacher-education institutions. A number of states have also passed laws requiring teachers to take an oath of allegiance to support the constitutional form of government.

ORGANIZATION The tendency in all national systems of education is toward a highly centralized organization with a hierarchy or military gradation of administration and supervision. The system is invariably headed by a national or state chief school officer with authority delegated downward through minor officials. In practically all countries, educational organization is centralized in a Minister of Education who is a member of the cabinet.

France has the most completely centralized system of education in western Europe. At the head of the entire system is the Minister of Public Instruction. He is assisted by an advisory council, known as the Higher Council of Public Instruction, and by three directors, one each for higher, secondary, and primary education. At the head of each of the districts or academies into which the country is divided, is a rector assisted by an academic council. The rector has authority over all three levels of education in his district with the exception of the appointment of teachers, which is in the hands of the prefect of the department. The efficiency of the entire system is assured by the maintenance of a complete corps of state and district inspectors, assisted by local school committees. Through this highly centralized organization, teachers are appointed, salaries fixed, pension systems maintained, curriculum and method controlled, and private instruction supervised.

Prussia, the forerunner of modern Germany, appointed a national school head with the educational reforms adopted by Frederick the Great. In 1817 the Bureau of Education was elevated to an independent ministry; and in 1825 the organization of a centralized state system of public instruction was completed by the establishment of provincial school boards, responsible to the Minister of Education, and intended to replace the church consistories in the local control of education. However, many of the members of the district school boards, which operated under the administration of the provincial boards, and many of the local school inspectors continued to be clergymen through the formation of the German Empire in 1871, its defeat in 1918, and until after the adoption of the new federal constitution of the Weimar Republic. In spite of the opposition of church officials and conservative Germans, every school regulation that was issued in Germany from the establishment of the Ministry of Education down to the end of World War II was in the direction of a more thoroughly centralized national control of education. Recognizing nationalistic education as the principal support of the state, not only Prussia, but other German states organized centralized national school systems. Germany, under Hitler, organized the schools even more thoroughly on a militaristic basis as a means of upholding his government, preserving the national culture, and satisfying the needs of the new industrial and economic life of the nation.

A similar tendency toward supernationalism occurred in pre-World War II Italy. Here, under the spell of another totalitarianism, leaders of education in Italy attempted, beginning in 1922, to develop nationalistic patterns in accord with fascism. The clearest statements of their ideology were made by GIOVANNI GENTILE (1875–1944), Mussolini's Minister of Education and author of the *Reform of Education*. Gentile believed that the practical aim of education is nationalism; that the means of education are the spiritual products of the past relived in the present. He asserted that the state, representing universal will or reason, is—as a whole— over and above the citizen. The state is universal and continuous, and the individual good must be identical with the state's good or else be sacrificed for the good of the state. The individual is an instrument of the state. The state has rights, but the individual has only duties. The individual participates in the benefits of government but not in the government. Education, by giving the pupil the common national language, history, and culture, evokes the common will. Thus Gentile developed a fascist conception of education—a nationalistic type even more pronounced than those of the monarchies and democracies we have already discussed. The schools of fascist Italy were radically re-organized and strictly controlled.

In the United States there has never been an organization of the school system on a centralized federal basis, and even in the states no move has succeeded to substitute a strongly centralized state school organization for local autonomy. Although the federal government had been making land grants for educational purposes to the states for several decades, it was not until 1867 that Congress made any effort to enable the federal government to do anything about education except to subsidize it. In that year, Congress established a Department of Education, but without cabinet rank, for the purpose of "collecting facts, statistics, and information as to schools and school systems to aid the different states in the establishment and maintenance of efficient school systems and otherwise promote the cause of education generally throughout the country." The Department was headed by a Commissioner of Education (Henry Barnard was the first appointee) who was to report annually to Congress. Thus the federal government adopted a policy of investigation and inspiration rather than a policy of administration and control.

Recently the Office of Education was placed under the Secretary for Health, Education, and Welfare but—with the decentralization suggested by the place of education in the United States constitution— Congress has from the first carefully contrived to keep most of the educational activities of the federal government out of the hands of the Commissioner of Education. When the Smith-Hughes Vocational Education Act was passed in 1917, setting up a national system of vocational training, the administration of the act was placed in the hands of a Federal Board of Vocational Education. Many other federal educational activities are scattered through various federal departments. When, in 1935, President Roosevelt set aside fifty million dollars for a national "Youth Movement," the administration of the fund was placed under the Treasury Department. Considerable effort has been made to establish a full-fledged Department of Education, with a Secretary of Education in the President's cabinet, but up to the present time these efforts have failed.

Although the organization of the school system varies considerably in the different states, there is a great deal of uniformity. Every state has a chief school officer, known variously as the Superintendent of Schools, Superintendent of Public Instruction, or Commissioner of Education. Often he is elected by the people, sometimes appointed by the Governor of the state, and sometimes chosen by a State Board of Education. Practically all the states have Boards of Education, but there is considerable variety in their scope and functions. Many states have educational control divided among different boards. In all states there is a greater or less degree of local autonomy. In some, the district is the smallest local unit; in some, the township; and in others, the county. There has been a distinct movement toward reorganization of the schools on a county unit basis; and, since 1929, there has been a strong tendency to centralize educational support and control in the hands of the state government, in order to provide greater equalization of educational opportunities.

City school systems often operate under special charters, quite independently of state authority. States usually delegate administrative responsibilities to county, township, district, and city boards of education. In some states county superintendents of schools are the executive officers of county boards of education, but more often they are elected by the people and work directly under the state board or state department. City superintendents, on the other hand, are universally appointed by the city boards of education as their professional executive officers. In some cities administrative responsibility is divided between the superintendent of instruction and the business manager. There is considerable agitation for reorganization in the direction of greater centralization of schools in the hands of the state and federal governments although opposition to either or both of these panaceas is strong and well-led.

As far as the organization of the levels of instruction is concerned, the trend has been in the direction of the ladder system as advocated by Comenius. Unfortunately, however, the arrangement of these levels has grown up on a basis of administrative convenience as well as through a careful study of child psychology and of educational needs.

In France, the child first enters the *école maternelle* and remains there until he passes into the *école primaire* at six. The primary school is compulsory until the age of fourteen. Above the *école primaire* is the *école primaire supérieure,* with a three-year course devoted to practical work of a vocational nature. There are also continuation schools, supported by the various districts and subsidized by the state, for agricultural and industrial education. The secondary schools are called *lycées,* national schools supported partly by the state, and *collèges,* maintained chiefly by the districts with some aid from the state. Children may transfer to these secondary schools from the primary school at the age of eleven, but usually are prepared instead in the preparatory departments of the *lycées* and *collèges* themselves. The completion of secondary education is crowned by a rigorous state examination, the *baccalaureate,* necessary for entrance to the university or the professions.

Following World War I there developed in France a movement to establish a common school for all, the *école unique.* This plan was to give to all children the same schooling from six to thirteen. The brighter pupils were to receive a secondary education from fourteen to seventeen, and finally a few selected students would at the age of eighteen be admitted to the institutions of higher education. All of this education should be free.

French progress was impeded by World War II and French education under German occupation stagnated although Nazi attempts to restrict the curriculum were only partially successful. Upon the liberation of Paris in August, 1944, the French government empowered Dr. Paul Langevin and Dr. Henri Wallon to suggest modifications in the education in keeping with the *école unique* idea. The new plan (only parts of which were enacted into law) calls for two levels that follow a single pattern. Three cycles make up the lower level: (1) personal development, 7-11; (2) orientation, 11-15; (3) determination, 15-18. Higher education for those who qualify begins at age eighteen.

In Germany, before 1919, there was no sign of the educational ladder as we have come to be familiar with it here in the United States. The children of the masses were educated in the *Volksschule,* which provided a course eight years in length, ending at fourteen, and not leading to any of the secondary schools. It was impossible for a graduate of the *Volksschule* to enter a secondary school even if he could pay the necessary fees. The only avenue open to him was common labor or attending the *Fortbildungschule* (continuation school) to become skilled in a trade. The prerequisites required for entrance to the secondary schools— the *Gymnasium,* the *Realgymnasium,* or the *Realschule*—were provided by private tutors or a *Vorschule* (private preparatory school), although many did go to the *Volksschule* for three years and then transfer to the secondary school. Secondary schools were for the children of the higher classes who were destined for the universities, the professions, and higher civil service.

The Constitution of the 1919 Republic did away with this dual system. The Common School Law of 1920 provided that a "public school system be constructed as an organic whole, the Middle and Higher schools to be extensions of a common school." A public four-year elementary school was organized as a common school for all, known as the *Grundschule*. The *Mittelschule* took pupils from the fifth year and carried them through the ninth or tenth years. In addition to the older patterns of secondary schools, two new types were established, the *Deutsche Oberschule* (vernacular high school) and the *Aufbauschule* (rural high school).

In Germany—as in France—a single track or *Einheitsschule* has been debated since 1919 but with little progress. Following the defeat in 1945 and subsequent occupation the schools of the Western Zone and West Berlin were modified somewhat. In the Eastern Zone, occupied by the U.S.S.R., they were modified too, but in the direction of Russian education.

In the west generally (although each state has a separate system) the *Grundschule* occupies four to six years, the *Volksschule* is from two to five years in length, and those capable of secondary school work (about 15 percent) enter one of the *Gymnasien* at age ten.

In the United States, the traditional ladder system has been organized on an 8-4-4 basis. The eight-year elementary school is followed by a four-year high school, and this in turn by a four-year college. Beyond this come the graduate and professional schools. Since 1910, certain interesting reorganizations have taken place.

As early as 1892 national committees were urging the reorganization of the 8-4 plan. Urging economy of time it was commonly thought that if the high school could begin at grade 7 rather than 9, students could be prepared for college and university somewhat earlier, thus allowing entrance into the professions at a more advantageous age. This idea was first furthered by offering high school subjects at lower levels, but in 1910 a clear break was made with the older organization in the creation of the junior high school, generally grades 7, 8, and 9.

The idea of economy of time soon was lost, however, and thus the junior high school came to be looked upon as a proper setting for orientation and academic and vocational guidance. Many arrangements were offered but the usual brackets were 6-3-3, 6-2-4, or 6-6.

The expansion of the public junior college at about the same time confirmed to many Americans that they had indeed achieved a democratic single ladder.[11]

METHODS The nationalistic conception of education has done little directly in the way of originating and developing new methods of instruction. School legislation, as a rule, does not concern itself very much with matters of methodology. Nevertheless, national and state

---

[11] See Robert Ulich, "The Legend of the Single Ladder," School and Society. Vol. 65, No. 1675 (February 1, 1947). Pp. 73-75.

educational leaders have done much in the way of introducing and encouraging the use of the methods developed by those active in the psychological and scientific educational movements described in later units.

Early in the nineteenth century, the Prussian government sent a number of young men to Pestalozzi's institute at Yverdon to observe the methods and try to catch the spirit of the Swiss schoolmaster; and upon their return they Pestalozzianized the state teacher-training system and thus introduced the new methods into their national system of instruction. Victor Cousin's *Report on the Conditions of Public Instruction in Prussia* described the methods as well as the organization; but it was the latter that attracted the greatest attention and had the most influence.

Conscientious state and national school officials in the United States have always tried to keep the teachers in their school systems up to the highest standards of pedagogy known in their day. Although Horace Mann confessed in his diary that he had never read a book on pedagogy at the time he was appointed secretary of the Massachusetts State Board of Education, he did much to familiarize his teachers with the best methods developed up to his time. Through his annual messages, especially the Seventh Annual Report dealing with European schools, he familiarized the teachers of Massachusetts with the best methods of instruction available. Henry Barnard's idea of teachers' institutes developed into a popular state agency for the dissemination of information about new teaching methods. His powerful *American Journal of Education* was another influence in the same direction. Placed in charge of early state normal schools, educators like CYRUS PEIRCE at Lexington, and DAVID PAGE (1810–1848) at Albany, gave considerable thought to the question of the improvement of instruction. Peirce's *Lectures on the Art of Teaching* and Page's *Theory and Practice of Teaching* were outstanding among the books presenting practical suggestions for the conduct of schools under the district system. The state normal schools were instrumental in introducing the actual use of Pestalozzian and Herbartian methods into the United States.

State Departments of Education and the United States Office of Education, through their bulletins and reports also have familiarized the local schools with the best educational methods and have been instrumental in the exchange of instructional experiences. The states, by legislation requiring teachers to take professional courses before they can secure certificates, are doing much to improve instruction in American classrooms.

Frequently those in charge of national school systems are not in sympathy with experimentation and innovation in methods of teaching, although they do encourage the adoption of those methods that have been proved practical and efficient. Most pioneering in method has been done in private schools and through the encouragement of associations of the teachers themselves.

On the other hand, the supernationalist philosophy regards a paramilitary spirit and organization as conducive to the development of the proper academic attitude, *i.e.,* minds receptive to the ideology of the state and indoctrination in the current mode of thought or presentation of whatever special facts or interpretations of history have been determined upon by the ruling clique. This entails the use of special methods or organization for its effectiveness; a rigorous discipline is enforced and the work of youth groups of the appropriate age level, both within and without the school, is considered another essential of learning. Such devices were much in evidence in pre-World War II Italy, Germany,[12] and Japan and presently flourish in all Communist-controlled areas, especially in mainland China and East Central Europe.

Thus, as far as discipline is concerned, national school authorities usually favor a condition of system, order, and obedience. They are seldom in sympathy with permissive doctrines or self-government. Under extreme nationalism the schools and its students are merely supports to its ideology.

FOR FURTHER READING

Arrowood, Charles F., *Thomas Jefferson on Education.* New York: McGraw-Hill Book Co., 1930.

Butts, R. Freeman, *A Cultural History of Western Education.* Second Edition. New York: McGraw-Hill Book Co., 1955. Pp. 267-337.

Cubberley, Ellwood P., *Public Education in the United States.* Revised and Enlarged Edition. Boston: Houghton Mifflin Company, 1934. Pp. 163-281.

Curti, Merle, *Social Ideas of American Educators.* New Revised Edition. Paterson, N. J.: Littlefield, Adams and Company, 1959. Pp. 101-168.

Doughton, Isaac, *Modern Public Education, Its Philosophy and Background.* New York: Appleton-Century-Crofts, Inc., 1935. Pp. 380-459.

Duggan, Stephen P., *Student's Textbook in the History of Education.* Revised Enlarged Edition. New York: Appleton-Century-Crofts, Inc., 1936. Pp. 373-475.

Eby, Frederick, and Arrowood, Charles F., *The Development of Modern Education.* New York: Prentice-Hall, Inc., 1934. Pp. 540-617.

Edwards, Newton, and Richey, Herman G., *The School in the American Social Order.* Boston: Houghton Mifflin Co., 1947. Pp. 322-385.

Good, H. G., *A History of American Education.* New York: The Macmillan Co., 1956. Pp. 81-170.

————, *A History of Western Education.* New York: The Macmillan Co., 1960. Pp. 292-295, 318-325, 344-356, 367-433.

---

[12] See Gregor Ziemer, *Education for Death, The Making of the Nazi.* (New York: Oxford University Press, 1941.)

Hansen, Allen, *Liberalism and American Education*. New York: The Macmillan Co., 1926. Pp. 44-104.

Kandel, I. L., *Comparative Education*. Boston: Houghton Mifflin Company, 1933. Pp. 1-22.

Knight, Edgar W., *Education in the United States*. Second Revised Edition. Boston: Ginn & Co., 1941. Pp. 192-407.

LaFontainerie, François de, *French Liberalism and Education*. New York: McGraw-Hill Book Co., 1932. Pp. 29-169, 311-378.

Mayer, Frederick, *A History of Educational Thought*. Columbus, Ohio: Charles E. Merrill Books, Inc., 1960. Pp. 247-262, 291-304.

Mulhern, James, *A History of Education*. Second Edition. New York: The Ronald Press Co., 1959. Pp. 422-435, 494-568.

Raup, Bruce, *Education and the Organized Interests in America*. New York: G. P. Putnam's Sons, 1936. Pp. 40-72.

Reisner, Edward H., *Evolution of the Common School*. New York: The Macmillan Co., 1930. Pp. 219-344.

Ulich, Robert, *A History of Educational Thought*. New York: American Book Company, 1950. Pp. 225-257.

————, *Three Thousand Years of Educational Wisdom*. Cambridge, Mass.: Harvard University Press, 1954. Pp. 426-479.

QUESTIONS FOR CLASS DISCUSSION

1. What has been the outstanding difference between the purposes of education in a democracy and those of a dictatorship or absolute monarchy?
2. Compose arguments for or against the adoption of a policy of greater centralization of educational control in the federal government of the United States.
3. What are the arguments for and against giving the public schools a monopoly in the education of the children of a state or nation?
4. To what extent do you believe that there should be local control in educational matters?
5. Why have so many contemporary governments assumed such a high degree of state control over teacher-education schools?
6. Present arguments for and against the conclusion that nationalism often leads to indoctrination through propaganda rather than furthering the teaching of the whole truth.
7. What do you consider the legitimate requirements that a state may set up as the basis for teacher certification?
8. Show how differences in the school systems of various countries illustrate differences in the national philosophies, aspirations, and needs of these countries.

9. Present arguments for or against the creation of a federal department of education in the United States.
10. What are the relative advantages of state universities and private or parochial institutions? To the student? To the state?
11. What do you consider proper subjects for school legislation? Should state educational legislation be permissive or mandatory? Federal legislation in so much as it applies to the schools?
12. Discuss the constitutional position of education in the United States. What are states' rights?

CHAPTER XV

THE PSYCHOLOGICAL CONTROL OF CHILD DEVELOPMENT

DEVELOPMENTALISM

While the nationalists were engaged in the organization of educational agencies that would be effective in the attainment of patriotic ideals, another group of thinkers and teachers, in the late eighteenth century and through the nineteenth century, concerned themselves with the reform of the educational process itself, hoping to bring it more in accord with the laws of human development. This endeavor is usually called the "psychological" movement, since it concerned itself primarily with the nature of the mind and its workings. It was based upon a "child-centered" point of view, and its findings grew out of a careful study of the child.

The psychological movement was greatly stimulated—especially in its later stages—by the theory of evolution, as developed by Lamarck, Darwin, and Huxley, and for that reason it is sometimes designated by the term "evolutionism." Since, however, its chief characteristic is the belief that education is control of the development of the child from within instead of an imposition of adult standards from without, the term "developmentalism" is perhaps preferable.

Education is the process of development which goes on in the individual human being as the result of his activity in and his reaction upon the environment, and which by giving meaning to experience progressively increases his power to direct subsequent experience.[1]

Teaching is the presenting of stimuli in order to produce desirable responses and the withholding of stimuli in order to prevent undesirable responses.[2]

These definitions clearly present the point of view of the psychological developmentalists. They are concerned primarily with the child and his development—a development which results only through continual interaction of the child with his stimulating environment. The complete conception and full significance of this idea came about only gradually through the contributions of many educational philosophers and experimenters, but its implications are now almost universally accepted. The psychological developmentalists have not brought about changes in the curriculum or in the organization and administration of educational agencies, so much as a revolution in the methodology of teaching, better training of teachers, and a better understanding of the whole educational process. Indeed it was in the effort to provide just this departure from the earlier traditional and disciplinary methodology that the developmental movement arose.

Rousseau's naturalism may be considered the antecedent of developmentalism in its proclamation that education is a matter of the free and unrestricted development of the natural powers and inclinations of the individual. Naturalism was a distinct reaction against the belief that the individual by nature was bad and thus had to be fashioned by nurture into a different being. It condemned all that was artificial, and took a negative and destructive attitude toward any school procedures that attempted to shape the individual to the institutions of human society. Developmentalism is a reconciliation of the two extremes—education as a matter of human nurture, and education as a matter of natural growth. The psychological developmentalist conceived of education as a natural process of growth, an unfolding of native capacities; but he believed also that this development—or organic growth—could be hindered or helped, and thus guided in desirable directions, by the methods with which the natural capacities and activities were treated.

The work of the psychologists was influenced considerably by the spread of the theory of materialistic monism. As long as the dualistic conception that the mind is distinct from the body prevailed discussion of mental phenomena necessarily remained in the realm of philosophy. But with the growing conviction that the body and mind are one metaphysical speculation gave way to careful observation and experimentation. One of the chief characteristics of developmentalism was this belief that observation and experimentation could lead to the discovery

---

[1] Isaac Doughton, *Modern Public Education*. (New York: Appleton-Century-Crofts, Inc., 1935.) P. 134. Reprinted with the permission of the publishers.
[2] Edward L. Thorndike, *The Principles of Teaching*. (New York: A. G. Seiler, 1906.) P. 7.

of psychological principles upon which educational procedures could securely rest. Late in the nineteenth century, developmentalism became linked with scientific determinism in its insistence that all educational procedures should be based upon a careful scientific study of the mind. As a result of this scientific study a new dynamic biological psychology replaced the older faculty psychology as a basis for educational theory and practice.

The influence of developmentalism was felt first in the elementary school. The earlier psychologists gave most attention to the study of the young child and to the beginning years of his development. Since education is a process of development the primary stages in this evolution were of greatest importance. As a result of this emphasis upon early growth elementary education supplanted secondary education as the chief interest of those concerned with educational thinking and practice. The reforms in educational procedures resulting from this psychological movement were confined for almost a century to the elementary schools.

There were many contributors to the development of this psychological movement in education, but in this chapter we shall consider primarily those philosophers and reformers who made the most outstanding contributions. The phases of the movement to which we shall give most attention are: (1) Pestalozzianism, (2) Herbartianism, (3) Froebelianism, (4) the child study movement of G. Stanley Hall; (5) the development of educational psychology under the leadership of William James and Edward Lee Thorndike; and (6) Behaviorism.

JOHANN HEINRICH PESTALOZZI (1746–1827) was born in Zurich, Switzerland. Unlike Rousseau, he received a careful rearing in a good home environment. His mother, although left a widow when he was only five years old, was able to send him through the Latin school and to the University of Zurich. As a youth he became greatly interested in the plight of the poor Swiss peasants. Influenced by his grandfather, pastor in a nearby town, he first studied for the ministry, but soon considered himself a failure in that career. He then studied law to prepare himself as a champion of the downtrodden masses. Here his revolutionary ideas brought him into conflict with the government, and his usefulness as a lawyer was at an end.

In 1769, he married and bought a farm, which he called Neuhof, where he launched an experiment to improve the dismal conditions of the Swiss farmers through education. He had read *Émile* and had tried to bring up his young son according to Rousseau's principles of naturalism. This experience convinced him that in practice naturalism needed some modifications; and so he took a group of ragged, vagrant children and attempted to give them instruction in the rudiments of reading, writing, and counting as well as in religion and morals, while they supported themselves by industrial work under the influence of a good home environment. The experiment was an educational success, but financially it was a failure and had to be abandoned when the reformer became bankrupt.

The next eighteen years of Pestalozzi's life were a period of literary production. In 1781, he wrote his great didactic novel, *Leonard and Gertrude,* a book which ranks among the educational classics. Later he published a sequel, *How Gertrude Teaches Her Children.* In these works, and in *The Evening Hour of a Hermit* (1780), he expounded his educational ideals and described the methods by which they were to be realized.

In 1798, Pestalozzi was given the opportunity to turn from the pleasant task of theorizing about education to the more thrilling and difficult task of practicing it. The Swiss government asked him to establish a school in an old convent at Stanz and entrusted him with the task of educating about eighty children orphaned by war. Here he began his experiments in educational methods which were later continued at Burgdorf, where he first acted as assistant to the head teacher in the village school and later established himself in a school of his own. With the aid of several loyal and efficient assistants, he continued his experimentation, and was able by the aid of voluntary contributions and government subsidies to open an institute for the training of teachers in his new methods. In 1805, the institute was moved to Yverdon where for twenty years he continued his experimentation and the teacher-training work begun at Burgdorf. As the fame of the institute at Yverdon spread students and visitors were attracted from other countries; and the Pestalozzian philosophy and methods were carried to other nations, particularly Germany, France, England, and the United States.

In his native country, Pestalozzian pedagogy was slow in gaining recognition. The most notable fruit of Pestalozzianism in Switzerland is to be found in the works of EMANUEL VON FELLENBERG (1771–1844), who established a school at Hofwyl designed to give a combined industrial and intellectual education. Fellenberg's school was very successful and attracted wide attention. His modification of Pestalozzianism found ready acceptance in the educational institutions of many countries beyond the borders of Switzerland.

Pestalozzianism was especially influential in Germany. German teachers were among the first to study at the institute at Yverdon. Under the influence of Fichte, the Prussian government early recognized the value of Pestalozzi's work, sent able young men to Yverdon to study, and placed Pestalozzian-trained men in charge of the public school system.

In France progress was made toward the adoption of Pestalozzianism, especially in the training of teachers, after the publication of Victor Cousin's *Report on the Conditions of Public Instruction in Prussia,* which attributed the remarkable educational progress of Prussia to the use of Pestalozzian methods. Pestalozzianism was introduced into England by Charles Mayo and his sister Elizabeth, who spent three years at Yverdon where they absorbed the mechanics of the methods, but not much of their philosophy and spirit. They opened a private school in

London for wealthy children, in which formalized Pestalozzian methods were used. A manual for teachers was prepared, called *Lessons on Objects,* which was greatly popularized by its adoption by the philanthropic Home and Colonial Infant School Society. This society—although it established model schools and a training college for teachers which had great influence in spreading the movement—fostered a type of Anglicized Pestalozzianism which was quite different from the German type and quite lacking in the true spirit of the great reformer.

The first attempt to introduce Pestalozzian methods to the United States was made as early as 1809, when a wealthy philanthropist brought Jospeh Neef, an associate of Pestalozzi, to Philadelphia to establish such a school. The effort met with little recognition, and Neef joined the communistic group at New Harmony, Indiana, after which his influence waned. Actually, educators in the United States first learned of the movement through the publication of WARREN COLBURN's *First Lessons in Arithmetic,* in Boston in 1821; and the bringing of ARNOLD GUYOT and HERMANN KRUSI from Switzerland to Massachusetts to lecture in the state normal schools, attracted some attention to Pestalozzian principles and methods. Articles in Woodbridge's *American Annals of Education* and William Russell's *American Journal of Education* also aroused some interest, but these early efforts affected the practices in the schools very little, and it was not until after 1860 that American schools really began to be Pestalozzianized.

It was the Oswego Movement that put Pestalozzianism into practice in the American schools. EDWARD A. SHELDON (1823–1897), superintendent of the schools at Oswego, New York, visiting at Toronto—across the lake in Canada—happened upon an exhibit of materials used for object lessons by the Home and Colonial Infant School Society. Greatly interested, he secured books and materials for this object study and persuaded one of the Society's teachers to come to Oswego and train his faculty in the new object-lesson teaching. A year later, he was able to employ Hermann Krusi, who spent the next twenty-five years in the Oswego Normal School, infusing American teachers with the spirit as well as the form of Pestalozzian method. The Oswego Normal School became the center of the movement, and the enthusiasm of its students carried the new methods to every state in the Union.

JOHANN FRIEDRICH HERBART (1776–1841) was a native of Oldenburg, in northwestern Germany. His background and career were just the opposite of Pestalozzi's. He came from a well-to-do family; his father was a learned public official, and his mother was a woman of exceptional intelligence, who carefully supervised the early rearing and education of her gifted son. Between the ages of twelve and eighteen, Herbart attended the *Gymnasium* of his home city, from which he was graduated with the highest honors. He entered the University of Jena to prepare for the practice of law. Studying under Fichte he was deeply influenced by the new humanism which prevailed there and by his associations with a brilliant group containing such creative geniuses as Herder, Goethe, and Schiller. Finding that he had little taste for the study of law, Herbart left the university to become private tutor to the three sons of the Governor of Interlaken, in Switzerland. While in Switzerland, he visited Pestalozzi's school at Burgdorf and wrote sympathetically of what he observed there. From 1802–1808 he lectured on education and philosophy at the University of Göttingen, where he published his famous *Science of Education*. For the next twenty-six years, he held the chair of philosophy formerly occupied by the great Immanuel Kant at the University of Königsberg. Here he founded a pedagogical seminar, a practice school for teacher-training and experimentation in methods of teaching, and in 1835 published *The Outlines of Educational Doctrine*, a clear and practical exposition of his educational ideas.

In Germany, the influence of Herbart was carried on into the second half of the nineteenth century by ZILLER, who headed the pedagogical seminar at the University of Leipzig, founded the Association for the Scientific Study of Education, and extended the Herbartian methods to elementary school instruction; and by REIN, a pupil of Ziller, who became head of the pedagogical seminar and practice school at the University of Jena, and made it the great center of German Herbartianism.

The Herbartian movement did not reach the United States until almost the close of the century. A group of young men from the Illinois State Normal at Bloomington studied at Jena and brought back with them the new science of educational method. CHARLES DE GARMO published *The Essentials of Method* in 1889, CHARLES A. MCMURRY published his *General Method* in 1892, and with FRANK M. MCMURRY, his brother, published *The Method of the Recitation* in 1897. In addition, the McMurrys published books on the special methods of teaching the various subjects stressed by the Herbartians. In 1892, the National Herbartian Society was organized in the United States, the name of the society being changed ten years later to the National Society for the Study of Education. Most of the normal schools—particularly in the Midwest—were soon won over to Herbartian principles and, through the teachers they sent to every section of the country, greatly influenced the practices of the elementary schools.

FRIEDRICH WILHELM FROEBEL (1782–1852) was born in the mountains of Thuringia in southern Germany. His father was the overworked pastor of an extensive parish. When his mother died in his infancy, he was left under the unsympathetic control of a harsh stepmother. His unhappy home environment made him deeply introspective and developed in him a tendency toward mysticism. Deprived of parental affection and congenial playmates, he turned to nature for companionship. From ten to fourteen, Froebel spent the only happy years of his youth living with a kindly uncle and attending the parish school, where he received the only systematic instruction of his whole life. At fifteen he was apprenticed to a forester and for the next eight years engaged in a variety of occupations, none of which gave him any satisfaction. In 1799, at the age of seventeen, he visited his brother who was studying medicine at the University of Jena, and there he was greatly impressed with the intellectual activity that centered about that institution and he conceived an interest in teaching that never left him. By a happy accident, he was invited to teach drawing in a Pestalozzian school at Frankfurt. Three years later he was engaged as a private tutor to three children and spent most of the time with his young charges at Pestalozzi's institute at Yverdon, where he studied the methods of the Swiss reformer and became one of his most enthusiastic disciples.

At the age of twenty-four, after a careful study of the works of Rousseau, Basedow, and Pestalozzi, Froebel opened an experimental school at Keilhau, in his native Thuringia, which was a pedagogical success but a financial failure. During the next few years, he taught in various schools in Switzerland and in 1826 published his epochal work, *The Education of Man,* which contains the best exposition of his educational philosophy. He was attracted to the writings of Comenius, and the description of the School of the Mother's Knee confirmed him in his belief that the earliest years of childhood were the most important in education. In 1837, he opened his "School for Little Children"—the first kindergarten—in the mountain village of Blankenburg. The remainder of his life was spent in developing games, plays, and songs for young children, the founding of kindergartens, the training of kindergarten teachers and further elaboration of his methods.

Froebel's preoccupation with early childhood education and his mystical nature alienated certain Germans and a reactionary government passed a law prohibiting kindergartens, a shattering blow which brought about his death in 1852. His ideas were taken up by BARONESS BÜLOW-WENDHAUSEN, and in 1860 the kindergartens were allowed to reopen in Prussia. In England the infant school, and in France the *école maternelle,* were influenced by the spirit of Froebel. In the United States, the first private kindergarten was established by MRS. CARL SCHURZ, in 1855, for German-speaking children at Watertown, Wisconsin. The first English-speaking school was founded by ELIZABETH PEABODY, sister-in-law of Horace Mann, in Boston, in 1860. The first American public kindergarten, taught by SUSAN BLOW, was opened by Superintendent WILLIAM T. HARRIS, as part of the St. Louis public school system, in 1873. In more recent years the Froebelian influence has been extended into the first and second grades of the elementary school in the new unified kindergarten-primary organization of early childhood education.

WILLIAM JAMES (1842–1910), one of the most influential American philosophers and psychologists, was born in New York City, but spent most of his youthful years in Europe. His early education was irregular and intermittent, partly because of constantly changing residence, and partly because of his father's desire that he should develop from within rather than represent the formal educational practice of the time. He acquired the fragments of a liberal education in schools and under private tutors in Switzerland, France, England, and America. During these years of study, in addition to his formal schooling, he stored up a fund of impressions which nourished his mind and stimulated his imagination. After a year engaged in the study of art, he was convinced that distinguished attainment in that field was not for him; and in the fall of 1861 he entered the Lawrence Scientific School at Cambridge, thus inaugurating the career in science and the connection with Harvard that continued until his death.

For thirty-five years, he taught in this university. He was instructor of physiology and anatomy for seven years, professor of philosophy for nine years, then professor of psychology until the last decade of his teaching, when he returned again to the teaching of philosophy. He was a prolific and gifted writer in the fields of philosophy, psychology, and education, and his influence upon the practice of education in American schools was exceptional. His greatest and most influential work, *The Principles of Psychology* (1890), soon became a classic. His concepts of education and his views concerning the work of the teacher are best summed up in his widely read *Talks to Teachers*. Through their popularity, these books exerted a powerful influence upon education and a whole generation of teachers.[3]

G. STANLEY HALL (1844-1924) was born in Ashfield, Massachusetts. Although non-professional, young Hall's family was one of unusual culture and intellectual superiority, and had sufficient funds to enable him to secure an extensive education at Williams College, Union Theological Seminary, and the Universities of Bonn and Berlin in Germany. For four years he taught English literature and philosophy at Antioch College, in Ohio. Resigning this position, he spent two years as a graduate student at Harvard studying under William James, the functional psychologist, and receiving the Ph.D. in 1878. He went to Germany again to study physiology at the University of Berlin, and psychology, under structuralist WILHELM WUNDT, at Leipzig. His unusually comprehensive education thus included specialization and study in theology, philosophy, psychology, physiology, anthropology, biology, anatomy, and neurology, under the most noted teachers of Germany and America. In 1880, in Boston, he made his famous study of the *Contents of Children's Minds on Entering School*.

Dr. Hall next taught psychology and pedagogy for six years at Johns Hopkins University and then for thirty years was the president of Clark University at Worcester, Massachusetts—one of the most unique and influential institutions of higher education in the United States during all that time. Here a small group of selected students, stimulated by Hall's scholarship and scientific spirit, explored hitherto unknown regions of genetic psychology, the laws of human development, and the

---

[3] See William James, *Talks to Teachers and Students*. (New York: Holt, Rinehart and Winston, Inc., 1900); for a vivid impression of James as a teacher see Chapter XVI, "Beloved Psychologist," in Houston Peterson (editor), *Great Teachers*. (New Brunswick, N. J.: Rutgers University Press, 1946.) Pp. 223-228.

laws of growth and learning. Clark University became noted as the acknowledged center for the study of child nature and development. Hall set forth his educational theories in some fourteen volumes, notable among which are his *Adolescence, Educational Problems,* and *Youth, Its Education, Regimen, and Hygiene.* In 1891, he initiated the publication of *The Pedagogical Seminary,* devoted to articles on child study and education from this new point of view.

JAMES McKEEN CATTELL (1860–1944), along with James and Hall, studied under Wundt in Germany. Born at Easton, Pennsylvania, he graduated from Lafayette before becoming the first assistant of the German structural psychologist. Returning to America, Cattell taught at the University of Pennsylvania from 1888 to 1891, here publishing his famous *Mental Tests and Measurements* (1890). At Columbia from 1891 to 1917, Cattell became associated with Thorndike with whom he had much in common. Of considerable importance in American psychology and extremely influential in spreading the influence of applied psychology and testing, Cattell utilized both the laboratory and statistics in his psychological excursions. He served as editor of *School and Society, Science,* and the *Scientific Monthly.*

EDWARD LEE THORNDIKE (1874–1949), eminent pupil and follower of G. Stanley Hall and William James, was born at Williamsburg, Massachusetts, and attended Roxbury Latin School. His undergraduate and graduate work was done at Harvard University, and his first teaching appointment was at Western Reserve University. In 1899, he became an instructor of genetic psychology at Teachers College, Columbia University, where he remained, playing a leading part in developing that institution into one of the foremost educational centers of the world. Although his greatest contributions were to the scientific movement, which we shall consider in the next chapter, his early work as a dynamic psychologist carried the developmentalist movement to its zenith. His *Principles of Teaching* (1905), his outstanding *Elements of Psychology,* published in the same year, and his monumental *Educational Psychology* (the "three gospels"—"Original Nature," "Individual Differences," and "Laws of Learning"), published in 1914, have had an immeasurable influence on teaching practice.

JOHN BROADUS WATSON (1878–1939) shared the popularity which psychology enjoyed in early twentieth century America. A native of Greenville, South Carolina, Watson took his Ph.D. at the University of Chicago where he taught from 1903 to 1908. Named Director of the Psychological Laboratory at Johns Hopkins he retained the post until 1920 when he entered private business. Relying heavily on Pavlov's conditioned reflex findings Watson became the "Father of Behaviorism," describing action in terms of psychological response to stimuli (rejecting the concept of conscious or unconscious mental activity). Celebrated for his work with infants Watson relied on three instincts (or unconditioned, unlearned responses), fear, love, rage, and believed implicitly in the supremacy of conditioning. "Give me the baby," he is reported to have said, for with this raw material he was confident that he could shape an intelligent, well-adjusted person. Watson wrote *Psychology from the Standpoint of the Behaviorists* (1919), *Behavior* (1925), and *The Psychological Care of Infant and Child* (1928).

KARL SPENCER LASHLEY (1890-   ) was a pupil and disciple of Watson at Johns Hopkins. Born at Davis, West Virginia, Lashley, following graduation, taught at Hopkins, Chicago, and Harvard. His experimentation relative to the structure and function of the brain is perhaps among the most significant carried on in the United States. Among his findings—through brain surgery with rats—Lashley determined that habits are not dependent upon specific neural pathways. He concluded, however, that the amount of uninjured brain tissue possessed by his subject is important and governed its action. This struck at the main contention of the connectionists. Following his tenure at Harvard, Lashley became Director of the Yerkes Laboratory of Primate Biology at Orange Park, Florida.

Significant for his role and influence in the reconstruction of the laws of child development was ARNOLD GESELL (1880-   ). Born in Salina, Wisconsin, Gesell studied at Clark University under G. Stanley Hall, winning his doctorate in 1906. After some preliminary teaching at Los Angeles, he moved to Yale in 1911, where he remained until 1948 as Director of the Clinic of Child Development of the Medical School. Upon retirement he organized and headed the Gesell Institute of Child Development in New Haven, perhaps the world's foremost child study center. Gesell's studies have been concerned with the development of children from birth through age sixteen and his observations and conclusions were largely instrumental in breaking the rigidity of former child-rearing methods. Gesell's writings include *The First Five Years of Life* (1940), *Studies in Child Development* (1948), and *Infant Development: The Embryology of Early Human Behavior* (1952).

With this brief introduction to the personalities who have contributed most to the movement of psychological developmentalism, we are now ready to analyze those theories that are pertinent to the various phases of educational practice.

EDUCATION AS A PSYCHOLOGICAL DEVELOPMENT

AIMS The psychological developmentalists were concerned more with the immediate individual aims of education than they were with the ultimate social objectives. They aimed at making the child the center of the educational process, and so addressed themselves primarily to the task of discovering the psychological laws of learning. They believed that teaching should direct itself toward the development of the child from within, and not toward an imposition of adult standards. Since education was a matter of directing and controlling growth and development, they believed that there must be continual observation and experimentation to determine the psychological principles upon which such an educational process could securely rest. Since the early stages of the child's progress were recognized as important factors in determining the course of his later development, they aimed particularly at a careful control of the elementary years of the child's schooling.

Pestalozzi believed that the genuine reform of society must begin with the reformation of the individual, and that the individual can be elevated only by putting into his grasp the power of helping himself. The only sure means of attaining the end sought is through the process of development. Although his aim was to secure a happier and more virtuous life for every individual, the process by which he hoped to bring about this desired end was "the natural, progressive, and harmonious development of all the powers and faculties of the human being." He felt that these powers lie dormant and latent in every child, merely awaiting an opportunity to unfold; education must furnish the opportunities for their unfolding. Pestalozzi liked to compare the education of the child with the development and growth of a plant. He writes, "Man, formed from the dust of the earth, grows and ripens like a plant rooted in the soil." Pestalozzi's main purpose was to discover the natural laws underlying the development of the head, heart, and hand of the child. Education is to provide the conditions under which this development can take place naturally and harmoniously.

Pestalozzi's ultimate goal was the social regeneration of humanity. He said that his sole end was to stop the sources of the misery in which he saw the people around him sunk. "I lived like a beggar," he writes, "in order to learn how to make beggars live like men." He desired to improve the desperate conditions under which humanity existed, but instead of depending upon new forms of religion, new types of government, or new systems of economic organization he turned to education for his solution of this age-old problem. He believed that it was possible to change society for the better through changing the individuals that make up society.

The winning of political, social, and economic rights meant little for the people unless these were accompanied by the development of their capacities to profit by and utilize their liberties. The right to individual development must be prior to and more fundamental than any other human right whatsoever. Without the development of a child's capacities, all other rights are useless and a mockery.[4]

---

[4] Frederick Eby and Charles F. Arrowood, *The Development of Modern Education.* (New York: Prentice-Hall, Inc., 1934.) P. 635. Reprinted with the permission of the publishers.

These ideas of Pestalozzi mark a striking change in aim. In the schools of his day teaching meant the giving of information. To Pestalozzi teaching meant the development of the child in accordance with his inborn faculties.

To teach a child properly it is necessary to know what his possibilities are, that is, what he should become, not merely what we should like him to be. Education then is continuous development. Education is the result of natural and spontaneous action of the mind. It is not something poured into the mind.[5]

Fellenberg, in his agricultural and industrial institute at Hofwyl, endeavored to carry out the Pestalozzian idea of developing the hand as well as the head and heart. This ideal of the symmetrical development of muscle, mind, and morals was brought to the United States and prevailed in our earlier manual-training shops and schools, in the self-help institutes of the Middle West, and later in the Y.M.C.A. and Y.W.C.A. movements. In company with Fellenberg, these American institutions aimed at educating the children of rich and poor together in order to develop a mutual sympathy and understanding.

According to Herbart, the ultimate goal of education is the development of moral character. He regarded dependable moral personality as the highest aim of humanity, and consequently of education. He rejected Rousseau's idea of allowing free expression to the native capacities of the child; he also rejected Pestalozzi's idea of the harmonious development of all the child's faculties and powers. Herbart believed that the ultimate goal of moral personality could be attained only through the development of a group of desirable, abiding, many-sided interests. The aim of education is to analyze the interests of man to discover which are best for individual and social living, and then by means of instruction to enable the individual to develop and apply these interests in the various situations of life. By producing a well-balanced many-sidedness of worthy interests, education endeavors to develop in the youth the will to be good and the desire to make sound moral choices. Thus a high degree of personal character and social morality will result.

The medieval and Reformation educators aimed at teaching morality through the use of preaching, precept, and the memorizing of moral maxims. Herbart believed that moral conduct must be based upon the development of the will, and that will-attitudes depend upon the accumulation of experiences, so organized as to express themselves freely and constantly in intelligent moral decisions. "We will what we know; we cannot will what we do not know." This is Herbart's justification of his aim of "many-sided interests." He maintained that the main purpose of education is the growth and development of ideas in the mind of the child, brought about in conformity with psychological laws.

---

[5] James F. Messenger, *An Interpretative History of Education.* (New York: Thomas Y. Crowell Company, 1931.) P. 193. Reprinted with the permission of the publishers.

Herbart aimed at the development of the adolescent rather than of the child, and, differing in this respect from most of the other developmentalists, concerned himself more with secondary than with elementary education. Most of his followers, however, applied his philosophy and method to primary education.

Froebel agreed with Pestalozzi and Herbart in the belief that the aim of education is the development of the child. He differed, however, in his conception of the nature of this development. According to the father of the kindergarten, the aim of education is the development of the inborn capacities and powers of the child—the latent powers of the individual. However, his conception of original nature was quite different from the pure naturalism of Rousseau. Froebel was the first real educational evolutionist. He believed that education is an essential element in the process of cosmic evolution. Education to him is the process by which the race and the individual evolve to a higher and ever higher level.

Froebel insisted that there is one underlying power in the universe, the Absolute, manifesting itself as force in nature and as consciousness in man—an original, active, energizing, creative, intelligent, self-conscious source of all being. Creation is a continuous process of productive activity, and the source of all created objects (including the child's nature) is this universal power which we call God. The forming crystal, the growing tree, the developing child—all reflect God's plan of creation, but under different manifestations. Therefore, any study of changes in the evolution of nature will throw light upon the nature of the development of man. All that man is ever to be lies hidden, however slightly revealed, in the being of the child. Froebel looked upon man as a human plant. The purpose of the educator is to control the growth of the child into a man, just as the purpose of the gardener is to control the growth of a plant to its full flowering and fruition. The aim of the teacher is to see to it that the development of the child is in accord with the original and logical course of human development. Failure in education consists of neglecting or preventing the development of certain sides of the child's personality causing "the distortion of originally good human powers and tendencies by arbitrary and willful interference."

If the child's nature has been marred it must be redirected into the original course of development; if the child displays activities contrary to the true principle of growth these must be watched for and corrected in order to keep the development progressing along the right lines. Thus, according to Froebel, education must be a controlled development by which the individual comes into realization of the life of the all-encompassing unity of which he is but a part, a development by which his life broadens until it has related itself to nature, until it enters sympathetically into all the activities of society, until it enters, said Froebel, into the achievements of the race and the aspirations of humanity. Education is but the realization in the individual human being of the evolutionary process at its highest stage. The work of the teacher is to bring about this unified evolutionary development.

G. Stanley Hall agreed with the European developmentalists that the aim of education was the development of the child's own nature, activities, capabilities, and interests. He, too, believed that education should be many-sided and lead to a well-balanced, normal personality; but he based his fundamental theories of development upon the principles of biological evolution rather than philosophy. He devoted his life to the study of genetic psychology, the evolution of mind, in order that an educational method could be perfected which would enable the child to realize its highest possibilities. Hall's fundamental thesis was that mental and physical life are always parallel; that there is "no psychosis without neurosis"; that mind and body have evolved together; that throughout the process of evolution mental life has been developing along with the development of the body and its biological activities. Hall attempted to trace the history of mental life just as Darwin had attempted to trace the history of physical life. Hall's aim was to educate the individual in such a manner that through him the race would continue its upward climb.

Earlier developmentalists believed that the human race has passed through certain stages which the unfolding life of the individual repeats, both physically and mentally. This theory, designated by the Herbartians as the "culture-epoch theory" and by the biologists as the "recapitulation theory," was accepted and elaborated upon by Hall as a basic principle in his educational aims. Hall was firmly convinced that "ontogeny repeats phylogeny" in the mental life as well as the physical. The teacher must discover through the study of genetic psychology the stages in the mental development of the race, and then so construct the curriculum and so build methods that the growth of the child will be in accord with the order of development. Hall urged educators to "develop nature's first intention and fulfill the law of nascent periods, or else not only no good, but great harm may be done." He believed that the teacher must, above all else, see that education does not obstruct, but rather facilitates, natural evolution. It must make the individual the fittest possible instrument for racial improvement.

On the surface, it would seem that Hall's recapitulation theory, although aiming at individual development, is nonprogressive in its social and racial outcomes. No longer does it aim at the "regeneration of society" or at the "process of cosmic development." It is more concerned with the development of the individual child as an end in itself.

Similarly, William James is essentially an individualist. Nowhere in his *Talks to Teachers* does he speak of education as a social function. To him education aims merely at "the organization of the instinctive tendencies of behavior and the acquired habits of conduct and action to fit the individual to his environment." Developmentalism comes to mean an organization of the elements of mental experience in order to prepare the individual effectively for the struggle of life. This concern with instinct and habit is a natural outgrowth of the study of animal psychology and the doctrine of biological evolution.

The great emphasis placed upon instincts, and the place given to them in education by James, led many of his disciples to the belief that one of the important ends of education was to allow the child to follow his instincts. Thus there came into educational theory the maxim, "Work with the instincts and not against them." The more careful could find in James' writings support for the modification of some of these instincts, but he undoubtedly was concerned more with the argument that the associationist psychologists were mistaken in failing to recognize the power of instincts in human life than with enshrining them.

James' doctrine of habit was highly individualistic and conservative in its implications. In spite of his admission that habits could be changed, his discussion seems to imply an "iron law of habit," and a belief that the main purpose of teaching is the early development of individual and class habits, in order to produce a more integrated society.

Habit is thus the enormous fly-wheel of society, its most precious conservative agent. It alone is what keeps us all within the bounds of ordinance, and saves the children of fortune from the envious uprisings of the poor. It alone prevents the hardest and most repulsive walks of life from being deserted by those brought up to tread therein. . . . It dooms us all to fight out the battle of life upon the lines of our nurture or early choice, and to make the best of a pursuit that disagrees, because there is no other for which we are fitted, and it is too late to begin again. It keeps the different social strata from mixing. . . . The man can by-and-by no more escape than his coat-sleeve can suddenly fall into new sets of folds. On the whole, it is best he should not escape. It is well for the world that in most of us, at the age of thirty, the character has set like plaster, and will never soften again.[6]

Thus, James maintained that the basis of all education is the fund of native instincts with which the child is endowed, and that the purpose of education is the organization of acquired habits on the part of the individual in such a way as to promote his personal well-being.

Thorndike, on the other hand, distinguished between the ultimate and proximate aims of education. He looked beyond the immediate psychological changes that the school is to produce in the individual to the ultimate social goals of education. Nevertheless, he insisted that one cannot change society without the proper development of the individuals that make up society.

Education as a whole should make human beings wish each other well, should increase the sum of human energy and happiness and decrease the sum

---

[6] William James, *Principles of Psychology.* (New York: Holt, Rinehart and Winston, Inc., 1890.) P. 121.

of discomforts of human beings that are or will be, and should foster the higher, impersonal pleasures. These aims of education in general—good will to men, useful and happy lives, and noble enjoyment—are the ultimate aims of school education in particular. Its proximate aims are to give boys and girls health in mind and body, information about the world of nature and men, worthy interests in knowledge and actions, a multitude of habits of thought, feeling, and behavior, and ideals of efficiency, honor, duty, love and service.[7]

According to Thorndike, education aims at satisfying the wants of all people in order to give each individual the fullest realization of his own desires. The chief aim of education is to realize the fullest satisfaction of human wants.

Thorndike, more than any of the earlier developmentalists, emphasized the importance of aiming not only at the development of the child for adult life and work, but also the development of the child in adaptation to the life of childhood itself. He held that we should strive more toward making children succeed with the problems and duties of childhood and less at fitting them for the problems and duties of twenty years after.

TYPES One can readily see, from the statement of their aims, that the developmentalists emphasized individual education rather than social education. Although they were concerned primarily with the child himself, it was the child as an individual, and not as a unit of society, that primarily interested them. Therefore, their education is far more a matter of individual approach and individual growth than a matter of socialization. Social education is left for another—and later—group of educational reformers.

Most of the developmentalists conceived of education as having a broad scope. Pestalozzi, with his aim of the "harmonious development of all the faculties," was concerned with: (1) intellectual education, the "training of the head"; (2) moral education, "the training of the heart"; and (3) industrial education, "the training of the hand." The Fellenberg movement was especially effective in connection with the industrial and agricultural types of education. Neither Pestalozzi nor Fellenberg considered these three types of training as entirely separate and distinct forms of training, but rather as phases of education as closely related as the three aspects of life for which they trained. Both of these reformers advocated a humanistic approach with general education for all, but in this general cultural education they insisted that training in practical activities must not be neglected. This practical education was not to be a narrow vocational preparation, a training for a job. It was to be a broad training in practical power, creativity, productivity—a "skill, readiness, or capacity for performance, for execution, or for production." Education was to prepare a man not only to think and feel, but also to act.

---

[7] Edward L. Thorndike, *op. cit.*, pp. 3-4. Reprinted with the permission of the publishers.

The three types of education emphasized by Pestalozzi and Fellenberg were those that developed the intellect, the moral-religious nature, and practical power.

Herbart (and the Herbartians) emphasized intellectual education beyond all else. This does not mean that they were ignoring the broad scope of life for which education must prepare. Unlike the faculty psychologists, however, they did not consider it necessary to provide for the separate cultivation of the intellect, the emotions, and the will. They did not believe that there are distinct forms of education—an intellectual education, a moral education, a practical education. The central idea of Herbartian psychology is that the only foundation of the whole structure of education is intellectual instruction, the growth and development of ideas in the mind of the child. All mental nature is a unity and therefore there is only one type of education, education by instruction or, more properly speaking, educative instruction. Through the development of the intellect comes controlled emotions and a purposeful enlightened willpower that expresses itself in desirable action and performance.

Froebel also insisted that man is a unity and not a duality, but he made productive activity the central factor in this unity. He, therefore, emphasized what might well be called creative education. It is a mistake to say that Froebel was concerned only with motor training, only with the development of the manual, vocal, or general muscular activities. He contended that in any creative activity the memory, the imagination, the perception, the reasoning, the will, and the feelings are all cooperating with the sense organs, the nerves, and the muscles. Since all these are exercised in unity, he considered the development of productive or creative activity the one important type of education. Froebel resorted to his religious concepts for a still more powerful sanction for his emphasis upon creative education. "God is the original unity from which the entire universe has evolved by virtue of His own creative self-expression." To develop the child's creative self-expression is to develop the most nearly divine attribute of the child.

Hall was interested in every type of training, every aspect of human growth. His own widespread education and his many-sided specialization gave him a comprehension and insight that enabled him to study education with considerable range and detail.

He emphasized every phase of human development, physical growth, emotional growth, moral and religious growth, and growth of the will and social nature. But of all the types of education he emphasized emotional training as the most important. He believed that the emotional life is far more fundamental than the intellectual; even that intelligence is a comparatively late development, while emotion is as old as life itself. He believed that the emotions motivate the development of the intellect; that all thought owes its origin to the emotions. Hall also stressed play as a type of education.

Play is the best kind of education, because it practices powers of mind and body which, in our highly specialized civilization, would never otherwise have a chance to develop.[8]

James and Thorndike, with their interest in habits and instincts, were primarily concerned with the development of behavior and conduct. Their emphasis, therefore, was upon dynamic education, training for the manifold activities of life. They urged physical training, intellectual training, and emotional or moral training, but they, too, conceived of the individual as a unit and not as a collection of faculties. Their emphasis, however, was upon practical training as the central feature of development. As Thorndike says:

With respect to the amount of emphasis upon different features . . . the best judgment of the present rates practical ability somewhat higher. . . . No sensible thinker about education now regards the ability to support oneself as a mean thing. Every one must gain power at school as well as at home to pull his own weight in the boat. . . . The best judgment of the present gives much more weight . . . to health, to bodily skill and to the technical and industrial arts. The ideal of the scholar has given way to the ideal of the capable man—capable in scholarship, still, but also capable in physique and in the power to manipulate things.[9]

Thus the developmentalists are concerned with as many types of education as there are aspects of the individual organism to be developed. Although all of the later developmentalists consider the individual as a unit, with the various types of training dependent one upon the other, some emphasize one phase and some another as the central factors in human development. For this reason, we see a difference of opinion as to which type of training is to be made central. We have seen, however, that the developmentalists as a whole neglect no part of the growth of the individual. Whatever neglect there is in the scope of their educational theory, is along the lines of social education and the development of society as a whole.

METHODS Since the educational philosophy of the psychological developmentalists placed greatest emphasis upon the child and his growth as the central factor of education, methodology played a larger part in their thinking than any other aspect of education. With them, content, organization, and agencies were all secondary to and dependent upon method. For that reason, in this chapter, we are changing our order of discussion and considering method before we deal with these other phases of education.

The period from Pestalozzi to Watson was marked by the de-

---

[8] G. Stanley Hall, "Play and Dancing for Adolescents," *The Independent,* Vol. 62, pp. 355-356.
[9] Edward L. Thorndike, *op. cit.,* pp. 4-5. Reprinted with the permission of the publishers.

velopment of new psychologies of learning. Pestalozzi based all his method upon the principle of pupil activity. There were two steps in his procedure, impression and expression; and both of these must be carried on by the child himself. He said, "Sense impression of nature is the only foundation of human instruction, because it is the only true foundation of human knowledge." He firmly believed that observation must be the basis of all learning. For this reason his instruction of children, especially in the early stages, consisted largely of having them observe, count, analyze, and name objects. He made use of the object lesson, where learning comes through sense experience rather than through words. He insisted on oral teaching of all subjects.

Like Rousseau, Pestalozzi believed that the child was not to learn from a book; the teacher was not to hear the child's recitation. The child's expression activities should come from the impressions gained from the observation of actual objects. Language expression, both oral and written, must grow out of the observation of objects presented to the various senses of the child. So it was with drawing. Geographical expression consisted of such activities as the modeling of landforms perceived on field trips. Arithmetical expression consisted of counting the windows in the room, measuring the distance across the room, and similar exercises in counting and measuring. Moral expression grew out of the incidents which arose in the daily lives of the children.

Pestalozzi likewise abandoned the older deductive methods (whereby teaching began with rules and abstractions), for the inductive methods, whereby children began with simple elements of experience which they combined into larger meaningful wholes. He recognized the principle that learning must proceed from the known to the unknown, which to him meant from the simple to the complex. He bitterly criticized the then prevalent method of "teaching the unknown by means of the uncomprehensible." He reduced all subjects to their simplest unanalyzable elements (their A B C's), and then taught these subjects by carefully graded steps. Nothing was to be learned which was not readily understood and easily mastered. The results of the application of this principle to the teaching of reading, drawing, and music has not been very effective, but its effect upon the teaching of arithmetic, language, geography, and elementary science has been most significant.

The principle which formed the core of the Pestalozzian method was that of proceeding from the concrete to the abstract, from the particular to the general. (This was, of course, not the method of Comenius.) He protested vehemently against teaching generalized ideas to the child in the form of meaningless words. He insisted that the child must express his own ideas as the result of the impressions gained from concrete observation and experiences. Pestalozzi's great contributions to the new educational methods were: (1) the study of real objects, (2) learning through the various senses, (3) individual expression of ideas. One of his limitations was that his efforts were spent largely in the perfecting of the elementary steps of instruction. The second was that he knew nothing about the psychological control of mental organization—that which went on in between impression and expression. It was along these lines that Herbart was to make his greatest contribution.

The English version of Pestalozzianism, with its textbook, *Lessons on Objects,* missed the spirit of Pestalozzi's method completely. The lessons were bookish, formal, and analytical, far beyond the comprehension of children.

For example, if common salt were the object of the lesson, the children would be expected to learn its chemical composition, its uses, how and where found in nature, how mined and refined, that its crystalline form is cubical, that it varies in color from white to bluish and reddish, that it is transparent to translucent, that it is soluble in water and saline in taste, that it imparts a yellow color to flame, etc., without more contact with a piece of real salt than seeing the 'specimen' passed around by the teacher.[10]

Charles Dickens has satirized the formal memorizing of the object lessons in the following passage taken from his *Hard Times:*

Sissy Jupe, Girl No. 20, the daughter of a strolling circus actor, whose life, no small share of it, has been passed under the canvas; whose knowledge of horse, generic and specific, extends back as far as memory reaches; familiar with the form and food, the powers and habits and everything related to the horse; knowing it through several senses; Sissy Jupe has been asked to define horse. Bewildered by the striking want of resemblance between the horse of her own conceptions and the prescribed formula that represents the animal in the books of the Home and Colonial Society, she dares not trust herself with the confusing description, and shrinks from it in silence and alarm.

"Girl No. 20 unable to define horse," said Mr. Gradgrind.

Girl No. 20 is declared possessed of no facts in reference to one of the commonest of animals, and appeal is made to one red-eyed Bitzer, who knows horse practically only as he has seen a picture of a horse or as he has, perhaps, sometimes safely weathered the perils of a crowded street-crossing.

"Bitzer," said Thomas Gradgrind, your "definition of a horse!"

"Quadruped, Gramnivorous. Forty teeth, namely: twenty-four grinders, four eye teeth, and twelve incisors. Sheds coat in the spring; in marshy countries sheds hoofs too. Hoofs hard but requiring to be shod with iron. Age known by marks in mouth." Thus, and much more, Bitzer.

"Now, Girl No. 20," said Mr. Gradgrind, "you know what a horse is."

Pestalozzi was opposed to the harsh, brutal discipline which for ages had characterized the schools, and tried to substitute for it a discipline of sympathy and love. He wanted to reproduce as far as possible the atmosphere of a good Christian home, gentle and refined. When a father visited his school house and said, "Why, this is not a school, but a family," Pestalozzi was very much pleased. His doctrine of "thinking love" was a natural outgrowth of his conception of education as the development of the child rather than the pressing of the child into

---

[10] E. P. Cubberley, *Public Education in the United States.* (Boston: Houghton Mifflin Company, 1934.) P. 353. Reprinted with the permission of the publishers.

molds of adult behavior that was present in most educational practice of his day.

The basic principle upon which Herbart's methods were based was the "doctrine of interest." He believed that interest is of first importance in good instruction; only that knowledge which is acquired with the warm glow of genuine interest will affect the will of the learner and pass over into appropriate action. Skillful teaching is marked by the ability to secure interest without resorting to force on the one hand or "sugar-coating" on the other. Herbart's whole philosophy is, in a sense, a summation of ways in which interest, the *sine qua non* of "educative instruction," can best be aroused.

Herbart took the principle that learning must proceed from the known to the unknown and elaborated it into the doctrine that new knowledge is always assimilated in terms of what the learner already knows. If the child is to be interested in new experiences he must have something in his mind which will cause him to listen. The pupil must be in the proper frame of mind to accept the new experience, and must have a stock of recalled related ideas which will enable him to interpret and respond to the new situation. Since Herbart called these related revived experiences "apperceptive masses," this principle is known as the "doctrine of apperception."

Herbart insisted that only large, connected units of subject matter are able to arouse and keep alive the deep interest of the child's mind. Therefore he devised a principle of teaching known as the "doctrine of concentration." Effective reactions of will and conduct come only when the whole of consciousness has been focused on one single unit of thought. Herbart, however, supplemented this doctrine of concentration with the "doctrine of correlation," which makes one subject central in the focus of attention, but organizes the learning situation so that this subject receives support from all other related subjects. These two doctrines, concentration and correlation, have played a prominent part in clarifying his conception of the principle of interest.

Herbart was the first to formulate the steps of a method based on psychological principles. He was the first to set forth a theory of the stages of procedure which enable the teacher to control all the learning processes of the child, including the process of mental organization, as well as the processes of impression and expression. The Herbartians recognized five steps as essential in the procedure of instruction. These, usually designated as the "five formal steps," were as follows:

(1) *Preparation.* This is the process of reviving in consciousness the related ideas from past experience, which will arouse a vital interest in the new material and prepare the pupil for its rapid understanding and assimilation.

(2) *Presentation.* This process involves the presenting of the new material, in concrete form unless there is already ample sensory experience, and in such a way that it is closely articulated with "the apperceptive mass," or past experience.

(3) *Association.* This is the process of assimilating the new experiences, by using analysis and comparison to point out points of likeness and points of difference between the new and the old, thus enabling the new idea to take its true place in the mind's understanding.

(4) *Generalization.* This is the process of forming general rules, laws, and principles from the analyzed sensory experiences, thus developing general concepts in addition to sensations and perceptions in the mind's structure.

(5) *Application.* This process consists of putting the generalized idea to work, sometimes merely to test it, sometimes to deepen the impression by expression, and sometimes to put the idea to use in a purely utilitarian sense.

John Dewey later was to challenge the "formal steps" of the Herbartians on the ground that thinking occurs only when the problem is real. The special weakness of the Herbartian method, however, was the attempt to use the formal steps in the planning of all types of teaching, in the lesson for skill and in the appreciation lesson, as well as in the thought lesson. Yet great credit is due to Herbart for developing a more complete educational psychology and a better organization and technique of classroom instruction. This has led to an even better understanding of educational psychology and method.

Froebel considered education to be a process of creative self-development. This development comes from what he called an "inner unfolding," and is brought about by means of spontaneous self-activity on the part of the pupil. He based his whole methodology on this principle of self-activity. He insisted that only when a child is actively creating, only when he is "making the inner outer," as he put it, is he really developing. Like Pestalozzi, Froebel contended that the child must learn by doing, but where the former depends upon natural objects from without to stimulate impressions the latter endeavors to draw out of the child, by means of self-prompted activities, every potentiality of his nature. Froebel did not believe that these activities should result from outer stimulation, or from an instinct to emulate, but that they should come as a process of natural evolution like the unfolding of the leaves of a tree. This principle of evolutional self-activity is succinctly expressed in these words in his *The Education of Man:*

All the child is ever to be and become, lies in the child, and can be attained only through development from within outward. The purpose of teaching and instruction is to bring ever more out of man rather than to put more and more into man.

According to Froebel, educative activity is to take place only when the child is ready for it, only when the child has a "certain felt need" for it. But this readiness is a condition of his inner nature and not of curiosity, interest, or past experience. The teacher must plan so that the child has the opportunity to engage in the activity when the "budding point" is reached, when there is a felt need.

Froebel was the first educational philosopher to perceive the

significance of socialization as a basic principle of teaching. He maintained that the inner nature of the child impels him to cooperative
activity with others. This was part of his central doctrine of unity in
creative evolution. The "morning circle" in his kindergarten, where the
teachers and all the children stood in a ring and joined hands for song,
prayer, and play, was a splendid method of socialization, a method of
instilling a unity of feeling and purpose into the group. Froebel felt that
it was the duty of the school to make possible the expression of cooperative social activity so that the children would develop better forms of
social living.

Froebel, in his insistence that educational method should be a
following of the natural course of the evolution of the child's innately
stimulated activities, did not impart any illuminating information regarding the true nature of this inner urge, and gave little definite information as to how one should proceed in the later developments of the
child's life. His conceptions were drawn largely from a metaphysical
symbolism which other teachers found rather difficult to put into practice, especially beyond the kindergarten stage of the child's development.
Hall rendered a service in clearing away some of the eccentricities of
Froebelian methodology. From his knowledge of biology, anthropology,
and child study he developed a coherent methodology for all the stages
of the child's development, formulating more definitely than either Herbart or Froebel the cultural-epoch theory and the law of recapitulation.

Hall interpreted the inner urge in terms of simple instincts or
tendencies inherited from the past of the race. He contended that these
innate traits were not connate—that is, operative at birth—but have under
normal conditions a definite order of appearance. He thought that, although the neural connections are fixed at birth the stimuli that set up
the excitations do not appear until later. (In some cases, the reacting
mechanism must await development if not full maturation.)

According to Hall, the appearance of these delayed instincts
follow the same order as the appearance of similar forms of activities
in the history of the race, that "ontogeny repeats phylogeny" in the
mental life as well as in the physical. He claimed that there was a fixed
period—or nascent stage—for each form of activity, corresponding to similar periods in the successive development of animals from lower forms
to higher and of man in his transition from savagery to civilization. The
teacher must strike while the iron is hot, and arrange that the child
engages in the appropriate activity when the nascent stage for that
activity is reached.

A startling aspect of Hall's theory, with important bearing upon
school discipline, is his "doctrine of catharsis," the doctrine that innate
tendencies must be allowed to run their course when they appear naturally in childhood, even though they are considered harmful in later life.
By being allowed to pass through their normal and natural development
they work themselves out and disappear. Thorndike later showed that

this theory was opposed not only to common sense but to science, when he advanced abundant evidence for his well-known law of learning that states that a capacity becomes more deeply ingrained through exercise. Other discoveries in the conditioning of reflexes and the sublimation of instincts have led educators to the view that undesirable tendencies can and must be weeded out as soon as possible.

Although psychologists disagree with him in many of his conclusions and question the reliability of his methods of research, Hall deserves credit for stimulating the study of child nature and inspiring an intelligent, sympathetic treatment of children. Largely as a result of his efforts, it has been realized that the teacher can do his best work only when he understands fully the nature of his pupils. Methods must be determined by that understanding; the school at each level must provide the type of activity best suited to the nature of the children at that level; the school must provide methods and facilities which will enable children to behave normally and naturally and to learn by means of that behavior.

The most influential contribution of William James to educational method was in connection with habit formation. He says:

The great thing, then, in all education, is to make our nervous system our ally instead of our enemy. It is to fund and capitalize our acquisitions and live at ease upon the interest of the fund. For this we must make automatic and habitual, as early as possible, as many useful actions as we can, and guard against the growing into ways that are likely to be disadvantageous to us, as we should guard against the plague. The more of the details of our daily life we can hand over to the effortless custody of automatism, the more our higher powers of mind will be set free for their proper work.[11]

In discussing the methods of habit formation, James set forth four basic principles:

(1) Launch yourselves with as strong and decided an initiative as possible.

(2) Never suffer an exception to occur till the new habit is securely rooted in your life.

(3) Seize the very first possible opportunity to act.

(4) Keep the habit alive by a little gratuitous effort every day.

Thorndike developed these principles further and applied them to all forms of associative learning in his famous "laws of learning":

(1) The *law of readiness*. The start of learning must be enthusiastic and motivated.

(2) The *law of exercise*. The more frequently a bond is exercised, the stronger it becomes.

(3) The *law of effect*. There must be some measure of progress so that the learner can gauge his success and thus gain a feeling of satisfaction.

---

[11] William James, *Briefer Course in Psychology*. (New York: Holt, Rinehart and Winston, Inc., 1923.) Pp. 144-145.

Thorndike was even more influential than James in formulating and putting into practice the principles of functionalist psychology. Through his elaboration of laws of learning he, more than any other psychologist, convinced teachers that learning consists of effecting changes in the nervous organization of the individual, that development comes with the building up of neural connections. His educational psychology is based upon the well-known Stimulus-Response Hypothesis. This means that when a given stimulus has been followed by a certain reaction or response, under satisfying conditions, a bond is created between the two. Learning is the result of the formation of these bonds, and development comes with the multiplying of these bonds into patterns of behavior. The teacher's work is to control the formation of these bonds. In the case of undesirable natural behavior the teacher must either withhold the stimuli, or so modify the neural organization that the stimuli will evoke responses different from those prompted by original nature. The ideal teaching methods, therefore, are those that develop within the child the neural organization that produces desirable responses.

In developing this methodology, Thorndike elaborated upon (1) the principle of self-activity, (2) the principle of apperception, (3) the principle of motivation, which had been formulated by earlier developmentalists. He added, however, an important fourth principle, the principle of individual differences.

Common observation shows that children differ greatly in their mental make-up. . . . The practical consequence of this fact of individual differences is that every general law of teaching has to be applied with consideration of the particular person in question. . . . The responses of children to any stimulus will not be invariable like the responses of atoms of hydrogen or of filings of iron, but will vary with their individual capacities, interests, and previous experience.[12]

Thus the educational thinking of the developmentalists led to the formulation of five basic principles of teaching:

(1) The Principle of Pupil-Activity (Self-activity)
    1. Psychological basis—learning comes from the pupil's own responses to stimulation.
    2. Law of procedure for teacher—control the activity of the pupil in the right direction.
(2) The Principle of Motivation (Interest)
    1. Psychological basis—the intensity of the learning response depends upon interest.
    2. Law of procedure for teacher—reveal interests in the stimulating situation.

---

[12] Edward L. Thorndike, *op. cit.*, pp. 68, 83. Reprinted with the permission of the publishers.

(3) The Principle of Apperception (Preparation and Mental Set)
    1. Psychological basis—the nature of the learning response depends upon past experience and present frame of mind.
    2. Law of procedure for teacher—present stimuli adapted to the experience and mental set of the pupils.
(4) The Principle of Individualization
    1. Psychological basis—learning responses are determined and limited by individual differences in ability.
    2. Law of procedure for teacher—adapt instruction to individual differences.
(5) The Principle of Socialization
    1. Psychological basis—every response has its social implications —"No one lives unto himself alone."
    2. Law of procedure for teacher—all learning responses must be developed in natural social settings.

Developmentalists maintain that these principles are universally applicable to all teaching situations and to all levels of instruction. The later Gestalt or field psychologists see learning somewhat differently; their contribution to educational psychology will be considered in Chapter XVIII.

During the second quarter of the twentieth century the Behaviorist school assumed a prominent position in structural and functional psychology. The American phase of this movement—an extreme development of functionalism—dates from the publication of John B. Watson's *Behavior: An Introduction to Comparative Psychology* (1914). Watson adopted the conditioned reflex principle made famous by the experiments of the Russian physiologist and psychologist IVAN PETROVIC PAVLOV (1849–1936), which stressed the mechanistic foundations of life.[13] Watson and his followers rejected both introspective methods and the concept of consciousness; they maintained that "scientifically valuable data cannot be obtained by introspection . . . [and] subjective observations (such as Hall's) are a strictly private affair."

The Behaviorists, Meyer in Germany and Watson and Lashley in the United States, emphasized stimulus and response, the concept of the conditioned reflex (or response)—as indeed had Thorndike's experimental use of connectionist psychology. They were interested chiefly in those processes and activities related to motor (muscular and glandular) responses of the organism to environmental stimuli. But the proponents of this school frequently disagreed in their premises and conclusions and Behaviorism soon reached its zenith—at least in the United States. Its effect on American educational methodology was not great.

Yet despite Behaviorism's exaggerated claims few of its theses have been scientifically disproved. What conditioning can do was demonstrated in the educational practices of Nazi Germany and Fascist Italy

---

[13] See Boris P. Babkin, *Pavlov: A Biography*. (Chicago: University of Chicago Press, 1949.)

and it is being utilized to the hilt presently in the entire Communist world. But Behaviorism denies the existence of the soul, mind, and consciousness and the American mentality does not favor a doctrine holding that behavior should be placed on a purely mechanical, stimulus-response, conditioning basis, and that only those aspects of human behavior which can be observed and analyzed should be studied.[14]

CONTENT   One of the obvious results of the educational theories of the psychological developmentalists was the broadening of the curriculum, especially at the elementary level. Some of the newer subjects were not covered by their conception of education, and had to be introduced later as a result of more recent movements. But the curriculum that they developed was much more extensive than any which had preceded their work. Moreover, the character of many of the older subjects was changed to such an extent that they were scarcely recognizable.

In general terms, Pestalozzi believed that the essential elements of an elementary education were language, number and form; that all the materials of instruction could be brought under this threefold classification. Yet in practice the Pestalozzians retained the traditional names of the various subjects in the elementary curriculum, only modifying each according to the Pestalozzian theory. Some of the subjects were changed for the better and some were not, but all came under their influence.

As a result of the Pestalozzian emphasis upon oral object teaching, certain subjects were emphasized much more than others; these were greatly improved in character. Arithmetic, geography, elementary science, and language were so enhanced. But, as a result of the extreme application of his principle of proceeding from the simple to the complex, other subjects did not fare so well. Drawing, music, reading, and writing suffered.

In connection with the teaching of object lessons, Pestalozzi and his followers made use of many materials used later in the teaching of the natural sciences. They usually designated such instruction by the term "object teaching," the phrase "elementary science" coming into use later, and the phrase "nature study" still more recently. Object teaching was at first of a rather informal nature, the teacher making use of materials in the children's environment in order to enlarge the scope of their impressions and provide the basis for language expression. Later, this objective teaching became more scientific and quite highly systematized. Collections of physical, chemical, mineralogical, botanical, and zoological specimens were made available for observation by the children, who were required to learn to describe them in scientific terms. Still later, especially among the English and American Pestalozzians, these

---

[14] From an unpublished paper by Joseph S. Roucek and Kenneth V. Lottich.

lessons in elementary science were looked upon as essential preparation for the advanced study of natural science and history in the secondary schools.

No subject in the curriculum was more completely changed by the Pestalozzian influence than geography. Before the time of Pestalozzi geographies were mere compendia of facts, arranged in encyclopedic manner. Even after the development of Pestalozzianism this dictionary-encyclopedic type of geography continued to be taught in many localities, and it is not uncommon to find traces of it in geographies today. This fact-geography involved the memorizing of all kinds of astronomical, physical, natural, and political data, usually presented in a catechetical, or question-and-answer, form. The pupils learned definitions, statistics, boundaries, capitals, products, exports and imports, population figures, etc., and the teacher "heard" the pupils recite these memorized facts.

The application of oral object teaching to geography changed this. A new study of home geography was introduced, based on the principle of proceeding from the simple and known to the complex and unknown. KARL RITTER, a German pupil of Pestalozzi, changed the emphasis from political and statistical geography to physical and human geography, with much attention to out-of-doors observation and the study of type forms. ARNOLD GUYOT, a pupil of Ritter, who came to America as an institute lecturer for the Massachusetts State Board of Education, wrote a geography textbook on the Pestalozzian plan, the purpose of which, he said, was "to fill the young with vivid pictures of nature in such regions of the globe as may be considered great geographical types." FRANCIS W. PARKER in his *How to Teach Geography,* and ALEXIS FRYE, with his geography textbook series, improved upon the earlier Pestalozzian content.

The third subject that was greatly improved as the result of Pestalozzian theory was arithmetic. Earlier arithmetic consisted largely of figuring on paper, and was commonly known as "ciphering." Rules were memorized and examples solved according to these fixed rules. Pestalozzi replaced such processes with rapid mental calculations in connection with the counting and measuring of objects. He tried to develop "number ideas" instead of meaningless words about numbers. These number ideas were gained by counting, measuring, grouping, and arranging concrete objects and lines. This type of arithmetic was popular down to the end of the nineteenth century. Mental arithmetic was the first of the Pestalozzian subjects to be introduced into the United States. In 1821 WARREN COLBURN published his *First Lessons in Arithmetic on the Pestalozzian Plan,* a book which represents the only phase of the Pestalozzian curriculum to receive any attention in the United States before the beginning of the Oswego movement in 1860.

Pestalozzi made oral language one of the outstanding features of his curriculum. He was the first to introduce the oral language lessons which became a prominent phase of elementary school study. Children were encouraged to tell what they had experienced after they had been filled with sense impressions through their observation of objects. Thus language came to be a free oral description based on sensory experience rather than a reproduction of words read in a printed text; correct speech usage came to be stressed instead of the formal rules of grammar.

Perhaps writing, drawing, and music should have been developed by Pestalozzi along with oral language as agencies for free expression. He did include these subjects in his course of study, but they were influenced unfavorably by his principle of procedure from the simple to the complex. Because of his attempts to reduce each of these subjects to its elements and to present it logically, they were taught in a mechanical, lifeless, and ineffectual manner. Children were started on learning to write by means of drills on lines, curves, and muscular movements. Years were spent on angles, geometric figures, and forms in preparation for drawing. In music, children were drilled on notes, scales, and tones.

Pestalozzi, in so far as he taught reading, was satisfied to continue in the traditional manner, beginning with drills on the alphabet, and then proceeding through drills on syllables and words to phrases and sentences. Now it is realized, as a result of the work of later educational psychologists, that the phrase or sentence is the simplest element to the child, and we begin the teaching of reading with these elements. Even arithmetic came under the influence of this mistaken principle. Grube, a German Pestalozzian, reduced arithmetic to its elements, and with intense thoroughness spent days teaching each of these elements. This idea was introduced into the United States by Louis Soldan, a teacher in the St. Louis Public Schools, and, unfortunately, found a wide acceptance in the last decade of the nineteenth century.

Pestalozzi's early use of industrial and agricultural activities found little place in his later work at Burgdorf and Yverdon. In fact, he never particularly stressed these activities as a form of vocational preparation. Even the Fellenberg institutes seldom used the results of training in these activities for any other purpose than self-support while engaged in the study of academic subjects. The Pestalozzians looked upon manual training as a form of developmental expression, as a part of the "harmonious development of the faculties." The early manual training movement in this country and much of the handwork in our elementary schools were in accord with this point of view.

Herbart outlined the materials of instruction in terms of his doctrine of interests, classifying all subject matter in terms of typical human concerns. Man's interests, he said, were derived from two sources: (1) his contacts with the real *things* of his environment, or sense impressions; and (2) his contacts with other human beings, or social intercourse. He believed, therefore, that the content of education should consist of two types of studies: (1) studies about *things,* such as sciences, mathematics, and fine arts; and (2) studies about people, such as languages, history, and mathematics.

The Pestalozzians, as indicated above, had already emphasized and developed the first group of subjects. Of the second group, however, Pestalozzi had concerned himself only with oral language. It remained for Herbart and his followers to introduce and foster history and literature as subjects of preeminent importance in the curriculum. Herbart was concerned primarily with the application of his theory to the study of languages, literature, and history in the secondary schools. Ziller, seeing the value of Herbartian-taught history and literature as a means for developing the morals of the child, made story material from history and literature the basis of the content of the elementary curriculum. The Herbartians have favored history as a study of primary importance in developing good human relationships and good citizenship. Partly as a result of the influence of the American Herbartians, history and literature have become important subjects in American elementary courses of study. Literature, originally used as models for expressions and taught by means of a few selected classics, is now taught for its moral and esthetic values with material drawn from the whole range of children's publications.

Froebel's curriculum was an activity curriculum. His content was made up of all types of self-expression activities. He encouraged language as the earliest and most fundamental means by which unfolding occurs. He believed that language must accompany all the other educational activities. He insisted that there must be a simultaneous development of language, song, gesture, and constructive activity. He included drawing and rhythm among the activities of the school, for he considered these as essential to expression as language. Handwork was looked upon as an opportunity for expression, an aid to further impressions, a training of the mind through the hand. Nature study, instead of being a study of classified specimens, became the examination of living and growing plants and animals.

Above and beyond everything else, Froebel emphasized play as the most valuable form of self-expression. He was interested in its social and intellectual implications rather than in its health values. He organized his play materials systematically and designated them by the terms "gifts" and "occupations." These were developed gradually and manufactured and sold for school purposes. Such materials as balls, a sphere, a cube, a cylinder, small blocks, sticks, and paper for folding were included—all for the stimulation of motor expression on the part of the child. He also developed many types of cooperative play and group games, minutely and systematically setting forth the songs and movements involved in each. While the idea that a spiritual meaning is intuitively grasped by the child from every gift and occupation may be somewhat fanciful, we must admit that Froebel enriched the curriculum—especially at the early elementary level—with a vast amount of most valuable educational material.

Hall was particularly influential in organizing the curriculum in terms of the stages of the child's development. First, he said, should come the training of the child in the use of his own physical endowments—training in walking, talking, and the movements and activities essential to comfort and self-preservation. Then attention should be given to the training of the senses, through activities of sensory observation and sense impression. Sensory activity should give way to imaginative activity when the child reached the proper stage. The reading of myths and poetic fancy should be encouraged and the child's imagination should be extended into the past and out over the world.

Next should come drill, memorization, and regimentation—the acquisition of the fundamental habits needed for adaptation to an integrated society. At this stage the subject matter should be made up of the so-called rudiments—the essential habits of daily life. Finally, at the adolescent stage, the child should learn to appreciate and understand the "whole world of nature and of man," by being brought into touch with all the cultural subjects of a civilized people. Even if we feel that Hall was wrong in his organization of the curriculum into fixed periods, one must agree that he advocated a most extensive and complete educational content.

The dynamic psychologists, under the leadership of James and Thorndike, although they retained somewhat the organization of the curriculum in terms of stages of development, were more inclined to classify and discuss the subjects of instruction in terms of types of teaching and learning. As a result of their influence, familiarity with the psychology of elementary and secondary school subjects came to be looked upon as an essential part of the teacher's preparation. These school subjects were approached from the standpoint of their psychological aims, and the content of the curriculum was analyzed in terms of skills, appreciations, and knowledge.

Thorndike, for example, said that the first six years of school life should be given over to the development of: (1) physical training and protection against disease; (2) knowledge of the simple facts of nature and human life; (3) skill in gaining knowledge through reading and in expressing ideas through spoken and written language, music, and other arts; (4) interests in the concrete life of the world; (5) habits of intelligent curiosity, purposive thinking, modesty, obedience, honesty, helpfulness, courage, and justice; (6) ideals and appreciations proper for children. School life from twelve to eighteen, he said, should be given over to the development of: (1) physical skills; (2) knowledge of the general laws of nature and of human life, and of the opinions of the wisest and best; (3) skill in the effective use of the expressive arts; (4) interests in the arts and sciences, and in human life as directly experienced and as portrayed in literature; (5) powers of self-control, accuracy, steadiness and logical thought, technical and executive abilities, cooperation and leadership; (6) habits of self-restraint, honor, courage, and justice; (7) the ideals and appreciations proper for youth.[15]

AGENCIES The psychological developmentalists set up few new agencies of instruction. As a rule they made use of existing institutions. The welcome that was given to their ideas by the nationalists made it unnecessary for them to break away and found new schools apart from those in the national school systems. The only new types of schools fostered by the developmental movement were the Fellenberg institutes and the Froebelian kindergartens.

Even the kindergarten was not an entirely new institution. The idea that attention should be given to the education of pre-school children is at least as old as Comenius, who advocated the "School of the Mother's Knee." JEAN OBERLIN had already founded the first *école maternelle* in France, and ROBERT OWEN had initiated "infant schools" in Great Britain. But both of these institutions were the result of a philanthropic desire to ameliorate conditions arising from social and economic maladjustments. Froebel was really the first to give a philosophical and psychological basis to such an institution.

The developmentalists considered the teacher to be the only truly effective agency for education. As an obvious corollary of their belief that teaching was a matter of psychological methodology, they continually emphasized the careful training of teachers in these methods. We cannot say that the first teacher-training institutions were started as a result of this movement, for we have already called attention to earlier institutions of this type. There is no quesiton, however, but that the psychologists stimulated the establishment and growth of teacher-training facilities as educational agencies more than any other group ever did. From the establishment of Pestalozzi's institute at Yverdon, down through the pedagogical seminars of the Herbartians, to teachers colleges in the United States, the psychologists have been instrumental in building thriving and effective teacher-education institutions. Not only have these schools presented the theories of developmentalism, but in their model schools and practice schools they have made it possible for teachers to learn to put these theories, as well as other later concepts, into actual practice.

ORGANIZATION The earlier developmentalists made no recommendations for changes in the established organization of the school system, either in regard to administrative control or in regard to levels of instruction. Pestalozzi was so closely concerned with elementary education, Herbart with secondary education, and Froebel with the

---

[15] See R. Freeman Butts and Lawrence A. Cremin, *A History of Education in American Culture*. (New York: Holt, Rinehart and Winston, Inc., 1953.) Pp. 343-347, 496-499, for a good interpretation of the contributions of Hall and Thorndike.

kindergarten, that they gave little attention to the problems of articulation and reorganization. It remained for Hall to make the first start in this direction.

He believed that educational development proceeds in distinct stages with somewhat abrupt changes at certain points. This is known as the saltatory theory of development as opposed to the gradual theory. He also believed that different phases of development begin at different stages rather than that all phases develop side by side. This is known as the serial theory of development as opposed to the concomitant theory. As a result of these theories, Hall suggested that there should be distinct levels of schools, organized on the basis of the changes in the child's life and the stages of his development. He divided this development into four general stages: (1) Infancy, (2) Childhood, (3) Youth, (4) Adolescence. Some of his later followers modified this into a five-fold division: (1) Infancy, (2) Early childhood, (3) Later childhood, (4) Early adolescence, (5) Later adolescence.

According to Hall, infancy is the period from birth to about four years of age. The stage of childhood extends normally from about four to eight years of age. Youth is the period from eight to twelve or thirteen years of age, the prepubescent stage. Adolescence begins with puberty and extends to full physical maturity at twenty-two to twenty-five years of age.

Probably this theory concerning the stages in the development of the child has been one of the most influential factors in bringing about such recent reorganizations of the American school system as those represented by the establishment of the Kindergarten-Primary, the Junior High School, and Junior College. At any rate, this reorganization came about largely as a result of attempts to bring the passing of the child from one level to another more closely in accord with the changes in his psychological nature.

FOR FURTHER READING

Burnham, William H., *Great Teachers and Mental Health*. New York: Appleton-Century-Crofts, Inc., 1926. Pp. 189-247.

Butts, R. Freeman, *A Cultural History of Western Education*. Second Edition. New York: McGraw-Hill Book Co., 1955. Pp. 383-406.

———— and Cremin, Lawrence A., *A History of Education in American Culture*. New York: Holt, Rinehart and Winston, Inc., 1953. Pp. 343-347, 496-499, *et passim*.

Cole, Luella, *A History of Education from Socrates to Montessori*. New York: Holt, Rinehart and Winston, Inc., 1950. Pp. 454-540.

Cubberley, Ellwood P., *Public Education in the United States*. Revised and Enlarged Edition. Boston: Houghton Mifflin Company, 1934. Pp. 340-366, 449-467.

Curti, Merle, *Social Ideas of American Educators.* Revised Edition. Paterson, N. J.; Littlefield, Adams and Company, 1959. Pp. 396-498.

Duggan, Stephen P., *Student's Textbook in the History of Education.* Revised Enlarged Edition. New York: Appleton-Century-Crofts, Inc., 1936. Pp. 22-268.

Eby, Frederick, and Arrowood, Charles F., *The Development of Modern Education.* New York: Prentice-Hall, Inc., 1934. Pp. 619-678, 755-855.

Ganz, Hans, *Pestalozzi, Leben und Werk.* Zurich: Origo Verlag, 1956.

Good, H. G., *A History of Western Education.* New York: The Macmillan Co., 1960. Pp. 225-291.

Graves, Frank P., *Great Educators of Three Centuries.* New York: Appleton-Century-Crofts, Inc., 1909. Pp. 122-233.

Knight, Edgar W., *Twenty Centuries of Education.* Boston: Ginn & Co., 1940. Pp. 356-369.

Mayer, Frederick, *A History of Educational Thought.* Columbus, Ohio: Charles E. Merrill Books, Inc., 1960. Pp. 264-287.

Messenger, James F., *An Interpretative History of Education.* New York: Thomas Y. Crowell Co., 1931. Pp. 182-227.

Monroe, Paul, *A Textbook in the History of Education.* New York: The Macmillan Co., 1933. Pp. 587-673.

Mulhern, James, *A History of Education.* Second Edition. New York: The Ronald Press Co., 1959. Pp. 462-481, 490-493.

Noble, Stuart G., *A History of American Education.* New York: Holt, Rinehart and Winston, Inc., 1954. Pp. 220-237.

Parker, Samuel C., *A History of Modern Elementary Education.* Boston: Ginn & Co., 1912. Pp. 273-484.

Ulich, Robert, *A History of Educational Thought.* New York: American Book Company, 1950. Pp. 258-291.

————, *Three Thousand Years of Educational Wisdom.* Cambridge, Mass.: Harvard University Press, 1954. Pp. 480-576.

QUESTIONS FOR CLASS DISCUSSION

1. What differences do you find between psychological aims and social objectives in education? Which are placed first today?
2. In what respects is the present emphasis upon visual education a continuation of Pestalozzian theories?
3. How does present-day teaching of the manual arts differ from that of Pestalozzi and Fellenberg?
4. To what extent do we still use object teaching in the elementary school?

5. Under present conditions, do you feel it would be wise or unwise to attempt to make the "development of individuality" the chief aim of education? Explain.
6. In what ways have contemporary schools extended Herbart's doctrine of correlation?
7. To what extent do William James' theories concerning the importance of habit formation still influence educational practice?
8. How do the methods used for "character education" and moral training in today's schools differ from those advocated by Herbart?
9. On what grounds were the culture epoch theory and the doctrine of recapitulation rejected?
10. Is play in contemporary schools fostered for the same reasons that were advocated by Friedrich Froebel? State Froebel's theory of child growth and development.
11. Why is lesson planning in terms of Herbart's "formal steps" now considered passé?
12. What theories of the psychology of learning presently are supplanting those of James and Thorndike? What are the essential differences?

CHAPTER XVI

THE SCIENTIFIC MOVEMENT IN EDUCATION

SCIENTIFIC DETERMINISM

The educational theories of the psychological developmentalists were formulated largely as a result of empirical and speculative thinking. At their best they were all too often based entirely upon the trial-and-error experiences of the educational reformer himself; frequently they were educational pronouncements based upon nothing more than philosophical speculation. These findings and speculations—although they added much to educational progress—lacked the reliability and adequacy which the scientific method of attack had already brought to pure and applied sciences during the great scientific advance of the latter part of the nineteenth century.

This great century was characterized by tremendous developments in the pure sciences, such as astronomy, biology, physiology, physics, and chemistry, and in the applications of science to agriculture, manufacture, transportation, and almost every other phase of practical life. Most of these advances took place outside the schools, and the scientific movement was carried on more in spite of education than because of it. Although the scientific awakening of the sixteenth and seventeenth centuries had been reflected in the sense-realistic movement in education, and a new impetus had been given to scientific curricular content by

Rousseau and Pestalozzi, scientific studies and the scientific methods were introduced into the schools slowly and against much opposition.

Within his century HERBERT SPENCER (1820–1903) was perhaps the most influential educational writer in stimulating a demand that the new scientific content and the new scientific method be given a more conspicuous place in the schools and colleges. In *Education, Intellectual, Moral, and Physical* (1860), he urged the introduction of the exact sciences into the school curriculum not only for their content values, but also for their method values. Yet even after the introduction of sciences into the curriculum, education itself was still far from being a science, and aims, content, organization, and methods were far from being scientifically determined.

Early in the twentieth century, however, the spirit of scientific inquiry and scientific experimentation began to push its way into the professional thinking of educators, and made significant contributions to educational progress. By 1910, the older empirical and speculative thinking of educational leaders had given way to inquiries made in a more rigid spirit and pursued by the accurate and precise methods of modern science. The educational mind had developed a new sensitiveness to suggested reforms based on scientific inquiry; it had become increasingly skeptical of proposals not based on scientific bases. This scientific approach to the problems of education was centered largely in the United States, in graduate schools of education such as those at Chicago, Columbia, and Stanford Universities, but these centers had been influenced to some extent by the work of other investigators in Germany, England, and France.

The scientific determinist insisted that all educational problems be approached in a scientific attitude, that educational practices and procedures be determined by investigations conducted in the scientific spirit and by means of the scientific method. In essence the scientific method is (1) objective, (2) impartial, (3) mathematically precise, and (4) subject to verification by any competent observer. Educational scientists thus should not only draw upon the basic sciences for their data, both in the form of facts and in the form of general principles, but they should also copy the laboratory and statistical investigation procedures of the exact sciences.

The scientific method was first applied in the field of psychology to determine the actual facts concerning the working of the mind. As early as 1879 Wundt established the first psychological laboratory at Leipzig. Other German psychologists, notably Weber and Fechner, began to develop a series of psycho-physical measurements, and by the turn of the century various psychological tests were being given in Germany, mainly limited, however, to the fields of sensation and perception. In England, FRANCIS GALTON and KARL PEARSON developed statistical methods of research and measurement in the fields of biology, heredity, eugenics, sociology, and psychology. Although these men were not educators they developed the statistical methods and originated the statistical principles and terms used later in connection with educational research. In the United States, J. McKeen Cattell came under the influence of the new science of anthropometry or biometry which had grown out of the statistical work of Galton and Pearson, and in 1890 at the University of Pennsylvania published his *Mental Tests and Measurements,* which was the first use of these terms. (The sketch of Cattell in Chapter XV lists his other publications and comments on his contributions to the scientific movement.)

Thorndike was the real originator of educational statistics, the first to apply the methods of quantitative research to educational problems. In 1902 he gave the first course in educational measurement at Columbia, and in 1904 published his epoch-making, *Mental and Social Measurements.* In the preface he said modestly, "It is the aim of this book to introduce students to the theory of mental measurements and to provide them with such knowledge and practice as may assist them to follow critically quantitative evidence and argument and to make their own researches exact and logical." (See Chapter XV.)

Thorndike stimulated his students to construct devices for the scientific measurement of the results of instruction. Although he is called by some the father of the movement, he was not the first to attempt a scientific measurement of the results of instruction.

The measurement movement in education really began in the United States with the work of Dr. J. M. Rice, who in 1894 made his famous study of the spelling attainment of over thirty thousand school children in various city and village schools. Using a single list of fifty words, he made the striking discovery that those who spent fifteen minutes a day on spelling were able to spell as well as those who had devoted forty minutes a day to the subject. His findings (although they attracted great attention) had little influence because school authorities, still largely dominated by the doctrine of formal discipline, insisted that it was foolish to expect to determine the value of the teaching of spelling by measuring the spelling ability of the pupils! Thus the principal importance of this pioneer study was the fact that it directed the attention of educational leaders to the feasibility of standardized tests for the objective and exact measurement of educational attainment.

A complete program of scientific educational measurement sprang from the genius of Thorndike. Utilizing the Cattell equal-distance theorem, he devised a scale unit for the measurement of educational achievement. Stone's Arithmetic Reasoning Tests, worked out under the direction of Thorndike in 1908, represented a transition from the Rice comparative test to the scaled tests advocated by Thorndike. Thorndike published his Handwriting Scale in 1909, and this was followed by the publication of the work of several of his students, such as the Hillegas Composition Scale, the Buckingham Spelling Scale, the Trabue Language Scale, and the Woody Fundamentals of Arithmetic Scale. Meanwhile, in Detroit, Stuart Courtis had been successful in experimenting with standardized tests, and was appropriately chosen to direct the testing in the first formal survey where scientifically constructed devices were used, the New York City Survey of 1911.

Other problems that could be studied statistically soon began to attract the attention of those interested in quantitative research. Thorndike's study entitled *Elimination of Pupils from School* appeared in 1907. Two years later LEONARD P. AYRES published *Laggards in Our Schools,* a study of retardation and elimination in city school systems, and in 1912 HARLAN UPDEGRAFF's *Study of Expenses of City School Systems* was published. These three studies were pioneer attempts to measure definitely by precise and rigid statistical methods just what the schools were accomplishing and what they cost. In 1913 Thorndike, in collaboration with GEORGE D. STRAYER, published *Quantitative Studies in Educational Administration,* in 1915 HAROLD RUGG his *Statistical Methods Applied to Education,* and in 1918 CHARLES H. JUDD published his *Introduction to the Scientific Study of Education.*

Yet the results obtained from the measurement of achievement did not have much significance until these results could be interpreted. The scales for measuring school accomplishment had to be supplemented by scales for measuring intellectual ability before any great progress could be made in the solution of educational problems. The beginning of objective mental testing had been made in 1905 when ALFRED BINET (1857–1911), a French psychologist at the University of Paris, devised a scale for the measurement of general intelligence in terms of mental age. The Intelligence Quotient, which offered a yardstick for mental testing, was developed in 1910 by WILLIAM STERN. Binet's scale was revised in 1908 and again in 1911. Translations of the Binet Scale were made and used in the United States by Goddard and others; but it was the revision and adaptation of the tests made by LEWIS M. TERMAN and several assistants at Stanford University and published in Terman's *The Measurement of Intelligence,* that gave the intelligence testing movement its impetus in this country. During World War I a group of psychologists devised the Army Alpha group intelligence scale for classifying soldiers for vocational purposes and for officer-training; thus was demonstrated the significance of measuring the intelligence of large groups. Following the close of this war, Otis, Terman, Haggerty, and others constructed similar group tests for measuring the intelligence of elementary school, secondary school, and college students.

In recent years, the study of the child has become more and more scientific. No longer is dependence placed upon the type of random observation and introspective questioning used by G. Stanley Hall and others. Thousands of scientific experiments and research studies have been made to determine the nature, not only of the child's intelligence, but also of his physiology, his personality, his emotional responses, his social responses, and his growth and development along intellectual, physical, emotional, and social lines. With the aid of endowment funds, systematic growth studies have been initiated, notably that at Harvard University under WALTER F. DEARBORN, at Yale under ARNOLD GESELL, and at the State University of Iowa under BIRD T. BALDWIN. The day has long passed since psychologists considered the child's body a lump of clay to be molded by parents and teachers in the shape demanded by the current fancy.

The school survey was a natural outgrowth of the scientific movement in education. Each survey made use of all the methods of quantitative research developed up to the time it was made. The first of these was made in 1910 in Montclair and East Orange, New Jersey. The reports on these surveys were composed largely of the personal observations and opinions of one experienced educational expert, PAUL H. HANUS, of Harvard University. In 1911, Hanus organized a staff to conduct a comprehensive study of the school system of New York City, in which Courtis used standardized tests for the first time in a school survey. Within a short time surveys became entirely objective, and were based upon precise statistical-research methods. The first of this type was the survey of the schools of Butte, Montana, conducted by Strayer. By 1915, when the extensive Cleveland Survey was made by a staff under the direction of Charles H. Judd, the technique had become standardized. The Cleveland Survey was financed by the Russell Sage Foundation, and the results were published in twenty-two monographs.

Educational experimentation under scientifically controlled conditions developed rapidly. Scientific curriculum construction and scientific determination of teaching technique have become an accepted technique of administration, a self-survey movement largely locally administered.

Beginning with New York City in 1913, Bureaus of Investigation and Research were established in school systems. The National Association of Directors of Educational Research was formed in 1916, the name later being changed to the American Educational Research Association, now an active and extensive department of the National Education Association. The work of these research specialists has rapidly expanded, from that of a general survey of accomplishment and of the conducting of testing programs, to include a wide diversity of scientfiic studies dealing with such problems as pupil placement, retardation, curriculum reorganization, salary schedules, school finance, legislation, and even school publicity and public relations. During the post-war years and the resulting great increase in school construction, school building scales and score-cards were developed, and school architecture and school construction were placed on a more exact and scientific basis. GEORGE D. STRAYER, of Columbia University, was most influential in the application of scientific methods to the solution of the problems of school administration and organization.

The Schools of Education at Ohio State University and at Harvard likewise were particularly active in this area. PHILLIP J. RULON at Harvard and RALPH W. TYLER at Ohio State were prominent in statistical analysis. T. C. HOLY at Ohio State conducted school organization surveys.

This brief review of the development of scientific education is merely indicative of the vast quantity of educational research carried on during the past half century, and mentions but a few of the leaders who have been active in the various fields of such scientific research. In the following pages we shall go into greater detail in our attempt to show the implications and effects of this doctrine of scientific determinism in respect to the aims, types, content, agencies, organization, and methods in the American educational system.

EDUCATION AS SCIENTIFICALLY DETERMINED

AIMS   The scientific determinist has little to say about the ultimate goals of education. His concern with the measurement of educational achievement and the measurement of capacity to achieve tended to divert his attention from an analysis of fundamental social aims and from much consideration of the ultimate objectives of education. There is little question, however, but that the scientific determinist had in mind a universe and a social order operating in harmony with universal natural laws—laws which always can be discovered by accurate and exact experimentation and research. The ideal social order for him is one that is in accord with the principles and laws which have been formulated by science; therefore he looks upon science as the only guarantor of social progress.

It is not difficult for the scientifically minded educator to agree with Karl Compton, former president of the Massachusetts Institute of Technology, when he said that the future safety and prosperity of our country depend upon the adoption of a national program based on scientific research and scientific principles, that we should attack the problem of agricultural overproduction scientifically, that we should find a scientific base for industrial functioning, and that we ought to develop our natural resources in such a way that scientfiic use will replace needless waste. Accepting this concept of the social order, the scientific educator aims to set up as the goal of education the development, in the first place, of skilled scientists who would discover, formulate, and apply these principles, and, in the second place, of a body of enlightened citizens who would be willing to accept and live according to these scientific findings.

THOMAS H. HUXLEY (1825–1895), who was active in promulgating the scientific point of view in England toward the close of the last century, expressed this concern very concisely in his definition of education: "Education is the instruction of the intellect in the laws of nature; under which name I include, not merely things and their forces, but men and their ways; and the fashioning of the affections and the will into an earnest and loving desire to move in harmony with those laws."[1]

One might well question the adequacy of such a concept of the ultimate goal of education. Many believe that in attacking our social problems, especially those involving intricate human relationships, complex social motives, and varied individual personalities, it is necessary to draw upon the methods of philosophy as well as the methods of science. Unfortunately, there has been a tendency to neglect the older fields of philosophical speculation in favor of an almost exclusive dependency upon the so-called scientific methods. Ross L. FINNEY has pointed out an error of this direction:

> Devotees of science, in their ardor to promote the prestige of their deity, are wont . . . to select problems for the solution of which there is a prospect of demonstrable conclusions, eschewing such problems as promise slight prospect of that sort. But such selection leaves large fields uncultivated. The cultivation of these neglected fields remains, therefore, to those who, because of the element of conjecture that must remain in whatever conclusions they are able to reach, are modestly willing, even in an age when science is exclusively the fashion, to call themselves philosophers. Their claim to recognition and respect lies, however, in the obvious fact that even the provisional findings of careful, critical, systematic work upon such problems are preferable to the obvious false beliefs that would otherwise prevail unchallenged. . . . Most of the practical problems of life are still left in the gray shadows of partial conjecture despite the amazing growth of scientific knowledge in many fields. . . . To formulate certain beliefs, and do it in such a way as to make them at least not inconsistent with what actual knowledge we do possess, is a very important and useful sort of intellectual labor, even though the certitude of its conclusions be somewhat less than scientific.[2]

The aim of education should be, therefore, to prepare us to supplement the findings of science, as far as they are at present available, with the findings of synthetic reasoning; to utilize, in addition to scientific factual research, that other method of investigation which consists of a careful, critical, systematic formulation of beliefs, with the aim of making them represent the highest degree of probabilities, in spite of the fact that adequate scientific data are not obtainable for strictly demonstrable conclusions. Of course, we should discourage dogmatic statements, hasty generalizations, *a priori* reasoning, and unwarranted conclusions; but the scientist, in condemning everything that cannot be scientifically determined, is unnecessarily limiting the scope of his educational objectives.

There is another point to be considered. This objective called science is dependent to a large degree upon slow and sometimes painful experimentation. A formula which looks well on paper or works well in

---

[1] Thomas Huxley, *Science and Education*. (New York: Appleton-Century-Crofts, Inc., 1910.) P. 83.
[2] Ross L. Finney, *A Sociological Philosophy of Education*. (New York: The Macmillan Co., 1928.) Pp. 3 ff. Reprinted with the permission of the publishers.

the laboratory cannot always be applied with equal success to human affairs. Scientists, of necessity, are patient people, willing to try a system and see how it works, to accept disappointments as they come and use them as stepping-stones to hoped-for ultimate success. The general public, however, is not so patient, and is likely to be particularly impatient with scientists pursuing scientific methods. It wants quick results, and failing to secure them, it wants to start all over again with something entirely different. To get the world's affairs placed on a scientific basis we must first get the world in a truly scientific frame of mind. And that is an educational objective that is big enough to engage the efforts of the best of the scientific determinists.

The scientific educator aims particularly at making education itself a science, and it is along this line that they have accomplished the most. Both Thorndike and Judd strongly insisted for over a quarter of a century that the chief duty of the serious student of education is to form the habit of scientific study and to learn the logic of statistics. Their predominant interest always was in the application of scientific method to education. Their influence in establishing and popularizing the fact-finding, statistical, and experimental technique in education was immeasurable. Inspired by their leadership, thousands of their graduate students have aimed at answering scientifically the question of how individuals may be changed through education.

The educational purpose of the scientific determinist has been to determine educational processes and educational results quantitatively; to make it possible for us to evolve, by the careful measurement of schools and school-children, standards of efficiency—time-and-effort evaluations of instruction—and standards of accomplishment—measuring-sticks for school work—standards which can be applied to schools everywhere to determine scientifically the economy or wastefulness, the efficiency or inefficiency of the work being done.

WILLIAM A. McCALL, another of Thorndike's followers, in his *How to Measure in Education*,[3] has set forth certain theses in justification of this aim. Briefly stated, they are as follows:

1. Whatever exists at all, exists in some amount.
2. Anything that exists in amount can be measured.
3. Measurement in education is in general the same as measurement in the physical sciences.
4. Not all measurements in the physical sciences are perfect.
5. Measurement is indispensable to the growth of scientific education.
6. Measurement in education is broader than educational tests.
7. There are other things in education besides measurement.
8. To the extent that the pupil's initial abilities or capabilities are unmeasurable, a knowledge of him is impossible.
9. To the extent that any goal of education is intangible, it is worthless.

---

[3] William A. McCall, *How to Measure in Education*. (New York: The Macmillan Co., 1922.)

10. The worth of the methods and materials of instruction is unknown until their effect is measured.

11. Measurement of achievement should precede supervision of teaching method.

12. Measurement is not an educational fad.

13. Measurement will not mechanize education or educators.

14. Measurement will not produce a deadly uniformity.

In aiming at such objectives, however, the scientific determinist should consider certain warnings. In the first place, he should remember that we cannot expect to perfect our measuring instruments in this world of intellect, emotions, and social relations in a few decades. In the second place, he must not reach the conclusion that only those things have value that can be measured "objectively" and concretely, and that we can safely throw overboard the work of the educational philosopher. In third place, he must never—however scientific he becomes—depersonalize and mechanize the work of the schools, and allow the child to degenerate into a mere tally in a frequency distribution or a number in a case-study. Scientific measurements and statistical studies should never be allowed to become ends in themselves, but always should be used as a means toward the more effective education of children.

One aim of the scientific determinist is to use his scientific measuring instruments to determine the classification of the child in school and his placement in the vocational world when his school days are over. WILLIAM C. BAGLEY, in an address before the National Education Association as early as 1922, on the topic "Democracy and the I.Q." bitterly assailed this aspect of the work of the determinists. He made a formidable attack upon their use of general intelligence tests for classification and vocational placement purposes. He held that determinists, by emphasizing the intellectual limitation of the masses and by openly disregarding the possibility of securing individual and social progress by environmental means, cast a shadow across democratic hopes.

Many leaders in the field of vocational guidance have begun to question the methods of scientific determinists in the field of vocational placement. Fred C. Smith, secretary of the National Vocational Guidance Association, in a critical address to the association, presented this viewpoint:

We have been maintaining an out-moded conception of the vocational capacities of individuals. Counselors, and especially writers on vocational psychology, have pictured the individual as the repository of a single vocational aptitude, a static entity to be discovered by means of psychological tests. There is a tendency to define our task as that of prediction, and to regard the counselor as a glorified fortune-teller. The available evidence shows that this conception is wrong, out of tune with facts. One of our immediate tasks is to correct our thinking about human capacities, and to enlighten the public concerning the more modest service that we can actually render.

Recent conceptions of the significance of testing for the I.Q. sometimes consider the results as measures of lost opportunities rather than as a definitive prediction for the future. Thus fitting the round peg into the round hole and the square peg into the square hole is not the easy task that the scientific determinists earlier judged it to be.

TYPES   The type of education predominantly favored by the scientific educator is utilitarian in character. Like the education of Bacon's sense realism and Rousseau's naturalism, it must face the pragmatic test, "Of what use?" The scientist is particularly concerned with efficiency in education, and he cannot consider any education efficient if it does not contribute to the attainment of a practical end—the utility of which has been scientifically determined. By careful and precise measurements, he attempts to discover exactly what directly affects conduct, improves life, and benefits man individually or socially. Because of this emphasis upon a utilitarian type of education, the scientific tendency has become a much more effective reaction against the disciplinary point of view than either the naturalistic or the developmentalistic movements.

There are some who claim that the scientific movement, because of this emphasis upon utility, is inclined to favor a narrow vocational type of education. The truth is that such prominent scientific educational leaders as Thorndike and Judd have really advocated an education that is much more truly liberal and cultural than that urged by those who call themselves "liberal" educators. The narrow curriculum pursued in the traditional academic course in high school and college and labeled as a liberal-culture course of study, is, in reality, perhaps "vocational" in that it prepares only for a few selected occupations, and in no sense fits the student for the whole of modern life. The scientists, with their interest in the natural and social sciences, consider those subjects cultural and liberal that develop the judgment and understanding, enlarge the vision and extend the intellectual horizon, broaden the human sympathies, train for efficient living, stimulate ambitions for individual and social progress. They believe that such subjects as human and economic biology, astronomy, economics, industrial chemistry and physics, commercial and industrial history, government and sociology, domestic science and household finance, can be as truly liberal and cultural as the traditional languages, literature, mathematics, and history that are so often looked upon as the only "cultural" subjects. Indeed the scientist believes that any subject can be either liberal or vocational, according to the use to which it is put by the individual student.

Scientific determinists are confident that they are providing types of education that are truly universal and democratic. By scientific job analysis of the needs of life, by scientific curriculum building, and by scientific classification of pupils, they feel that they are presenting education fitted to the needs of every individual. Differentiation of instructional content and method, they think, provides the most democratic type of education, in that each individual is thereby enabled to attain the maximum of his potentialities with the least emotional disturbance and the least expenditure of time and effort. Thus they believe they are opening wide the door of opportunity to every child.

On the other hand, the enemies of scientific determinism bitterly assail such devices as ability-grouping and differentiated curricula as examples of undemocratic class discrimination. Some maintain that the propaganda of the intelligence-testers and the resulting glorification of the I.Q. has only led the schools to cater still further to the superior child, with a consequent neglect of those of lower mental abilities. Others claim that the scientific emphasis upon the study of handicapped children—the blind, the deaf, the crippled, the physically weak, the feeble-minded, and other types of defectives—has led to a serious neglect of the gifted child.

CONTENT The rapid increase in scientific knowledge during the later decades of the nineteenth century and the constantly growing interest in scientific investigations and applications brought about many additions of scientific subject matter to the curriculum of the schools. HERBERT SPENCER, especially, was influential in adding the natural and physical sciences to the course of study. In his discussion of *What Knowledge Is of Most Worth,* he contends that there are five types of knowledge which are of supreme importance:

(1) Knowledge which leads directly to self-preservation and produces physical well-being, including the knowledge to be obtained along these lines from such sciences as physiology, hygiene, biology, physics, and chemistry.

(2) Knowledge which leads indirectly to self-preservation through the building up of sufficient vocational capacity to secure food, clothing, and shelter, including the vocational knowledge obtainable from the sciences of mathematics, physics, chemistry, and the various practical and applied sciences.

(3) Knowledge which leads to parenthood and the rearing of offspring, including the knowledge valuable for these ends to be secured in such sciences as biology, physiology, and psychology.

(4) Knowledge which leads to the proper use of leisure and the enjoyment of the finer things of life, including the knowledge that is to be found in the sciences underlying the fine arts, such as physiology, physics, and psychology.

(5) Knowledge which leads to citizenship and which helps one to become a good neighbor and a useful member of the community, including primarily the political, social, and economic sciences, but not neglecting the knowledge to be obtained from psychology.

Spencer emphasizes the fundamental importance of the natural sciences and gives them precedence over both the social sciences and the humanistic arts. Both Spencer and Huxley urged the abandonment of much of the traditional in favor of a more useful scientific curriculum. Regardless of this extreme position, these men were well ahead of their time in the advocacy of training in science.

Yet there were many so-called scientific subjects in the curriculum of elementary school, secondary school, and higher school, both in the

United States and abroad, before the development of the modern laboratory type of science at the close of the nineteenth century. All of these studies, however, were quite bookish and speculative. In fact, the most commonly taught subjects were known as "natural history" and "natural philosophy." Scientific study had not really shifted from the bookish-demonstration type, as developed by the sense realists and the Pestalozzians and Froebelians, to the modern laboratory type until the very end of the nineteenth century. Actually the present curricular offerings in the natural and physical sciences have had their greatest development in the last few decades. (The earlier scientific studies, as taught in the colleges and universities, the academies and *Realschulen,* and even the elementary schools, were often justified on the basis of the disciplinary conception of education and defended more because of their difficulty than because of their usefulness.)

Germany has been a pioneer in the introduction of modern experimental science in the curriculum. The scientific spirit developed by Francke at the University of Halle as early as 1695, and by Hecker in the *Realschule* in Berlin in 1747, was never lost, and eventually flowered into the modern scientific methods and techniques which made the Germans the early leaders in applied science. Laboratory work by students was probably first begun about 1826 by LIEBIG at Giessen. As early as 1823, technical schools were established in Nuremberg, with the scientific and mathematical subjects taught as the bases for the applied sciences. In 1852, the *Realschulen* began to teach physics, chemistry, mineralogy, and physical geography with a new emphasis upon the use of scientific material as a basis for industrial activity.

In the United States, laboratory experiments were not performed by the students themselves—even in the universities—until after 1850, and not until the close of the century in the high schools. It was not until the 1850's that laboratory methods were introduced into the universities of England; even now in both England and France, the best scientific work is done in the technical and special schools rather than in the older universities and colleges. In all countries, however, the various physical and natural sciences are included in the curriculum of at least some of the schools at practically every level of instruction, and taught with an ever-increasing recognition of the true scientific spirit and of the precise scientific methods of controlled experimentation.

The scientific educators would include science in the curriculum as a core subject for every pupil. They believe that the facts of science and the scientific spirit and method should be imparted to all citizens. Boyd H. Bode, of Ohio State University, has said:

The development of science is evidence that man can control his physical and social environment for his own ends. There is every reason to believe that this control will become more extensive and more complete as time goes on. Science with all its triumphs is still in its infancy. The prophets and seers of the race have seen visions and dreamed dreams; we look to science for the means by which these visions and dreams will be brought to fruition. The culti-vation of science, therefore, is a collective enterprise, a common concern.[4]

The influence of the scientific movement upon the curriculum, however, has gone far beyond the inclusion of the sciences into the course of study. Its greatest contribution has been along the lines of a scientific study of the curriculum and scientific curriculum construction. Up to the beginning of the twentieth century, the curriculum had de-veloped slowly. Additions had been made by force of opinion and authority, or by the fortuitous accumulation of knowledge. Very little had ever been subtracted once it had become a part of the educational offering. Even when a subject, once definitely needed and useful, had outgrown its original usefulness, it was kept in the curriculum because of the force of custom, or because teachers wanted to teach it, or because parents felt that their children should be taught what they themselves had learned.

The scientific movement in education brought about a system-atic objective analysis of curricular materials in order to determine scientifically just what should be taught to satisfy the actual needs both of the individual and of society. DAVID SNEDDEN, FREDERICK G. BONSER, WERRETT W. CHARTERS, and FRANKLIN BOBBITT were prominent repre-sentatives of this movement for scientific curriculum reconstruction.

Snedden made the scientific determination of the sociological objectives of education the basis of his concept of curriculum construc-tion. He furthered development of a fully-worked-out science of educa-tional objectives, made up of a series of scientifically validated specifica-tions for the school curriculum based on a scale of social values objec-tively determined by the techniques of sociological science. His scientific procedure consisted of the following steps:

(1) The scientific determination of social objectives.

(2) The scientific determination of the social objectives that could be attained by education—the educational objectives.

(3) The scientific determination of the educational objectives that could be attained by the school—the school objectives.

(4) The scientific determination of the kinds and amounts of subject matter that could be utilized to attain the school objectives—the curricular objectives.

(5) The scientific determination of the differentiation needed to enable each individual to attain the maximum potentialities of his intellectual capacity and his specific talents—the pupil objectives.

Snedden considered all the objectives of education in terms of the needs of adult life, physical, vocational, civic, and cultural. These needs are to be considered both from the standpoint of the producer and performer, and from that of the consumer and enjoyer—all the general

---

[4] Boyd H. Bode, *Modern Educational Theories.* (New York: The Macmillan Co., 1927.) P. 288. Reprinted with the permission of the publishers.

objectives to be scientifically analyzed into specific goals of knowledges, habits, powers, and interests.

Bonser—particularly interested in the construction of the elementary curriculum—was concerned with the scientific determination of the integrating habits and skills, attitudes and appreciations that every individual must have in order to bring about a unified, harmonious, and stable social order. Through a process of scientific job analysis, he would construct an elementary curriculum made up of such integrating activities.

Charters emphasized the scientific analysis of the ideals, activities, and ideas of efficient social living. He set forth four essentials in scientific curriculum building:

(1) The scientific determination of the ideals that sway socially efficient individuals.

(2) The scientific determination of the physical and mental activities that are needed for a socially efficient life.

(3) The scientific determination of the ideas that control the specific activities of socially efficient living.

(4) The scientific determination of the order in which these ideals, activities, and ideas are to be presented to the pupils.

Bobbitt's book, *How to Make a Curriculum,* was the forerunner of many others on the subject, and has had great influence upon school practice. Bobbitt believes that scientific curriculum making should begin with a careful analysis of the shortcomings of children and adults—a human survey, as he calls it. Through objective scientific studies he would determine what the general fields of human life and action are, and he would then analyze these major areas into ever finer units. Thus the school, provided with detailed lists of socially desirable activities drawn from life, and with scientific knowledge of skillfully diagnosed individual deficiencies, would be able to select, from a rich store of experiential knowledge, suitable remedies psychologically matched to the age and ability of the pupils.

It is a recognized principle of scientific curriculum building that three types of experts should cooperate in the selection of subject matter for school use. First, there should be an expert in the subject itself, with a complete mastery of the subject, who should be responsible for the reliability and truth of the facts that make up the content of the subject. Second, there should be an expert supervisor or administrator, with a sound sociological training and point of view, who should be responsible for the selection of subject matter necessary for the satisfaction of community needs. Third, there should be the expert teacher, with a thorough knowledge of child psychology and the individual child, who should be responsible for the selection of subject matter adapted to the age, capacity, and interests of each pupil.

In scientific curriculum building these experts would reject:

(1) Irrelevant and obsolete details, and facts that are unreliable or questionable.

(2) Materials that are not related to the real needs of life.

(3) Materials that are not within the child's comprehension and that do not appeal to the child's interests.

ERNEST HORN has pointed out that it is rather difficult to make any adequate scientific analyses of the real values of life; thus—since we must necessarily limit our analysis largely to the functioning of particular subjects in life outside the school—most of the practical work in scientific curriculum revision has been along the lines of adapting existing school subjects more closely to the needs of that outside life. Ayres' study of the frequency of use of words and the frequency of misspelling of words as a basis for the spelling curriculum, Charters' study of grammatical errors as a basis for the language curriculum, and Wilson's study of the arithmetical calculations actually used in home, store, and shop, as a basis for the arithmetic curriculum, are examples of this practical type of scientific curriculum building. Yet this is one of the weaknesses of the whole movement; too much of the work in curriculum making is directed toward an analysis of society as it is instead of toward an analysis of society as it ought to be.

AGENCIES   Those interested in the teaching of the sciences have usually succeeded in introducing their subjects in the existing schools, and few new schools have been established primarily for scientific instruction at the elementary and secondary levels. In some cases, technical schools have been introduced at the secondary level for the purpose of providing instruction in pure and applied sciences that could not be obtained in the conventional schools. At the college and university level, separate scientific schools have been more common, because of the hesitancy with which the traditional colleges formerly introduced scientific subjects.

The earliest special scientific school in the United States at the collegiate level was the Rensselaer Polytechnic Institute, founded at Troy, New York, in 1824, which has been the pattern for many similar institutions. The charter of this school provided that the students were not to be taught by seeing experiments and hearing lectures according to the usual methods, but were to experiment under the immediate direction of a professor or competent assistant—thus to become practical scientists. The Lawrence Scientific School was organized in connection with Harvard College in 1847, to provide instruction in science leading to the Bachelor of Science degree. A similar institution, the Sheffield Scientific School, was organized at Yale in 1860. The Morrill Act of 1862 brought about the establishment in each state—either as a separate college or as a branch of the existing state university—an institution in which the sciences were to be studied in their application to the agricultural and mechanical arts. One such institution, Cornell University, at Ithaca, New York, founded in 1867, has been especially active in scientific and technical research.

The movement to make education a science furthered the

establishment of a number of schools of education in connection with the leading universities in the United States. It is in these schools or colleges that the scientific study of education has been most success-fully carried on, and the most effective research in educational problems has been developed. The influence of these schools has been felt not only in our own country but also in many foreign lands; indeed students from other countries come to them in order to train themselves for serv-ice in scientifically attacking the educational problems of their home-lands.

One of the most influential of these institutions has been Teach-ers College, founded in 1887, and now a part of Columbia University in the City of New York. The University of Chicago had a "Department of Education" from the time of its establishment in 1892. In 1909, the School of Education was formed, with CHARLES H. JUDD as director, and here some of the most outstanding scientific research work in silent and oral reading, arithmetic, and penmanship was carried out. Other promi-nent centers of scientific research developed at the School of Education of Stanford University with ELLWOOD P. CUBBERLEY as Dean, and the Graduate School of Education at Harvard University under the leader-ship of Dean HENRY W. HOLMES. At present most large universities maintain professional schools for the scientific study of education. In addition, the "normal schools," now usually designated as teachers col-leges or sometimes as "state colleges," also have become imbued with the spirit of scientific research in the study and practice of education.

The Graduate School of Education at Harvard also has the dis-tinction of pioneering the professional doctorate in education. With the belief that the Doctor of Philosophy degree does not lend itself to prepa-ration for teaching or careers in the schools, the Ed.D. was developed as the professional degree. Differing from the Ph.D. primarily in its broader scope, candidates are required to present "such special preparation in foreign languages, mathematics, or other tools of research, as may be necessary for proper handling of the thesis problem."

The scientific movement in education has been marked by the appearance of a new force in school work—the educational research spe-cialist. Directors of Research are found in many of the larger school systems and most of the State Departments of Education, and National and State Research Committees are constantly at work on a great variety of scientific studies in various educational fields.

Such functions are being carried out by the various committees of the National Education Association, especially the American Associa-tion of School Administrators; the American Association for Educational Research; the National Society for the Study of Education; the National Society of College Teachers of Education, and similar organizations. Various surveys conducted under the auspices of the United States Office of Education are also steps in the same direction. Yet the educational laboratories of the larger universities remain the centers for most of the scientific experimental work in education.

There are many who believe that every educational worker should be equipped with the tools of scientific research. As McCall pointed out, experimental education cannot expect to cope with its great task until superintendents, principals, and teachers are equipped to solve their own problems. Every teacher should be a scientist; every classroom should be a laboratory; the whole school staff should be experimentally minded.

Not only is it the duty of administrators and teachers constantly to examine critically and scientifically their own practices, but it is the duty of every school system to help in the discovery and organization of scientifically determined procedures. This does not necessarily mean that educators should "be always trying something new." They should be, nevertheless, constantly and systematically testing the value of their procedures and systematically searching for better ways of doing things. Every administrator and teacher should cultivate the scientific habit of thought.

The practice of scientific experimentation in a school or school system pays in terms of an altered attitude on the part of the entire staff, willingness to consider new proposals, and an alertness for new methods and devices. Experimentation ploughs up the mental field. Teachers join their pupils in becoming question-askers. It is the absence of just such stirrings of the mental soil which, in all probability, is responsible for the supposed fact that teachers fail to improve after a few years of experience.[5]

ORGANIZATION The scientific study of the pupil has led to many reorganizations of the school system designed to adjust the school more carefully to the needs of the individual pupil. These reorganizations have been supplemented by many extensions to the older school arrangement. Attempts have been made to take care of the individual differences of the pupils by means of flexible grading systems, ability groupings, differentiated courses, individualized laboratory plans, qualitative instead of quantitative markings, and similar reorganizations of the school machinery.

New functions have been assumed in the direction of supervision of student activities, playground management, and the supervision of health. Special rooms have been provided for problem cases. Special classes have been established for over-age, non-English, low mentality, speech-defective, and disciplinary cases. Open air rooms have been built for those who need such an environment. Special state schools have been established for the feebleminded, the deaf, the blind, the crippled, the incorrigible, and the neglected children. Scientific study of these various types of handicapped children has made possible the organization of a system of special education adapted to the needs of all these exceptional cases, and great progress has been made in the scientific treatment of these special cases and problems.

---

5 William A. McCall, *How to Experiment in Education.* (New York: The Macmillan Co., 1923.) P. 3. Reprinted with the permission of the publishers.

The study of school architecture has brought about many changes in school buildings and equipment. Buildings have been made fireproof; heating, lighting, and ventilation have been standardized according to scientific principles, and toilets and drinking fountains are now constructed according to scientifically determined laws of sanitation. Custodial service has become a science in itself, and the construction and maintenance of school buildings are based on scientifically determined rating scales, such as those devised by Strayer and Englehardt, of Teachers College, Columbia University. Even the financial support of the schools has felt the impact of science. Under the leadership of such research workers as F. H. SWIFT and PAUL R. MORT, the problems of school taxation and school budgeting were approached scientifically.

One of the most important results of the scientific study of education has been the reorganization of the units of the educational system. The traditional 8-4-4 organization of elementary school, secondary school, and college, has been broken up into new units. The nursery school, the junior high school, the senior high school, the junior college, the senior college—these are terms designating units of school organization developed largely as a result of attempts to adjust the school system to the findings of educational research in human growth and evolution.

Scientific determinism has added a new branch to the organization of education, the division responsible for the carrying out of the inspectorial function. The school survey movement was the first attempt to perform this function in a scientific manner. It was an effort to evaluate in terms of objective standards and scientific principles the various factors involved in educational labors. It aimed at analyzing the school organization and its activities into specific elements, and measuring the efficiency of each of these elements. There is a permanent need for the carrying on of such a task. That which the survey attempts to do is something the need of which will continue—a stock-taking of results, an inspection of each factor in education to see whether it should continue or not, and if not, by what it ought to be replaced.

The functions of educational organization have come to be divided into three classes: (1) legislative, (2) administrative, and (3) inspectorial. This is true in the organization of the general civil government as well as in the organization of the schools. To anyone who has followed closely the recent tendencies in governmental policies, it is clear that a new function of government, the regulatory function, has been added to the traditional legislative, administrative, and judicial functions, and that this function of government is becoming of greater and greater importance as is evidenced by the innumerable investigation committees that have sprung up through the force of public opinion.

Historically, in the development of the school system, the school board came first; the superintendent came later. More recently, within the past few decades, came the supervisor of special subjects. The newest development in this evolution of school organization has made its appearance—the Bureau of Research, with inspectorial functions of scientific investigation and appraisal. The responsibilities of school government are now shared by these three groups:

(1) The legislative body in school affairs is the school board. It is the policy-determining body. It determines the conditions under which the educational work must be carried on. It determines the educational needs of the community and fixes educational policies to meet these needs. It appropriates and distributes the school funds. The board is not to administrate, but gives over this task to those who are skilled in the doing of what it has decided must be done.

(2) The administrative and executive labors are performed by the superintendent and those under his direction, the business manager, the principals, the supervising heads.

(3) The board must, in some way, scientifically determine whether the work is being done efficiently and according to their wishes and policies. Accurate and reliable inspection must be had to determine the adequacy of the work. This inspection is of two sorts: first, antecedent inspection of what is to be done before work is started, as in the cases of plans for buildings, or of records of prospective teachers; and second, subsequent inspection of results after the work is done. Research workers measure the adequacy of conditions, the waste or inadequacy of financial outlay, the efficiency of instruction in the various subjects, and many other factors similarly important. There are three ways in which this inspectorial function has been performed: (1) by a specially employed outside survey staff, from national or state departments of education, or from higher institutions of learning; (2) by a permanently established Bureau of Research within the local school system; or (3) by a self-survey committee of supervisors, teachers, and others within the school system, working under the direction of the superintendent in addition to their regular administrative and instructional duties.[6]

The scientific movement in education has greatly increased the number of administrators and supervisors in the school system. Specialists of all kinds have been added to the administrative staff, especially in the various state and city school organizations. There is some danger that this may result in the relegating of the instructional function to a secondary role.

METHODS Scientific research—the mere sound of the word often appalled the teacher. But when the concept is explained as "the solution of a problem on the basis of the facts," a great deal of the mystery of the term is removed. Scientific method in education is simply a procedure of solving educational problems by means of statistical and experimental techniques.

In the treatment of sense realism, we pointed out the way in which Bacon and Comenius introduced the method of inductive reasoning into the solution of problems. Today, the scientific educator makes

---

[6] Elmer H. Wilds, "The Inspectorial Function," *Wisconsin Journal of Education*, Vol. LI, No. 1, pp. 12-16.

use of this same inductive process, which is the solution of problems through the formulation of generalizations out of data pertaining to concrete and specific cases. In order to develop sound generalizations, it is necessary to gather facts and to organize them into usable form. The gathering of data usually involves careful quantitative measurement, and the organization of data involves statistical tabulation and treatment. The scientific method of educational research, therefore, has particularly emphasized *quantitative measurement* and *statistical manipulation*.

Most of the workers in the field of educational research have been captivated by the mathematically precise quantitative techniques of the inductive process, and have concentrated most of their effort on measurement and statistical analysis. As a result, since World War I, they have set forth an almost complete quantitative description of American education in all its phases. The zeal for quantitative measurement and tabulation has brought about the collection and classification of facts concerning such educational factors as:

(1) School Buildings—standards of design, materials, equipment, and arrangement—unit costs.

(2) School Finance—sources, budgeting, expenditures—accounting systems.

(3) Teaching Staff—personality, training, and experience—salary schedules and tenure.

(4) School Curriculum—content of textbooks and courses of study—appraisal of results.

(5) School Population—social and economic background of pupils—distribution by age, grade, sex—retardation and elimination.

(6) Pupil Achievement—skills, knowledge, appreciations—marking and promotion systems.

(7) Pupil Traits—physical, emotional, intellectual, and social—anatomical, physiological, and mental growth.

The advances in the field of educational measurement have been particularly striking. Instead of the traditional measurement by the methods of subjective judgment of teachers, various types of scientifically constructed and standardized tests are now in use. An examination of the lists of such pioneer test publishers as the World Book Company and The Public School Publishing Company will reveal the large number of such measuring devices now offered.

Most schools and teachers are utilizing objective achievement tests, either in the standardized and published form or in the home-made form, as these have been constructed and are available for practically all subjects. By means of standardized achievement tests, we are able to determine the pupil's Educational Age and Educational Quotient, the latter being the ratio between Educational Age and Chronological Age. Thus:

$$E.Q. = \frac{E.A.}{C.A.}$$

Many different scholastic aptitude or intelligence tests, both of the verbal and of the nonverbal or performance types, have been made available; some of these must be administered individually while others can be administered to a group. From these tests the pupil's Mental Age and Intelligence Quotient can be determined. The I. Q. is usually expressed in terms of 100 (the quotient for the normal child) and is computed as follows:

$$I. Q. = \frac{M.A.}{C.A.} \times 100$$

It is also possible to measure the pupil's effort by obtaining the ratio of his Educational Quotient to his Intelligence Quotient, a result which has been somewhat misnamed the Achievement Quotient. Hence:

$$A. Q. = \frac{E. Q.}{I. Q.}$$

Work has been done likewise in the development of methods for measuring both general and special aptitudes. The Stenquist Mechanical Aptitude Tests and the Thurston Clerical Aptitude Tests are examples of the general type, and the Rogers Prognostic Tests in Mathematics and the Wilkins Prognostic Tests in Foreign Languages are examples of instruments for measuring special aptitudes and talents.

Attempts have been made, with some success, to develop methods for measuring personality and character traits. The Downey Will Temperament Tests and the Allport A. S. Reaction Tests are examples of personality tests; the work of Hartshorne and May, and of Voelker, pioneered in the construction of character tests, of which the Haggerty-Olson-Wickman Behavior Rating Scales are good examples. Some progress is also being made in the development of techniques for the measurement of the pupil's anatomical, physiological, and social growth.

Every scientific worker must keep an accurate record of his data. Educators now realize this, and efforts have been made to develop comprehensive and cumulative records and report systems, for the accumulation and preservation of facts essential to scientific investigation and experimentation. The scientific educator takes the position that a large proportion of the school's time, energy, and resources should be expended in the careful study of the pupil and in organizing this information into readily accessible records and reports, before the school's energy and resources can be used effectively in teaching.

Quantitative facts are meaningless unless they are treated statistically. HAROLD O. RUGG's *Statistical Methods Applied to Education*, published in 1917, was the first of a series of books designed to familiarize school administrators and teachers with the statistical technique available for the organization and interpretation of quantitative facts. The normal frequency curve has appeared so frequently on the blackboards of classes in education that someone has facetiously called it "the coat-of-arms of the teachers college." Measures of distribution, measures of central tendency, measures of deviation, measures of reliability, and measures of correlation—all these have been applied in educational statistics. Most school workers of today are familiar with such terms as median, quartile deviation, standard deviation, probable error, and coefficient of correlation. Progress in the collection of quantitative facts and in the statistical treatment of these facts has reached goals undreamed of only a few decades ago.

Striking advances have also been made during the last few decades in the field of educational experiments. The experimental laboratory methods of the basic sciences have been taken over by educational workers. The physical and chemical scientists have developed a scientific method of experimental problem solving consisting of the following steps:

(1) The realization and recognition of the problem.

(2) The venture of an inference or tentative hypothesis.

(3) The testing of this inference or hypothesis.

(4) The modification of the hypothesis in the light of the findings of the testing.

(5) Further testing and modifications until a valid theory is established.

(6) A verification of the theory and its acceptance as a verified law, rule, or principle.

(7) The application of the accepted generalization to all relevant situations.

Educational experimenters have developed and established techniques in connection with each of these steps. By means of these techniques experimental investigations have been carried out for the purpose of evaluating practically every aspect of educational method, educational materials, and educational aims. One or the other of two methods of attack is usually followed. The first is to start with one or more causes (the experimental factor or factors) as the hypothesis, and then determine the absolute or relative effects upon the situation involved in the problem.

The second is to start with some desired effect, and then determine whether the hypothetical causes are the real causes, and just how much each of several hypothetical causes contributes to produce the desired effect. In all such experimentation the experimental factor must be isolated and its effect carefully measured, or the experimental method will be unreliable. Experimental conditions must be controlled, or false conclusions may be reached.

Those engaged in educational research must remember that the obvious purpose of scientific measurement and experimentation is problem solving. All too frequently research workers in education stop with the collection of data by survey or experimentation, and fail to interpret these data specifically or to apply them to the solution of a problem. The three processes, diagnosis, interpretation, and verification are much more important steps in the scientific method than the mere collection, tabulation, and manipulation of data.

One of the most fruitful results of this scientific study of educational problems has been the improvement of teaching methods. Classroom method is no longer a matter of guesswork, but has been scientifically determined on the basis of its effectiveness in directing the learning of the pupils. As a result, the quality of teaching methods has been greatly improved, with a corresponding decrease in the time expended in the process. Experimentation in teaching method has brought about an increased recognition of the fact that specific method is more important than general method; that each subject has a special methodology that must be utilized. This has placed a new emphasis upon the psychology of the school subjects, and the method used in practically every subject of the curriculum has been undergoing continual experimentation and resulting revision during recent years.

The scientific movement has increased the attention given by teachers to the problem-solving methods of teaching. The development lesson, the problem lesson, and the project method are emphasized and given a prominent place in all school work. Laboratory methods play a large part in all scientific instruction and are being extended even to the social studies. Exercises in reflective thinking and problem solving now have a definite place in almost every subject. JOHN DEWEY's *How We Think* has had a great influence upon educational methodology. Improved drill techniques have made possible a quicker formation of the essential integrating habits, thus giving the pupil more time for vital problem solving; improved reasoning techniques have made possible the solution of more of the pupil's immediate problems, thus preparing him for the solution of his later life-problems. Scientifically determined educational psychology is bearing fruit in considerably improved and effective teaching methods.

As far as methods of discipline are concerned, the traditional rules governing classroom management and the control of pupil conduct have given way to a scientific treatment of problem cases on the basis of a thorough scientific study of the physical, emotional, and social nature of the individual child. The detention period and the principal's office have given way to the clinic and the psychological laboratory of the psychiatrist. The rod has been replaced by guidance.

Yet educational experimentation, if it really is to succeed, must be not only a school but a community affair. Each community must solve its problem cooperatively and in the light of local conditions. Scientific experimentation in education will not be effective until the public has come to have the same confidence in the science of education that it now has in the science of medicine and surgery, the science of engineering, agricultural science, or any of the other sciences that have so richly benefited mankind.

FOR FURTHER READING

Bode, Boyd Henry, *Modern Educational Theories.* New York: The Macmillan Co., 1927. Pp. 171-192, 329-348.

Butterweck, Joseph, and Seegers, J. Conrad, *An Orientation Course in Education.* Boston: Houghton Mifflin Company, 1933. Pp. 203-238.

Butts, R. Freeman, *A Cultural History of Western Education.* Second Edition. New York: McGraw-Hill Book Co., 1955. Pp. 554-584.

Clough, Shepard B., *The Rise and Fall of Civilization.* New York: McGraw-Hill Book Co., 1951. Pp. 217-264.

Cole, Luella, *A History of Education from Socrates to Montessori.* New York: Holt, Rinehart and Winston, Inc., 1950. Pp. 548-562.

Cubberley, Ellwood P., *Public Education in the United States.* Revised and Enlarged Edition. Boston: Houghton Mifflin Company, 1934. Pp. 688-704.

Curti, Merle, *Social Ideas of American Educators.* New Revised Edition. Patterson, N. J.: Littlefield, Adams and Company, 1959. Pp. 542-580.

Doughton, Isaac, *Modern Public Education.* New York: Appleton-Century-Crofts, Inc., 1935. Pp. 207-339.

Douglass, Aubrey A., *The American Public School System.* New York: Farrar and Rinehart, Inc., 1934. Pp. 271-302.

Duggan, Stephen P., *Student's Textbook in the History of Education.* Revised Enlarged Edition. New York: Appleton-Century-Crofts, Inc., 1936. Pp. 271-285.

Good, H. G., *A History of American Education.* New York: The Macmillan Co., 1956. Pp. 313-341.

————, *A History of Western Education.* New York: The Macmillan Co., 1960. *Passim.*

Graves, Frank P., *Great Educators of Three Centuries.* New York: The Macmillan Co., 1912. Pp. 274-284.

Mayer, Frederick, *A History of Educational Thought.* Columbus, Ohio: Charles E. Merrill Books, Inc., 1960. Pp. 420-429.

McCall, William A., *How to Measure in Education.* New York: The Macmillan Co., 1922.

————, *How to Experiment in Education.* New York: The Macmillan Co., 1923.

Messenger, James F., *An Interpretative History of Education.* New York: Thomas Y. Crowell Company, 1931. Pp. 228-243, 327-343.

Meyer, Adolphe E., *An Educational History of the American People.* New York: McGraw-Hill Book Co., 1957. Pp. 291-313.

Misawa, Tadasu, *Modern Educators and their Ideals.* New York: Appleton-Century-Crofts, Inc., 1909. Pp. 223-243.

Monroe, Paul, *A Textbook in the History of Education.* New York: The Macmillan Co., 1933. Pp. 677-703.

Monroe, Walter S., editor, *Encyclopedia of Educational Research.* New York: The Macmillan Co., 1941.

Mulhern, James, *A History of Education*. Second Edition. New York: The Ronald Press Co., 1959. Pp. 435-446, 510-523.

Myers, Alonzo F., and Williams, Clarence O., *Education in a Democracy*. New York: Prentice-Hall, Inc., 1937. Pp. 122-158.

Noble, Stuart G., *A History of American Education*. New York: Holt, Rinehart and Winston, Inc., 1954. Pp. 468-482.

Quick, Robert Herbert, *Educational Reformers*. New York: Appleton-Century-Crofts, Inc., 1904. Pp. 439-469.

Randall, John H., *Making of the Modern Mind*. Boston: Houghton Mifflin Company, 1926. Pp. 439-469.

Reller, Theodore Lee, *The Development of the City Superintendency of Schools in the United States*. Philadelphia: Published by the Author, 1935.

Thwing, Charles F., *Education According to Some Modern Masters*. New York: Platt and Peck, 1916. Pp. 131-178.

Trow, William Clark, *Scientific Method in Education*. Boston: Houghton Mifflin Company, 1925.

Ulich, Robert, *A History of Educational Thought*. New York: American Book Company, 1950. Pp. 337-349.

Valentine, P. F., *Twentieth Century Education*. New York: Philosophical Library, Inc., 1946. Pp. 155-326, 327-371.

Wender, Herbert, *The Growth of Modern Thought and Culture*. New York: Philosophical Library, Inc., 1959. Pp. 115-179.

Woelfel, Norman, *Molders of the American Mind*. New York: Columbia University Press, 1933. Pp. 81-118, 178-200.

Woody, Clifford, and Sangren, Paul V., *Administration of the Testing Program*. New York: World Book Company, 1933.

QUESTIONS FOR CLASS DISCUSSION

1. How is it possible to solve the problems of social science to the same extent that the problems of chemistry, physics, medicine, and engineering have been solved?
2. What fields of human activity can fruitfully enlist the cooperation of both philosophy and science?
3. Do you see a contemporary tendency in the high school to emphasize the value of science over that of literature and the arts? Explain.
4. What types of pupil characteristics are not yet being measured with scientific accuracy? Do you consider them possible of such measurement?
5. To what extent do you agree with the contention that the normal or average child is presently neglected in favor of the gifted or handicapped child?

6. What changes have taken place in the teaching of reading, penmanship, and spelling as a result of the scientific movement in education?
7. Do you believe that educational experimentation should be carried on by classroom teachers or by experts devoting full time to the task?
8. Present the advantages and disadvantages of standardized objective tests over the traditional essay examination. Do you feel that there is any further use for the essay type?
9. Cite some of the problems in the field of education that do not lend themselves readily to scientific research.
10. Discuss some of the recent developments that are making school administration a more scientific profession. Is there a danger that school administration may become too efficient?

CHAPTER XVII

AN EMPHASIS UPON SOCIALIZATION

THE SOCIAL MOTIVE

The most commonly accepted educational theories and practices
of the twentieth century have been strongly influenced by sociology.
During the closing decades of the nineteenth, psychology reigned
supreme as the dominating factor in educational thinking; with the turn
of the century, however, the contributions of the sociologist were added
to those of psychology. Today we have an educational sociology as well
as an educational psychology, both characterized to a considerable degree
by the spirit and methods of the scientific determinists. Although August
Comte—the founder of modern scientific sociology—gave little specific
attention to education, his followers have had much to say about its
place in social organization and social progress. Now educators concern
themselves with the social implication and social outcomes of education;
they approach the study of educational issues from the standpoint of
their social, political, and economic significance.

Yet the point of view of the educational sociologist is not necessarily antagonistic to that of the psychological developmentalist and the
scientific determinist. The psychological movement and the sociological
movement in education complement each other. The difference in the
two tendencies is a difference in emphasis. The psychologist is concerned
with education from the standpoint of the development of the indi-

vidual; the sociologist, and indeed the social anthropologist, are concerned with both the individual and his relationship to the social structure; he is interested in education for its contributions to the preservation and progress of society. Each needs to realize, however, his dependence upon the other. For the development of the individual is conditioned by his social environment; cultural integration and social progress depend upon the habits, skills, attitudes, and reasoning powers that have been developed in the individuals who make up a given society.

Nor is there any conflict between the sociological tendency and the scientific tendency in education. The sociologist is eager to adapt the techniques of the natural and physical sciences to social science just as the psychologist was willing to make use of the scientific methods in the development of a psychological science. In fact scientific method is barren of results unless it is directed toward the attainment of both psychological and sociological objectives. The scientific worker in education makes a great mistake when he thinks that his scientific technique is supreme and utterly fails to realize that in it he has only tools. The three most recently developed tendencies in educational thinking—the psychological, the scientific, and the sociological, or cultural—must be synthesized in the building up of a complete and adequate educational philosophy.

Sociological educationists consider the ultimate aim of education as social rather than individualistic. Few believe that the school's purpose is to prepare the individual merely for the attainment of his own security, welfare, happiness, or power. Socializers distrust the idea that education is to help the individual prepare himself to play a lone but effective hand in a world of competitive struggle. Narrow individualistic aims in terms of "bread and butter," "knowledge," "polish," or even "character" are being recognized as only partial. Many educational leaders are emphasizing as never before that the formation of habits and skills, the inculcation of ideals, attitudes, and appreciations, the acquisition and utilization of knowledge, are not ends in themselves; but only means to the greater end of preparing individuals to fit into the general social organization and to serve the general social welfare. In the sociological conception of education, the ultimate goal is almost universally accepted as cooperative.

There is a real justification for this tendency. No man "lives unto himself alone"; he must play his part in the social structure; this is much more true today than it was in the past. There is an increasing interdependency in human relationships.

Society has become in fact corporate. Its interests and activities are so tied together that human beings have become dependent upon one another, for good or for harm, to an unprecedented degree. This is a statement of fact, whether the fact be welcomed or deplored. This interdependence is increasing, not lessening. It must be taken into account by education. We must not only educate individuals to live in a world where social conditions, beyond the reach of any one's individual will, affect his security, his work, his achievement, but we must take account of the total incapacity of competitive individualism to work anything but harm in this state of interdependence in which we live.[1]

Nevertheless, in our earlier history, conditions favored a belief in "rugged individualism" and competitive acquisitiveness. The individualistic ideal of the early nineteenth century, asserting the right of individuals to equality of opportunity and freedom of action unhampered by social control, is an understandable doctrine. The belief that social welfare and social progress are best advanced by the personal choice, personal initiative, and personal action of the individual was supported by the economic conditions that then prevailed.

Population was sparse and land was abundant and available in many areas of the world. Enormous stores of natural resources were unappropriated, inviting human exploitation. New continents were still to be conquered, an opportunity presenting a challenge to all but the most lazy. Under such conditions, it seemed desirable to educate individuals to win in the race of life through the development of their own competitive ability and industry. Furthermore, under these earlier economic conditions, individual prowess and success seemed to go hand in hand with the satisfaction of the needs of society. Those who discovered new lands, cleared forests, cultivated fields, built roads, developed cities, and invented machines, were conscious of a service they were rendering to society as well as to themselves. Personal success was not a private affair; it was a contribution to social welfare and progress. Educating a pupil for success in life was automatically considered a service to society, even though no study was made of social needs, nor thought given to social objectives. Preparation for the attainment of personal rewards and satisfactions brought with it a sense of service to society.

Because of changed economic and industrial conditions during the last few decades, training for acquisitive individualism has lost some of its earlier social significance. The impact of World War II and the consequent all-out effort to build an "arsenal for democracy" put the emphasis on cooperation and teamwork, and a new climate of opinion which regards group judgment as generally superior to that of one man or woman likewise has served to recondition educational thinking.

But social goals of education are not new. Primitive education was socializing in its adjustment of the child to group characteristics. Oriental educational systems were devised for the preservation of social stability. The ancient Hebrews, Greeks, and Romans saw the social significance of education. Jesus presented a most advanced social goal, a goal that unfortunately was lost sight of by many followers. In the twentieth century, however, a new and more pronounced interest has

---

[1] John Dewey and John L. Childs, *The Educational Frontier.* William H. Kilpatrick, Editor. (New York: Appleton-Century-Crofts, Inc., 1933.) P. 68. Reprinted with the permission of the publishers.

been aroused in education for social purpose; progressive thinking has concerned itself with the nature of social organization and social needs and the ways in which education can serve them.

Leaders in world thought are coming to see clearly that in spite of the inadequacy of the individual man, there is a way out. In the arithmetic of co-operation, an I.Q. of 100 added to an I.Q. of 100 makes a combination which by teamwork can solve problems which demand an I.Q. of 125. Singly, each man proves to be hopelessly inadequate and fails. Jointly, men may form a larger, more powerful individual who can triumph over material limitations. Today the major issues of life have far outstripped the powers of individuals to cope with them successfully; modern civilization must master a new technique of co-operative thinking and action or die.[2]

Largely as the result of the work and writings of JOHN DEWEY (1859–1952), sociological objectives and actual socializing techniques came to be emphasized as never before. When Dewey left the University of Michigan in 1894 to become head of the Department of Philosophy and Education at the newly established University of Chicago, he found himself in a position favorable to the inauguration of a new movement in education—at a time when it was greatly needed. In 1896, he established his "Laboratory School," now often spoken of as "The Dewey School,"[3] where he was able to put into practical experimentation his theories of a socializing education. Here, during the years between 1896 and 1903, his social philosophy of education crystallized. The practices and experiments of this pioneer venture in socialized education had more to do with giving impetus to the new movement than any other previous endeavor.

Out of his work in this school, Dewey developed the ideas presented first in that influential educational classic, *The School and Society* (published in 1899), and later in his epochal work, *Democracy and Education* (1916), which is the most complete statement of his educational philosophy. Dewey had many disciples, among the most influential of whom were WILLIAM H. KILPATRICK, BOYD H. BODE, THOMAS H. BRIGGS, ROSS L. FINNEY, and GEORGE S. COUNTS. These so-called "Molders of the American Mind" have not been in complete agreement in all phases of their thinking, but they have been alike in their common emphasis of a social philosophy of education.

Dewey's Laboratory School was the precursor of many other such schools. In Europe, appeared such experimental agencies as the German country-home schools of HERMAN LIETZ, the French *École des Roches* of EDMOND DEMOLINS, and the Belgian progressive schools founded by OVIDE DECROLY. In the United States, the Francis W. Parker School of

---

[2] S. A. Courtis, "Achievement of the Impossible," *Michigan Educational Journal,* Vol. 8, No. 5, p. 211.
[3] K. C. Mayhew and A. C. Edwards, *The Dewey School.* (New York: Appleton-Century-Crofts, Inc., 1936.) See also Lawrence A. Cremin, "John Dewey and the Progressive Education Movement, 1915–1952," *The School Review,* Vol. 67, No. 2 (Summer, 1959), pp. 160-173, for a new interpretation of Dewey's place in the "movement."

Chicago, the Meriam School at the University of Missouri, the Lincoln School and the Speyer School at Columbia University, the Fairhope School—these are just a few of the great number of experimental schools. The Progressive Education Association in the United States and the New Education Fellowship in Europe were organized to further the cause of this new type of socializing schools.

In the interpretation of the ultimate social goal, there is still considerable confusion and wide variation of opinion. In setting up the social objectives of education, four possible alternatives are suggested:

(1) Education should prepare for the *status quo,* for social life and institutions as they now exist, by integrating the pupils into the established social order and indoctrinating them in the accepted traditions of their inherited culture;

(2) Education should attempt to anticipate the changed social conditions that come about through a natural drift along the paths of least resistance, and prepare the pupils for these anticipated new needs;

(3) Education should accept the vision of a new social order in all its details, mold the pupil for this preconceived society, and, through propaganda, help bring about this preconceived society; or

(4) Education should prepare thinking individuals to play an intelligent part in a cooperative social planning toward an ever improving social order, only dimly conceived in its vague outlines by farseeing prophets.

In looking over these alternatives, we find that the first three involve what we could call "social adjustment," whereas the fourth involves "social guidance." Education for the first three would demand the methods of indoctrination and propaganda; in the fourth, instruction in the sense of training the intelligence for problem solving and social responsibility is needed.

In the discussions of the social implications of education, the principal conflict is between those who would train for the accepted social standards and those who would educate toward a solution of debatable (and controversial) social issues. Since the two points of view are not necessarily antagonistic, it is desirable to prepare the pupil for both the constants and the variables of society. For convenience and clearness, however, we shall discuss each of these concepts under a separate heading: (1) Social Traditionalism and (2) Social Experimentalism.

THE DOCTRINE OF SOCIAL TRADITIONALISM

Tradition is the record of man's accomplishments and the accumulation of human experience. Each individual comes into the world with a social as well as a biological inheritance. Each generation has acquired and transmitted the collective cultural tradition of the past, has made an effort to preserve the continuity of the common social tradition.

There is no question but that much of this social inheritance is extremely desirable. Survival is usually a test of value. Traditional ideas, customs, and institutions are considered by many to be as valuable today as when they first developed. It is possible, however, for an idea, a custom, or an institution to outlive its usefulness and become ill-adapted to changed conditions. That is why it may be a mistake to accept all social traditions blindly and unquestioningly without a careful study of their adaptation to the present age. Unquestionably there are certain things that are permanent in society—social constants—and there are other things that are changing in society—social variables. The careful educational thinker must learn to distinguish between the constant and the variable, between that which is universally accepted and that which is ephemeral. He must learn to make the distinction between the task of adjustment and the task of guidance.

AIMS   The social traditionalist aims at giving all pupils an insight into their social inheritance—into the ideals, institutions, conditions, and customs of society. He aims at arousing a knowledge of, an interest in, and a sympathy toward all branches of society. He aims at giving a practice in social communication and social service. He aims at the development of social efficiency and the adaptation of the individual to society.

"Education," said NICHOLAS MURRAY BUTLER, "must mean a gradual adjustment to the spiritual possessions of the race. The child is entitled to his scientific, literary, esthetic, institutional, and religious inheritance."

"To educate a person," says W. C. RUEDIGER, "means to adjust him to those elements of his environment that are of concern in modern life, and to develop, organize, and train his powers so that he may make efficient and proper use of them."

William C. Bagley has continuously advanced the doctrine that the development of the socially efficient individual is the ultimate aim of education. He would develop (1) economic efficiency, or ability to "pull one's own weight" in economic life; (2) negative morality, or willingness to sacrifice one's own desires when their gratification would interfere with the general social efficiency; (3) positive morality, or the willingness to contribute directly or indirectly to social efficiency.

These educators would adjust the child to his social inheritance largely for the benefit of the child himself rather than for the benefit of society. Other writers, however, are free from this emphasis upon the individualistic use of social tradition. Dewey has said:

> Social efficiency as an educational purpose should mean cultivation of power to join freely and fully in shared or common activities.[4]

---

[4] John Dewey, *Democracy and Education* (New York: The Macmillan Co., 1916), p. 144.

Thorndike held that the socially efficient individual is one who (1) leads a useful and happy economic, civic, and domestic life, (2) has good will to others, and (3) engages in harmless enjoyments. Betts says that the socially efficient person has (1) a spirit of artistry in work and achievement, (2) a spirit of social good will and service, and (3) a capacity for fine appreciations. Undoubtedly most child developmentalists would agree with these objectives. The aim of Pestalozzi, Herbart, and perhaps Arnold Gesell, would surely be in harmony with the goal of the social educationists.

There have been many attempts to analyze this ultimate goal of social efficiency into specific social objectives. Perhaps the most familiar of these enumerations is that adapted from Spencer and known generally as the CARDINAL PRINCIPLES OF EDUCATION: (1) Health, (2) Command of Fundamentals, (3) Citizenship, (4) Worthy Use of Leisure, (5) Vocations, (6) Worthy Home Membership, and (7) Ethical Character.

A more complete and more consistently expressed enumeration would be the following:

    (1) Physical efficiency
    (2) Vocational efficiency
    (3) Avocational efficiency
    (4) Civic efficiency
    (5) Domestic efficiency
    (6) Social efficiency
    (7) Moral efficiency
    (8) Religious efficiency

Bobbitt has set forth a list of ten types of social activities to which the pupil must be adjusted:

    (1) Language activities—social communication
    (2) General social activities—meeting with others
    (3) Health activities
    (4) Citizenship activities
    (5) Parental activities
    (6) Religious activities
    (7) Mental and emotional activities—mental hygiene
    (8) Spare-time activities
    (9) Unspecialized practical activities
    (10) Practical activities of one's calling

Thus, the social traditionalist conceives the aim of the school as a preparation for all the phases of social life; a balanced effective participation in all social institutions. He believes that social welfare depends upon men and women finding and filling their places in all phases of life.

The social traditionalist is primarily interested in social integration; he seeks social efficiency through social harmony. One of the purposes of education is the formation of the common habits of social life, so that the individual can participate smoothly and harmoniously with his fellows. The more one has acquired the universally accepted habits and attitudes of his social group, the less friction there will be in his social relationships. One can not object seriously to such an aim, providing these common habits are not socially undesirable. We may criticize, however, any limitation of education to this one integrating function.

There are certain social standards that the sociologist would have education help maintain. The pupil must be so trained that he will adjust himself to these. He must be educated away from crime, poverty, disease, unemployment, and all such recognized social evils. The social traditionalist believes that society has the right to demand an education that will maintain its standards, safeguard its traditions, and preserve its institutions. He defines education as a process of developing in the individual the power of adaptation and adjustment to his social environment.

TYPES   Those who are interested in the adjustment of the child to the accepted standards and institutions of society have much to say, of course, about social education. Some confusion is likely to arise in the use of this term. Social education, in its broadest sense, covers all types of education that prepare the pupil for living with his fellows. Social training, in its narrower meaning, refers to the formation of the skills of social communication through language, and the building of the etiquette of harmonious and frictionless human relationships. Social training, in this latter sense, is merely one of many types of training in a long list including physical training, vocational training, civic training, domestic training, avocational training, moral training, and religious training—all considered essential in the development of complete social efficiency.

The results of the medical examinations of conscripted men during American participation in World War I stimulated intensified interest in physical education. The appalling number of physical defects and the low standard of health revealed by these examinations aroused demands for health education and physical training in the schools. Industrial accidents led to the passing of workingmen's compensation laws in many states. Manufacturers joined with the insurance companies in a campaign to teach safety in the schools. In recent years, the phenomenal increase in automobile accidents has strengthened the movement. The National Safety Council, and the American National Red Cross, through its Junior Red Cross, are enlisting the cooperation of the schools in an extensive program of accident prevention.

Vocational education has been particularly emphasized by the social educator. With the development of modern manufacturing methods in all parts of the world, the old apprenticeship system broke down, and a new demand arose that the schools should train industrial and agricultural workers as well as those who were to go into business and the professions. Germany, France, and Denmark led the way in building schools for the teaching of the practical arts. The United States was slow in responding to this new need, largely because of the influx of technically educated workers from Europe. With new immigrants furnishing both cheap unskilled labor and technical trained workers, the schools continued to devote themselves to preparation for white-collar jobs.

During the past half century, however, we have at last turned our attention to the vocational training of our factory and farm workers. The National Commission on Vocational Education, set up by Congress in 1913, made a comprehensive study that ultimately resulted in the passage of the Smith-Hughes Bill in 1917. This act provided for a Federal Board of Vocational Education to cooperate with the states in furthering high school instruction in industrial trades, agriculture, home economics, and commerce. With the growth of vocational high schools and the introduction of prevocational courses in the elementary schools, vocational education in the practical arts is now being provided for the large proportion of our population that must engage in industrial, agricultural, clerical, and domestic occupations.

Closely connected with vocational education has come the development of vocational guidance. Not only are students to be trained for jobs, but they are also placed advantageously. The movement began in this country in 1907, when a bureau was opened in Boston for the placement of youth in vocations best fitted to them. This grew into the Bureau of Vocational Guidance, which later was taken over by Harvard University. Through the influence of its director, JOHN M. BREWER, this bureau became the center of the movement, which spread rapidly to every section of the country. The study of occupations became a part of the curriculum of almost all schools.

Recreational training also has received a new emphasis. Especially since the great depression new attempts have been made to train the pupil for his leisure hours. Even the courses in the practical arts have been increasingly given, not as a training for vocations, but as a training in hobbies and leisure occupations. Play and playground activities have been encouraged, as have been all forms of wholesome recreation.

Much has been done in the training for a better home life. In addition to the teaching of the household arts, instruction is being given in sex hygiene, infant care, and other phases of parenthood. Sex education and parental education have been taken over by many schools as a definite part of their responsibility.

The attempts to introduce more civic education, moral education, and religious education into the schools have met with difficulties, due to the controversial issues involved. The social traditionalist is inclined to follow the lead of the nationalist in respect to the content and methods of civic education. He stresses conformity to American ideals of Democracy, Christianity, and Capitalism. As a result, his teaching of civic, religious, and moral questions is likely to be a matter of indoctrination rather than a serious attempt to build understanding, allegiance, and loyalties.

Since social efficiency demands the adjustment of every indi-

vidual to the social organization, social traditionalism is committed to a
policy of universal education. This education, however, must be differentiated to meet the needs of various groups in the social structure.
Because they consider education in terms of its benefits to the social
order, the traditionalists are as insistent upon compulsory education as
are the nationalists, and have been active in extending the compulsory
attendance limits to higher levels. In a few states the leaving age has
been increased to eighteen years, although the usual limits are fourteen
and sixteen.

CONTENT   John Dewey stated many years ago that the
school is not a preparation for life, but is life itself. The school curriculum, therefore, must be made up of the activities of real social living;
the school cannot be a preparation for life except as it presents the conditions of social life. This point of view has led to the present emphasis
upon the "activity" or "project" curriculum, consisting of exercises and
problems drawn from the fields of actual social conduct. The social
motive in education demands that all the materials of the school be
drawn from the varied activities of social, political, and economic life,
rather than from what social educators consider the abstractions of an
academic world far removed from actuality.

There seems to be a general agreement that the elementary
school should provide the essential tools of social living and the common
integrating habits of human relationships; that the intermediate school
is to present opportunities for the exploration of the world of nature and
the world of man so that the pupil can find himself and his place in
society; that the secondary school must provide specialized training for
the individual's specific needs once they have been determined.

The elementary school is performing its function by drills in the
essential integrating habits of arithmetical calculation, oral and written
speech, hygiene, and social manners, supplemented by much constructive
and cooperative work, together with music, art, and other forms of
esthetic appreciation and recreational participation.

Most junior high schools are attempting to give an exploration
of the various aspects of life through courses in General Science, General
Mathematics, General Language, Social Studies, General Fine Arts,
General Practical Arts, together with such exploratory agencies as general
shop, tryout courses, and classes in occupations.

The most satisfactory solution, according to some social educators, would be to have the junior high school curriculum organized in
terms of social objectives. Instead of courses in Mathematics, Science,
English, and History, courses in Vocations, Health, Moral Conduct,
Home Life, Leisure Occupations, Educational Opportunities, and Social
Communication, with accompanying tryout opportunities should be
offered. Undoubtedly some progress in this direction will come eventually but, in the meantime, teachers are doing what they can to socialize
the traditional subjects.

As a result of this new emphasis, there has been a growing tendency for the high schools to get away from a narrow propaedeutic curriculum, dominated by college entrance requirements, and to offer a curriculum fitting boys and girls directly for the specific activities of life. Vocational subjects have gained in importance akin to that of the academic subjects. Even in the colleges the social sciences, such as history, government, economics, and sociology, and the applied sciences are encroaching upon the domains of the humanities and the pure sciences.

Many colleges and universities are moving away from the traditional academic curriculum by requiring that a part of the student's time be given over to socially useful work, travel, and study. Such developments have been especially noteworthy at Antioch, Bennington, Olivet, the General College at Minnesota, and the New College at Columbia. High school and college curricula are becoming better adapted to the satisfaction of social needs.

One of the most striking results of the social emphasis in education has been the recognition of the place of extracurricular activities in the school program. These activities, once looked upon with indifference if not with open hostility by teachers and administrators, are now accepted as valuable educational assets. Although these activities have been carried on by pupils for generations, it has only lately that they have been taken over as part of the school's educational program.

Extracurricular activities—when properly controlled and directed —are of the utmost value in providing experiences through which training may be obtained for the various phases of life. These activities are effective instruments for the achievement of the social objectives of education. For each objective there are some activities that contribute, and some contribute to many or even all. Moreover many of these contributions can come only through these activities. In them may be recognized values not ordinarily found in the routine of the classroom. These activities are an effective means of training young people to live together on the highest plane. Social training, vocational training, civic training, training in leadership, moral training, training for leisure—all are provided through participation in the modern extracurricular program.[5]

Athletic activities, public speaking activities, dramatic activities, journalistic activities, musical activities, school councils, dances and parties, clubs, assemblies, homeroom activities are providing fruitful sources of training for the various aspects of social life. They are furnishing an adjustment that is seldom secured through traditional school subjects.

The content of the traditional subjects, the social educationists feel, can be socialized and enriched by the addition of new materials.

---

[5] See Elmer H. Wilds, *Extra-curricular Activities*. (New York: Appleton-Century-Crofts, Inc., 1926.) Pp. 17-35.
One of the latest texts in this area, by Robert W. Frederick, is entitled *The Third Curriculum*. (New York: Appleton-Century-Crofts, Inc., 1959), a recognition of the increasing importance of this guidance field.

Much of the deadwood inherited from the past can be removed from the curriculum; much can be replaced by content drawn from the experiences of life. Vocational life, home life, the social life of the community —these should be the sources of a functional curriculum that adjusts the child to his environment and satisfies his assured immediate and future needs.

AGENCIES   Within the social educationist philosophy the school is looked upon as the primary agency for adjusting the individual to his place in society. Whenever and wherever other agencies have failed to prepare the child for any of the aspects of social life, the school, and particularly the public school, must assume this task as its proper function. This point of view has given to the school a new importance as a social institution. Since society will be harmed by any failure to adjust the child to his social environment, a new obligation is placed upon society to support the school by public taxation. Society must contribute to the support of public schools in order to protect itself from maladjusted individuals.

This recognition of the social responsibility of the school has brought about many extensions of public education, particularly at the secondary and college levels. The former college-preparatory emphasis has given way either to the comprehensive high school with its multiple curriculum, or to a system of specialized high schools in which each school adjusts the pupil to a particular career. The junior college has been established to extend secondary education over a longer period. At the University of Minnesota, a General College was founded to take care of those students who do not have the capacity or inclination to follow the traditional college curriculum. During the depression many states established junior colleges in local communities for those young people who were unemployed and yet unable to go away to college. In most countries, there has been an extensive increase in technical and professional schools to fit young men and young women more adequately for the various trades and professions.

Since it is usually difficult for the public schools to secure up-to-date machines and other forms of industrial and commercial equipment, many are now advocating the turning over of much of our vocational training to factory schools, store schools, and corporation schools. In recent years, there has been a great increase in these schools. A National Factory School Association is active in promoting vocational education in this manner. The schools are desirable agencies for vocational education if any tendencies toward the exploitation of youth for the profit of the corporations are promptly checked.

One of the striking developments of recent years has been the provision of opportunities for adult education. Schools have been established for both the employed and the unemployed. Evening schools have existed for many years. Originally these schools were established to give vocational education that would lead to promotion or to better jobs.

More recently, evening schools have devoted themselves mainly to the task of providing general education to the employed solely to enrich their lives and make them better members of society. The Folk Schools of Denmark have led the way in this movement to raise the cultural level of the people.

During and immediately after the first World War, adult education in the United States was largely confined to the Americanization movement, through which the foreign-born was taught the use of English in his common speech, and prepared for naturalization by training in the history and principles of our government and the traditions and standards of American life. The widespread unemployment of depression years and the increased amount of leisure time intensified the demand for new types of adult education. There was an increased effort in this direction; the federal government made a large appropriation for the establishment of Adult Education Forums to be conducted in various cities under the direction of the United States Office of Education. Public lectures, motion pictures, and radio programs were used as agencies of adult education. A wider use of the school plant made the school a community center for adult education and recreation.

Nation, state, and local communities assumed a new responsibility for the education of out-of-school youth. The educational work of the Civilian Conservation Corps was a demonstration of what can be done. The National Youth Administration made it possible for many to attend school who otherwise could not do so. States established short unit courses and correspondence and extension courses, even for those in penal institutions. Guidance Bureaus and Placement Offices undertook the task of readjusting and re-educating the youth already at work.

The social motive in education not only developed new agencies of education, but brought about a cooperation between the school and other institutions and organizations. The Y.M.C.A. and Y.W.C.A., the scouting organizations, and similar youth groups are active in the work of adjusting youth to their social responsibilities. The National Congress of Parents and Teachers has organized Parent-Teacher Associations throughout the country as active and effective educational agencies. Women's Clubs, Chambers of Commerce, and the various service clubs have added educational activities to their programs. Education has become the business of every citizen.

The task of adjusting the child to social living makes necessary a new type of teacher. Teachers must have a social vision; the effective preparation of pupils for the opportunities and responsibility of social participation demands a broader preparation on the part of the teacher than is required for the mere dispensing of knowledge. The teacher must have a broad background of social knowledge gained largely through varied contacts with life itself. In teacher education new emphasis is placed upon the social studies. A knowledge of biology, social psychology, sociology, economics, and government is considered as essential for the teacher as an acquaintanceship with the subjects taught and the methods for teaching them. The two-year normal school has given way to the four-year teachers college, with professional subjects postponed until after the prospective teacher has been given a broad general background; graduate schools of education are requiring a broad general education as a prerequisite to specialization in education. If the teacher is to be a social agent, he must have a thorough knowledge of social institutions and social organization.

The new socialized school is much less dependent upon books than were the older schools. Visual materials, in the form of photographs, transparencies, and motion pictures, give the child a vicarious contact with life. Television and radio programs bring the child very close to the activities of life and give him a clearer picture of social institutions. School excursions and trips give him actual contacts with different phases of community endeavors. The curriculum, especially at the elementary level, is growing less bookish. Life is now the book from which the pupil reads.[6]

ORGANIZATION   The increasing interdependencies of social living have made necessary the organization of education on a much larger scale. When each little community was self-sustaining and self-contained, the organization of the schools on a small district basis was satisfactory. The ease with which people today can move from place to place has made a larger group consciousness of the problems of education inevitable. Lack of educational opportunity in any one locality is likely to reflect on any part of the state or nation; educational benefits flow over a wide expanse of territory. In order to satisfy local needs, it is not necessary to have a school unit smaller than the trade area surrounding a town or village.

If larger educational opportunities are to be provided for communities, school finance likewise must be organized on a statewide or even a nation-wide basis. The social motive has led to increased state aid to schools. Realizing that certain states are unable to finance the type of education needed to maintain the desired social standards, demands are being made upon the federal government to appropriate large sums to the states on the basis of need. Unless additional sources of support are found schools in many areas will lag behind the better financed schools, and the nation as a whole will be unfavorably influenced. The problem facing us is to secure equalizing centralization of support without a hampering centralization of control.

METHODS   In teaching the child to live with others, the method used is that of social communication, social cooperation, and social service. The socializing method gives experiential education in social

---

[6] See Harold Rugg, *American Life and the School Curriculum.* (Boston: Ginn & Co., 1936), for a thorough exposition of this social and progressivist educational philosophy. Pp. 215-237.

groupings. The teacher works with the various social interests of the pupils such as gregariousness, cooperation, altruism, and emulation. Informal conversation, group discussions, group assignments, dramatizations, and construction projects are used as socializing devices for the development of the social virtues and the elimination of antisocial tendencies. Socialized school management, through the use of student participation in school housekeeping and school government, is an effective aid in training the pupils for social life. The various school enterprises and extracurricular activities—if conducted in the proper social spirit—provide plentiful opportunities for initiative, leadership, responsibility, and cooperation.

Children are encouraged to work for each other rather than for themselves. They are taught to face the class instead of the teacher and to have a lively sense of communication. They are given many opportunities to work together in helpful cooperation, and individual pupils and small groups are held responsible for definite contributions to the class.

Teachers have little difficulty in perfecting a technique for the development of the social virtues. The difficulty is in determining what the social virtues are. The social traditionalist is inclined to be overzealous in the preservation of the social heritage; he is likely to try to standardize children in the commonly accepted social patterns. Their immaturity and the authoritative position of the teacher make the method of domination over social activity much easier than guidance in social choice. The plasticity of youth stimulates the use of the methods of indoctrination and coercion. The direction of the teacher, which is necessary in the rapid and accurate formation of the integrating skills, is often carried over into the realms of alternatives and controversial questions.

Conformity to the officially approved social behavior is often considered the acme of social virtue; the youth is not encouraged to examine critically into the approved social order. Only a few teachers are able to strike a balance between coercion and coddling. They either give the child so much freedom that it becomes license, or they swing to the other extreme of domination, regimentation, and indoctrination in order to make sure that the child is adjusted to the approved social patterns. They are inclined to support a school discipline that brings the pupil in conformity to law and order. They insist that if every student is trained to meet these requirements, which they consider necessary to normal home and social life and business and professional employment, the school will have made a forward step in establishing a better attitude toward law and order and in checking the growing spirit of lawlessness.

These principles of the traditionalists are indeed those of essentialism, although essentialists generally require a more rigid program of studies than did the social traditionalists of the depression and early postwar era.

THE DOCTRINE OF SOCIAL EXPERIMENTALISM

The social traditionalist, as we have just pointed out, is primarily concerned with the adjustment of the individual to the existing social order. At his best, he would use the school to adapt the pupil only to those elements in the social organization that are universally accepted; in the extreme form, he would perpetuate all traditional social beliefs and practices by processes of complete pupil indoctrination and coercion. Social traditionalism is not concerned sufficiently with social change. In its failure to meet the necessities of progress, it falls short of a complete socialization of the individual.

In recent years, particularly between the two World Wars and during the world-wide depression, there was an increasing realization that the social order does change and that change is necessary and desirable. Although there are still some who adhere to a philosophy of complacency—who are willing to believe that "this is the best of all possible worlds" and who insist that the traditional institutions of the established social order are permanently valuable and infallible—many groups in various parts of the world, are convinced that the developments of modern science and modern technology have made certain old customs, traditional beliefs and standards, and inherited institutions ill adapted to modern times.

Social, economic, and political institutions must change and are changing. The social order continues to change. The society of tomorrow will be very different from the society of today. What is to be the attitude of education toward this inevitable social change? Surely, they say, the school can never be satisfied with preparing the child for his assured immediate needs. His future needs under changed social conditions must also be considered.

Some contend that change comes about as a natural evolution; that nothing can be done about it one way or another except to let it drift. They say that we live in a genetic society haphazardly changing through the chance reactions of its elements. Thus they would have the school anticipate this social drift and prepare its pupils for a drifting society. In attempting to adapt the pupils to this naturally changing situation, the teacher would have to play the role of a clairvoyant. To chart such a drift would be difficult; it would take wise men indeed to anticipate the needs of the future.

Under the spell perhaps of the social science of Spencer and Comte or of the mathematical certainties of J. M. Cattell and Edward L. Thorndike, others would map out an ideal social order in all its details, and use education to help bring it about. It is undoubtedly possible to achieve a preconceived society, but the school must use the same methods of indoctrination and coercion that are used to preserve an existing society. The schools can change society by changing the individuals who make up society. During the great depression several works appeared whose purpose was to blueprint the shape of a new and better society. GEORGE S. COUNTS' *New Social Order*[7] and HAROLD RUGG's *Great Technology*[8] are not the first "total visions" to be revealed. More recently THEODORE BRAMELD has offered, as a "reconstructionist" philosophy, a design for a new school and method of education which had, as its inception, the necessity for remaking the social order. Many utopian societies have been projected from Plato to H. G. Wells. Are educators willing to adopt any one of these as a universially accepted goal? It is obvious that a preconceived society can be looked upon by some as bad or can be considered by others as good; that it can be the object of condemnation as well as praise.

The social experimentalist is attempting to steer a course between the Scylla of social traditionalism and the Charybdis of social preconception. He tries to cling firmly to a doctrine of progressive democracy in the midst of appeals from reactionary conservatives on the one hand and ultra-liberals on the other, each promising short cuts to social perfection.

Almost a generation ago Glenn Frank, President of the University of Wisconsin, predicted the danger to the school from extreme forms of social experimentalism:

> Until recently few, if any, Americans could be found who did not think the enslavement of the schools to a formula was utterly dangerous. Lately, however, from the widely separated quarters of the Right and the Left have arisen Americans who demand that the schools be made agencies of propaganda. Those on the Right want the schools to become agencies of propaganda for their particular conservative concept of the traditional social order. Those on the Left want them to become agencies of propaganda for their particular brand of a new social order based on some measure of collectivism.[9]

AIMS Social experimentalists believe that the task of the school is to prepare for a progressive reconstruction of the social order. Both Dewey and Kilpatrick insisted that the environment of the school should be such as to direct the pupil in learning how to meet the progressively developing demands of a changing society; to develop in the pupil a social motive and a social intelligence that will enable him to play his part in solving the problem of a changing civilization. They are called instrumentalists because they believed that social institutions and science should be used only as instruments in the development of new and better ways of life.

The social experimentalist believes that the school can play an

---

[7] George S. Counts, *Dare the School Build a New Social Order?* (New York: John Day Co., 1932.)
[8] See Harold Rugg, *The Great Technology.* (New York: John Day Co., 1933.) Also *Now Is the Moment.* (New York: Duell, Sloan & Pearce, 1943.) See Theodore Brameld, *Patterns of Educational Philosophy.* (Yonkers-on-Hudson, New York: World Book Company, 1950.) Pp. 569-620. Also *Toward a Reconstructed Philosophy of Education.* (New York: Holt, Rinehart and Winston, Inc., 1956.) *Passim.*
[9] From an address by Glenn Frank at St. Louis on February 20, 1936.

effective part in a telic society, purposively self-directing itself forward and onward to a better social order, even though the exact nature of the ultimate achievement is only dimly perceived. As examples, HENRY W. HOLMES advocated for many years a social policy in education that would set up the creation of a purposive society as the goal of endeavor, and ROSS L. FINNEY, in his *Sociological Philosophy of Education,* urged the adoption of a teleological function in education. It appears that this aim is the only one possible if we are to preserve a true democracy, in which each one contributes freely and to the maximum of his powers to the general welfare. Dewey has pointed out that our national democratic tradition includes the following:

(1) The right of every mature citizen to participate in the government of his locality, state, and nation, on the ground that such participation both makes the individual a better citizen and helps insure that the government will serve the public good.

(2) The equal right of every individual for opportunity to make his own career and develop his personality, on the ground that by such a development he can best serve the general social welfare.

(3) The right of peoples to change their institutions when they find that they are failing to meet the common need, even to the extent of revolutionary action, in the belief that government is an affair of voluntary organization for the common good.

(4) The right to individual inventiveness and adaptability, based on a conception of change as an omen of future good rather than a sign of degeneration from a superior past.[10]

Can the school help to insure the preservation of these rights? Must the school follow society, or is it possible for the school to lead society? It has been said that "schools cannot be made better until society is made better and society cannot be made better until the schools are made better." This statement sounds like a hopeless enigma of "lifting ourselves by our own boot-straps," but indeed there is some truth in it, especially under the present restrictions placed upon the publicly supported and controlled schools. Still if there are a few strong, thoughtful leaders who can envisage needed steps in the direction of an improved society, and if our teachers can only produce thoughtful citizens ready to evaluate, accept, and put into practice these improvements, and also develop additional leaders for the future, then there are strong prospects for the survival of democracy and the Judaeo-Christian ethic.[11]

Social, economic, and political leaders are getting a vision of the general goals toward which society must gradually move forward step by step. Educational leaders are aware of these general social objectives. A committee of the National Education Association set forth the following as the "Social-Economic Goals of American Education":

---

[10] John Dewey, *The Educational Frontier.* William H. Kilpatrick. (New York: Appleton-Century-Crofts, Inc., 1933.) Pp. 42-43.
[11] See Harold Rugg, *American Life and the School Curriculum,* pp. 263-327.

(1) Hereditary strength—everyone has a right to be well-born and under conditions which will conserve his innate strengths and capacities.

(2) Physical security—everyone has a right to protection from accident and disease.

(3) Participation in an evolving culture—everyone has a right to share the skills, standards, values, and knowledge of the race.

(4) An active, flexible personality—everyone has a right to conditions which foster the development of initiative, ability to weigh facts, resist prejudice, and act cooperatively.

(5) Suitable occupation—everyone has a right to whatever joy the most fitting work can bring.

(6) Economic security—everyone has a right to a minimum income that will provide a reasonable standard of living.

(7) Mental security—everyone has a right to trustworthy information from unprejudiced, unbiased sources.

(8) Equality of opportunity—everyone has a right to the fullest possible development.

(9) Freedom—everyone has a right to the widest sphere of freedom compatible with the equal freedom of others.

(10) Fair play—everyone has a right to expect others to act in conformity with the highest good of all.

TYPES The social experimentalist would include in the schools all the types of education included by the social traditionalist, but with different emphases. Training for intelligent cooperative social planning in all phases of human activity naturally makes certain types of education particularly significant.

Intellectual training is again raised to a place of prominence in education. The pupil must be trained in the intellectual processes indispensable to the cooperative functioning of society. He must learn the sources of factual information about the realities of social conditions and social problems; he must gain skill in selecting, checking, and verifying these sources for their authenticity and reliability. He must be taught to discover and state the various sides of controversial issues; he must develop skill in weighing and evaluating these issues through group discussion and thinking. To be effective, the pupil must be taught to think; to make wise decisions in his choice of alternatives and sound conclusions in reference to controversial issues. In the training of the emotions, emphasis is placed upon the elimination of fear, prejudice, and the crowd emotions that lead to unintelligent and irresponsible social action.

Social-moral or character education is placed upon a new basis— the motive of social service. It involves the development of a love for the truth, an appreciation of the clean and beautiful, a disposition toward law and order. There must be created in the pupil a desire and a will to use his knowledge and reasoning powers for beneficial social results.

In the new type of civic training, emphasis is placed upon intelligent participation and cooperation in civic affairs instead of a blind allegiance to national patriotism or party loyalty. The social experimentalist believes that instead of training yes men to take orders from headquarters, the school must develop thinking citizens who will critically examine every proposal made and act on the basis of social intelligence rather than social emotionalism, on the basis of facts and reason rather than mass demonstrations and propaganda. It must develop citizens who are willing to adhere to the democratic principle of having matters decided by the majority, and yet who are willing to give minorities the advantages of free speech, free press, free instruction, so that each minority may use every legitimate device for becoming the majority. James Bryce has said:

> The good citizen is one who will have sense enough to judge of public affairs; discernment enough to choose the right officers; self-control enough to accept the decisions of the majority; honesty enough to seek the general welfare rather than his own at the expense of the community; public spirit enough to face trouble or even danger for the good of the community.[12]

A broader conception of vocational training has been developed by the social experimentalist. Pupils must be trained for much more than the "automatic repetitiousness of machines." Vocational education must be broad and comprehensive and integrated with cultural and intellectual education, so that, in the inevitable monotonous work hours, the imagination might be able to feed upon the interesting materials of art, literature, and science instead of being, as Dewey states it, "frittered away upon undisciplined dreamings and sensual fancies." The pupil must be taught the importance of his task and its place in the general scheme of industrial and social life. Beyond all else, he must be trained for the social relationships of his job. Brewer has pointed out that most discharges in industry are due, not to failures in performing the vocational tasks, but to failures in human relations.

CONTENT   The social experimentalist devotes his attention largely to the development of the part of the curriculum that includes what are now known as "the social studies." The report of the Hoover Commission on Recent Social Trends and the work of the Commission on the Social Studies of the American Historical Association aroused the educational world to a new interest in the social studies.[13] In 1932, a committee of the Department of Superintendence of the National Education Association was appointed to prepare a yearbook on the *Social Studies Curriculum* which was published in 1936 as the fourteenth yearbook of that department.

Particular emphasis has been placed upon the teaching of controversial issues. Differences of opinion and clashes of interest are common in all phases of economic, social, and political life. The presentation

---

[12] James Bryce, *Promoting Good Citizenship*. (Boston: Houghton Mifflin Company, 1913.) P. 3. Reprinted with the permission of the publishers.
[13] The report of the Hoover Commission on Recent Social Trends was published by McGraw-Hill Book Co., and the Report of the Commission on the Social Studies was published by Charles Scribner's Sons in sixteen volumes.

of these controversial issues must necessarily be a part of the social studies curriculum. Instead of limiting social studies to history and geography, the social life of the past and the far-away, current social issues and the social problems of the pupil's own community are now being emphasized. History and geography textbooks are being reinforced by the current issues of newspapers and magazines.

The social, economic, and political activities of the local community are used as materials of instruction. Actual community experiences are far superior to vicarious experiences derived from books. Through extensive programs of field trips and directed classroom study, the pupils can engage in an analysis of the social structure of their community and gain a better understanding of the problems and issues of community life. It is even possible for the pupils to participate in certain of the simpler aspects of community social planning.

The extracurricular activities of the school also furnish abundant opportunities for training in social planning if they are properly administrated but teachers should avoid domination in their sponsorship of these exercises. They should at all times be largely pupil-initiated, pupil-planned, pupil-organized, pupil-conducted, and pupil evaluated. Cooperative school activities should be substituted for the recent excess of competitive contests. To prepare pupils for social planning, the school must educate more in the direction of cooperation and less in the direction of competition. Cooperative activities could be substituted for competitive activities even in interschool relationships. Certain substitutions have already been developed. The National High School Orchestra and Band, All-state Orchestras and Bands, the National High School Chorus, music festivals, decisionless debates, play days and athletic festivals, all-school student councils, press conferences, school tours—all these have been developed and their success offers much promise in the direction of interschool cooperative planning. In these activities the students of different schools work with each other instead of against each other and usually for the benefit of others as well as themselves. If these substitutions and others like them gain headway in our schools and come to supplant the traditional interschool contests, the motif of interschool relationships can well cease to be competition for personal and institutional renown and become instead, cooperation for community and social service.

AGENCIES Social experimentalism strongly supports a free public school system as the only safe agency for education. It is distrustful of any type of school that is likely to exploit the pupils for the benefit of a privileged class or to indoctrinate the pupils in the dogmas or prejudices of a single group. The social experimentalist, however, would extend the public school system to include the general education of adults and there are many evidences that this is occurring.

Such a conception of education demands a free teacher in addition to a free school. One of the last volumes to appear in the publications of the American Historical Association's Commission on the Social Studies, Howard K. Beale's *Are American Teachers Free?* raises grave questions in regard to the academic freedom of American teachers as well as—under certain circumstances—their personal freedoms.[14] The National Education Association, through its annual conventions and various subsidiary bodies, attempts to provide the same type of protection for public school teachers that the American Association of College Professors furnishes college teaching personnel.

During the great depression (and again following World War II), the question of academic freedom became prominent. In 1935 at the Denver meeting of the N.E.A., stirred by the passage of the so-called "gag laws" in state after state, and by the efforts of certain newspapers and patriotic organizations to pin the "red" label upon many classroom teachers, the liberal element among the delegates determined to commit the Association to a strong declaration for academic freedom and the protection of teachers unjustly accused of "subversive teaching." The resulting resolution placed the Association squarely on record in affirming a policy of academic freedom. It read:

The National Education Association believes that administrators, teachers, and schools should have full opportunities to present differing points of view on any and all controversial questions in order to aid students to adjust themselves to their environment and to changing social conditions.

Among the activities which the N.E.A. set itself to perform in this connection were the following:

(1) To make known to teachers and other friends of education any proposed legislation against freedom in teaching, and to take necessary steps to combat such legislation.

(2) To investigate and to report upon cases of discharge of teachers in violation of the principle of academic freedom.

(3) To cooperate with other reputable and recognized national organizations which are actively engaged in maintaining the principles of academic freedom.

In 1941 the National Education Association organized the National Commission for the Defense of Democracy Through Education to help develop understanding of the important relationship between a better education for all of the people and the maintenance of American democracy and way of life, and to bring to the teaching profession greater strength and unity in working for increased democracy in and through education. The functions of the National Commission for the Defense of Democracy Through Education, as stated in 1958 by the Representative Assembly, are:

(1) To defend teachers, schools, and the cause of education against unjust attacks; to investigate controversies involving teachers, schools, educa-

---

[14] Howard K. Beale, *Are American Teachers Free?* (New York: Charles Scribner's Sons, 1940.)

tional methods and procedures justly, fearlessly, and in the public interest; to issue appropriate reports of its activities.

(2) To gather information about the various individuals and groups who destructively criticize or oppose education, and to make résumés of their activities.

(3) To investigate alleged subversive teaching and to expose any teacher whose actions are found to be inimical to the best interests of our country.

(4) To develop among members of both the teaching profession and the public a better understanding of the issues and problems in the area in which the Commission operates.

This principle of academic freedom places an important obligation upon all teachers in service and prospective teachers in training. One of the most sincere and sensible objections to academic freedom is that the ordinary teacher is not sufficiently prepared to use it wisely. Some fear that the inadequately educated teacher will merely substitute propaganda in new and untried theories for the customary interpretation of the accepted political, social, and economic theories. True academic freedom implies that the teacher be permitted to teach all the truth and not a factional selection of the truth. This means that teachers must have a broad background of social information and experience.

Another volume in the American Historical Association's Commission on the Social Studies series, Merle Curti's *The Social Ideas of American Educators*[15] confirms the necessity for a truly social education and for social thinking on the part of American teachers and administrators. Professor Curti believes that in many cases educational leaders have not really led but have been too much influenced by economic and political considerations to be able to give an objective appraisal to the real goals of education in our American democracy.

In order to prepare pupils for social planning, it is necessary to have teachers who have come out of the sheltered academic cloisters and are living in the active social world. Teachers must be more familiar than they generally are with the social sciences. In addition to the usual educational requirements for a teacher's certificate as set up in the various states, there should be established requirements covering thorough training in the various social subjects. Teachers should also be encouraged to participate in the various social, economic, and political activities of their community, state, and nation. In this way they will study at first hand the controversial issues of the day, and be able to secure practice in the cooperative social planning needed to meet them.

Experimentalist belief suggests that schools and teachers alone cannot furnish all the education needed to prepare for social planning. The community must be used as a laboratory. Some plan of cooperation should be worked out between the school and the community by which

---

[15] Merle Curti, *The Social Ideas of American Educators.* (Paterson, N. J.: Pageant Books, 1959.) A re-issue of the 1935 edition with the addition of a new chapter on contemporary issues.

the pupils can be given a larger share in the responsibility of solving the problems which arise locally. The practice of withholding the right of citizenship until the age of twenty-one is a survival from the period when adults ran the world, and the periods of childhood and youth were supposed to be spent in preparing for adult citizenship. We realize now that citizenship can be developed through practice only. Many opportunities should be offered through which young people can participate in the responsibilities of community life. High school and college students could certainly make many contributions to the solution of social problems if they were given a chance to do so. Every age level should be allowed to play its part, however slight, in this enterprise of cooperative social thinking.

ORGANIZATION   Social education teaches that in order to prepare for a democratic society, it is necessary to have a democratic school organization. Authoritarian and dictatorial methods of administration and government are out of place in a school that pretends to develop democratic ideals. The militaristic and hierarchical system of organization should give way to a cooperative government in which all those concerned play a part.

Autocratic school government by boards of education and superintendents has been superseded by systems of administration in which teachers and even pupils participate. Faculty councils and student councils are becoming more common. A still more democratic scheme would suggest a school council in which students, teachers, administrators, parents, and citizens—in fact, every group concerned with the school—should be represented. Here practice could be obtained and an example set in intelligent cooperative social planning.

Teachers are participating in the administrative problems of school organization to a greater degree than ever before. The National Education Association and the various State Education Associations have taken steps to place the classroom teachers on a par with administrators in the management of Association affairs. These organizations, together with the American Federation of Teachers, are working together for a more democratic school organization. Indeed, the National Education Association, with its affiliated organizations, represents more than one million American teachers and, therefore, is in a position to speak for the teaching profession of the United States.

In democratic social planning and action, it is necessary to have the cooperation of two types of people. We need inventive leaders and intelligent followers. The school should be so organized that all would be provided with the equivalent of sixteen years of education. During these years the school would: (1) guide the pupil in the discovery, development, and control of his mental, physical, and emotional tools; (2) guide the pupil in the formation of the commonly accepted habits, skills, and attitudes; (3) guide the pupil in the acquisition of sensory and perceptive experience and the broadening of his horizons; (4) guide the pupil in the interpretation of the world of nature and the world of man, thus developing insight, wisdom, and a philosophy of life. For those capable of leadership, a higher school should be organized. The purpose of this school would be to guide each student in the mastery of some specialized form of expert leadership, preparing him to discover and formulate new laws and principles and invent new devices and institutions for the social welfare. Such a system of education could bring about a situation whereby popular mass understanding would cooperate with expert leadership in bringing about intelligent social action.

Upon his retirement from the faculty of the Graduate School of Education at Harvard, Dean Henry W. Holmes joined Dr. John W. Mahoney in establishing the Civic Education Project at Tufts University (1948). Their view that "education for citizenship in a democracy must remain faulty and inadequate unless it results in serious attention on the part of young people in school to the problems that democracy must work at and try to solve," implemented through the activities of the Civic Education Center, did much to make civic education a major concern in American high schools. Under their direction, the Center published a series titled *The Living Democracy,* dealing with social, economic, and political issues, which have been used extensively in American schools. Holmes and Mahoney likewise played a part in effecting the appointment of a Director of American Citizenship in the Massachusetts State Education Department.

METHODS If the goals of the social experimentalist are accepted, teachers must abandon traditional classroom methods. They must educate their pupils for an intelligent and cooperative participation in this gradual redirection of society. If the teacher uses the right methods, social planning will be possible.

If this reconstructionist philosophy is followed teachers must accept the responsibility of building up intelligent and willing participants in a work of social cooperation. The method to be used, both in the classroom and in the extracurricular activities of the school, is the method of guidance. Guidance means helping the pupils to solve their own problems; to make intelligent choices when alternatives are presented. Guidance means helping the pupils to find all the available facts and also helping them to develop the reasoning powers needed to use these facts wisely in the solution of social problems. Teachers must—beyond everything else—teach pupils all the facts rather than a partisan selection of facts; teach them how to think rather than what to think. All the work of the school should be cooperative. There must be developed in the pupils a sense of the values implicit in a society where cooperative action directed toward social security for all is the basic characteristic of living. The pupils must be alerted to the fact of social interdependence and of the need for intelligent cooperation in all social situations. Teachers must fit their pupils for an intelligent planning together of democratic procedures by which life for all may be stable and satisfying. This can best be done by pupil-planned and pupil-executed exercises and activities in the school. Teachers must develop in their pupils methods of thought and action which bring traditional theories up for reevaluation and reconstruction as changing conditions demand new attitudes and procedures.

The social experimentalist believes that social guidance should be substituted for discipline as a method of establishing order and good behavior in the school. The pupil should be taught to see that he can best satisfy his own legitimate desires by refraining from any action that will thwart the legitimate desires of others. Self-control is established by the development of the social motive, by the substitution of the cooperative for the competitive basis of action. Recognition of the rights of others is the surest source of good conduct. When a pupil refrains from a certain act because he sees that it is inimical to the welfare of the group, he has been started on the road to good behavior outside the school as well as in it.

The guidance objective is to set in motion—through the progressive development of individual intelligence—the unlimited play of intelligence in a progressive, cooperative planning for world betterment. Some of our social problems may never be solved, but most are more likely of solution if attacked by men and women who have been trained to do honest and intelligent thinking; have been given both the ways and the will for cooperation; have been taught to believe in the greatest good for all.

At the beginning of the present era in educational revision a splendid note was struck by President Glenn Frank, of the University of Wisconsin. Indeed it is still pertinent.

In a democracy the major business of the schools is to train the exceptional man for leadership and to cultivate in the vast and seething majority a capacity for understanding the trends of the time and sensing the human meaning of the policies that leaders propose. Democracy falters only when leadership is laggard and popular understanding is darkened.[16]

FOR FURTHER READING

Bode, Boyd H., *Modern Educational Theories*. New York: The Macmillan Co., 1927. Pp. 73-139, 223-266.
Bonser, Frederick G., *Life Needs and Education*. New York: Teachers College, Columbia University, 1932. Pp. 69-219.

---

[16] Glenn Frank, *op. cit.*

Butts, R. Freeman. *A Cultural History of Western Education.* Second Edition. New York: McGraw-Hill Book Co., 1955. Pp. 338-382.

———— and Cremin, Lawrence A., *A History of Education in American Culture.* New York: Holt, Rinehart and Winston, Inc., 1953. Pp. 461-499.

Curti, Merle, *The Social Ideas of American Educators.* (New Revised Edition). Paterson, N. J.: Littlefield Adams and Company, 1959. Pp. 499-591.

Dewey, John, *Democracy and Education.* New York: The Macmillan Co., 1916. Pp. 94-129.

————, *The School and Society.* Chicago: University of Chicago Press, 1899.

Doughton, Isaac, *Modern Public Education, Its Philosophy and Background.* New York: Appleton-Century-Crofts, Inc., 1935. Pp. 341-377, 464-505.

Duggan, Stephen P., *A Student's Textbook in the History of Education.* (Revised Edition). New York: Appleton-Century-Crofts, Inc., 1936. Pp. 345-365.

Faunce, Roland C., and Bossing, Nelson L., *Developing the Core Curriculum.* New York: Prentice-Hall, 1958.

Finney, Ross L., *Sociological Philosophy of Education.* New York: The Macmillan Co., 1928. Pp. 116-131.

Good, H. G., *A History of American Education.* New York: The Macmillan Co., 1956. Pp. 345-407.

Hart, Joseph K., *Creative Moments in Education.* New York: Holt, Rinehart and Winston, Inc., 1931. Pp. 449-463.

Justman, Joseph, *Theories of Secondary Education in the United States,* T.C.C.U. Cont. to Ed. No. 814, New York: Bureau of Pub., Teachers College, Columbia University, 1940.

Mayer, Frederick, *A History of Educational Thought.* Columbus, Ohio: Charles E. Merrill Books, Inc., 1960. Pp. 351-366.

Mead, Margaret, *The School in American Culture.* Cambridge, Mass.: Harvard University Press, 1951. 48 pp.

Meyer, Adolphe E., *An Educational History of the American People.* New York: McGraw-Hill Book Co., 1957. Pp. 314-329.

Mulhern, James, *A History of Education.* (Second Edition). New York: The Ronald Press Co., 1959. Pp. 633-667.

Myers, Alonzo F., and Williams, Clarence O., *Education in a Democracy.* New York: Prentice-Hall Inc., 1937. Pp. 164-227.

Noble, Stuart G., *A History of American Education.* New York: Holt, Rinehart and Winston, Inc., 1954. Pp. 482-493.

Randall, John H., *Making of the Modern Mind.* Boston: Houghton Mifflin Company, 1926. Pp. 594-638.

Raup, Bruce, *Education and Organized Interests in America.* New York: G. P. Putnam's Sons, 1936. Pp. 179-229.

Rugg, Harold, *Now is the Moment.* New York: Duell, Sloan & Pearce, Inc., 1943. 262 pp.

Russell, Bertrand, *Education and the Good Life*. New York: Boni and Liveright, 1926. Pp. 1-83.

Shaw, Charles G., *Trends of Civilization and Culture*. New York: American Book Company, 1932. Pp. 368-394, 596-653.

Snedden, David, *Sociological Determination of Educational Objectives*. Philadelphia: J. B. Lippincott Co., 1921.

Tugwell, Rexford G., and Keyserling, Leon H., *Redirecting Education*. Vol. I. New York: Columbia University Press, 1934. Pp. 2-112.

Ulich, Robert, *A History of Educational Thought*. New York: American Book Company. Pp. 315-336.

————, *Three Thousand Years of Educational Wisdom*. Cambridge, Mass.: Harvard University Press, 1954. Pp. 577-614.

Valentine, P. F., *Twentieth Century Education*. New York: Philosophical Library, Inc., 1946. Pp. 3-155, 372-456.

Van Waters, Miriam, *Youth in Conflict*. New York: Republic Publishing Co., 1925. 293 pp.

Wender, Herbert, *The Growth of Modern Thought and Culture*. New York: Philosophical Library, 1959. Pp. 183-213.

Woelfel, Norman, *Molders of the American Mind*. New York: Columbia University Press, 1933. Pp. 50-81, 118-153, 157-178, 200-220.

QUESTIONS FOR CLASS DISCUSSION

1. What are some commonly accepted customs and standards to which the child should be adjusted?

2. Do you believe that the schools should train pupils for competition or cooperation? Which of these seems to be emphasized more in contemporary schools?

3. Do you think that the schools should follow the procession or lead the way in social reconstruction?

4. Describe some of the recent economic and industrial changes in the United States that have made it virtually impossible for an individual to achieve personal success without affecting the security and welfare of others.

5. What are the relative values of philosophy and science as instruments of social planning? Was this as true in the ancient world as in the modern?

6. To what extent is the average teacher in present-day public schools socially minded? To what degree should he be?

7. To what degree should the teacher be free to teach? What are some of the common misconceptions of the principle of academic freedom?

8. What are some contemporary controversial issues of the presentation

of which may result in criticism for the teacher? How can such criticism be avoided?

9. By what means may a minority group legitimately place itself in a more favorable position? Do you consider teachers a minority or majority group?

10. Which do you consider the better motive for morality—the social or the religious motive?

11. To what extent is the doctrine of social experimentalism in accord with the teachings of Jesus? The teachings of the Hebrew prophets?

CHAPTER XVIII

AMERICAN PROGRESSIVISM IN THE THIRTIES

EDUCATION AND ADVERSITY

The economic depression which came with startling suddenness to the United States in the fall of 1929 was part of a world economic collapse which had its roots in the disruptions growing out of the World War of 1914–1918. It was felt more deeply here than elsewhere because it was preceded by a postwar decade of greater prosperity. Probably because of this era of good times and the confidence and faith of our people in education, the results of the depression did not affect the schools at once.[1]

By 1931, however, the severe economic dislocations had begun to have serious effects upon the cultural agencies of our country—including the schools. Educational appropriations were greatly cut, teachers' salaries were drastically reduced, building programs were abandoned, teaching load and size of classes were increased, school terms were shortened—in many cases from ten months to six—and educational economies of all kinds were attempted.

But more serious than the slashing of educational budgets and

---

[1] See Dixon Wecter, *The Age of the Great Depression* (New York: The Macmillan Company, 1948), for a comprehensive and penetrating account of the various aspects of this unique period in American history.

the resulting crippling of educational efforts was the wave of criticism that swept over the schools and their work. Public authorities seized upon the few instances of waste of public school funds, of expensive and ornate public school buildings, of fads and frills in educational practice, as excuses for "intelligent economy" in education. Even teachers and administrators, failing to realize that the lessening of financial support for education was due to the three D's—debt, deficit, and depression—began to have a sense of guilt, to fear that perhaps all this was a punishment for their educational sins. Education was criticized not only by press and pulpit from without but by educational leaders within the fold. Educational theories and practices were questioned as never before.

The educational hired men and women of the community were severely censured by the high priests of education—those who set the pedagogical styles for school teachers and managers. These professional experts condemned, often out of hand, about every feature of the democratic theory and practice of education which had so long been one of the proud boasts of the United States. The elementary school was attacked for its low standards of discipline and the chaos of its curriculum, as well as its inadequately trained teachers and the fact (apparently only then discovered) that most of them were women. The secondary school was assailed as an educational fetish and an arid and purposeless luxury, which was every year costing the American public immense sums. Higher education was condemned as positively degenerate.[2]

The educational misery of the country was reflected in the nature of the discussions carried on in state and national educational meetings, and in the appointment of various educational councils, commissions, and committees to deliberate on policies and practices. There developed many earnest efforts not only to get out of the financial mess into which the schools had fallen but—more importantly—to place education upon a surer and sounder foundation.

The criticisms and lack of faith in education were perhaps a reflection of the existing confusion regarding the aims of life among the peoples of the world. The general confusion in educational thinking indicated the absence of a consistent philosophy from which the educational aims of a country are derived. These educational commissions, therefore, attempted to formulate an educational philosophy and to establish educational policies adapted to the economic and social conditions of the times.

In 1932 the National Education Association established a Joint Commission on the Emergency in Education. This agency inaugurated a program of action designed to meet the educational difficulties growing out of the depression. It undertook "to exert the full force of the million members of the teaching profession and the millions of parents and citizens interested in the preservation of the idea of free public education and of making that idea increasingly articulate in improving

---

[2] Edgar W. Knight, *Education in the United States*. (Ginn & Co., 1941.) Pp. 580-581. Reprinted with the permission of the publishers.

schools and colleges." The work of this commission was most effective in stimulating sound thinking about educational problems.

In December, 1935, an Educational Policies Commission was established by joint action of the National Education Association and the Department of Superintendence. The commission was empowered to hold meetings, call conferences, conduct studies, issue pronouncements, and adopt such procedures as would be necessary for the accomplishment of its purposes. The work was financed by a grant from the General Education Board. Upon its organization the commission set up the following objectives:

(1) To stimulate thoughtful, realistic, long-term planning within the teaching profession, looking toward continued adaptation of education to social needs.

(2) To appraise existing conditions in education critically and to stimulate desirable changes in the purposes, procedures, and organization of education.

(3) To consider and act upon recommendations from all sources for the improvement of education.

(4) To make the best practices and procedures in education known throughout the country and to encourage their use everywhere.

(5) To develop understanding and cooperation among all organized groups interested in educational improvement.

The Educational Policies Commission sought through cooperative means to develop long-term policies for American education, which would merit the united support not only of the profession, but of all citizens.

Many sincere and able efforts to adapt education more effectively to the needs of a world in a period of great change were made by an organization known as the Progressive Education Association—later called the American Education Fellowship. Actually this group was part of a world-wide association of educational liberals whose goal is the development of the newer methodology and a life-centered curriculum. Internationally the movement is represented by the organization called The New Education Fellowship, which, beginning in 1915, has held a series of international conferences in such widely scattered places as Heidelberg, Locarno, Elsinore, and Ann Arbor. (In the United States the movement began with the establishment of the Progressive Education Association in 1919).[3]

These organizations grew out of the success of a number of experimental schools in both Europe and the United States. In its early years, the movement was confined largely to private schools and its influence in public education was negligible. But during the depression decade, the influence of these organizations as agencies for improving

---

[3] See William O. Stanley and others, *Social Foundations of Education*. (New York: Holt, Rinehart and Winston, Inc., 1956), p. 597, for a concise statement of the history and purposes of this organization.

the schools to meet the world emergency was quite pronounced. The movement made rapid progress in the public schools, especially in the wealthy suburbs of large centers of population. The movement throve on the attacks of its opponents, especially after the meeting of the American Association of School Administrators in Atlantic City in 1938, when the controversy between the progressives and the essentialists first broke into the open, and the proponents of progressivism felt called upon to defend their theories and practices before the bar of public opinion.

In an attempt to adapt education to the needs of a world in depression and war, two seemingly conflicting philosophies of education emerged from the thinking and discussion of educational leaders. It is true that the old conflict between the philosophy of totalitarian education and the philosophy of democratic education, which was discussed in the chapter on nationalism, has continued. But this older conflict based on differences of political ideology appeared to be less violent than the newer controversy raging in the ranks of education between what we shall call "naturalistic progressivism" and "realistic essentialism." While the world was in the throes of economic depression, progressivism seemed to be in the ascendancy, at least in our own country. But with the advent of World War II—especially after the entrance of the United States in December of 1941—essentialism gained ground.

This reversal was not without hazard, however. The gravest danger that confronts a democracy in the exigencies of war—or, more recently, cold war—is that the people may lose their democratic right to utilize their mature intelligence in determining what the experiences of the race have demonstrated as the "essentials" in which youth is to be trained, both for war and for peace.

THE CHALLENGE TO DEMOCRATIC EDUCATION

The American Association of School Administrators meeting in Atlantic City in February, 1941, had already stressed the growing concern of educational leaders for the cause of democracy and national defense. The general theme of the convention was "provision for the common defense, the promotion of the general welfare, and the safeguarding of the blessings of liberty." The convention agreed that the safety and welfare of the nation was "largely dependent upon the success to which our young people are taught to be loyal to our institutions and freedoms, upon their understanding of democracy, its strengths, weaknesses, and enemies, upon the efficiency of their vocational training and upon their willingness to sacrifice for the common good."

Who is to determine the essentials for which training is to be given? In totalitarian nations the dictatorial leaders determine these essentials on the basis of their own interpretation of experience. The Soviet system of Russia, the Fascist system of Italy, the Nazi system of Germany—all were advanced by their authors as preconceived utopias. Each of these nations educated its children for and into a preconceived social structure. Is such a goal desirable for a democracy?

In a democracy, it is the responsibility of education not only to provide the actual training in the essentials, but also to help develop a realization on the part of all that these types of education are essential, and thus produce a willingness to enter voluntarily into the needed training. If democracies are to be able to resist the might of totalitarian powers, they must do more than develop the skills that make resistance possible. They must arouse a spirit that will inspire that resistance by making evident the background of the struggle, the underlying causes, and, above all, the aims that are to be attained. When this is done, the training is not only initiated but the results of this education are used with conviction based upon understanding rather than emotion. It is essential to know what is essential, and this, too, is the task of education in a democracy.

Thus, the prosecution of the war entailed grave dangers. Would it be possible so to organize and indoctrinate for victory and yet not lose the democratic spirit which had begun to characterize the schools during and after the Great Depression? This was the challenge.

As one democracy after another in Europe and Asia lost their sovereignties and were enslaved by the onward march of the totalitarian powers—Germany, Italy, and Japan—educational leaders became more and more concerned with those phases of education that were essential to the preservation of what they called "the democratic way of life." Even the isolationists who wanted America to remain neutral and to take steps only for its own defense advocated an education that would build and preserve a true democracy that would shine as a light in a darkened world. During the early months of World War II the emphasis in educational discussions was on education for democracy. The Educational Policies Commission published a series of books and pamphlets under such titles as *The Unique Function of Education in American Democracy, The Purpose of Education in American Democracy, Education and the Defense of American Democracy, The Education of Free Men in American Democracy,* and *Learning the Ways of Democracy.* The Commission also held a series of regional conferences early in 1941 devoted to the discussion of ways in which youth could be better educated for the responsibilities of American citizenship.

With the adoption of the Lend-lease policy and the resolution to make the United States the arsenal of democracy, schools began to realize that the greatest need in the emergency was for realistic training in the essential skills needed for industrial production. Farsighted educational leaders saw clearly that our national policy was carrying us inevitably toward actual participation in a shooting war, and the educational slogan became "Education for National Defense." Education now concerned itself with the basic essentials required in an all-out war effort. In the autumn of 1940 the impact of the immense rearmament program of the government began to be felt in the schools. Congress established the National Defense Training Program under the direction of the Federal Security Agency, and schools, the N.Y.A., and state employment agencies cooperated in inaugurating within and outside the schools Defense Training Classes devoted to the development of the essential skills needed in industry.

The United States Office of Education issued many publications on this theme and urged the schools to incorporate elements essential to education for democracy into their curriculum, and to stress these essentials as steps in the forward march of democracy.

The year 1941 was a difficult one in the schools and the colleges. The Selective Training and Service Act had been passed, and the colleges were uncertain as to the policy they should follow in connection with the deferment of students to complete their education. The schools found it difficult to harmonize the instructional needs of their pupils with the demands of governmental agencies for defense training. There still was a majority concerned not only with the defense of the nation but with the defense of democracy as well; who not only wished to preserve America, but desired also to preserve the American way of life. There were many who feared that in a war to save democracy we might lose our own heritage. They felt that it was not enough to train our people to repulse the aggressor nations who would destroy the democracies by force, but that we must educate our people to understand the meaning of democracy, to love it and to practice it.

At Pearl Harbor, on December 7, 1941, this period of uncertainty and ambiguity ceased. By December 11, Congress had committed the nation to a war with all of the axis powers. With this action the conflict between education as usual and the defense training for war efforts ended. The schools and colleges through their leaders quickly pledged all educational resources to the prosecution of the war and the attainment of victory.

Since progressivism had become the leading educational philosophy in the period directly preceding the return to war, it is appropriate to turn now to a more specific discussion of the Progressive Movement and its relationship to the new essentialism before, during, and immediately following World War II.

NATURALISTIC PROGRESSIVISM

It is a cardinal principle of progressivism that it is concerned with the development of personality, and that its primary regard is for wholesome human growth and development. Essentialism is more concerned with the preservation of our ways of life and the adaptation of education to the maintenance of our established institutions and practices. Which is to be the dominant philosophy of the future, history alone can tell. Here we can merely analyze these opposing points of view—as revealed in the course of recent events—and examine their effects on the various aspects of education.

It has been said that progressive education is not so much a philosophy of education as a philosophizing about education. Within the membership of the Progressive Education Association there were wide differences of position and conviction. Progressive education is at once a protest and a vision. In its beginnings it was a protest against the deadening subordination of the individual to mass methods of education, the regimentation of minds, and the standardization of education through the efficiency methods stimulated by the determinism and mechanism of educational science.

Critiques of progressivism (and, to some degree, of its offspring, reconstructionism) have generally alleged that this doctrine has no distinctive philosophy of its own; that although it purports to be child-centered and speaks in terms of the training of the whole child, in reality it represents merely an opposition to traditional methods and philosophies; in this sense it is said to present a negative rather than a positive face toward education.

Many critics have assailed the movement as being neither progressive nor educational. Other criticisms have been in terms of harm done to the pupils. It is charged that progressive education is soft, that it is responsible for the relaxation of discipline in American life, that it allows too much freedom to children who need careful adult direction, and that it develops egotism, cockiness, impertinence, and disregard for the feelings of others.

One of these critics has written as follows:

> One thing that makes it difficult to reach an understanding with certain proponents of the "new education" is their apparent unwillingness to stick to the point, or to come out with any clear statement of position. On the negative side, we understand that they are against whatever can be stigmatized as "formal," "conventional," "traditional," or "subject-matter," but with all candor and good will it is sometimes difficult to see just what they stand for positively. Thoughtful and honest examination of the general principles as set forth by Kilpatrick will show how constantly the philosophy of the new education takes refuge in obscurity. . . . It seems clear to some of us that it is not really new, that it is not education, and that—whatever else it may be—it is certainly not philosophy.[4]

Yet it may be—and it certainly should be—remembered that, during the doldrums of the Great Depression, it was the dynamic force

---

[4] Lewis Foley, "The Philosophy of the New Education: A Reply to Professor Kilpatrick," *School and Society,* Vol. 55, No. 1411 (January 10, 1942).

of progressive education that gave much of the strength and meaning to community life. That its attempt to counteract the effects of those lean years by fostering an education aimed at developing human personalities and individual character was not entirely unsuccessful, is frequently forgotten by critics in their zeal to disestablish progressivism.

Lester Dix, in 1939, as a foreword for *A Charter for Progressive Education,* gave his optimistic appraisal of the future of the progressive ideology in glowing terms, ". . . that democratic education which is not yet, *but destined to be,* both the invigoration and decoration of the great American society which will ultimately emerge on this continent."[5] His conception of the foundation of this motive—as well as a partial definition of progressive education—is revealed in the imperatives set for progressivism. First, says Dix, this education will be organic; "it completely abolishes the old separation of mind and body, and robs of reality any assumed separation of physical, emotional, and intellectual activities"; next, education must be evolutionary—"The best things that man can know and do have not all been done; his behavior may continue to evolve without limit into more efficient, more satisfying, and more beautiful forms"; thirdly, "It will be dynamic. . . . Life, growth, and learning do not proceed in the absence of actual activity on the part of the individual, and they cannot go on in the absence of purpose and choice"; and, finally—perhaps most significantly—the modern conception of learning will view it as Life and Growth: "One cannot live without learning and growing. . . . (young people) will learn what they do, not what they are told, or what they see others do."[6]

As illustrated by Dix's interpretation, the progressive movement was at first dominated by those who wished to move away from regimentation and mechanization toward free child-centered activities in real life situations. Many of its early leaders—influenced consciously or unconsciously by the basic theories of Rousseau, Pestalozzi, Herbart, Froebel, and Hall—advocated an educational procedure based on the "natural inner urge of growth," the "unfolding of self," and the child's "immediate interests," not always distinguishing carefully between these and childish whims and caprice. Naturalism is one of the characteristics of the movement; for one of the familiar slogans of progressivism is to "work with and not against the pupil's instincts."

Since naturalism is still popular, it is well that we attempt an evaluation of this conception, particularly in its application to present-day conditions and in the light of its contemporary meaning. The modern psychologist admits that the child comes into the world with certain natural biological and psychological predispositions; but he insists that these are modifiable by processes of conditioning and sublimation, and

---

[5] Lester Dix, *A Charter for Progressive Education* (New York: Bureau of Publications, Teachers College, Columbia University, 1939), p. iii. Italics are mine.
[6] *Ibid.,* pp. 25-28.

even subject to elimination and substitution. It is true, as the naturalists have wisely contended in their protests against meaningless formalism in education, that the child is educated only by his own responses to stimulation. There is no doubt but that the child would be educated by turning him loose to respond to natural situations in the environment. But there is a desirable education and an undesirable one, and certainly many of these natural reactions would be socially undesirable and would educate in socially undesirable directions.

The modern exponents of naturalism and freedom praise the qualities of self-direction, self-control, and creative originality. These are most desirable goals. The mistake is made in thinking that these characteristics are "natural." The truth of the matter is that children even find it tiresome and confusing to have their own way at all times. The fallacy of the doctrine of freedom in education is revealed by the remark of a child in one of the ultramodern progressive schools who is reported to have asked, "Teacher, do we *have* to do just what we want to all day today?"

There is a distinct place for the school and the teacher as controls of stimulation. The teacher has a duty "to present stimuli that will produce desirable responses and withhold stimuli that will produce undesirable responses." Complete freedom would undoubtedly result in many undesirable instinctive and habitual responses—many that were undoubtedly originally useful, but are no longer useful and desirable under modern civilized conditions. Thus, in practice, the natural has to be seriously modified.

This earlier stage of the progressive education movement, however, had a great influence on education throughout the world. It helped to change the school from an institution concerned with the learning of the facts of a narrow curriculum and the development of a few basic skills, to an institution devoted to the development of the whole child, both psychologically and as a social organism.

American psychology, as noted in Chapter XV, owes much of its impetus and inspiration to European sources. During the second quarter of the twentieth century this debt was to be doubled with the arrival from Germany of four outstanding practitioners of the experimentalist group. Their researches were destined to be among the most significant in the reorganization of American educational psychology during the depression years and following.

MAX WERTHEIMER's (1880–1943) influence was barometric in the development of organismic (Gestalt) psychology. From professorships at Berlin and Frankfurt Wertheimer came to the United States in 1933, where he held positions at Columbia and at the New School for Social Research. He had discovered (1910–1912) the *phi* phenomenon (which concerns the illusion of motion) and thus may be considered the "Father of Gestalt Psychology." His approach to the study of psychological problems has been called macroscopic (as opposed to microscopic). The latter years of his life were devoted to the study of the problem of learning and in 1945 his *Productive Thinking* was published posthumously.

KURT KOFFKA (1886–1941) was born in Germany and secured his Ph.D. at Berlin. After serving as visiting professor at Cornell and Wisconsin, Koffka located permanently in the United States at Smith College in 1928. In company with Wertheimer and Wolfgang Köhler he contributed much to the development of Gestalt psychology. Koffka's *Growth of the Mind* (1924) dealt with organismic principles and created considerable interest. He published *Principles of Gestalt Psychology* in 1935.

WOLFGANG KÖHLER (1887–   ), another product of the University of Berlin, served as Professor of Psychology at Göttingen and at Berlin. His experience as Director of the Anthropoid Station at Tenerife in the Canaries resulted in the famous *Mentality of Apes* (1925). His relationship to Wertheimer and Koffka has already been suggested and Köhler's interpretation of field or organismic psychology appeared as *Gestalt Psychology* in 1929 (Revised edition, 1947). In America he took a post at Swarthmore (1935–1955) and, following this, became affiliated with the Institute for Advanced Study at Princeton, New Jersey.

KURT LEWIN (1890–1947) was born at Mogilno, Prussia, and graduated in 1914 from the University of Berlin where he taught before coming to the United States. After holding posts at Stanford (1932–1933) and Cornell (1933–1935), Lewin affiliated with the University of Iowa. In harmony with his connection with Wertheimer, Koffka, and Köhler, he was interested in experimental, theoretical, and social psychology. Lewin was perhaps foremost in the area of group dynamics and his *A Dynamic Theory of Personality* (1935) and *Principles of Topological Psychology* (1936) represent salient contributions to American psychological literature.

Gestalt (from *Gestalten,* visual shapes) psychologists interpret phenomena as organized wholes rather than masses of distinct parts. Their theoretical and experimental contributions have buttressed the more progressive educational methodology, sustaining as they do the view that the whole child is involved in every educational process. In maintaining that "the whole is greater than the sum of all of its parts," the Gestalt entrée to motivation offers an excellent basis for projects which begin with the child's natural, unpracticed, spontaneous interests; also as a rationale for those educational routines which proceed from the general to the particular.

Beginning in Germany the movement passed to the United States with the arrival of the leading Gestaltists mentioned above about 1930. In addition to Wertheimer, Koffka, Köhler, and Lewin, Gestalt in America has been espoused by George W. Hartmann, Robert M. Ogden, and Raymond H. Wheeler. Its central feature rests on the whole and unitary aspect of organismic behavior and considers *insight* as the salient factor in learning. Gestalt maintains that perception and memory are invariably concerned with the wholes which determine the meaning of their parts.

Two underlying laws are adduced by the Gestaltists: (1) each element of a pattern or configuration, through dynamic participation, alters its individuality; and (2) the dynamic attribute of self-fulfillment permits small gaps or incompletions which may properly be ignored through perception of the whole. Gestalt criticism of the mechanistic stimulus-response interpretation of behavior has greatly influenced changes to teaching practices which abet the unity or integratedness of experiences. Although Gestalt psychology was not concerned exclusively with educational method, its advent served to stimulate reevaluation of pedagogical practices and to reemphasize the necessity for a consideration of the whole child.

After Dewey the most influential champion of the progressive doctrine was WILLIAM HEARD KILPATRICK (1871–   ). He was more instrumental than anyone else in formulating its philosophy and developing its practices. As a distinguished professor of education, lecturer, writer, and editor, he popularized the movement among classroom teachers as well as educational leaders. He taught at Teachers College, Columbia University, from 1909 until his retirement in 1938. He was a guiding force in the Progressive Education Association and the John Dewey Society for the Study of the School and Culture. He is the author of such influential and popular books as *Foundations of Method, Education for a Changing Civilization,* and *Education and the Social Crisis.* Kilpatrick edited *The Educational Frontier* and *Frontiers of Democracy,* an organ of the progressive movement. A reading of his books, magazine articles, and editorials is perhaps the best avenue to an understanding of the philosophy of progressivism and its implications in the various aspects of education.

With the death of Dewey in 1952 progressive education lost its strongest voice although, of course, Kilpatrick still was vocal. George Counts and Harold Rugg as well as Harold Hand and Lester Dix continued the crusade, but it seemed the spark was gone. The tide of essentialism was running stronger and at the University of Illinois, long a center of progressivist activity and the headquarters of the journal, *Progressive Education,* Arthur Bestor maintained his—for a time—one-man vendetta against the movement.

The most common complaint against progressive education has been—although it does not deal with the idea adequately—that it glorifies the means at the expense of ends. Yet the fact that the essentialists adopted many of the methods of the progressives—grafting them on their own system—indicates that the means frequently were very good.[7]

Leadership in the progressive movement over the half-century of American life just completed includes the names of Boyd Bode, William H. Burton, George Counts, Lester Dix, Harold Hand, Sidney Hook, Gordon Hullfish, Alice Keliher, William H. Kilpatrick, Doris and J. Murray Lee, Harold Rugg, Carson Ryan, Harold Taylor, William Van Til, Carleton Washburne, and Carolyn Zachery. Although differing moderately among themselves all have given adherence to the principles enunciated in the writings of John Dewey and to the pragmatic spirit of William James.

AIMS The progressive education movement, influenced as it was by followers of Dewey's social philosophy, has always been conscious of the social implications of education. It has never been entirely limited to an exclusive concern with the child-centered concept. The serious threat of the economic depression and the rise of totalitarianism in the world, however, brought this social concern to the forefront in its thinking. Faced with the serious economic evils of the depression, the Progressive Education Association in 1933 appointed a Committee on Social-Economic Problems which formulated a policy under the title, "A Call to the Teachers of the Nation." Teachers were asked to recognize the corporate and interdependent character of the contemporary economic order and transfer the democratic tradition from individualistic to cooperative economic foundations, to a productive and distributive system managed in the interests of all who labor, to a society dominated by the ideal of guaranteeing to every child born into the nation the fullest opportunities for personal growth. The continuation of depression conditions, the spread of totalitarian thought, and the reappearance of world war caused the progressives to turn to the possibilities of designing an education that would lead to the creation of a new society nearer to man's dreams and desires.[8]

In 1941, with democracy facing extreme dangers if not destruction, the Progressive Education Association attempted a formulation of its philosophy in a report entitled, "Progressive Education: Its Philosophy and Challenge." In this report, the association not only rejected the idea of education being based alone on the natural growth and interests of the child, but also the concept of education for a planned society. It set forth its educational aims in these words:

The committee holds that the dominant ideals of our democratic culture, continuously reinterpreted and defined, provide the direction for educa-

---

[7] For a good analysis of progressive education and its post-World War II problems, see Frederick L. Redefer, "What Has Happened to Progressive Education?" *School and Society,* Vol. 67, No. 174 (May 8, 1948), pp. 345-349.

[8] The earlier aims of progressive education are fairly represented in Harold Rugg and Ann Shumaker, *The Child-Centered School* (Yonkers-on-Hudson, New York: World Book Company, 1928).

tion. . . . Democracy is not a mere association of individuals whose purposes and acts are individualistic in the *laissez-faire* sense. It is an intelligent use of co-operative means for the progressive attainment of significant personalities. Significant personalities cannot be unfolded from within; they must be acquired by individuals in union with other individuals intent upon a similar quest.

Here then we see the aims and purposes of progressivism—the development of significant human personalities as an end, through the means of social democracy. Two ideals are visioned—respect for human personality, and cooperative social participation—and are recognized as reciprocal. The more we respect human personality, the more we will organize our social institutions to promote its development; and the more we share in the activities of our cooperative social institutions, the more we will enhance the development of our individual personalities.

Progressive educators, as a rule, advocate a personalistic philosophy of education. They insist that education cannot be effective in the development of the individual and the development of society unless it facilitates growth in all phases of the pupils' lives. A personalistic point of view is an evolutionary philosophy which emphasizes the individual pupil and his all-around development as a person and not his intellectual training alone. In this its proponents are in accord with the point of view of a long line of educational philosophers running from Socrates to Dewey. They believe that the basic purpose of education is to assist individuals to achieve that whole personality which is within the range of their potentialities. Intellect alone is not enough to cope with the complexities of modern industrial-social organization. Progressivism demands the education of the whole man, the development of a personal character that involves physical, emotional, and social worth as well as intellectual. Progressives talk much of "human growth and development"; they are interested in attitudes, emotions, and interests, the nonintellectual as well as the intellectual aims of education. They believe that significant personalities are whole personalities.

TYPES   Progressivism, in its recognition of the pupil as a complete, dynamic, living organism, emphasizes the necessity of a continual use of every type of education. The progressives realize that the child is at all times a unity, and they recognize the dangers involved in a preoccupation with only one aspect of growth or one phase of behavior. They know that there are both physical and cultural requisites for healthy growth into individually satisfying and socially valuable personalities. They believe that education results from the interaction between the individual and the culture in which he lives, and therefore must include every element in a changing dynamic culture. The schools must make use of every type of growth-inducing experience and activity to be found in our present culture. These are the principles of the new Gestalt psychology.

Progressive education recognizes, as it has seldom been recognized before, the dominant role that emotion plays in human life, and has emphasized the great need for an education of the emotions and feelings. It believes that the education of the emotions is as essential as the education of the intellect. Emotions, however, are not conceived as separate and distinct entities but rather as aspects of the various biochemical and biophysical processes of the organism. Emotional education, therefore, is not something apart from mental and physical education; all three are phases of the unitary functioning of the organism.

The earlier progressives believed to a greater or less degree in the doctrine of naturalism. They held that the goal of education is an adherence to natural law; they insisted that education is for the benefit of nature, to provide opportunities for natural growth, and to remove all influences and restrictions hampering the natural evolution of the individual and of the race. Preaching a gospel of freedom in education they were exponents of the naturalistic movement initiated by Rousseau; refined and elaborated upon by Pestalozzi, Herbart, and G. Stanley Hall; accepted in part by the early educational psychologists; and popularized by John Dewey and his followers.

Present-day progressives give social education and individual education equal consideration. Their concept of the interaction of the individual and the culture upon each other prevents any exclusive or excessive preoccupation either with the individual and his desires or with the culture and its patterning. They are equally concerned with the development of the individual who will fulfill his potentialities for social contribution and the development of a social culture that will provide the fundamental requisites for the best possible growth and functioning of the individual. They see the futility of setting up social and individual values as natural antagonists. Their interest in social conditions, however, is that these may be educative, facilitating the best possible growth of the individual at every stage of his development.

In attempting to achieve their aim of developing significant whole personalities, the progressives neglect none of the types of education. They emphasize the necessity for work experiences, the development of occupational skills and proper work attitudes. But they also recognize the need for the rich and full development of the non-money-earning aspects of life. They give abundant attention to training for adequate recreational and leisure activities, the development of hobbies and of abiding esthetic interests. They place emphasis on those sports and recreational pursuits that have continuing value. Education should be pleasant; people's mutual enjoyment of each other is considered as important as purely academic training. The expressive activities associated with esthetic interests are made a vital part of education. Most of the work of the progressive schools—and much of the activity of most of the pupils—has been devoted to the development of interest in creative and esthetic achievement.

Progressivism in education has emphasized functional activity rather than passive receptivity. It does not merely teach items of knowledge or fix habits of response. It strives to provide experience opportunities of every type for its students. It provides opportunities for expression in more than verbal ways. Practical experiences and activities, esthetic experiences and activities, and social experiences and activities are emphaszed equally with intellectual experiences and activities as agencies for the significant development of whole personalities.

To be sure, certain educational liberals have taken positions further to the left than the generality of the progressives. Especially to be noted are the reconstructionists. Spearheaded by Theodore Brameld this movement retains many of the attributes of early progressivism, particularly the emphases developed by Counts (*Dare the Schools Build a New Social Order?*) and Rugg (*Now is the Moment*). Reconstructionism is indebted likewise to naturalism and stands much in the same relationship to progressivism and pragmatism as essentialism does to idealism.

Paraphrasing the words of Brameld, reconstructionism directs its chief attention to the future, here being indebted to the best in utopianism. The potential in American and world culture is its goal. Thus, it projects its thinking well beyond the ways of living to which we are accustomed for it strives with "imagination and audacity to design novel cultural patterns upon the solid basis of scientific knowledge of nature and man"; it strives also to develop workable methods of achieving them.

The guiding goal of reconstructionism is then, the enunciation of beliefs demanded by the revolutionary age in which we live. At the same time, they are beliefs that aim to be both concretely grounded in experience and attainable in practice.[9]

While most of the reconstructionists tolerate the more conservative progressivism, they generally reject and frequently denounce the educational ideologies of the right—essentialism and classic idealism (perennialism).

CONTENT   Progressivism insists upon a curriculum made up of life experiences; it abandons completely the idea that educational content consists of the words and ideas provided by a textbook or a professor's lectures. "Learning takes place when any part or phase of experience, once it has been lived, stays on to affect pertinently further experience; we learn what we live and in the degree that we live it."

The progressives condemn the older curriculum which was made in advance and handed to teachers who in turn assigned it in lessons to pupils. Its bookish content was divided logically into separate subject-matter areas, airtight compartments, often remote from the rapidly changing world and the actual life the pupil was living. The pupils memorized the information contained in the lessons and repeated it to the teacher in oral recitations and written examinations, success being determined in terms of the degree to which the pupil returned what

---

[9] Theodore Brameld, *Patterns of Educational Philosophy* (Yonkers-on-Hudson, New York: World Book Company, 1950), pp. 396-397.

had been given to him. Progressives maintain that when the pupil did succeed in retaining to greater or less degree this mass of organized information, its value usually was purely pedantic.

The progressive curriculum, on the other hand, consists of the experiences of actual living. What the child actually lives he builds into his character and personality; the school is to foster the kind of living which fits into the building of good character and significant personality. This curriculum cannot be built in advance and handed down to teachers and pupils. The curriculum consists of both richness of living and all-aroundness of living; it includes "distinctions made, knowledge used, consideration for others sensed, responsibilities accepted"; it covers all the aspects of daily living—practical, social, moral, vocational, esthetic, and intellectual.

Progressivism accepts the newer organismic psychology which rejects the idea that only the child's mind is educated, and insists that whenever any learning takes place the whole organism learns. Thus learning does not come about through repetition, but through the interaction of the individual organism and the culture in which it moves.

Field theory psychologists reject the mechanistic views of the functionalists. *Insight,* for them, is the central factor in learning. This concept is also central to the later progressivist thought. Frederick Mayer has stated the significance of configuration, as follows:

> Gestalt psychologists like Wertheimer, Lewin, and Köhler are correct when they point to pattern as the fundamental fact of existence. The whole does determine the structure of the parts. Our achievements, in part, are products of the *Zeitgeist,* the spirit of our times.[10]

Thus, the task of the school is to make available all the elements of the culture for this process of interaction. There are three results of this interaction between the individual and his environment, namely: expansion, differentiation, and integration. Children are expanding, differentiating, integrating individuals. The expanding individual, as he reacts to his environmental culture, is continually picking up experiences here and there. The growing organism participates in activities all the time, but he is not progressively advancing unless he is differentiating and integrating these separate experiences toward a meaningful and purposeful goal. This is the only true learning. The older subject-matter curriculum destroys this wholeness (say progressives), actually disintegrates the individual. The progressive curriculum preserves and promotes integration by providing the pupil with rich and varied opportunities to select and engage in his own goal-seeking activities. Progressives realize that the school can provide only part of the materials of an integrating curriculum—that only part of the work can be done in the classroom.

---

[10] Frederick Mayer, *Philosophy of Education for Our Time* (New York: The Odyssey Press, Inc., 1958), p. 18. See also I. N. Thut, *The Story of Education.* (New York: McGraw-Hill Book Co., 1957), pp. 267-282, 327-350.

The educational sociologists attempted to break away from the traditional subject-matter curriculum in the direction of a curriculum adapted to social needs by moving first toward a course of study made up of the broad fields of learning, such as General Mathematics, General Science, General Language, and so on. Then they advocated the core. In their conception of the core curriculum the position was taken that a core of common materials was necessary for all children in a given school period. In the elementary school, the whole curriculum was a core; nothing was to be put in that was not needed for social ends. In the secondary school, the core consisted of those subjects or experiences required by society, and the rest was left to individual choice as electives. Both of these approaches to curriculum building involved a concern with objectives, scope, and sequence—terms carried over from the subject-matter curriculum and the authoritative philosophies of education and not in accord with the general philosophy of progressivism.

Progressives moved still farther away from the subject-matter curriculum by organizing the curriculum in terms of what they called units of work, based on the structure of society and its aims. Units of work were built up around the major functions of social living and the structures and processes through which these functions were carried out. Society has such institutions as the government, the family, and the church, and their functions are such things as food getting, production, consumption, transportation, protection of life and property, experiencing religion, esthetic expression; the processes are economic, political, and social. Attempts have been made to vitalize the curriculum and make it more functional by organizing units of work around such topics. The Virginia Curriculum Program, the Wilmington Program in Delaware, and the unit-of-work program of the Horace Mann-Lincoln School are examples of attempts in this direction. Here again, as in traditional treatments, we have a concern with aims, scope, and sequence in curriculum building.

The experience-integrating curriculum of present-day progressivism generally does not attempt to analyze or set up aims in terms of social objectives, for the true progressive fears that by setting up specific aims they may become static. He believes that the child himself determines the scope and sequence of experience getting. As the child integrates his experiences into a meaningful whole, we have what Dewey calls "relevancy"; and as he expands and grows purposefully, we have what the progressives call "continuity." Thus instead of the scope and sequence of the subject-matter curriculum, the integrating curriculum has relevancy and continuity.

The curriculum under progressive education is made up of all of a child's activity, the sum total of his experiences; its scope is the extent of human living. Its function is one of so integrating experiences that the child will have an opportunity to expand and grow into a significant personality—with attitudes and ways of conduct that will make his life individually satisfying and socially desirable.

AGENCIES For the task of developing personalities the schools have been found to be insufficient, especially when they attempt to work alone. The serious plight of American youth, particularly during the depression, was revealed by many studies, notable among which was that of the American Council on Education in 1938.[11] The reports of such studies revealed the fact that, without assistance from other organizations, the schools could not meet the economic, social, recreational, and health needs of American youth, but that many agencies would have to cooperate in solving the problem.

Progressive education has recognized education's need to cooperate with other social agencies. These agencies are also providing educative experiences useful in the development of character and personality and frequently in areas not commonly served by the program of school activities. Adult education groups, churches, leisure-time and recreational groups, the Y.M.C.A. and the Y.W.C.A., and many other agencies are positive educational forces with which the progressive schools are working to bring all educational efforts into a more unified pattern centering upon a common task.[12]

In 1933 the federal government started to participate in the work of meeting the needs of American youth with the establishment of the Civilian Conservation Corps (C.C.C.) which was organized (1) to relieve distress through the employment of idle young men on constructive conservation projects, (2) to aid in the rehabilitation of youth, and (3) to assist in the general administrative drive for economic recovery. In 1935, the National Youth Administration (N.Y.A.) was established as an independent division of the Works Progress Administration (1) to provide funds for the part-time employment of needy students, whether high school, college, or graduate students, sixteen to twenty-four years of age, so as to enable them to continue their education, and (2) to provide funds for the part-time employment of youth for relief families on work projects designed not only to give young people valuable work experiences, but also to benefit the community in which they lived. These governmental agencies were designed not only to give financial aid to needy youth, but also to improve their morale and help develop them into useful workers and well-rounded personalities.[13]

The leaders of progressive education, however, along with all farsighted educational leaders, have recognized the fact that of all the agencies of education, the teacher is the most important. Through its annual national meeting and its various regional meetings, the Progressive Education Association made every effort to imbue teachers with the progressive philosophy and to instruct them in the techniques of personality development. Its leaders have stated that the hope for the

---

[11] Howard M. Bell, *Youth Tell Their Story* (Washington, D. C.: American Council on Education, 1938); see also Dixon Wecter, *op. cit.*, especially Chapter IX, "Youth in Search of a Chance," pp. 178-199.
[12] Wecter, *loc. cit.*
[13] Wecter, *op. cit.*, Chapter II, "New Design for Living," pp. 25-40.

progressive advancement of democratic education in our schools lies in
the reconceiving and reconstruction of our present practices in the education of teachers.

Teachers, of their own accord, have done very much toward
clarifying their philosophies and improving their methods, in spite of
conditions that would have completely discouraged a less loyal and
conscientious group. During the lean years of the depression, many
teachers of America demonstrated their loyalty to the cause of education. With salaries pared to the bone, with thousands actually unpaid,
they worked on at their tasks patiently—even attempting improvements
in their work in the face of discouraging difficulties. In spite of their
own financial plight, they retained their belief in the importance of the
education of boys and girls. They saw how easy it was for material possessions to slip away. They came to believe as never before in the worth
of their job of developing imperishable and indestructible human personalities. Whatever materialistic philosophies that had swayed them in
the prosperous era following the war were stripped away and were replaced by a dedication that glorified their work with a new meaning.
Teachers, through their organizations, began to formulate a philosophy
for the emergency which expressed a new belief in the improvability of
human character and destiny.

Teacher-training institutions have undergone a process of redirection and reorganization. Under the leadership of such organizations
as the American Association of Teachers Colleges and the National
Society of College Teachers of Education, this problem of teacher education has been attacked rigorously since 1933. The multiplication and
duplication of courses in teachers' colleges which developed during the
post-war decades has been checked. Many closer ties have evolved between departments of education and academic subject-matter departments for the better training of teachers. Courses in education have been
more closely integrated with the social sciences in order that teachers
might be led to see the relationship of education to the social order as a
whole. Educational sociology and cultural anthropology have been added
to the curriculum.

In 1938, the American Council on Education projected a study
of teacher education in the United States. This undertaking was made
possible by grants from American educational foundations. The Commission of Teacher Education, set up by the Council, with KARL BIGELOW
as director, inaugurated a far-reaching study of teacher education. The
underlying principles of this study, as set forth by the directors, were
based on the assumption that the adequate education of the teachers of
the country was a social obligation of increasing importance in the
existing emergency of recession and imminent war. "What teachers are,
what they know, and what they do, will be factors of critical importance
for individuals and society alike. Teachers should be viewed as human
beings and attention should be paid to their needs as men and women
and citizens as well as their needs as teachers. The good teacher must

first be a good human being." Reports from the cooperating institutions revealed that improvements had been projected in the education of both in-service and prospective teachers along lines of guidance and personnel work, general education, and professional education. The belief is growing that to develop significant personalities teachers themselves must become significant personalities.

The Progressive Education Association took the lead in the development of a new agency for the training of teachers, known as the summer workshop. The first of these workshops was held at Ohio State University during the summer of 1936, under the auspices of the Commission on the Relation of School and College of the Progressive Education Association. Thirty-five teachers, carefully selected by the staff of the Commission and by local educational authorities, attended. In the summer of 1937, a workshop was held at Sarah Lawrence College, Bronxville, New York, attended by 126 teachers from a wide range of subject-matter fields. In 1938, the Progressive Education Association held four workshops in four different sections of the country, attended by over five hundred teachers. In 1940, the Commission on Teacher Education organized workshops for college and university teachers who were cooperating in the study of teacher education. By 1941 the establishment of summer workshops had spread widely throughout the country, almost every teacher-training institution having organized one or more. In Michigan alone thirteen different workshops were in operation.

Basically, a workshop is a group of teachers working, under flexible laboratory conditions, on problems that are immediate and practical for the participants and the schools they represent. A workshop differs from a course in that a course is pre-arranged and taught as a systematic overview of a certain area, while a workshop is organized around the problems which students bring in. Each member of the group takes as his special task the solution of a problem or the completion of a project related to his own teaching or administrative position. The major part of his time is spent working on his problem in individual conferences with staff members or in small seminars or conferences of those working on similar problems.

The characteristics and values of the workshop techniques are as follows:[14]

(1) The participant brings a specific interest or problem which has arisen out of his experience as a teacher or administrator, and is afforded an opportunity to make an intensive study of the interest or problem at a place where superior library, advisory, and other resources are available to aid him.

(2) The participant may have not only easy access to the services of various staff members and consultants representing a variety of kinds of assistance related to his problem, but a ready contract with other members of the group who have problems akin to his own.

---

[14] K. L. Heaton, W. G. Camp, and P. B. Diederich, *Professional Education for Experienced Teachers: The Program of the Summer Workshop* (Chicago: The University of Chicago Press, 1940).

(3) The participant has formal and informal association with those of varied background, an association which contributes to his thinking on his specific problem, broadens his general professional orientation, and provides training in cooperative social thinking and action.

(4) The participant's total experience as he studies his specific interest or problem tends to prepare him for future solution of other professional problems.

(5) The participant, through the workshop's supplementary program of social and recreational activities, is given opportunities to improve himself as an individual personality in addition to the opportunities to solve his professional problem.

The leaders of progressive education realize that their philosophy can never be adequately applied until the program of teacher education is reorganized. Hope lies in the revision of traditional practices in the education of teachers. The beginning teacher usually is inclined to teach as he has been taught, unless teacher-education institutions catch the vision of including new areas of social education in their preparation of teachers. The educational experiences of teachers should include contacts with many community undertakings. Provision should be made for responsible participation on the part of teachers in various community activities. Opportunities for contacts with children should be a dominant part of the teacher-education program, so that both through knowledge and through experience the teacher may acquire an understanding of the principles of human growth and development. Most of all, the various phases of his professional education must be synthesized and integrated into a meaningful whole—a philosophy of education in the light of which all educational practices will be continuously reexamined and evaluated.

ORGANIZATION   Since the primary concern of progressivism is with the growth and development of the individual, as an integrated human personality, from his prenatal stage to maturity, the organization of the school into distinctly separate units and levels is discouraged. The progressives agree that a certain degree of organized division of responsibility is necessary for administrative convenience, but they fear that too frequently the mechanics of organization interfere with the real function and purpose of the school. In fact, each level of the school has frequently gone its own way in working out its program, and as a result great gaps have occurred in what should be a continuity of growth and development. Under the influence of the progressive movement, the rigid system of school organization, with its emphasis upon distinct stages of development, has been broken down to a considerable extent, and a close articulation among the units and levels of the school organization has been perfected. The overemphasis upon the division of education into pre-school, early elementary, later elementary, junior high, senior high, junior college, and senior college levels has been checked, and the only division recognized in many quarters now is that between elementary, secondary, and higher education. Even here the progressives have urged greater articulation, attempting to bridge the breaks in the continuous development of the pupil.

The progressives do recognize certain differences in the task of educating children and the task of educating youth. As Goodwin Watson says: "In childhood are laid foundations for emotional poise or instability, for social adjustment or isolation and for life-long patterns of behavior. . . . During the years of adolescence new strengths, new hungers, new associations, new insights and new social demands bring a Renaissance to personality. Sometimes the childhood patterns persist; usually they are modified; occasionally they are transformed for better or for worse." But the progressives insist that the elementary and the secondary school must work together most closely in this total task of personality building.

The most unique contribution of the Progressive Education Association along lines of articulation was the work of its Commission on the Relation of the Secondary School and College, which began in 1932 an eight-year experiment with thirty secondary schools and a large number of colleges, under the direction of Wilford M. Aiken. Twelve public schools, twelve private schools, and six university schools were included in the experiment. The purpose was to determine whether the graduates of secondary schools that had not followed a set curriculum of college entrance requirements could do as well in college as those from traditional schools. Two hundred and fifty colleges and universities agreed to waive their technical requirements for admission for graduates of the thirty schools and to enroll these students on the basis of scholastic aptitude and intelligence plus achievement in a broad field. The thirty schools were left free to revise their curricula on the basis of what they considered the interests and needs of the students.

The results of the investigation, published in 1942,[15] revealed that preparation for a fixed set of entrance requirements was not the only satisfactory means of fitting a student for profiting most from college, and that the stimulus and initiative which the less conventional approach to secondary education afforded produced better human material for the colleges than had obtained in the past. In 1937, the Southern Association of Colleges and Secondary Schools initiated an experiment, similar to that of the Progressive Education Association, in which schools and colleges agreed to modify their instruction to meet more nearly the abilities and needs of youth. These experiments are tending to break down the domination of the colleges over the high school curriculum, and have helped the high schools to break the chains

---

[15] Wilford M. Aikin, *The Story of the Eight-Year Study* (New York: Harper & Brothers, 1942). For several revelant evaluations of the Eight-Year Study see Kenneth V. Lottich, "Democracy Begins in Progressive High School Classrooms," *The Social Studies*, Vol. 42, No. 4 (April, 1951), pp. 162-166. The writer questions the technique of the study as well as the significance of its conclusions, defending at the same time the necessity for, and purpose of, the experiment.

of the sixteen-unit organization in which they have been bound for so long. But more than anything else they illustrate the way in which schools and colleges are being stimulated into bringing their organization closer together, each group giving up some of its cherished prerogatives.[16]

Another educational trend growing out of the depression is the emphasis placed upon the "community school." The community school may be considered as a descriptive term applying to that type of educational organization which recognizes the partnership concept in public education, the continuity of the educational process through the adult level, and the integration of the school with the community of which it is a part.

In 1937, the Committee of Secondary Schools of the Society for Curriculum Study issued a report[17] in which it recommended that the school be organized as a definite and integral part of the community. The school should be the organized agency for the participation of teachers and pupils in the life of the community. The community school increases the amount of community responsibility in education; it puts compulsion on all members of the community to participate in the work of developing the children of the community; it brings greater reality into the classroom. Progressive education urges that the whole community be organized into a program for the education of childhood and youth with the goal of seeing to it that every young person in the community gets the help he needs in building up physical strength, getting a job, enjoying leisure, participating as an intelligent citizen in the affairs of the world, and, most of all, developing a well-adjusted personality. The Committee on Adolescence of the Progressive Education Associaion, the Regents' Inquiry in the State of New York, the American Youth Commission, and similar organizations have issued reports emphasizing the necessity of such an organized community effort for the education of American youth in the direction of self-realization as well as social service.[18]

Although the community school movement flourished during the the decade of World War II in such diverse settings as Holtsville, Alabama, Kings Ferry, New York, and the Desert Queen School, located in the San Bernardino Mountains of California, its uniqueness and drive now seem to have been absorbed into the regular curriculum or into adult education programs. Yet the idea of school and community work-

---

[16] See R. Freeman Butts, *A Cultural History of Western Education* (New York: McGraw-Hill Book Co., 1955.) Pp. 569-584, for a thorough-going review of progressive practices and professional activities on each educational level: elementary, secondary, and higher.

[17] Samuel Everett, *The Community School* (New York: Appleton-Century-Crofts, Inc., 1937.)

[18] See Edward G. Olson, *School and Community Programs* (New York: Prentice-Hall, Inc., 1949); also Richard Waverly Poston, *Small Town Renaissance, a Story of the Montana Study* (New York: Harper and Brothers, 1950), for illustrations of an interesting approach to community education.

ing in harmony and sharing educational experiences offers infinite possibilities for school and cultural renaissance.

The immense publicity received by "life-adjustment"[19] served to crystallize public opinion and to divide the progressive and essentialist camps more sharply. The most persistent criticism of progressive education has been that it neglects the essentials of training needed for the realities of actual living—in essentialist terms, these are the traditional learnings rather than mere personal development or adjustment. As noted earlier, some critics claim that the progressive movement is intangible and indefinite; that it is far removed from the realities of life; and that it is therefore difficult to know what it actually stands for or does. Others charge that its aspirations are merely utopian dreams, that its practices have often increased the evils with which we are faced.

METHODS   The progressive classroom, like the socialized classroom, provides for the participation of each individual in group activities and situations, and provides for the contribution of each member of the group. But these activities are selected in terms of the extent to which they enable each individual through his interaction with others to acquire personal as well as social status and growth. All the exercises of the classroom are centered in and directed toward the individual as an organized personality. The methods are socialized in order to bring each group progressively toward the acceptance and skilled use of dynamic procedures as the truly democratic way of protecting individual interests. Progressive education emphasizes conference, consultation, planning, and participation as essential elements of a teaching procedure that provides maximum learning.

The methodology of progressivism is experiential as well as social. Abundant and varied opportunities must be provided for pupils to experience. Students must be given the chance to express themselves in more than verbal ways in order to attain complete status as persons. Practical experiences, social experiences, esthetic experiences, emotional experiences, as well as intellectual experiences should be emphasized, and these should always be evaluated in terms of their capacity to bring about the most significant development of each individual. The basic principle of progressive method is that vital personalities can be developed best through active participation in varied life activities.

The basic premise of progressive learning is called the "wholeness of method."[20] Learning is one whole experience, a single thing that branches and grows. Skill comes from experiences in original writ-

---

[19] See *Life Adjustment Education for Every Youth,* Bulletin No. 22, Federal Security Agency, Office of Education (Washington, D. C., 1951). The plan for this shift in curriculum requirements from the more formal program to certain immediate needs was based on the "Prosser Resolution" of May, 1947, which described the conventional high school curriculum as "unrelated to the everyday needs of life."
[20] A. Gordon Melvin, *Method for New Schools* (New York: The John Day Co., 1941).

ing and creative expression in the arts. Knowledge is the fruit of experience with a world of *things*. Understanding comes through the experiences of social living. Experiences are learned when they have become
fused into the wholeness and goodness of an individual's life, his personality, and his character.

The progressives accept the principles of motivation and apperception as formulated by the earlier psychological developmentalists, but
express them in newer and simpler terms. Kilpatrick says:[21]

> I learn each response in the degree that I feel it or count it important,
> and also in the degree that it interrelates itself with what I already know. All
> that I thus learn I build at once into character. . . . The presence of interest
> or purpose constitutes a favorable condition for learning. Interest and felt
> purpose mean that the learner faces a situation in which he is concerned. The
> purpose as aim guides his thought and effort. Because of his interest and con-
> cern he gets more wholeheartedly into action; he puts forth more effort; what
> he learns has accordingly more importance to him and probably more meaning-
> ful connections. From both counts he is better learned.

The argument is advanced that the first requisite of learning is
a pupil who recognizes that what he now wants to do cannot be done
until he possesses further knowledge or skill. All learning leads to some
goal. Thus the teacher must analyze the pupils he teaches; he must
know "what values these individuals now hold, what cultural deficiencies
now confront them, what driving interests now intrigue them, what
personal conflicts now distress them." The teacher, to be effective, must
discover the uniqueness of each child and understand its significance.

The method of instruction is largely that which earlier was
called the project—the carrying on of pupil-needed, pupil-planned, pupil-
organized, and pupil-evaluated activities. Situations are to be created
through which pupils can learn to gain control of themselves and of the
conditions that face them. The test to be applied in the selection of
instructional materials is the extent to which these are educational
experiences—in the sense that the pupils need them in order to live fully
developed and integrated lives. The principles of Gestalt psychology
are commonly used.

The prevailing criticism of the progressive classroom is that it
is lacking in discipline, that the pupils are being spoiled. This is the
same criticism that was raised against socialized education. It is perhaps
justified in those cases where teachers have misunderstood the principles
of progressive education and have allowed liberty to degenerate into
license; and whim and caprice to be followed instead of purpose and
interest. A school where children are living and working together in
order to develop in themselves and each other wholesome personalities
and good character can be nothing other than a well-disciplined school.

---

[21] William H. Kilpatrick, "The Case for Progressivism in Education," *The Journal of the National Education Association*, Vol. 30, No. 8 (November, 1941), pp. 231-232.

This discipline is the positive rather than the negative type. The basic characteristics of a disciplined democracy are a love of justice and a respect for human personality; these can best result from greater freedom and more responsibility on the part of pupils in the activities of the school.

It is in this last feature that the reconstructionists feel that their planning and organization is superior to that of conventional progressives. Governed by the urge to develop a utopian society, they consider their motivation more purposeful and self-directive.

HAROLD HAND, in a manual for school evaluation, suggested that the community's interest (and stake) in the school must be analyzed in social terms and that "thumbs-up" and "thumbs-down" groups are its vital concern. Under such headings as "How Parents Feel about the Way Their Children Are Treated by the Other Pupils" and "How Pupils Feel about the Help They are Getting with Their Personal Problems," Hand attempts to show how the social setting influences the tone and work of the school.[22]

Nevertheless, for reasons mentioned earlier in this chapter, the progressive movement in America appears to have lost much of its early drive. The necessities of conflict, the growth of essentialism, and the cold war threat have contributed greatly to its decline. Yet the fact remains that many of its methods—and much of what it preached—were assimilated by schools which carried a traditional label and by leaders who chose to consider its ideas their own.[23]

Professor L. A. Cremin has epitomized the decline of the progressive movement and the death, in 1955, of the Progressive Education Association, as the "end of an era in American pedagogy." "Somehow a movement which had for half a century enlisted the enthusiasm, the loyalty, the imagination, and the energy of large segments of the American public and the teaching profession became, in the decade following World War II, anathema. . . ."[24]

---

[22] Harold Hand, *What People Think About Their Schools* (Yonkers-on-Hudson, N. Y.: World Book Company, 1948) pp. 96-99, 111-114. For a delightfully visionary approach to the relationship of two mythical communities to their schools, see *Education for All American Youth*. Washington: Educational Policies Commission of the National Education Association, 1944. Pp. 23-170, 171-338. See also Theodore Brameld, *Ends and Means in Education: A Midcentury Appraisal* (New York: Harper & Bros., 1950).

[23] David Lawson, in "Two Views of the Child's Education for Freedom," *The Educational Forum*, Vol. XXIV, No. 3 (March, 1960), pp. 345-350, offers an attempt at reconciliation of the presumed differences between the naturalists and the idealists. His arguments are well chosen and are pertinent to the progressivist controversy.

[24] Lawrence A. Cremin, "What Happened to Progressive Education?" *Teacher's College Record*, Vol. 61, No. 1 (October, 1959), pp. 23 ff; also Cremin, "The Progressive Movement in American Education: A Reappraisal," *Harvard Educational Review*, Vol. 27, No. 4 (Fall, 1957), pp. 251-270, and "John Dewey and the Progressive Education Movement, 1915-1952," *The School Review*, Vol. 67, No. 2 (Summer, 1959), pp. 160-173; William H. Kilpatrick, "Personal Reminiscences of Dewey and My Judgment of His Present Influence," *School and Society*, Vol. 87, No. 2159 (October 10, 1959), pp. 374-375, emphasizes the indigeneous features in Dewey's educational philosophy.

Perhaps this is too severe; yet interest in the "movement" did wane and the journal *Progressive Education* itself suspended operations in 1957. However—and this in no way disagrees with Cremin's thesis— two pertinent factors must be mentioned here. *First,* the progressive movement itself was much more diffuse than usually considered and, to attribute progressivism largely to the activities of the Progressive Education Association compounds this error. Part of the general reform movement in the United States following its coming of age at the turn of the century, progressivism appears to be as natural a product as slum clearance, purer food and drugs, and municipal reform. To attribute solely to John Dewey that which—to a large degree—resulted spontaneously is, of course, unhistorical and oversimplified.

Second, although the movement has subsided, progressiveness in education is anything but dead. Its famous methods: the use of problems and projects, unit teaching, provision for individual differences, the guidance function of education, and the reorganization of the school whereby these things should be accomplished are still very much in evidence. So, too, is the utilization of an organismic psychology of education.

FOR FURTHER READING

Alberty, Harold and Others, *Progressive Education: Its Philosophy and Challenge*. New York: The Progressive Education Association, 1941.

Bayles, Ernest E., *Democratic Educational Theory*. New York: Harper and Brothers, 1960.

Beard, Charles A., *The Unique Function of Education in American Democracy*. Washington: Educational Policies Commission of the National Education Association, 1937.

Bode, Boyd H., *Progressive Education at the Crossroads*. New York and Chicago: Newson and Co., 1938.

Brameld, Theodore, *Patterns of Educational Philosophy*. New York: World Book Company, 1950. Pp. 167-208, 508-526.

Butts, R. Freeman. *A Cultural History of Western Education*. New York: McGraw-Hill Book Co., 1955. Pp. 569-584.

————, and Cremin, Lawrence A., *A History of Education in American Culture*. New York: Holt, Rinehart and Winston, Inc., 1953. Pp. 515-562.

Carr, William G., *The Purposes of Education in American Democracy*. Washington: Educational Policies Commission of the National Education Association, 1938.

Counts, George S., *The Education of Free Men in American Democracy*.

Washington: Educational Policies Commission of the National Education Association, 1942.

————, *The Social Foundations of Education*. New York: Charles Scribner's Sons, 1934. Pp. 1-30, 252-282.

Edwards, Newton, and Richey, Herman G., *The School in the American Social Order*. Boston: Houghton Mifflin Company, 1947. Pp. 730-735.

Good, H. G., *A History of Western Education*. New York: The Macmillan Co., 1960. Pp. 536-606.

Hand, Harold C., *What People Think about Their Schools*. Yonkers-on-Hudson, New York: World Book Company, 1948. 219 pp.

Justman, Joseph, *Theories of Secondary Education in the United States*. (T.C.C.U. Cont. to Education No. 814.) New York: Bureau of Publications, Teachers College, Columbia University, 1940. Pp. 12-54.

Kandel, I. L., *Conflicting Theories of Education*. New York: The Macmillan Co., 1939.

Knight, Edgar W., *Education in the United States* (Second Revised Edition). Boston: Ginn & Co., 1941. Pp. 576-669.

————, *Twenty Centuries of Education*. Boston: Ginn & Co., 1940. Pp. 583-608.

Life Adjustment Education for Every Youth, Bulletin No. 22, Federal Security Agency, Office of Education. Washington: Government Printing Office, 1951.

Mason, Robert E., *Educational Ideals in American Society*. Boston: Allyn and Bacon, 1960.

Mayer, Frederick, *Philosophy of Education for Our Time*. New York: Odyssey Press, Inc., 1958. 198 pp.

Melvin, A. Gordon, *Method for New Schools*. New York: The John Day Company, 1941.

Meyer, Adolphe E., *An Educational History of the American People*. New York: McGraw-Hill Book Co., 1957. Pp. 396-426.

————, *The Development of Education in the Twentieth Century*. New York: Prentice-Hall, Inc., 1939. Pp. 1-124.

Myers, Alonzo F., and Williams, Clarence O., *Education in a Democracy*. New York: Prentice-Hall, Inc., 1937. Pp. 228-360.

Park, Joe (Ed.), *Selected Readings in the Philosophy of Education*. New York: The Macmillan Co., 1958. Pp. 55-150.

Ulich, Robert, *A History of Educational Thought*. New York: American Book Company, 1950. Pp. 315-345.

Valentine, P. F., *Twentieth Century Education*. New York: Philosophical Library, Inc., 1946. Pp. 42-68, 89-113, 482-654.

Washburne, Carleton, *A Living Philosophy of Education*. New York: The John Day Company, 1940.

Weber, Christian O., *Basic Philosophies of Education*. New York: Holt, Rinehart and Winston, Inc., 1960. Pp. 239-285, 303-322.

Wecter, Dixon, *The Age of the Great Depression*. New York: The Macmillan Co., 1948.

QUESTIONS FOR CLASS DISCUSSION

1. Although a period of adversity, a number of positive achievements in education occurred during the Age of the Great Depression in the United States. Cite several of these and comment on their significance.
2. What arguments may be presented against the establishment by the federal government of educational agencies supplanting or even duplicating the work of the public schools? Are there no arguments favorable to federal cooperation?
3. To what extend do you agree with the critics of progressive education who consider it intangible and indefinite?
4. What features in American political and economic life reflect those same pragmatic influences which many interpreters consider the original basis for progressivism in the schools?
5. How much emphasis do you feel that the schools should give to the development of specialized skills and competencies? Explain.
6. What are the significant points at issue between progressivism and essentialism or traditionalism? Do you believe that these seemingly conflicting philosophies of education can be harmonized?
7. Present arguments pro and con for the adoption of a Reconstructionist philosophy of education. What leading figures champion this new direction for the American schools?
8. Comment on the philosophy of Lester Dix as it is revealed in his statement of objectives for the Horace Mann-Lincoln School. Do you consider this an extreme form, or merely a moderate progressivism? Defend your position.
9. Compare or contrast John Dewey's instrumentalist educational philosophy with Rousseau's naturalism. Do you believe that the social ideas of Dewey and Rousseau are comparable?
10. Account for the spread of progressive education to several of the countries of western Europe. To the U.S.S.R.

CHAPTER XIX

AMERICAN ESSENTIALISM IN THE WAR DECADES

VICTORY WITHOUT PEACE

Victory for the West implied that the democratic idea (and education in democratic principles) had prevailed. With the cessation of hostilities in 1945 the totalitarian governments of Germany, Italy, and Japan were overthrown and democratic regimes instituted. The educational systems likewise were revised in accordance with democratic principles; although in each case the organization was slightly more class-oriented than that in the United States.

But the danger from totalitarianism was far from vanquished. By the end of the European phase of World War II the U.S.S.R. had moved its army and institutions into ten countries in East Central Europe and (although under the terms agreed upon by the Grand Alliance) occupied the eastern section of Germany; here another People's Democracy—a carbon copy of the Soviet system—was created. The Communist brand of totalitarian education was imposed in each of these settings.[1]

---

[1] See Winston S. Churchill, *Triumph and Tragedy* (Boston: Houghton Mifflin Company, 1953). The overrun countries in East Central Europe—the so-called Iron Curtain countries—are Esthonia, Latvia, Lithuania, Poland, Czechoslovakia, Hungary, Romania, Bulgaria, Albania, and Yugoslavia (although the last frequently operates independently of Moscow.)

Politically the situation worsened and by as early as 1947 a cold war was said to obtain between the Soviet-controlled bloc and the Western democracies. When the former Republic of China (the island of Formosa excepted) became Communist—adopting Marxist collectivism—the peril became increasingly greater.

Indeed it appeared to many educational thinkers in the United States that the aims fostered in the stress of World War II were the only guarantee against softness and inefficiency should a deteriorating international situation result in another appeal to arms—a terrifying third world war.

The resurgence of the Communist idea of the world state—especially since 1944—has led to apprehension (and conservatism) in the United States. Professor Merle Curti notes the "great gulf between Communism and the western form of democracy" which has produced the cold war.

This in turn has been in part responsible for the conservative mood of America in the postwar era. It has expressed itself, so far as education goes, in many ways. One has been the closer relations between American business and education . . . but the chief example of the relation between the conservative mood of the country and education has been the retreat of the idea that the school can and should take the lead in initiating and implementing social reform.[2]

This explicit reference to that sector of the social educationists who, at the time of the great depression, suggested that the school act as an advance agent for social and political planning clearly indicates the changing educational climate of postwar years.

Although World War II had been fought to obliterate totalitarianism and its thought-control tactics, the upsweep of Communism, both in East Europe and in Asia, which followed presented nothing less than an ominous picture. By the end of 1949 all of mainland China had fallen under Communist control; a Soviet-type People's Republic had been set up; and in 1950–1953 the Korean War occurred as the Soviets attempted to drive United States and United Nations forces from that peninsula.

The threat of Communism to objective truth and to democratic education as the West understands it must be grasped by students of education. Indeed—grave though the political aspect of Communism appears—this menace is far greater in that it attacks the mind as well as the body. The so-called brain-washing tactics heavily utilized during the Korean War are well known; that this species of thought-control is inherent in Communism and in its system of education is less familiar.

In order to visualize the power of this Communist drive through the senses one must review the materialist origins of the movement. Although indebted to Marx, groundwork for a Communist state on

---

[2] Merle Curti, *The Social Ideas of American Educators,* Revised Edition. (Paterson, N. J.: Pageant Books, Inc., 1959.) Pp. xxxii, xxxiii.

utopian lines had already been conceived by nineteenth century Russian revolutionary leaders. Its necessity was a new man—"possessed neither of patriotism nor of pity; his only faith in the revolution itself, and in this fanatic . . . a man who regarded himself as expendable, who followed blindly the leader and the party line, and who if need be would lie, cheat and murder to gain his objective."[3] In this aspect, then, Communism became—and is—a secular faith and from this fact springs its power.

Ivan Sergeyevich Turgenev, the Russian novelist, has put this peculiar fascination of Marxist extremism into words:[4]

—To you who desire to cross this threshold, do you know what awaits you?
— I know, replied the girl.
—Cold, hunger, abhorrence, derision, contempt, abuse, prison, disease and death!
—I know, I am ready, I shall endure all blows.
—Not from enemies alone, but also from relatives, from friends.
—Yes, even from them. . . .
—Are you ready to commit a crime?
—I am ready for crime, too.
—Do you know that you may be disillusioned in that which you believe, that you may discover that you were mistaken, that you ruined your young life in vain?
—I know that too.
—Enter!
The girl crossed the threshold and a heavy curtain fell behind her.
—Fool! said someone gnashing his teeth.
—Saint! someone uttered in reply.

Communism thus assumes the status of a religion to its followers; since the education systems of the Communist bloc are designed for the perpetuation of Marxist principles and world revolution, the West faces a grave threat. This, as noted earlier, has already partially conditioned educational thinking away from the prewar emphases on progressivism and child-centeredness.

NEW DIRECTIONS IN EDUCATION

Within the United States—following the Second World War—opposition to progressivist and popularist tendencies made greater head-

---

[3] Alan Moorehead, *The Russian Revolution.* (New York: Harper and Brothers, 1958.) P. 33. Reprinted with the permission of the publishers.
[4] *Ibid.,* Quoted from *The Threshold.* Reprinted with the permission of the publishers. See also *I Want to Be Like Stalin*, by B. P. Yesipov and N. K. Goncharov, Translated by George S. Counts and Nucia P. Lodge (New York: John Day, 1947). Chapter II, "For Bolshevik Character,"—The Principles of Moral Education, pp. 42-52, stresses the development of the Communist mentality.

way. A new group of critics appeared and venerable Harvard herself produced a lengthy study indicating the need for a stemming of the tide of popularism.[5] The two forces in American education are sometimes designated as Jeffersonian—for the more traditional, idealistic and academic tendency; and Jacksonian—for the pragmatic, vocational, and popular at its most extreme stage. In general the essentialists may be said to be Jeffersonian, and the progressives, Jacksonian.[6]

Jacksonianism—far from dead—was especially visible in the vogue for "life adjustment," a development originally fostered at the close of the war by the division of vocational education of the United States Office of Education. Charles A. Prosser, a member of one of the groups called for the purpose of formulating the platform and objectives of the movement, introduced a resolution indicating that the consensus of the conference was that at least 60 percent of the students of secondary school age could not find opportunity for the training they needed in the conventional schools. This appeared to demand an entirely new program for secondary education; at a later time the use of percentages was dropped and the request for "Life Adjustment Education for Every Youth" was made general.[7]

This is not to say that Jacksonianism had again gained the ascendancy. Life adjustment, however, gained enough adherents to serve as an agency for crystallizing educational thought and thus contributed to the necessity for a thorough reappraisal of American educational practice.

A second result of pressure from without (although this direction may indeed owe much to the social doctrination of the earlier depression years) was the new accent on anti-individualism and conformity. Curti notes that "in becoming increasingly corporate in character American life and values stressed the importance of teamwork, of conformity to the group norm, of reducing conflict in personal and group relations . . . summed up in such slogans for 'other-directedness,' 'the organization man,' and 'togetherness'."[8]

The thesis of this new direction—first cited by David Riesman[9] several years ago—simply put, is this: Three stages in value formation

[5] *General Education in a Free Society* (Cambridge: Harvard University Press, for the President and Fellows of Harvard College, 1948).

[6] *Ibid.,* pp. 27-35. *General Education in a Free Society* expresses the view that the Jeffersonian-Jacksonian terminology is perhaps "unfair to Jefferson's express interest in the citizen-farmer and artisan" but goes on to emphasize his attachment to selection of the ablest through education as revealed in his famous plan for Virginia proposed in 1779.

[7] See *Life Adjustment Education for Every Youth,* Bulletin No. 22, Federal Security Agency, Office of Education (Washington, D. C., 1951); also Harl R. Douglass (ed.), *Education for Life Adjustment: Its Meaning and Implementation* (New York: Ronald Press Co., 1950).

[8] Curti, *op. cit.,* p. xxxvi.

[9] David Riesman, Nathan Glazer, Reuel Denney, *The Lonely Crowd, A Study of the Changing American Character.* (New Haven: Yale University Press, 1950.) David Riesman and Nathan Glazer, *Faces in the Crowd* (New Haven: Yale University Press, 1952.) David Riesman, *Constraint and Variety in American Education.* (Lincoln, Neb.: University of Nebraska Press, 1956.)

may be detected throughout the past thousand or so years of Western civilization. The first, tradition-centered, lasted until around 1500; it was replaced by an inner-directed urge based on individualism and inner-compulsion (this appears to have been the wellspring of Puritanism—the Calvinistic ethos); however, within recent years, reports Riesman (and this may have incubated at the depression period between the great wars, or in the early post-1944 era at the latest), a third orientation has gained ground. This is "other-directedness," seemingly a reversal of the value formation index of earlier American life.

Riesman is not alone in his perception of other-direction—especially as applied to the business world in the United States; this is revealed by the spate of contemporary novels and motion pictures which deal with these phenomena in realistic fashion. The reader is directed to the offerings of John P. Marquand, Cameron Hawley, Sloan Wilson, Frederic Wakesman, William H. Whyte and others for this contemporary view.

That this philosophy, which undoubtedly owed a debt of some kind to one of the various existential movements, found favor with the younger adults and some adolescents is admitted. The presence of the "world-owes-me-a-living" type, the Beatnik, the "Blackboard Jungle-ite," and the general feeling of "living for today" prevalent in certain sectors of American life in the sixties seems to corroborate Curti's diagnosis.

That other-directedness has already conditioned American schools is not admitted although the recent vogue for so-called life adjustment courses rather than the conventional elements of the more formal curriculum may be submitted as evidence of a tendency to anti-individualism.

There are, nevertheless, new American educational leaders who view education from the strictly Jeffersonian vantage point. And in the present mood of conservation and caution their advice may be followed.

James B. Conant,[10] former President of Harvard, and Paul Woodring,[11] the Ford Foundation (formerly Western Washington College), offer plans for the reorganization of American public education. In deference to the broadness of the essentialist definition they too may be placed in this camp. Woodring's design is far to the right and Conant, too, would remove many of the tendencies to soft elections in the high school through a stricter series of required subjects and prerequisites. Arthur E. Bestor's Council for Basic Education, organized in 1956, stands even further to the right and would, in effect, revive most of the curriculum and practices of the early twentieth century.

Leadership of the essentialist camp (comprising, for our purposes, both idealists and realists) has included William C. Bagley,

---

[10] James B. Conant, *The American High School Today*. (New York: McGraw-Hill Book Co., 1959.)
[11] Paul Woodring, *A Fourth of a Nation*. (New York: McGraw-Hill Book Co., 1957.) See also his *Let's Talk Sense about Our Schools*. (New York: McGraw-Hill Book Co., 1953.)

Arthur E. Bestor, Franklin Bobbitt, William W. Brickman, Thomas H. Briggs, Harry C. Broudy, James B. Conant, Harold Clapp, Michael J. Demiashkevich,[12] Hermann Harrell Horne, Robert M. Hutchins, Charles H. Judd, Isaac L. Kandel, Henry C. Morrison, Robert Ulich, and Paul Woodring.

Now, having devoted the previous chapter to naturalistic progressivism in the prewar and postwar periods, the rising influence of essentialism, traditionalism, and perennialism within this era of world crisis must be our next consideration.

ESSENTIALISM AND PERENNIALISM

While it is easiest to identify the opponents of progressivism (and reconstructionism) as traditionalists, a sharper definition would characterize those at the extreme right as perennialists and the moderate traditionalists as essentialists, and this is in recognition of their philosophical position as well. By the older terminology, both moralists and disciplinists would be included with the traditionalists; naturalists, of course, would share the progressives' position on the more liberal left. The Jeffersonians are the traditionalists and the Jacksonians are the advocates of popularism in education.

Progressivism ran strongest before and during the great depression. With the threat of war, essentialism appeared to gain ground. Thus, when war actually began in Europe in the fall of 1939, and the democracies were threatened with destruction by the totalitarian powers, the doctrine of essentialism was greatly strengthened and given new support.

WILLIAM CHANDLER BAGLEY (1874–1946), who was recognized as the leader of the essentialists in education in 1938 when the controversy between the progressives and essentialists first appeared in national discussion, championed his position as a necessity for a nation faced with possible ruin from the strongest combination of powers yet to oppose the democratic tradition.

Bagley said:

The essentialists are sure that if our democratic society is to meet the conflict with totalitarian states, there must be a discipline that will give strength to the democratic purpose and ideal. If the theory of democracy finds no place for discipline, then before long the theory will have only historical significance. The essentialists stand for a literate electorate. That such an electorate is indispensable to its survival is demonstrated by the fate that overtook every unschooled democracy founded as a result of the war that was 'to make the world

---

[12] Although Bagley was perhaps the most prominent of the "Essentialists," credit for the origination of the term (in 1935) usually is granted to Michael John Demiashkevich.

safe for democracy'. . . . Essentialism provides a strong theory; its competing school offers a weak theory. If there has been a question in the past as to the kind of educational theory the few remaining democracies of the world need, there can be no question today.[13]

Bagley, though far from being a reactionary or an extreme conservative, stood in opposition to radical and extreme tendencies in American education. It was noted in an earlier chapter that he was influential in checking the extremes of the scientific measurement movement. He was respected and followed because of his long years of educational leadership and accomplishment. He was Professor of Education and Dean of the School of Education at the University of Illinois from 1908 to 1917, and at Teachers College, Columbia University, from 1917 until 1940, when he retired from active teaching. He is the author of such influential books as *The Educative Process, Classroom Management, Educational Values, School Discipline, Determinism in Education, Education, Crime, and Social Progress,* and *Education and the Emergent Man.* Bagley was editor of the Modern Teachers' Series published by The Macmillan Company, and was for many years editor of *Educational Administration and Supervision.* In 1939, he was instrumental in the organization of the Society for the Advancement of American Education, becoming its secretary. He was the editor of its official publication, *School and Society,* and a member of its "Essentialist Committee."

Although picking up strength during and following World War II, the essentialist cause suffered serious losses in leadership with the deaths of Bagley, Judd, and H. H. Horne in 1946; Morrison had preceded this illustrious trio in 1945. Influential men remained, in KANDEL, HUTCHINS, and ROBERT ULICH of Harvard, but for a few years opposition to progressivism did not flourish. In the next decade, however, the former controversy burst forth with a vengeance.

Among those who sought to indict what they felt were contrary currents in the schools, especially the fad for "life adjustment" courses, were Albert S. Lynd, Mortimer Smith, John Keats and Arthur E. Bestor. Lynd's account "Quackery in the Public Schools," drew a great deal of attention; Smith wrote *And Madly Teach;* John Keats deplored *Schools Without Scholars.* Arthur Bestor, a Professor of History at the University of Illinois, attacked in several new directions:[14] the "certification racket," by which he meant required education courses; the growing hierarchy of administrative personnel in the public schools; and he cited instances of poor teaching and subject matter dilution.

In the last instance Bestor followed the lead of the generally accepted essentialist philosophy. While, as could be expected, significant

---

[13] William C. Bagley, "The Case for Essentialism in Education," *The Journal of the National Educational Association,* Vol. 30, No. 7 (October, 1941), pp. 201-202.
[14] See Arthur E. Bestor, *Educational Wastelands.* (Champaign, Ill.: University of Illinois Press, 1953.) *The Restoration of Learning.* (New York: Alfred A. Knopf, 1955.) See also William W. Brickman, "Essentialism Ten Years After," *School and Society,* Vol. 67, No. 1742 (May 15, 1948), pp. 361-365, a plea for rejuvenated leadership in the essentialist cause.

variations in philosophy exist among the essentialists they are as one in prescribing the following rubrics for their educational program:

1. A fixed curriculum;
2. Certain minimum "essentials": literature, mathematics, history, etc.:
3. Preconceived educational values; and
4. Education as individual adaptation to an absolute knowledge which exists independently of individuals.

Although it will be easily seen that items three and four especially identify the idealistic wing of essentialism, the realists, by no means, eschew inherent values, although they usually choose to emphasize content and organization.

The interpretation of realism as supplied by HARRY S. BROUDY (which he calls "Classical Realism") may be noted here for it provides considerable assistance in producing an understanding of what has been labeled "Essentialism" in this text. Broudy's emphasis "accepts as regulative principles the idea of a truth independent of the knower, and the idea of structures in the universe, man, and society that are normative for man's striving toward the good life and for the education that will help him achieve it"; its foundation, "the fundamental notions about the structure of human personality, its goals, and its destiny are adaptations of the theories of Plato and Aristotle." Broudy maintains that "this role does not point to the traditional school, but rather to a curriculum, organization, and methodology that tries to take account of the contributions of psychology, the science of education, and the more basic contribution of Dewey's Instrumentalism."[15]

Perhaps this identification serves as well as any to pull together the various interpretations and positions of those we have denominated essentialists.[16] Clearly the differences in orientation are of much less significance than their agreements.

One of the most vocal opponents of American education as it developed during and after the great depression was Vice-Admiral H. S. Rickover. His suggestions for improvement included the rigid program advocated by all essentialists plus tougher courses and teaching procedures. Rickover, in order to strengthen the program still further, called for the imposition of "national standards," a device quite foreign to conventional American thinking.[17] Bestor was vocal too and most influential

---

[15] Harry S. Broudy, *Building a Philosophy of Education.* (New York: Prentice-Hall, Inc., 1954.) P. viii.

[16] See Christian O. Weber, *Basic Philosophies of Education.* (New York: Holt, Rinehart and Winston, Inc., 1960.) Chapter 3, "Essentialism and Traditionalism," pp. 35-45; also Robert E. Mason, *Educational Ideals in American Society* (Boston: Allyn and Bacon, 1960), pp. 41-51; for a thorough discussion of the currents of American educational philosophy during the years which followed World War II, the student is directed to the January 17, 1959, issue of *School and Society,* Vol. 87, No. 2145. Especially valuable are accounts by Ernest E. Bayles, Theodore Brameld, J. Donald Butler, Harry S. Broudy, and Foster McMurray.

[17] See his "European vs. American Secondary Schools," *Phi Delta Kappan,* Vol. 40, No. 2 (November, 1958), pp. 60-64, and *Education and Freedom.* (New York: E. P. Dutton and Company, 1959.)

in establishing the Council for Basic Education—an organization devoted to popularizing the ideas of Bestor, Mortimer Smith, and others.

If Rickover and Bestor may be noted as the best propagandists, then James B. Conant may be considered the most effective agent in securing public and professional acceptance of the essentialist views. Conant's background as an educator and public figure lent stature and dignity to his part of the movement; his thoroughness and obvious devotion to the preservation of the American public, state-controlled, junior and senior high school were convincing; it appeared that many of his ideas for improvement would be put into practice.

The position of Hutchins, Ulich and of idealism generally, will be discussed in a later section.

AIMS   The essentialists, like the realists of the seventeenth century, have as their ultimate aim "to fit the man to perform justly, skillfully, and magnanimously all the offices, both private and public, of peace and war." Indeed, there are those who would designate this movement as the "new realism," setting up as the purpose of education "the adjustment of the pupil to the actual demands of a real external world." For example, FREDERICK S. BREED says:

> The problem of education, as of life, becomes that of establishing for the individual the most effectual relationships with an environing world. . . . The demands of environment, of life, of society, of school and curriculum. . . . are easily seen to represent in essence the independent objects postulated by the realist, the scientist, and the common man. . . . They are taken deeply to heart if one starts with realistic premises. The source of compulsion and requirement in education . . . is found ultimately to originate in the independent reals with which personality must deal and to which it must make the most endurable and satisfactory adjustment.[18]

Bagley stated the fundamental issue as follows: "Should not our public schools prepare boys and girls for adult responsibility through systematic training in such subjects as reading, writing, arithmetic, history, and English, requiring mastery of such subjects and, when necessary, stressing discipline and obedience?"

The essentialists do not believe that the essential skills, knowledge, and attitudes needed by the individual in making his adjustment to the realities of life will fall into his lap incidentally. The essentialist insists that adult direction of the immature is necessary; that it is inherent in human nature; that it is the real meaning of the long period of dependency on adult care and support on the part of human offspring; that it is this plastic period of dependency that furnishes opportunities for inducting the young into the heritage of culture. The indispensable cultural objectives of humanity, commonly referred to as essentials, are goals that must be achieved—sometimes incidentally—but

---

[18] Frederick S. Breed, *Education and the New Realism.* (New York: The Macmillan Co., 1939.) Pp. 123-124.

more often by direct instruction. The essentialist insists that teachers must be responsible for systematic programs of studies and systematically planned activities in order that the recognized essentials be acquired.

Most essentialists agree that informal learning can share in the attainment of such objectives, but believe that this should always be supplementary and secondary. Most of these essentials are more exacting; they generally require more effort and attention than is provided in the project or activity curriculum. Judd advocated "wise guidance of immature minds" as the aim of education, and raised the question, "Why should we deny children the right and even the duty to adopt the orderly mental arrangements that the race has given to the experiences of life?"

The essentialists, as realists, are concerned with the building up of "competencies" in the individual, competencies of mind and body and spirit to meet all the needs, even the emergencies, of life. With the outbreak of hostilities in Europe, and especially after the United States entered the war in 1941, the emphasis upon a more competent people became pronounced in our country. The Educational Policies Commission declared:

> American education faces a momentous decision. . . . It can, if it will, come to grips with the needs of the hour, and direct its vast resources to the task of increasing the understanding, the loyalty and the competence of millions of citizens, with speed and efficiency matched to the exigencies of the time. . . . The defense which the American people must now organize, requires a strategy which is more subtle than the blunt appeal of armed might. It requires, to be sure, close attention to direct military preparedness, as such. It requires also the training of every worker to the highest possible level of effectiveness, and the useful employment of every worker in tasks of importance. It requires confidence in the sincerity and reliability of one's fellow citizens and comradeship in the common search for the solution to the nation's problems. It requires, above all, the common understanding of aims and procedures which lead to united and effective action. Of such elements is the defense of our democracy to be built. In the building of it the schools of America are ready and determined to play their part.[19]

Thus the philosophy of essentialism had its aims greatly reinforced by a realistic recognition of the needs of a people faced with world conflict. The school, as well as the nation as a whole, set up as its goal the preservation of democracy and directed its whole attention toward developing the skills, knowledge, and attitudes essential to this tremendous task—a necessity which was to continue during the decades of cold war.

At about the same time New York State completed a comprehensive study of education known as the Regents' Inquiry, directed by an agency of the state education department. The results were included

---

[19] Educational Policies Commission, *Education and the Defense of American Democracy.* (National Education Association, 1940), pp. 20-21.

in a twelve-volume report and suggested a greater need for guidance, adequate background in reading, oral and written expression, and arithmetic, as well as some preparation for after-high-school cultural and vocational adjustment.[20] Since the various reports appeared at approximately the beginning of the Second World War it is probable that their influence was somewhat curtailed.

The perennialist views education as a recurring process based on eternal truths, and as such his essentials include the traditional materials of the curriculum. He believes that the literature and the art, the social life and political life, of the peoples of the past will throw much light upon our problems of the present. ROBERT MAYNARD HUTCHINS, formerly President of the University of Chicago, believes that the study of the great classics serves this purpose. In our zeal for the more immediate essentials of education, we must not neglect these broader and more general needs of our students.

Roman Catholic and other parochial educationists adhere firmly to perennialism but utilize religious philosophy and subject matter in their teaching. Their view that the truth is the same yesterday, today, and tomorrow and that its verities have been revealed through the sacred presence makes them intolerant of naturalist, pragmatic, and social education. Catholic thought especially opposes the teaching of history on economic or strictly political grounds, citing the "need to associate the Divine Tradition with the legitimate heritage of human values and human culture . . . saving the world from the demolition of Voltaire and Marx." It considers entrepreneurial theories of history as debased and stresses the superiority of moral judgment over economic judgment; presents history as "philosophy teaching by examples."

TYPES   Basically, the essentialists were concerned with a revival of efforts in the direction of teaching the fundamental tools of learning as the most indispensable type of education. Since investigations had suggested that many high school and college students were woefully weak in such fundamental skills as reading, spelling, penmanship, and arithmetic, schools were urged to make this their dominant concern. With the development of the emergency, this type of training continued to be emphasized as of primary importance in the defense of democracy, but other kinds of education were also recognized as essential for this purpose.

In response to many requests from teachers and administrators regarding the types of education to be stressed during the emergency, the United States Office of Education in July, 1941, issued a bulletin in its series on education and national defense under the title, "What the Schools Can Do." Action along six fronts was recommended to schools planning to adapt their programs to the needs of the times: (1) health

---

[20] See Francis T. Spaulding, *High School and Life: Report of the Regents' Inquiry.* (New York: McGraw-Hill Book Co., 1940.)

and physical education; (2) education for citizenship; (3) education in community, national, and international relationships; (4) education in the conservation of national resources; (5) education for work; and (6) education for personal adjustment.

The creation of physical health has long been recognized as an essential type of education, although it is only in recent decades that the schools have assumed much responsibility for its development. The early Greeks, John Locke in the seventeenth century, and Spencer in the nineteenth made sound physical health one of the basic essentials of their educational programs. War always highlights the need for marked attention to the health, physical well-being, and mental hygiene of children and of youth. War-minded nations never neglect this type of education. Health and physical fitness is an absolute essential for military service both at the front abroad and behind the lines at home. The physical examinations of 1939 selectees revealed the deplorable prevalence of physical defects in our American youth that was discovered in World War I, and aroused our schools to the necessity for increased attention to this type of education. Health, however, is always an essential for human happiness and efficiency and must continue as a definite part of our educational program.

In the summer of 1940, the federal government made appropriations for a summer training program in schools and colleges for workers essential to defense industries. Late in the fall of the same year additional appropriations were made for the training in vocational schools, rural schools, high schools, colleges, and universities of both youths and adults for defense production. Established vocational and trade schools made their facilities available for defense classes and many new schools were established by the federal agencies. Most of these schools operated on a twenty-four-hour, six-days-a-week basis. Instructors were usually selected on the basis of their practical experience in the trades, and adult trainees were recruited from unemployed men registered with government employment services and from W.P.A. employees. The Civilian Pilot Training Program contributed much to the training of the military flying forces.

From the beginning the essentialists insisted upon the provision of craft experiences for American youth as an essential part of the school's task. Vocational education—especially training in the mechanical trades—is now recognized as a requisite to an effective national defense.

One of the most essential types of education for the cold war is civic education. It has been the chief concern of our educational leaders in the past few years to promote civic education, not because other types of education are not vital and important, but because civic enlightenment and citizenship training are now of crucial importance. Without it we are very likely to lose our freedom and slip over into a regimentation that is as totalitarian as the forces that presently menace our democracy. Civic education of all our people is just as essential for the preservation of democracy as the industrial and military training of workers and fighters is essential to the defeat of our enemies. Civic education is the first essential of internal defense.

We are likely to overlook the fact that the so-called cultural types of education are also essential. The schools must always seek to raise the educational level of the people by providing training to both youth and adults in music, the fine arts, literature, architecture, and home decoration. Cultural education and education in the humanities, are doubly essential in times of stress and strain. It is essential that we then impart something of the vital experiences of the human race so that our people may be better able to solve their common problems. The study of history "may so accumulate years to us as though we had lived from the beginning of time."

CONTENT   The essentialists emphasize the need for a curriculum that transmits significant race experiences, and they believe that this racial experience should be presented to the pupils largely through organized subject-matter courses. They would use individual personal experiences merely as a means toward the end of interpreting this organized racial experience. While it is not their purpose to go back to the formalism and verbalism of an earlier day, they do believe that subject matter can be logically organized and still be presented psychologically, and that there is a definite place in education for exact and exacting studies. They are particularly concerned with the fundamentals of education, the skills and knowledge without which a person cannot be either individually or socially efficient.

Yet there is great variation as to what these essentials comprise among those educators which we have considered traditionalist as opposed to the progressive left. Hutchins and Adler would seek the essentials for living in the "Great Books." Morrison developed a curriculum, broad and extensive, based upon what he considered the essentials for common living. Parochialists base their content on the eternal verities. The moderates, led by Judd and Bagley, took a realistic view.

Bagley said:

There can be little question as to the essentials. It is no accident that the arts of recordings, computing, and measuring have been among the first concerns of organized education. Every civilized society has been founded upon these arts, and when they have been lost, civilization has invariably collapsed. Nor is it accidental that a knowledge of the world that lies beyond one's immediate experience has been among the recognized essentials of universal education, and that at least a speaking acquaintance with man's past and especially with the story of one's country was early provided for in the program of the universal school. Investigation, invention, and creative art have added to our heritage. Health instruction is a basic phase of work in the lower schools. The elements of natural science have their place. Neither the fine arts nor the industrial arts should be neglected.[21]

---

[21] William C. Bagley, "The Case for Essentialism in Education," *The Journal of the National Education Association,* Vol. 30, No. 7, (October, 1941). P. 202.

Thus reading, writing, arithmetic, grammar, history, geography, hygiene, elementary science, drawing, language, art, manual training, domestic arts—all the traditional subjects of the elementary school—are given a new justification and a new emphasis as basic essentials in the training of children.

In a democracy everyone should be able to read and write, yet we have known for years that a shocking amount of illiteracy has existed in our country. The revelation of the facts of the selective service examinations in two world wars has awakened us again to the importance of this problem in relation to national defense. In one state 35,000 young men had to sign their registration cards for selective service with a mark; in some areas nearly half of the Negroes and a quarter of the whites were excluded from the armed services on account of illiteracy. Those too illiterate for military service are undoubtedly also too illiterate for successful civilian life. It would be well for us to have a new emphasis on the necessity of teaching every child at least to read and write. This is the lowest minimum essential of education.

The essentialists first turned their attention to the elementary school curriculum, and it was much later that the high school and college curriculum was influenced by the Jeffersonian point of view. In the final report of a six-year investigation by the American Youth Commission, under the title, *Youth and the Future,*[22] the Commission reaffirmed its recommendations for curriculum revision presented in a preliminary announcement, originally issued as *What the High Schools Ought to Teach*. Emphasis was given to the importance of continued instruction in reading as a much neglected element in the high school curriculum. Special emphasis was given to actual experience as a phrase of general education second in importance to none. Instruction in the social studies and instruction to prepare young people to meet major personal problems were also stressed as essential elements in a reorganized curriculum.

Science and technology advanced rapidly during the pressure of war and cold war. The first atom bomb appeared in 1945 in the closing days of the conflict with Japan. A little later the hydrogen (fusion) bomb was developed. The use of the jet engine in military and civilian planes caught on rapidly. There was a veritable communications revolution. The first artificial satellite (Sputnik) went into orbit in 1957. Automation brought vast changes in factory organization and personnel needs. Engineering of all kinds made great strides. The development of rockets and missiles went on apace. Chemistry flourished as never before, while plastics and other synthetic products monopolized fields previously held by metals and natural and plant resources. It was inevitable that the schools would be expected to keep pace with such progress.

A new look at science in the curriculum was demanded by

---

[22] American Youth Commission, *Youth and the Future.* (American Council on Education, 1942.)

Bestor of Illinois, Woodring, and Dr. James B. Conant. Science courses had become essential to the preservation of the nation as well as necessities by which intelligent citizens might be prepared for an understanding of the present together with an anticipation of the future. While it was not expected that every student could profit from rigorous scientific study, levels were established and gradations within them made the basis for suitable offerings. Nor should each student continue further work in science after the basic and exploratory courses. By the same token, the able must be encouraged to reach their maximum development both for the sake of insuring their highest potential as well as adding to the brainpower reserve of the nation. In general, the public—science conscious as never before—agreed.

Woodring called for a whole new organization of the American school system placing the accent on a rigid course of study and thorough work. Several groupings should be made, he said, thus allowing the able to pursue uninterruptedly a rigorous study of algebra and geometry, for example; thus make a proper preparation for college entrance and professions requiring this knowledge. Woodring believes that if honor rolls are retained in high school their basis should rest on proficiency in the conventional high school courses, including science, mathematics, language, etc., rather than on the softer courses frequently utilized to secure higher grade point averages.[23]

Conant's prescription for the high school curriculum, while allowing course-space for the less able and medium-ability student, suggests rigorous programs for the scholastically able. He proposes three levels of instruction indicating that aptitude may cause a particular student to rate the highest section in one subject while obtaining lower positions in others. In the highest type course, however, the program should be thorough. He would require prerequisites for admission to these higher classes. All students would take science but the course appropriate for them would be determined by their aptitude and previous record. Two types of chemistry and two of physics should be offered for students of different abilities. Dr. Conant prescribes foreign languages for the able and insists that not less than four years in one language should be the standard.[24]

Hutchins has always favored the approach through the classics and, as such, may be classed with the perennialist wing of the traditionalists. While concerned—at least in his tenure at Chicago—with college and university education primarily, his conclusions on general education betray his allegiance to the classical on even lower levels as well. In *The Higher Learning in America* (quite appropriate for the sixties although originally published in October, 1936), Hutchins maintains that a general education must be given to all young Americans until

---

[23] Paul Woodring, *A Fourth of a Nation.* (New York: McGraw-Hill Book Co., 1957.) Pp. 149-150.
[24] James B. Conant, *The American High School Today.* (New York: McGraw-Hill Book Co., 1959.) Especially pp. 49-50, 69-73, 73.

about their twentieth year. One problem is how to handle the "hand-minded and functionally illiterate" in such a program; another is the adaptation of "the intellectual virtues" for it is here that men become citizens and here also that the specialists can, Hutchins hopes, meet on common ground.[25] His premise that education should draw out the elements of common human nature is reciprocated in the axiom that these elements are the same at any place or in any time; hence the same education should obtain everywhere just as the same truth is everywhere present. Truth and knowledge are reciprocals. Obviously, Hutchins favors the Seven Liberal Arts and their classic repositories for such a general education.

Roman Catholic thought considers CHRISTOPHER DAWSON's philosophy of history as the authentic treatment of the facts of anthropology, history, and education; Dawson maintains that "great religions are the foundation on which great civilizations rest." Catholic educational content includes the history of the church and its saints as well as the general content of an essentialist curriculum.

Robert Ulich speaks of the "consciousness of the transcendent" by which he invokes the universal and the eternal; he calls for persistence and the "Seeing of Relationships" although it may indeed be that few can qualify—adults as well as adolescents—here.[26] Yet Ulich's contention that secondary schools should so organize instruction need not be entirely lost. The direction can be set even if the goal remains far over the horizon.

The emergency gave reinforcement to all those areas in the curriculum which, as we have shown before, have always been utilized by the nationalists. The teaching of history, and civics particularly, is again being emphasized as essential to national welfare. The social studies are essential in times such as this, but in ways not ordinarily recognized. They meet needs of many sorts; needs that are immediate and needs that are more remote. Some of these needs are obvious; others are harder to see. The latter, involving the larger aspects of national and international life, the rise and growth of nations, the causes of war and the bases of peace, are the more profoundly significant. On the adequacy with which these subjects meet all of these needs depend not only military victory but—equally important—permanent peace. Trained leaders, thoroughly educated in the culture of the Western world, possessed of the sharp tools of an educated mind, aware of the complexities of the world order, and inspired by the nobler possibilities open to man, are urgently needed. The social studies are essential.

Intercultural education has replaced the Americanization movement of the first World War. By furthering understanding of the contributions of many diverse people to the culture of America, intercultural

---

[25] Robert Hutchins, *The Higher Learning in America* (New Haven, Conn.: Yale University Press, 1936), pp. 61-85.
[26] Robert Ulich, *Crisis and Hope in American Education*. (Boston: The Beacon Press, 1951.) Pp. 94-100.

education in the school curriculum attempts to advance national unity and morale, to unite the various races and nationalities who have come from the four corners of the earth into a great united nation. A recent study in intercultural education[27] deals with what should be done and what is being done in the schools under such headings as building concepts of racial democracy, conserving cultural resources of various culture groups, rediscovering folkways of various peoples, and cultural emphases in foreign language classes. Committees on intercultural understandings are being organized in many states.

In war and in crisis there is a tendency for high schools and colleges to mobilize their efforts toward the special uses their curricula may have for military and defense values. History and geography departments, English and speech departments, biology, chemistry, physics and science in general, the commercial and industrial departments, mathematics and physical education all select and teach those items and materials that have immediate preparedness values. While from the nationalistic standpoint this is commendable, there is a grave possibility that the larger implications of an education may be brushed aside or sidetracked by such an approach. Thus, in the zeal to provide for defense or to compete in the cold war, it is probable that, through the inclusion of new, specific, and *ad hoc* items, other more permanent essentials of the curriculum will be neglected.

For example, there is a special danger in connection with the industrial arts curriculum. Vocational instructors in the past have tried to give their students basic training in the general skills of a trade, and a broad acquaintanceship with various phases of work in an industry, so that the worker could more readily adapt himself to a new task when necessity demanded it. But in defense training classes speed is essential. No attempt can be made to give broad trade training; the trainee is merely given the skills necessary for him to work on a specific job such as milling machine operator, lathe operator, drill press operator, punch press operator, shaper, grinder, arc welder, wing assembler, cable splicer, fabric applier, and so on. This is true whether the job is in the area of precision instrument making, tool making, aircraft, missile, or boat construction, tank building, or any other of the many fields involved in war production. In such a program of highly specialized training for all-out production, some means must be devised for preserving the broader vocational training of the earlier industrial schools.

Totalitarian nations prepare their youth for war by means of a curriculum that develops blind devotion to their leaders, passionate feelings of patriotism for their countries, and a fervent belief that they are fighting a holy crusade. There are some who insist that the same kind

---

[27] *Americans All.* Studies in Intercultural Education. Yearbook sponsored by Department of Supervisors and Directors of Instruction, National Council of Teachers of English, and Society for Curriculum Study. (National Education Association, 1942.) See also, John A. Rademaker, *These Are Americans.* (Palo Alto, Calif.: Pacific Books, 1951.)

of education is essential to a fighting democracy. Such a recommendation is based on a misconception of the true nature of democracy. We can accomplish more by developing a genuine loyalty based on intelligent understanding and calm reasoning. We can best create a national unity, a willingness to sacrifice and serve, a supreme confidence in a durable peace, by teaching the truth instead of spreading propaganda, and by developing calm, straightforward thinking instead of intense national fanaticism.

May we add another essential—the need to discover the road to a more united world, a world of free nations maintaining governments of their own choice based on their individual cultures, voluntarily co-operating in a world organization which will promote the common good of all through law based upon justice. This can come only through a careful study and thorough understanding of all peoples.[28]

AGENCIES   An education in the essentials, particularly those needed for the preservation of democracy and national welfare, cannot confine itself to children and youth in formally organized schools. It must reach the significant body of adults who actually will determine public policy and practice. The Educational Policies Commission in its bulletin, *A War Policy for American Schools,* emphasized the fact that foreign and domestic policies are debated and major decisions of public policy made by adults and not by children. Unwise judgments on the part of these adult voters will adversely affect the role that America plays in this postwar period. Adult education becomes, therefore, a central rather than a marginal responsibility.

There are many agencies for the education of adults. The broadcasting companies have cooperated with educational leaders in providing various types of educational programs for adults as well as for children in the schools. Public evening schools, established in the nineteenth century, are developing more and more into agencies for adult education. The most promising agency for the education of adults is the forum or discussion group.

Opportunities must be provided also for various forms of cultural, technical, and individual training for those men and women who were denied these opportunities in youth. We need to realize the neglected truth that education is a continuous process, and provide extended educational opportunities to all adults. Schools and school libraries must serve as community centers to which adults must turn as places for discussion, information, and other aids to help them intelligently decide on the issues of the hour. Books must be prepared that are not only informative and useful but that are easy to comprehend. The Readability Laboratory of the American Association of Adult Education devoted

---

[28] Robert Ulich, mentioned earlier, is a strong advocate of international education. See his *History of Educational Thought.* (New York: American Book Company, 1950.) Pp. 349-350E.

much effort to this problem and recently issued its first experimental series of books, the eleven volumes called *The People's Library*. LYMAN BRYSON (1888–1959), its director and one of the outstanding leaders in the field of adult education, said:

Up to this time, most of the informative books have been written for the intellectuals. That would be all right if this were to be a government of, by, and for the intellectuals, but it is not that. As a democracy it is supposed to be of, by, and for the people. That means that books that say something have got to be written for the people in language they can understand if they are going to do a good job of running this country.

Another development in adult education, somewhat different from that fostered by Dr. Bryson, but in harmony with its idea, is the Great Books study groups. Operating in many sections of the country, meeting in public libraries, churches, or homes, under the leadership of intelligent men and women, either professional or lay, these assemblies read and discuss the masterpieces of literature, past and present. Generally founding their study on the great Greek classics, they move through Rome and the Middle Ages to Renaissance and Reformation and so on to the contemporary scene. Such a search for the meaning of life is essentially perennialist and the vogue for this study must indeed gladden the heart of Robert M. Hutchins and his colleagues in neo-scholasticism. (Although the method is Jacksonian, its purpose is Jeffersonian.)

Throughout the earlier crisis, the Office of Education was an active agency in stimulating the schools to give serious attention to the essential educational needs of the emergency. Early in 1941 an Information Exchange on Education and National Defense was organized as a "defense education clearing house for the federal government." Schools, colleges, and communities throughout the nation dispatched to the Exchange publications and reports on defense education activities and services. Organized by educational subjects and school levels, this material was gathered into loan packets which constantly circulated over the country.

The Office of Education was active also in helping to mobilize all the educational forces of the nation into a cooperative defense and war effort. On December 23, 1941, all educational institutions and organizations of the country were united in a Wartime Commission to take up the consideration of such important questions as: (1) hastening graduation of students by lengthening school weeks and school terms, shortening vacations, and modifying curricular content; (2) utilizing colleges and universities for training various types of military personnel; (3) removing educational handicaps for men rejected in the draft; (4) establishing nursery schools for children of mothers employed in war industries; (5) improving the health and physical vigor of all our people; (6) planning for postwar educational readjustments.

The National Education Association continued its fine educational leadership by promoting the essential educational needs of the crisis. As noted earlier, its legislative assembly established a Commission on the Defense of Democracy through Education, made up of representatives from the various states, to aid in developing statewide programs of education for democracy and to counteract the forces that were inimical to such programs. In cooperation with the American Council of Education, it organized the National Committee of Education and Defense in which the efforts of sixty or more national educational organizations and agencies were coordinated in the task of adapting education to the essential needs of the war without sacrificing long-term educational objectives.

In January, 1942, this National Committee on Education and Defense, in cooperation with the Office of Education, sponsored a National Conference of College and University Presidents to deal with the problems of higher education in wartime. At this conference the institutions of higher education offered their "united power for decisive military victory, and for the ultimate and even more difficult task of establishing a just and lasting peace." Such a widespread cooperation of all the educational agencies of the nation in a common cause is something never before accomplished.

During the great depression the federal government became increasingly concerned with education, particularly along vocational lines, and set up many agencies to aid in the training of youth. The war accelerated this concern and participation. The National Committee on Education and Defense recommended that no agency be developed through federal funds that paralleled or duplicated existing educational facilities, but that existing agencies be adjusted, expanded, and utilized to meet the needs of the times. This cautious attitude has, of course, been fostered by the long history of decentralization in American education and, possibly, by the strict separation of church and state demanded by the federal constitution.

As we have stated many times in earlier chapters, there is no agency in education more important than the teacher. Yet, initiated by the war and the consequent demand in defense industries and aggravated by the inflationary period which followed World War II, the teaching profession found itself placed in a new situation. Scarcity of personnel rather than abundance obtained and, while salary rises stabilized the condition temporarily, the problem of securing good, well-qualified teachers was one that soon plagued many boards of education.

The difficulty was compounded by the immense enrollments rising from the higher birth rate of the forties. The first pinch, of course, was felt in the elementary schools, but after a few years, secondary education likewise was hard hit. The shortage was most acute in rural and village schools and in certain areas such as science, mathematics, home economics, industrial education, and business practice. That State Departments of Education would be called upon to "let down the bars" and issue temporary or sub-standard certificates was expected and this indeed was done in many instances. On the whole, however, standards were adhered to remarkably well considering the pressures involved.

ORGANIZATION   The urgencies of war and of cold war en-hanced rather than diminished institutionalism in education. There is more of a tendency than ever before to organize all educational endeavors within the framework of a closely knit public school system. The economic depression, followed by the heavy taxation imposed by the demands of war and the resulting inflation has made the position of independent private schools and colleges rather precarious. Both the American Youth Commission and the Educational Policies Commission suggested the need for a unified public policy that will bring together all the educa-tional functioning of nation, state, and local community into one power-ful organization of effort.

Certain reorganizations that were proposed earlier have been stimulated by the saturation of the existing conventional agencies. One of the most frequently discussed proposals is the extension of the public school upward through the fourteenth grade for all boys and girls. For years the junior college duplicated the work of the first two years of the traditional liberal arts college. A usual justification was the fact that it was making part of a liberal college education available to high school graduates in their home communities, making it unnecessary for them to leave their own locality. Now the junior college is becoming an institu-tion for "terminal" education, providing essential training for such occu-pations as secretarial work, retail selling, and other types of technical and clerical pursuits and college training as well. Many public junior colleges and technical schools are being incorporated into the school system of the local school districts. It is urged that all students with the requisite abilities should not only be required to attend throughout the fourteen grades, but that they should be enabled to do so by means of such forms of school aid, including part-time work-education programs, as may be necessary. The recent provision of scholarships, from both public and private sources, is a step in this direction.

It was gratifying to find that most of the national defense pro-gram was organized around the existing public school program of voca-tional education. The entire program of defense training in no way supplanted or conflicted with the regular occupational training con-ducted in the public schools and subsidized by the federal government through funds made available by the Smith-Hughes and George-Dean Acts. As in the First World War, the nation's schools were given primary responsibility in training workers for defense employment. The public vocational schools provided preemployment training in the occupations designated by the War Production Board as essential to national defense. In addition to such preemployment training, public schools provided up-grading courses for employed workers which made possible their pro-motion to jobs requiring higher skills.

The colleges reorganized their programs to meet the needs of the return to world conflict. Most of these rearranged their year's work on a three-semester plan so that students might, by enrolling in this accelerated program, complete the regular college course in much less than the usual four years—soon enough for many to get their degrees before they reached the minimum draft age of twenty. Some colleges admitted students before they finished high school. Professional schools shortened their programs and many admitted students before they received their bachelor's degrees. Spring vacations were eliminated and Christmas holidays shortened in this attempt to streamline college education.

Although there was some apprehension that acceleration might lower the standards of higher education generally this appears not to have happened. However, as a matter of precaution, the executive committee of the North Central Association of Colleges and Secondary Schools issued a statement to members of the association concerning the "attitude of the association toward special adjustments within schools and colleges to meet emergency conditions." Emphasizing that it expected every school and college to devote their energies and resources to the service of the nation, it also dwelt on the necessity for adhering to certain fundamentals: (1) that where acceleration of programs was adopted, every effort be made to insure that there was no loss in the quality of work; and (2) that in any program of speeding up school and college work there must be no dilution, but that which was regularly required to be done should be thoroughly completed. A further condition mandated that all reorganization and readjustment to meet the war emergency must adhere to the same basic educational principles that hold true whether a nation is at war or at peace.

That the foregoing has more than historic interest was soon to be shown. Although the prescriptions noted were conceived for the benefit of institutions operating under the rigors of war and defense conditions, peace brought no relief but a serious aggravation of the problem. First, the so-called "G-I Bill" offered college education to thousands who had been unable to attend because of the interruption due to the war and to others who—except for the terms of this most remarkable instrument—could never have financed the operation. As a result the colleges and universities virtually burst at the seams. Secondly, the baby boom mentioned earlier, brought the promise of an ever increased enrollment within a matter of a few years. It was predicted that college attendance, based on the enrollment of the early forties would double by 1960 and quadruple by 1970.

Thus the problems of college organization, difficult in wartime, had become even more potentially worrisome in peacetime. Already the University of Chicago had, however, adopted an interesting reform. Under President Robert M. Hutchins the university had decided to award the bachelor's degree at the end of the sophomore year, not merely as an emergency measure, but because Hutchins believes that the baccalaureate should mark the completion of general education. Dr.

Hutchins held that it was foolish for a scholarly student to remain in college for four years to secure a degree that might as well be conferred a year or two earlier. This was consonant with his famous Chicago Plan, whereby a student could secure his degree just as soon as he had demonstrated that he had satisfied the requirements, regardless of the elapsed time.

Regardless of the merits or demerits of Hutchins' program, upon his retirement from the university Chicago reverted to the familiar four-year plan for the first degree. Nevertheless, there are many who agree with Hutchins that too much of the student's time is being wasted in college and that students, by eliminating certain overlapping, can begin their specialized preparation for the professions at least two years earlier, as has always been the custom in the European universities.

Increased enrollment and inadequate facilities must force some decision in these matters of college and university education. And it is easily seen that the conflict between popular Jacksonianism and the more rigorous Jeffersonianism which has reached even the Teachers Colleges is not confined to secondary school curriculum.[29]

Nevertheless, complaint about educational philosophy is a chronic thing and certainly need not be confined to the present generation. A point which many critics fail to grasp is that the real wonder may be that the American schools—especially the high school—are as good as they are. A quick summary of the new climate in the secondary school, through its population change, will suffice to demonstrate this.

By 1870 there were scarcely 70,000 students in the American public high school although it was already in its fiftieth year; in 1900 the number had reached 700,000; by the decade of the fifties the pupil population had zoomed to 7,000,000. Coupled with this prodigious growth in numbers was the problem of staff, housing, and administration, to say nothing of the evolution of the curriculum and academic standards.

Yet, regardless of controversy over organization or philosophy the American people are considerably proud of their public school system. Single track or no (reference here is made to the existence of a number of private, academy-type schools in the East, South, and Far West and to the fact that virtually each high school beyond hamlet-size offers a variety of curricula, four courses being a frequent organization, with usually only one of these leading to college preparation), Europe did not err when educational statesmen saw something more than quantity and chance in the American fetish of universal education.[30]

Professor Kenneth Richmond, University of Glasgow, finds a uniqueness here that is unparalleled. He concludes a worthwhile study

[29] Karl W. Meyer in "The Passing of the Teachers College," *School and Society,* Vol. 87, No. 2160 (October 24, 1959), concludes that "the transition of the normal schools into comprehensive institutions is not without its dangers and problems." Pp. 416-417.
[30] In an unprecedented decision (Brown *vs.* the Board of Education) the United States Supreme Court, in 1954, declared segregation in the nation's schools to be unconstitutional and illegal. The court ordered the removal of every such restriction with "all deliberate speed," this decree to be interpreted by the regional federal judiciaries.

with the following happy phrases: "The Jacksonian lion and the Jeffersonian lamb will lie down together and although their natures are opposed, agree, for strange as it seems, the two are of one flesh."[31]

METHODS   Present-day differences between the methodology of the essentialists and that of the progressives are mainly those of degree; neither group giving exclusive emphasis to one extreme or another. The essentialists emphasize habituation more than experience, guidance more than incidentalism, discipline more than freedom, effort more than interest, and self-examination more than expression. They believe also that the realities of environment place distinct limitations on individual freedom and individual interest.

The environment demands from the pupil the performance of certain acts and the inhibition of others. The price of genuine freedom from want, fear, superstition, and error is the surrender by the learner of a certain amount of his liberty, especially the freedom to learn what he pleases and when he pleases. The systematic mastery of the culture that has been acquired by mankind through its long struggle upward from primitive barbarism is the best source of real freedom. The knowledges and skills, the customs and manners, the attitudes and appreciations, built up through centuries of civilization, are our most precious heritage and the best aids in meeting the emergencies now confronting humanity. The essentialists believe that it is unwise to waste time in building up generalizations by the slower method of induction when the general laws and principles discovered and formulated by generations of thinkers can be acquired by the properly guided pupil in a few hours or days; then used deductively in the solution of immediate and pressing problems.

The essentialists, therefore, first believe that there is a distinct place in our schools for the teaching of inhibitions, the forming of habits, and the development of skills. They agree, to this extent, with William James, who many years ago in his classic chapter on habit, said, "The great thing, then, in all education is to make . . . automatic, as early as possible, as many useful actions as we can." There are certain essential reactions that the realities of life demand of all of us, and certain other reactions that our place in life requires from us individually; there is no good reason why these should not be made automatic and habitual so as to lessen the toll on our time and energy. The daily routine tasks of our lives should be made as effortless as possible, and the repeated acts of our occupations should become skills; habits raised to a high level of accuracy and speed. The most effective methods of forming habits and developing skills are of great concern to the essentialists, and drill is finding a place in our classrooms again.

In the second place, since the essentialist emphasizes the neces-

[31] W. Kenneth Richmond, *Education in the U.S.A., A Comparative Study.* (New York: The Philosophical Library, Inc., 1956.) P. 223.

sity of teaching pupils how to think systematically and effectively, we are witnessing a return to the "reasoning lesson" to our schools. Judd said, "What children need, if they are to get in a short time what the race has evolved in a long time, is guidance in systematic thinking." We cannot do effective thinking by looking at the world en masse, or by picking up knowledge piecemeal in encyclopedic fashion. We must make use of the methods of systematic analysis and systematic synthesis. The essential elements of knowledge must be separated from the worthless chaff, and these essentials must be organized into meaningful wholes, with close attention to the interrelationship of each of these entities. In teaching the pupil to think we must so guide his learning that (1) he will come into mental possession of the important elements of truth, the most reliable knowledge available; (2) he will be able to use this knowledge in the solution of the real problems that confront mankind; and (3) he will get enough practice in the actual techniques of thinking and learn to escape the pitfalls and errors of faulty reasoning. The pupil must be disciplined in the acquisition and use of "coherent compilations of related content," but the teacher must not make the mistake of insisting that the completed organization of knowledge by the mature scholar be the first material to confront the child.

H. H. Horne, one of the leading exponents of the idealist wing of essentialism, complained that the progressives failed to appreciate the real significance of intelligence by limiting "the formation and free play of both intellectual and ethical ideas." [Dewey's] "naturalistic view of intelligence is both inadequate in itself and insufficient as a basis of school procedure. It is inadequate in itself because the course of nature is not its own object; yet it is the object of intelligence."[32] Essentialists strongly advocate subject matter and experiences calculated to both challenge and develop the student's mental capacity and ethical realizations.

The essentialists accept the guidance function as a responsibility of the teacher. Yet often, possibly, they misunderstand the true meaning of guidance; they think it means telling the pupil what he must do. Guidance is helping pupils to make their own choices and decisions. Obviously, the prime characteristic of democracy is freedom of thought and action on the part of all people within the democracy. Freedom of choice and freedom of action are the fundamental requisites for the democratic way of life, but this alone does not make a *good* democracy. A people could be free to be depraved, free to be diseased, free to be dishonest, free to exploit; freedom can easily become a state of anarchy. If a democracy is to be efficient and worthy, freedom must be intelligent and socially minded. Intelligence and good will must be concomitants of freedom. A true democracy, then, rests upon these relevant conditions: (1) freedom of choice in thought and action; (2) intelligence of choice in thought and action; (3) socialization of choice in thought and action.

---

[32] Herman Harrell Horne, *The Democratic Philosophy of Education.* (New York: The Macmillan Co., 1932.) P. 532. Reprinted with the permission of the publishers.

Freedom must operate within the laws of intelligence and social welfare
if democracy is to succeed and function beneficially for all. The teacher
must so guide the pupils that they will come to make not only free
choices, but intelligent and socially desirable choices. By helping the
pupils seek out all the relevant truth about themselves and the alternatives from which choices are to be made, teachers will guide the pupils
toward choices that have all three characteristics. This sort of guidance
is essential if democracy is to be preserved. Nor should it ever be forgotten that the ultimate goal is self-guidance. The good counselor is
one who soon makes himself dispensable.

Essentialism, like progressivism, recognizes the fact that interest
is a strong motivating force in learning. Learning, however, that is not
immediately interesting and appealing to the child should not be entirely eliminated from our education. The more valuable and more
permanent interests may grow out of efforts that are at first disagreeable
and monotonous. Very often the pupil will find a deep and abiding
interest in something that did not at all attract and hold his attention
at first. It is the duty of the teacher to help the pupil grow into these
higher interests rather than limit all school activities to those ephemeral
things that appeal only to natural and childish interests.

When the essentialists urge that we bring discipline back into
our schools, they are often misunderstood. They do not refer to a blind
obedience to a tyrannical authority when they use this term which has
become displeasing to many young teachers. They feel that the basis of
all true authority lies in the realities of life. All the desires, projects,
and proposals of men are subject to the veto power of reality. We must
teach our children to face realities; to discipline themselves to the
actualities of the world of nature, and the world of men. We must teach
them to relinquish sentimental and romantic dreaming. True wisdom
comes when we have brought ourselves in harmony with the realistic
laws of physical and human nature. Self-discipline is the goal, but imposed discipline is essential for a while. "The truth will make us free,"
but in the immature years of childhood and youth we need competent,
sympathetic, and firm teachers to help us see the truth and to help us
adjust ourselves to inexorable facts. This is discipline as the essentialist
understands it.

Perhaps the most important goal of the schools is to teach
people to live together in peace. If we learn to be friendly, neighborly,
and brotherly in the small-group relationships of the school and the
home, then shall we not be more inclined to be friendly, neighborly, and
brotherly in our large-group relationships of community, state, and
nation, and eventually in our relationships with the other nations of
the world? Experiences in cooperative school living must begin at home
and in the school on a relatively small scale. Family quarrels, neighborhood jealousies, class struggles, racial animosities, and sectional rivalries

—these are the things that will destroy the spirit of the good neighbor and make easier the development of the envies, jealousies, and hatreds that breed wars. Peaceful relations on a small scale may help to bring about peaceful relations on a large scale. If every teacher in every school-room in the world could somehow teach the pupils the gospel of brotherly love, then perhaps the day would come when the whole world would remain at peace.

In an address formally opening the golden anniversary White House Conference on Youth and Children, President Eisenhower declared that the faith of the American people in peace with justice is an absolute. "So," he continued, "among the things we teach to the young are such truths as the transcendent value of the individual and the dignity of all people, the futility and stupidity of war, its destructiveness of life and its degradation of human values."[33] The advocacy of this principle is not the monopoly of the essentialist; it is the property of all democratic societies and the goal of all true education.

In the past decades the civilized world has been staggered by two terrible blows. A world depression followed by a world at war has left its mark upon education. Along with many other cherished aspects of our civilization, education has been endangered by the ill winds of adversity and the ravage of hot and cold war. But fortunately those in charge of education have not surrendered to a defeatist philosophy. They realize, as never before, the importance of education in such emergencies, and insist that the task of education is greater because of the great crisis through which the world is passing.

The schools of each nation must develop in its people an understanding of and empathy with the people of other nations. Most wars are the result of mutual misunderstanding and mistrust. The study of languages of other peoples will help to eliminate this. How much of our friendship and support of Great Britain is due to our use of a common language? When one understands the speech of those of another country and reads their literature, a firmer basis is laid for understanding and rapport. The study of the vital interests and cultural forces of foreign nations in our schools should serve as an effective means for diminishing the danger to international peace. If we place before our students the materials pertaining to a foreign land—ethical, esthetic, historical, economic, political, and cultural materials compiled by scholars and authors representative of that nation, we are building a common bond of understanding and fellow-feeling which should help preserve peace between our nation and theirs.

Schools and colleges must make clear that permanent peace depends upon equality of opportunity and freedom of action in all world relationships. Threats to that freedom precipitated the last war and have forced nations into the present cold war. This deadly cycle must be

---

[33] Associated Press release, College Park, Maryland, March 27, 1960.

changed and we must learn how to change it. Scientific discovery, rapidity of communication, complexity of human wants, increase of knowledge—all these have made world cooperation essential if the present level of civilization is to continue. Perhaps the United Nations and its cultural agencies may prove to be the answer. Whatever the medium, the effort must be made.

A recent commentator in viewing the threat both to existence and interpersonal relationships among mankind has said (and this thought may well be a goal for modern education):

> In projecting the idea of brotherhood, we might each paraphrase a great American poet, and say to ourselves: Each man's folly diminishes me. Since man's worst folly is his inhumanity to his fellow man, we cannot, in our own interest, ignore our responsibility to our fellow man. Brotherhood is not the noble prerogative of a select, dedicated few; it should be the prevailing signpost of every waking hour of the daily life of each person who breathes the air of God's world.[34]

FOR FURTHER READING

Adler, Mortimer J., and Mayer, Milton, *The Revolution in Education.* Chicago: The University of Chicago Press, 1958.

Bayles, Ernest E., *Democratic Educational Theory*. New York: Harper and Brothers, 1960. 259 pp.

Bestor, Arthur, *The Restoration of Learning*. New York: Alfred A. Knopf, 1955.

Brameld, Theodore, *Ends and Means in Education: A Midcentury Appraisal.* New York: Harper & Brothers, 1950.

————, *Patterns of Educational Philosophy*. New York: World Book Company, 1950. Pp. 265-288, 351-386.

Breed, Frederick S., *Education and the New Realism*. New York: The Macmillan Co., 1939.

Broudy, Harry S., *Building a Philosophy of Education*. New York: Prentice-Hall, Inc., 1954. Pp. 3-26.

Butts, R. Freeman, and Cremin, Lawrence A., *A History of Education in American Culture*. New York: Holt, Rinehart and Winston, Inc., 1953. Pp. 515-562.

Conant, James Bryant, *Education and Liberty*. Cambridge, Mass.: Harvard University Press, 1953.

————, *The American High School Today*. New York: McGraw-Hill Book Co., 1959. 140 pp.

---

[34] Dore Schary, *The Stereotype.* (Medford, Mass.: The Tufts Civic Education Center, Tufts University, in cooperation with the Massachusetts Committee, Catholics, Protestants, and Jews, 1960.)

Crosser, Paul K., *The Nihilism of John Dewey*. New York: The Philosophical Library, Inc., 1955.

Curti, Merle, *The Social Ideas of American Educators*, New Revised Edition. Paterson, N. J.: Pageant Books, Inc., 1959. Pp. xxv-xliv.

Demiashkevich, Michael, *An Introduction to the Philosophy of Education*. New York: American Book Company, 1935. Pp. 381-440.

Edwards, Newton, and Richey, Herman G., *The School in the American Social Order*. Boston: Houghton Mifflin Company, 1947. Pp. 720-723, 840-863.

General Education in a Free Society. Cambridge, Mass.: Harvard University Press for the President and Fellows of Harvard College, 1945.

Horne, H. H. *The Democratic Philosophy of Education*. New York: The Macmillan Co., 1932.

Hutchins, Robert Maynard, *The Higher Learning in America*. New Haven, Conn.: Yale University Press, 1936. 119 pp.

Maritain, Jacques, *Education at the Crossroads*. New Haven, Conn.: Yale University Press, 1943. 118 p.

Mason, Robert E., *Educational Ideals in American Society*. Boston: Allyn and Bacon, 1960. Pp. 41-51.

Mayer, Frederick, *Philosophy of Education for Our Time*. New York: Odyssey Press, Inc., 1958. 198 pp.

Meyer, Adolphe E., *An Educational History of the American People*. New York: McGraw-Hill, 1957. Pp. 396-426.

Mulhern, James. *A History of Education,* Second Edition. New York: The Ronald Press Co., 1959. Pp. 668-721.

Park, Joe, editor, *Selected Readings in the Philosophy of Education*. New York: The Macmillan Co., 1958. Pp. 155-353.

Redden, John D., and Ryan, Francis A., *A Catholic Philosophy of Education*. Milwaukee: Bruce Publishing Co., 1942.

Richmond, W. Kenneth, *Education in the U.S.A.* New York: The Philosophical Library, Inc., 1956. 227 pp.

Riesman, David, Glazer, Nathan, and Denney, Reuel, *The Lonely Crowd*. New Haven, Conn.: Yale University Press, 1950.

Scheffler, Israel, editor, *Philosophy and Education*. Boston: Allyn and Bacon, Inc., 1958. Pp. 263-271.

Ulich, Robert, *A History of Educational Thought*. New York: American Book Company, 1950. Pp. 292-314, 345-350E.

——, *Crisis and Hope in American Education*. Boston: The Beacon Press, 1951. 235 pp.

——, *Three Thousand Years of Educational Wisdom*. Cambridge, Mass.: Harvard University Press, 1954. Pp. 577-614.

Weber, Christian O., *Basic Philosophies of Education*. New York: Holt, Rinehart and Winston, Inc., 1960. Pp. 35-87, 91-156, 159-236.

Whitehead, Alfred North, *The Aims of Education and Other Essays*. New York: The Macmillan Co., 1929. 247 pp.

Woodring, Paul, *A Fourth of a Nation*. New York: McGraw-Hill Book Co., 1957. 255 pp.

QUESTIONS FOR CLASS DISCUSSION

1. Enumerate what you believe to be the essentials of education in a democracy. Defend your position.
2. What potential dangers exist in an overextended zeal to develop the competencies needed in wartime, or cold war, at the expense of other more permanent essentials? Identify some of the latter.
3. Does your personal educational philosophy incline in the direction of Jeffersonianism or Jacksonianism as the mode for America's contemporary educational effort? Explain.
4. What arguments can you advance to show that the appropriations for school support during a period of crisis should be greatly increased? Would you extend your approval to assistance from the federal government?
5. Would you justify or criticize the emphasis placed by the essentialists on the removal of illiteracy in the United States?
6. Advocates of a perennialist philosophy maintain that its goals are no less significant in crisis or wartime than in peace. Assume the perennialist point of view and try to buttress this claim.
7. Recapitulate the life activities of William C. Bagley. What consistent pattern may be seen in his devotion to essentials and essentialism?
8. Discuss and evaluate some of the recent trends in teacher education and suggest additional ways through which you believe that the education of teachers could be improved.
9. Produce a short essay defending the need for international and inter-cultural education as a positive device for reducing the tension of political rivalries and cold war.
10. Contrast the position of the individual citizen under Communism and as a member of one of the Western democracies. By what means is it possible for the West to achieve the efficiency of the totalitarians without sacrificing democratic goals or methods in education?

CHAPTER XX

CONTEMPORARY IDEOLOGIES
AND EDUCATION

CHANGING POLITICAL SCENES

Any real assessment of the results and significance of World War II—like its predecessor in 1914–1918—can be made only in terms that are basically nonmilitary. In this analysis three foci immediately suggest themselves: (1) a host of new and resurgent nationalisms; (2) a new and extraordinary type of satellitism; and (3) powerful new recourses to education.

Since it is not the purpose of this chapter to deal with political processes except to the extent that they *affect* educational philosophy— and since the developments in nationalism and satellitism, oriented both to the U.S.S.R. and the U.S.A., are well known[1]—we shall consider directly only those new responses to education having their wellsprings in the lately changed circumstances so apparent throughout the world after 1945.

The post-1944 period does indeed present changed ideologies in education—both philosophically and in practice—and supranational in scope; the coverage of our chapter being of necessity limited, we shall

---

[1] See J. A. Lukacs, "The American Imperial Disease," *The American Scholar*, Vol. 28, No. 2 (Spring, 1959), pp. 141-150.

attempt to survey primarily the newer relationships only in England, France, Germany, the U.S.S.R., Czechoslovakia, mainland China, and coincidentally, the United States.

This is not to say that dynamic developments are not occurring in Africa, the Near East, Latin America, and Japan. However, for reasons which will be quite apparent to the reader, it seems appropriate to deal here only with a typical representation from the West—the free world— and an equal number from the Marxist orientation.

THE SINGLE LADDER

About—and immediately following—1944, the American school system was increasingly scrutinized by the newer nations of the world as well as by the directorates of the other great powers, together with certain of those countries in the process of transition from former greatness to a less demanding status in world polity.

Possibly because of American success, militarily and industrially, in winning the war, and doubtless because of the contemporary period of American hegemony, beginning sometime after the conclusion of World War I and becoming self-evident in 1945, the structure—and what was taken to be the American educational philosophy—gained a respectful attention almost everywhere.

Indeed, what has come to be called the "Single Ladder" or one-track system in the United States began to evoke, at least rudimentary, adherence in many European countries and here and there throughout the world. To illustrate: the French *école unique,* the German *Einheitsschule* idea, the Italian *scuola unica,* and one of the underlying purposes in British reform under the Education Act of 1944, led patently in this direction.[2]

That the United States had in practice qualified its Single Ladder somewhat either was not known or was blithely disregarded in the haste to show a democratic orientation. This last was in keeping with the new tide that had begun to run strong during the closing years of the conflict and especially after V-E and V-J Days. Such an outlook had sprung from popular desires in the new nationalisms and grass-roots movements which had come to the surface during the war's dark hours; it was a response to the demands of a popular front.

It was reasoned (perhaps rightly) that America's victory in the war was—to a large degree—a resultant of her system of universal education. Moreover, the protestations of the Atlantic Charter and the well-publicized principles of the lately born United Nations served to imple-

---

[2] Arthur H. Moehlman and Joseph S. Roucek, *Comparative Education.* (New York: Holt, Rinehart and Winston, Inc., 1952.) P. 9.

ment these desires and demands throughout the Western and—to a great and even remarkable concurrence—the Eastern world as well as a rising Africa.

In addition to notions concerning the one-track system, American progressivism, too, had come in for scrutiny, and, to a certain extent, imitation. This had already been true (for a time) in the Soviet Union; now French and Italian cabinets felt disposed to concede—along with lip service to the single track—that new methods, and even purposes, were proper responses to the demands for broadening the base of popular education. That these methods usually were conditioned on some sort of pragmatic philosophy which lent itself to mass education was understood. That many Americans and American schools were becoming more highly traditional and essentialist in outlook was—if this were apprehended at all—glossed over.

Among the patterns expressing the organization as well as the method was that of the "modern" school in Britain. This is the new popular secondary school, which, together with the grammar and technical schools, offers an alternate route in the education of adolescents. Yet not even in America (although the British organization did greatly resemble some phases of the progressive American junior high school) was the program brought down so to the level of the mass; indeed—speaking in scholastic terms—it hardly could be called a level, so diluted was the content and so nondirective the methodology applied.

EDUCATIONAL PHILOSOPHY AND METHOD

In the United States the forces at work in education have been identified as Jeffersonian—for the more traditional, idealistic and academic tendency; and Jacksonian, for the pragmatic, vocational, and popular. That pragmatic methods applied in the Jacksonian phase is a natural conclusion; they had to. Nor did the so-called classically oriented school eschew progressivism completely. Frequently one found the pragmatic method grafted upon a fairly rigid association of subject matter. Yet circumstances varied, and those Jeffersonians who used progressive methods hardly ever spoke of them as such.

In order to properly understand the development of educational ideology in the United States one has to consider the history of the American nineteenth century: the unique development of the American states; their constitutional independence—in education, at least; the existence of the frontier; the impact of the industrial revolution; rugged individualism; and the radical political philosophy (for the century that gave them birth, that is) to which they gave assent. All of these must be considered in their educational perspectives.

It is easily possible that many Europeans did not fathom the conditions under which American education had undertaken progressivism for they were many and various. Perhaps the name itself caused much of the confusion.

For progressivism in the schools was but part of that great social and intellectual uplift in American life and culture known historically as "The Progressive Movement." Its roots led to the quest for redress from the sweating slum that accompanied the rise of the city, the aspirations of labor, relief from political rings and bosses, the problem of the farmer with his crushing obligations to the mortgage holder, and indeed, even the sterility of the common public school of the late nineteen hundreds with its lockstep (or as some preferred, goosestep); together with the remoteness of the celebrated American High School—emphasizing almost solely the propaedeutic, through a curriculum only a step from the class-conscious traditional Latin-Grammar School still flourishing under private auspices in the older culture areas of the United States.

To the foregoing must be added the reorganization of American secondary education with junior and senior divisions—the 6-3-3 plan— and the advent of the public junior college—grades 13 and 14.[3] When these are viewed in relationship to the "American Dream" as conceptualized by the historian James Truslow Adams, it appears immediately that—what with industrialization, urbanization, America's new role in world affairs, and the spectacular rise in population, through both immigration and natural causes—it hardly could have been possible that the American people should fail to be powerfully affected by the currents of change which they saw all about them. That similar developments in education should accrue was but a foregone conclusion.

Quite probably what Europe saw so vividly was only the most evident phase of American nationalism and pragmatism. It squared, however, with the myth of the American Dream and with the glamor of popular single-track Jacksonianism in education. Method, too, except in the citadels of New England privatism where the model in old England of the high British Public School discouraged innovation, veered almost one hundred eighty degrees until, if what Europe saw in American schools of the pre-Potsdam decades was progressivism, then Europe saw not too incorrectly.[4]

Yet, in Europe, academic thought—like that of the Ivy League university in the United States generally—has traditionally considered

---

[3] See Edmund A. Ford, "Organizational Pattern of the Nation's Public Secondary Schools." *School Life,* Vol. 42, No. 9 (May, 1960). Pp. 10-12. Ford reports that, as of 1959, eighty-two percent of the total secondary school population was attending a "reorganized school." Specifically, 32% were in 6-6 organizations; 25% in a separate junior high plan; 15% in a 6-3-3 organization; and 10% in a 6-2-4 reorganization.

[4] As mentioned in Chapter XVIII, Wilfred S. Aikin, *The Story of the Eight-Year Study* (New York: Harper and Brothers, 1942) recapitulates the experiment whereby progressive experience in secondary education was made more popular and thus brought to the attention of the American public. That this picture is presented as a glowing one should not be unexpected. However, following World War II, something of the bloom was extracted from this flower as certain more critical analyses of the results of the study were given wide publicity by the essentialists.

the art (or science) of education as a mere technical occupation; as such, having little claim to recognition by prestige institutions: the classical secondary school and the humanistic university. The most honored educational theory of Western Europe can be described, in simple terms, as philosophically idealistic. It is concerned largely with abstract ideas; it is generally intolerant of the scientific method in education and of its findings in educational sociology and social psychology. Educational experimentation and the utilization of practical problems are rare—if usually nonexistent—recourses. That any modification, particularly of the type suggested earlier, should be permitted to enter such a system of thought represents a veritable revolution in educational theory.

Speaking of the roots of European educational thought, Martin Levit establishes this philosophical base even more definitely.[5] "In the main . . . (educational theorists) reach back into, and stay within, the philosophical categories derived chiefly from ancient Greece, the Christian tradition, the rationalism of the Enlightenment, and the idealism of Hegel and Kant." Moreover, in certain areas where theory leads to sharing particular developments with the existentialists, "many theorists seem to be defending the ultimate efficacy of the human will against the influence of external conditions."

EDUCATION IN FRANCE

For these and other reasons, European philosophy, especially in France, finds many reasons for not entering wholeheartedly into the reform contemplated under the Langevin-Wallon recommendation of 1947, attempting, insofar as practicable in France, a one-track system of public education.

Edmund J. King, a close observer of the French educational scene, comments, "Judged by modern standards in more experimental countries like the United States and Britain the system in France is excessively formal and bookish. It bears little relationship to the everyday life of the average French community . . . takes pitifully small account of France's urgent need for greater industrialization."[6]

As is well known, the French system is highly centralized; it is secular and compulsory between the ages of six and fourteen and this is being gradually raised to sixteen; it is uniform throughout France although pupils have the option of attending either a public or a private school; under the 1947 legislation three levels (*degrés*) were conceived: elementary, secondary and higher; the state maintains a monopoly of

---

[5] "Educational Theory in the USSR and West Europe," *School and Society*, Vol. 87, No. 2145 (January 17, 1959), pp. 23.
[6] Edmund J. King, *Other Schools and Ours*. (New York: Holt, Rinehart and Winston, Inc., 1958.) P. 45.

approved examinations which are centrally supervised. Even in Roman Catholic schools the same examinations are administered from Paris.[7]

King reports that "The French people are fully conscious of their problems. They try to make the school less formal. (Even) 'new methods' are officially encouraged and demonstrated by the Ministry of National Education. 'Pilot classes' are to be found in all regional centers, and 'experimental *lycées*' are maintained at six points. (It will be remembered that the '*classes nouvelles*' were to be a special feature of the new legislation in 1947)."[8] Such experimentation in a country with as national a system as France's is unusual, to say the least.

There are, of course, the usual difficulties with the public. The religious faction calls any education except the classical "Godless"; the prosperous call practical education "communistic." It would seem that the United States and Britain have no monopoly on educational kibitzers.

French examinations, especially the *baccalauréate* (*bachot,* for short) are notoriously difficult. However, since the end of 1947 children have been increasingly selected (or rejected)—at the age of eleven—on their previous teacher's recommendation; only those whose status is unclear are now required to take the written examination. (The *bachot* itself, under deGaulle, has been shorn of its oral section.)

It is alleged that, regardless of the fact that only about 14 percent of French children are admitted to secondary education, "a surprising number without this would outplay the average American collegian in nimbleness of wits." French educators, it has been said, "for all their insistence on knowledge, are not primarily interested in factual learning; they insist that 'the intellectual faculties shall be developed' and that children's minds shall be 'trained, enriched, and broadened'."[9] Thus, it would appear that, the future of progressivism, except in miniature, as well as the implementation (in spirit, at least) of the Wallon reform still is dependent upon the European—and French—concept of philosophical idealism.

Nevertheless (recall the concessions that are being made to a more modern viewpoint) contemporary education in France is not quite fossilized. The most astonishing development—in the light of past French educational history—is that a new look is being taken of the *baccalauréate* examination itself. That this *bête noir* of generations of French secondary school students is to be modified is almost as fantastic as Jules Verne's *Autour de la Lune.* Yet this, together with a reconsideration of amount of study per week that *lycée* students must endure, suggests progress. However, lest it be thought that a loosening of standards is contemplated, such reforms in France are always to be achieved within the existing scholastic framework!

[7] See *The French System of Education.* (New York 21, New York: The French Cultural Services, 972 Fifth Avenue, 1958.) Pp. 5-18.
[8] King *op. cit.,* p. 63.
[9] *Ibid.,* p. 37. See also Theodore L. Reller, "Success and Failure of the Reforms of French Secondary Education," *Educational Administration and Supervision,* Vol. 42 (October, 1956), pp. 329-342.

EDUCATION IN BRITAIN

As noted earlier, the British Educational Act of 1944,[10] in addition to attempting to provide a one-track board school (public) to countervail the existing—and venerable—Public School influence, set up alternate routes for its secondary school program. The break comes at age eleven when the British public school student (or his parents) must make a significant decision which may—indeed, probably will—affect the remainder of his three-score years of life.

G. Z. F. Bereday comments as follows on the inequity within the present British system: "Such proposals as there were for one-stream secondary education which preceded the framing of the 1944 Education Act in England were defeated by the enactment of the tripartite division of secondary schools into grammar, technical, and modern. . . . The inequities and stress inherent in assigning children only eleven years old to definite school careers irked the opponents of the system."[11]

Among the opponents must be classed the British Labour Party whose advocacy of the comprehensive school (a British version of the multicurricular high school) has, generally speaking, postponed its acceptance at this time.

The problem of selection for the swank secondary school has been a particularly difficult one and the methods used have aroused much opposition to the tripartite system, at least from those on the lower socio-economic levels. Although election differs community-wise, a usual basis for selection has been on an I.Q. test plus papers on arithmetic and English composition. "The I.Q. cutting point for grammar schools varies from district to district but seldom falls below 110 and is usually between 114-120."[12]

As alleged by Allison Davis and others in the United States,[13] the relationships between socio-economic status and success in securing a higher I.Q. evaluation has not been overlooked by British writers. Himmelweit and Whitfield, for instance, suggest that at least twenty points in a standardized I.Q. instrument depend on class status—upper, that is.[14]

An idea of the dilemma faced by the average British parents

---

[10] *Education in Great Britain*, I. D. 606 (Revised), (45 Rockefeller Plaza. New York 20: British Information Services, Reference Division, May, 1958.) Pp. 7-23.
[11] G. Z. F. Bereday, "Equal Opportunity," *Journal of Education* (London), Vol. 90, (Feb. 1958), p. 47.
[12] Joel B. Montague, Jr., "Some Problems of Selection for Secondary Schools in England—Implications for the United States," *Journal of Educational Sociology*, Vol. 32, No. 8 (April, 1959), p. 375.
[13] See Allison Davis, *Social-class Influences upon Learning*. (Inglis Lecture, 1948, Cambridge: Harvard University Press, 1948.) Also *Intelligence and Cultural Differences*, by Kenneth Wells, Allison Davis, Robert J. Havighurst, *et al.* (Chicago: University of Chicago Press, 1951.)
[14] H. T. Himmelweit and J. Whitfield, "Mean Intelligence Test Scores of a Random Sample of Occupations," *British Industrial Medicine*, Vol. 1 (1947), quoted in Montague, *op. cit.*, p. 376.

when their offspring reaches the 11+ of decision is reported in inimitable fashion by Professor Kenneth Richmond.

It is to be imagined that Mr. and Mrs. A. (of Muddlewick, Lancs.) are going to have much difficulty in deciding whether their son shall go the Muddlewick Alderman Smith modern high school or, given half a chance, to Eton College. At one (the old senior school writ large) he would in all probability get on very well, but he would leave it—how shall we say?—without social allure. At the other he might be like a dog without a tail, but wouldn't he be "made" for life? And Eton would give him that indefinable quality which Muddlewick held in admiration and awe—poise.

[But] to be perfectly honest, what they would *really like* best of all (other things being equal) would be for him to go to Muddlewick Queen Elizabeth Grammar School: It was nice to know French and Chemistry and things . . . and the blazers were so smart. Possibly Dad had a sneaking idea that his son would be better off at a technical school. If so, he either repressed it or thought better to keep it to himself knowing Mrs. A.; anyway the lad hadn't shown any noticeable inclination for that sort of thing . . . though he *did* like his Meccano.[15]

Another problem faced by the new British education is that of the Public Schools themselves. Under the heading "Old Bow Tie" Editor Ford (of a leading British education publication now unfortunately suspended) offers some tidbits concerning Public School status.

The Bow group proposals to "save the public schools" by converting up to half their intake into wards of the Chancellor of the Exchequer have not met with an enthusiastic reception in the Press. This may surprise Sir Robin Williams, author of *Whose Public Schools,* for he writes with an unquestioning conviction of the value of even a minor public school education. . . . But it is not on intellectual grounds that Sir Robin wishes to link the public schools with the state system. As Sir Robin himself admits, there are a growing number of maintained grammar schools which are doing a better job than some public schools. The main basis of Sir Robin's argument is that hoary old chestnut still offered without self-consciousness, "character-building." . . . It would be very difficult to establish that, if the public school does anything for a boy which the grammar school cannot, it is the kind of thing the taxpayer should provide.[16]

In the citation noted, Sir Robin continues, and, at the end, states, bluntly enough, that "to have a son in a public school is a recognized symbol of success." Nevertheless, Bereday comments that, "While England [and perhaps France] revels in the high intellectual training of its elite, its common man is being out-educated not only by the American but also by the German and Russian counterpart. The concentration

15 W. Kenneth Richmond, *Education in England* (Harmondsworth, Middlesex, England: Penguin Books, 1945), p. 160.
16 Boris Ford, "Old Bow Tie" (Editorial), *Journal of Education,* Vol. 90 (February, 1958), p. 41. See also Joel B. Montague, Jr., "The Eleven-Plus Battle in Education in England," *The Clearing House,* Vol. 32, No. 5 (January, 1958), pp. 259-262, and "Are Eton and Rugby Doomed by Socialism?" *The Clearing House,* Vol. 32, No. 6 (February, 1958), pp. 333-335.

on education of the most neglected seems to do much more for the overall dynamics of a country than the concentration on the most highly endowed in the hope [shades of John Locke!] that they will lift the rest by their genius."[17]

As indicated earlier, public interest now is being focused on the possibilities of the comprehensive school and should Labour return to power (if their election platform is to be taken at all seriously), there is the strong possibility that this plan may be given a trial. Three of the present difficulties might become more susceptible of solution in this event. These are: (1) insurance of equality of opportunity; (2) the reduction of social disparities; and (3) provision of alternate patterns of achievement. Bereday thinks that "the lessons of the American high school confirm the proposition that mixing children of different social classes can lead to a greater feeling of Equality."[18] While this has not always occurred in practice in American schools, it may be noted that Dr. Bereday wisely used the potential.

Nor is it clear that there is a definite commitment to social equality in England at this time. Richmond argues that "the fact that the comprehensive school is the center of such a bitter controversy in England provides the clearest indication that a fluid society is by no means acceptable by everyone in this country as a desirable ideal."[19]

Having accented the comprehensive school question in Britain it may now be asked if the success or failure of the "modern school" is an issue. Generally speaking, it appears that the modern school problem in England is not dissimilar to that confronting the large city multi-lateral or vocational high school in the United States. The American problems have been aired in films, novels, magazines, and newspapers for some time. Compare an English modern school teacher's dilemma with that depicted in *Blackboard Jungle, Rebel Without a Cause,* or *High School Confidential,* popular films dealing with adolescent delinquency connected with American schools.

Ruth, British, age fifteen, a modern school student, was prevailed upon to express her attitude toward her wishing-to-remain-anonymous mentor. Ruth wrote:

> There was an old Hag
> Who took from her Bag
> All the Books of the Old Hag
> And then
> She made us wear out our fountain pens.
> She was a BITCH
> Who looked like a WITCH
> Who also had a big SNITCH. . . .

---

[17] Bereday, *op. cit.,* p. 47.
[18] *Ibid.*
[19] W. Kenneth Richmond, *Education in the U.S.A., A Comparative Study.* (New York: Philosophical Library, Inc., 1956.) P. 144.

She would cackle at us
And make a fuss
And her face was like a
Back of a bus.
And when she had a broom-stick
She looked like the NICK.[20]

It is easy, of course, to dismiss the problems of dealing with the mass—especially those with substandard mentality or even those of differing socio-economic levels as being merely issues of valuation. However, until these—frequently antagonistic—strata meet, there is little possibility of *education* (although there may be a certain amount of "schooling").

EDUCATION IN GERMANY

Somewhat of a paradox is offered by the educational arrangements in contemporary Germany. In Communist East Germany the organization of the schools on an 8-4 basis gives—on the surface—the appearance of a single track; in Western Germany the system is more conventional although it varies, of course, in the several *Länder* (states).

While progressive school reform had marked the inauguration of the Weimar republic in 1919, the older forces of German authoritarianism—the upper social classes, the Junkers, and the military bodies—had, by the 1930's (and the advent of Adolf Hitler), restored much of the former practice. Under National Socialism, although recession from the intellectualism of pre-World War I had become a cardinal principle in the training of an ideologically correct population, regimentation, in terms of "scientific" theory (biology and race hygiene) and through the creation of paramilitary organizations for both boys and girls, had merely changed the emphasis and authority of educational practice—not its rigors.

Nevertheless the *Einheitsschule* or common track idea which had flowered during republican days was not dead. Following the surrender of Germany the Allied educational missions in each of the Western Zones—British, American, and French—advocated a pattern designed to encourage the development of equal educational opportunities. That a single track was not accomplished need not be taken as a sign of absolute failure. The autonomy of each of the *Länder* plus the strong class tradition provided a situation completely dissimilar from that obtaining east of the Elbe where class lines as well as provincial boundaries were

---

[20] "Portrait of a Secondary Modern School in England," *Journal of Education*, Vol. 90 (March, 1958), pp. 87-89.

eradicated by government ukase under the cloak of "democracy," as a basic strategy in the creation of a Communist state.

Recent developments in the German Federal Republic (West Germany) suggest that modification is in the offing and that the old solidly elite system has lost some ground at least to the common track concept. Several *Länder* possess the equivalent of the 8-4 system and legislation concerning a *Rahmenplan* (master plan) has been attained. In the German Democratic Republic (East Germany) educational preference ostensibly is nonexistent; actually the children of workers and peasants, party members in good standing, and well-recommended members of certain youth groups—notably the "Organization Ernst Thaelmann"—have priority in securing the opportunity for an education higher than the basic eight or ten years or for the university.

EDUCATIONAL REFORM IN THE U.S.S.R.

An example of a solution to the prestige problem—the holding of several equally recognizable standards rather than one, and only one, absolute—is offered by the Soviet Union.[21] According to Bereday, in contrast to the situation in Britain and France, "the Soviet school system has significantly re-valued the traditional conception of prestige between liberal arts men and 'engineers.' Even more telling is the superior social position of Stakhanovites in comparison with the lower white-collarworkers."[22]

Indeed, a recent report from the U.S.S.R. indicates an even more drastic foreshortening of the gap between mental and manual labor. Soviet comment on the recent move which introduces a practical work program into each phase of Russian education, not only serves to justify this departure but reveals a great deal of Communist strategy as well.

This is a time of tremendous Soviet progress. The country's economy driving full speed ahead, science and culture are experiencing an unprecedented growth, the working people's living standards are rising steadily. In every field of economic and cultural development the Soviet people—truly masters of life and makers of history—have won outstanding victories they are justly proud of, which are bringing joy and hope to the hearts of millions of friends of peace and socialism and fear and despair to enemies of the working class. . . .

V. I. Lenin taught that the training and education of the young generation, the preparation of highly qualified cadres for all branches of the national economy, science and culture, must always be a matter of central concern for the Communist Party and the Soviet State. . . .

---

[21] See George Z. F. Bereday, William W. Brickman, Gerald H. Read (Eds.), *The Changing Soviet School*. (Boston: Houghton Mifflin Company, 1960.) Pp. 186-270.
[22] Bereday, "Equal Opportunity," p. 47.

Speaking at the 13th Congress of the Young Communist League, N. S. Khrushchev said, in this connection: "Every boy and girl should know that while studying at school, they must prepare themselves for working, for the creation of values useful to people, to society. For each one of them, regardless of the position of his or her parents, there should be only one road—to study, then having learned, to work." [23]

In this connection—and stripping the report of its overt propaganda—it will be recalled that, a few years ago, a group of leading Soviet medical authorities published a long letter in the *Literaturnaya Gazeta* charging Soviet educational authorities with "endangering the health of school children" by overloading them with lessons and homework. "Chronic over-exhaustion, frequent headaches, weakened memory and vision, proneness to infectious diseases with various complications, result in a general weakening of the child's organism." They complained of the "unbelievable over-burdening" of school children. Children of eleven to thirteen were averaging, including homework, from eight to ten hours a day; and students of fourteen to seventeen, from ten to twelve hours. [24]

Since in the U.S.S.R. nothing is presumed to happen by chance, this move may be suggested as the preliminary to a reduction in the academic part of the Soviet public school program, which was done in September, 1956. That the present move—undoubtedly to counteract the tendency which was developing in Soviet secondary education (compare with the British problem) of placing prestige on academic attainment in the upper classical and scientific schools—is a way to retreat gracefully from an untenable program is sure. That it was impossible for all to succeed in them; and that the prestige factor was seen as inconsistent with Soviet ideology make logical explanations for the proletarian turn.

To return to the new program.

Public education must be reorganized along lines that will allow the secondary and higher schools to play a more active role in all of the creative activity of the Soviet people. . . . One of the major defects in the old society was the gulf between physical and mental labor. . . . Marxist teaching has dispelled the bourgeois myth of the inevitable and eternal existence of a grey mass of people, on the one side, whose destiny is submission and grinding physical toil, and on the other, a handful supposedly called by nature herself to do the thinking and ruling, to develop science and literature and the arts. . . .

The idea of uniting instruction with productive labor has long at-

---

[23] "On Strengthening the Bonds of the School with Life, and the Further Development of the Public Education System in the Country. Theses of the Central Committee of the Communist Party in the Soviet Union and Council of Ministers of the U.S.S.R.," *Soviet Education* (an English translation of the U.S.S.R. monthly journal, *Sovetskaya Pedagogica,* Journal of the Russian Academy of Pedagogical Science), Vol. 1 (Feb., 1959), pp. 3-5. See also George S. Counts, *Khrushchev and the Central Committee Speak on Education.* (Pittsburgh: University of Pittsburgh Press, 1959.)
[24] Quoted in Robert J. Havighurst, "Is Russia Really Out-Producing Us in Scientists?," *School and Society,* Vol. 86 (April 26, 1958), p. 190.

tracted progressive thinkers. Such Utopian Socialists as Campanella, Fourier, and Owen, and the great Russian revolutionary democrat, Chernyshevsky, already in this day, picturing the society of the future, spoke of the close bond of instruction with physical labor under socialism.

The 20th Congress of the CPSU pointed out, as a serious shortcoming in our schools, the fact that instruction is, in a certain measure, divorced from life, and that graduates are ill-prepared for practical activity.

In order to strengthen the bond of the schools with life, it is not only necessary to introduce new subjects into the school curriculum . . . but also to involve them systematically in work at enterprises, collective and state farms, experimental school plots, and school workshops. The curriculum for secondary schools should be revised in the direction of a greater specialization in production so that young people who complete the ten-year (complete secondary school) have a good general education opening the way to higher education, and at the same time, prepared for practical activity, since the greater part of the graduates will at once start work in the various branches of the national economy.[25]

Two stages in providing the new program are envisioned. First, a compulsory eight-year school (to replace the present seven) from which "the youth as a whole must become involved in socially useful work at enterprises, or collective farms, etc." The second plateau involves continuation schools, secondary general educational labor polytechnical schools, and technical schools with the complete secondary education program. Beginning in the 1959-1960 school year there were to be boarding schools and specialized secondary education programs.[26]

The philosophy of the new move is fairly well revealed in the concluding statement of the directive adopted November 12, 1958. "In mastering these qualities, the study of the social sciences plays an important role. A knowledge of the fundamentals of Marxism-Leninism is essential for specialists in all fields. . . . Our youth must be trained in a spirit of implacability towards bourgeois ideology and any manifestation of revisionism."[27]

Such a monolithic attack on the problem which badgers England, Germany, and even the United States confirms the view of George S. Counts, an American interpreter of the Russian educational world for many years. "Teacher and education as such, moreover, are essentially technicians who translate into practice the general and specific directives formulated by the party leadership." And, "The goals of Soviet education are to be found in the Bolshevik conception of history, the nature of the social structure, the controlling purposes of the party, the cultural heritage from Old Russia, and the shifting tides of change among the nations."[28]

---

[25] "On Strengthening the Bonds . . . ," p. 5.
[26] *Ibid.*, pp. 6-7.
[27] *Ibid.*, p. 14.
[28] George S. Counts, *The Challenge of Soviet Education.* (New York: McGraw-Hill Book Co., 1957.) Pp. 50-51; 32.

Indeed the present turn might well be a paraphrase of Lenin himself. "In the field of people's education," he said, "the Communist Party sets itself the aim of concluding the task begun by the October Revolution of 1917 of converting the school from a weapon for the class domination of the Bourgeoisie into a weapon for the destruction of this domination, as well as for the complete destruction of the division of society into classes. The school must become a weapon of the dictatorship of the proletariat."[29]

One would, of course, be naive to expect that each of the words quoted above should be taken in its literal meaning. At the same time the problem in the Soviet Union and in the satellite states is to devise a working arrangement as between Communist ideology and the needs of the Soviet national state. "It seems evident that a growing number of Soviet intellectuals recognize the mythological function of certain elements of the official ideology," surmises Martin Levit in a recent paper on educational theory in the U.S.S.R.

At the same time, the influence of the Marxist-Leninist legacy is strong; it colors even the objections of dissenters. Nevertheless, a reciprocity of influence is discernible between it and other forces—historical Russian traditions, four decades of an embracive Soviet enculturation process, international problems, the development of a giant industrial power, and an increasingly complex social class structure.[30]

A higher Russian birth rate than the United States before Pearl Harbor, together with a school system geared to university requirements, had led to a surplus of academically trained young people which the facilities of the state were unable to assimilate. More students were being graduated from the complete secondary school, still largely propaedeutic, than could be enrolled in higher educational agencies. The paramount need was that of developing a larger, occupationally skilled, and more variegated middle class. This is the prime reason for the Soviet shift to polytechnicalization—not student eyestrain.

REFORM IN CZECHOSLOVAKIA

The above dilemma was also one in the Soviet satellites;[31] and since their educational policies are controlled by Moscow, developments within these Iron Curtain countries—and Czechoslovakia offers a good example—serve to indicate the completeness with which the move has been formulated.

---

[29] Quoted in Counts, *op. cit.*, p. 47.
[30] Levit, *op. cit.*, p. 22.
[31] See Chapter XIX.

The Czech reforms begin with the usual Communist polemic:

All affairs of public education and the school system of the Czechoslovak Republic have undergone profound changes during the years the democratic regime has existed. From a school of the bourgeoisie, based on social and
property inequality, from a servile weapon of the ruling clique of exploiter-
capitalists, the Czech schools have been transformed into a really public school
which educates conscious builders of socialism.[32]

Then the "extenuating circumstances" leading to the change are
retold.

Although certain reforms were established in Czechoslovakia on the
basis of "The Law of the Unified School" by the National Assembly in May,
1948, and the April, 1953, Act reducing the term of compulsory instruction from
nine to eight years and the term of instruction in the complete secondary school
from thirteen to eleven years, some dissatisfaction with the program still existed.
Among the chief reasons appended for change were (1) overloading and extended homework; (2) failure of the school to enroll sufficient numbers of
children for the worker and peasant background; and (3) the adolescent was
found, at age 14, in many cases incapable of correctly choosing a future vocation
(in this the school could not help him, since almost no kind of work in vocational guidance was conducted).[33]

Having considered the U.S.S.R., this is a familiar refrain.
The Kasvin-Shibanov report continues and details the expedient
chosen.

[Thus] the Central Committee of the Communist Party of Czechoslovakia at the 11th Congress proposed a series of measures which will contribute
to the further development of public education in the country and to the regulation of the school system with the object of bringing it closer to the needs of
socialist construction. . . . In his speech to the Congress, Comrade A. Novotnyy
said, "The chief task of our school must become the training of thoroughly
developed people, who possess the basic facts of knowledge in the field of science
and technology and at the same time are trained for skilled physical labor and
conscious participation in the construction of communist society. To create
such a truly socialist school means, by all possible methods to join teaching in
school increasingly more tightly with the productive labor of pupils so that they
acquire not only working habits, but in the senior classes of the secondary
schools, also gain a basic skill in the field of some kind of working occupation". . .[34]

For reasons of clarity, and because of its current significance, tables

---

[32] G. A. Kasvin and A. A. Shibanov, "The Reform of the Schools in the Czechoslovak
Republic," *Soviet Education*, Vol. I, No. 4 (February, 1959), pp. 64-70.
[33] *Ibid.*, p. 66.
[34] *Ibid.*, p. 67. See also E. P. Gusarov, "Labor as a Factor in the Pupil's Upbringing,"
Soviet Education, Vol. 1, No. 5 (March, 1959), pp. 29-32. Contains anecdotes and an-
thropometrical studies.

of the new program (from the Kasvin-Shibanov report) are appended. The system of training pupils for labor contains three grades as follows:

TABLE I: THE FIRST LEVEL, "LESSONS IN HANDIWORK" (CLASSES I-V)

Kinds of work	Number of lessons by years of study					
	I	II	III	IV	V-1	V-2
Work with small objects used, for example, in teaching safety, to clean up the workplace, etc.	6	0	0	0	0	0
Work with paper and cardboard	10	10	10	10	0	10
Work with plastics and clay	6	6	4	4	0	4
Work with fabrics	0	6	12	12	0	12
Work with wood and metal (soft tin, wire, etc.)	0	0	6	6	26	6
Work in nature corner and on garden plot	7	7	18	18	24	18
Socially useful labor	4	4	10	10	10	10
Excursions connected with handiwork lessons	0	0	6	6	6	6
Total	33x	33x	66	66	66	66

x lessons per week, all others 2 lessons per week

(The following table represents a combination of two indexes, the agricultural and the industrial. Where paired figures are shown, the first refers to the emphasis given in agricultural regions, the second in industrial areas; otherwise the program is similar. The labor lessons are included in a study plan called "bases of production.")

TABLE II: THE SECOND LEVEL, "BASES OF PRODUCTION" (CLASSES VI-IX)

Sections of "Bases of Production"	Number of hours by years of instruction, by semesters							
	VI		VII		VIII		IX	
Bases of technology, ind.	11	0/0	0/0	0/8	0/15	15/15	23	23
Work in craftshops, ind.	29	0/0	0/0	0/30	0/26	33/26	33	33
Socially useful labor, ind.	4	0/0	0/0	0/6	0/4	10/4	3	3
Talks, industrial emphasis	2	0/0	0/0	0/2	0/2	4/2	2	2
Trips, industrial	4	0/0	0/0	0/3	0/3	4/3	5	5
Bases of technology, ag.	0	7/7	7/7	7/0	15/0	0/0	0	0
Work in craftshops, ag.	0	30/30	25/25	25/0	33/8	0/8	0	0
Socially useful labor, ag.	0	6/5	10/10	10/0	10/5	0/5	17	16
Talks, agricultural	0	2/3	3/4	3/0	2/1	0/1	0	0
Trips, agricultural	0	4/4	5/4	4/0	6/2	0/2	0	0
Totals	50	49/49	50/50	49/49	66/66	66/66	83	82

It will be noted that two basic plans have been set up for use (1) in predominantly agricultural regions, or (2) in industrial areas, although every student is given some contact with each at some time during his study in years VI-IX. Likewise the yearly totals progress from 99 hours per year of instruction in class VI to a total of 165 hours in class IX.

In the third grade, Classes X to XII, the general polytechnical education is combined with production training in specialties of a wide range. Training in cities is in the bases of machine-building, of the leading branches of heavy industry, in the bases of textile production and in the bases of the construction industry. In the agricultural areas, the program is indicated in the tabulation below. The new program is planned to be in complete effect by September 1, 1961.

TABLE III: THE THIRD LEVEL, "GENERAL POLYTECHNICAL" (CLASSES X-XII) Cities

Component parts of production training	Number of hours per week by years of study			
	X	XI	XII	Yearly total
Technology	2	2	3	222
Mechanical engineering	2	2	0	132
Production practice and productive labor	6	7	9	700

TABLE IV: THE THIRD LEVEL, "GENERAL POLYTECHNICAL" (CLASSES X-XII) Rural

Component parts of production training	By years		By semesters		Yearly total
	X	XI	XII		
Crop raising	2	1	1 or 2	0	132
Livestock raising	2	1	2 or 1	0	132
Mechanical engineering	0	2	0	3	156
Production practice and labor	6	7	9	9	700

So may the new polytechnical program (which serves as a complement to the lightened academic phase), in the ancient land of John Amos Comenius, be outlined. Broad in educational outlook though the grand old Moravian was, it is doubtful that he could have approved such a curriculum, disagreeing—if for no other reason—with its materialistic base. Nevertheless, in deference to their greatest educational prophet—indeed, possibly the world's greatest—the Czechoslovakian Academy of Science published, in the tercentenary of his epocal work, a photolithic edition of the Amsterdam imprint.[35] The introduction (given in the national language, Latin, Russian, English, French,

---

[35] Joannes Amos Comenius, *Opera Didactica Omnia (Editio anni 1657 lucis ope expressa)*, 3 volumes. (Prague: Academia Scientiarum Bohemoslovenica, MCMLVII.) See William W. Brickman, "Three Centuries of Comenius' Contributions to Education," *School and Society*, 86 (April 26, 1958), pp 193-194, for other publications under Czech auspices of Comenius' great contributions to the science of education.

German and Spanish) reads as follows: "After three centuries in Komen-sky's native country, there arise the conditions that will make possible the realization of even his most daring plans. The socialist society real-izes the unified school system from the primary school up to the highest school standard, as Komensky has proposed it; in the socialist society all children are given a general education without any discrimination of sex, social origin, and property as it was Komensky's idea." Other tributes to Comenius follow along with a schedule for republishing his basic peda-gogical works.[36]

Only time can reveal whether the Marxist myth is adequate or satisfactory for the stabilizing of the new 1958 system; but given the conditioning which has already occurred and is being perpetuated by the various youth organizations and paramilitary fronts perhaps the trans-formation will not be found an impossible one.

CHINESE PEOPLE'S REPUBLIC

Turning now to mainland China for another example of the Com-munist ideology in education, we find the vocational motif again in evi-dence. In Red China, as in every other Communist country, the monopoly of education is vested in the state. However, it is possible—theoretically at least—for private schools to exist if they accept control and inspection and if they provide curricula drawn up by the state authorities. Eighty per cent of the total costs are provided by Peking; the remainder must be furnished by the provincial governments or the municipalities. Ac-cording to J. A. Lauwerys,[37] three ministries are concerned with educa-tion: (1) The Ministry of Culture, which looks after museums, broad-casting, the theatre, and so on; (2) the Ministry of Higher Education, which is in charge of all technical institutions, research institutes, uni-versities and colleges; and (3) the Ministry of Education proper, which controls all elementary and middle schools, all teacher training, all gen-eral education provided in part-time schools, and, in addition, runs special schools for handicapped children, of which there are at present, 62 with 65,000 pupils and 960 teachers. The Minister of Education is in charge also of the rapidly growing systems, for infants, of nursery schools and kindergartens. Truly, an awe-inspiring task.

This highly organized educational program is in keeping with Communist China's "Great Leap Forward," by which the Marxist leader-ship hopes to overtake the Western democracies through a crash program

---

[36] In the Western world perhaps the most significant recognition of Comenius' ter-centenary was the Paris publication in 1957 by UNESCO of *Selections, John Amos Comenius.* Introduction by Jean Piaget.
[37] *Journal of Education,* Vol. 90, No. 1064 (March, 1958), pp. 97-98; see also *Soviet Education,* Vol. 1, No. 4 (February, 1959), pp. 57-64.

on the farms and in her factories. Millions of Chinese of both sexes have been taken from their homes, organized into battalions of farm workers, housed in barracks, and their children placed in the hands of the state. The development of manufacturing in the towns and cities is being fostered too—with special emphasis on the creation of metals and other heavy industries.

Vocational middle schools exist in the large towns where there also are polytechnics, normal schools, pre-medical and trade schools. Without going into the program which, recently, has been developing in the fashion indicated in Czechoslovakia and the parent U.S.S.R., it may be indicated that an ideology is being constructed which, no doubt, will result in the creation of further practicalism.

> A difficult point of policy, at present unsolved, is whether it would be wise at the moment, to encourage the increase in the number of the "general schools" or to concentrate resources upon the vocational school. Public opinion among parents favors the former. Economics needs the latter.[38]

Delicately put!

More blunt, but with the same intention, are the remarks of Lin Ting-yi in "Education Must be Linked to Productive Work,"[39] "The majority of bourgeois educational specialists consider that only book knowledge is knowledge . . . that practical experience is not knowledge. . . . Theirs is a blind alley!"

Dr. Oskar Anweiler, Hamburg, sees an apparently unanticipated problem in the shift to "polytechnic emphasis" in the schools, from primary through university, in the Communist-oriented bloc—the U.S.S.R., mainland China, and the People's Democracies of East Central Europe: Bulgaria, Czechoslovakia, East Germany, Hungary, and Romania (but with the exception of Poland).

In addition to certain objections raised by factory managers bent on efficiency and the necessary provision of school buildings with special space for workshops and technical equipment to say nothing of the retraining required to produce adequate school staffs, Anweiler maintains that:

> Here the aim is to preserve the scientific structure of the various disciplines, whilst at the same time paying special attention to their practical applications . . . the children's age, their attitude to work and their participation in "workers' collectives" also present various problems with respect to the methods of teaching and giving work experience.
>
> Seen as a whole, the main educational problem consists in the conflict between, on the one hand, the forms of life and teaching suited to children and young people and, on the other, the early adaptation to and preparation for the adult working world which it is sought to achieve.[40]

---

[38] Lauwerys, *op. cit.*, p. 98.
[39] Source noted under 37, *Soviet Education*, p. 58.
[40] Oskar Anweiler, "School Reform Problems in Eastern Europe," *International Review of Education*, Vol. VI, No. 1 (1960). Pp. 34-35.

Western-trained (Cambridge) T. C. Cheng comments on the new half-work, half-study plan in Communist China, suggesting a note of warning to the West:

It would be folly to ignore the basic challenge posed by the Peiping regime in terms of its aims, industrialization, military prowess, and educational achievement. In spite of the fact that the so-called Communist institutions of higher education are little more than vocational schools, and Communist schools hardly compare with the schools of the Free World as regards their academic standards, they already claimed in 1958 that 93.9 per cent of all school-age children on the mainland was enrolled in primary schools, and that illiteracy was to be wiped out in five years. . . . [Yet] it remained to be seen whether or not the institutions and ideology of Communist China may eventually succeed in blending the unlettered laborers with the intellectual elite in the years to come.[41]

Obviously, Red China presents both a promise and a threat!

A CONTEMPORARY VIEW

While admittedly in kaleidoscopic fashion, educational ideologies in six countries have been considered. Comparisons and contrasts are easily suggested, three of these countries being among the leading "democracies" of the Western world, the second trio representing members of the Communist-oriented bloc.

Speaking in philosophical terms, these ideologies vary from the idealism tinged with rationalism of the western European setting through the idealism and pragmatism of American education to the frank dilectical materialism of the Soviet group. Yet there is also a peculiar inverted idealism in the Marxist camp and there are strong pragmatic leanings in Britain and elsewhere in western Europe. The Progressive Education Association in the United States has withered but there is a New Education Fellowship in western Europe that is not dead. Both England and France are engaged in a certain amount of experimentation and in America the essentialists have absorbed much from the pragmatic methodology of the progressives. In Western Germany the popular emphasis finds more support.

But how to assess the new directions in education more visible since 1944 than at any time previously? Has Pandora's box been opened or do the developments in popular education represent progress? What have the rising nationalisms of Asia and Africa to offer? And is the national-

---

[41] T. C. Cheng, "Half-Work and Half-Study in Communist China," *History of Education Journal*, Vol. IX, No. 4 (Summer, 1958), pp. 88-92.

ism of the captive East European countries dead? Is communism as a new world force to destroy the democratic achievement of the world to date or is it in turn to be liquidated by the very currents it has contrived to liberate? Perhaps such questions are too difficult of answer without further experience with the new ideologies in education.

There is change—if not progress—and this in itself is a healthy sign; the people themselves (although this must be a relative phenomenon) are making their wishes in education (and sometimes in politics) known; education as an abstract term is being redefined; and— although free, mandatory, universal education has not been achieved in most of the world—the levels of literacy, under the twin spurs of nationalism and independence, are rising rapidly.[42]

Summing up, several tendencies may easily be observed: (1) the new demands for literacy, from either nationalistic or monolithic motives; (2) the de-accentuation of class bias in the provision for a greater range of educational opportunities at all levels; (3) the broader base assumed by education in the Soviet orbit through the utilization of work experience plans; (4) a noticeable willingness to educational experimentation, especially by the Western European democracies; (5) the strengthening, particularly in the United States, of educational philosophy and method leading to a synthesis of many of the better features of essentialism and progressivism; (6) the increasingly dominant role now being played by students and youth organizations throughout much of the world; and (7) fresh urges to education, both scientific and academic, springing in large part from the grass-roots of societies and from the natural dignity of the newly created, independent nations on the older continents, where anticolonial movements (while not without a certain peril) offer great promise.

Brotherhood has, of course, not been reached—and the millennium is still far away—but the picture is infinitely brighter (except for the threat, political and ethical, offered by world communism) than, say, in 1939, when it appeared that the overthrow of an entire civilization with a return to primordial tribalism was immediately imminent. The new world literacy movement—as well as a surer awareness of totalitarian tactics—implies that the "wave of the future" will not flow from utopian illusion but from democratic realities founded on the long history of the races in their struggle for individual freedoms and a higher existence than that of an ant-hill society. It is education's role to assure this reality.

---

[42] Robert E. Belding in a small volume, *Students Speak Around the World* (Iowa City, Iowa: State University of Iowa, 1960), highlights this inclination. Speaking of Britain (pp. 15-25), France (pp. 26-33), and the USSR (pp. 54-63), together with Latin America, Scandinavia, Western Germany, and Japan, Belding points up the newer tendencies through illustrations of influences which presently are providing non-class education to a greater degree than ever before. Moreover, the influence of the student mind is providing a significant new force.

FOR FURTHER READING

Adler, Mortimer J., and Mayer, Milton, *The Revolution in Education.* Chicago: University of Chicago Press, 1958.

Belding, Robert E., *Students Speak Around the World, A Book of Contemporary Cases.* Iowa City, Iowa: State University of Iowa, 1960. 74 pp.

Bereday, George Z. F., Brickman, William W., and Read, Gerald H. (Eds.), *The Changing Soviet School.* Boston: Houghton Mifflin Company, 1960.

Bestor, Arthur, *The Restoration of Learning.* New York: Alfred A. Knopf, 1955.

Conant, James Bryant, *Education and Liberty.* Cambridge, Mass.: Harvard University Press, 1953.

Counts, George S., *Khrushchev and the Central Committee Speak on Education.* Pittsburgh: University of Pittsburgh Press, 1959. 66 pp.

————, *The Challenge of Soviet Education.* New York: McGraw-Hill Book Co., 1957.

Cramer, John Francis, and Browne, George Stephenson, *Contemporary Education.* New York: Harcourt, Brace and Company, 1956.

Crosser, Paul K., *The Nihilism of John Dewey.* New York: The Philosophical Library, Inc., 1955.

Davis, Allison, *Social-Class Influences upon Learning* (Inglis Lecture, 1948). Cambridge, Mass.: Harvard University Press, 1948.

Education in Great Britain (I. D. 606, Revised). 45 Rockefeller Plaza, New York 20: British Information Services, Reference Division, May, 1958. 43 pp.

The French System of Education. 972 Fifth Avenue, New York 21: The French Cultural Services, 1958. 46 pp.

General Education in a Free Society. Cambridge, Mass.: Harvard University Press for the President and Fellows of Harvard College, 1945.

Hoover, J. Edgar, *Communist Illusion and Democratic Reality.* Washington: United States Department of Justice, Federal Bureau of Investigation, July, 1959. 22 pp.

Kandel, I. L., *The New Era in Education, A Comparative Study.* Boston: Houghton Mifflin Company, 1955.

King, Edmund J., *Other Schools and Ours.* New York: Holt, Rinehart and Winston, Inc., 1958.

Moehlman, Arthur H., and Roucek, Joseph S., *Comparative Education.* New York: Holt, Rinehart and Winston, Inc., 1952.

Myers, Edward D., *Education in the Perspective of History.* New York: Harper and Brothers, 1960.

Richmond, W. Kenneth, *Education in England.* Harmondsworth, Middlesex, England: Penguin Books, 1945.

————, *Education in the U. S. A.* New York: The Philosophical Library, Inc., 1956.

Riesman, David, Glazer, Nathan, and Denney, Reuel, *The Lonely Crowd*. New Haven, Conn.: Yale University Press, 1950.

Truscott, Bruce, *Red Brick University*. London: Faber and Faber, 1943.

Ulich, Robert, *Fundamentals of Democratic Education*. New York: American Book Company, 1940.

————, *Crisis and Hope in American Education*. Boston: The Beacon Press, 1951.

Yesipov, B. P., and Goncharov, N. K., *I Want to be Like Stalin* (Translated by George S. Counts and Nucia P. Lodge). New York: The John Day Company, 1947.

QUESTIONS FOR CLASS DISCUSSION

1. Comment on the following definition of comparative education: "Comparative Education is the systematic examination of cultures and in particular their system of education in order to discover resemblances and differences." What in your estimation can such study offer to students of education generally?

2. The use of myth is a significant factor in the development of a state—especially one of the totalitarian type. Find examples of such usage and point out their utility in terms of educational theory and practice.

3. Try to account for the differences in secondary education found in Britain, France, and the United States.

4. Do you agree that the United States has a single-ladder type of educational opportunity? If not, explain your position.

5. Present a number of arguments pro and con relating to the question, "Is the European High School Really Better?"

6. Do you think that nationalism itself is a cause of war? Comment upon some of the relationships between nationalism and education.

7. If you do not feel that the United Nations in its present form is adequate to keep the peace of the world, what steps, changes, or additions would you recommend? Do you agree or disagree that a study of UN and UNESCO is a proper elementary and/or high school function?

8. What are your views regarding language study in a world divided as it now is into several ideological and economic camps? Should this emphasize reading knowledge or speaking abilities? What other possibilities are entailed in language study? Would you expand or contract present tendencies?

9. Do you believe that the work-study plan presently being initiated in the Communist-oriented bloc is psychologically sound? If not, what do you consider its vulnerable points?

INDEX

Date Due

	PRINTED IN U. S. A.	CAT. NO. 23231			